Contents

GW00492759

133 entering Cahirciveen on the morning mixed train in May 1949. This train left Farranfore at 6.15am as a goods train, but was advertised as having passenger accommodation from Killorglin. It terminated at Cahirciveen at 11am, one of only two trains a day at this time on the branch following the coal shortages brought on by World War Two.

The photographer John Dewing, now blessed to be in his 91st year, was on a cycling holiday and was determined to concentrate on enjoying the scenery rather than the trains. Nonetheless he achieved both in this shot, one of the very few railway photographs which he took on his visit. He remembers being almost seduced by the prospect of a run up the line behind 182, but he did remain in the vicinity to see what was coming the other way, which proved, in his own words, to have been "a very lucky decision"!

133 had been built at Inchicore in 1885 and was exhibited at the Dublin Exhibition of that year. She was one of the first of the class to be built new with vacuum brakes and to have her cylinders cast at Inchicore. She remained almost as built, apart from the 4' 4" boiler which she received in 1904, until she was scrapped in 1963.

Foreword

The first of Ireland's most numerous type of steam locomotive began work in 1866. Of the 119 members of the type, two remain in the custody of the Railway Preservation Society of Ireland (RPSI). One of them, 186, has been restored to working order and is reminding a new generation what capable machines these nineteenth century veterans were. This event provoked a suggestion to the London Area of the Irish Railway Record Society (IRRS) that it might help with fundraising to keep the newly restored locomotive going by publishing a new edition of *'Steaming Through a Century'*, first published in 1966 by the IRRS in Dublin to celebrate the centenary of these ubiquitous engines.

Dr Patrick Flanagan edited that book and we should be grateful to him that he persuaded such a notable group of experts to tell the different parts of the class's story. Kevin Murray wrote many papers on Irish railways and notable histories of the Dublin and Kingstown Railway and the Great Northern. He held several posts within the IRRS over many years and was its founding chairman. R.N. ('Bob') Clements was a familiar face on the footplate and the practical knowledge obtained there, along with much original research, resulted in dozens of well argued papers on Irish locomotives. His knowledge of the subject remains unsurpassed. He was the first editor of the IRRS's *'Journal'*. J.J. ('Jackie') Johnston was Assistant Mechanical Engineer (Technical) of CIE at the time the original book was written and had day-to-day experience of the last couple of decades of steam. Jack O'Neill is a footplateman from Waterford whose enthusiasm for, and working knowledge of, the '101' class continued unabated into the preservation era, when he often encouraged 'foreign' crews how to get the best from these sturdy little engines.

The words of the original authors have been left unchanged – except where the passage of time has rendered some parts no longer correct. To do otherwise would have been an injustice, for each in his own way demonstrated an unparalleled knowledge of the subject.

Those who first wrote that story in 1966 could hardly have imagined that the history of these remarkable machines had further to run. Since that time the World has changed greatly, but remarkably two of the class survive and one of them at least will haul passenger trains into the Twenty First Century.

In this new book the opportunity has been taken to explain to the reader just how important a part of our Industrial Heritage the two surviving members of the '101' Class are, by placing them in the wider context of locomotive development throughout Ireland. The remarkable story of their new life, which followed a narrow escape from the scrapyard, is told by Joe Cassells, author of two histories of RPSI trains. Finally, the project to restore 186 to working order is detailed and will give the reader the inside story of the myriad parts which must be maintained to keep a relatively simple machine working.

We have included many more illustrations than was possible in the original book, to show the class during a century of 'company' work and their remarkable second life in preservation. On these pages you will find a hundred and one of the GS&WR locomotives and the two from the D&BJR.

A word about the way these engines are referred to. The Great Southern and Western Railway classified their locomotives by the number of the first locomotive of the type, numerically, but not in order of building, hence the '101' Class: but to-day most people refer to them by the later Great Southern Railways classification – 'J15'. However, the original authors of the centenary history used the older term throughout and we now do the same. Whether you think of 184 and 186 as '101s' or 'J15s' we hope that you will enjoy reading about them and enjoy travelling behind 186, still running well in her third century.

We have dedicated this book to the late Robin 'Bob' Clements, the doyen of Irish steam locomotive experts. Locomotive enthusiasts owe a great debt of gratitude to Bob for the comprehensive records he left us on many aspects of the subject. You can read some of his work here in the book and much more in the *Journals* of the IRRS. It was he, on the night on which the RPSI was founded, who set the nascent society on the right path. He broke into a fairly heated debate on what should be preserved and simply stated "I have come here tonight from County Kildare to say one thing and one thing only. If you are going to preserve anything, it should be a member of the '170' series of the Great Northern (the 'S' class 4-4-0s) and a member of the '101' series of the Great Southern and Western". And, as they say, "the rest is history"!

Irwin Pryce
Leslie McAllister

The Irish 0-6-0

A Classic Locomotive Type

By Irwin Pryce

For a large part of the past two centuries the casual traveller arriving anywhere in Ireland would probably have found his train headed by a modest 4-4-0 and if he cared to look at any goods trains these would almost certainly have had nothing more than an 0-6-0 hauling them. Indeed many less important passenger trains would also have been worked by these maids of all work.

The reason for this was not difficult to see, for patterns of traffic throughout the island of Ireland - where passenger trains were lighter than in many other countries and there were no heavy flows of coal or mineral traffic, combined with the shorter distances involved - meant that these two types of locomotive accounted for the largest part the locomotive fleet on almost every Irish railway company. The state of penury in which some companies existed also meant that many engines were blessed with a long life, indeed the locomotives which form the subject of this book approached a period of 100 years in daily service.

No.63 and 128 seen at Limerick Junction in 1900 illustrate the two types which were to dominate Irish railways for a century. In their heyday the '60' class were as highly thought of by railwaymen as the 101 class and speeds into the 70s were recorded with them. The two engines present a study in elegance here.

No.63 will run through the station and, in time honoured fashion, reverse into the platforms. The singular layout of Limerick Junction always provided diversion for enthusiasts.

Locomotive and General Railway Publishing Co./NRM

This fact in itself is remarkable, but even more so is the fact that they carried out their designed task so effectively throughout this period until the very end of the steam age.

Twelve years before the appearance of number 112, which was to become the first of that numerous and long lived class which forms the subject of this book, the first Irish 0-6-0 appeared from the Great Southern and Western Railway's Inchicore Works. Other Irish railways rapidly took up the type and well before the end of the 19th century the 0-6-0 had established itself as the main source of power for goods traffic in Ireland, a position it was not to finally relinquish until the dieselisation of railways in the 1960s.

Family Features

As a goods locomotive, the classic Irish inside-cylindered 0-6-0 had many virtues which endeared it to operators. Firstly, 100% of the locomotive's weight was available for adhesion. Carrying wheels, whether a bogie or pony truck contribute nothing to a locomotive's ability to grip the rails. Enginemen appreciated the surefootedness of the type, while in poor conditions sand could be applied to the rails to assist adhesion, either by gravity feed or assisted by steam in later designs.

Similarly, once locomotives were equipped with brakes, all of the locomotive and tender weight was available for braking. This was an important factor in the days when the only brake power on a goods train was the engine's brake and a hand brake in the guard's van at the rear. The working of a loose-coupled goods train, where the weight of the train itself could be ten times the weight of the locomotive, depended on the skill of the driver and a close working relationship with the guard. Both of these men would have had an intimate knowledge of the gradients of all the lines over which they worked; however such skills are no longer required on the modern railway, where goods trains run at near passenger speeds and have brakes throughout the train.

The basic layout of the type allowed for a deep firebox and an adequately sized ashpan to be placed between the driving and trailing axle. The cylinder block at the front provided strong bracing for the frames, the motion plate which supported slide-bars and the valve gear braced the centre, and a solid drag box at the rear made for a strong and rigid arrangement with consequently low maintenance costs.

Combined with a driving wheel of about 5ft diameter, such an engine was able to run comfortably at speeds in excess of 50mph and indeed with a more adventurous approach from crews, speeds in excess of 60mph were regularly attained. This capability was valuable to the Operating Department, enabling the type to be used for passenger work when required.

No.30 of the Belfast and Northern Counties Railway was built in 1880 and bears the unmistakeable stamp of her makers, Beyer Peacock. The BN&CR, and more particularly its successor the LMS(NCC), made modest use of the type. By the time the LMS had begun the delivery of the 'Moguls' during the 1930s, vintage machines such as this were consigned to the scrap heap. By the 1960s, three individualistic but excellent engines known as the 'Heavy Goods' were the sole survivors of the genre.

Bill Scott Collection

The Belfast and County Down Railway had four 0-6-0s. No.26, seen at Ballynickle between Comber and Ballygowan near the family farm of the photographer, has empty carriages for a later Orange special on 12th July 1931. The weekly notice containing instructions for these trains would remind those responsible that "ample van space is to be provided for band instruments etc". Adequate space seems to be available here.

William Robb

The Great Northern Railway was another company to appreciate the value of the 0-6-0. Here SG3 class No.6 of l920 is being oiled prior to her next turn of duty. This class incorporated the best design features of their time making them arguably the finest heavy goods engine to run in Ireland. Trains of seventy-five wagons were considered quite normal for these splendid machines.

Irwin Pryce collection

The final 0-6-0 to be built by any Irish railway was No.149, a UG class which was delivered to the Great Northern by Beyer Peacock in 1948. No.149, by then numbered No.49 by the Ulster Transport Authority, waits to leave Antrim for Belfast with the daily goods train in August 1960. These modestly sized engines confirmed the inherent virtues of the 0-6-0, handling goods and passenger trains all over the system. They had a considerable turn of speed, although the highest recorded speed of 67mph has been slightly exceeded by their older GS&WR rivals.

Irwin Pryce

Close agreement in major dimensions, nominal power and speed capacity was evident in Irish 0-6-0s by the turn of the 19th century. A representative locomotive of this period might have used steam at a pressure of 160 to 175 psi and had a narrow firebox between the frames. Cylinders of about 17in (diameter) by 24in (stroke) were fed with saturated steam by slide valves driven by Stephenson valve gear and were invariably inside due to simplicity of construction and loading gauge restrictions. A wheel diameter of about five feet was common and weights were in the range of 35 to 40 tons. The 101 class is as close to the typical goods and mixed traffic locomotive of the period as you can get.

Combined with conventional Victorian views on locomotive style, which dictated that low running plates and an absence of clutter were called for, even at the expense of convenience, this led to a family resemblance between the 0-6-0s of all the major Irish railways. Each company did of course have an individual approach to matters of cosmetic appearance and the enthusiast could identify this from a considerable distance.

None of this of course prevented railwaymen and enthusiasts developing a highly partisan view of the capabilities of their steeds and among those who remember the days of steam arguments will still develop at the drop of a hat! It would be fair to say that the humble 101 was universally respected and admired wherever it went, and that was literally from Derry to Kerry. Frank Dunlop, then Locomotive Inspector in Belfast once looked at 186 and said "Just look at that wee engine, look at the way she's put together, everything you want is there!"

Development

Throughout the 20th century the Irish 0-6-0 gradually increased in size and power, though the mould had been clearly set by existing designs. The type developed from the simple machines of the 1850s to its apogee in the powerful SG3s of the Great Northern. The last of the breed was not finally built until 1948, when the final batch of five UGs were turned out for the Great Northern.

In the original steam engine, the steam generated in the boiler is said to be 'saturated', in that, being in contact with boiling water, it contains moisture. As this steam passes through pipes and into the cylinders, expansion of the steam and contact with the cooler metal surfaces of these causes water droplets to form, which create a resistance to the moving pistons in the cylinders, with subsequent reduction of power and efficiency.

If one single development can be said to have caused a quantum leap in locomotive design it must have been the introduction of superheating. Essentially the wet steam in contact with the boiling water, at a temperature of 375 degrees Fahrenheit and at a pressure of say 175psi, is passed through a series of tubes in direct contact with combustion gases thus raising its temperature to as high as 600 degrees. The moisture in the wet steam is converted to yet more steam and, thanks to the high temperature achieved in the 'superheater', the steam does not fall below 'saturation' level until after it has been used in the cylinders. Thus the efficiency of the engine is improved through the reduction in condensation. The superheating of the steam also causes it to increase in volume, so giving more power for a given amount of original wet steam. This effectively increased the capability of a given size of boiler to generate more power.

The first effective superheater was developed by Wilhelm Schmidt in Germany in 1898 and in 1906 had been applied to both Lancashire and Yorkshire and Great Western Railway locomotives. Such was the effectiveness of the device that by 1910 few saturated locomotives were built anywhere. With superheated steam at about 650 degrees economies of 15%-25% in coal and 25%-35% in water consumption were attainable. For some railway companies, annual savings of tens of thousands of tons of coal were achieved, so superheating was applied to many existing designs and most new engines incorporated it.

However, the advantages of superheating were not obtained without cost, as beyond about 550 degrees difficulties were to be expected with the lubrication of slide valves and packings. Three main ways were open to designers to overcome the difficulties in applying superheating to an existing engine.

1) Retain the slide valves but use only a moderate degree of superheat.
2) Use a lower boiler pressure and apply superheat. This option clearly negated some of the advantages obtained in the first place, but did reduce boiler maintenance costs.
3) Apply high superheat, use piston valves and an adequate system of lubrication.

The third was the preferred option but involved major expenditure on new valves and cylinders and as the new layout usually meant raising the pitch of the boiler there were additional costs here. If, as in some designs, the frames were already weak then the additional power of which the engine would be capable could lead to problems.

George Glover on the Great Northern was an early advocate of superheating and all new engines built after 1913 were built with superheaters and piston valves. Older classes were gradually rebuilt with superheaters as boilers became due for renewal. After some attempts to combine superheating with slide valves, Glover went for extensive rebuilding with piston valves. The main exceptions being the small goods engines of the PGs and QGs classes which retained slide valves.

The GS&WR and its successor the Great Southern Railway were less convinced than the Great Northern of the value of high superheat and, no doubt with financial strictures, did not superheat any 101 until 1930. When the process began, Inchicore went for the first option with the 101s and probably got the balance just right. As boilers became due for replacement, the new Z type boiler with 12 superheater elements was used along with the existing slide valves. Most other classes on the Great Southern followed the pattern of combining moderate superheat with slide valves.

186 in her present state represents this stage of development, having been superheated in 1932, while her sister 184 remains in the unsuperheated form and is a precious link in the story of locomotive development.

The Third Century

Of all the 0-6-0s to run on Irish railways the two 101s in the care of the RPSI are the sole survivors of that hardy breed. With the restoration to working order of 186 a new generation will be given a unique insight into the world of the 19th century when she, and others like her, hauled their trains of small, unbraked, loose-coupled wagons round a railway system which reached hundreds of tiny stations now forgotten by the towns they served.

Curious onlookers will be fascinated by a machine where the elemental simplicity of its working is clearly visible and they will certainly notice the scant attention given to the comfort of the crew. The mechanically-minded may look at the well thought out design and sound construction of the engine and wonder at the skill of those who put it together over a hundred and twenty years ago. Others may simply ponder on just how well the engine still continues to do the job it was built for.

We can be grateful to those in the RPSI who by their efforts have made sure that at least one of these remarkable survivors will continue to be seen at the head of a train in the 21st century.

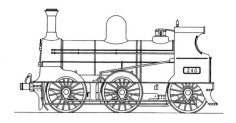

A classic scene captured at Tullow on 17 June 1939, shows two of McDonnell's most celebrated locomotive types. No.59, of his '60' class originally built to haul the GS&WR's mainline passenger services, is on the 4.15pm passenger train to Sallins, while 132 deals with the goods. She is making up an interesting goods train, the second wagon of which is an open cattle wagon, while a couple of 'convertible' wagons are also visible.

Courtesy the Stephenson Locomotive Society

The engine which gave the class its name, 101, was actually the 78th member to go into service. She is seen at Inchicore where she was built in 1882, the last year of McDonnell's reign. When built, she was one of the first to have a steel boiler, but one of the last to have been fitted with a handbrake only. McDonnell's successor, John Aspinall, began fitting vacuum brakes to the entire class, a task completed in 1887 after he had moved on to greater things as CME of the Lancashire and Yorkshire Railway. Her 4' 4" boiler dates this scene before 1942, when she received a 'Z' type.

Lance King Collection

Alexander McDonnell (1829 -1904)

A Profile by K A Murray

Alexander McDonnell was, distinctively, an Irishman who did his best work in Ireland; a doctor's son, born in Dublin in 1829, he went to Trinity College in 1847, taking his M.A. degree in 1852. He then went to learn his chosen profession in England and, after his pupilship, worked under Charles Liddell on railway building in the West of England and Wales. But he tended towards the mechanical side of engineering and in 1857, at the age of 28, became the Locomotive Superintendent of the Newport, Abergavenny & Hereford Rly., having 26 engines to keep in order. When that line became part of the West Midland Rly., McDonnell stayed on for a short time but, in 1862, went to Eastern Europe to set up the locomotive department of the Danube & Black Sea Rly. This experience did not, surely, come amiss; his life was to take on a quite definite locomotive aspect very soon, for early in 1864 he came to Inchicore Works.

Alexander McDonnell, M.A., M.I.Mech.E.
1829 - 1904
Courtesy Coras Iompair Eireann

In the *IRRS Journal* No.12 Mr RN Clements has described the state of things which prevailed at Inchicore before McDonnell loomed up. From 1851, George Miller had held the posts of Civil and Locomotive Engineer, but engine matters would seem to have been left mainly to John Wakefield, the Running Superintendent. Wakefield left after him the legendary impression of a man not burdened with technical knowledge, but who could push the work along by robust personality. As a result, the Inchicore workers were possibly inclined to accept more easily whatever forceful treatment might result from a new man at the top. Certainly, innovations were necessary; the original fleet of engines, to makers' designs and good enough for their time, had been enlarged slowly with Inchicore additions and the resulting flock was a mixture. It was time that the effect of a single mind should be perceived.

Miller died in office in January 1864 and the civil and loco departments were separated, McDonnell taking charge of the engines within a month or so. There is a legend that a kinship with the Chairman of the GS&WR, Sir Edward M'Donnel, led to his getting the job, but a little consideration of dates, etc., shows that the story is probably groundless; but it may reflect some abiding tradition of the coming of McDonnell to Inchicore.

To design new engines to replace the mixed bag he inherited was beyond McDonnell's powers, but he *was* able to organise the workshop facilities so as to get the best from them, and to get from somewhere something which would serve as a pattern for locomotive practice on the GS&WR. There can be little doubt that he acted rightly when he obtained first a design for a simple and strong goods engine. Given that, in sufficient numbers, he could play his part in keeping the trains moving. The design he got was by Charles Beyer (who had learned his business with Sharps of Manchester) and its Sharp/Beyer pedigree was perfect.

Once the good seed was sown McDonnell had only to adapt, although it is not in his passenger classes that the design is sharply apparent all through. However, he had begun well and given Directors and men engines which were reliable and up to their duty. For years, indeed, economy laid down that whatever materials could be salved out of broken-up engines should be re-used in 'new' ones. Time, as was natural, got rid of these adapted parts, and the locomotive stock became standard in its details, to the Company's benefit.

But we should not think that the GS&WR attained to a dull, if profitable, sameness of locomotive aspects. In fact, McDonnell combined with his bent for order an awareness of what was going on around him. He brought into use in 1869-70 the first single-boilered 'Fairlie' engines, and although the pattern was not perpetuated, it gave him a basis for a useful class of tank engines, built largely by him and his successor. He put on rails the first 0-6-4T engines, for heavy goods-assisting jobs; he imported from America the principle of the swing-link bogie, later used everywhere; he experimented in burning peat fuel in locomotives; he tried steel for fireboxes; and made other trials of whatever seemed likely to yield good results. He was certainly no hide-bound slave to the accepted way of doing things.

Inchicore in his time must have been capable of providing locomotive power at the lowest cost attainable, for McDonnell reorganised the place, and got a great deal more work out of the shops. In little things he showed practical sense; where brass had been used (in bushes of side-rods, for instance) he put in cast iron - it was not so cheap to machine, but was less attractive to the light-fingered. Things like this were not due to a desire for economy; his principle was to use the best material in hand, and when the material lasted longer, it was really the cheapest - a simple and logical approach. Also, he could show the effect of his practice, for he insisted from the start on the keeping of accurate and detailed accounts and every pound spent could be shown to have its due results - when an Irishman really gets down to watching the money, there is no better man.

In 1882 McDonnell went away to England to take charge of the locomotives of the North Eastern Railway. His sad story in that field is, fortunately, not our business now; again, he took over a beggar's-bag of engines and once more tried to get things in order. But, the men he had to work with were less amenable than those he had tackled at Inchicore, and his NER career was short and stormy. He did not again venture on railway service, but seems to have been rather more concerned with armaments. He remained much respected in his profession, and was freely consulted by his colleagues and others who wanted counsel of value on technical matters.

Thus he lived on, until he was 75. In December 1904, not well, he was travelling to Ireland for his brother's funeral, and was taken ill at Rugby. Persisting in his journey, he died in the Holyhead Railway Hotel on 4 December and he is buried at Kilsharvan in Co. Meath. Except among a few of his brethren in his profession, his passing was little regarded; McDonnell had outlived most of his fame.

Alexander McDonnell deserves, even so late as now, honour for doing well the task which came to his hands so long ago. The men who drew the design, the men who made the metal into the engines, the men who set them on the rails and watched them for the first time ascend to Clondalkin with their trains of boxy little wagons - none of these could have dreamed of the kind of world which would surround the survivors of the class when a century would have gone by.

A London and North Western Railway 'DX' class, attributed to John Ramsbottom, but with decided Beyer Peacock features. There are some undoubted similarities to the 101 class, although Irish drivers must have been thankful to have been given some sort of cab roof!

Michael Bentley Collection

Peter Rowledge has added the following information, having gained access to other sources after 1966, when Bob Clements wrote the original paper.

Bob makes reference to the apparent likeness between the 101 and the L&NWR 'DX' class. Beyer Peacock produced many examples of straightforward soundly built inside-cylinder 0-6-0 goods engines before the GS&WR placed an order for four in March 1866 and McDonnell would have been familiar with very similar engines supplied to the Danube & Black Sea Railway in 1859-62. In the case of one order for that railway, four were diverted to the London & North Western Railway in 1859 and became Nos. 199 and 200 (Northern Division) and 321 and 322 (Southern Division); it seems reasonable to believe that these four became the pattern for the famous 'DX' class of that railway, which exceeded in number all other classes in Britain. The 101 class, destined to become the largest in Ireland, was likewise part of this large family, born on the drawing office tables in Manchester.

An examination of the dimensions shows significant differences, but also shows a Beyer Peacock family likeness. The dimensions for the Danube & Black Sea locomotives, which would have been familiar to McDonnell, are also quoted. These and those for the GS&WR engines are taken from Beyer Peacock records. *From a table produced by Peter Rowledge*

	Danube & Black Sea Railway	GS& WR 101 class	L&NWR 'DX'class
Cylinders	16in. x 24in.	17in. x 24in.	17in. x 24in.
Coupled wheels dia.	5ft. 0in.	5ft. 1½in.	5ft. 2in.
Wheelbase	6ft. 9in. + 7ft. 1in.	7ft. 3in. + 8ft. 3in.	7ft. 3in. + 8ft. 3in.
Boiler Barrel	3ft. 11in. x 10ft. 0in.	4ft. 0in. x 9ft. 10in.	4ft. 2in. x 10ft. 6in.
Tubes No./dia.	168 x 2in.	174 x 2in.	190 x 1¾in.
Heating surface: tubes firebox	927 sq. ft. 82 sq. ft.	922 sq. ft. 95 sq. ft.	1,002 sq. ft. 92 sq. ft.
Grate area	14 sq. ft.	19½ sq. ft.	15 sq. ft.
Boiler pressure	Not quoted	140 p.s.i.	120 p.s.i.
Weight	25 tons 3 cwt.	32 tons 12 cwt.	27 tons 0 cwt.

The 101 Class

Evolution and History

By R N Clements

In the original article, published in 1949 in the S.L.S. Journal, of which this is a much-revised version, I suggested that the 101 class had stood the test of time better than any other type in the history of the steam locomotive. At that time I was not aware that *all* the standard 0-6-0 engines of the Northern Railway of Spain, of which 86 were built from 1859 to 1864, were still in service, with the sole exception of four engines sold in 1873. Some of them, and a number of the Norte 0-8-0 engines of 1864, as well as quite a few centenarians on other Spanish lines, worked on for a few years after the last of the 101 class had been withdrawn from company service. So, as far as simple longevity in service is concerned, our engines cannot rival these. On the other hand, the Spanish engines had been, for some years, mainly confined to pilot duties. The real distinction of the 101 class is that over 90 years after their introduction they were still a *standard* engine, used on all classes of traffic, including much passenger work at relatively high speeds; also that for no less than 87 years, from 1873 to 1960, they were the most numerous class in the country. There can be little doubt that, but for dieselisation, they would still retain these two distinctions, and both, I believe, are quite unique in the history of the steam locomotive.

It has often been suggested that the design derived from Ramsbottom's 'DX' engines for the LNWR, but I am fully satisfied that this was not so, and that they were a pure Beyer Peacock engine. Although the size of cylinders, wheels and wheelbase were the same as the DX, and there was a certain external likeness, comparison of the remaining proportions of the engines, and of constructional and mechanical details, shows that the two classes differed at almost every point. Very significant is what Richard Cronin told Mr KA Murray many years ago (and he had been on the GS&WR in McDonnell's time) that when McDonnell came to Inchicore, being primarily a civil rather than a mechanical engineer, he got Beyer Peacock to design a goods engine for him. More conclusive still is the earliest 101 class general arrangement drawing in Inchicore, which shows the engines exactly as first built, save only the cab, which has a roof the full length of the footplate supported by corner pillars, but with no side sheets. Now this was exactly the type of cab used on engines supplied by Beyer Peacock to the 5' 3" gauge

Victorian Railways; however, none of the Victorian engines correspond to the 101 class, for those of 1859, with inside frames, were much smaller, whilst an 1865 batch, of roughly 101 size, had outside frames. Still, I have no doubt that this was the drawing submitted by Beyer to McDonnell for his approval; whether it was one already submitted to Victoria as an alternative to the outside frame design, or whether Beyer's draughtsmen just copied the cab from a drawing of the Australian engines, we cannot now tell. But the design was accepted by McDonnell with no alteration, save for the cab, which was made shorter in the roof but with side-sheets. There is just one possible slight connection with the DX. McDonnell's works manager, John C Park[1], had been at Longsight under Ramsbottom when the first DX was built there. It could be that on his advice McDonnell might have said to Beyer "Let the engine be an improved DX", but, if so, it was improved out of all recognition.

So the first completely new engines of the class were 147-150, delivered by Beyer Peacock in May and June 1867. They had the following dimensions:- cylinders 17" x 24", wheels 5' 1¼" diam., boiler 4' 0" diam. x 9' 10" barrel, pitched at 6' 8" and with 140 lbs. pressure, firebox casing 5' 7" x 4' 6", grate area 19.5 sq. ft., 174 tubes 2" diam., heating surface 102 + 919 sq. ft. They were followed by four identical engines by Beyer in 1868. Comment on other details of the engines will be found in the comparisons of the Southern and Midland engines.

That was 1867, yet we celebrated the centenary of the class in 1966. McDonnell wasted nothing he could use, and on 30 June 1866 a rebuilt engine, No.112, left the shops - not yet a standard goods engine but destined, in the course of time, to become one. It is not easy to say how far McDonnell, at this stage, was consciously aiming at his future standard engine. Iron and copper plates for the boilers of the rebuilds were ordered in the autumn of 1865, five months before the Board authorised him to get tenders for new engines. Yet it is quite possible that he may already have been in touch with Beyer Peacock, so as to decide the type of engine he thought suitable before applying to the Board to sanction them. Thus the Beyer drawing may already have been at Inchicore when those for the rebuilds were made.

At any rate, this 0-6-0 No.112 had started life in 1850 as a 0-4-2 (No.53) by Rothwell, with cylinders 16" x 24", coupled wheels 5' 0" diam., wheelbase 7' 2¾" + 6' 9½", boiler 4' 0" x 10' 11½", and firebox casing 4' 3" x 4' 3". In the rebuilt 112, only the boiler, firebox and trailing wheels and axles were new, all other parts coming from the old engine, though not necessarily original; thus the cylinders dated from 1859 and the crank axle from 1860. The new boiler was probably of the same dimensions as the original (but with wider firebox), or it may have been like that of 118 (see below); the old smokebox was retained. After running 136,000 miles in this form, the engine went into the shops in February 1872 and came out nine months later with

112 which began the 101 class story in 1866. The details to be seen in the photograph seem to match those known for the two original engines as built, so we can be fairly sure that the photograph was taken before 1889 when she received a new boiler. Although she did receive a 4' 4" boiler around 1911, she was an early casualty in 1929. 113, also built at Inchicore from an old 0-4-2 in 1866, succumbed in 1930 and seems to have eluded the camera.

Locomotive and General Railway Publishing Co./NRM

148 was the second Beyer Peacock engine and is here seen in immaculate condition, after 1892 when she received her second boiler. By now she had also been fitted with engine brakes and a directly connected reversing screw instead of the old Ramsbottom arrangement. The technically-minded may find it rewarding to compare this shot with that of 154, taken when she was built.

Real Photographs/NRM

The Beyer Peacock quartet of 1868 all enjoyed long useful lives.

In 1928, 151 sits at Inchicore beside one of her 'improved' sisters. 151 was built with lever reverse, but changed to Coey's pattern of screw reverse with directly connected rod in 1891. Curiously the GS&WR favoured screw reverse rather than the lever reverse used on many lines. A day's work shunting, with constant changes of direction (six and a half turns each time), might have convinced the designer of the advantages of a lever. 151 was superheated as late as 1950.

Kelland Collection 23061, courtesy the Bournemouth Railway Club

From the long rake of cattle wagons behind her, 152 appears to be making up a fair special. She saw 91 years of service as a saturated engine.

Simmons, IRRS collection

153 was another of the batch from Beyer Peacock in 1868. In this view of Waterford in 1911 the immaculate condition of both passenger and goods engines is notable. The lavish provision of labour which made this possible could not withstand the harsh economic pressures the railways found themselves in from the 1920s on. In 1929 the Great Southern sacked drivers over 60, many junior men were reduced in grade and large numbers of cleaners found themselves jobless.

Kelland Collection, courtesy the Bournemouth Railway Club

A typical Beyer Peacock product of the time, with sloping smokebox, tapered chimney and the maker's plate on the splasher. The records show 154's life with the GS&WR beginning in March 1868, but the builder's plate clearly states 1867! As the plate simply states that 'Beyer, Peacock & Co. Manchester' were the builders, the puzzle may simply be answered by the possibility that they had some of the previous year's plates left over and were saving money! The photograph is that held in the Beyer Peacock archives and has all the appearance of a Builder's Photograph, suggesting that it was taken in the year 154 was built. However, the livery carried here is more ornate than that previously thought to be in use at that time (see page 40). Instead it appears to be that believed to date from around 1873 - olive green, with black bands lined by a light green line each side, with a thin red line in between. This photograph suggests that this new livery was carried earlier than previously thought. 154 was to enjoy a long life until 1962 and carried three different boilers.

F Moore

standard frames, cylinders (17"), wheels and axles, but with the boiler still non-standard as to length of barrel and firebox. This was finally replaced by a standard boiler in 1892, bringing the engine completely into line with the rest of the class. The official building date was always 1866, though actually after 1892 there was nothing dating from earlier than 1872.

No.113 (ex Rothwell's 54 of 1850) was similarly rebuilt in December 1866, but in this case the cylinders were new and perhaps 17" diam. This engine is recorded as getting new frames and motion in December 1872, and new wheels in 1874: finally, a standard boiler was fitted in 1889. No.118, turned out in May 1867, had originally been an 0-4-2 engine built at Inchicore in 1852 as No. 58, having 15" x 24" cylinders, 5' 0" coupled wheels, wheelbase 8' 3½" + 6' 10½", boiler 4' 0" x 11' 7", and firebox casing 4' 3" x 4' 6". The new boiler was shorter than the original, being 4' 0" x 11' 0" with 4' 8" firebox casing, and the 17" cylinders were new. In this case new frames were provided in October 1870 (after 93,000 miles), standard except at the front, where retention of the old motion involved the cylinders being set 3" further forward than the normal position. This engine was scrapped in 1890, still with the old Wakefield motion and non-standard boiler.

Two completely new engines, 103 and 111, were built at Inchicore in 1868, differing only very slightly from Beyer's engines. The sandboxes were removed from below the top framing and put inside the smokebox, with a view to keeping the sand dry; the dome was jointed towards the top instead of at the bottom and the arc of the cab side-sheets was altered to what was to be Inchicore's standard shape. The odd thing about these engines is that 103 is shown as having cylinders only 15" diam. till replaced by 17" ones in 1870: no figure is given for the original cylinders of 111, but as cylinders for both were ordered at the same time from Beyer Peacock, they were probably the same. Nos. 105 and 110 of 1868 were similar, except that they had standard 17" cylinders.

The next four engines, 114 and 115 of 1868 and 155-6 of 1871 had the firebox casing only 5' 1" long, and the wheelbase at the trailing end was correspondingly reduced by 6". Firebox heating surface was only 86 sq.ft. The cylinders, at first, were only 16" diam., later replaced by the successively standard 17" and 18" ones. The boiler centre line was raised to 6' 8¾" and the motion plate no longer attached to a bracket on the underside of the boiler barrel, as it had so far been. Three of these were scrapped unchanged, but 156 (after 6 years as the only engine retaining the 4ft. boiler) got new frames in 1936. The drawing of 114-5 shows plain axle-boxes, but that of the rebuilt 118, dated April 1870, shows adjusting wedges fitted, as remained standard practice till their use was abandoned, probably in the 1920s.

It is likely (though not certain) that the other engines built in 1871 were the first to have what was to be the standard firebox for 30 years - the same length as the last, but with a deeper grate, flat instead of sloping, giving a

156 is seen at Limerick in 1930, still carrying her second 4ft. boiler. She was one of the engines built in 1871 with a shorter firebox and in 1889, when she received her second 4ft. boiler, her 17" cylinders were replaced by 18" ones. This boiler was to last her for 46 years, so that she had the double distinction of being the last engine in the class to retain this type and the only one to go straight from the 4ft. boiler to a 'Z' type.

Real Photographs/NRM

159, seen here at Limerick, was an Inchicore engine dating from 1871, when she received an out-sourced boiler from the Worcester Engine Company. She received a 'Z' boiler in 1933, only to be scrapped in 1949. Inchicore was noted for careful housekeeping and the boiler would no doubt have been used in another engine.

Locomotive and General Railway Publishing Co./NRM

heating surface of 101½ sq.ft. , very little less than the original Beyer box, though the grate area came down to 17½ sq.ft. Four engines of 1871 were unusual in having the boilers bought complete from outside, instead of being made at Inchicore; those of 159-60 came from the Worcester Engine Co., and of 161-2 from the Yorkshire Engine Co. Also till 1871, probably, McDonnell lightened the frames, which he had already been making only 1" thick instead of Beyer's 1⅛" by also reducing their depth, except at the motion plate.

It was probably in 1871 or 1872 that screw reverse replaced the lever of the earlier engines; it had already been used for several years on passenger engines. Several other changes were made about 1871-3, but cannot be exactly dated. One is only known for Sharp's six engines of 1872-3, though it may have applied to some others of the same date; this was the use of laminated trailing springs instead of volute, but the standard volute springs later replaced them. These, too, were the last engines to have the sandboxes inside the smokeboxes, as they were now combined with the leading splashers and the older engines altered to this arrangement.

By 1873 the eccentric rods were coupled to the top and bottom, instead of the back, of the expansion link. Till 1873 the chimneys, of Beyer's copper-top design, were bought outside. Then, for a few years, similar built-up chimneys (but without the copper-top) were made at Inchicore; these, in turn, soon gave way to cast-iron ones, still of the old Beyer shape, tapering inwards to the top. The Beyer engines of 1867-8 had rectangular brass numberplates attached to the cab side-sheets, but for some years thereafter cut-out brass figures were attached to the side of the smokebox. These, too, disappeared along with the copper-topped chimneys, for the first drawing of the familiar Inchicore numberplate is dated May 1873; at first it was (as in later days) made of cast iron, but before long it was changed to white metal.

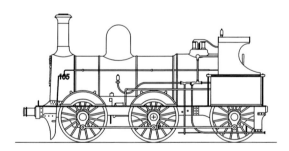

105 as originally built with number on smokebox

Patrick O'Sullivan 2005

This year, too, saw a new tube arrangement which was to be standard for 20 years. On seeing the change, one first thinks of steaming troubles. However, the provision of 1¾" tubes in 168 and 1½" in 167, instead of the 2" hitherto standard, may show that the real motive was economy, smaller tubes

163, seen here at Cork, was built by Sharp Stewart in 1872. The two pipes along the boiler come from the large and small vacuum ejectors described by Jack O'Neill. The engine had two whistles, one of which was used for 'crowing' to staff on the ground during shunting.

Real Photographs/NRM

167 spent part of her later career at Waterford, but is seen shunting at Killarney on 15 April 1955. She was the subject of an unsuccessful experiment with $1^1/_2$" tubes when built in 1873.

Henry Casserley

being cheaper in spite of the greater number required. No doubt 167 was found not to steam well, so the £17 saved on a set of 1½" tubes over the cost of 1¾" ones was a false economy.

In July 1874 a major change was made by the increase of the cylinder diameter from 17" to 18", the steam ports being increased at the same time from 1⅜" to 1½". Till 1885, however, most engines requiring new cylinders had 17" ones fitted. It may well have been thought that the 1⅜" ports would have been too small for the 18" cylinder, and the use of 1½" ports would, of course, involve altering the eccentrics which operated the valves. It can be assumed that all 17" engines not noted in the statistics table as altered retained the smaller cylinders to the end of 1891; after that date details are no longer available, but ultimately all engines got 18" cylinders. It was probably at the same time as 18" cylinders were introduced that the pressure was raised from 140 to 150 lbs., but the exact date is unknown.

In March 1875 JAF Aspinall arrived from Crewe to succeed Park as Works Manager. McDonnell being mainly interested in administration and economics, and rarely visiting the drawing office, the development of the 101 class during the following years seems mainly to have been in Aspinall's hands. The first change was the standardisation of cast-iron, instead of wrought-iron, wheels in 1877 (not, as usually stated, in 1882). Their introduction, however, had been earlier than this for 3' 6" and 4' 6" wheels, and there had been one isolated application to the 101 class, cast-iron wheels having been put under 113 in September 1874.

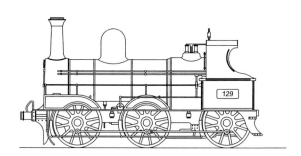

GS&WR No.129 with cast-iron wheels.
Patrick O'Sullivan 2005

Next, and this we may be certain was due to Aspinall, we have the 1878 batch, 143-146, fitted new with the simple vacuum brake, though at first this move was not followed up. The next vacuum engine was 188 of 1882, specially fitted on account of being sent (with a carriage) to the Dublin Exhibition of that year in Rutland (now Parnell) Square. Then came more handbrakes-only before three old engines got vacuum equipment, 183 in 1883, 139 and 141 in 1884. In 1885 all new engines were fitted, and the

28

addition of vacuum brakes to the whole class was completed in 1887. I have suggested the Board's unwillingness to provide money as the reason for delay, but there may have been another factor. It is noticeable that immediately after McDonnell's departure at the end of 1882 progress began to be made: probably as soon as Aspinall, with his greater interest in vacuum brakes, was officially appointed Locomotive Superintendent and so with direct access to the Board, he pushed the matter harder than his former chief had done.

A cheery wave from fireman Jim Murphy as tidy-looking superheated 144 passes the photographer at Rathpeacon on the outskirts of Cork. The make up of the train with a 'metal van' next to the engine suggests a relief to the Rosslare Express which usually carried fish for export from Lismore. The crew usually dined well that evening.

By the time she was built at Inchicore in 1878, Aspinall was the works manager and probably his influence caused her to be one of the first of the class to be built new with the simple vacuum brake. She was a fairly early casualty, being withdrawn in 1954.

Kelland Collection 23060, courtesy the Bournemouth Railway Club

Turning back to 1879, up-to-date drawings were made of various parts, but only the frames showed any real change, being made almost the same as the Beyer frames of 1867, but ½" deeper and still only 1" thick instead of 1⅛". Though this drawing (which shows also the bracket for the engine brake shaft) is dated March 1879, it was not till just three years later that such frames appeared, and these were iron, though previously a batch of the lighter type McDonnell frames had been made of steel.

Steel plates for boilers had been introduced in 1881 and remained standard; we cannot tell whether it was then or a little later that pressure was raised to 160 lbs. In 1882 provision of new boilers for some of the older engines began; it is surprising how few of the old iron boilers were provided with new fireboxes, though four of the large Beyer fireboxes were renewed to the original size. From 1882 a spiral spring was used to balance the weight of the links, in place of the counter-weight on the weighbar shaft, and about the same time steel buffer plates replaced the old 6" oak beams. Steel frames (of the improved type) finally became standard in 1885; this, no doubt, would have happened sooner, but there had been no new engines built since the end of 1882. By 1885, when a second engine, 133, was exhibited in Dublin, there were 81 engines in service.

In 1886-90 seven old engines, with an average mileage of 428,000, were broken up and replaced by new ones in 1889-91. Even apart from the few items known, a certain amount of other old material must have gone into these, so one's faith in the accounting system is rather shaken by finding them shown to cost only 6% less than the new engines of 1888. They included two modifications made by HA Ivatt, who had succeeded Aspinall in 1886. The cabs were lengthened at the *front* only, bringing the front corner level with the rectangular plate below, and (except 103, 147 and 149) they had the improved footsteps introduced with the 1888 batch. Nos. 103, 114 and 149, as also 129 (built with them), had the standard 185 tubes, but only 139 of these were of the usual brass, the other 46 being of copper-coated steel.

In March 1891 Ivatt experimentally converted 165 to a two-cylinder compound. The left-hand cylinder was replaced by a low-pressure one 26" diam., the frames being suitably strengthened at the front and the valves placed over the cylinders. As with the passenger compound (No. 93), the number of tubes was reduced, in this case to 165. Writing in 1917, Joynt[2] (who had been in the drawing office at Inchicore for much of the period while the 101s were being built) described 165 as economical in coal and water, though 15 years later, telling of his own experience on her on the Nenagh goods, he stated the exact opposite. Both accounts agree that she was weaker than the simple engines, but better than the passenger compound. From the conversion of 93 after three years experience of 165, it seems that the latter must have been thought to show, at least, some promise. A cracked cylinder led to her reconversion to simple in 1896.

Nos. 105 and 116, built in 1896 just after Robert Coey had succeeded Ivatt, were the first new engines to have the directly connected reversing screw instead of the old Ramsbottom arrangement. The only engines altered to this pattern were 148 and 151-4, obviously not altered from lever to screw till after 1891, the others having been altered earlier; 157-8 and 143-4, of which the former pair might possibly have had levers originally, but the latter, definitely built with screw, I cannot explain. The type of wheel used for these engines is not known. There is also uncertainty as to their tube arrangement, for the date of change to 173 tubes (standard thereafter) was April 1896, by which time their boilers may have been finished.

Coey's eight engines of 1898-9 had all these details, with the addition of cast-steel wheels with balance weights, single slidebars and marine big-ends.

Experimentally converted to compound working, 165 never received a 'Z' boiler and was withdrawn in 1945. On 19 May 1939 she called at Palace East with the 3.15pm 'Mail' from Waterford to Macmine Junction, where the train connected into the 2.55pm ex Harcourt Street to Wexford. The open door in the fine clerestory coach and the poses of the railway staff suggest that they are waiting for the photographer to take his shot and rejoin the train!

Charles Friel Collection

116, built in 1896, was the second of Coey's 101s. Seen here at Inchicore, she received a 4' 4" boiler after about ten years and was to retain one until her withdrawal in 1964. Boilers would have been rotated through the locomotives of the class over time, so that in the course of her life an engine would carry several different ones. The more modern looking, vertically fronted smoke-box with a dished door, as carried by 116 here, dates from after 1922 and must have been a boon for enginemen, used to struggling to keep the archaic double-doored variety airtight. The tender has had 'rails', in this case a solid plate, added to increase coal capacity.

John Edgington

When Coey built her in 1898, 192 was one of the last engines to receive the old four foot boiler. She appears to have been built without a dedicated tender and like many of the class would simply have inherited a spare one from another locomotive. She got her first 4' 4" boiler ten years later, but had to wait until 1950 to be superheated, in which form the march of progress overtook her quickly and she was withdrawn in 1956.

Real Photographs/NRM

The front of the cab in this batch was returned to the normal position, but the roof was extended 6" at the rear and the curve of the side-sheets altered to give better protection. Though these were the last engines built new with them, construction of 4 ft. boilers for rebuilding continued until September 1900.

The new standard goods boiler first appeared early in 1901 on the four 217 class 0-6-0T engines; in October 1901 one was put in 124. It was 4' 3" (front ring) and 4' 4" diam. (rear ring, which by convention is usually quoted as the boiler diameter) and the firebox casing was 5' 7" long with a flat grate of 19.3 sq.ft. area. Heating surface with 200 tubes was 116 + 925 sq. ft., but the number of tubes was later reduced to 194. Centre-line was 6' 10⅞" above the rails, and pressure unchanged at 160 lbs.

This boiler was used for the last of the 101 class, 12 engines built in 1902-3. These included some further minor alterations: the sandboxes were enlarged, a footstep (later removed) was provided for access to the motion, and though the upper part of the cab was the same as in 192-9, the rectangular lower panel was suppressed. Some had Crosby pop safety valves when new, and they were the last engines built with the old cast-iron chimney.

For nearly 30 years then, change was confined to bringing the engines gradually up to date. The 4' 4" boiler replaced the 4ft. one on all but the short-frame engines 115 and 155. They were made at Inchicore, with the exception

232 was one of Coey's final 1903 batch of the class, seen here, little changed, at her birthplace in 1930. Note the Coey features of enlarged sandboxes and the straight fronted cab, with its partial splasher over the rear driving wheel. She retains her handsome, tapered cast-iron chimney. Her 4' 4" boiler lasted throughout her sixty years.

Real Photographs/NRM

Coey's last dozen members of the class were built with the then new 4' 4" boiler and remarkably only four were ever superheated. None of the 1902 quartet was ever modified apart from the smokebox and all succumbed by 1957. 241 is at Inchicore shed, shortly before withdrawal.

L Marshall

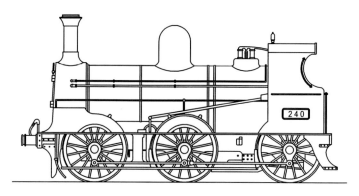

GS&WR No.240 as built by Coey.

Patrick O'Sullivan 2005

of eight from the Vulcan Foundry in 1903-4 and fifteen from Robert Stephenson in 1921. After 1905, the first 4' 4" boiler put in an engine was often a second-hand one, and in these cases it is only possible to give approximate dates. The last 4 ft. boiler (except for the short-frame engines) disappeared in 1927-8. Cast-steel wheels replaced cast-iron and wrought-iron. Built-up chimneys became universal and cab roofs and side-sheets were extended, the roofs being steel instead of timber. Smokeboxes with vertical front and circular door date from 1922 and no doubt the few boilers made after this time had them. A few additional 101 class boilers were required after the Amalgamation for reboilering DSER 2-4-2Ts.

The Belpaire superheated 'Z' boiler introduced in 1930 was, at first, the same as the 4' 4" saturated boiler in all overall dimensions and, despite appearances, it was pitched at the same height. The tube arrangement was 12 superheater flues $5^{1}/_{4}$" diam. and 107 tubes $1^{3}/_{4}$" diam. After the first few boilers had been made, the foundation ring was widened from $2^{1}/_{2}$" to 3" reducing the grate area to $18^{3}/_{4}$ sq.ft. The heating surface was then $112 + 662 + 112$ sq.ft. (firebox, tubes and superheater). In many cases new frames were provided for the superheated engines.

The only other point to be mentioned is the conversion of some engines for oil-burning in 1947-8. These were 102, 107, 110, 138, 140, 149, 153, 160, 166, 171, 182, 185, 198, 255 and 256, all superheated. All had the Inchicore type of Weir burner except 185 which was experimentally fitted with Laidlaw-Drew apparatus. A sudden improvement in the coal situation led to all being reconverted by June 1948. Further experiments with oil were made in 1954 when 197 was fitted with an improved type of Laidlaw-Drew burner.

I have not wasted space quoting weights, nominal figures often being so

197 was one of the first of the class to receive the new 'Z' boiler and is seen in 1954 at Inchicore, when she had been experimentally fitted with an improved type of Laidlaw-Drew oil-burner. The exercise does not seem to have warranted further conversions, especially as by this time the decision to dieselise had been taken.

Charles Friel Collection

Here we see 255 in oil-burning guise at Inchicore in 1948. Note the fire extinguisher! The coal available at the time was so poor that journeys were punctuated by long and frequent stops for fire cleaning, or 'baling out', which had become a feature of almost every journey. The white circle was intended to let signalmen know that they could confidently give the engine a clear path.

Henry Casserley

far from reality, but it is worth noting that the standard 101 class of the 1870s was given as weighing about $30\frac{1}{4}$ tons, while the final superheated version was about $37\frac{3}{4}$ tons.

Tenders of all engines to 1898 were of the 1,864 gallon Beyer Peacock design. Comparison of tender with engine dates shows that they generally corresponded, but that 13 engines built between 1866 and 1875 must have run for some time with old tenders. The dates when corresponding new tenders were built are: 1875, 157; 1880, 110 and 146; 1881, 112-3, 142, 148-9; 1882, 105, 111 and 150; 1887, 103; and 1890, 118. It will be noted that these include the Beyer engines of 1867, with which no tenders were supplied (though they were in 1868). The tenders for 163-6 by Sharp were made at Inchicore, but at the same time as the engines. There were no tenders numbered 116 or 192-3, and those numbered 194-9 in 1899 were of the 3,345 gallon type, being the first built of this design. These, however, were almost certainly put straight behind passenger engines, releasing small tenders for the 101 class. No new tenders can be traced for the engines of 1902-3, which no doubt got spare 1,800 gallon ones. As well as the 2,730 and 3,345 gallon tenders put behind the 101 class in later years, one spare MGWR 3,000 gallon tender was altered in 1938 to run with them. There was also one 1,800 gallon tender rebuilt with a 2,150 gallon tank.

122 is seen, fully lined out, in the Kingsbridge goods yard early in the twentieth century, after she received her 4' 4" boiler. She is remarkable here in having steel wheels on her driving (centre) axle and 'H' section cast-iron wheels on the others. Coey had introduced cast-steel wheels in 1898. The fine lines of the class and the well-matched 1,864 gallon tender are well in evidence.

Sean Kennedy Collection

143 and a sister engine, both dwarfed by their 3,345 gallon tenders, head a Race Special past Inchicore works in the 1950s. A train of this size might have benefitted from a larger locomotive, but of course once off the main line (to Naas, or into The Curragh siding) a light axleload was essential.

Kelland Collection 23059, courtesy the Bournemouth Railway Club

105, coupled to a 2,730 gallon tender, shunts oil wagons at the west end of Tralee station on 11 June 1958. The layout here was similar to many GS&WR stations, with one platform only and a run-round encompassed by a short overall roof.

A E Bennett

There were 119 101 class engines on the GS&WR but 121 altogether in Ireland, for Beyer Peacock supplied two to the Dublin & Belfast Junction Railway in 1872, absolutely identical with the first batch for Inchicore. They were the DBJ Nos. 21 and 22, later GNR Nos. 40 and 41.

Notes

[1] John Carter Park was works manager at Inchicore from 1865 until he moved to the North London Railway as locomotive superintendent in 1875. He remained at Bow Works of the NLR until retirement in 1893 and produced 4-4-0 tank locomotives for passenger work and 0-6-0 tanks for goods. One of his engines, No.76, an 0-6-0T built at Bow in 1880, is being returned to steam on the Bluebell Railway in Sussex. Like most railway engineers of the Victorian period, he had a remarkably diverse career which began in Italy, where he served his engineering pupilage, and included service as an officer in the Sardinian navy during the Crimean War. It was after this that he worked with Ramsbottom at Lonsight, followed by a superintendent role for five years in Canada before his move to Ireland.

To separate him from James Crawford Park, who became mechanical engineer of the newly unified GNR(I) in 1876, John is usually known to railway history as 'JC (North London) Park'!

[2] Ernest Edwin Joynt (Eamon de Siunta) was born in 1874 in Ballina, Co. Mayo, was educated at Methodist College, Belfast (1888-1892) and became chief draughtsman at Inchicore. After railway service he became Principal of Bolton St. Technical School in Dublin. He wrote a notable series of articles on Irish locomotive matters in the Railway Magazine and the Locomotive Railway Carriage and Wagon Review in the 1930s. He is also noted for translating *'Pilgrim's Progress'* into Irish.

Barely recognisable as a 101, but hidden under all that classic Great Northern apparel is a rebuilt ex-Dublin and Belfast Junction Railway No.21, built by Beyer Peacock to the same design in 1872. She was rebuilt twice by the GNR(I) in 1889 and 1913 and was withdrawn in 1937. As No.40, she is hauling a local train near Dunmurry. The four-wheel van is a Class Y3, followed by a first/second class composite coach and then two of Park's standard six compartment third class coaches.

Bill Scott Collection

D&BJR No.22 is seen at Adelaide on 8 August 1930, now as GNR(I) No.41. She was also rebuilt twice, in 1888 and 1913, so that resemblance to her southern cousins is hard to distinguish by now. She lasted 62 years until withdrawal in 1934. While 60-plus years of useful life would be considered good for any railway equipment today, it was modest in 101 class terms. However, on the Great Northern Nos.40 and 41 were but a class of two and that richer railway had many fine, newer 0-6-0s.

Henry Casserley

Liveries carried

In his original paper, Bob Clements did not cover the subject of the liveries carried by the locomotives. Early liveries carried by locomotives present a problem and even photographic evidence can be deceptive, as early emulsions did not pick up red and sometimes even black, but Peter Rowledge has determined the following from his researches.

In the period 1870-5 some changes were made to the livery which until then had been a dark olive green, lined with only a fine yellow line so far as is known. About 1873, black bands lined by a light green line each side, with a thin red line in between were added. Frames were painted red-brown. Tenders were lined in two or three panels, reduced after a few years to a single panel.

With the dawn of the Twentieth Century, a black livery replaced the more colourful one, with vermillion lining edged in white and this can be seen on 158 opposite. In 1919, plain unlined battleship grey became the order of the day and in service this soon degenerated into black. Nonetheless, Inchicore finished many engines in black, but Limerick generally favoured grey.

Until 1870 the number consisted of brass block figures on each side of the smokebox as seen in the drawing of 105 on page 26. The Beyer Peacock engines of 1867-8 had plain brass rectangular numberplates, as seen on 154 on page 23. What became the standard numberplate was introduced with a drawing dated May 1873 and presumably they were used from that date. It had the lettering 'G.S.&W.R.' above the number and 'INCHICORE WORKS (date)' below, as seen in the photographs here. Similarity to the numberplates used by Crewe Works and the London & North Western Railway has often been mentioned - Crewe's drawing is dated March 1873!

119 of 1877 is seen very much as she was built, although the provision of brake gear to the driving wheels date this picture in the 1880s. Here we see a 101 in the all her glory in the full GS&WR livery of the period. *Hamish Stevenson Collection*

40

A fully lined 134 is seen with a smartly dressed member of staff.

Real Photographs/NRM

158 hauls a modest but varied goods train past Inchicore in 1914. Splendid in her lined black livery, she was already on her third boiler and would see one further upgrade in that department and new frames, extending her working life to a useful 85 years.

Ken Nunn Collection, courtesy the Locomotive Club of Great Britain

186 has a long association with the town of Waterford and since preservation has visited the lines around there several times. Here she waits to leave with the 2.45pm to Macmine Junction via Palace East on 15 August 1958. The 'tin van' at the front of the train is the most modern vehicle and looks somewhat incongruous beside the more spartan accommodation provided for the passengers. In No.2 bay, along with an 'A' class diesel-electric, is an oil tank wagon containing fuel for the newly arrived diesels.

Late James L Stevenson

168 arrives at Waterford with a passenger train on Saturday 6 June 1953. The loco is passing over the 'scissors' crossing leading to the Rosslare end of the platform while the Mail to Limerick waits to leave from the other end. One particular Guard on the Rosslare train would alarm passengers by telling them they would be at the platform as soon as he got the scissors. Note the starting signal for eastbound trains, hung from the station canopy.

Charles Friel Collection

An Engineman's Tribute

by Driver Jack O'Neill, Waterford

An era has ended - the passing of steam on Irish railways is regretted by all small boys between the ages of eight and eighty, and in particular by the 'small boys ' who achieved the universal ambition, the footplate men. A new breed of driver has taken over the new machines. Gone is the corpulent, pipe-smoking, overall-clad driver; his place has been taken by the clinically clean, classroom-trained young man who regards his diesel engine not as a friend but as a pay packet.

With many others, I regret the passing of the different types of locos - the good, very good, and not too bad. But most of all I miss the great and versatile '101', Inchicore's finest achievement. This very numerous class gripped the imagination from one's first introduction to it. No job or branch line was too difficult for it, and it survived to the end in almost its original appearance. I am not going to talk of its mechanical make-up but will try to give some idea of what it was like to work these beautiful machines.

The 101s came in three distinct forms and the performance of each was vastly different. (I should make it clear here that I only refer to the 'Southern' engines). As most enginemen did, I divided the locos as follows: saturated, superheated, and marine big-end fitted. The saturated were by far the fastest of the three types and seemed to last out longer between general repairs. All saturated 101s carried the long chimney on the short and very crowded smokebox and were equipped with the GS&WR type of vacuum brake which had small ejector, large ejector and application handle separate from each other - not a very good arrangement. The small ejector was on the top steam manifold, the large one was a handle at the driver's side of the boiler which was pulled out to work, and the application handle was situated in a very awkward position, midway on the trailing wheel splasher, and to operate it one had to stand out from under the canopy, not very pleasant in rain! The nuts of both ejectors often blew out with constant use and a very wet and uncomfortable cab was the result. Despite this, it was an efficient brake and application could be augmented by pulling out the large ejector handle - a practice frowned on by loco inspectors.

These locos worked all types of trains: goods, for which they were built, branch or main line passenger. Not infrequently, they worked the Cork-Rosslare express and they were to be seen on the DSE section suburban trains. In all this they excelled and in the words of the late Driver Jimmy Byrnes of Bray, "they refused no rotten train". The saturated engines were faster-running, particularly 'shut off', than their superheated sisters. I cannot give a reason for this, but old drivers maintain that saturated steam acted as a lubricant and I heard one old driver (long since gone to his reward) refer to superheated steam as 'burnt steam'. Some of the saturated locos remain vividly in my memory because of some peculiarity or other. Loco 150 was the only one I saw fitted with the Gresham & Craven combination vacuum brake. I first saw her working on the Castlecomer branch with the leading parts of her outside rods removed and a timber cab built over the bunker plate for protection in tender first working. The rods were removed because of the terrible curves on this hilly line. 150 spent nearly all of her working life in the Waterford area and was by far the heaviest on coal and water.

I seem to recall that 134 spent nearly all her time on passenger working. New from the shops, she was put on the Waterford-Kingsbridge morning train and after a few months was transferred to the Macmine branch trains. This run always managed to slack out an average 101 in three to six months but 134 managed it on and off for two years. She was truly a remarkable engine and her memory is pleasant indeed. But no engine in Waterford was as well known or universally loved as 111 - known locally as 'The Sergeant' or sometimes as 'Nelson'. I won't explain the nick-names as the first is obvious and the second vulgar! She was the last of the class I worked as a driver. She was on the 5 a.m. goods from Wexford to Waterford and I took over at Palace East. The fireman and myself cleaned the boiler at Palace and the faceplate on the long run down into New Ross, and we left there with a gleaming loco at the head of 22 wagons. I can still feel her footplate vibrating under me, and see her long shining boiler, as we headed up Glenmore Bank.

Among the saturated engines I recall at Waterford are 187, 116, 157, 167, 190, 240, 242, 243 and, of course, 111, 134 and 150. Life could be interesting - 167 arrived one day on the Waterford down line and her back axle promptly broke in halves! In September 1954, 157 was involved in a collision at Dromkeen due to her driver not noticing he had a short section staff, rather than the long section one from the Junction to Killonan. As a result, 157 had to get a complete new cylinder block and from then on was never a good steaming engine. Nos. 240, 242 and 243 were fitted with marine big-ends and single slidebars and blocks. They were sluggish compared to the engines fitted with the strap big-end and the conventional four slidebars and two blocks to each side of the motion. Very soon after their general repairs the big-ends began to knock. They tended to roll more than the strap fitted locos and a constant watch had to be kept on the gudgeon nuts securing the crossheads - these constantly slacked out as did the big-end nuts. The only redeeming feature of these engines was that they had metallic packing

Although 134 latterly seems to have been a Waterford favourite for passenger work, on 2 July 1938 she was engaged in more mundane, but probably more profitable, goods work. She received a 4' 4" boiler in 1922 and carried one until withdrawal in 1961. Note the handles for securing the smokebox door - easier to use than the usual wheel.

Henry Casserley

157 is seen at Kilkenny's loco shed on 19 May 1939, fifteen years before her accident at Dromkeen.

W A Camwell, courtesy the Stephenson Locomotive Society

in their piston and spindle glands and so saved the fireman the very messy and uncomfortable job he had with the saturated locos fitted with 'soft' glands, which were filled with salamander packing. The unfortunate fireman was allowed 15 minutes to pack a soft gland - a task which usually took 45 minutes and was the most hated duty in a running shed.

Now for the very controversial superheated 101s! In Waterford the engines that spring to mind are 114 (the last of the class in Waterford to be superheated), 118 (a gazelle), 130, 144, 147 (Waterford's No. 1 special engine), 151, 163, 164, 174 (a beauty), 182, 183, the unlucky 188 and the pride of Waterford, 186 - now preserved in Belfast, and a loco I hope to see run again, if only to give a thrill to children who have never seen the magnificence of a steam engine at speed. These locos were never idle and their only rest was for a washout or a major repair. One of them was prepared and sent to Waterford station every night at 8.30 p.m. when the Rosslare express was running, to be available if the train engine needed assistance or to work an auxiliary train in case of necessity. If not needed for either duty, this engine acted as coaching pilot until 10 p.m. when it either left with the Limerick goods or relieved 'Jumbo' as yard pilot.

147, seen here with several sisters at her home shed on 2 July 1938, was deemed to be Waterford's number one engine, light on water and coal, but capable of doing the heaviest work. Built in 1891, she took the number of the first Beyer Peacock engine which was withdrawn in 1888. In time, she went through the whole range of 101 boilers but was not to receive her 'Z' type one until the dark days of 1941. In 1956, no doubt deemed to be superfluous, she fell victim to that year's dieselisation programme.

Henry Casserley

144, with her crew of Driver Joe Hodgens and Fireman Joe Kennedy ("Smokey Joe"), is seen at Waterford on 6 May 1949. Her tender has been graced with the CIE 'flying snail' logo, which was not universally applied to goods locomotives. The tender itself was used originally on the 710 class and had a 2,800 gallon tank fitted onto the original frames of the 1,864 gallon type. It had a higher bunker than previously, which must have saved the firemens' backs. Experimental piston and valve packing were tried on her while at Waterford.

John Dewing

164 has arrived at Limerick Junction with a train from Limerick on 8 July 1955. The fireman is engaged in one of his regular tasks – bringing coal forward from the back of the tender to the bunk at the front where it will be accessible for firing. The driver meanwhile is attending to the lubrication of the big ends. The GS&WR made life easier for crews in that many oiling points had a sprung button on each one and the use of a long feeder meant that it was not necessary to get under the engine to carry out this job.

Lance King

These engines were to be seen almost every Sunday piloting some 4-4-0 or even a Woolwich on excursions, and it was not uncommon to have two 101s working heavy Knock pilgrimage trains to Limerick, returning in the evening. The 'All-Ireland' specials from Waterford via the DSE line were always piloted by a 101 and I recall a very pleasant trip on 174, piloting 342. 174 was the freest steaming engine in Waterford and was very strong on a bank. 147, when available, worked the cattle specials and was a remarkably light engine on both coal and water. I remember running non-stop from Cahir to Waterford with 147 with a special of 33 wagons of stock from Cahir Fair and with a tender holding 1,800 gallons of water. On arrival at Waterford, water was still in the bucket cock and roughly two bunkers of coal had been burned - a fine performance. This was in 1948 when the coal was just starting to improve and I was in my second year as fireman.

Loco 188 was considered unlucky and was very much disliked. She was involved in many minor mishaps and one major one which almost claimed the lives of her crew. Working the 3.05 p.m. from Cork to Waterford in July 1945, she left the rails on the curve approaching the Suir Bridge - two miles from Waterford, and buried herself in the steelwork of the bridge, trapping Driver J Cleary and Fireman Harry Flynn in the cab. The driver was pressed against the reversing wheel and trapped there by the tender box. The steam manifold blew out its packing nuts and steam started to condense in the enclosed space on top of the unfortunate driver. The fireman climbed out through the front spectacle window (the 'spec') and onto the top girders of the bridge some 80 feet above the river, where he was able to crawl to safety. Later, no matter how many times he tried, he could never fit through an engine spec! After a three-hour ordeal, the driver was freed after acetylene burners had been used to cut away the wreckage. He spent a year in hospital but was not to work again. Truly, 188 deserved its bad name.

On a happier occasion 188, even with a superheated boiler, presents a scene of delightful antiquity as she trundles along the banks of the Slaney with the 6.15pm mixed train from Wexford to Enniscorthy on 17 August 1957. The present day motorist would hardly beat even this humble train as he attempts to extricate himself from traffic in both congested towns.

Late James L Stevenson

Right and opposite

Rogue engine, 188, after the accident at the Suir Bridge, while hauling the 3.05pm Cork – Waterford train, via Mallow on 24 July 1945. Jack tells the full story on the page opposite.

Jack O'Neill Collection

When built in 1882, she was fitted new with vacuum brakes, being one of the first of the class so equipped. Like so many of the class, she carried every type of 101 boiler, but never received new frames.

The Waterford crews must have been glad to see the back of her when she was withdrawn, fairly early, in 1959.

There were many differences between the saturated and superheated engines. The former had Ramsbottom safety valves, while the latter carried the Ross Pop type. Lubricators and injectors also differed: the saturated engines having a single feed lubricator (the 'luber') and top steam valve injectors; the superheated engines had Detroit two or four feed lubers and wheel valve injectors. The exhaust of the saturated locos sounded like a soft cough while the others had a sharp clear bark. The types also differed in coal and water consumption, the superheated being much the lighter on fuel but taking longer to heat up; they would not begin to give their best performance until they had run about 10 miles. But, saturated or superheated, the class were the best all-round engines in these islands and, with reasonable maintenance, would have lasted another 10 years.

The beet season placed a terrible strain on the 101s as they worked nearly all the specials over the Thurles branch. This was necessary because of axle-load restrictions. The turnabout of these engines when in good repair was remarkable, as they usually ran from Rosslare to Thurles without firecleaning, though they stopped long enough in Waterford to take on a bucket or two of coal and to have the sandboxes filled. For their size, they handled enormous trains of beet with very smart sectional running. But in 1957 CIE apparently decided to permit the engines to be worked to death. I would prefer not to remember them as they were then, dirty, badly maintained and very sluggish in running.

For a short two-year period, some of the superheated engines were converted to burn oil and they proved very efficient. But I firmly believe that this conversion reduced the life of the boilers and fireboxes by at least 5 years. They constantly leaked and firehole rings started to blow. It has been said that the crude type of burner used was responsible. 153 was by far the most efficient of the oil-burners while 166 was the worst and most dangerous. She had the bad habit of flashing back her flame under the tender and a coaching shunter was badly burned at Waterford as a result of this. Oil-burning was a short-lived experiment and it seems a pity that it was not continued with an improved burner.

There was another class of engine I haven't referred to before. This was the 700 class, surely the most despised, ugliest and most inefficient steam locos in Ireland. We had two based at Waterford - 700 and 702 - and I never heard anyone say a word in their favour. No matter what the train was, they had to be flogged with a full regulator to get anything approaching speed from them. They steamed freely but should have had mechanical stokers as, in the words of the coalmen, "they ate coal". One day, working a goods from Waterford to Kilkenny, I put on 700's injector passing Gouldings and didn't shut it off till we stopped at Ballyhale to fill the tank, all the way shovelling coal into a hungry firebox. Needless to remark, they worked passenger trains only in time of dire necessity. I am led to believe that the designer tried to

153 is propelling wagons from the Clover Meat factory siding (just visible behind the last wagon) to Waterford on 14 April 1953. This would have required some care, as the siding is nearly a mile and a half out of the city on the line to Rosslare Harbour and the fireman is clearly keeping a good lookout.

Robin Linsley Collection

166, waiting at Wicklow on a Rosslare train, was one of the six Sharp Stewart engines, dating in this case from 1872. In the course of her 91 years, she carried every kind of boiler and had been reframed for ten years by the time she was superheated in 1933. She was one of the class to be temporarily converted to oil-burning, in which form she caused a shunter at Waterford to be badly burned. She has acquired the Coey pattern of directly linked reversing rod and the platform end observer could note from its position that the cut off was set well out. The climb of $8^{1}/_{2}$ miles ahead, much of it at 1 in 80, will not allow much opportunity for expansive working!

Drew Donaldson

make a cross between a 101 and a Midland 'E' class when building the 700s. All he succeeded in doing was putting an excellent cab on a heap of scrap and having all kinds of misfortune wished upon him by the crews who manned his follies.

On Saturday, 12 January 1963, steam traction ended on the lines out of Waterford, and the gallant 101s ended a long association with that city. The locos on the last day of working were 116, 179, 183, 186 and 253, with 187 on the North Wharf pilot duties. Their memory still lingers and will continue to do so as long as the present generation of footplatemen live. Whenever our retired brethren gather for a relaxing pint, the talk turns to these gallant engines and the company relives past times when the footplate had romance and glamour.

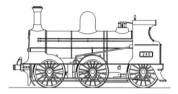

A grubby 253 is shunting at Limerick on 28 August 1957. She appears very much as built in 1903, except that she now has a smokebox with a vertical front with circular dished door. The trio of engines on these two pages were among those working at Waterford on the last day.

Late James L Stevenson

The porter steps forward to greet the 10.50am from Waterford to Limerick on 28 March 1956 as 179 runs into Pallas. A burnt smokebox door is usually a sign that the engine has been doing some hard work and the seventy-seven mile run, stopping and restarting at all stations, was a man-sized job for a modestly sized engine such as this.

The use of poor quality coal made the job of keeping the smokebox doors tight a difficult one. Like most engines, 179 has acquired a set of clamps, known as 'dogs', around the circumference of the doors to prevent air being drawn in and spoiling steaming.

Charles Friel collection

When built in 1883, 183 was one of the first 101s to be fitted with vacuum brakes by Aspinall when he became chief. She was a long term resident of Waterford and was working on the last day of steam there. Her other claim to fame was as one of the four locomotives to haul the 1964 'Grand Tour'. At Abbey Jct. she takes the line to New Ross and Macmine Jct. with a train to Wexford. By 1960 this working had been taken over by AEC railcars, a big change from this train of a six-wheeler, a bogie coach and a ubiquitous 'tin van'!

Courtesy Stephenson Locomotive Society

Seen here at Grace Dieu in Waterford is 180 of 1875. She was withdrawn as early as 1928, so this is a rare record of the engine. She received this boiler, with a raised firebox, in 1898 during her first rebuilding.

The bearded driver is sporting a bowler hat – not very practical on such an exposed footplate but a statement of the status and authority that engine drivers enjoyed in Victorian times.

Real Photographs/NRM

Would anyone deny Martin Atock his place as an artist among locomotive engineers? No doubt, as was usually the case, his able Chief Draughtsman, James Rowe, had some input to the final appearance, too.

L class No.95, *'Bulldog',* was built by Robert Stephenson and Co. in 1876. She is seen in 1895 in the emerald green livery with black and white lining which was introduced in 1889.

Locomotive & General Railway Photographs/NRM

THE STANDARD GOODS ENGINES OF THE GS&WR AND MGWR

A Comparative Evaluation of the 101 Class and the Lm Class

by R N Clements

By May 1876 the GS&WR had already 41 standard goods engines in service, though varying somewhat in dimensions and details, as I have outlined earlier; in discussing them here I shall refer, in general, only to the engines as built in 1876 and afterwards. The date May 1876 is mentioned as being the date of the first of the MGWR 'L' class standard goods engines which I now propose to compare with their Southern equivalents.

Two Locomotive Families

The first contrast is in the origin of the two designs, for whereas the GS&WR engines were a product of Beyer Peacock's drawing office, the MGWR ones (though the first batch were built by R. Stephenson) were to drawings prepared, to the last rivet, at the Broadstone under Martin Atock and his Chief Draughtsman, James Rowe, whom he had brought with him from Limerick in 1872.

Though the GSW engine was nominally more powerful, the MGW one was considerably larger, as was perhaps natural from the ten years difference in date. Both, in view of the necessity of working many specials of stock as well as goods trains, had relatively large wheels, 5' 1¾" diam. on the GSW and 5' 3" on the MGW; thus they were able for all but the fastest passenger trains, though the MGW engines, at any rate, did very little passenger work till many years later. Though Inchicore was by now using 18" cylinders for new engines, Broadstone was content for the moment with 17", both sharing 24" stroke; this in spite of Broadstone providing a considerably larger boiler, 4' 3" against 4' 0" diam.

The MGW boiler was 1½" shorter in the barrel, increased to 4" shorter between tubeplates by Atock's use of a drumhead tubeplate slightly recessed in the barrel. At the firebox end the boilers differed greatly. The GSW firebox casing was raised 2½" over the barrel, which made the grate slightly wider than the MGW one as well as being an inch longer, both engines having flat grates. The crown of the GSW firebox was flat, with girder stays, whereas Atock always used a slightly domed firebox crown with direct stays. McDonnell used a firehole ring, whereas Atock flanged the copper and iron plates together at the fire hole.

Both engines had a sliding firedoor with handle on the driver's side. This allowed him to open and close the doors between each shovelful of coal using his right hand. The rhythmic movement was done without taking his eyes off the road and remained a feature of CIE locomotive work long after the practice died out on other railways. The placing of the handle on the driver's side remained a feature of locomotive designs all over the British Isles until the end of steam.

Inchicore had experimented with various combinations before deciding on their arrangement of 185 tubes of 1¾" diam.; this gave less paper heating surface than Atock's 222 of 1⅝" diam., but it probably provided more steam, though the Atock boiler may have gained a little by its slightly better water spaces (2½" at the sides, but 3" front and back, where Inchicore used 2½" all round). Though Inchicore used a 4½" blastpipe top, the Broadstone one was at first 5", later reduced to 4⅝" and the MGW engines must have required very careful firing, but should have been economical in coal.

Though the Broadstone boiler was, if anything, the stronger of the two, it worked at only 130lbs pressure against Inchicore's 140 or 150lbs. Both boilers were made in three rings, butt-jointed. Though both had spark-arresters, they were as different as possible; Inchicore's was a circular wire one extending from the blastpipe top into the base of the chimney, but Broadstone divided the smokebox horizontally by a grid level with the top of the blastpipe. Both engines had this, as was then usual, just above the top row of tubes. Inchicore had recently changed from the horizontal to the vertical Giffard injector - a typical McDonnell detail was the use of injectors (perhaps made at Inchicore) of cast iron, only the cones being brass. Broadstone used Gresham & Craven ashpan injectors, then more up to date.

McDonnell used frames only 1" thick, whereas Atock's were a very solid 1¼" and were also deeper than Inchicore's; both were iron. Both classes had wrought-iron wheels, McDonnell's unbalanced (though Beyer's engines of 1867-8 had had the driving wheels, at least, balanced), whilst Atock's had small balance weights. McDonnell used steel for all axles, but Atock for the crank axles only, his straight axles being iron; both classes had steel tyres.

L class No.94 *'Badger'* was built by Robert Stephenson and Co. in 1876. This is almost certainly a builder's photograph taken with the locomotive in 'workshop grey'. Worthy of note is the generous provision of sanding gear, including 'back-sanding' behind the rear wheel, a feature absent in the 101s.

Locomotive & General Railway Photographs/NRM

L class No.60 *'Lough Owel'* was built at Broadstone in 1885 replacing an 0-4-2 of the same number and name and is seen in her original state before she received a new boiler in 1915.

Harold Fayle, IRRS Collection

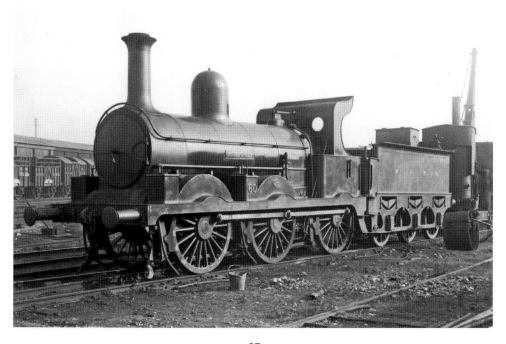

Inchicore used cast-iron axleboxes, with slightly better bearing surfaces than Broadstone's gun-metal ones, and the GSW boxes had adjusting wedges, never used by the MGW for small engines. Cast-iron was also used by McDonnell for coupling rod bushes.

Suspension of both classes was by overhung laminated springs to the leading and driving wheels and volute springs at the trailing end, but the arrangement of the latter was very different. Whereas Inchicore continued the simple Beyer arrangement of three volute springs over each trailing box, placed on the footplate, Atock secured better riding at the cost of accessibility by connecting his trailing boxes by a transverse beam supported by seven volute springs.

Both engines had the classic arrangement of vertical slide valves between the cylinders, and Stephenson link motion, the MGW one having a trifle more space in the steam chest as the cylinders were $\frac{1}{2}$" further apart. Both had $1\frac{1}{2}$" steam ports, 14" long on the MGW against $13\frac{1}{2}$" on the GSW engine; for the exhaust ports, Inchicore followed the usual practice of making them more than twice the width of the steam ports ($3\frac{1}{2}$"), whereas Broadstone was content with 3". With both engines having $\frac{7}{8}$" lap, Broadstone's longer valve travel ($4\frac{1}{2}$" against $3\frac{3}{4}$") gave wider steam port openings and no doubt the 6" longer eccentric rods were an advantage - but the GSW engine would gain a little by having a 4" longer connecting rod. Both engines had four slidebars per cylinder, extending from the back cover of the cylinder to the motion-plate. The valve rods, in each case, were supported by swing-links, but the GSW arrangement was the better, the links (attached to the motion-plate) being suspended from above, whereas Broadstone, for no very apparent reason, placed them below.

At first sight McDonnell's cab would appear to give much better shelter than Atock's, but the firebox projected so far into it that Atock's high upswept roof actually extended further back from the faceplate, though the GSW cab gave better side protection; this advantage was partially nullified by what looked like a typical McDonnell economy, the side-sheets (perhaps really due to Beyer) had no beading to their edges, so an elbow could not be rested there with comfort. The GSW cab had the fault, surprising in a railway which served Tipperary, Cork and Kerry, of being too low in the roof. It was distinguished, however, by its unusually large rectangular specs (with economical bay-wood frames) which gave a wonderful view ahead, even from a sitting position. The round MGW spec, though very adequate, was not as large.

Inside the cab the GSW used an ordinary upright regulator handle, but the MGW a butterfly one, with, however, rather short handles. The GSW regulator was of the ordinary sliding type, whereas Broadstone's was a circular butterfly valve capable of much finer adjustment. It was, also, a two-valve regulator; Inchicore then used one valve only, though two became standard some years later. Each line provided one gauge-glass only (placed on the right in each case, though the engines drove from opposite sides) and two try-cocks (which allowed the water level to be checked if a gauge glass burst). Both classes had screw reverse, the MGW arrangement being the more modern, with the pointer moving over a neat brass strip over the wheel. On the GSW the levers of the earlier engines had given way to the original Ramsbottom arrangement of screw, in which the wheel was solid with the screw and itself moved forwards and backwards; also it was so coupled as to move back to put the engine into forward gear. The only indication of its position was a strip attached to the side-sheet of the cab and it could only be locked by putting a hook, attached to a chain, round the appropriate spoke. It is, perhaps, debatable whether screw reverse was of much advantage to either class, seeing the amount of shunting they had to do, but it was standard on *all* Inchicore and Broadstone engines. There was a lot to be said for the GNR practice of screw for passenger and lever for goods engines.

Both engines, as was then usual, relied entirely on the tender hand-brake. Though the GSW had made some experiments with steam brakes a few years before, they had abandoned them, but about this time Aspinall, at Inchicore, was studying the question of vacuum brakes for passenger trains. On the MGW, so far, the handbrake had not been challenged.

The GSW tender, of 1,860 gallons, had a typical Beyer underframe but I think the arrangement of the bunker had been subsequently redesigned at Inchicore. It might have been intended for the special infliction of penance on firemen - not only a very low shovelling plate, but also a most inadequate bunker which had continually to be refilled. The 1,600 gallon MGW tender, of Atock's very handsome design with the springs inside but accessible through slots in the frameplates, had an equally low shovelling plate, but at least the bunker, once filled, held a reasonable amount of coal.

So we find that the 1876 position is that the GSW is building to a design ten years older than the MGW, but partly brought up to date; very small, and with a regard for economy which verges on parsimony. Atock's new design is larger and in many (but not all) respects more up to date; it is the reverse of McDonnell's in being solid and well-finished almost to the point of extravagance. A contrast, very minor in itself, but not without deeper significance, is the extensive use of snap-headed rivets by Inchicore, compared to their complete absence from any visible part of the Broadstone engine.

Ln class No.567, formerly No.53 *'Duke'* built in 1880 at Broadstone, is seen at her birthplace in July 1931. She was fitted with a Cusack-Morton superheater in 1919, but as seen here has reverted to a saturated boiler from Cusack and Morton's early days and the 1915-designed cab critically alluded to here.

Locomotive & General Railway Photographs/NRM

The Classes Develop

We can now proceed to compare the further development of the two types, dealing first with the Broadstone engines of 1879-80. These six engines, known as the 'Ln' class, and the first built there, were like earlier Inchicore practice in including parts of old 0-4-2 engines (supplied by Fairbairn in 1860). There was this major difference, however, that the old parts retained in the new engines were intended to be kept until the next major renewal, instead of being replaced after a short time. The old leading and driving wheels were used, hence the non-standard diameter of 5' 1½". Parts of the old motion were used also, a point I shall return to later. Cylinders were made 18" diam., and the 14 tubeplate stays of the L class were replaced by tubes, making 236.

The most important alteration was the provision of a steam brake. The arrangement of a three-way cock for applying the brake to engine and tender or either, or shutting it off, was just as it remained to our own times, and immediately above it was a handwheel which controlled the steam valve. Though all right for working a train, it was very inconvenient for shunting to have the brake controlled from the middle of the faceplate. So the operating wheel was replaced by a short crank, connected to a rod, screwed at the end, which extended across the faceplate to the fireman's side, where a bracket carried a handwheel through which the screwed end of the rod passed. This fully adjustable steam brake must have been a delight to work on the road, and very much superior, for controlling goods trains, to the GSW's vacuum, though it would not be at all as handy as the vacuum for shunting. The placing of the brake on the fireman's side of goods engines, though unusual, was not unique (the Caledonian, at least, also did so); no doubt it arose from its always having been the fireman's duty to work the handbrake. The GSW had, in fact, been just ahead in the brake question for, following Aspinall's start on fitting passenger engines with vacuum brakes in 1876, four goods engines built in 1878 were also fitted. Thereafter, though the MGW soon fitted all their Stephenson L class engines with steam brakes like the Ln, the GSW returned to the handbrake for several years; this, I think, was not due to any fault in the working of the vacuum, but probably to the GSW board's unwillingness to spend money.

Aspinall, therefore, had to be content for the moment with such minor improvements as he could make to the engines. From 1877 he used cast-iron wheels of the Crewe type, from 1881 steel boilers, and in the same year the first steel frames were used. These seem to have been experimental only, for next a return was made to iron frames, but deeper; finally, in 1885, this improved frame was made in steel. Webb injectors had, by this time, been standard for some years in place of the old Giffards. Aspinall seems finally to have won his point about brakes towards the end of 1884, for in the years 1885 to 1887 practically the whole 101 class were fitted with the simple vacuum.

The 1885 batch of 101 class were the first to have their cylinders cast in Inchicore, where that work was first undertaken about 1883. Till that time most GSW cylinders had been got from Grendon, though occasionally they were bought from England. At Inchicore the pair of cylinders were made in one casting, though Grendon had always cast them separately. There never was an iron foundry at the Broadstone and MGW cylinders came mainly from Grendon till they closed, and in later times mostly from Ross & Walpole.

Nor were there any but detail changes in the twenty L class engines built at Broadstone from 1885 to 1889, which were almost the same as the 1879 engines, save for having standard 5' 3" wheels; these were unbalanced probably because the unbalanced wheels of the Ln class had been found quite suitable; thus both companies had started with balanced wheels and then changed to unbalanced. Broadstone, however, never reversed the position as far as the small goods engines were concerned, though Inchicore reintroduced balance weights later. The handles of the regulator were lengthened, making them handier for shunting, and (just like Inchicore a few years before) Atock replaced the old built-up chimneys by cast-iron ones.

All but two of these 20 engines were replacements, which retained their old Caledonian-type tenders, with their flat 1,600 gallon tanks extending right to the front, so that the shovelling-plate was conveniently at about the same level as the firehole. These brought the MGW to a total of 35 engines, whilst by 1889 the GSW had ninety of their 101 class, since 1886 the only goods tender engines on the line.

In 1889 Atock undertook a major re-design of his standard engines, passenger and goods. Goods engines to the new standards began to appear in 1891. Apart from external details and the use of steel for frameplates (still $1^1/4$" thick), wheels and straight axles, the changes were confined to the boilers and motion. The boilers were of steel, with $^9/_{16}$" plates and pressure increased to 150 lbs (though Inchicore, by now using 160 lbs pressure, was still content with $^1/_2$" plates). The firebox was as before, but the barrel being now joined to it by a butt instead of a lap joint gained 1" in diameter. The number of tubes, still $1^5/_8$", was slightly reduced to 230. At the front end these boilers had Atock's patent elastic tubeplates, involving the use of a corrugated ring, intended to equalise the expansion of the steel barrels and brass tubes; these are outside the scope of the present account, beyond observing that the boiler therefore consisted of four rings instead of three. The sliding firedoor was replaced by a door with a flap, curiously placed at an angle of 30° from the vertical. Modern faceplate injectors replaced the old ashpan type.

The redesign of the motion included two quite different aspects. Firstly, the slidebars were moved back clear of the cylinder covers and supported at their centre by a strong cast-steel motion-plate incorporating valve spindle guides to replace the swing-links. The slidebars, formerly very close together, were moved apart to make room for a larger cross-head. Marine-type big ends were used. This layout of the motion was exactly as used for many years by Dougald Drummond and was undoubtedly a very great improvement.

For the rest, a peculiarity of the Ln class was standardised. In these, the old 5' $9^1/_2$" radius expansion link of 1860 was retained, coupled to standard eccentric rods only 4' $6^5/_{16}$" between centres, and coupled top and bottom instead of at the back of the link. The throw of the eccentrics was unaltered, so valve travel was reduced to the same $3^3/_4$" as the Southern engines. This arrangement, presumably accidental in origin, was most unorthodox, but its adoption as standard was clearly the result of ten years experience of it in the Ln class.

Lm Class No.84 *'Dunkellan'*, was built at Broadstone in 1891.

Harold Fayle, IRRS Collection

The only other change in the new engines, classed 'Lm', was an improved cab. Cylinders, frames, wheels, suspension, etc. were all identical with the old L class. Tenders of the ten engines built 1891-3 were again secondhand ones of Caledonian type.

Proceedings of 1889-91 at Inchicore were very much out of normal character, for in these years the old 101 class engines were broken up and replaced by new ones. So unusual was this on the GS&WR that I long thought the record of it must be merely some trick of the accountants, but the details show that the total of old material recorded in the renewal of the seven engines was no more than one set of wheel centres, one set of straight axles and two crank axles, though no doubt other minor parts were used as well. One more old engine was similarly replaced in 1896.

Most of these engines included a minor improvement already made in 1888 - the replacement of the singularly awkward Beyer engine footstep by one designed for the natural use of the feet. About 1891 another improvement was made. In the replacement of the lever reverse of the older engines by a screw, the old Ramsbottom arrangement was at last abandoned, and the reversing rod was directly connected from screw to weighbar shaft. The wheel now had a proper catch and a sliding indicator. Both these alterations were merely the provision on the 101 class of details which had been standard on other classes for many years; the retention for so long of the old features on the goods engines appears a case of standardisation gone mad. Nor, I should add, were these details altered on any but a very few of the old engines, though included in all new construction.

As I mentioned accountants above, it is appropriate to refer to the very detailed accounts kept by the Loco Accounts Office at Inchicore ever since McDonnell's time, in which the cost and life of every item was carefully entered. At the same time, it is clear that this was accountancy performing its proper function - recording, summarising and supplying information to those qualified to judge its value. I can see no trace of the modern tendency, particularly prevalent in a neighbouring country, of accountants dictating policy on technical matters quite outside their competence. There is no evidence of the keeping of any such detailed records by the MGWR.

On the Midland, in 1894-5, the old Stephenson L class engines of 1876 were renewed as Lm, with new boilers, motion and cab, but the old frames, etc. Then more Lm class were built outside in 1895 and had improved boilers, at first pressed to 160 lbs. By slightly lengthening the front corrugated ring, it became possible to make the rest of the boiler in one ring 6' 9" long.

For these engines a new tender was designed with a 2,000 gallon tank. Evidently Atock, by this time, had seen the advantage of the flat tank in saving the fireman from lifting the coal, so he adopted this, but as the larger tank would have been too high, he made a recess in the front of it to form a convenient shovelling plate. From that time on, all Broadstone tenders had a convenient shovelling level, but it was to be 40 years before the same consideration was given to Inchicore firemen. By 1895 continuous brakes were required for passenger trains, so on these engines a vacuum ejector was supplied in combination with the steam brake, still placed on the fireman's side.

Both GSW and MGW vacuum arrangements had their peculiarities; the former require a full-length study, and all we need notice now is the placing of the large ejector high in the smokebox ahead of the blastpipe; the small ejector was in the cab and was completely separate, the application valve being again quite separate from both. Atock used normal combination ejectors, but his ejector exhaust arrangement was unusual; the upper part of the blastpipe for about 12" from the top was annular, the ejector exhausting through the central part, and the engine exhaust through the outer ring only.

In 1896 Robert Coey took over at Inchicore, the fourth successive locomotive superintendent to build the 101 class. The chief change he made was the introduction of single slidebars and marine big-ends, as used by

Ivatt for tank engines since 1892. Marine big-ends were also used in the MGW Lm class. Single slidebars were being used by Broadstone at this period on passenger engines; but were very soon rejected, whereas the GSW continued to use them for forty years. Coey's other alterations included cast-steel wheels, with balance weights, reducing the number of tubes to 173, and a slightly improved cab. His eight engines of 1898-9 were the last built of the 101 class with 4 ft boilers and in the same year the MGW rebuilt the Ln class of 1879 so as to correspond to the Lm class in everything except wheel diameter; at the same time 2,000 gallon tenders replaced the old Fairbairn ones.

By 1901 the 101s were obviously too small and Coey rebuilt two of them. The larger boiler fitted had been introduced for the 0-6-4T engines of 1876, and it is surprising that it was not sooner applied to the standard goods engines. It derived simply from matching the barrel directly to the existing firebox casing wrapper-plate; thus it was 4' 4"diam., but being now made in two telescopic rings; the diameter of the front one was 1" less. The firebox casing returned to the 5' 7" diameter of Beyer's engines, but with the deeper flat grate.

Fitting of these boilers continued steadily over the years, but the process was not finally completed till 1936. In 1902-3 the last 101 class engines were built, twelve with the larger boiler, but otherwise unchanged save for a few external details. These were the last engines built at Inchicore with the old rectangular-section side-rods, made (since 1896) to a slightly heavier section than before. Fluted rods had been introduced in 1900 and in the course of time replaced the older type on all engines. The MGW also used plain rods (slightly fish-bellied) but, as usual for the same duty, Broadstone made them to a heavier section than Inchicore, and these rods lasted till the end.

The engines of 1902-3 brought the 101 class up to the final maximum figure of 111 engines at any one time; on account of the replacements of 1889-96 the total number of engines involved was 119.

So back to Broadstone again, where the changes were greater, due to the retirement in 1900 of Martin Atock, and with him James Rowe. Edward Cusack became Locomotive Engineer, with the young WH Morton as his Chief Draughtsman; in mechanical matters only Morton counted.

The L class were due for reboilering, but with the larger MGW boiler no increase in size was necessary, though the other changes were considerable. The major change was the use of a Belpaire firebox. The barrel was in two butt-jointed rings; there was no longer a corrugated ring at the front, but Morton followed Atock's practice of making the rings of unequal length, so as to keep the dome in its central position (Inchicore's two rings were of roughly equal length, with the dome on the second one). Morton replaced the flanged firehole by a ring; at Inchicore, at just the same time, the ring hitherto used gave way to a flanged firehole.

At first there was a parallel with the 1866-72 period at Inchicore, in the experimenting with different numbers and sizes of tubes, and size of fireboxes, though the variation in the latter was in depth only; they were finally made 2¼" deeper than the old ones, but otherwise the same size. The tube arrangement decided on was 200 of 1¾" diam., a close parallel to Coey's 200/194 for the same size of barrel.

The old motion was retained in improved form. Atock had started the process by increasing the distance between top and bottom slidebars and providing larger crossheads. Now the swing-links were moved from below to above, and a few engines also got heavier slidebars. The result was not quite as good as the Lm motion, but it was a cheaper alteration, and probably no-one thought, at the time, that the engines would last another 50 to 60 years.

The much larger cab, with full-length roof and corner pillars, had been introduced by Atock just before he left, but a backward step was the use of a single upright regulator handle. Atock's annular blastpipes were abandoned and the ejector exhaust brought straight to the chimney. Alterations (hardly necessary) were made to splashers and sandboxes. The rebuilding of the L class was completed in 1913, and from 1914, when new fireboxes or copper tubeplates were required, the number of 1¾" tubes was further reduced to 166, a complete reversal of Atock's tendency to overcrowd the boiler with tubes. Though most engines had had 160 lbs pressure at first, all finally settled to 150.

One would have expected these boilers to be provided for the Lm class also, but when their reboilering started in 1917, Atock-type round top boilers were used, changed only at the front ring, firehole ring and in the tube arrangement - now 179 of 1¾" diam. No external changes were made, and though a new cab had been designed in 1915 it was not used at this time.

I said that during the twenty years from 1903 to 1923 nothing had happened to the 101 class, but one general development affected them in particular, as the most numerous class on the GS&WR. This was the pooling of boilers, introduced, I think, about 1904 or 1905, and it then became a common thing for an engine in shops to get a change of boiler (though a 4 ft. boiler never replaced a 4' 4" one). Though Broadstone started the provision of a few spare boilers about 1908-9, the system never developed to the same extent.

At Inchicore in 1922-3 three 101 class engines were rebuilt, and I have heard it said that this was done specially for working the Rosslare Express, then running via Macmine. They got new and deeper frames, but the novelty was the provision of new smokeboxes, vertical in front and with dished

Three engines, 143, 158 and 174, were altered in 1922-3 with a more up to date smokebox with a single dished door to improve steaming for working the diverted Rosslare to Cork boat trains over the more hilly D&SER tracks between Wexford, Macmine Junction and Waterford after the Taylorstown viaduct, on the usual route, had been blown up during the Civil War.

143 is seen as rebuilt with new frames and a new vertical-fronted smokebox with conventional circular door. This shot at Inchicore was taken before she received her 'Z' boiler in 1936. The burnished steel of the coupling and reversing rods shows a high standard of pride in appearance.

Real Photographs/NRM

174 appears to be taking water after being turned at Shillelagh on 26 August 1938. In the summer of 1938, the $16^3/_4$ mile branch had a service of three trains per day, but was a casualty of the Second World War and its consequent fuel shortage. The short section to Aughrim, where there was a siding to Fogarty's mill, survived until 1953.

Henry Casserley

circular doors instead of the old Inchicore folding type. Attractive as the old doors were to look at, it must be admitted that by this time they were almost unbelievably old-fashioned; yet (to go a little ahead of our time) no large-scale replacement of them took place till twenty years later, when they proved unable to stand up to the 'Duff'. I should mention that they were a purely Inchicore design, for Beyer's engines of 1867, though with the sloping smokebox front, had ordinary dished doors.

Great Southern Days

In 1925 came the Amalgamation, which, naturally, involved no change in the GSW engines (as the GSW's chief – JR Bazin - took the top job in the GSR) but considerably affected the MGW ones. The Lm class were, due to the war, overdue for reboilering. Apart from three which got spare L class boilers, the reboilering proceeded as already described, and Morton was preparing, once he had finished dealing with the small passenger engines, to add superheaters to these boilers, but Bazin, who showed great reluctance to apply superheating to an existing engine, stopped that.

Soon the construction of the new boilers was transferred to Inchicore, where they were made in GSW style, telescopic instead of butt-jointed, and with the dome set back. The domed and direct-stayed Broadstone firebox gave way to the flat-topped Inchicore crown with girder stays. Most Lm class engines shopped at Inchicore got GSW type cabs, at first with very low roofs. Broadstone at last fitted some with the 1915 design of round cab, but apart from being more 'modern-looking', it had little merit. The roof was short and its low corners might have been specially designed to inflict maximum damage to drivers' heads.

When Morton succeeded Bazin in 1929 he could at last proceed with the intended superheating of the Lm class, but he did not, now, fit superheaters to any of the existing Lm boilers. Instead, a complete range of new standard superheated boilers with Belpaire fireboxes was designed to suit all classes, of which the 'Z' type went into the 101 class, and 'X', identical with it save for length of barrel and firebox, fitted both L and Lm classes.

These superheated boilers first appeared towards the end of 1930, and a surprising detail was that those for MGW engines were at first arranged for the brake on the fireman's side. The barrel was 4' 3" diam., the same as the 101 and a trifle less than the L and Lm. The fireboxes, save that after the first few the foundation ring was increased from $2\frac{1}{2}$" to 3", were respectively the same as the 101 and L, so the Lm engines gained a little in depth. The 5' 7" long Z box had a much greater grate area than the 5' 1" X, but the latter being deeper there was not much difference in nominal heating surface. The larger smokeboxes made it necessary to move the leading springs of both GSW and MGW engines to below the axleboxes.

Lm class No.612, formerly No.75 *'Hector',* illustrates the class as evolved into the Inchicore house style, but still with a saturated boiler. In this 1951 view she is, appropriately, by the Inchicore coaling stage.

Sean Kennedy

L class No.608, formerly No.70 *'Ballinasloe',* is seen with her 'X' boiler at Broadstone in CIE days. By this time the Midland engines had been re-boilered with the Inchicore 'X' type boiler which conformed to the established practice of the former GS&WR.

G R Sharpe, Charles Friel Collection

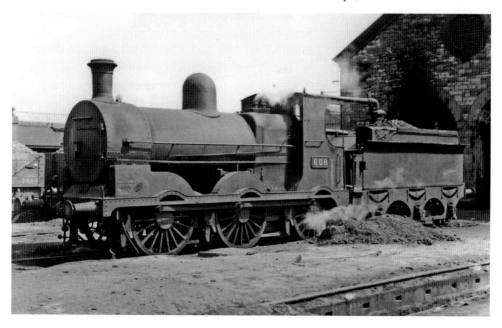

There was no other alteration, save for the provision of GSW cabs for all but two of the Lm class; the L class cabs were not altered. The slightly lower-pitched boilers and the wider cabs of the GSW engines still left room for a very good front spec, but the MGW engines became rather deficient in this respect.

Many of the GSW engines required new frames as well as boilers, and these were made to the 1923 pattern, but none of the stronger MGW frames required renewal. Even 85 years after the introduction of the 101 class, the intended locomotive renewal programme of 1951 provided for 25 new sets of frames for the class, which, had it not been cancelled, would have eliminated all the surviving iron frames of the lighter McDonnell type.

Superheating was the last major development and was never completed; in 1952, 33% of the GSW and 15% of the MGW engines still had saturated boilers.

Before passing to the last part of this article I must mention a contrast in the matter of the withdrawal dates. This, really, is a contrast between the two companies' practice, with the MGW - and this in spite of the more solid construction of their engines - always inclined to replace them by new ones at the earliest possible moment, while GSW engines tended to be practically everlasting with the minimum of change. Ignoring three MGW and one GSW Civil War casualties, twenty of the MGW engines were withdrawn between 1923 and 1928, due to their replacement by mixed traffic and Woolwich engines; but after that there were no more withdrawals till 1954, when dieselisation had been decided on. The first normal GSW withdrawal was not till 1926, but between then and 1953 a further sixteen engines were withdrawn from time to time.

Working at lower speeds, goods engines take longer than passenger engines to accumulate big mileages, and probably none of the 101 class quite achieved 2,000,000 miles, though 150, 151 and 153 may just have done so; the exact figures are lacking. However, about forty engines had exceeded 1,750,000 miles by 1956, and the average for the whole class would be about 1,600,000.

The Midland could not approach these figures, for the engines were not as old, nor was their yearly mileage as big. The best was 575, the only survivor of the 1876 batch, with over 1,500,000, while the others, excluding those scrapped before 1928, averaged about 1,250,000.

The Classes at Work

So far this has been all discussion of the past, known only from paper; now I approach the end with a comparison of GSW and MGW engines on the road. I hope that in dealing with the paper work I have been reasonably impartial - should that prove harder in dealing with personal experience of live engines, it is well known on which side my preference lies (Bob, as all who knew him will appreciate, had a deep affection for all things Midland).

It is only fair to admit, for a start, that it was possible to find a few Midland men who thought the GSW engines were the better, but I never knew a Southern man say that of the MGW engines. In a debate, I might just argue that it only proved the greater adaptability of the Midland men; but there were solid reasons for the fact. Midland men were already used to driving and firing from either side, and to the vacuum brake, but a Southern man on an MGW engine found himself on what was (to him) the wrong side, and faced with the use of a completely unfamiliar steam brake. Of course he didn't like it. It is worth quoting a Southern man's description of 602 when she was at Waterford in unchanged MGW condition - "the engine with the lever on the fireman's side and the letter-box fire-door".

Though the Southern men could sometimes be impressed too. The 'Slasher' Morgan (I think it was) was once in Newcastle West with the cantilever train. His Southern conductor warned him he'd never bring it up Barnagh Bank unassisted, but the 'Slasher' would go anywhere there were rails under him, so off he went. The Southern man could hardly believe his eyes when 590 just walked away with it, and no trouble to her.

Whenever possible, I like a neutral opinion of an engine, and here the best I can get is that of a Limerick & Waterford man (his own description, though it must have been at least ten years after the 1901 Amalgamation when he joined the railway - the inversion of the WLR's official title was invariable in the Tuam area). "The Midland", he used to say, "had wonderful engines, but they weren't made to steam". There I think he put his finger on it; with its bigger grate the GSW engine could (and did) burn more coal, and, the boiler barrel being the same, it was bound to make more steam. You would feel the difference all the more on a passenger train, where the extra demand of the ejector might be just too much for the MGW engine. There was another reason, too, for the 101's better steaming. An MGW engine, properly set, was and would remain straight in the valves, but it was unusual to find one of the GSW engines really straight, and they were often very crooked, which is always good for producing steam. On the other hand, when you got an MGW engine that had not her four even beats, you would feel at once that she was working against herself, whereas the GSW engine would hop along just as happily on three beats as on four.

The GSW engines had the reputation of being speedier on passenger trains, but this, I think, was only partially true. No doubt it was getting rid of the steam that limited the maximum speed of both classes, so the larger exhaust ports of the 101 should have given them an advantage which, in ordinary first-valve working, they certainly had. But though the MGW engines were inferior in these conditions, if pulled up tight and the second valve opened to suit, they became very much more lively, and worked this way there would be little to choose between an Lm and a 101, though an L might not do quite as well.

There could be no doubt at all about the very much smoother running of the MGW engine with its heavier frames and better springing; it was, probably for that reason, a freer engine to run shut off (fortunately, as it was more inclined to require a shut-off). I think that in the higher ranges of speed its lower internal resistance may just have balanced the 101's greater freedom of exhaust. The latter was an altogether rougher engine, developing, in particular, a side-to-side motion at the trailing end which must have increased its resistance - this may have been due to the removal (at a date unknown) of the collars from the trailing axles.

I have left the above as originally written, since it shows the conclusions I came to from personal experience of both classes; they are no doubt influenced by the fact that I have travelled (downhill) at 68 mph on an MGW engine, but never myself noted more than 64 mph with a GSW one. But the conclusions require amendment in the light of information supplied by Mr RM Arnold who noted a speed of 69 mph with a GSW engine; the really significant thing is that this was not down a steep bank, for it was at Straffan, where the fall is only at 1 in 450 for about five miles. On this occasion, 198, with a train of 5 bogies, would, unchecked, have run the 25$^1/_2$ miles from Newbridge to Kingsbridge in 29$^1/_2$ minutes start-to-stop, which I do not think even the best of the MGW engines could have done; nor, indeed, many of the GSW ones either. So, for speed, it seems established that the GSW engine was the better.

For heavy slogging on steep banks, on the other hand, the MGW engines were definitely stronger, within the limits of their steaming. They were also much better to keep their feet, partly because they were heavier, but more, I think, on account of their better valve events, which more than overcame such advantage as the GSW engines may have gained from their balanced wheels. It was well that this was so, for the sand gear of the Broadstone engines was much inferior to the Inchicore arrangement, though, in the days when they had it at all, the MGW engines had better back-sand. Most of the GSW engines, too, had screw dampers (a screw adjustment to the damper doors which controlled the admission of air below the fire bed), which were introduced in 1882, though eighty years later there were still a few engines not fitted with them. These were enormously better than the notched rods by which all MGW dampers (except for one or two engines altered when they were oil-burners) were controlled.

I have said that the screw reverse was a bit of a nuisance for shunting; of the two, the Broadstone wheel was the more inclined to get stiff (and even occasionally to jam) but you had under five turns of it to make, and with your right hand, whereas the Inchicore wheel took $7^1/_2$ turns, and with the left hand. The latter, if it was stiff, was really heart-breaking, for it was out in front of you and you could only pull it round by the spokes. (When a '101's reverser wheel is in 'reverse', it is right forward in an inaccessible position and the handle cannot be gripped to get purchase and the driver must resort to turning the spokes). The Broadstone wheel had no spokes to help, but you could get *beside* it where you had power at the handle. In latter days all the old Broadstone butterfly regulator handles had gone, so in neither engine could you have your hand on the regulator while watching the shunter.

Brakes, very largely, are a matter of what you are used to, and my personal preference is for a steam brake on an engine, as being simpler and more reliable, as well as using less steam than the vacuum. The old MGW steam brake must have been a real beauty, but once it had to be combined with the vacuum ejector it lost the virtue of being able to be graduated as you wanted it. I should mention that I have always heard it said that after the Amalgamation the MGW steam brake was considered too severe, and that the size of the steam pipe to the brake cylinder was reduced, but I could never get firm confirmation of this. What is certain is that in latter days the steam brake gear was removed from all MGW tenders.

Whatever about the relative merits of steam and vacuum, there can be no doubt about the very great superiority of the GSW brake gear. With an MGW engine in poor condition it was no uncommon thing to find the blocks rubbing when the engine was working hard on a bank; and usually this would be the very engine that would have the worst stopping power when you wanted it. And there was nothing you could do about it, for adjustment of the brake was definitely a fitter's job. I never knew this trouble occur with a GSW engine, and should any adjustment of the brake be needed, it was only a matter of a couple of minutes to do it, and no need to go underneath her either.

In comfort, no doubt, the MGW engines had it every time. Always smooth and steady, whereas the GSW engines (the superheated ones in particular) were nearly as hard on the ankles as a Woolwich. All the various types of MGW cab provided reasonable shelter but the apparently longer 101 class cabs covered as much of the firebox as of the footplate. Even when the 101 class got big tenders, they were almost all of the abominable Inchicore type, whereas the big MGW tenders were surely the most comfortable ever seen in Ireland.

I would imagine that the MGW engines, with their very solid frames (and in the Lm class, better motion) should have been lighter in maintenance, but I have never seen any comparative figures. With standard goods engines forming a large part of each company's stock, it is tempting to make deductions from the comparative costs of repair for 1924 - 2.19 shillings. per mile on the GSW and only 1.73 shillings per mile on the MGW. But the latter figure would be much affected by the large proportion of new, or nearly new, engines in stock at that time.

So there you have it - the GSW engine definitely better for steam (a good one could stand up to unmerciful abuse that no MGW engine could take), a little faster, and superior in many fittings. The MGW engine better in the frames and (the Lm at any rate) in the motion, a stronger engine for heavy slogging, and far more comfortable. On the whole, and in spite of my personal preference for the MGW engines, I think that probably the GSW was the better engine, but by very little. If the MGW engine had been long enough in the wheelbase to take the 5' 7" firebox, it might just have reversed the position.

But - a final thought - the GSW may have been very lucky. The first four engines built with the shorter firebox had the wheelbase correspondingly reduced, but then McDonnell changed his mind, and returned to the original wheelbase. Whether he did so with an eye to the future, or for some other motive, we shall never know; but if he had not had second thoughts about the wheelbase, there could have been no 5' 7" firebox without new frames (unless a very shallow one with sloping grate to clear the trailing axle) and probably the 5' 1" box would have remained standard.

A Valuable Asset

A Professional Appraisal of the 101 Class

by J J Johnston, MIMechE, MILocoE,
former Assistant Mechanical Engineer (Technical), CIE

The former Great Southern & Western Railway had in their locomotive fleet a group of engines classified as 'Standard Goods', but more commonly referred to as the 101 class. They were of the 0-6-0 wheel arrangement, the original weight being about 31 tons; later rebuilds scaled approximately 38 tons. Over the years the class was modified and rebuilt by the addition of new and heavier frames, heavier cabs, improved smoke-boxes, larger boilers and so on. The net result of these modifications was to improve the efficiency and power of the original locomotive, but it is fair to say that the original conception and 'bones' still remained throughout the many years the class was in active service.

The original designs have always been very favourably commented on by previous Chief Mechanical Engineers and several of them endeavoured to improve the basic design by using the modern concepts of their time and, in time, the class received different types of improved boilers, as well as being fitted with such refinements as superheaters. Working pressures were increased and the introduction of larger tenders extended the operational range of the engines.

As an operating unit the 101 was always very popular and it formed the backbone of the freight services, having an amazing capacity to haul its allotted load of over 500 tons, equivalent to 45 wagon units. It proved most reliable in service and drivers spoke very highly of the class as it had a very high recovery margin and was not at all sensitive to the various types of coals which were burned in it over the years. I shall have more to say about the wide variety of fuels used in the 101s later, but suffice it to say now that using a good Welsh steam coal a 101 proved complete master of its job.

On a railway network such as that in Ireland, with much of the track mileage consisting of relatively lightly-laid rural branch lines, a very important property of a locomotive is its axle-loading. In this respect the 101 was ideal; its low axle-load of approximately 12 tons allowed it to work almost any place on the system. To the Operating people this was a great advantage and meant a lessened burden in making out rosters and timetables. It was also of benefit to the Permanent Way Department as each year a 101 could be allocated to the weed-spraying train which could then be worked at ease throughout the system without having to worry about the route availability of engine power.

Their operation on branch lines showed the class up to great advantage, as the engines could be manned and operated very cheaply. Their coal and oil consumption was very low and there was great competition between the Districts as to how low the coal and oil figures could be brought. While in later years the 101s could be found on many branches, on some lines they worked for many years, for example on the long and mountainous Valencia branch.

On the question of hauling heavy trains on gradients the 101 was very capable indeed. Due to its wheel diameter of 5' 1³/₄" it had the ability to negotiate gradients easily, and it had a turn of speed to enable the boiler to keep a sufficient supply of steam to the cylinders. As regards curves, it had a locomotive rigid wheelbase of 15' 6" and with a thin flange on the middle drivers it could easily negotiate the sharpest curves and turnouts in complete safety. Due to its combination of laminated and volute springs the 101 was a very safe locomotive at all speeds within its working range of up to approximately 60 mph.

198 lasted until 1965 and in the early 1960s was a familiar sight for passengers coming off the Holyhead – Dun Laoghaire ferry as she took them on the last leg of their journey.

Here she heads a goods train through Clondalkin. The steep climb for the first few miles out of Dublin would not have taxed 198 today with her 20 or so wagons.

Charles Friel Collection

The wheel arrangement and power classification of the 101 was very much to the liking of the Civil Engineer as it did not create any major problem for him as to balancing and to punishment of track. The consequential hammer-blow was well within acceptable limits and the speed of the class did not cause any trouble in this regard. The dimensions of the engines were such that the class could go into any loading-bank or goods store and no complicating restrictions were imposed. The total wheelbase of approximately 35ft meant that the engines could be turned on even the smallest turntable usually found. In the odd case where exceptionally small tables were sited, extension rails were readily fitted to accommodate the class.

Much could be written on the upkeep, repairs and maintenance of the class, but suffice it to say that, in general, the 101 was an easy unit to maintain, both in shops and in running sheds. The axleboxes, motion, pistons, valves, etc. could be repaired and maintained easily and, due to the good accessibility of the design, the engine could be 'stripped down' very quickly and faulty or worn components replaced much more speedily than with the other classes. The wearing parts were few and, once tyres were turned at 50,000-60,000 miles and axleboxes and motion tightened up, a 101 could give an economic mileage of about 150,000 between general repairs. This was considered quite satisfactory. Most running sheds and small depots carried a sufficiency of springs, brake blocks, crosshead slippers, piston rings, etc. to enable a locomotive to be refurbished and put back to service without undue delay. The 101 was a very convenient locomotive to lift in any depot to change wheels or boxes, and it was not unusual on a visit to find a fitter and his mate handling a job in a road outside a running shed.

A handy gadget which allowed the buffer beam to be supported and moved out to gain access to the valves and pistons. The left piston is visible and the slide valve chest has been opened up by the fitters. The observant will note that 140 still had an oak buffer beam!

Real Photographs/NRM

On the operating side, the class was used for a very great variety of jobs and it is quite true to say that it was the mainstay of the Operating Department, which required an engine capable of carrying out yard shunting, banking, freight and transfer work, passenger and cattle special working, assisting of heavy passenger trains, overload and beet special working, to name but some of the duties assigned to this extremely versatile class.

It is worth commenting on some of these duties in a little greater detail, for the main advantages of the class when used on a particular type of work may not be at all obvious at first glance. For example, with cattle specials, availability for working all yards and cattle-banks is vital, as is manoeuvrability. With the 101s on the job very few traders complained of injury to animals because of rough shunting. The job of marshalling a train was smoothly carried out, as was the actual running of the train to its destination. This was also true of overload specials and, indeed, the one potential restriction on the class where through running was concerned was the limiting factor of the coal and water capacity. The 101s were selected for the bulk of the freight workings and trains were made up on the basis of 45 wagons, to suit the class. Once they had received assistance up the heavy banks from North Wall or Kingsbridge, they could go anywhere with this sort of loading.

On beet specials throughout the winter months the class was at its best. Train rosters were prepared well in advance and the engines were 'tightened-up'. Then, night after night, for three or four months, the 101s would haul full specials of beet from countryside to factory, returning quickly to be ready for another run the next night. Only the toughest of locomotives could stand this type of punishment, but the 101 lived up to it manfully.

Train assisting was another 101 'speciality'. There are many who will remember the days when a 400 class 4-6-0 hauled the Day Mails out of Cork with a 101 heading up the train. The practice continued for quite some time and it was only decided to discontinue this form of assisting when it was deemed undesirable to have a higher-speed train engine, with a 6' 7" diameter driving wheel, running with a much smaller-wheeled 101. Another very familiar task for the 101s was the working of special passenger trains. Besides working football or pilgrimage trains up such lines as the Newmarket or Cashel branches, the class was also in evidence for the Naas race specials. To the end of the 1950s it was a rewarding sight to watch two of the class, polished and gleaming, double-head a race train down the Southern main line to Sallins Junction.

I have previously mentioned the reaction of the class to different fuels, but it must be stated that in the war years, when every alternative to coal had to be considered, the behaviour of the 101 was again excellent. Satisfactory results were obtained both on test and in service. Besides the normal soft

A big source of traffic for railway companies throughout Ireland was the regular, usually monthly, fairs held in towns all over the system. In the days when cattle were transported 'on the hoof' they were carried after sale by train to the nearest port for shipping to the United Kingdom. The operation was organised with military precision by the railway and the first item of business in the Weekly Notices of the GS&WR and its successors was *always* that week's livestock arrangements. Cleaned empty wagons were worked out in advance of the fair, often, as in this case, having accommodation provided for engine crews, loaders and drovers. 196 here tackles the 1 in 85 gradient through Inchicore with an empty train from Cabra on 8 May 1953. Note the AEC railcar, which first went into service a year earlier.

Charles Friel Collection

Pilot engine 154 and the train engine, a Woolwich mogul, both show signs of effort as they heave the Rosslare Express through the tunnel leaving Cork. 154 would normally have been detached after six miles at Blarney, leaving the Woolwich to tackle the remaining seventy miles alone.

David Murray, IRRS Collection

An exceptionally heavy 3.50pm 'Up Mail' needed three engines on this day. The train was made up of eight fairly new steel coaches, four older wooden ones and the Post Office sorting carriage seen behind the train engine – 52 axles, around 400 tons. An unidentified 101 was the pilot, which came off at Blarney, and she certainly looks to be pulling her weight. Following her is No.322, a member of Coey's celebrated '321' class, while the train engine is No.402 one of Watson's less successful '400' class. Both of these engines worked through to Dublin.

J A Hogg, IRRS Collection

In April 1955, 152 pilots No.401 on the Up Day Mail from Cork, seen here emerging from the tunnel which begins at the platform end at Cork. Even a capable engine such as this rebuild of the disastrous '400' class would be allowed assistance as far as Blarney on this gruelling climb. Nominally, the load for an unassisted '400' class was "equal to 24", which equated to 6/7 bogie coaches. Assistance was, however, available on request to a driver who felt he needed it and the 101s were by far the most regular performers on this type of duty.

Kelland Collection 23063, courtesy the Bournemouth Railway Club

139 pilots a '700' class 0-6-0 at Rathpeacon, heading to Fermoy with a lengthy train of six wheelers on Sunday 25 June 1939. Another locomotive to have carried every kind of 101 class boiler, she survived until 1961. Interesting to see a 101 working together with one of her less successful descendants, which certainly seems to be trying to do her share of the work here, probably at the cost of the fireman's back!

That day, Cork played Waterford in the Munster Hurling Championship at Fermoy and the GSR provided the GAA with four specials from Cork at a fare of 2s 8d. Waterford's supporters were accommodated in three specials from that city and a further one from Mitchelstown. The railway used to carry thousands of supporters to Gaelic football and hurling matches every Sunday during the season and for this particular event a page and a half of the Weekly Notice was taken up with the arrangements; right down to the names of the inspectors attending, including two from Kingsbridge! Even to-day, the National Finals in Dublin see many specials run, although specials for purely local games are less common.

140 and 131 head another of the specials with an almost identical train that day.

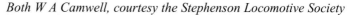

Both W A Camwell, courtesy the Stephenson Locomotive Society

Welsh steam coals, for which the class was designed, hard Yorkshire coal and, in the days of the 'Coal-Cattle War', Polish and American nuts were tried. Some use was also made of anthracite nuts and smalls from the mines near Kilkenny. All these coals were burned quite satisfactorily after certain modifications were made to blast pipe caps, and the firebar spaces adjusted to suit each type of fuel. Coke was also used and again a new form of draught arrangement was employed. Liquid pitch was likewise tried on the 101s but, while the experiment was quite satisfactory, the difficulty of keeping the pitch liquid ruled it out as a suitable fuel for a transport unit.

The use of turf, both in the hand-won and briquette state, was also tried and it was found that, if supplemented by timber in log form, this fuel was usable in the 101s. Several locomotives of the class were 'adapted' for turf burning by having cages built up on the tender to hold the large quantity of fuel needed. A spare wagon of turf was also necessary and an adjustment had to be made to the draught.

Quite apart from the fuels mentioned there was the Duff, which we had to use during the war when coal just was not available. Its use was most trying, but when it was combined with turf, wood, etc. it could be burned with quite reasonable results. Later it was found that the Duff could be briquetted and centres for the production of rectangular briquettes and oval 'ovoids' were established at Inchicore and the Broadstone. Pitch was used as a binder. It can be fairly stated that the railway was enabled to carry on during a very difficult period by the use of very large quantities of briquettes. These burned well in the fireboxes of the 101 class - yet another example of the adaptability of these engines.

I think I have said enough to indicate to those who were familiar with the 101s and to those for whom the interest in the class is academic, just how valuable an asset these engines were on our railway system. Certainly, from the large variety of duties assigned to them, they were thoroughly appreciated. Truly, the 101 class was the mainstay of the GS&WR locomotive fleet in its heyday - an honour retained until very recently indeed.

198, seen here at Inchicore, was a common sight around Dublin for decades. The ground is covered with the briquettes, made from low grade fuel bound together with a variety of materials including pitch and even cement, which kept services of a sort going during the fuel crisis. In the background is the mechanical coaling plant.

198 was a candidate for preservation but made her way to the front of the scrap siding and into the abyss while a decision was made about preserving one of the class. This locomotive is credited with the highest recorded speed with the class, 69mph at Straffan on only a modest downgrade. Perhaps a record for any Irish 0-6-0?

L Marshall

Mr Johnston mentions the class's value as cheap-to-run motive power for branch lines. Here, 156 sits in the bay platform at Headford Junction with the branch mixed train to Kenmare.

Rev John Parker, Photos from the Fifties 3021

J15a (or '700') class No.701 at Inchicore in 1933. Their designer, Bazin, attempted to improve the ageing 101 class but the result has been described as "A good cab on a bad engine." The use of saturated steam in an engine of this vintage was remarkable. Having an axleload 1.35 tons heavier than their predecessors restricted their use on some lines and their tractive effort was identical with McDonnell's older engines.

Locomotive and General Railway Publishing Co./NRM

J15b (or '710') class No.713 at Inchicore. This was another unsuccessful attempt to improve McDonnell's original design. Morton incorporated some elements of Midland practice into the engines but the tractive effort remained the same as the 101 class while the axleload was now 14.85 tons, about two tons heavier.

Frustrated crews complained of poor steaming, an inconveniently long cab for firing, an excessive appetite for coal and an inability to run freely when shut off. Many designers of locomotives carried out their craft quite unconcerned, it appears, with the lot of those who had to work on them. At least the cab provided some protection from the elements!

Locomotive and General Railway Publishing Co./NRM

The Descendants

The 700 and 710 Classes of the GSR

by R N Clements

Though the introduction of much larger goods engines by the GS&WR in 1903 looked like the end of new building of the smaller type, two much later classes require attention; the 700 class was a direct descendant of the 101 class, and the 710, closer in size, a modernised equivalent.

First, the 700 class of 1929 which, if my interpretation of events is right, was designed around the boiler. In 1924-5 Inchicore built 8 boilers, described as '60 and 101 class Belpaire', apparently with the intention of rebuilding the classes mentioned. Only one of these boilers was, in fact, put into a 60 class engine, and none into a 101 class, the other 7 remaining spare for several years, till the 700 class were built to use them. The boilers were, as was inevitable in Bazin's time, saturated, though they had Belpaire fireboxes and slightly extended smokeboxes. The barrel was 4' 5³/₄" min. inside diam., like the 351 class, but the length of barrel and firebox casing were the 9' 10" and 5' 7" of the 101 class, though the firebox was deeper with a slightly sloping grate. With only 188 1³/₄" tubes (223 in the 351 class) there was plenty of room for water in the boiler, and heating surface was 126 + 887 sq. ft. Pressure was the standard 160 lbs.

Wheels, axles, cylinders and motion were identical to the 101 class, the latter, of course, the final form with single slidebars. These must have been the last engines built with the old swing-links for the valve rods. The 1" frames were deeper than any of the 101 class varieties, and the suspension was quite different, coil springs for the driving axle and the others laminated, all being underhung. The axleboxes were not provided with wedges, the use of which had been abandoned by Inchicore.

Externally the change was complete - not only the larger and higher-pitched (7' 9") Belpaire boiler, but a large and excellent cab with extended roof and corner pillars, and the platforms raised clear of the side-rods. Tenders were at first 3,300-gallon ones from scrapped 362 class engines, but the usual changes occurred later. Within the limits of Bazin's addiction to saturated boilers, the 700 class were quite good engines, perhaps an improvement on a saturated 101; but their reputation suffered in comparison with the superheated 101s, which began to appear less than two years after them and were universally preferred to them.

The 710 class, of which five were built in 1934 and another five in 1935, were much further away from the original 101 class design, though all the main dimensions were the same, save only the height of the boiler, pitched at 7' 9 7/8". All essential features of the design had appeared in the 670 class 0-6-2T engines built in 1933, and it was a natural development to produce a tender version of these, with 5' 1 3/4" wheels instead of the 5' 6" of the tank engines. The boiler was the same Z as was used for superheating the 101 class, but otherwise everything was very different, and it is interesting to note that several features of Broadstone practice were included in the design. As the 710 class were built new with superheaters, 8" piston valves were provided instead of slide valves. So far, both Broadstone and Inchicore had used rocker-arms for all their piston valve engines, but these were now avoided by placing the valves at an angle of 1 in 8 to the cylinders, which made direct drive possible. This was similar to Glover's GNR arrangement, but the even more steeply inclined valves allowed the pulling links and valve spindles to be set in the same plane, whereas Glover's were slightly offset. Though the old swing-link had reappeared in the 700 class, it had been standard practice at Inchicore since 1900 (and at Broadstone long before that) to use guides attached to the motion plate for the pulling links, so the adoption of this arrangement was natural. The use of four slidebars, centrally supported in the motion-plate, quite clearly derived from Broadstone.

Externally, the conventions set by the 700 class were followed, except for the use of a heavy cast-iron chimney in place of the standard built-up one. It is hard to see why the frames were lengthened at the trailing end, resulting in a cab so long as to be inconvenient not only for the fireman, but also for the driver, who could not reach the firedoor handle from his seat which was set right back. The reversing screw and bracket in the cab were of Broadstone type, having the reversing rod connected to a die-block which moved on the screw, whereas Inchicore attached the reversing rod direct to the screw, the latter moving through the reversing wheel. The actual reversing wheel, however, was the large Inchicore one with a single handle, much more convenient than the two-handled Broadstone one. An innovation (on the Southern) was steam-sanding gear.

There was a clear attempt in this design to combine the best features of Inchicore and Broadstone practice. The idea was excellent but, as has often happened in the history of the steam locomotive, the result was quite the reverse; though the 670 class tanks were sometimes well spoken of, I never heard a good word said for the 710 class, which were the most universally despised engines on the GSR. They were, indeed, poor feeble things, with a considerable appetite for coal, but quite disinclined to show any result for it. It may well be that their greatest fault lay in the one feature not previously used by either the Southern or the Midland. I have commented elsewhere on the poor results of inclined piston valves, with their great difference between the length of front and back steam passages, on the GNR. I am, therefore, all

No.717 has just worked a local train into one of the 'Loop' platforms at Dublin, Amiens St., on 13 August 1956. The general lack of ability of these engines would have been concealed to some extent on such stopping trains on the Dublin and South Eastern section.

Charles Friel Collection

No.717 has steam to spare as she rolls into Dun Laoghaire with a train for Bray, a service on which, latterly at least, the class saw some use. The advert for Kingston Shirts reminds us of the town's former name, while Ireland's first railway, the Dublin and *Kingstown* Railway, terminated in the platform behind the name board proclaiming the town's name since 1922. The splendid colonnaded building in the background belonged to the Commissioner of Irish Lights.

David Murray, IRRS Collection

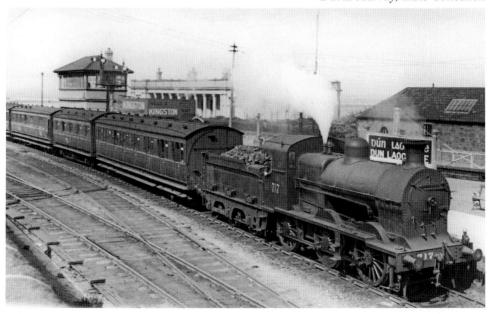

the more interested to see this very point considered by Inchicore, for in 1945 drawings were made of proposed new cylinders for the 670 and 710 classes, with the valves parallel to them. The arrangement was simple, with the valve spindle supported at the back by a guide bracketted to the motion plate; the pulling links worked through guides parallel to the centre line of the cylinders, and the vertical distance of $15^{3}/_{4}$" between pulling links and valve spindles was bridged by a fixed distance piece. The motion plate was to be set further back, and a single slidebar of standard Inchicore type, supported at both ends, was to be used. The alteration, involving new cylinders and extensive modification to the motion, would have been an expensive one, but was not proceeded with; probably this was as well, for, as it turned out, the life of the engines was not to be long enough to justify the expenditure; but it would have been most interesting to see its effect.

132, driven at full cry by Joe Bowe of Inchicore, takes the Waterford line at Cherryville Jct with a beet special/goods train from Kildare. The train's designation 'BC35' indicated that it was bound for the Carlow factory on 28 October 1961.

During the annual beet campaign, a number of crews would be based temporarily at Bagenalstown (or Muinebeag as it was commonly called then). 172 arrives with a special in October 1961, to be greeted by a relief crew. Note the typical impedimenta of a locomotive crew at the time – the can of oil and the basket containing the crew's meal, tea cans etc. The locomotive shed is on the right.

both Conrad Natzio

After the exams were over at Trinity College in Autumn 1961, Conrad Natzio made good use of his leisure time to capture some of the last steam workings. Here he gets a wave from the fireman of 197 as she drifts downhill on beet empties on the ill-starred Bagenalstown (Muinebeag) – Palace East line on 28 October. Mount Leinster in the background. The white disc on her tender signifies that it had once been converted for use by an oil-burning locomotive.

The same train makes an impressive arrival at Palace East, the junction with the North Wexford line from Waterford to Macmine Jct. For the final mile into Palace East, the GS&WR and D&SER lines ran parallel – this was not a double-track section.

both Conrad Natzio

172 rolls into Macmine Jct with an empty beet train on 11 November 1961.

Later she made her way along the River Slaney between Killurin and Wexford.

both Conrad Natzio

In October 1961 there was a three-day ballast working to the D&SER section from Lisduff. On the first day of the cycle, 195 was hurrying the empty train along the main line from Thurles to Lisduff quarry. Templemore was a superb example of Sancton-Wood's mainline stations, in dressed stone, with typical GS&WR low platforms and rounded off by a campanile.

On arrival at Lisduff, she propelled her train back into the ballast sidings for loading.

both Conrad Natzio

195 pulls out of the ballast yard at Lisduff, en route for Inchicore, where the night will be spent. In silhouette can be seen the aerial ropeway from the quarry and the crusher/hopper structure.

195 passes the Cherryville up home signal en route for Inchicore while working Day One of the ballast train cycle.

both Conrad Natzio

On the second day of the cycle, 195 travelled from Inchicore to the D&SER main line, where she is seen powering through Glenealy. After discharging ballast as required, the empty train will stay overnight at Wexford and return to Lisduff on the third day. The crew slept in sleeping vans which were a feature of CIE rolling stock for many years.

183 and 116, with steam to spare, attack the three miles of Ballyanne bank, between New Ross and Rathgarogue, while hauling a ballast train in September 1962. Even as the death knell rang for steam on CIE these little engines were still literally pulling their weight.

both Conrad Natzio

170 stands at platform 2 at Cork with a train of antique six-wheelers and the inevitable 'tin van' on the 2.30pm Sunday excursion to Youghal on 9 July 1960. By this time, the Cobh suburban trains and the less-intensive service to Youghal, for long the preserve of the 101 class, had succumbed to the AEC railcars, one of which can be seen in platform 4.

The late AG Cramp, courtesy Colour-Rail

A smart 137, with a tender from a withdrawn '342' class locomotive, has just arrived on the D&SER side at Amiens Street with a suburban train from Bray in the 1950s. She was associated with at least three different tenders during her last years before withdrawal in 1960.

The late Reggie Ludgate, courtesy Colour-Rail

The smart lines of the saturated 101 class were evident in this portrait of 191 at Thurles shed 3 July 1961.

John Dewing

162 was shunting at Limerick on 15 March 1961. Oil traffic from the Foynes is very evident.

Colour-Rail

The IRRS used to run an annual tour on St Patrick's Day and during the 1960 tour, 184 in her green livery was heading north at Enniscorthy after a journey which included 'Mott's Line' from Bagenalstown to Palace East.

John Dewing

In March 1963, the school railway society of the Royal Belfast Academical Institution (hence 'RBAI' on the rather oversize headboard) ran a special from Dublin to Ballylinan, Palace East via 'Mott's Line', Macmine Jct and returned to Dublin by the D&SER main line – impressively late, as it turned out! 151, seen running round her train at Athy after the visit to Ballylinan, was one of the second batch of Beyer Peacock locomotives and the oldest remaining member of the class.

Colour-Rail

The preserved 101s on Company service, before and after preservation. 184 became something of a pet when CIE hosted a meeting of the Institution of Locomotive Engineers at Inchicore in 1958. She had previously been displayed as part of the celebrations for the belated launch of the 'A' class diesel-electrics. In a livery similar to the original Great Southern and Western green of the previous century she made an eye-catching sight as she continued to carry out her daily tasks around the capital city. Here she passes through Islandbridge Junction on 19 March 1960 with a transfer goods.   *John Dewing*

The extensive dockyard system of the Belfast Harbour Commissioners generated much traffic for all three railway companies in Belfast. On 2 June 1967, while officially stored at York Road for the RPSI, 186 was appropriated by NIR to act as station pilot and to collect coal traffic from the docks. The class therefore saw company service a century after being introduced.

Irwin Pryce

The Sheriff Street Lift Bridge over the Grand Canal into the Spencer Dock provides an unusual foreground for this view of 136 shunting near Newcomen Bridge Junction in Dublin. The bridge is unusual as the lifting beam is at 90° to the direction of the tracks and the bridge, when open, is lifted completely clear of its foundations, not the normal 'drawbridge' format. It is illustrated in the open position in Donal Murray's *'Rails around Dublin'* (page 68).

David Soggee

Rathdrum bank is a stern test of a locomotive which faces an eight mile climb south from Wicklow. Northbound trains face a similar challenge with an ever-steepening ten mile climb out of the Vale of Avoca. On 10 April 1976, we see 186 on this climb returning to Dublin.

Irwin Pryce

Before and after. Inside Mullingar shed, 186 had already visited the make-up department to be repainted for her static role in the film *'The First Great Train Robbery'*. Sister 184 remained externally in a semi-derelict state as RPSI volunteers continued with her 'fast track' restoration.

Now heavily disguised as 'South Eastern Railway No.134', 184 waits at Moate which stood in for Ashford, Kent in the film.

both Charles Friel

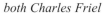

A view of 184's footplate during the filming of '*The First Great Train Robbery*'. Driver Joe Byrne, Fireman Paddy Reeves and Inspector Eamon Lacken seem quite unperturbed as they make their way from Castletown to Mullingar, pursued by a helicopter!

Irwin Pryce

Surely a pinnacle in RPSI history was on 11 June 1978, when no less than three of the Society's locomotives were in steam together at Limerick Jct on a gloriously sunny Sunday afternoon? 186 had just completed her stint on the two-day tour and with 184 was about to run light engine to Cork for further work on '*The First Great Train Robbery*'. No.4, built in 1947, provides a modern contrast with her older mixed traffic sisters.

Charles Friel

After the making of '*The First Great Train Robbery*', the two stars remained for a time in the green livery used and it was in that guise that they headed the 1979 two-day tour. On 27 May, the saturated 101 pilots the superheated one as they head away from Ballinasloe.

"From Derry to Kerry". Still in 'film green', on 1 September 1979, 186 makes her first acquaintance with the city of Londonderry – the furthest north that a member of the class has ventured!

Both Charles Friel

The RPSI has run 'Santa' specials both North and South for many years, but never with the effect of the first year we tried them in the Republic. The night before, it snowed! 184 approaches the 46th Mile Box on 12 December 1981. To split the long section between Killucan and Mullingar, the MGWR inserted this block post, which once had a loop and a siding.

Once NIR had accepted her, 186 began to do her share of RPSI work, an early example being the northern 2004 'Santa' trains. She is seen crossing the Dargan Bridge over the Lagan.

both Charles Friel

186 and her train sit in the autumn sun amid much modern railway paraphernalia at the now-closed Adelaide container base at Belfast, prior to her big occasion – the special train to Cultra to celebrate the 40th anniversary of the foundation of the RPSI.

Alexander McDonnell could not in his wildest dreams have visualised one of his locomotives in a scene such as this. In her third century, 186 returns to Whitehead, skirting Belfast Lough and passing through the modern engineering wonders of an electricity generating station powered variously by coal, oil and natural gas. When the first 101 was built in 1866, electricity was still an undeveloped source of heat, light and power.

both Charles Friel

The Class at Work

By Leslie McAllister
and Irwin Pryce

When Alexander McDonnell came to Inchicore in 1864, goods traffic on the GS&WR was handled mainly by several types of 0-4-2 tender locomotives and the eight 0-6-0s which the company had by then. When he re-numbered the stock that year, he classified 47 locomotives in all as 'goods', so he included a few 2-4-0s, but these did not survive long into his reign. These locomotives hauled trains made up of small, fairly light, wooden-bodied wagons, of which the railway had some 700 in the 1850s, some of which would have served departmental needs such as locomotive coal and permanent way materials.

As their numbers increased, the 101s inexorably took over an ever-greater proportion of the goods traffic. By 1880, when some sixty of the class were in use, only a dozen of the 0-4-2s were still on the books and the 0-6-0s had all gone. By 1890, when over ninety of the class were in use, they ran virtually all the GS&WR's goods services.

An indication of the growth and nature of the company's goods traffic is the Report of the Directors for the half-year ending 30 June 1904, when the company had 6,867 goods vehicles: 2,445 covered, 2,536 open and 1,327 cattle wagons. By the First World War this had risen to a total of 8,400. In the Twentieth Century, wagons were now of a heavier type, typically weighing about 7 tons and with 10 tons capacity.

To cope with the increasing demand, Robert Coey first rejuvenated the existing standard 0-6-0s, by the introduction of the 4' 4" boiler. Even this was insufficient and he introduced a heavier class of 0-6-0 in 1903, although they were converted to 2-6-0s within a few years. After an unsuccessful experiment with some 4-6-0s for goods work, he built a further four 2-6-0s in 1909 before returning to the tried and tested 0-6-0 for two further batches of a dozen locomotives in all. Finally, in GS&WR days, Bazin introduced the '500' class 4-6-0s for mainline goods traffic, but No.500 proved to be so good on passenger work, and the 400 class were so unsuccessful, that the three members of the former type seldom worked the trains for which they were intended.

So the heaviest mainline goods work passed to these newer 0-6-0 and 2-6-0 locomotives, but there is ample photographic evidence that they never completely banished the smaller 101s from the main line. Such 101s as were displaced went to work on the branches, on some of which they took over both goods and passenger services from tank locomotives.

At the end of 1921 there were 25 of the class in the Northern District, 44 in the Southern, and 21 each in the Limerick and Waterford Districts. After 1925 the class naturally remained mostly at former GS&WR sheds and their use in the Midland Section (former MGWR) was infrequent as there were plenty of similar sized goods engines inherited from that railway. It was only on extension of Southern Section workings that they normally penetrated into the Midland area; such workings were Limerick to Galway passenger trains. On the Eastern Section (former D&SER) a few were used at Wexford and Enniscorthy where their duties included goods trains to Dublin. It was the crisis with the D&SER engines in January 1925 that caused an immediate transfer of several engines onto suburban work, Nos. 103/18/22/8/36/45/65/72/83/98 all being used in the years 1925 to 1928. Afterwards they were used only intermittently on these trains until the withdrawal of former D&SER passenger tank engines after 1950 made it necessary to move several to the suburban services. Their performance was often very lively and they gave nothing away to any of the passenger classes.

In mid 1930, after a reduction in number to 99, there were 21 allocated to the Northern District (with four still at D&SER sheds), 37 on the Southern, 19 in the Western and 22 in the Eastern Districts. There was little change by 1938 the district totals being 19, 36, 22 and 21 respectively. The number in stock was reduced very slowly. No. 173 going in 1933, No. 129 in 1940, No.165 in 1945 and then No. 159 in 1949. Over the next decade 31 were withdrawn, leaving 64, or no less than 58 per cent of the maximum, at the beginning of the last three years of CIE steam. At the middle of that decade a list of 1954 shows that there were still 20 in the Northern District, 33 in the Southern, 20 in the Western and 19 in the Eastern Districts. As more and more diesel locomotives were put into traffic during the late 'fifties and early 'sixties so the numbers steadily decreased but new ground was covered in 1959-63 when a few of the class were sent to the former Great Northern Railway shed at Amiens Street (the sole Dublin steam shed by then). Use on branch lines, working all trains, continued until either the branch closed or diesels took over. At the beginning of 1963 with only three months of regular steam working left there were still 39 in service (including the green No. 184) and even at this late stage the number exceeded by a handsome margin the next most numerous class of steam locomotive in Ireland.

It was during the fifties and early sixties that most of the photographs of the class were taken, as enthusiasts took the opportunity to capture them on film, while they could. Thus the Kerry branches, the Thurles to Clonmel line and the lines around Waterford became unlikely tourist attractions. Right up until the early sixties, the class shouldered much of the burden during the annual autumn beet campaign. They also continued to act as yard and station pilots right up to the eleventh hour.

An interesting point to relate is that after the GNR had been dissolved in 1958 and some of its locomotives came into CIE ownership that they found their way to far-flung parts of the southern system, whereas the contrary was not the case. A 101 did reach Belturbet and 172 worked the weed-killing train from Cavan to Dundalk after passenger traffic had ceased on that line. The unexpected appearance of this train, complete with 'Southern' locomotive and crew caused near apoplexy in Dundalk and after a pilotman was found, it was hurriedly despatched southwards. An unusual trial, involving the use of 136 on GNR metals, is described on page 140.

When steam officially ended on CIE in 1963, eighteen locomotives (104, 106, 109, 116, 118, 124, 125, 130, 132, 151, 164, 172, 179, 183, 186, 195, 197 and 198) were retained should they be needed for the seasonal beet traffic. Outposts such as Drogheda and the former tramcar sheds at Sutton were used to store locomotives, although the reliability of the newly delivered General Motors diesels meant that they were not required and so made their way to the scrap bank at Inchicore, Mullingar or Dundalk.

During the winter of 1963/4 Amiens St shed turned out one of the class each day, chosen from 130, 151 and 197, to heat the stock of out-going trains. In the summer of 1964; 130, 183, 186 and 198 provided power for a tour of much of the Irish railway system, organised by the SLS/RCTS and the IRRS. It fell to 183 and 198 to write what might have been the final chapter as they double-headed the train back from Dundalk to Dublin, reaching a creditable 55mph on the way.

In her early days as a preserved locomotive, 186 spent some time stored at Adelaide, Ballymena and York Road. Eventually, the staff at the latter shed found the temptation to try out a potentially useful machine irresistible and she was to be found for most of the summer of 1967 acting as station pilot at York Road. So the class can truly claim to have been employed on company service for a hundred years.

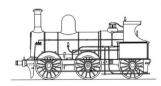

Inchicore shed about 1890. On the left is the pay carriage with its locomotive 'Sprite', then 103, 124, No.77 (0-4-4T), 160, 136, another 101 and No.35 (0-4-4T). We can be sure of the date, as 103 entered service in August 1889 and No.35 was withdrawn in 1892, being replaced by a 2-4-2 tank.

IRRS Collection

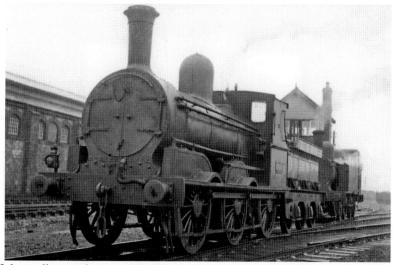

Seven of the earliest engines were scrapped when Ivatt was in charge at Inchicore and were replaced by him in 1889-91. He later scrapped the original 105 in 1895 and she was replaced by Coey in 1896, so that while 119 of the class were built, the actual number on the Company's books never exceeded 111.

103 is being shunted, out of steam, by a 2-4-2 tank at Tralee, suggesting that the photograph was taken just before the First World War, when these tanks were working the Valencia line. Her predecessor was built in 1867 and scrapped in 1886.

Real Photographs/NRM

Henry Ivatt had been trained at Crewe, like his predecessor Aspinall, and had been District Locomotive Superintendent at Cork where he must have had plenty of experience of the 101s in service. He obviously was satisfied with the type, adding a dozen during his ten years in the chair. Like many of Inchicore's top men, he was to progress to the top of his profession, becoming the CME of the mainland Great Northern Railway in 1896. His successor, Robert Coey, was a Belfast man who had spent most of his professional life at Inchicore, entering the drawing office in 1873 and being appointed works manager in 1886. He retired through ill-health in 1911.

It was he who built the final 21 locomotives of the class, starting with 105, which was the first to have a directly-connected reversing screw and one of the last to receive a 'Z' boiler, which lasted her until withdrawal in 1963. She was shunting at Castleisland on 24 May 1958. The branch had been closed during the fuel shortage of 1947 and apart from occasional specials, did not see regular, if sparse, goods traffic again until 1957. It finally closed in 1977 and was lifted in 1988.

John Edgington

110 was built in 1890 to replace the fourth 'true' 101 to be built at Inchicore in 1868, largely identical to the two batches of locomotives which Beyer Peacock built in 1867 and 1868. The original engine lasted just 21 years, but this 110 was to last 72 years. Little wonder that Hamish Stevenson, son a famous photographer father James, should have grown up as an enthusiast, for when he took this photo on 16 August 1958, while accompanying James on a foray to Ireland, he was but ten years old! 110 is shunting at Thurles and appears slightly dwarfed by '351' class No.252, which has a '257' class boiler!

Hamish Stevenson

114 was another of the replacement engines, built in 1889. Now with her second, a 4' 4" boiler, she is seen with her proud crew at Rosslare's shed at Ballygeary. The 'GS' wagons date this picture as after 1925.

Real Photographs/NRM

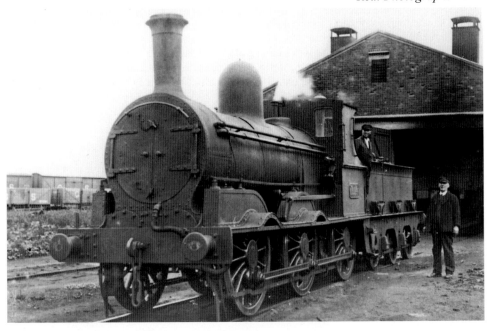

118 was the last steam locomotive left in Cork on 28 August 1965 when John Langford photographed her. In the background C211, in CIE's green livery, is smokily carrying out the station pilot duties formerly the preserve of 118 and her sisters. She had replaced an 1867 'hybrid' locomotive of that number when she was built in 1891. Obtaining a 4' 4" boiler about 1928, she only had one for about 5 years before upgrading to a 'Z' type which she carried until officially withdrawn in 1966.

John Langford

149 replaced one of the 1867 built Beyer Peacock engines when she was built in 1889. She had carried a 4' 4" boiler for 30 years when she received her first 'Z' boiler in 1933. In this guise, she is seen at Inchicore shed in the mid-thirties. For some unknown reason, the vacuum ejector and application handle have been placed in an unusual position outside the cab, evidently operated by an extension rod from the footplate. The flush smokebox with counter-sunk rivets also offers a diversion from the normal Inchicore practice.

Locomotive and General Railway Publishing Co./NRM

Ivatt used this photograph of 135 in articles which he wrote to describe the standard goods design. She is seen with her four foot boiler and 'H' section cast-iron wheels, with cast numberplate proclaiming that she was built at Inchicore in 1885. She is fully lined out, although the reader should be reminded that the photographic emulsions of the period did not pick out black or red very well, so that the lining appears to be simply the double light green lines! The central black band is just discernable in the original photograph.

Official GS&WR, D McNamara, courtesy Sean Kennedy

A rare view of a 101 class in almost original condition. 'H' section spokes, raised firebox and the absence of vacuum brakes date this photograph as 1887 or earlier. The vehicle being shunted in this view of the Kingsbridge yard is a 'birdcage' brakevan. The idea of this design of van was that the guard could see over the top of the train from his perch. The North American caboose follows the same principle.

Locomotive and General Railway Publishing Co./NRM

108, built in 1875, had already received her second boiler when she was recorded at Mallow in 1901. She was one of the first of the class to be built with the larger 18" cylinders and was to survive until 1957.

170 is being prepared for her next task at Inchicore on 2 September 1901. She retains the early Ramsbottom screw reversing arrangement, which connected to the weighbar shaft by means of an intermediate pivoted link and shaft. She does not appear to have any any lining, or other adornment, but despite that she was maintained in gleaming condition.

Both Ken Nunn Collection, courtesy the Locomotive Club of Great Britain

A goods train ready to leave Kingsbridge with 149 at the head. The variety of wagon types in this long train is a reminder of the role the class filled in the transport of the necessaria for daily life at the time. There are several 'convertible' wagons at the front of the train - such wagons had a removable tarpaulin in the roof, allowing it to become a wagon ventilated for use in transporting cattle.

The GS&WR used a complex lamp code to show the type of train, for a goods train this was two green lamps, one over each buffer. This was later simplified and by 1935 a goods like this one would have carried one white lamp over the left buffer. In CIE days most trains carried two white lamps.

Robin Linsley Collection

163 photographed at Limerick shows many features of the original design. During her 83 years she carried four different types of boiler and two types of frame, reminding one of the hundred year old axe which had three new heads and four new handles. The driver is wearing a bowler hat – a common status symbol among persons of such elite standing.

Ken Nunn Collection, courtesy the Locomotive Club of Great Britain

138 with a short train of horseboxes and a six-wheel passenger brake in the Military Platform at Kingsbridge during 1914. We can only speculate as to just what sort of operation she was involved in. Remounts for the Curragh? A race meeting? Horses destined for the Front? The next few years were to see mighty changes for Ireland, Britain and the continent of Europe, but 138 was to soldier on for almost another half century oblivious to all of this.

Ken Nunn Collection, courtesy the Locomotive Club of Great Britain

The two classic types of Irish locomotives are seen in the 1880s at Banteer on the Mallow to Tralee line. 187 is piloting '2' class No.8. These 4-4-0s were also a McDonnell design and were Ireland's first class with this wheel arrangement. The theory expressed about such a pairing was "an 0-6-0 for pulling and a 4-4-0 for speed". The 101 class engine has not yet been fitted with a vacuum brake as she has no connections on the buffer beam. The train may well be a Killarney excursion, although the lack of facilities in the six-wheel coaches may well have taxed the endurance of some passengers.

H H Coghlan, Real Photographs/NRM

Bearing in mind that the 101s were goods engines, there are relatively few photographs of them doing the work for which they were intended! The reason may be that the times of passenger trains were publicly available to the photographer?

If the Inchicore cab gave little protection for the enginemen, they were at least better off than in the open roofed wagons provided for livestock. Legislation later demanded that roofed wagons be provided for animals, though engine crews did not benefit from similar consideration.

Lance King Collection

242 was one of the last twelve members of the class, built 1902-3. With their marine big-ends, they were deemed sluggish compared with their more conventional sisters. Built new with a 4' 4" boiler, she retained one all her working life. She is seen on arrival at Waterford with a goods train from Mallow on 24 April 1956, a year before withdrawal.

John Edgington

The Wexford Goods was the preserve of what were the pride of the erstwhile Dublin and South Eastern Railway, the inside cylindered Moguls Nos.461 and 462. With only two of the larger engines available and strict weight restrictions on the line a 101 was the likely alternative when either of them was not available and here 135 pauses at Rathcool with the Wexford Goods.

The Inchicore engines, being in Group J for goods trains, were allowed to take only 33 wagons over the D&SER against the 45 allowed for the Moguls which were placed in Group C. Furthermore, the large cab with sliding side sheets and overall roof on Nos.461 and 462 were enough to convince local enginemen that the mighty Inchicore had something to learn from Grand Canal Street.

Drew Donaldson

Athy has always been a busy town for the railway. In the 1950s it was served by the Dublin - Waterford goods and another which terminated there. On most days during its time in Athy the engine would have made its way to Ballylinan to pick up any traffic offering there. Beyond Ballylinan the line extended to serve that rarity in Ireland - a colliery.

Working back from Athy in August 1955 we see 172 joining the Dublin - Cork Main Line at Cherryville Junction. The fireman can be seen holding the single line token as the signalman prepares to catch it.

David Murray, IRRS Collection

The 101 class were regularly used to assist other locomotives on steep sections of the railway and nowhere more so than the 1 in 78 straight off the platform-end *and in a tunnel* at Cork.

110 pilots 4-4-0 No.306 out of the Cork tunnel on the 1.25pm train to Tralee and Waterford on 28 June 1951. The train split at Mallow, one half going on to Waterford, with a connection to Rosslare Harbour and the other offering a connection to Kerry off the 10.45am Dublin - Cork express.

Cedric H S Owen

Another strenuous two miles at 1 in 60 up to Rathpeacon still faces this pair, as 171 pilots a 'Woolwich Mogul' out of the tunnel and past Kilbarry on the 'Rosslare Express', which ran via Mallow, Dungarvan and Waterford to the port from which it took its name. The crew of the train engine would have hoped for the pilot engine to have done a bit more than their share of the work before detaching at Blarney.

The Woolwich Moguls (2-6-0s) were assembled by the MGWR (the first one only, as No.49 of that railway) and then by the GSR at Broadstone and Inchicore in 1925-7 from parts manufactured at the famous arsenal after World War One. In an endeavour to keep the large workforce busy for a period after the Armistice, locomotive manufacture was tried; but only the Southern Railway bought complete locomotives - no great surprise as they were to the design of their CME Richard Maunsell when he was in charge at Ashford on the South Eastern and Chatham Railway. An Irishman, Maunsell had earlier been 'in the chair' at Inchicore.

David Murray, IRRS Collection

The difficult climb out of Cork was a trial for engines and men. Even to-day, when greater power is available at the push of a button, it is not unknown for trains to get into difficulty. In the days of steam, loose-coupled goods trains, known as the 'Runs of Goods', were worked up to Rathpeacon where they were made up into larger trains for the easier road thereafter. The Working Timetable included about ten paths each day for these trains in the 1950s.

As they arrived at Rathpeacon, 130 at the front seems to have just shut off, while a sister engine banking at the rear is still hard at work.

David Murray, IRRS Collection

Even No.328, one of Coey's splendid rebuilt '321' class, would have been grateful for assistance from a lesser engine in the shape of 108 for the heavy climb out of Cork. They are bringing their own train into Glanmire Road from the sidings, ready to pick up the passengers and set about the climb. This was almost certainly the Waterford and Tralee train which left Cork about 1.15pm.

L Marshall

Members of the class intermittently saw use on the suburban trains to Bray, from both Westland Row and Harcourt Street, in GSR and CIE days.

114 quenches her thirst at Harcourt Street between duties on suburban trains. A fine selection of coaches in CIE's 1950s two-tone green livery suggest that this was not long before the line was closed in 1959 after 105 years of operation, happily to have been reborn as part of LUAS in 2004.

Dr Neil A McKillop

121 is sitting in the 'Dog's Home Siding' at Grand Canal Street shed on 27 July 1936. The siding took its name from the cat and dog home below. Behind the tender can be seen Boland's Mills, famous as Eamon de Valera's command post during the Easter Rising in 1916.

She carried this 4' 4" boiler for about fifty years until she was withdrawn in 1963. The GS&WR had a complex whistling code for communications between drivers, signalmen and shunters. Thus, the engines carried two whistles of different pitch, one being used for shunting moves. The two can be clearly seen on the cab roof.

R G Jarvis, courtesy Midland Railway Trust

An immaculate 200 at Bray on 6 June 1932. She remains exactly as she had been built 29 years earlier, complete with those archaic double smokebox doors. She would not swop her original 4' 4" boiler for the new 'Z' type until 1942. It would appear that Henry Casserley was not sufficiently attracted by the magnificent Compounds which the Great Northern had just put into service to ignore this attractive local train. In the event, the Compounds came and went, and life went on for the humble 101 class.

Henry Casserley

200 is about to leave the 'Loop' platforms at Dublin, Amiens Street, with the 12.53pm to Dalkey on 14 August 1958. By this time the short reign of the AEC railcars on mainline services was all but over and they were being cascaded onto some suburban services.

Late James L Stevenson

132 is seen on the turntable at Bray with her 4' 4" boiler, replaced by a 'Z' type in 1941. The 101s worked on the ex-D&SER local services after the Amalgamation of 1925 and again in the 1950s until the dieselisation of these services late in decade. Being tender engines, the crew had the chore, after each relatively short journey, of turning their engine.

Hamish Stevenson Collection

254 awaits passengers from the Holyhead boat at Dun Laoghaire Pier on 9 June 1958. As can be seen, the station was being reconstructed, but the old signal cabin on the platform was still in place. An interesting feature from an earlier era is folk *carrying* their luggage, long before the days of suitcases with wheels!

A E Bennett

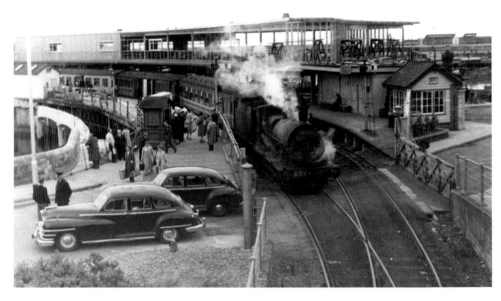

The other commuter flow often served by the 101 class was the line from Cork to Cobh, and to a more limited extent, to Youghal. Services on the Cobh line have prospered, but the line to Youghal has been dormant for some time. However, in recent times, the potential value of the Youghal line and even the main line to Mallow has begun to be appreciated as a sensible way of relieving congestion in the city.

In 1957, 140 heads a train of four bogie coaches, with a clerestory brake carriage at the rear, through the city outskirts to Cobh

Courtesy the Stephenson Locomotive Society

181 heads a most diverse rake of coaching and goods stock on the 3pm from Cork to Cobh on 29 May 1955.

C Saunders, R K Blencowe Collection

108 had steam to spare while energetically getting away up the stiff climb from Cobh on the 4.20pm to Cork on 30 May 1955. Her train is mainly of elliptically roofed GS&WR stock, although the final coach is a 1930s 'Bredin'. The line from Cork to Cobh was probably the nearest thing that the GS&WR had to a commuter line. Residents of the transatlantic port had just over a dozen trains a day at this time.

Even with just twenty minutes between trains, 108 had visited Cork's turntable to be turned before hauling the 5.20pm to Cobh, seen here near Fota. Eight passenger vehicles of an older vintage for this train, including two six wheel brake thirds. Munster was obviously enjoying a fine warm May day, judging from the lowered sash windows.

Both C Saunders, R K Blencowe Collection

An excursion train hauled by 128 passes Dunkettle, en route for Youghal on 9 July 1958. Despite the cloudy sky, it was obviously a warm summer's day, to judge from the number of open windows in the old bogie and six wheeled stock. Heads are out of the windows enjoying the fresh air and the view. By now, 128 was on her third type of boiler, which lasted her thirty years until her withdrawal in 1963.

Roy M B Crombie

Already an octogenarian, 104 will have her work cut out as she sets off from Youghal with a return excursion for Cork on 3 July 1955. The train is a heavy nine coaches and the efforts of her crew are attracting the critical gaze of their colleagues on another of the same class on a following train. Cork folk returning from a day at the seaside were well served by trains on a Sunday at 7.20pm, 8pm and 10pm.

L Marshall

There were few comers of the Irish railway system that were not penetrated by Drew Donaldson, but the Valencia Harbour line held a special affection and Cahirciveen was featured on his famous 'O' gauge model railway. Drew was never one to tread lightly through the world and both men in the photograph seem fascinated by the photographer - as well they might. Here he has recorded 241 at Castlemaine with the 2.15pm mixed from Valencia to Farranfore on 30 May 1955.

The rugged nature of the line from Farranfore to Valencia is apparent in this view from the train as 126 crosses Gleensk Viaduct between Mountain Stage and Kells. Thanks to Drew we have a complete log of this journey on 23 August 1954; the load of two bogies, a six wheeler and a van did not tax 126 too much, although another log shows 107 being well stretched with a bogie and twenty five wagons. Remarkably this view has changed little today, the viaduct and the track bed remain as a mute testimony to the rugged engines and men who worked the line.

The railway staff wait at Cahirciveen for Drew to take his photograph of 126 before she continues on her journey. His logbook shows how most of the uphill sections brought speed down into the 'teens, the 6¼ miles from Cahirciveen to Kells taking 22m 53s and the next 7 miles to Mountain Stage taking 19m 35s. The burns on the smokebox door bear testimony to the hard work involved on this line. The nature of the line excited comment in the Appendix to the Working Time Table under the heading 'Special Instructions re Particular Places' to the effect that "Drivers will be held responsible for their brake being in perfect working order". In the 40 odd miles of the branch there were six restrictions to 10mph due to 10 chain curves, five to 20mph and one to 5mph and in case anyone felt tempted to indulge in anything too adventurous there was a note that " Running times must be strictly adhered to"!

Drew Donaldson

Furthest West. On 14 April 1955, 127 has just arrived at the most westerly point served by the steel rail in Europe – Valencia Harbour. In the background, apparently in mist, one can just perceive Valencia Island. There were great, but alas unrealised, hopes for this line when built; both that it might become a Trans-Atlantic port and that it might bring prosperity to this remote area. Reenard Point, where a fisheries pier with sidings was planned, is behind the building to the right. There were just two trains a day each way on the line at this time and 127 has brought the afternoon passenger train the 39? miles from Farranfore.

Hamish Stevenson Collection

179 enters Killorglin in 1954 with the afternoon train from Tralee to Valencia Harbour, the only down train to traverse the whole line. It offers a remarkable variety of coaching stock, including what appears to be a former six-wheel saloon behind the engine. Little wonder that this branch was a magnet for enthusiasts!

141 waits at Glenbeigh with a train of six-wheelers en route to Farranfore sometime in the early 1940s. Corrugated iron was quite adequate for the 'Gents' on the platform, but the stationmaster might have hoped for something better for his residence on the left.

Both courtesy Stephenson Locomotive Society

133 has steam to spare as she gently follows what was surely one of the most scenic sections on all of Ireland's railways - the coastal section of the Valencia Harbour branch near the Drung Hill tunnels, seen behind the train. She is working the 11.35am train ex-Valencia Harbour on 28 August 1938. She was one of the locomotives involved in lifting the line following closure in 1960.

H B Priestley

Money was obviously short by the time that the line to Valencia Harbour was completed, as corrugated iron was used freely in station buildings and for the shed at Cahirciveen. 135 (left) and 195 await their next turn of duty on 24 April 1938.

W A Camwell, courtesy Stephenson Locomotive Society

The long branch from Headford Junction to Kenmare was an enthusiast's delight, running through wild and remote country. 133 is seen at Loo Bridge with the 3.30pm train from Headford Junction on 24 May 1955. Usually on branches an attempt was made to provide one bogie coach for those not wishing to sample the rigours of six-wheel travel. Even the introduction of diesel locomotives could not long delay the closure of this line, which succumbed on 1 January 1960.

John Edgington

On 20 August 1957, 130 awaits departure time at Kenmare on the 1.20pm to Headford Jct, with two bogies, a six wheel brake and a handful of wagons. Such antiquarian delights for the traveller were soon to disappear, though 130 herself survived to take a major part in the All Ireland tour in 1964. The Kenmare Branch was one of several with a 14 ton axleload restriction. The 101 class were well suited to a line with curves, steep gradients and weight restrictions.

Late James L Stevenson

107 brings the 8.15am train from Tralee into Limerick on 5 July 1955. This train was a 'mixed' and has a tail of no less than three horseboxes to complement the vintage passenger accommodation.

L Marshall

111 was a replacement for one of Beyer Peacock's 1867 locomotives, when she was built in 1891 and was a particular favourite at Waterford. She is making up a train in the Dungarvan line bay platform at Mallow. She never received a 'Z' type boiler and remained as seen here until withdrawal in 1963.

John Edgington Collection

131

On Friday 7 July 1950, John Edgington concluded his first trip to Ireland with a journey from Skibbereen to Swansea! He started on the 8am Skibbereen to Cork, the only through passenger service on the Cork, Bandon and South Coast line at that time. He had plenty of time to walk from Albert Quay to Glanmire Road to catch the 1.15pm train to Waterford and Tralee.

The 10.45am 'Kerry' passenger train from Dublin arrived at Mallow at 2.10pm and a shining 4-6-0 No.405 has just come off and been replaced by 146 and 4-4-0 No.336, which will depart at 2.15pm. Passengers off the Dublin train could connect to stations along the South Wexford line through Dungarvan to Waterford at 2.20pm as John was about to do; or continue to Cork by joining the 8am 'Perishables' train from Dublin, which the 10.45 overtook here, and which would depart at 2.25pm. A busy quarter of an hour at Mallow: the short post-war Indian Summer of steam on the Dublin - Cork mainline was in full swing but destined to end with the delivery of the AEC railcars from 1952 onwards. *John Edgington*

193 was at Blarney with a down train, mainly of six-wheelers, on 9 July 1934. Blarney, of course, had two railways with the Cork and Muskerry terminating in the town square adjacent to the grounds of the famous castle. One suspects that Henry was taking the opportunity of a ride on that line, which closed at the end of the year.

Henry Casserley

When this photograph was taken on 24 August 1957 steam had already been relegated to secondary work. The 101 class became a more familiar sight on passenger trains as passenger locomotives were rapidly withdrawn and the more utilitarian mixed traffic types were retained. 104 is at Mallow with the 7.20pm Saturdays-only to Tralee, which gave a connection from the 3.40pm train from Dublin.

Late James L Stevenson

A septuagenarian helps out the newcomer. A leaky and workstained 131 removes a failed diesel-electric from a Tralee train at Mallow in May 1962. The unreliability of the earlier diesels gave steam an extended life, as engines were kept standing-by waiting for an event such as this. At this time, Mallow still had two steam pilots on almost continuous duty, one at each end of the station. The shunter's pole, carried on the front buffer beam, was at one time a familiar sight as these men nimbly used them to hook and unhook the three-link couplings.

Oatway, Charles Friel Collection

On 22 June 1939, No.322 has arrived at Thurles with the 5pm Dublin to Limerick train, scheduled a three minute stop at 7.16pm. 114 is waiting with the connecting 7.30pm train to Clonmel. The low platforms were a characteristic feature of GS&WR stations and even with the double footboards on the six-wheelers of 114's train must have provided a challenge to the less agile.

Courtesy Stephenson Locomotive Society

191 is clearly ready to depart from Clonmel with the 8.10am to Thurles on 4 April 1958. Lance King, for years the Chairman of the London Area of the IRRS, had spent the night there, having arrived with the previous evening's connection from Thurles. By this time steam was all but a memory on the main line, but for the enthusiast, there were some steam-hauled trains on secondary lines. The cross-country line to Clonmel offered two such trips each day and was a magnet for British enthusiasts. When built in 1885, 191 was one of the first to be built new with steel frames and to be fitted with vacuum brakes. Her 4' 4" boiler was to last her 48 years until withdrawal in 1962.

Lance King

138 was shunting at Clonmel on 21 March 1960. The shorter smokebox on saturated engines left more room to stand at the front for the job of emptying the smokebox of char. The records appear to show that this engine received a 'Z' boiler in 1947, but in that case clearly she reverted to an older saturated one at a later date, as the photograph shows! An exchange of boiler would have been common as a locomotive underwent a major overhaul, but a reversion such as this must have been rare. At this period Clonmel had engine crews based there and driver Jack Dunphy strikes a proud pose, despite the battered appearance of his engine. The goods to Thurles remained steam, but the connections into the mainline trains were now handled by an AEC railcar.

John Dewing

On 4 July 1938, at Cahir, 171 heads a very varied train, including a bogie coach, some six-wheelers and a 'tail' of vans on a train from Waterford to Limerick.

Hamish Stevenson Collection

119 enters Athenry with the 11.55am Galway to Tuam train on 15 September 1956. The first coach, a six-wheeler brake third, probably dates from the 1880s, but the following bogie vehicles are much newer, the first is a 'Bredin' from the Thirties and the second, a 'Park Royal', is barely a year old. Salubrious accommodation for such a modest service, which is presently the subject of an energetic campaign for reinstatement.

At the period, CIE, unlike other railways almost worldwide, always made an effort to include some modern accommodation in most trains. The brake vehicle was often a six-wheeler - the guard sometimes perplexed by enthusiasts preferring to travel in that vehicle! One such, requesting that a compartment be unlocked, discovered that it had (unmistakably) been regularly used for the conveyance of greyhounds!

Lance King

At the time Laurie Marshall photographed 121 at Sligo on 9 July 1955 (his birthday!), the shed would have hosted engines from the MGWR, GS&WR and SL&NCR. 121 would have reached this northern outpost via the 'Burma Road' from Claremorris. On the left is one of two 0-6-4 tank engines delivered to the SL&NCR in 1951.

L Marshall

On 7 July 1955, 124 leaves Athenry with the 9am Limerick – Tuam goods which called here for an hour at 5pm. A further pair of trains between Limerick and Sligo catered for the goods needs of stations north of Tuam. By now, the single daily passenger service between Limerick and Sligo was provided by an AEC railcar set, but the Limerick – Galway passenger train remained steam.

L Marshall

Athenry was a rarity in Ireland – a four-way junction. The MGWR Dublin to Galway line crossed the WL&WR Limerick to Sligo line. Allowing for long section block working, the signalman had no less than six different patterns of single line staff to contend with.

The next day, 123 is seen during her two hour stop at Ennis with the Athenry to Limerick goods. A mixed train from Tuam connected into this train at Athenry. The 60 miles from Athenry to Limerick occupied around ten hours as the train served almost every station and most would have had wagons to be attached or detached. The lazy progress of the loose-coupled goods train is a thing of the past on today's railway, but was bread and butter work for the 101 class during nine decades.

Lance King

114 awaits departure time at Wexford North with the 6pm to Rosslare Harbour in 1958. There were two of these local services each way on weekdays, with an additional train on Thursdays and Saturdays. This short ten mile run was a magnet for enthusiasts while it remained steam, especially because of the diversion of chasing cars, etc while traversing the quays on the way to Wexford South!

To this day, Wexford Quay continues to offer excitement for cars, bikes, pedestrians and trains alike. 114 is seen shortly afterwards sharing the quays with a vintage assortment of road vehicles.

Both courtesy the Stephenson Locomotive Society

The same service on another day in 1958 was hauled again by 114 which was a regular performer around Wexford at this time. The passenger accommodation was provided by two older ex-D&SER passenger vehicles: a 45 foot bogie coach with centre lavatories and a six wheeler. As before, any parcel traffic offering was generously provided for by two 'tin vans'.

A traveller nowadays could easily miss the site of Macmine Jct – once a place of some importance in South Wexford. Country junctions were places where long periods of tranquillity would be rudely awakened by a burst of activity and one is unfolding here in this 1957 scene. 135 has arrived with the afternoon train from Waterford. At the island platform, another 101 waits with the connection back to that city and the afternoon mail train from Rosslare to Dublin is signalled. A small pile of mail sacks for the Dublin direction from 135's train is ready by the waiting room. The normal calm will be restored in about ten minutes time and so things will remain for another five hours.

135 was withdrawn shortly after this and was shipped, with 107 and 158, to Spain for scrapping.
Both courtesy Stephenson Locomotive Society

Here 101 is waiting to cross the main Cork to Limerick road on 15 August 1957 while working a construction train for the Castlemungret branch. Serving a cement factory, the branch was a late addition to the system, leaving the Foynes Branch from a junction on the outskirts of Limerick. From 1968 the connection was made closer to Limerick.

Drew Donaldson

With the demise of the Great Northern Railway in 1958, CIE inherited a substantial number of capable locomotives in good order. This proved a blessing, as the first generation of diesel locomotives had by then demonstrated an embarrassing degree of unreliability. While Great Northern locomotives were used in various places throughout the system, no corresponding use was made of Great Southern ones north of Dublin.

In this unique view, on 13 May 1961, 136 is seen passing East Wall Jct. with seven Great Northern bogie coaches. She is returning from Dundalk after a test run to try out Polish coal. Whatever conclusion was reached regarding the coal, the use of the class on the Great Northern lines does not appear to have been repeated.

Courtesy Stephenson Locomotive Society

The Dublin and South Eastern Railway was another Irish line with severe weight restrictions and the climb of Rathdrum bank was a demanding task for the small engines allowed on the line.

In 1951, 254 and 172 head an up Wexford hurling special through Lord Cloncurry's private bridge, swimming pavilion and slipway near Blackrock. The bridge dates from 1833 and its exotic style reflects the sensitivity of many members of the aristocracy to having a railway built anywhere near their land and, indeed, the price they demanded for such a right of way. The ten coach train features GSR, CIE, D&SER and MGWR stock.

The leading engine, 254, was derailed during the Civil War while hauling the 11.55am goods from Maryborough on 30 November 1922. She stayed upright, but buried herself pretty well in the ballast, with the tender and following six wagons smashing into her and becoming derailed as well.

Another GAA special on the Dublin and South Eastern as 188 and 143 hurry a special south past Killiney in 1953. One wonders if any of the supporters (willingly) opted for the six-wheel brake/third at the front of the train?

Both Sean Kennedy

Ballyvoyle Viaduct was situated at Milepost 50 at the end of a three mile bank descending from Durrow on the Waterford to Mallow line. 189 had been on a ballast train and was returning to Waterford when she was intercepted at Durrow before being sent driverless towards the viaduct which had one arch blown up. The train demolished most of what remained of the viaduct (see inset) and the hapless 189 was so badly damaged that she was scrapped. She was retrieved by laying a temporary section of track and being hauled back up to the line. This photograph was taken on 31 January 1923.

Bill Scott Collection

James Tuohy, who was a locomotive foreman at Maryborough (Portloaise) at the time of the Civil War, left a small album of railway photographs entitled "Derailments on the GS&WR".

174 was derailed at milepost 4½, between Conniberry Junction and Abbeyleix, while working the 11.55am goods from Portlaoise on 8 March 1923. Happily she survived her ordeal and was to serve the railway for another 30 years. One wonders, indeed, if her presence in the works for inspection and repair after this derailment led to her being fitted with a circular dished door for use on the Rosslare to Cork boat trains.

James Tuohy Collection, IRRS

Variations on a theme. 106 pilots No.239 (formerly WL&WR No.58 *'Goliath'* of 1897) at Limerick Jct on 30 June 1938. Their respective designers' careers were to take very different paths. McDonnell went to the North Eastern Railway at Gateshead, but did not prosper and left the railway service. JG Robinson, on the other hand, went from Limerick to the Great Central Railway, where he earned no little glory with a succession of handsome, effective designs, of which the 'Directors' were probably the most famous. It has been suggested that Robinson copied the elegant cast iron chimney from the GS&WR and eventually applied the design on the Great Central.

Henry Casserley

125 calls at Birdhill on the Ballybrophy to Limerick line on 6 June 1961.

W A C Smith

Twice during the final years of steam in the Irish Republic was a major 'All-Ireland' rail tour run, in 1961 and in 1964. They were jointly organised by the IRRS and the British societies: the Stephenson Locomotive Society and the Railway Correspondence and Travel Society. Just as the RPSI today relies on British support to successfully run its ambitious annual 'International Railtour', British support was imperative to back-up Irish support for these tours which travelled the length and breadth of the island.

While both tours could call on ex-GNR(I) and LMS(NCC) locomotives on the northern part of the itinerary, it fell to the versatile and ubiquitous 101s to carry the major burden elsewhere.

Both tours involved CIE in a major effort to ensure success on what was, by then, a dieselised railway. Both tour trains included a dining car where the crews, by prodigious efforts, fed and watered the participants.

131 energetically departs Mallow for Tralee on 5 June 1961.

Late James L Stevenson

109 enters Gortatlea on the 1961 'Grand Tour'.

Courtesy the Stephenson Locomotive Society

For many years, the IRRS ran a trip to celebrate St Patrick's Day. 1962 saw an ambitious trip when Great Northern 4-4-0 No.207 *'Boyne'* made a lively run to Cork where 193 took over for a trip to Youghal. Cork shed had turned out 193 beautifully and she looks a picture here, though within a year she was scrapped. As was common in this area at the time 193 is painted grey. The Inchicore cab was perhaps politely described as distinctive and the engines had no frills or refinements, even beading on the cab was considered unnecessary. Enginemen often made their own modifications and the piece of wood here wedged behind the handrail made a more comfortable armrest.

John Dewing

Sisters meet at Limerick Junction. 118 is rolling into the rear bay platform with a train from Limerick to Waterford in the 1930s. As was usual for such trains, she will run behind the station building and reverse to her platform, taking up the position in which you can see 164 on page 47. Her diverse train is made up of a four-wheel passenger brake van, a four-wheel goods van, a six-wheel coach and a bogie coach – something for everybody (or everything!). On the main line face of the platform, 165 is shunting a horsebox and some vans.

232 was one of the last batch of the 101 class to be built in 1903 with modifications by Coey. Her train of two six wheelers is a perfect period piece. The leading vehicle provided First and Second Class accommodation, the former in generously spaced eight-seater compartments. The second vehicle provided Third Class seating and space for luggage and the Guard.

She is seen here at Birr the terminus of the branch from Roscrea. The station shows the pride which the stationmaster here took in the condition of his platforms. The company provided him with a substantial dwelling, which in nineteenth century rural Ireland must have reflected the considerable status of his post and the self-confidence of the railways at the time. The branch closed on 1 January 1963.

Both W A Camwell, courtesy the Stephenson Locomotive Society

A less romantic part of the steam age is evident in this photograph at Limerick as a cleaner emerges from the pit having raked the contents of the ashpan into the pit, to be shovelled into a wagon later. 106 has an unusual and inelegant stovepipe chimney.

Henry Casserley

Photographs by that inveterate traveller Henry Casserley appear throughout this book, but it was his son, Richard, who recorded 106 in 1955, by now superheated and carrying a form of spark arrester intended to avoid the risk of fire with oil traffic. As we have seen elsewhere, engines without spark arresters quite happily handled oil traffic from Foynes, where this photograph was taken.

Richard Casserley

A task which often fell to the 101 class, especially in the latter years of steam, was shunting or 'pilot' work and here we see some of the class executing this important work.

A view of Dublin familiar to passengers on the Great Northern, as 122 shunts the Midland Yard at North Wall alongside the tidal part of the Royal Canal on 28 June 1960. Even at this late date, the pilot engines here were still booked steam, with no fewer than four turns in the GS&WR yard and six in the Midland. Gas holders, commonly miscalled gasometers, were a familiar sight in the dockside skyline of both Belfast and Dublin as town gas was generated from coal brought in by sea.

Lance King

This busy scene at North Wall on 15 June 1962 reminds us of the level of freight traffic the railway once handled. Obviously 184's period of glory was over by this time as she looks well worn and has been attached to a black 3,345 gallon tender. She was not destined to see the year out in service, but did escape scrapping.

The progressive and adventurous O V S Bulleid was the designer of the corrugated wagon in the foreground. One wonders at his thoughts on finding so many veteran machines in the locomotive fleet he inherited on coming to Inchicore in 1949? However, his priority was to reduce the huge number of locomotive types on CIE by scrapping less numerous classes, so the Company's largest (and most useful?) class was to survive right to the end of steam.

Late James L Stevenson

127 shunts the carriage shed at Cork in July 1958. The handsome full brake next to the engine was one of two such vehicles designed by the GS&WR and built at Inchicore in 1924, the last year of the company's independent existence.

Dr E M Patterson

At the Cobh end of the station, 182 shunts vehicles on to a train in the main departure platform at Cork on 3 July 1955. Her clean appearance, even on so humble a duty, reflects the continuing pride which locomotive men took in their steeds. The diesel era had begun and while many mainline trains were now formed of railcars, it was not until this month that the first of a substantial order of diesel locomotives arrived on CIE. The lines in the left foreground provided a means for goods trains to avoid the two main passenger platforms.

L Marshall

A work worn 161 shunts at Ennis on 19 October 1954. When built in 1871, she received a boiler made by the Yorkshire Engine Company, an example of Inchicore out-sourcing components when required. Like many members of the class in latter years, she had acquired a larger tender by the time she reached the scrap line at Mullingar around 1962.

George Ellis

143 is seen at Inchicore in her final form with heavy frames and a superheated boiler. The man on the right is Paddy Leonard who was the fireman on No.406 in the Portarlington accident.

Sean Kennedy

150

106 at Tralee on 13 July 1934 as seen through the camera of "Cam" Camwell, one of Britain's most travelled railway photographers. Like many enthusiasts from the other island, he found Ireland's railways a source of fascination and this photograph captures the period perfectly. Tralee still retains the characteristics of many GS&WR stations with its overall roof covering one platform.

W A Camwell, courtesy the Stephenson Locomotive Society

181 of 1879 at Cork in 1931. She, too, went through the whole series of 101 boilers, getting new frames when she was upgraded to a 'Z' in 1937. She was still based at Cork at the end of her days in 1959.

Locomotive and General Railway Publishing Co./NRM

A fine portrait of three shining locomotives at Inchicore on 1 April 1956. Their appearance is a great credit to the shed staff, as by now the 'Indian Summer' had ended and steam hauled a mere ten percent of trains on the former GS&WR mainline. The 4-6-0 No.403 was originally built by Watson as a four-cylinder engine, but was converted to a more successful two-cylinder arrangement by Harty. The 4-4-0 is No.328 of Coey's much-praised '321' class, while 197 is an 1899 built member of the class which is the subject of this book. None of this fine trio was to last very long, even 197 succumbing within five years.

W A C Smith

200, seen here at the former Midland Great Western shed at Broadstone, was one of Coey's engines of 1903. The photograph shows the distinguishing features of the final engines of the class. The sandbox is larger and the reversing rod is connected directly to the valve gear rather than by a rocking lever attached to the front of the cab which is flush. This arrangement of the reversing rod would have meant that the reverser operated the opposite way to other engines, but was avoided by having a left hand thread on the screw. The roof and side sheets provide slightly better shelter for the crew than the older engines. Not apparent from the outside is the marine type of big ends favoured by Coey and the metallic packing used for the piston glands. While at Broadstone the GS&WR engines and men were regarded as outsiders and Midland engines took priority when it came to covered accommodation.

R S Carpenter

The camera-shy 102 was found behind the loco shed at Cork, Glanmire Road on 26 April 1956. It is notable that she has a screw coupling at the front, rather than the usual three-link version. Tender-first working was fairly unusual, except for short distances, as the GS&WR was well served by turntables. The working timetable indicated those stations so equipped.
John Edgington

117 was built in 1874 with 17" cylinders and received new, by then standard, 18" cylinders ten years later. An early casualty, she was withdrawn in 1930 just a year after this photograph was taken at Cork. This rear view underlines the almost total lack of creature comforts for the crew offered by the 101 class cab – not even beading on which to rest an arm. It is just possible to see the degree to which the firebox encroached into the cab, so that what appears to be a generous roof in fact covers as much equipment as crew!
Henry Casserley

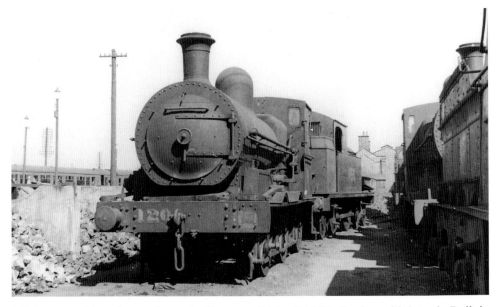

120 is seen, without her tender, at Inchicore on 24 April 1955 after her withdrawal. Built in 1877, she had carried every type of 101 boiler, her 'Z' type lasting her 20 years. One assumes that she had been coupled to a tender in good condition and that this had now been married up to a luckier sister.

Henry Casserley

129 is seen at Cork in the 1930s. She had just received her 'Z' boiler in 1933, but it was not to last her long, as she was withdrawn in 1940. She was a solitary withdrawal at this time and the reason seems lost in the mists of time. However, whether it was cracked frames, or another major defect deemed uneconomic to repair, we may be sure that good use would have been made of the usable parts and no doubt her boiler went on to be carried for another twenty years by a more fortunate sister.

Real Photographs/NRM

160 awaits her fate at Sallins on 29 August 1957, despite having been officially withdrawn in June 1955. Built in 1871, when she received a boiler made by the Worcester Engine Company, she saw many changes during her long life, carried every kind of 101 class boiler and received new frames when she got her 'Z' type in 1932. She had even been one of the locomotives converted to oil-burning in 1947-8. There can't have been much original left at the end!

A grubby 162 rests inside Limerick shed on 17 August 1958. Despite her forlorn appearance, CIE got more work out of her and she was not withdrawn until 1963.

Both the late James L Stevenson

175 has been fully modernised with a superheated boiler, though running with a tender still without the coal rails or subsequent built-up sides. Barely a trace remains today of Woodenbridge Junction on the Dublin to Rosslare line where 175 sits in the Shillelagh branch platform.

Simmons, IRRS Collection

176 was one of the two Sharp Stewart engines of 1873. She got new frames when she was equipped with a 4' 4" boiler in 1922. She is seen ready for more work at Cork on 27 June 1951.

Charles Friel Collection

A spotless Sharp Stewart-built 185 of 1879 is seen at Broadstone, probably in the 1930s. She received her 'Z' boiler in 1933, but unusually received new frames after that event. She was converted to oil-burning during the fuel crisis. Her tender is notable as it appears to be a completely unmodified relic from the earliest days.

Lance King Collection

190 was one of the ten 101 class to come from Beyer Peacock of Manchester and is seen at Cork on 3 July 1955. The photographer found her four days later at the opposite end of the country at Claremorris, an indication both of the class's ability to go anywhere and just how hard they were worked. In the background is a rake of six-wheelers retained for excursion traffic.

L Marshall

The crew of 194 busy themselves while waiting for the right away from the north end of Mallow on 10 June 1954. A train has been signalled away on the main line.

Charles Friel Collection

A well worn looking 195 sits beside one of her less successful cousins at Inchicore. Locomotive Inspector Bill McDonnell suggested that the '700' class remained mechanically tight longer than their older cousins – but that this was probably because foremen avoided sending them out if any hard work was needed! As the saying goes "handsome is as handsome does."

Simmons, IRRS Collection

199 at Limerick in 1932 shortly after receiving a superheated 'Z' boiler. The smokebox with countersunk rivets and flush-fitting door is in contrast to the normal Inchicore practice of using snap headed rivets and a door closing onto the front of the smokebox, often secured by 'dogs' round the periphery. Unusual also is the use of the more convenient two handles to hold the door rather than the almost universal Irish practice of using a wheel. The 4-4-0 in the background is No.298, formerly WL&WR No.55 '*Bernard*'.

Kelland Collection 23070, courtesy the Bournemouth Railway Club

223 was shunting stock at Headford Jct. on 15 April 1955. This busy little station, with an array of sidings and the junction for the Kenmare branch, survived until 1963 three years after the branch had closed.

Henry Casserley

Another engine never to be superheated, 229 of 1903 was being coaled at Tralee on 21 August 1957.

Late James L Stevenson

Sadly, the only photograph to come to light of 243 is after her working days were over and she was resident in the scrap line at Inchicore, between two passenger engines – No.60, 'name engine' of the noted 4-4-0 class and No.403, one of Watson's less-celebrated '400' class.

Charles Friel Collection

Mullingar seemed to be in danger of being overwhelmed by the tide of engines coming for scrap during the 1960s. Dundalk received many CIE engines for scrap in an effort to reduce the backlog. On 3 June 1961, 141, withdrawn two years previously, is being brought to meet her end by a more fortunate ex-GNR No.171 *'Slieve Gullion'*.

Late James L Stevenson

Mullingar marked the end of the line for many of the class. Engines for scrapping were stored under the gantries previously used for loading track panels onto the Bretland tracklayer train, designed by a former MGWR civil engineer. Here 232, 160, 253 and 190 await the end.

John Langford

On the evening of 10 June 1964, 186 leads 130 into Swinford, on the Burma Road, during that year's All Ireland railtour. This was 186's last passenger train in CIE service and, but for the intervention of the Railway Preservation Society of Ireland, she would have gone to the breaker's yard with her sister, whose last train was to be the next day double-heading the tour, with 198, into Amiens Street.

The train was formed of a full brake van at each end; with an ex-GS&WR dining car to feed the inner man and three of CIE's more modern bogie coaches. Those brake vans were very different with a lovely ex-GS&WR six-wheeler, complete with full length double step boards, clearly visible behind 130, and a new 'tin van' now sporting the 'black and tan' livery at the rear.

David Murray, IRRS Collection

186 was officially handed over to the RPSI in a ceremony at Dublin's Connolly station on 4 May 1968. Afterwards she hauled a tour to Arklow, when the train included the former Great Northern Railway directors' saloon which provided suitably distinguished accommodation for the guests. Here 186 passes under Kerr's Bridge on the climb to Milepost 96 (between Lurgan and Moira) heading north on the return empty working with the saloon and a brake first.

Drew Donaldson

The Preserved Engines

By Joe Cassells

Everyday steam ended on CIE in February 1963, but the last steam operation under CIE auspices was the 'Grand Tour' of Ireland in June 1964 for the IRRS/SLS/RCTS when 186, along with sisters 130, 183 and 198 worked the tour train over most of the CIE system, mainly double-headed. 186 spent her normal working last days in Waterford. Her connection with the Railway Preservation Society of Ireland began indirectly in June 1965 at a luncheon held to mark the presentation of Guinness No.3 to the society. A tentative request during the meal to Mr Frank Lemass, then chairman of CIE, led him to suggest that the RPSI might write to his board directly and ask for the present of a J15 – just like that! Within a week the letter had been sent and the reply received, and by September 186 had been chosen for the society. She was hauled to the former Great Northern shed at Adelaide, Belfast, on 11 December 1965, having cost the society only the £27 which CIE charged for the diesel haulage from Dublin!

In the spring of 1966, she was moved to Ballymena and later to Belfast's York Road depot where she received some works attention in anticipation of a film contract. The steam engine sequences of '*Journey to the Moon*' were never made, but the society funded the completion of the work. In early 1967 she found 'Company' employment as the York Road station pilot, also on a series of ballast workings on the Larne line and the mainline as far as Kingsbog Junction. Her mainline tour debut came on 13 May 1967 and gave her a day's work on the Portrush branch which at that time was closed during the winter timetable.

In what the society prophetically billed as the beginning of a new era of long distance steam railtours in Ireland, 186 worked a special from York Road to Dundalk Barrack Street via Antrim and Lisburn on 9 September 1967. Just over a week after this tour 186 was moved to the RPSI's new depot at Whitehead for the first time.

1968 saw a major expansion of the RPSI's operations and 186 was very much the flagship engine. The official handover of the engine to the RPSI by CIE took place at Dublin Connolly on 4 May, following which she worked a tour to Wicklow, visiting both the passenger and the now-closed Goods station. On 14/15 September 186 was involved in the society's first ever 'two-day' tour, double-heading 'Jeep' No.4 (then still a company engine) from Connolly to Enfield and then taking the train forward to Athlone and Ballinasloe. The following morning she did a short working to Roscommon before working the tour to Portarlington and finally following No.4 into Dublin with a train of dining cars which had provided the luncheon catering.

Returning cross-channel passengers were worked forward by 186 to Dun Laoghaire Pier – possibly the shortest branch she has ever traversed? On 29 September she was hired by the IRRS for a day excursion from Dublin Heuston to Kilkenny. On 3 November she should have made a first appearance in Derry, but due to heavy flooding which washed away a bridge at Glarryford the night before, the tour was reorganised at 5.30 in the morning! So 186, together with Jeep No.50 found themselves working from York Road to Dundalk via Antrim and Lisburn instead. A classical example of the flexible and friendly way NIR and CIE/IE have helped the society down the years.

1969 was a quiet year for 186, but on 20 March 1970 she was used on a 'local' tour from Belfast to Portadown and then to Larne Harbour. Two months later she covered the Kingscourt branch on a special which began in Dundalk and finished in Dublin. 186's first substantial outing in 1971 was on 17 April, from Belfast to Dublin, taking in the Ardee branch and the cement factory at Drogheda. The following day she worked out to Portlaoise and covered the surviving stub of the former Kilkenny line as far as the Coolnamona turf factory. At this period, 186 had a Southern base in the goods yard at Sallins, later replaced by the former shed at Mullingar. On 11 September she worked out of Dublin again, heading down the D&SER once more to Arklow, and on return to Dublin made an extensive tour of the Dublin dock lines.

The only passenger train to have visited the Cement factory at Boyne Road in Drogheda was worked by 186 while on the way from Belfast to Dublin with the *Slieve Gullion* railtour on 17 April 1971. *Courtesy the Stephenson Locomotive Society*

The June 1972 two-day tour was unique in that it started and finished in Limerick. 186 worked over the North Kerry line to Tralee and back, visiting FOUR branch lines over the two days – Castlemungret Cement Factory, Fenit pier, Foynes and Castleisland. She returned to Belfast in October working from Dublin to Dundalk via Southern Point Yard and the Howth branch. The journey back to Whitehead continued with the RPSI's recently acquired first coach, the twelve-wheeled No.861.

On 13 May 1967, 186 worked her first RPSI outing, the *'Dalriada'* railtour, double-heading WT class No.55 from Ballymena to Coleraine in preparation for a busy afternoon of shuttles on the Portrush Branch. Here they are seen at the closed Macfin Junction, where the former Derry Central Railway once joined the B&NCR main line - an opportunity to compare Ireland's oldest working steam locomotive with one which marked the final chapter of conventional steam locomotive building for the island. Both, incidentally, deemed to be 'mixed traffic', but what a contrast!

In 1967, an Irish preserved branch line was but a dream, but on this day Drew Donaldson, then the RPSI's Railtours Officer, persuaded NIR to let the Society take over the Portrush branch and run a shuttle service of trains, powered alternately by No.55 and 186. 186 is seen departing from Portrush.

Both the late James L Stevenson

A feature of early RPSI tours was the 'runpast' which allowed passengers to descend at a station and record the engine working hard as she passed through. Engine and crew usually played to the gallery and here 186 darkens the sky at Ballinderry, Co Antrim, on 28 October 1967. The Scotsman, James Stevenson, who clearly had a love for Celtic steam away from the highlands and lowlands of his native land, catches that 'glint' effect, provided by a setting sun, much treasured by railway photographers.

Late James L Stevenson

186 crosses Ballyvoyle Viaduct between Durrow and Dungarvan on the highly scenic line from Waterford to Mallow with the *'Three Rivers'* railtour on 16 September 1973. Seen here returning from Ballinacourty to Waterford, she worked through to Belfast that evening. This was a distance of some 290 miles, surely a record day's mileage for the class?

When the viaduct was blown up in 1922 during the Civil War, classmate 189 was damaged beyond repair and scrapped the following year.

Tim Stephens

1973 saw 186 share the honours on the two-day tour with the society's ex-GNR(I) No.171. On the Saturday she worked from Dublin to Rosslare, whence No.171 worked the train across to Waterford. 186 followed light engine and hauled an evening trip to New Ross and back. Next morning, No.171 suffered a serious mechanical failure and it was left to 186 to haul the train out to Ballinacourty on the remains of the Waterford to Mallow 'Scenic Line' and then back – to Belfast! 186's marathon 290 mile day was almost certainly a record for a modest 0-6-0 in main line preservation.

The following year 186 took a short tour to Larne in April, before working the two-day tour in September with the newly restored Jeep No.4, rescued when NIR finished with steam in 1970. No.4 took the longer stretches on the main line, while 186 worked the train from Limerick Junction to Clonmel and back. Next day she double-headed the train with No.4 from Limerick to Silvermines, but then she suffered a hot tender axlebox and after arrival at Ballybrophy with No.4, she toddled gently back to her southern home at Sallins.

This depot was soon to disappear and on 24 January 1975 she travelled to her new home at Mullingar, which had become the Southern base of the RPSI. That year's two-day tour saw her work the train from Castlerea to Claremorris and then over the exotically-named 'Burma Road' to Sligo and back the next day, the last steam train over this route. On the Sunday morning she worked the train out along the quays at Sligo – almost certainly further than had been planned!

Apart from a day trip to Wexford in April, 186's only major mileage in 1976 took her from Cork to Youghal and back as part of the two-day tour. She then recreated a scene from times past when she double-headed this train up the steep gradient out of Cork and on to Mallow.

1977 was a big year for her beginning with a local excursion from Mullingar to Galway in April – the first of the RPSI's *'Claddagh'* trains. June saw her working from Limerick to Galway via Ennis and Athenry on the Saturday of the two-day tour. On the Sunday she took the train single-handed from Galway to Claremorris via Athenry and then double headed No.4 to Woodlawn. To end the year, she was involved in a Dublin – Drogheda outing, connecting with a working which brought No.171 from Bangor. During the day, she banked No.171 from Navan Junction to Tara Mines at Nevinstown and then worked by herself from Navan to Kingscourt, double-heading back to Drogheda before returning solo to Dublin.

Now came the year of *'The First Great Train Robbery'*, starring Sean Connery, Donald Sutherland, Lesley-Anne Down and 184, supported by 186! The 'star' 184's story is told later, but 186 still had a supporting actress role to play, before temporary retirement in 1980.

186 hauled the *'Claddagh'* to Galway in May and, between film shots, was used on the two-day tour in May with No.4. She double-headed the train from Carrick-on-Suir to Waterford, with the 'traditional' run up to New Ross in the

evening, then next day took the train on alone to Rosslare, double-heading back to Limerick Junction. Here 184 was waiting, having run down light engine after spending a restful weekend at Thurles shed. So on this gloriously sunny Sunday afternoon it was possible to photograph three RPSI engines in steam together. It was one of the high points of the RPSI's history – you had to have been there! While No.4 took the tour train back to Dublin, the two 0-6-0s slipped down the main line to Cork for their next date with the filmmakers. To crown a busy year, 186 worked three return trips from Dublin to Bray in September, the first of a long series of the RPSI's short steam trips from the Capital.

In a break with its tradition of using at least one express locomotive, the RPSI ran its 1979 two-day tour with two 'small' engines. 184 and 186 hauled the train from Mullingar to Westport and Ballina, returning to Athlone. Much less arduous was a short working from Whitehead to Belfast as part of the RPSI's Open Day. The year ended when 186 became the first 101 to visit Londonderry's Waterside station, confirming the class's 'go-anywhere' status. 1980 saw her work two short tours from Belfast to Carrickfergus and Whitehead and that might well have been the concluding chapter of 186's service in RPSI ownership.

184's story can be more briefly told, but after languishing unloved for many years, she was to have her fifteen minutes of fame!

In December 1966, CIE announced their intention to preserve three steam locomotives: ex D&SER No.461; ex GNR(I) No.131 and ex GS&WR No.184. After some time in store at Inchicore Works, 184 was overhauled for a film contract in 1968. The scenes for *'Darlin' Lili'* were shot on the ex-GNR(I) Navan branch, though assistance was provided by a diesel locomotive disguised as a coach! This was followed by appearances in steam at the then-annual open days at the Works in 1968 and 1969. However, by November 1975, 184 and No.461 had been moved to Cork for storage, while No.131 was placed on a plinth at Dundalk.

However, 184 and No.461 were not destined for plinths, as both were placed on long term loan to the RPSI. When a film company approached that society seeking a steam locomotive from the period of the Crimean War, they were, in effect, told that if they paid to restore 184, they could have it looking whatever way they wished!

Thus 184 was substantially overhauled in double-quick time by a team of RPSI volunteers working full time against the clock. The film company retained the late John Bellwood, Chief Engineer of the National Railway Museum at York, as consulting engineer and by all accounts he was suitably amazed when after just eight weeks, 184 hauled three coaches at 40mph to fulfil her mechanical reliability test!

Now with copper-topped chimney, a huge brass dome, outside framing covering her driving wheels and without a cab roof to save the crew from the elements, she really looked the part. Crewed by CIE men, she performed nearly faultlessly in scenes at Kingsbridge, Cork and Moate, to say nothing of being memorably filmed at speed on the closed line between Mullingar and Athlone by Oscar-winning cameraman Geoffrey Unsworth. In the colour section you can see just how well she looked, but you just have to see the film!

It was during 184's run to Cork that the meeting of the two preserved 101s took place at Limerick Junction. 186, also re-painted for the film, played a modest, static supporting role. The full story of this contract, too detailed to more than summarise here, appeared in the RPSI's magazine *'Five Foot Three'*. The RPSI gained valuable funds, but even more, now had two operational 101s – albeit painted in a totally fictitious green livery – and 184 took her place in the main line tour programme. A new life beckoned.

In the spring of 1979, 184 was in demand again for film work, shot between Bray and Greystones and this was followed by the two-day tour already mentioned above. September saw her hauling three shuttles between Dublin and Bray and the following Spring saw her repeat this performance on two dates. Although the 1980 tour was largely hauled by No.171, 184 ran a connection from Dun Laoghaire Pier on the Saturday and on the Sunday worked the last-ever steam working over this branch, before it closed as part of the DART modernisation.

184 has starred in several films. In 1968 some scenes in *'Darlin' Lili'* were filmed on the line from Drogheda to Navan where she is seen crossing the River Boyne. The smoking van behind the engine was in fact a disguised 'A' class diesel locomotive, as 184 was in poor condition. She retired to Inchicore afterwards until, having been handed into the care of the RPSI, she was restored to a condition fit to work trains unassisted again.

Charles Friel collection

1981 was a more adventurous year for 184 and began with the *'Claddagh'* working to Galway in June, supplemented with a local trip to Athenry, so that the people of Galway could sample the delights of an RPSI steam train. The two-day tour in September saw 184 hauling the train from Mullingar to Sligo, double-headed with No.171 to Longford, then on her own to Ballymote while a mechanical problem on the bigger engine was sorted out. At Ballymote No.171 caught up and both engines double-headed into Sligo. At Colloney Junction, just outside Sligo, the RPSI celebrated its coverage of the entire Irish railway network – and 184 had the satisfaction of covering a section of track (from Mullingar to Colloney) which her older sister has yet to cover in RPSI service! Fitting, too, that the 'junior' member of the RPSI's main line team should be there to help complete a unique achievement - for no other national preservation society, world-wide, has covered its entire native railway network, steam-hauled.

Christmas 1981 and the following Easter saw 184, as the resident Mullingar engine, working seasonal shuttles. There were Santa trains to Multyfarnham, Killucan and Castletown *in the snow*! *'Easter Bunny'* trains are an RPSI fund-raising vehicle, since copied by other preservation societies. The 1981 trains ran from Mullingar to Multyfarnham and Castletown. Just a week later, 184 was off on *'Claddagh'* duties to Galway. In May she worked the two-day tour from Athlone to Limerick via Athenry on the Saturday. Sunday saw her working to Foynes and back, before double-heading the train with No.171 as far as Roscrea. Christmas saw her working for Santa again, taking him from Athlone to Moate and back, having worked empty from Mullingar. That town's folk got their turn next day when she worked to Multyfarnham, Killucan and Castletown.

'Easter Bunny' trains and a *'Claddagh'* began 184's year in 1983, then came her appearance on the two-day tour. This time she worked from Kilkenny to Waterford, with an evening trip for local people to Campile and back. The day was not over, as she now had to run to Rosslare and back, simply to turn on the turntable there! The following day she took the tour train from Waterford to Limerick Junction. She hauled a private charter from Mullingar to Athlone in June, then a series of Dublin – Bray shuttles in September. October saw her used in filming for the TV series *'An Irish RM'* and a day's filming for *'A Painful Case'* in December finished a busy year.

Next year began with a Dublin – Enfield return excursion. There were two further Enfield shuttles in September. 184's contribution to the May two-day tour was to work the train from Claremorris to Galway via Athenry. A combination of train-splitting and double-heading the following day took her all the way from Galway to Athlone, before a light engine run back to the Mullingar depot.

The 1985 two-day tour took 184 to Cork and she worked two local trips to Cobh before the arrival of the main tour. Sunday saw her double-head No.171 to Mallow, before working on to Limerick Junction as part of a train-splitting

184 on tour duty at Dun Laoghaire Pier on 17 May 1980. She was picking up passengers off the Holyhead boat and other participants who had spent the night in a hotel at Booterstown. Her return trip to Dublin Connolly turned out to be the last ever steam-hauled passenger train to leave the station.   *Irwin Pryce*

operation. She returned home to Mullingar via Portarlington and Athlone. Dublin – Maynooth shuttles in October and Mullingar – Castletown Santa trains completed her year's work. In 1986, her work was limited to three appearances: May saw her double-heading with No.4 from Athlone to Westport on the two-day tour and heading a Claremorris – Tuam 'branch connection' on the Sunday. A *'Claddagh'* in July and a series of shuttles from Dublin to Maynooth in August completed her year's work.

1987 was more eventful for 184 and began in June with an empty carriages working from Mullingar to Ennis for two days of shuttles between Ennis and Gort for a local festival. In August there was a series of shuttles from Dublin to Clonsilla, repeated in September. This was followed by several days' operation for a further film contract, *'Echos',* in September. Over the course of a busy week's filming she covered the route from Dublin to Waterford, via Rosslare, then out to Carrick-on-Suir and back, on to Limerick via the Junction and finally back home to Mullingar via Athenry and Athlone. More filming between Mullingar and Moate in October ended a profitable period of work!

1988 was 184's last year of service – so far anyway. In May the two-day tour took her to Limerick, whence she ran a trip for the public to Birdhill and back before taking the tour train from Limerick to Tipperary on the Saturday. Next day she worked the train from Limerick to Athenry, but her work was not finished yet, as she finished with further local trips from Athlone to Clara and Clonydonnin, before returning to base at Mullingar.

That would have been the end of the 101 story, except that the decision was taken to restore 186 again and ensure that the Class would be seen steaming in its third century.

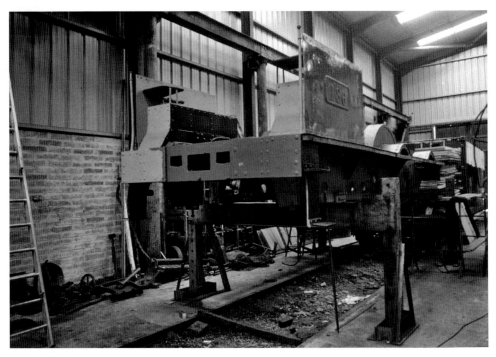

To give some idea of the fundamental nature of 186's restoration, these two photographs show parts of her in the process of the overhaul. Above can be seen the locomotive's frames, jacked up so that the wheels can be re-profiled, etc and the bearings attended to. The boiler, firebox and smokebox have all been removed for separate attention.

Charles Friel

Jim Rainey drives a threaded copper stay into the firebox. Once securely home the ends will be rivetted over. Hundreds of such stays hold the copper firebox and the steel outer wrapper plate against the boiler pressure.

Irwin Pryce

The Restoration of 186

By Irwin Pryce

By 1980, 186 was beginning to show her age and entered what many thought would be a short period of retirement. Eight years later 184 announced, that at the age of one hundred and eight, retirement was also beckoning. Pressures on the RPSI to overhaul other locomotives pushed both of them to the back of the queue and despite their historical significance there they remained until the year 2000 when a serious effort began to restore 186 to full working order. The RPSI is, of course, a voluntary, non profit-making organization and relies greatly on fund-raising schemes and grant aid (when this can be obtained) to further its restoration projects. Restoration of either locomotive was going to be an expensive job, so funding had to be in place before the project began.

The society has built up a volunteer and professional workforce and with a well-equipped workshop at its Whitehead base was well able to tackle the job from beginning to end. While the basic simplicity of the locomotive has been emphasised earlier in this book, modern requirements and standards have imposed new demands on the engineers carrying out the restoration. The task demonstrates the remarkable degree of knowledge and craftsmanship which resides in the restoration team at Whitehead, including a willingness to carry out the hard, dirty and downright unpleasant work involved in the repair and operation of steam locomotives.

Throughout all the society's restoration work the need to preserve the historical integrity of its charges is recognized. Modern methods may be cheaper and more convenient but the importance of these engines, as examples of engineering design and the methods of their period, cannot be ignored. So the retention of traditional skills such as riveting and hand fitting of bearings is a feature of the work at Whitehead. In addition to all of this, the operating requirements of the modern railway require an application of up-to-date technology to ensure safe operation. In the past, for example, drivers were not provided with a speedometer; electric lights were unknown and once they left a station they were left without any communication with the world outside the confines of their own footplate. All of these are examples of modern refinements which had to be sympathetically included in the restoration.

Boiler and firebox

At the centre of any locomotive is its boiler. As a pressure vessel, its overhaul and operation is subject to the most rigorous monitoring in every respect. In the past each railway company employed boiler inspectors specifically to monitor the operation of its boilers. These gentlemen had, single-handedly, the power to demand that certain jobs be carried out or indeed to withdraw an engine from traffic. Their knowledge had been built up from long experience and this, combined with a well-developed intuitive feel for their charges, secured safe operation of the company's locomotives. Much of their work used nothing more than a hammer, which in their experienced hands could detect a broken stay or wasted plate. Less accessible parts were examined with a burning oily rag attached to a piece of wire, while more accessible parts would have had the luxury of an oil 'duck lamp.' It is a tribute to the skills of these men that the safety record of Irish railways is impeccable in this respect.

It is here more than anywhere that modern technology has eliminated any element of rule of thumb, which may have existed in the past. Extensive use is made of ultra sonic techniques to ascertain the thickness of plates and the stays which support them. Early indications were that the boiler was in reasonable condition, without any need to renew the inner copper firebox. Several dozen of the copper stays which support the copper firebox did require replacement and were made and fitted at Whitehead, while many wasted rivets required renewal.

A complete set of foundation ring rivets was required – these secure the inner copper firebox to the outer steel wrapper plate. The lap joint rivets, which secure the joints in the corners of the firebox, were life-expired and replaced by copper patch screws with the heads rivetted over.

The front tubeplate of the boiler was however beyond economic repair, and though a major job, similar replacement has been carried out previously on other locomotives. The stays which run the length of the boiler securing the tubeplate to the firebox at the rear have also been replaced. Finally, the tubes which carry the hot combustion gases through the water space of the boiler have also been replaced, though this task is almost a matter of routine in the world of locomotive preservation. It might be mentioned that on a regular basis the boiler is examined in order to meet the strict legal requirements placed on the operation of all pressure vessels.

Frames, wheels and motion

The mechanical parts of the locomotive, though they attract more attention from the casual observer, often present less of a problem in a restoration project. Again each part was examined in minute detail using magnetic particle inspection and ultra sonic techniques to detect any possible flaws.

Beginning with the locomotive's wheels, the steel tyres were restored to the correct profile using the wheel lathe at Whitehead. This machine, now

Bill King-Wood examines the cylinder block after removal from the engine. The white markings show where magnetic particle inspection has been used to detect any possible flaws in the casting.

The driving wheels are seen mounted in the wheel lathe for reprofiling. The crank axle is an interesting piece of machinery as it was made as a single piece!

Both Irwin Pryce

175

A new front buffer is cast. A variety of trades would have been involved in such a job: the patternmaker would have made the wooden replica of the part, the moulder then packed sand around the pattern then withdrawing it leaving a hollow in the sand before pouring molten iron into the mould. The fettler removed the casting and chipped it clean (making it "in fine fettle"), passing it on to the turner for machining true. Finally the fitter would attach it to the engine. Peter Scott, the RPSI's Locomotive Officer, is scraping off the slag, while John Ferguson and Billy McConnel are pouring the molten iron into the mould.

Jim Rainey is machining a large end bearing to size in the lathe.

Both Irwin Pryce

unique in Ireland, is itself a remarkable piece of engineering history having been moved to Whitehead from the railway workshops at York Road in Belfast. This huge machine is capable of turning seven foot diameter wheels.

At an early stage in the work it was apparent that severe corrosion between the cylinder block and the locomotive's frames had caused the frames to become misaligned. The effect of this would have been to make accurate setting up of the axleboxes difficult. The entire cylinder block was removed to allow the frames to be trued up. The cylinders themselves revealed signs of long standing cracks so the opportunity was taken to have these professionally repaired by the 'Metalock' process. Refitting the cylinders involved the use of individually fitted bolts in accurately reamed-out holes in the block and frames. The two cylinders fortunately did not require re-boring to restore them to a uniform diameter; though the means to carry out this task is available at Whitehead. New piston rings were cast and machined at Whitehead – again another example of 'in house' expertise.

The frames are supported by two stretchers. The front one provides the means of mounting the slidebars on which the crossheads run, and is also the main support for the valve gear. Both stretchers showed evidence of some very rough and ready repairs dating back to her last days in company service when corners would have been cut in matters of maintenance, since steam was seen to have no long term future. The opportunity was also taken to attend to this as a much longer term future is now envisaged.

All bearings have been re-metalled to reduce clearances back to an acceptable level. White metal (a tin-based alloy) is used for this purpose. Each bearing surface was individually machined and finally bedded in by hand.

The crank axle through which all the power of the engine is transmitted is a remarkable example of the craftsmanship of the age. The entire axle which incorporates two huge cranks, set at 90 degrees to each other, was manufactured in one piece, a wonderful tribute to the skill of the men who forged this massive part. The crank-pins themselves needed attention to restore them to a true cross-section and this absorbed many hours of patient toil before a satisfactory finish could be obtained.

The valves, which control the admission and exhaust of steam in the cylinders, were set. Setting the valves on a 101 class loco has always been a hit and miss procedure since the only way of setting the timing was to lengthen or shorten the valve rods by heating and forging – a blacksmith's job. It is hardly surprising that a 101 with a completely even exhaust beat was a rarity. Bob Clements refers to this and to the fact that the engines would quite happily "three-leg it". It was indeed a popular belief among enginemen that the engines would not steam properly if the valves were set correctly. (A myth no doubt spread by the fitters to cover up their deficiencies in this respect!). 186 used to be noted for her lop-sided exhaust beat, which from the lineside was noticeable in the strange loops left in the exhaust across the skyline. It remains to be seen if any improvement results from this overhaul!

Brakes

The vacuum braking system in the 101 class is an archaic arrangement whereby the upper and lower chambers of the brake cylinder are divided by a rubber diaphragm, rather than a piston and rolling ring which became standard on other railways. Considerable difficulty was experienced in sourcing replacements for this diaphragm, and this one item was a significant part of the cost of the overhaul.

As first built the engines had only a simple hand brake, soon replaced by the non-automatic vacuum brake, activated by *creating* a vacuum in the brake cylinders on each vehicle. However, the railway companies were coming under increasing pressure to install systems which were 'fail-safe' - that is, if a vehicle should become detached from the train or the system become defective in any way then the whole train would automatically be stopped. Indeed after the dreadful Armagh disaster of 1889 in which 80 people were killed, Parliament made such a system a legal requirement.

The then GS&WR engineer Mr John Aspinall (later Sir John), displaying typical Inchicore ingenuity and economy realised that by making a modest change to the older system that it could be made automatic and this is the system which is installed in 186. In simple terms, a vacuum is *always* maintained in the brake cylinder and the brake pipes which run the length of the train. When required, the driver applied the brakes by using a valve on the engine activated by the brake lever. This let air into the pipes and through them the brake cylinders causing the brakes to come on. It can be seen that any break in the system would likewise cause air to enter the pipes and cylinders, destroy the vacuum, and apply the brakes throughout the train, so that it became fail-safe. The system proved so successful that this type of brake was at one time widely used in the U.K. and in parts of Europe.

Other work

A host of other jobs had to be attended to - the injectors which feed water to the boiler were overhauled; a new ash-pan made; a new smokebox and door made; new main steam pipes fitted; springs were overhauled and the weight distribution on the wheels adjusted.

A new set of firebars were cast at Whitehead and the drop-grate made. This is a useful device whereby ash and clinker remaining at the end of the day's work can be pushed forward and down into the ash pit, rather than having to be removed through the firebox door with a ten-foot-long clinker shovel! It was introduced to the class during the post war fuel shortage when all that was available for locomotive use was 'Duff', a term covering anything held to be even slightly combustible! The use of this fuel could extend an eight hour journey into one occupying several days, but the drop grate did at least make the job of 'baling out' every few miles a little easier for the enginemen.

The tender

The tender presently used with 186 is not her original one. The 101s had much smaller tenders when built and throughout most of their working lives, as can be seen in many illustrations. However, as an engine was overhauled, it would quite often swop tenders. Her present tender would have seen service with a variety of passenger engines. The large capacity of this type of tender was a valuable feature to the Operating Department and ensured that when they became available during the 1950s, as the older passengers engines were scrapped, they were frequently transferred to mixed traffic locomotives.

Areas of corroded platework have been replaced and all the running gear attended to, as with the locomotive itself. It was fitting that much of the platework was carried out at Inchicore Works of Irish Rail, assisted by grant aid.

Lastly, steam heating for the passengers, which had long ago passed into disuse, was reinstated. Today's passengers are less hardy than those of a few generations ago!

Running-in

The culmination of four year's work came in January 2004 when 186 took her first hesitant steps after 25 year's rest. Then followed a period of tentative running-in so that the behaviour of each part could be carefully monitored.

By a popular vote within the RPSI, the livery chosen was the grey favoured by the Great Southern Railway and as used right to the end by Limerick shops.

So, the engine was ready for formal re-commissioning at Whitehead on 23 July 2004. With due ceremony, Keith Moffatt, Managing Director of Translink, drove 186 through a banner proclaiming her re-birth and he then handed over the all-important paperwork to allow her to enter traffic again.

The significance of the restoration was recognised by the Heritage Railway Association which presented the RPSI with the John Coiley Award for 2004. This is awarded to a project which has demonstrated a high degree of excellence in the restoration of an item of great historical significance and this was the first time the award had been made outside the British mainland.

Once in traffic, the engine visited places as far apart as Portrush, Bangor, Rosslare, Limerick and Killarney, where she made a comeback as a film star!

During the RPSI's International tour in 2005, she triumphantly returned to her spiritual home – Waterford.

Perhaps more significantly, the engine has demonstrated a capacity for hard work and reliability, those very features which made the class such an important part of the Irish railway scene in two centuries.

As 186 steams confidently into her third century, one can be sure that Alexander McDonnell would have been proud.

The overhauled boiler has been returned to the frames and wheels, the cylinders have been refitted, a new smokebox and door have been made. All that remains now is for the pistons and motion to be assembled and the rebuilt tender to be attached.

Irwin Pryce

The finished job! Almost a traditional works photograph, except that the cramped nature of the RPSI's base at Whitehead does not allow the photographer to get back far enough to take a pure side elevation beloved of works' photographers of old.

Charles Friel

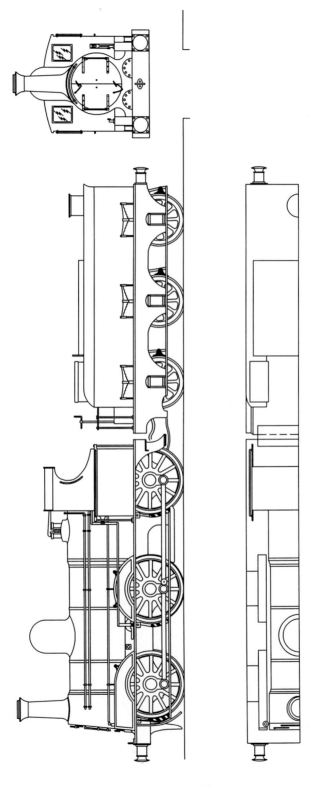

G.S.&W.R. 101 Class Locomotive as at 1888

Redrawn from original drawing by Bob Clements

Not to scale

Patrick O'Sullivan October 2005

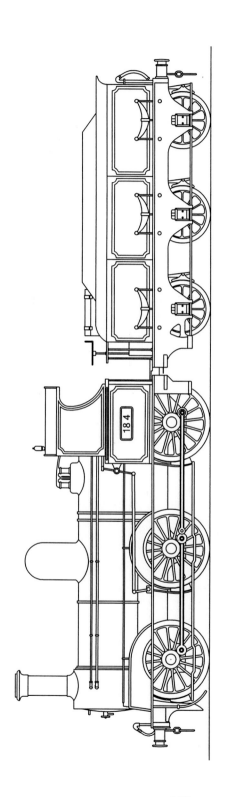

G.S.&W.R. 0-6-0 tender locomotive No.184 as fitted with a 4' 4" boiler

(This is how she is today)

Not to scale

Patrick O'Sullivan October 2005

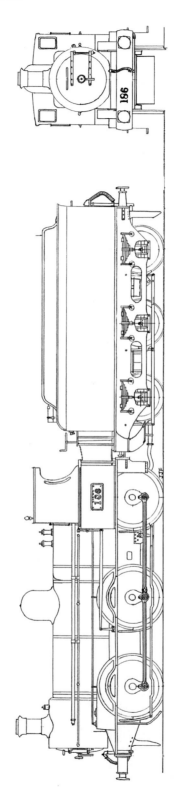

G.S.&W.R. 0-6-0 tender locomotive No.186 as fitted with a 'Z' type boiler

(This is how she is today)

Not to scale

Original drawing by James Friel 2004

THE '101' CLASS - The Statistical Details

Compiled by R N Clements

EXPLANATION OF TABLE:

Types:

A	'Hybrid' engines - see text
B	Beyer's engines, 5' 7" firebox, 1⅛" frames
C	As B, but 1" frames and 15" cylinders
D	As C, but 17" cylinders
E	5' 1" firebox, short wheelbase, 16" cylinders
F	As E, but 17" cylinders
G	As F, but flat grate, standard wheelbase, lighter frames
H	As G, but 18" cylinders
I	As H, but steel boiler
J	As I, but steel frames
K	As H, but deepened iron frames
L	As K, but steel frames
M	As L, but single slidebars, etc.
N	As M, but 4' 4" boiler
a	Cast-iron wheels

Tubes : **2" diam.**, **z** 157 ; **y** 158 ; **x** 159 ; **w** 160 ; **v** 172 ; **u** 174 ; **t** 175
(These are the numbers of tubes actually charged to each of the Inchicore engines, but perhaps all had either 160 or 174).
1¾" **diam.**, **s** 185 ; **r** 175 ; **q** 173 ; **p** 200.
1½" **diam.**, **o** 234.

Makers: All built at Inchicore except those marked **B**, Beyer Peacock's 747-750, 780-3, 1251-2 & 2029-30 and **S**, Sharp Stewart's 2155-8, 2310-1 & 2837-8. Numbers quoted are works numbers.

New 4'
Boilers: **x** Boiler from another engine, sometimes with new firebox.
b Supplied by Bolton Iron & Steel Co. All others made at Inchicore.

4' 4"
Boilers: * Date doubtful

Note on withdrawal dates: These are very uncertain, as few, if any, 101s worked in company service after 1962. Some did train heating in 1963 but were towed to do it. For the 1964 'Grand Tour' four 101 class were specially prepared. Thus the withdrawal dates shown in the table may have included many months of lying rusting in a siding.

No.	Type Tubes		Date Maker	New Boiler	4' 4" Boiler	New Frame	'Z' Boiler	Withdrawn	Remarks
112	A	z	6/66	1889	1911-2*	—	—	1929	
113	A	y	12/66	1889	9/1903	—	—	1930	
118	A	y	5/67	—	—	—	—	1890	
147	B	u	5/67B	—	—	—	—	1888	F'box 1878; 18" cyl. 1879
148	B	u	6/67B	1892	1907	—	1932	1953	F'box 1874.
149	B	u	6/67B	—	—	—	—	1887	
150	B	u	6/67B	—	1916-21	—	—	1957	F'box 1884.
103	C	x	8/67	—	—	—	—	1886	17" cyl. 1870.
111	C	y	9/67	—	—	—	—	1888	17" cyl. 1871.
151	B	u	3/68B	1883b	1904	—	1950	1965	
152	B	u	3/68B	1882	1901	—	—	1959	
153	B	u	3/68B	1890	1904	—	1932	1954	
154	B	u	3/68B	1890	1914-5*	—	1941	1962	F'box 1872; 18" cyl. 1877
105	D	t	5/68	1885x	—	—	—	1895	
110	D	y	7/68	—	—	—	—	1890	18" cyl. 1877.
114	E	v	8/69	—	—	—	—	1885	17" cyl. 1874.
115	E	v	10/69	1889	—	—	—	1929	17" cyl. 1876.
155	F	t	2/71	1882	—	—	—	1929	18" cyl. 1878.
156	F	t	4/71	1889	—	1935	1935	1961	18" cyl. 1889.
159	G	u	9/71	1889x	1912	—	1933	1949	
160	G	u	10/71	1891	1907	1932	1932	1955	
161	G	u	10/71	1886	1925-7	—	—	1963	
162	G	u	12/71	1891	1909	—	—	1963	
157	G	u	3/72	1889	1911-8*	—	—	1963	
158	G	u	4/72	1889	1905	1923	1941	1957	
163	G	u	7/72S	1889	1922-3	1936	1936	1955	
164	G	u	8/72S	1890	1924	1932	1932	1963	18" cyl. 1886.
165	G	u	8/72S	1891	1921	—	—	1945	
166	G	u	8/72S	1892	1923	1923	1933	1963	
102	G	w	1/73	1892	1904	—	1947	1962	
104	G	w	1/73	1892	1913	—	1930	1965	
167	G	o	3/73	1895	1915-6*	—	—	1960	
168	G	s	4/73	1892	1912-21	1935	1935	1962	
175	G	s	8/73S	1892	1924	—	1933	1956	18" cyl. 1878.
176	G	s	8/73S	1891	1922	1922	—	1959	
177	G	u	12/73B	1892	1921	—	—	1927	
178	G	u	12/73B	1894	1908-9*	—	—	1926	
106	G	s	1/74	1894	1921	1937	1937	1964	18" cyl. 1884.
117	G	s	3/74	1893	1904	—	—	1930	18" cyl. 1884.
169	G	s	3/74	1890x	1921	—	—	1928	
170	G	s	4/74	1890x	1917	—	1941	1963	
171	H	s	7/74	1896	1922-4	—	1933	1961	
172	H	s	8/74	1897	1906	—	1949	1964	
173	H	s	9/74	1893	1902	—	—	1933	
174	H	s	11/74	1889	1925-7	—	1933	1953	
108	H	s	2/75	1897	1922	1937	1931	1959	
142	H	s	3/75	1893	1907	—	—	1928	
179	H	s	4/75	1894	1920	1933	1933	1963	
180	H	s	5/75	1893	1912	—	—	1928	
109	Ha	s	1/77	1896	1912	—	—	1964	
119	Ha	s	1/77	1897	1925-6	—	—	1962	
120	Ha	s	2/77	1896	1916-21	—	1935	1955	
121	Ha	s	2/77	1896	1909-13	—	—	1963	
143	Ha	r	12/77	1889x	1906	1923	1936	1960	
144	Ha	r	2/78	1897	1910	—	1932	1954	
145	Ha	r	2/78	—	1922-3	—	—	1926	
146	Ha	r	2/78	1895	1912	—	1930	1955	
181	Ha	s	8/79	1897	1920	1937	1937	1959	
185	H	s	8/79S	1898	1914-8	1936	1933	1959	
182	Ha	s	9/79	1897	1925-7	—	1939	1962	
186	H	s	11/79S	1898	1908-10	1935	1932	—	**Preserved by RPSI**
183	Ha	s	1/80	—	1925-7	—	1932	1965	
184	Ha	s	2/80	1899	1921	—	—	—	**Preserved by RPSI**
107	Ha	s	2/81	—	1919-21	—	1935	1957	

No.	Type	Tubes	Date Maker	New Boiler	4' 4" Boiler	New Frame	'Z' Boiler	Withdrawn	Remarks
139	Ia	s	4/81	1898	1909	—	1932	1961	
140	Ia	s	5/81	**1894**	1909*	—	1942	1961	
141	Ia	s	5/81	**1894**	1922-3	—	1939	1959	
189	I	s	5/81**B**	—	1904	—	—	1923	
190	I	s	5/81**B**	—	1911-8	—	—	1963	
123	Ja	s	7/81	1899	1907-11*	—	1932	1963	
124	Ja	s	9/81	—	1901	—	1948	1965	
125	Ja	s	10/81	—	1915	—	1949	1965	
126	Ja	s	11/81	—	1901	—	1938	1959	
127	Ja	s	2/82	1900	1909-17	—	1931-3	1963	
128	Ka	s	3/82	—	1914	—	1933	1963	
187	Ka	s	3/82	—	1925-7	—	—	1957	
188	Ka	s	7/82	1899	1922-3	—	1932	1959	To traffic 12/82.
101	Ka	s	9/82	—	1924	—	1940	1962	
122	Ka	s	9/82	—	1901	—	1942	1963	
130	Ka	s	12/82	—	1902	—	1947	1965	
131	Ka	s	12/82	—	1909*	—	—	1963	
133	Ka	s	6/85	—	1904	—	—	1963	To Traffic 12/85.
134	La	s	6/85	—	1922	—	—	1961	
135	La	s	9/85	—	1903	—	—	1957	
191	La	s	10/85	—	1914	—	—	1962	
132	La	s	12/88	—	1905*	—	1941	1965	
136	La	s	12/88	—	1905	—	1931	1962	
137	La	s	12/88	—	1902	—	1931-3	1960	
138	La	s	12/88	—	1903	—	1947	1962	
103	La	s	8/89	—	1921	—	—	1957	
114	L	s	8/89	—	1907	—	1948	1961	
129	La	s	9/89	—	1907	—	1933	1940	
149	La	s	10/89	—	1903	—	1933	1962	
110	La	s	12/90	—	1922	—	1930	1963	
111	La	s	3/91	—	1912-3*	—	—	1963	
118	La	s	5/91	—	1927-8	—	1933	1966	
147	La	s	5/91	—	1907*	—	1941	1956	
105	L		6/96	—	1910	—	1949	1963	
116	L	q	8/96	—	1906-8*	—	—	1964	
192	M	q	9/98	—	1908	—	1950	1956	
193	M	q	9/98	—	1910	—	1948	1963	
194	M	q	11/98	—	1908	—	1933	1959	
195	M	q	12/98	—	1909	—	—	1965	
196	M	q	5/99	—	1911	—	1953	1961	
197	M	q	6/99	—	1911	—	1930-1	1961	
198	M	q	6/99	—	1910*	—	1933	1965	
199	M	q	11/99	—	1911-2*	—	1931	1954	
240	N	p	10/02	—	NEW	—	—	1957	
241	N	p	12/02	—	,,	—	—	1957	
242	N	p	12/02	—	,,	—	—	1957	
243	N	p	1/03	—	,,	—	—	1955	
200	N	p	2/03	—	,,	—	1941	1960	
223	N	p	2/03	—	,,	—	—	1960	
229	N	p	3/03	—	,,	—	—	1960	
232	N	p	3/03	—	,,	—	—	1963	
253	N	p	-/03	—	,,	—	—	1963	
254	N	p	-/03	—	,,	—	1933	1961	
255	N	p	-/03	—	,,	—	1936	1964	
256	N	p	-/03	—	,,	—	1931	1959	

Abbreviations and Explanations

B&CDR	Belfast and County Down Railway
B&NCR	Belfast and Northern Counties Railway
CIE	Coras Iompair Eireann
CB&SCR	Cork Bandon and South Coast Railway
D&BJR	Dublin and Belfast Junction Railway
D&SER	Dublin and South Eastern Railway
GNR	Great Northern Railway of Ireland
GS&WR	Great Southern and Western Railway
GSR	Great Southern Railway
	(union of MGWR, CB&SCR and GS&WR in 1924)
	Great Southern Railways after the full Amalgamation of 1925
LMS(NCC)	London Midland and Scottish Railway
	(Northern Counties Committee)
L&NWR	London and North Western Railway
MGWR	Midland Great Western Railway
NIR	Northern Ireland Railways
Psi	Pounds per square inch (usually boiler pressure)
SL&NCR	Sligo Leitrim and Northern Counties Railway
WL&WR	Waterford Limerick and Western Railway

Last but not least. The final member of the class, 256, was built new with a 4' 4" boiler but was one of the first to receive a superheated one in 1931. Apart from that enhancement, she is seen very much as Coey built her, with the final version of the cab and extended sandboxes. She was withdrawn in 1959.

Lance King Collection

Bibliography

Writings which cover the development and activity of the 101 class may be found in many places and the reader who wants to know more about this notable class could have many years of happy study.

The first source for any student of Irish railway affairs is of course the IRRS *Journal* published three times a year offering both a review of the present Irish scene and historical papers. It has been published since June 1947 and there are many references to the class therein. *Irish Railfans' News* was published from 1955 to 1973, covering the day-to-day activities on Irish railways, included many references to the class at work in the latter years of steam. The RPSI's magazine *Five Foot Three* has covered the lives of the two preserved engines and offers other historical articles with a steam slant.

Books referred to by the compilers and commended for further reading include: *Decade of Steam* (Donaldson, McDonnell and O'Neill), *Great Southern and Western Railway* (Murray and McNeill), *Irish Steam Loco Register* (Rowledge), *Locomotives of the GNRI* (Johnston), *Johnson's Atlas and Gazetteer of the Railways of Ireland* (to find out where some of the photographs were actually taken!); to read a little more about Martin Atock and his locomotives - *Midland Great Western Railway* (Shepherd). Patrick O'Sullivan's *The Farranfore to Valencia Harbour Railway* (2 volumes) offers many photographs of the class at work on that line. *Forty Shades of Steam* (Cassells and Friel) covers the first forty years of the RPSI and includes many fine colour photographs of the preserved locomotives on tours.

J E Chacksfield has written biographies of two of the engineers involved in the 101 story – *The Coey/Cowie Brothers* and *Richard Maunsell*. John Marshall's excellent *Biographical Dictionary of Railway Engineers* offers pen portraits of the engineers involved in the 101 story.

This photograph by Tony Burgess of 240 at Wexford came to light, just as we were about to publish. Thus she became the 101st '101' which we could include in this book. She had just taken over the 7.20am Dublin (Westland Row) to Rosslare Harbour train on 6 April 1953. She also appears in his recently published book *'Chasing the Flying Snail'* (Colourpoint).

Acknowledgements

The original book tracing the history of the 101 Class was published by the IRRS in Dublin and we are grateful to the current committee of the Society for their agreement to use the original text and for their support.

From the outset, it was our intention to tell the story in pictures as well as words, so it is a pleasure to acknowledge the generosity of many individuals who provided a cornucopia of wonderful illustrations. Of the 119 GS&WR engines, they ensured that we could present no less than (appropriately) a hundred and one, plus the two from the D&BJR. For the record, the 'missing' are: the original 103, 105, 110, 111, 114, 118, 147 and 149, all of which were replaced by engines of the same numbers in 1889 -1896; then engines scrapped in the 1920s and 1930s – 113, 115, 142, 145, 155, 169, 173, 177 and 178. The real mystery is how 150, withdrawn in 1957, eluded the photographers.

So we are very grateful to: Tony Bennett, RK Blencowe, Anthony Burgess, Roger Carpenter, Roy Crombie, Hugh Davies ('Photos from the Fifties'), John Dewing, John Edgington, Charles Friel, Sean Kennedy, Lance King, John Langford, Robin Linsley, Laurie Marshall, David Murray, Conrad Natzio, HB Priestley, Bill Scott, GW Sharpe, Bill Smith, David Soggee, AG Weaver (Midland Railway Trust) and Ron White ('Colour-Rail') for the use of their own photographs or access to their collections. Thanks are simply insufficient to give Richard Casserley and Hamish Stevenson who allowed very generous use of their late fathers' collections. The custodians of three society collections - Reg Carter, Graham Stacey and Mike Smith are thanked for access to the collections held by the SLS, the LCGB and the Bournemouth Railway Club respectively. Patrick O'Sullivan did marvels on the computer to produce the drawings, some from the original booklet. James Friel, following in the enthusiast footsteps of his famous father Charles, drew 186 as she is today.

Peter Rowledge generously gave permission for the use of extracts from his unpublished opus on GS&WR locomotives, while some biographical details have been copied from John Marshall's excellent *Biographical Dictionary of Railway Engineers*.

Others who helped in various ways include Phil Atkins, Des Coakham, Bruce Heaven, Norman Johnston, Norman McAdams, Terry MacDermott, Alan O'Rourke, Edward Talbot and Keith Thomas.

The IRRS's Honorary Archivist, Brendan Pender, must be singled out for willingly solving many problems, by expertly delving into the treasure trove under his care. Robin Linsley read through the final work and helped with the often-tedious task of proof reading.

It is fitting that in this, the IRRS's sixtieth year, that among the contributors are names from the IRRS's earliest membership lists – 'Mac' Arnold, Henry Casserley, Bob Clements, Drew Donaldson, Harold Fayle, Lance King, Sean Kennedy, David Murray, Kevin Murray, Ted Patterson and William Robb; while RK Blencowe, whose father (FA Blencowe) was an early member, permitted us to use photographs from his collection.

Index

(**Bold** indicates an illustration, or reference within a caption)

The Railway Preservation Society Of Ireland

The Society is a registered charity and was formed in 1964 to operate and preserve in working order steam locomotives and coaches which were disappearing rapidly from the Irish Railway system.

Today the Society owns and operates a fleet of nine steam locomotives and around 20 vintage carriages on public trains. The Society is a non-profit making organisation and all funds from ticket sales, membership fees or donations go directly to keeping Ireland's steam railway heritage running for future generations.

The RPSI is a limited liability company registered in Northern Ireland, having its registered office at

RAILWAY PRESERVATION SOCIETY OF IRELAND
P.O. BOX 171
LARNE
COUNTY ANTRIM
NORTHERN IRELAND
BT40 1UU

The society operates steam trains throughout the year from both Dublin and Belfast.

Locomotives and carriages are also available for corporate hire and film contract work.

Tickets for Belfast based trains can be obtained from Belfast Welcome Centre, Donegall Place (028) 9024 6609, Carrickfergus (028) 9336 6455, Bangor or Lisburn Tourist Information Centres. Tickets for Dublin based trains can be obtained from "Ashgrove House", Dublin. (01) 280 9147

Our office fax number / recorded message phone number is 2826 0803 (within Northern Ireland). If phoning from Great Britain, prefix with code (028). If phoning from the Republic of Ireland, prefix with (048).

For full details of all the society's activities, or to join us, write to the address above, or access our website at

www.rpsi-online.org

Library and Information Service

Library materials must be returned on or before the last due date or fines will be charged at the current rate. Items can be renewed by telephone, email or by visting the website, letter or personal call unless required by another borrower. For hours of opening and charges see notices displayed in libraries.
Tel: 03333 704700
Email: libraries@lewisham.gov.uk
www.lewisham.gov.uk/libraries

Apr 2018

GW00480666

Zu sem Buch

Oh rinnerung an die vergangenen Stunden kommt Kri-
mi errat Alexander Gerlach im Krankenhaus zu sich. Es
sch als sei er in einem noblen Heidelberger Viertel vom
Ra ürzt, doch seine Verletzungen passen nicht recht zu
ein nfall. Und was wollte er dort überhaupt? Bruch-
stü erinnert er sich daran, von einem Mann gestoßen
w u sein. War es Fred Heergarden, der Gerlach vor
we Tagen in seinem Büro aufgesucht hatte, um den
M einer eigenen Frau zu gestehen? Doch Vicky Heer-
ga r vor vielen Jahren bei einem Unfall ums Leben
ge , nichts deutete damals auf Fremdeinwirkung hin.
G schließt, Heergardens Behauptung auf den Grund
zu ls er ihn aufsucht, wirkt er verwirrt, doch Heer-
ga eint sich sicher zu sein, dass der Tod seiner Frau
se aligen Nebenbuhler anzulasten ist. Hatte er sich
n ezichtigt, um das Verfahren wieder ins Rollen zu
b ann kehrt allmählich auch Gerlachs Erinnerung
zu

W *Burger,* geboren 1952 im Südschwarzwald, ist
p er Ingenieur und hat viele Jahre in leitenden Posi-
ti Karlsruher Institut für Technologie KIT gearbei-
te rei erwachsene Töchter und lebt heute in Karls-
ru egensburg. Seit 1995 ist er schriftstellerisch tätig.
D der-Gerlach-Romane waren bereits zweimal für
d ch-Glauser-Preis nominiert und standen mehr-
fa *SPIEGEL*-Bestsellerliste.

Wolfgang Burger

DIE DUNKLE VILLA

Ein Fall für Alexander Gerlach

Mehr über unsere Autoren und Bücher:
www.piper.de

Von Wolfgang Burger liegen im Piper Verlag vor:
Alexander-Gerlach-Reihe:
Heidelberger Requiem
Heidelberger Lügen
Heidelberger Wut
Schwarzes Fieber
Echo einer Nacht
Eiskaltes Schweigen
Der fünfte Mörder
Die falsche Frau
Das vergessene Mädchen
Die dunkle Villa
Tödliche Geliebte
Drei Tage im Mai
Schlaf, Engelchen, schlaf
Die linke Hand des Bösen

MIX
Papier aus verantwor-
tungsvollen Quellen
FSC
www.fsc.org   FSC® C083411

Ungekürzte Taschenbuchausgabe
ISBN 978-3-492-30569-3
1. Auflage 2015
3. Auflage 2017
© Piper Verlag GmbH, München/Berlin 2014
Umschlaggestaltung: Eisele Grafik-Design, München
Umschlagabbildung: Gandee Vasan/Riser/Getty Images (Katze),
Image Source/Getty Images (Zimmer)
Satz: Kösel Media GmbH, Krugzell
Gesetzt aus der Sabon
Druck und Bindung: CPI books GmbH, Leck
Printed in Germany

Für Rebecca

1

Dieser hohe reine Ton in meinem Kopf ...

Das überirdisch helle Licht ...

War ich tot?

Plötzlich wurde es wieder dunkel. Der seltsame Ton blieb, klang jedoch nicht nach Sphärengesang oder Engelsjubel. Jemand drückte grob an mir herum. Ein Arzt? War ich beim Arzt? Und wenn ja, warum? Inzwischen konnte ich auch wieder sehen. Verschwommen zwar, aber immerhin. Einen altertümlichen Kronleuchter sah ich, eine gemusterte Tapete in Brauntönen, dunkelgrüne Samtvorhänge – nein, das war keine Arztpraxis und auch kein Krankenhaus. Aber es fummelte eindeutig jemand an mir herum, wie Ärzte es tun, brummelte medizinisches Fachlatein dazu, ein Daumen zog herzlos mein rechtes Augenlid hoch, wieder knallte das grelle Licht auf die Netzhaut.

»Oho«, sagte eine gemütliche Altmännerstimme, »wir sind ja aufgewacht!«

Ich hätte es vorgezogen, weiter bewusstlos zu sein, denn mir war speiübel. Dazu die mörderischen Kopfschmerzen, ein Hirn aus Watte. Irgendwer hatte jemanden umgebracht, das wusste ich noch. Ich versuchte, etwas zu sagen, brachte jedoch nur ein jämmerliches Keuchen zustande.

»Heißen Sie Gerlach?«

»Das Licht ist so hell«, krächzte ich.

»Versuchen wir bitte mal, dem Licht mit den Augen zu folgen.«

Die künstliche Sonne bewegte sich langsam hin und her. Ihr zu folgen war ein Kinderspiel.

»Hm«, brummte der Arzt befriedigt. »Ohrgeräusche?«

»Was?«

»Hören Sie irgendwelche Geräusche?«

»Nein. Aber das Licht! Bitte!«

»Schon vorbei.«

Wie wunderschön Dunkelheit sein konnte.

»Ihr Name ist also Gerlach?«

»Ja«, erwiderte ich und vermied es, dabei zu nicken.

Der Mann, der offenbar wirklich Arzt war, knetete weiter an mir herum, als wäre ich ein Rinderbraten, dessen Garungsgrad zu testen war.

»Vorname?«

»Alexander.«

»Was für einen Tag haben wir heute?«

Offenbar wollte er mit seinen dämlichen Fragen meine Hirnfunktionen testen.

»Samstag. Siebter Februar.«

»Und was sind wir von Beruf?«

»Bei Ihnen tippe ich auf Arzt.«

»Oho, er macht schon wieder Witze! Sie meinte ich natürlich.«

»Polizei …« Ich musste mich räuspern, was in meinem Magen eine kleine Rebellion auslöste. »Ich bin Polizist. Kripo.«

Etwas Hartes schlug sacht gegen meine rechte Kniescheibe. Gehorsam zuckte das dazugehörige Bein. Ich zwang mich, die Augen wieder zu öffnen, versuchte, das Bild klar zu stellen, aber es wollte mir immer noch nicht gelingen. Das mittlerweile wieder gedämpfte Licht schmerzte dennoch in den Augen, und alles, was ich ansah, verschwamm sofort wieder.

Das Wenige, was ich erkannte, verstärkte jedoch meinen anfänglichen Verdacht: Wo immer ich hingeraten war – eine Arztpraxis war es nicht. Arztpraxen waren üblicherweise hell und pflegeleicht eingerichtet, und von den Decken baumelten eher selten Kronleuchter mit nachgemachten Edelsteinen.

Eine Frau.

Irgendjemand hatte seine Frau umgebracht.

Und etwas stimmte dabei nicht. Wenn ich nur gewusst hätte, was.

»Sie sind sogar der Chef, nicht wahr?«, fuhr mein Quälgeist mit dem Hämmerchen fort. »Wir haben uns erlaubt, einen Blick in Ihre Geldbörse zu werfen, während Sie weg waren.«

»Was ist überhaupt los? Wo bin ich? Ist mir …« Wieder musste ich mich räuspern. »… was passiert?«

»Sie sind vom Rad gestürzt. Und haben sich dabei anscheinend eine zünftige Commotio cerebri zugezogen. Eine Gehirnerschütterung, wie der Volksmund es nennt. Und der Raum, in welchem Sie gerade allmählich wieder zur Besinnung kommen, ist mein Wohnzimmer.«

Der alte Mann schob sein Gesicht in mein Blickfeld. »Ich habe mich noch gar nicht vorgestellt, verzeihen Sie. Kamphusen. Dr. Kamphusen, Internist im schwer verdienten Ruhestand.« Seine Augen blickten trotz der ernsten Miene freundlich. Das Haar war voll und schlohweiß. Jetzt lächelte er sogar. Allzu schlimm schien es nicht um mich zu stehen. »Und das da drüben, das ist Svantje. Seit vierzig Jahren und elf Tagen meine bessere Hälfte und noch ein gutes Stück länger die gute Seele meiner Praxis.«

»Hallo«, sagte ich heiser. »Freut mich.«

Demnach konnte er nicht der Mann sein, der seine Frau umgebracht hatte. Ich versuchte den Kopf in die Richtung zu wenden, in die er blickte. Aber in meinem Magen wurde daraufhin unverzüglich Großalarm ausgelöst. Seufzend gab ich den Plan fürs Erste auf. Svantje Kamphusen konnte ich mir auch später noch ansehen. Ich schloss wieder die Augen. Dunkelheit. Nichts war im Moment schöner als Dunkelheit und Ruhe.

»Svantje hat Sie nämlich gefunden, müssen Sie wissen. Vor fünfzehn Minuten erst. Nur ein paar Meter von unserer Haustür entfernt.«

»Ich kam gerade vom Einkaufen«, fügte eine erstaunlich jung klingende Frauenstimme eifrig hinzu. »Und dann haben Sie dagelegen. Einfach so auf dem Gehsteig. Auf Ihrem Rad. Bewusstlos.«

»Nicht ganz, mein Schatz«, korrigierte der Arzt mit sanfter Strenge. »Herr Gerlach war ja ansprechbar und konnte sogar aus eigener Kraft gehen. Obwohl Sie über starke Sehstörungen geklagt haben.« Nun sprach er offenbar wieder mit mir. »Aber dann sind Sie uns plötzlich zusammengeklappt. Sie waren nur für wenige Minuten weg. Eine mittelschwere Gehirnerschütterung, würde ich nach der ersten, zugegeben flüchtigen Anamnese sagen.«

»Ich war mit dem Rad unterwegs? Wo sind wir eigentlich?«

»Sie können sich nicht erinnern?«

Bloß nicht den Kopf schütteln!

»Kein bisschen.«

Dr. Kamphusen erhob sich und packte sein Hämmerchen weg. »Die üblichen Symptome bei einer Commotio cerebri. Ansonsten ist alles heil geblieben, wie es scheint. Ein paar Schrammen und Prellungen, das vergeht rasch in Ihrem Alter.«

In meinem Alter – das hatte schon lange niemand mehr zu mir gesagt. Zumindest nicht in diesem angenehmen Sinn. Immerhin würde ich in wenigen Jahren fünfzig werden. Ein Umstand, der mir in letzter Zeit manchmal zu denken gab. Die Malaisen des Alters rückten mit jedem Tag unaufhaltsam näher: Prostataprobleme, Erektionsschwäche, Inkontinenz.

Der Arzt raschelte außerhalb meines Sichtfelds geschäftig herum. »Die Erinnerung wird mit der Zeit zurückkehren. Vielleicht nur zum Teil, vermutlich alles. Man wird sehen. Und nun lassen wir Sie ins Uniklinikum bringen ...«

»Ich ...«

»Keine Sorge, nur für ein paar Tage und nur zur Beobachtung. Ich habe dort einen alten Freund, der ...«

»Klinik ist nicht nötig«, fiel ich ihm ins Wort. »Mir geht's schon wieder prima.«

Er zögerte. Brummte etwas, das ich nicht verstand. »Ich kann Sie nicht zwingen. Aber mein Rat als Arzt ...«

Es gelang mir, meiner Stimme eine gewisse Festigkeit zu geben, als ich sagte: »Keine Klinik.«

»Sie hätten einen Helm tragen sollen«, meinte Frau Kamphusen schnippisch. Offenbar nahm sie mir übel, dass ich mich nicht der Autorität ihres Göttergatten fügte. »So etwas kann leicht böse ausgehen, glauben Sie mir.«

»Gibt es jemanden, den wir benachrichtigen können?«,

fragte Dr. Kamphusen. »Eine Frau? Kann jemand Sie abholen? Sie dürfen in den nächsten Tagen nicht ohne Aufsicht sein. Es kann zu Komplikationen kommen. Plötzliche Bewusstlosigkeit, zum Beispiel.«

Nein, eine Frau gab es nicht, beziehungsweise doch, aber die konnte mich unmöglich abholen, weil sie mit einem anderen Mann verheiratet war. Beaufsichtigen konnten mich meine Töchter, die waren jedoch zu jung zum Autofahren. In ein Krankenhaus wollte ich auf gar keinen Fall. Ich bat meine Retter, mir ein Taxi zu rufen. Der Vorschlag wurde rundweg abgeschmettert.

Schließlich, als ich wieder halbwegs normal sehen und ohne Hilfe stehen konnte, ein starkes Schmerzmittel geschluckt und mir einige tausend Ermahnungen und Belehrungen angehört hatte, fuhr der betagte Arzt mich in seinem alten Ford nach Hause. Hoch und heilig musste ich versprechen, dass ich in den nächsten Tagen und Nächten keinen Augenblick allein sein würde.

»Ich habe zwei praktisch erwachsene Töchter zu Hause«, erklärte ich meinem Retter während der Autofahrt durchs nördliche Heidelberg und – in der letzten Abendsonne – über die Neckarbrücke. »Sehr zuverlässig. Sehr gewissenhaft. Außerdem geht's mir schon wieder viel besser.«

»Sie sind ein erwachsener Mann. Ich kann Ihnen nur Ratschläge geben.«

»Was ist eigentlich mit meinem Rad?«

Svantje hatte mein geliebtes Motobecane-Rad mit Dreigangschaltung in der Garage untergestellt, erfuhr ich.

»Das können Sie abholen, wenn Sie wieder auf dem Damm sind. Ihr Bedarf an Radtouren dürfte fürs Erste gestillt sein.«

Wie recht er hatte! Immer noch war mir schwindlig und ein wenig übel. Trotz der Tablette hämmerten die Kopfschmerzen in meinem Schädel, als müsste er von innen ausgebeult werden. Die Augen hielt ich die meiste Zeit geschlossen, weil das gemeine Licht so schmerzte. Warum musste ausgerechnet heute die Sonne scheinen, nachdem es zwölf Wochen lang nur grau, nass und trüb gewesen war?

»Wir werden uns umgehend ins Bett legen, ja?«, gab mir Dr. Kamphusen noch mit auf den Weg, als wir uns an der Haustür verabschiedeten. »Sollten sich neue Symptome einstellen oder die alten zurückkehren, dann rufen Sie bitte diesen Kollegen hier an.« Er kritzelte eine Telefonnummer und die Anschrift in ein Notizbuch mit glänzenden Messingbeschlägen, riss das kleine Blatt aus und überreichte es mir. »Jonas ist ein alter Freund von mir, praktiziert nicht weit von hier in der Weststadt und ist ein erfahrener Allgemeinmediziner. Zudem ist er einer der wenigen, die heutzutage noch Hausbesuche machen. Sollten sich keine neuen Symptome einstellen, wovon ich ausgehe, dann gehen Sie morgen trotzdem zu ihm.« Er schüttelte kräftig meine Hand, sah mir ein letztes Mal besorgt in die Augen. »Bei Jonas sind Sie in guten Händen. Die meisten Doctores sind ja heutzutage technikverrnarrte Quacksalber und willenlose Sklaven der Pharmaindustrie.«

Minuten später lag ich in meinem Bett und war heilfroh, wieder in der Waagerechten zu sein. Die Treppe war eine schwere Herausforderung gewesen. Natürlich ging es mir bei Weitem nicht so gut, wie ich behauptet hatte. Meine Töchter waren bei meinem Anblick mehr interessiert als beunruhigt gewesen. Ihr gefühlloser Kommentar hatte gelautet: »Zu uns sagst du immer, wir dürfen nicht ohne Helm fahren.«

Samstag, der siebte Februar. Das war mir immerhin ohne Anstrengung wieder eingefallen. Ein ungewöhnlich warmer, sonniger Tag für diese Jahreszeit. Deshalb hatte ich nach dem Mittagessen spontan beschlossen, eine kleine Radtour zu unternehmen, ein wenig Winterspeck wegzustrampeln, frische Luft in die Lungen zu pumpen nach dem ewigen Wintermief. In Richtung Norden war ich geradelt. Aus der Weststadt heraus, über den Neckar, durch das weitläufige Gelände der Unikliniken, am Zoo vorbei, über die noch völlig kahlen Felder zwischen Handschuhsheim und der Autobahn. In Ladenburg hatte ich später einen Cappuccino getrunken. Auf einer proppenvollen sonnigen Terrasse am Marktplatz. Und das Anfang Februar!

2

»Nette Beule haben Sie da«, stellte Dr. Jonas Slavik am Sonntagvormittag fest. Zuvor hatte er mich einer oberflächlichen und, wie ich fand, ziemlich herzlosen Untersuchung unterzogen.

Eigens für mich hatte er seine Praxis aufgeschlossen, die zum Glück nur wenige hundert Meter von meinem Krankenbett entfernt in einer schönen Jugendstilvilla untergebracht war. »Wie haben Sie das eigentlich angestellt? Am Hinterkopf?«

»Keine Ahnung«, erwiderte ich wahrheitsgemäß. »Warum?«

»Weil Radfahrer normalerweise nach vorne fallen, über den Lenker. Deshalb haben sie ihre Beulen üblicherweise an der Stirn oder an der Seite. Sie müssen einen sensationellen Salto hingelegt haben. Und Helme sind ja nichts für echte Männer wie uns, was?« Sein Lachen klang unangemessen schadenfroh, fand ich.

»Es geht da ziemlich abwärts«, versuchte ich mich kraftlos zu verteidigen. Das hatte ich gesehen, als ich in den alten Ford seines noch älteren Freundes und Kollegen stieg. Immer noch regte sich nichts in meinem Kopf, wenn ich versuchte, mir die Minuten vor dem Sturz ins Gedächtnis zu rufen. Da war nur eine schwarze Wand. Keine Bilder. Nicht der flüchtigste Schatten einer Erinnerung an den Unfall oder die Zeit davor, so sehr ich mich auch bemühte.

»Sonst alles heil geblieben?«, erkundigte sich Dr. Slavik.

»Im Rücken tut's auch ein bisschen weh.«

»Dann mal das Hemd hoch, bitte … ooh, ah, schön, sehr schön …Da haben Sie aber mal ein hübsches Hämatom. Sehr sauber abgegrenzt. Ganz symmetrisch. Und wunderbare Farben. Sind Sie auf was Hartes gefallen? Einen Stein vielleicht?«

»Keine Ahnung«, wiederholte ich meinen derzeitigen Lieblingssatz.

»Schön, sehr schön.« Er lachte befriedigt, erlaubte mir, das Hemd wieder in die Hose zu stopfen. »Das wird alles wieder. Reflexe sind im Rahmen des in Ihrem Alter Üblichen.«

In meinem Alter, schon wieder. Aber dieses Mal war es wohl anders gemeint als bei Dr. Kamphusen.

»Jetzt machen wir noch einen kleinen Sehtest, und dann sind wir auch schon fertig. Sie sind privat versichert?«

»Ich bin Beamter.«

»Schön. Sehr schön.«

Am Morgen waren die Zwillinge eifrig ihrer Aufsichtspflicht nachgekommen. Sie hatten mich genötigt, wenigstens einige Stückchen Toastbrot zu frühstücken und ein Glas handgepressten Orangensaft zu trinken, wegen der Vitamine. Meinen zaghaften Einwand, Vitamine würden gegen Gehirnerschütterungen vielleicht nicht helfen, hatten sie resolut vom Tisch gewischt. Später hatten sie hin und wieder überprüft, ob ich nicht etwa plötzlich ins Koma gefallen war, und jedes Mal nachgefragt, ob ich nicht doch etwas essen wolle.

Was ich jedoch am allerwenigsten hatte an diesem Sonntagvormittag, war Appetit. Vielleicht würde meine so unsanft und peinlich geendete Radtour am Ende auf ganz unerwartete Weise doch noch zur Reduktion meines Körpergewichts beitragen? Die Kopfschmerzen waren inzwischen erträglich, wenn ich regelmäßig meine Tabletten nahm und ruckartige Bewegungen vermied.

Mittlerweile schienen Sarah und Louise ihren Krankenpflegerinnenjob schon langweilig zu finden, denn als ich vom Arzt zurückkehrte, fragten sie umständlich an, ob es vielleicht okay wäre, wenn sie vielleicht ein klein wenig in die Stadt … Freunde treffen und so. Nur für ein Stündchen oder zwei oder so. Ich hatte nichts dagegen einzuwenden. Sie legten mir Handy und Telefon neben das Bett, stellten eine Flasche Wasser und zwei liebevoll belegte Brötchen daneben und verkrümelten sich erleichtert.

Zigarettenrauch!

Im Halbschlaf, aus dem Nichts, war plötzlich eine Erinnerung da: Zigarettenrauch hatte ich gerochen, kurz bevor es Nacht wurde um mich. Jemand hatte geraucht.

Am Nachmittag kam Theresa vorbei, brachte ein Sträußchen lachsfarbene Rosen mit sowie eine Flasche Sekt, die wir irgendwann auf meine Genesung leeren würden. Die Zwillinge hatten sie angerufen und über meinen beklagenswerten Zustand aufgeklärt. Sie trug heute einen Rock, der nicht ganz bis zu den Knien reichte, setzte sich neben mein Bett, roch gut und bemitleidete mich ein wenig. Da ich als Gesprächspartner nicht viel taugte, begann sie bald, mir die Zeit zu vertreiben, indem sie von diversen Unfällen erzählte, die sie im Lauf ihres bewegten Lebens mehr oder weniger glücklich überstanden hatte.

Ich versuchte tapfer zuzuhören, dämmerte jedoch immer wieder für Sekunden weg.

»Ich weiß bis heute nicht, wie ich das fertiggebracht habe«, hörte ich sie sagen. »Fünfzehn oder sechzehn muss ich damals gewesen sein – und zack, liege ich auf einmal im Graben. Leider war da so ein furchtbar stacheliger Busch, und davon habe ich diese hässliche Narbe hier an der Innenseite des Oberschenkels …«

Sie sprang auf, stellte den linken Fuß auf mein Bett, zog unbekümmert den Jeansrock hoch, und mir wurde vorübergehend wieder schwindlig. In diesem Moment begann das Telefon auf meinem Nachttisch zu trillern.

Theresa ließ den Rock fallen und sah mich auffordernd an. »Möchtest du nicht …?«

Ich schüttelte matt den Kopf. Nein, ich mochte nicht. Schließlich, als es partout nicht aufhören wollte, nahm ich das Telefon doch in die Hand und schaute aufs Display. Wie ich befürchtet hatte, war es Doro.

»Nein«, sagte ich und lege das Telefon wieder zur Seite.

Endlich verstummte das blöde Ding. Allerdings nur, um Sekunden später erneut loszulegen.

»Wer ist es denn?«, wollte Theresa wissen.

»Eine …« Ich hustete. Mein Kopf dröhnte. Das Telefon trillerte. »Eine alte Schulfreundin.«

Theresas Blick wurde sofort inquisitorisch. »Wie alt ist sie denn, diese Schulfreundin?«

»So alt wie ich ungefähr. Und du wirst mir jetzt bitte keine Eifersuchtsszene machen.«

»Hätte ich denn Grund dazu?«

»Natürlich nicht.«

»Du hast mir nie von ihr erzählt. Wie heißt sie denn?«

Dieses Mal schien Doro nicht aufgeben zu wollen. Ich brauchte dringend ein neues Telefon mit Anrufbeantworter.

»Dorothee. Doro. Ich habe sie erst im Dezember wiedergetroffen. Bei dieser Sache mit dem verschwundenen Mädchen. Du erinnerst dich?«

Theresa nickte mit immer noch hochgezogenen Brauen.

»Nach fast zwanzig Jahren. Wusste gar nicht, dass sie auch in Heidelberg lebt …«

»War sie eine gute Schulfreundin, diese … Doro?«

Niemand ist imstande, einen Namen mit so viel Verachtung auszusprechen wie eine eifersüchtige Frau.

»Im Gegenteil. Sie war eine Zicke. Ich konnte sie nicht leiden.«

»Und deshalb ruft sie dich am Sonntagnachmittag an?«

»Theresa, Herrgott!« Ich mäßigte meine Stimme sofort wieder und sank in mein Kissen zurück. »Wir waren in derselben Klasse, das war's auch schon.«

Endlich verstummte das nervtötende Getriller. Theresa entspannte sich. Beäugte misstrauisch noch ein wenig das Telefon. Vor den Fenstern brach die tief stehende Sonne durch die Wolken.

»Wärst du so nett, die Vorhänge …?«, fragte ich mit betont leidender Miene. »Das Licht …«

Sie sprang auf und zog die dunkelblauen Vorhänge zu. Setzte sich wieder.

»Hast du in den letzten Tagen von einem Fall gehört oder gelesen, bei dem jemand seine Frau umgebracht hat?«, fragte ich vorsichtig.

»Seine Frau umgebracht?«, fragte Theresa verdutzt zurück.

»Solltest du als Kripochef so was nicht am besten wissen?«

»Ich habe so ein ... ich weiß nicht. Du hast also nichts gehört?«

Sie zuckte die Achseln. »Nö.«

Die nächsten Sekunden verstrichen schweigend. Es war ein zähes Schweigen voller unausgesprochener Fragen.

»Da fällt mir ein«, sagte Theresa schließlich und warf mit einer schnellen Bewegung ihre honigblonde Lockenpracht zurück, »damals war ich noch Studentin. Es gab da jemanden, er war Assistent, ein ganz knuddeliger Typ. Ich hatte vielleicht ein bisschen zu hohe Absätze an dem Tag ...«

»Willst du jetzt aus Rache mich eifersüchtig machen? Ich bin Rekonvaleszent, Theresa. Ich brauche Schonung und Verständnis.«

»Ich bin nicht im Geringsten eifersüchtig. Er hat das ganze Semester lang den Prof vertreten, und wie ich ihm also nach dem Seminar hinterherlaufe, um ihn noch irgendwas zu fragen, da knicke ich um, und zack. Er hat mich sogar in die Klinik gefahren zum Nähen. Aber es ist trotzdem nichts daraus geworden. Ich war wohl einfach nicht sein Typ.«

Wieder stellte sie den linken Fuß auf mein Bett, wieder rutschte der Rock so weit nach oben, dass ich freie Sicht auf die geheimsten Stellen ihres wohlgebauten Körpers hatte.

»Diese Narbe hier am Unterschenkel. Man sieht sie kaum noch, findest du nicht auch?«

Die seidenweiche Innenseite ihrer Oberschenkel. Der bordeauxrote, fast durchsichtige Slip, der meine Blicke im Gegensatz zur unsichtbaren Narbe am Unterschenkel magisch anzog. Meine Kopfschmerzen wurden sofort wieder stärker. Sicherheitshalber schloss ich die Augen.

»Du siehst ja gar nicht hin!«

»Mir ist gerade ... ein bisschen schwindlig.«

»Denkst du an deine Doro?«

»Theresa, bitte entschuldige, aber ich kann es im Moment nicht freundlicher ausdrücken: Du spinnst.«

Minuten später verabschiedete sie sich mit einem kühlen Kuss auf den Mund, um sich für einen lange geplanten Theaterbesuch am Abend hübsch zu machen. Im Mannheimer

Nationaltheater gab man Goethes Faust, Teil eins. Sie würde zusammen mit ihrem Mann hingehen.

Als hätte Doro geahnt, dass ich jetzt allein war, legte das Telefon erneut los.

»Was machst du nur für Sachen, Alexander?«, fragte sie aufgebracht. »Du bist vom Rad gefallen?«

»Mache ich hin und wieder ganz gern. Hält die Reflexe auf Trab.«

»Rede keinen Unsinn. Du hast eine Gehirnerschütterung, habe ich gehört.«

»Von wem?«

»Von deinem Sohn.«

»Henning? Und woher …?«

»Von wem wohl? Von deinen Töchtern. Hast du ihnen endlich …?«

»Rufst du mich an, um mir Vorwürfe zu machen?«

»Aber nein.«

»Du könntest mich zum Beispiel fragen, wie's mir geht.«

»Wie geht es dir?«

»Schlecht. Ich habe mörderische Kopfschmerzen. Bei der kleinsten Bewegung wird mir schwindlig. Ich liege im Bett und blase Trübsal.«

»Das tut mir leid, Alexander. Du gehörst eigentlich in ein Krankenhaus. Und trotzdem solltest du allmählich …«

»Ich werde mit ihnen reden. Heute noch. Wenn ich es irgendwie hinkriege. Spätestens morgen.«

»Was ist denn überhaupt passiert? Wieso bist du gestürzt?«

»Wenn ich das wüsste. Ich muss irgendwie einen Purzelbaum über den Lenker gemacht haben. Aber ich kann mich an überhaupt nichts erinnern. Der Arzt sagt, es sei normal bei einer Gehirnerschütterung, dass man anfangs kleine Gedächtnislücken hat.«

»Du musst endlich mit deinen Töchtern reden, Alexander. Sie müssen es wissen. Henning muss es wissen. Ich möchte ihn aber nicht aufklären, solange du nicht …« Sie seufzte. »Ich will, dass zwischen uns endlich Klarheit herrscht.«

Ich zog es vor zu schweigen.

»Ich bin diese Heimlichtuerei so leid«, fuhr sie fort. »Außerdem werde ich in letzter Zeit das Gefühl nicht los, dass Henning etwas ahnt.«

»Ich werde es meinen Mädels sagen, sobald es irgendwie passt.«

»Es scheint nie zu passen bei dir.«

»Herrgott!« Nein, nicht aufregen! Die Kopfschmerzen steigerten sich sofort wieder ins Unerträgliche. Ich zwang mich zur Ruhe. Atmete flach. »Ich kann doch nicht einfach beim Frühstück sagen: Mädels, gute Neuigkeiten, ihr habt seit Neuestem einen Bruder.«

»Einen Halbbruder.«

»Juristisch gesehen ist Henning ja überhaupt nicht mein Sohn.«

»Alexander, jetzt hör mir bitte mal zu. Es interessiert mich einen feuchten Kehricht, wie die Juristen das nennen. Ich habe achtzehn lange Jahre darunter gelitten, dass ich Henning seine Herkunft verheimlichen musste. Wie sehr ich gelitten habe, weiß ich übrigens erst, seit ich dich wiedergetroffen habe.«

Bei den Ermittlungen im Dezember hatte ich – allerdings ohne ihr Zutun – herausgefunden, dass ich vor fast zwei Jahrzehnten bei einem Klassentreffen und unter Alkoholeinfluss einen Sohn gezeugt hatte.

»Wenn du nicht Manns genug bist, deine Töchter aufzuklären, dann werde ich es eben selbst tun.«

»Bei der Polizei nennen wir so was Erpressung!«

»Es interessiert mich nicht, wie man das bei der Polizei nennt. Ich werde es tun.«

»Ich rede ja mit ihnen. Bald. Fest versprochen.«

»Du hast es schon fünfmal fest versprochen.«

»Zählst du etwa mit?«

»Natürlich.«

»Sobald ich wieder auf den Beinen bin, okay?«

Wieder seufzte sie. »Und nächstes Mal setzt du bitte einen Helm auf, wenn du aufs Rad steigst. Ich will nicht, dass Henning seinen eben erst wieder aufgetauchten Vater gleich wieder verliert.«

Die nächste Frau, die mich an diesem elenden Sonntagnachmittag anrief, um mir Vorwürfe zu machen, war Sönnchen, meine Sekretärin.

»Sie machen ja Sachen, Herr Gerlach! Wie geht's Ihnen denn?«

»Steht es jetzt schon in der Zeitung? Oder ist es in den Fernsehnachrichten gekommen?«

»Meine Nichte hat mich vorhin angerufen und gesagt, Sie hätten einen Fahrradunfall gehabt.«

»Ihre Nichte?«

»Facebook, Herr Gerlach.«

»Ich glaube, ich muss mal ein paar ernste Worte mit meinen Töchtern reden.«

»Sie haben nicht verraten, was genau passiert ist. Bloß, dass Sie einen Fahrradunfall gehabt haben und das Bett hüten müssen.«

»Weiß die Welt auch schon, wie lange ich noch liegen muss? Das würde mich nämlich auch interessieren.«

»Ein paar Tage bestimmt. Mit einer Gehirnerschütterung ist nicht zu spaßen, das weiß ich auch ohne Internet. Sie liegen doch hoffentlich brav im Bett?«

»Im Moment ja. Aber morgen, spätestens übermorgen bin ich wieder im Büro.«

»Das werden wir ja sehen. Was ist denn eigentlich passiert?«

»Ich weiß es nicht. Irgendwie bin ich vom Rad gefallen und habe mir den Kopf gestoßen. Und wenn Sie jetzt auch nur ein Wort zum Thema Helm sagen, dann haben Sie einen neuen Feind auf der Welt, Frau Walldorf!«

»Sie haben also wirklich keinen aufgehabt?«

»Was genau bedeutet das Wörtchen ›wirklich‹ in Ihrer Frage?«

»Bei Facebook wird behauptet, Sie seien ohne Helm unterwegs gewesen und …«

Meine Kopfschmerzen schwangen sich zu ungeahnten Höhen auf. »Ich werde meinen Töchtern das Internet abklemmen«, stieß ich durch die Zähne hervor. »Sobald ich aufstehen kann, klemme ich ihnen das Internet ab.«

»Gar nichts klemmen Sie ab. Sie bleiben jetzt erst mal im Bett. Und Sie kommen morgen auch nicht ins Büro. Ich werd Sie krankmelden. Sie müssen sich um gar nichts kümmern. Sie bleiben einfach nur im Bett und werden wieder gesund. Und keine Angst, die Welt geht schon nicht unter ohne Sie.«

Der Tag war noch nicht zu Ende. Tage, die man im Bett verbringt, sind überhaupt erstaunlich lang.

Noch eine dritte Frau rief mich an. Diese allerdings erst, als es draußen schon dunkelte, und erstaunlicherweise wusste sie noch nichts von meinem blamablen Unfall.

»Mama, du?«

»Ja, ich. Wie geht's dir, Alex?«

»Prima. Und dir? Wie ist das Wetter bei euch in Portugal?«

»Mir geht es gut. Sehr gut, danke.« Ach herrje, da gab es offenbar ein Problem. »Windig ist es. Seit Tagen schon. Sehr windig.«

»Soll im Winter am Meer hin und wieder vorkommen. Du bist doch nicht etwa krank?«

»Krank?«, fragte meine einundsiebzigjährige Mutter, als wäre das eine ganz und gar weltfremde Frage. »Wie kommst du denn darauf?«

»Du klingst so … Du klingst nicht, als würde es dir gut gehen, ehrlich gesagt.«

»Ich bin kerngesund. Mir geht es wunderbar.«

Nein, da stimmte etwas ganz und gar nicht. Meine Mutter rief mich üblicherweise zweimal im Jahr an, seit sie mit Vater zusammen ihren Wohnsitz an die Algarve verlegt hatte. Einmal an Weihnachten und einmal zu meinem Geburtstag. Sie zählte nicht zu der Sorte Mütter, die in ihrer Rolle aufgehen.

»Und wie geht's Papa?«

»Dem geht es auch gut. Sehr gut sogar.«

»Mama, raus mit der Sprache – was ist los? Du rufst mich doch nicht einfach so an.«

»Wieso denn nicht? Man wird als Mutter doch einfach mal sein Kind anrufen dürfen. Dir geht es wirklich gut?«

»Mir geht es wunderbar.«

»Und Sarah und Louise?«

»Denen geht es sowieso immer gut. Obwohl, in zwei Wochen gibt's Zeugnisse, und dann wird sich das wahrscheinlich ändern …«

»Sind sie immer noch in der Pubertät?«

»Mittendrin. Aber das meiste Geschirr ist noch heil.«

»Fehlt ihnen die Mutter denn gar nicht?«

»Doch, natürlich.«

»Und wie sieht es aus …?«

»Wie sieht was aus?«

»Gibt es vielleicht eine neue Frau in deinem Leben?«

»Nein. Ja.«

»Ja? Wer ist sie? Ist sie nett? Mögen die Kinder sie?«

»Ja, sie ist nett. Wenigstens meistens. Und ja, die Mädels mögen sie.«

»Habt ihr vor zu heiraten?«

»Davon ist momentan keine Rede, Mama.«

Dass Theresa bereits verheiratet war, brauchte meine Mutter nun wirklich nicht zu wissen. Sonst würde sie vermutlich ab sofort täglich anrufen.

»Werdet ihr uns endlich mal besuchen hier unten im Süden? Es ist wirklich schön hier.«

»Ich weiß, Mama. Irgendwann kommen wir ganz bestimmt. Und du wirst auch meine neue … Partnerin kennenlernen. Ihr werdet euch mögen, da bin ich mir sicher. Du hast doch nicht etwa Heimweh, Mama? Das Wetter hier im Norden, ich kann dir sagen …«

»Heimweh? Um Gottes willen, nein! Ich bin heilfroh, dass ich nicht mehr in Deutschland bin. Wie hoch liegt der Schnee zurzeit?«

»Hier liegt kein Schnee. Vorhin hat sogar ein bisschen die

Sonne geschienen. Und gestern war's so warm, dass ich eine kleine Radtour gemacht habe.«

»Mit den Mädchen? War die ... Frau auch dabei? Wie heißt sie eigentlich?«

»Erstens: Für pubertierende Mädchen gibt es nichts Uncooleres als Radtouren mit ihrem Papa. Zweitens: Sie war nicht dabei. Drittens: Sie heißt Theresa. Und viertens: Du wirst auf deine alten Tage ganz schön neugierig, Mama.«

Mein Scherz kam nicht gut an.

»Man wird sich als Mutter doch wohl noch dafür interessieren dürfen, wie es dem eigenen Fleisch und Blut geht!«

»Natürlich, Mama. Aber ... du willst mir wirklich nicht sagen, was los ist?«

»Was soll los sein?«

»Papa geht's auch gut?«

»Sehr gut geht es dem sogar. Sehr gut.«

Ein bisschen klang es wie: zu gut. Da unten im windigen Süden hing der Haussegen offenbar gewaltig schief. Aber heute würde ich nicht erfahren, was mir die ungewohnte Anhänglichkeit meiner Mutter bescherte. So plauderten wir noch ein wenig über das Wetter in Mitteleuropa im Speziellen und die Klimaerwärmung im Allgemeinen und legten schließlich auf im Einvernehmen darüber, dass es uns allen – von Kleinigkeiten abgesehen – sehr gut ging.

Nun war es dringend Zeit für die nächste der Schmerztabletten, die Dr. Kamphusen mir mitgegeben hatte. Alle sechs bis acht Stunden durfte ich eine davon nehmen. Ich hatte die Dosis eigenmächtig ein wenig erhöht, denn schließlich hatte ich keine Lust, ewig im Bett zu liegen und mit dröhnendem Kopf die Decke anzustarren.

3

Am Montagmorgen hielt sich mein Drang, aus dem Bett zu springen, immer noch in Grenzen. Wie ich es auch drehte und wendete, so sehr ich es auch hasste – ich war vorübergehend außer Gefecht. So wählte ich um Viertel nach acht meine eigene Nummer in der Polizeidirektion. Sönnchen nahm nach dem zweiten Klingeln ab.

»Meine Cousine hat am Samstag übrigens auch einen Salto über den Lenker gemacht«, war das Erste, was sie zu erzählen wusste.

»Am Samstag war anscheinend halb Heidelberg mit dem Rad unterwegs«, brummte ich.

»Wenn sie keinen Helm aufgehabt hätte – ach so, das Wort darf ich ja nicht ...«

Wir gingen die Termine des Tages durch und sicherheitshalber auch gleich die des Dienstags. Zu meiner Erleichterung war nichts dabei, was keinen Aufschub duldete. »Sönnchen, Sie wissen doch alles, was in Heidelberg passiert. Ist Ihnen irgendwas bekannt geworden von einem Mann, der in letzter Zeit seine Frau umgebracht hat?«

»Seit der Geschichte in Hirschberg letzten November nicht. Wieso?«

»Nur so.«

Der Gattinnenmord in Hirschberg hatte zu den aus kriminalistischer Sicht eher einfachen Fällen gezählt: Arbeitslosigkeit, Krankheit, Hoffnungslosigkeit, Geldsorgen und Alkohol. Nachdem der Täter wieder halbwegs nüchtern und bei Sinnen gewesen war, hatte er selbst die Polizei gerufen, den Kollegen die Tür geöffnet, ihnen die Waffe ausgehändigt – ein kleines Beil, das er sonst zum Holzhacken benutzte – und sich widerstandslos festnehmen lassen. Nein, das war nicht die Geschichte, die ich suchte. Der Mann saß längst im Gefängnis und wartete auf seinen Prozess.

»Sind Sie diesen komischen Kerl am Freitag eigentlich ohne Probleme wieder losgeworden?«, fragte Sönnchen.

»Welcher komische Kerl?« Noch während ich die drei Worte aussprach, fiel es mir wieder ein: Ein älterer, groß gewachsener und sehr hagerer Mann war kurz vor Dienstschluss in mein Büro geplatzt, ohne Termin, ohne Anmeldung, aufgewühlt und zornig. Nicht einmal Sönnchen hatte es geschafft, ihn aufzuhalten. Der Name des Besuchers war mir dummerweise entfallen.

»Sie können sich nicht mal daran erinnern? Da muss es Sie ja schlimmer erwischt haben ...«

»Natürlich kann ich mich erinnern! War eine ziemliche Nervensäge, der Kerl, aber nachdem er eine Weile rumgeschimpft hat, ist er freiwillig wieder abgezogen.«

»Tut mir leid, dass ich losmusste, wie er noch bei Ihnen drin war. Aber ich hab einen ganz dringenden ... Was hat er eigentlich gewollt?«

Ja, was hatte er eigentlich gewollt? Fettige, viel zu lange Haare hatte er gehabt, im Nacken zu einem dünnen Schwänzchen gebunden. Eine nicht mehr ganz saubere und schon ziemlich verblichene Jeans hatte er getragen, dazu ein kariertes Hemd und eine abgewetzte schwarze Lederjacke mit vielen Taschen und ohne Ärmel. Und kolossalen Mundgeruch hatte er gehabt. Und außerdem hatte er nach Rauch gestunken. Die Finger der Rechten waren gelb gewesen vom Nikotin. Sollte er etwa ...? Natürlich!

Plötzlich war alles wieder da. Seine Stimme. Seine Worte. Meine Erinnerung kehrte zurück. Nur der Name. Der Name fehlte noch.

»Er hat behauptet, er hätte seine Frau umgebracht«, sagte ich.

»Und da rennt er schnurstracks zur Kripo und macht ein solches Tamtam? Wenn ich eine Mörderin wäre, dann würde ich ein bisschen bescheidener auftreten, ehrlich gesagt.«

»Der Mord ist vor einer Ewigkeit passiert, hat er gesagt. Angeblich war er lange im Ausland.«

»Und jetzt plagt ihn auf seine alten Tage das Gewissen?«

»Ungefähr so hat er es formuliert, ja: Sein Gewissen lässt ihm keine Ruhe.«

»Sie haben ihm die Geschichte doch nicht etwa geglaubt? Wenn das stimmen würde, dann müssten wir ja irgendwo einen ungeklärten Mordfall haben. Oder ... soll ich vielleicht sicherheitshalber mal im Archiv ...?«

»Ich weiß nicht. Er hat nicht gewirkt wie ein Verrückter, auch wenn er sich zeitweise so aufgeführt hat. Ich wollte sogar einen Blick in die Akte werfen, damit er sich beruhigt. Aber der Fall – falls es ihn überhaupt gibt – ist so alt, dass auf unseren Servern nichts darüber zu finden war.«

»Digital haben wir die alten Sachen ja nicht. Wenn's diese Akte überhaupt gibt, dann liegt sie im Keller.«

»Ich habe ihm versprochen, mich darum zu kümmern, und da ist er schließlich wieder abgezogen.«

»Wenn Sie mir jetzt noch den Namen verraten, dann flitze ich runter zur Gerda. Mit der wollt ich sowieso schon seit Ewigkeiten mal wieder ein Schwätzchen halten. Ihr Mann ist letztes Jahr ganz plötzlich gestorben.«

»Das ist leider das Dumme: Der Name fällt mir nicht ein. Ist aber bestimmt nur eine Frage der Zeit.«

»Vor dreißig Jahren, hat er gesagt?«

»Ungefähr.«

»So viele Morde haben wir ja zum Glück nicht in Heidelberg ...«

Wie wohl es tat, sich wieder zu erinnern! Ich bettete den kaum noch schmerzenden Kopf auf mein gemütliches Kissen und schloss die Augen. Inzwischen sah ich das knochige, von tausend Falten zerfurchte Gesicht des angeblichen Gattinnenmörders deutlich vor mir. Die tief liegenden, wässrigen, unentwegt zwinkernden Trinkeraugen, die rekordverdächtigen Tränensäcke, das fettige und schon ziemlich schüttere Haar. Fast roch ich noch den Schweißgeruch seines lange nicht gewaschenen Hemds. Seinen fauligen Atem. Und dazu den Gestank nach hunderttausend gerauchten Zigaretten, der aus allen seinen Poren zu dringen schien. Nur nach Alkohol hatte er merkwürdigerweise nicht gerochen, obwohl das gut gepasst hätte. Seine Hände hatten ziemlich gezittert.

Der Mann hatte – wie die meisten Menschen, die von einer fixen Idee besessen sind – eine enorme Hartnäckigkeit an den Tag gelegt. Er hatte insistiert, war laut geworden, am Ende sogar beleidigend. Auch mein Ton war schließlich nicht mehr so freundlich gewesen. Irgendwann war er mitten im Satz aufgesprungen und türenknallend davongestürmt.

Wenn mir nur sein Name wieder eingefallen wäre …

Am Morgen hatte es eine kurze Diskussion gegeben, ob meine jungen Pflegerinnen angesichts meines bejammernswerten Zustands nicht besser die Schule schwänzen sollten.

»Die Noten stehen doch eh schon alle fest.«

Zu ihrer Enttäuschung hatte ich mich geweigert, die vorbereiteten Entschuldigungen zu unterschreiben. Ich brauchte keine Aufsicht und keine Krankenpflegerinnen mehr. Verglichen mit dem Vortag ging es mir schon wieder blendend. Als ich allerdings aufstand, um mir aus der Küche einen Apfel zu holen, schwankte plötzlich die Welt, und ich musste mich schnell irgendwo festhalten. Auch das Sehen wollte noch nicht wieder zuverlässig funktionieren. Ganz abgesehen von diesen verfluchten Kopfschmerzen! Helles Licht konnte ich nach wie vor nicht vertragen.

Der Apfel wurde schließlich im Liegen und nur zur Hälfte verzehrt. Dann war mir der Appetit schon wieder vergangen. Eine Weile lag ich ganz still, betrachtete zum ersten Mal seit Langem wieder die beiden silbern gerahmten Bilder, die über meinem Bett an der Wand hingen. Stiche, die meine Heimatstadt Karlsruhe zeigten und aus dem Haushalt meiner Eltern stammten, die natürlich beim Umzug nach Portugal vieles hatten aussortieren müssen. Ich fühlte, wie der Schwindel nachließ, die Kopfschmerzen schwächer und schwächer wurden, lauschte auf die Alltagsgeräusche von der Straße. Und dann wurde mir langweilig.

Lesen kam nicht infrage, aber meine Mädchen hatten mir netterweise ein kleines Radio neben das Bett gestellt. Ein knatterbuntes, pausbäckiges Kinderradio mit erbärmlichem Ton. Ich fand einen Sender, der Musik brachte.

Meine Gedanken trudelten ziellos herum. Das Gedudel im Radio war einschläfernd, aber ein anderer Sender ließ sich nicht sauber einstellen. Wencke Myhre gab mir den Rat, nicht in jeden Apfel zu beißen. Daraufhin aß ich auch die andere Hälfte meines kargen Frühstücks.

Vor dem Fenster war es heute wieder so grau wie in den langen Wochen zuvor. Hin und wieder schien es ein wenig zu regnen. Meine Augenlider sanken herab. Und immer noch gelang es mir nicht, mich an den Namen des merkwürdigen Kerls vom Freitag zu erinnern. Oder daran, auf welchem Weg ich dorthin gelangt war, wo ich ziemlich genau vierundzwanzig Stunden später auf dem Gehweg ...

Auf dem Gehweg?

Plötzlich war ich wieder wach. Ich tat alles Mögliche mit meinem Rad. Befuhr manchmal Einbahnstraßen in der falschen Richtung, missachtete sogar die eine oder andere rote Ampel. Aber niemals fuhr ich auf dem Gehweg. Zumindest nicht, wenn die Straße daneben so wenig befahren war wie die – wie hatte sie noch geheißen? Mir wurde klar, dass ich nicht einmal wusste, wo genau ich eigentlich verunglückt war. Neuenheim jedenfalls. Hanglage. Dort, wo die Häuser groß und die Grundstücke weitläufig waren. Dort, wo der wohlhabende Teil der Heidelberger Bevölkerung wohnte. Und immer wieder kehrten meine herumschweifenden Gedanken zu dem verrückten alten Kauz zurück, der angeblich seine Frau ermordet hatte.

Wenn mir nur der Name endlich wieder eingefallen wäre!

Irgendwann im Lauf des endlosen Vormittags rief ich, nur um wieder einmal eine menschliche Stimme zu hören, Sönnchen an und fragte sie, wie der Laden lief, so ohne den Chef. Ein winziges bisschen enttäuscht war ich schon, als sie gelassen erwiderte: »Keine Probleme. Alles im grünen Bereich.«

Außerdem richtete sie mir bei dieser Gelegenheit von meinem Vorgesetzten und allen Kolleginnen und Kollegen die allerherzlichsten Genesungswünsche aus.

»Würden Sie mir einen Gefallen tun, Sönnchen?«

»Fast jeden.«

» Würden Sie auf meinem Schreibtisch nachsehen, ob ich mir vielleicht den Namen dieses Kerls irgendwo notiert habe? «

Das tat ich üblicherweise, da ich schon immer dazu geneigt hatte, während eines Gesprächs den Namen meines Gegenüber zu vergessen. Dieses Mal hatte ich es offenbar unterlassen, denn Sönnchen fand nichts.

» Wie war das eigentlich, als er reinkam? «

» Es hat geklopft, ziemlich laut, und dann ist er auch schon vor mir gestanden. Er will zu meinem Chef, hat er gesagt und mich ganz bös angeguckt. Ich hab gesagt, so geht das aber nicht. Er hat gesagt, doch, das geht, weil, es ist wichtig. Ich bin dann aufgesprungen, weil er einfach weitergehen wollt. Da hat er mich ganz finster angeguckt und gesagt, ich wär nicht die erste Frau, die er abmurkst. «

» So hat er das gesagt? Abmurkst? «

» Wörtlich. Und eine Sekunde später ist er bei Ihnen drin gewesen und hat mir fast noch die Tür an den Kopf geknallt. «

Warum beschäftigte mich die kuriose Geschichte so? Weshalb kehrten meine Gedanken wieder und wieder zu diesem nicht allzu langen, wenn auch äußerst ungemütlichen Gespräch zurück? Nicht nur wütend war er gewesen. Auch verzweifelt. Hoffnungslos. Obwohl die Frau schon seit dreißig Jahren tot war.

Angeblich.

Ich wusste ja weder, ob diese Frau jemals existiert hatte, noch, ob sie tatsächlich tot war.

Auf dem Gehweg ... Wie mochte ich nur auf den Gehweg geraten sein? War ich vielleicht gegen den Bordstein gefahren und über den Lenker ...? Oder hatte mich jemand abgedrängt, ein entgegenkommendes Auto vielleicht? Dann hätte Svantje Kamphusen mich auf dem rechten Gehweg gefunden und nicht auf dem linken. War mir ein Kind in den Weg gesprungen? Eine Katze?

Ich versuchte, mich an die Stunden und Minuten vor meinem Sturz zu erinnern. Systematisch, von Anfang an. Ladenburg, Sonne, der Cappuccino auf dem Marktplatz. Gegenüber die kleine Buchhandlung, in deren Fenster ein buntes Plakat eine Lesung ankündigte. Den Namen der Autorin hatte ich nie zuvor gehört. Später war ich weitergeradelt, in Richtung Norden. Durch Heddesheim, genau, mit den beiden Hochhäusern am östlichen Ortsrand. Im höheren der beiden hatten wir vor einem Jahr eine ermordete Frau gefunden. Dann ein Golfplatz. Nördlich von Heddesheim gab es einen Golfplatz, wo Anfang Februar natürlich kein Betrieb herrschte. Ich erinnerte mich an einen Parkplatz, wo vereinzelte teure Autos herumstanden, und an Arbeiter, die auf dem weitläufigen Grün werkelten, das noch gar nicht richtig grün war. Warm war es gewesen. Viel zu warm für Anfang Februar.

Vor den Fenstern goss es jetzt in Strömen, wurde mir plötzlich bewusst, und es schien von Stunde zu Stunde dunkler statt heller zu werden.

Ich erhob mich vorsichtig, blieb ein Weilchen auf der Bettkante sitzen, bis mein Gehirn sich mit der neuen Lage angefreundet hatte, und schlurfte wie ein Achtzigjähriger zur Toilette. Anschließend suchte ich meine Radwanderkarte und fand sie nicht. Konnte ich auch nicht, fiel mir dann ein, denn die steckte immer noch in der Lenkertasche meines Rads, das immer noch in der Garage des Ehepaars Kamphusen stand.

Ein See! An einem kleinen Badesee war ich vorbeigekommen, am Rand von Weinheim. Gut gelaunte Enten, würdig watschelnde Gänse, keifende Möwen, Spaziergänger in der Spätwintersonne, viel zu warm angezogene Kinder, die das Federvieh begeistert fütterten. Ein Weilchen hatte ich auf einer Bank gesessen und dem bunten Treiben zugesehen.

In Hirschberg hatte ich sogar mit mir gerungen, ob ich mir ein Eis gönnen sollte. Das hätte jedoch mit meinem Vorsatz im Widerspruch gestanden, durch meine sportliche Betätigung ein wenig abzunehmen, und so hatte ich tapfer widerstanden. Später in der schon tief stehenden Sonne die Strahlenburg über Schriesheim, Weinberge, blattlose Rebstöcke, an denen noch vereinzelt verschrumpelte Trauben baumelten. Und dann – nichts mehr. Die restlichen sechs Kilometer und zwanzig Minuten blieben hartnäckig im Dunkeln.

Ich erwachte, als die Zwillinge aus der Schule kamen. Zwei Stunden lang hatte ich tief geschlafen. Ich fühlte mich frisch und ausgeruht und kerngesund. Außerdem hatte ich etwas geträumt. Normalerweise erinnere ich mich nicht an meine Träume, aber dieser war wohl zu aufwühlend gewesen: Ein großer, dunkler Mann hatte vor mir gestanden und mich bedroht. Breite Schultern, Anzug und Krawatte, was gar nicht zu seinem groben und vor Wut geröteten Gesicht passen wollte. Rekordverdächtige Tränensäcke. Nein, das konnte nicht sein. Der Kerl mit den Tränensäcken war zwar groß gewesen, aber schlank, fast dürr. Und im dunklen Anzug konnte ich ihn mir beim besten Willen nicht vorstellen. Weshalb verfolgte mich diese dumme Geschichte nun auch noch bis in meine Träume? Nun ja, es gab momentan nicht viel Aufregendes in meinem Leben ...

Ich bat meine Töchter um einen Cappuccino.

»Darfst du das denn?«

»Wer will es mir verbieten?«

»Der Arzt.«

»Den frag ich einfach nicht.«

»Willst du nicht erst mal was essen? Wir machen Pfannkuchen.«

»Ein bisschen vielleicht.«

»Wir machen Pfannkuchen mit Blaubeermarmelade, und dann isst du mit uns.«

Die Pfannkuchen schmeckten, als hätte ich sie selbst gebacken, und beim Essen kehrte plötzlich mein Appetit zurück. Die Zwillinge waren stolz auf sich und auf mich, und am Ende bekam ich zur Belohnung sogar meinen Cappuccino. Danach fühlte ich mich wiederhergestellt und beschloss, das Bett vorläufig zu verlassen.

Dr. Slavik hatte vollkommen recht, überlegte ich in der Langeweile des verregneten Montagnachmittags, während ich durch meine Vierzimmeraltbauwohnung tigerte. Wenn man mit dem Fahrrad stürzt, kann man sich an allen möglichen Stellen Beulen und Blutergüsse zuziehen, aber kaum am Hinterkopf. Den

Bluterguss am Rücken zu besichtigen gestaltete sich schwierig, aber es ging. Der dunkelblaue Fleck mit Stich ins Grüne war klein und kreisrund. Ein Stein vielleicht, kleiner als eine Kinderfaust? Mein Kopf rebellierte heftig gegen meine Gymnastikübungen vor dem Spiegel. Das aus dem Boden ragende Ende eines Rohrs?

Schließlich kam mir eine Idee: Ich bat meine Töchter, die in Sarahs Zimmer gemeinsam über ihren Hausaufgaben brüteten, mein Hämatom zu fotografieren und mir außerdem einen ihrer beiden Laptops zu überlassen. Sarahs neues Smartphone wurde gezückt, und eine Minute später konnte ich meinen lädierten Rücken ohne Verrenkungen begutachten. Der Bluterguss war nicht nur rund, er hatte sozusagen Flügel. Oben und unten zwei gleich große, jedoch deutlich schwächere Abdrücke. Vollkommen symmetrisch. Vollkommen seltsam. Das war weder ein Stein gewesen noch ein Rohr, das konnte nur ... ja was?

Im Internet sah ich mir den Norden Neuenheims aus der Vogelperspektive an, entdeckte jedoch nichts, was irgendwelche Erinnerungen ausgelöst hätte. Ich versuchte, die Anschrift von Dr. Kamphusen herauszufinden, fand aber nur die Internetseite seiner ehemaligen Praxis, die er vor fünf Jahren einem Nachfolger übergeben hatte. Ich rief dort an und stieß bei verschiedenen jungen Damen auf konsterniertes Unverständnis, gewürzt mit einem ordentlichen Schuss offener Ablehnung. Schließlich wurde ich an eine ältere Sprechstundenhilfe weitergereicht, die noch unter dem Vorgänger gedient hatte.

»Ja, der alte Herr Doktor«, seufzte sie wohlig und mit verhaltener Stimme. »Das waren noch andere Zeiten. Damals ist es noch um Patienten gegangen und nicht nur um Fallzahlen und Praxisbudgets. Zum Glück haben sie jetzt endlich diese dumme Praxisgebühr wieder abgeschafft. Was wollen Sie denn von ihm?«

»Ihm und seiner Frau einen Blumenstrauß schicken.« Ich erzählte ihr von meinem Unfall und der herzlichen Fürsorge des alten Arztes, der mir sozusagen das Leben gerettet hatte.

»Wegen der Gehirnerschütterung kann ich mich aber blöderweise nicht an die Adresse erinnern. Und hinfahren mag ich nicht ...«

»Sollten Sie auch nicht, wenn das erst vorgestern gewesen ist. Haben Sie etwa keinen Helm aufgehabt?«

»Der ist mir leider beim Sturz runtergefallen.«

»Dann sollten Sie nächstes Mal den Riemen straffer ziehen. Wenn der Riemen nicht straff sitzt, nützt der ganze Helm nichts.«

Diesen nützlichen Hinweis versprach ich künftig unbedingt zu beachten. Daraufhin diktierte sie mir Straße, Hausnummer und zur Sicherheit auch noch die Telefonnummer ihres verehrten alten Chefs. Anschließend klagte sie noch ein wenig über geldgierige Ärzte und neunmalkluge junge Kolleginnen, und am Ende verabschiedeten wir uns wie Komplizen, die soeben einen fetten Coup ausgeheckt hatten.

Mithilfe ihrer Angaben fand ich das Haus des alten Arztes im Internet mit zwei Klicks. Es lag am steilen Westhang des Heiligenbergs. Unterhalb grenzte ein weitläufiges, fast parkähnliches Grundstück an den auch nicht gerade kleinen Garten des Ehepaars Kamphusen. Die Frau war vom Einkaufen gekommen, als sie mich fand, war also die Straße heraufgekommen, an dem dicht bewachsenen Nachbargrundstück vorbei. Und irgendwo dort musste ich gelegen haben. Mitten in dem kleinen Park stand ein großes, dunkles Haus, das wegen der Bäume in der Satellitenansicht nur schlecht zu sehen war. Eine Villa, fast ein kleines Schloss. Regte sich da etwas in meinem Kopf?

Nein. Nichts regte sich.

Ich klappte den Laptop zu und gönnte meinen erschöpften Augen Erholung. Versuchte, mir meinen Traum noch einmal in Erinnerung zu rufen. Der große, breite Mann im dunklen Anzug. Seine drohende Miene. Seine Hand an meiner Brust. Offenbar hatten wir eine Auseinandersetzung gehabt. Weshalb? Weil ich auf dem Gehweg geradelt war? Wohl kaum. Was war es dann? Und weshalb projizierte ich immer wieder die Augen des angeblichen Gattinnenmörders ins Gesicht des Schlägertyps im Anzug? Je mehr ich mich anstrengte, mir die Bilder ins Gedächtnis zu rufen, desto verworrener wurde alles. Am Ende war ich fast überzeugt, dass es einfach nur ein Traum gewesen war. Dass es nichts zu bedeuten hatte.

Ich brachte Sarah ihren Laptop zurück, der ziemlich verstaubt war, weil Computer aus der Mode gekommen waren, wie ich erst kürzlich gelernt hatte. Laptops taugten heutzutage nur noch für Hausaufgaben und für Opas. Moderne Menschen nutzten ihre Smartphones.

4

Mitten in der Nacht schrak ich aus einem unruhigen, schweißtreibenden Schlaf hoch. Wieder war ein winziger Schnipsel Erinnerung an die Oberfläche getrieben.

Meine Frage hatte gelautet: » Wann? Wann genau soll das denn gewesen sein? «

» Fünfundachtzig «, hatte der alte Mann mit den Trinkeraugen geantwortet. Er hatte mir vermutlich auch das genaue Datum genannt, aber an diesen Teil des Gesprächs konnte ich mich wieder nicht erinnern. Da war noch etwas gewesen. Etwas Ungewöhnliches. Die Frau hatte einen Beruf gehabt, einen nicht alltäglichen Beruf.

Ich konnte nicht mehr einschlafen, wälzte mich im Bett herum, grübelte und schaltete schließlich meinen alten Rechner ein. Aus der Küche holte ich mir ein Glas Orangensaft, stöberte lange und erfolglos im Internet nach Meldungen aus jener Zeit vor fast dreißig Jahren, in denen eine gewaltsam ums Leben gekommene Frau vorkam. Und fand nichts. Jetzt half nur noch das Archiv der Polizeidirektion weiter, das um diese Uhrzeit natürlich noch verwaist war.

Inzwischen war es halb fünf, zeigte mein Radiowecker mit grün leuchtenden Ziffern. Ich holte mir ein zweites Glas Orangensaft, legte mich wieder ins Bett, konnte immer noch nicht einschlafen. Die Zeit bis zum Sonnenaufgang kam mir wie eine Ewigkeit vor. Ab halb acht rief ich alle fünf Minuten in der Direktion an. Beim siebten Versuch nahm Sönnchen ab, noch ein wenig atemlos von den Treppen. Ich sagte ihr das Jahr, das der namenlose Besucher mir genannt hatte.

»Die Gerda kommt immer erst um halb neun«, wurde ich aufgeklärt. »Sonst geht's Ihnen gut?«

»Nein. Wir haben im Schnitt drei, vier Mordfälle im Jahr. Und so gut wie alle werden aufgeklärt.«

»Ich geh nachher gleich in den Keller. Sobald ich was habe, hören Sie von mir.«

Nach dem kurzen Telefonat fühlte ich wieder den Puls in den Schläfen. Die Kopfschmerzen waren zurück. Nicht mehr so stark wie am Sonntag, aber sie schienen mir eine deutliche Warnung zu sein. Aufregung tat mir nicht gut. Sogar telefonieren überforderte meine Kräfte.

Frustriert schleppte ich mich in die Küche und traf dort auf meine schlaftrunkenen Töchter, die angeblich erst zur zweiten Stunde Unterricht hatten.

»Lehrermangel«, klärte man mich auf. »Seit du den Plako in den Knast gebracht hast, fällt andauernd Mathe aus.«

Ich nahm eine Tablette und wankte zu meinem Krankenlager zurück. Mir war wieder schwindlig wie am ersten Tag. Und so übel, dass ich für kurze Zeit fürchtete, mich übergeben zu müssen. Ich beschloss, bei Gelegenheit meinen alten Fahrradhelm abzustauben und griffbereit an die Garderobe zu hängen.

Im Dämmerschlaf hörte ich die Zwillinge die Wohnung verlassen, die ich im Zuge von Ermittlungen wegen eines Verkehrsunfalls mit Todesfolge um ihren Mathematiklehrer gebracht hatte. Opfer war eine junge Radfahrerin gewesen, von der ich nicht wusste, ob sie einen Helm getragen hatte. Jedenfalls hätte er sie nicht gerettet, denn sie war an inneren Blutungen im Bauchbereich gestorben. Vielleicht sollte man ja wie die alten Ritter im Blechpanzer …

Um zwanzig vor zehn lärmte mich das Handy aus dem Tiefschlaf. Ich brauchte einige Sekunden, bis ich wieder wusste, wo ich war und was diesen Radau veranstaltete. Es war Sönnchen.

»Unaufgeklärte Mordfälle haben wir fünfundachtzig gar keine gehabt«, verkündete sie. »Das genaue Datum hat er Ihnen nicht gesagt?«

»Wenn, dann kann ich mich nicht erinnern.«

»Wissen Sie irgendwas über die Frau?«

»Nur, dass sie einen ungewöhnlichen Beruf hatte.«

»Filmschauspielerin vielleicht?«

»Das könnte sein. Doch, da klingelt was.«

»Da hätte ich nämlich was. Viktoria Hergarden, eine Filmschauspielerin. Allerdings war's kein Mord, sondern ein häuslicher Unfall mit Todesfolge.«

»Heergarten war der Name?«

»Vorne mit einem e und hinten mit d statt t.«

Hergarden.

Hergarden?

Je öfter ich den Namen vor mich hin murmelte, desto bekannter kam er mir vor.

»Das passt«, entschied ich schließlich. »So hat er geheißen. Sie sind ein Schatz, Sönnchen. Was genau ist damals passiert?«

»Laut Protokoll ist die arme Frau in ihrem Wohnzimmer ausgerutscht und mit dem Kopf auf den Couchtisch geknallt. Eine Nachbarin hat sie am nächsten Tag gefunden.«

»Wie alt war sie?«

»Jahrgang siebenundfünfzig – demnach war sie achtundzwanzig.«

»Fremdverschulden ist ausgeschlossen?«

»Absolut. Sie war allein in der Wohnung. Die Tür war abgeschlossen. Der Schlüssel hat innen gesteckt. Keine Spuren von gewaltsamem Eindringen. Die ist eindeutig über ihre eigenen Füße gestolpert. War übrigens eine Hübsche. Es sind Fotos dabei. Auf einem sieht man eine leere Sektflasche.«

»Wären Sie so lieb, mir die Akte in der Mittagspause vorbeizubringen?«

»So weit kommt's noch! Sie sind krank und müssen sich schonen. Ich will mir später keine Vorwürfe machen müssen.«

»Dann schleppe ich mich eben zu Ihnen ins Büro, und Sie sind dann schuld, wenn es Spätfolgen gibt.«

»Das ist jetzt aber die ganz fiese Tour!«

»Sönnchen, ich bitte Sie! Wenn ich mich hier zu Tode langweile, werden Sie sich später auch Vorwürfe machen.«

Sie seufzte wie eine vielgeplagte Mutter. »Na gut. Wenn es Sie glücklich macht und Sie schön brav im Bett liegen bleiben, dann sollen Sie in Gottes Namen Ihre Akte kriegen, Herr Dickkopf.«

Ich bedankte mich ausführlich. Aber sie blieb reserviert.

»Sie sollten sich lieber um Ihre Gesundheit kümmern als um alte Mordgeschichten. Nach dreißig Jahren kommt's auf einen Tag mehr oder weniger doch nicht an.«

Damit hatte sie zweifellos recht. Aber wie sollte ich das Denken abstellen? Indem ich Radio hörte, zum Beispiel. Mich ablenkte. An etwas Schönes dachte. Theresa eine ordentlich schwülstige SMS schrieb. Die postwendend beantwortet wurde. Meine Liebste versprach, mir demnächst einen Krankenbesuch abzustatten und in meinem Elend ein wenig Gesellschaft zu leisten.

»Bringe selbst gebackenen Marmorkuchen mit und koche dir einen feinen Kamillentee.« Den letzten Teil las ich mit leichtem Grausen.

»Seit wann backst du Kuchen?«, schrieb ich zurück.

»Seit drei Wochen. Vermutlich die ersten Anzeichen der Wechseljahre. Bücher schreiben kann ich ja offenbar nicht.«

Theresa war vierundvierzig und in letzter Zeit oft gedrückter Stimmung wegen des ausbleibenden Verkaufserfolgs ihres neuen Buchs. Kurz vor Weihnachten war es erschienen, eine unterhaltsam zu lesende und dennoch lehrreiche und sachlich solide Abhandlung über die Entwicklung des Terrorismus über die Jahrhunderte. Ich hatte gleich meine Zweifel gehabt, ob die Menschheit sich nach einem solchen Buch gesehnt hatte. Und nun lag es in den Regalen der Buchhandlungen wie Beton.

Schon eine halbe Stunde später war sie da und füllte mein Schlafzimmer mit dem Duft eines neuen Parfüms, sprühender Energie und guter Laune.

»Dior«, wurde ich aufgeklärt. »Magst du es?«

»Ich fürchte, mir wird schlecht davon«, erwiderte ich kläglich.

Wortlos kippte sie ein Fenster. Dann setzte sie sich auf die Bettkante und sah mich prüfend an.

»Kann es sein, dass du mich und mein Leiden nicht ganz ernst nimmst?«, fragte ich.

»Eine Gehirnerschütterung ist nichts, woran man stirbt.«

»Woher willst du das wissen?«, stöhnte ich. »Du hast gut reden.«

»Ich hatte selbst mal eine. Im Turnunterricht vom Barren gefallen. Mein größtes Talent im Fach Sport war nämlich, von etwas möglichst Hohem möglichst ungeschickt herunterzufallen.«

Aufgeräumt erzählte sie, dass sie in ihrer Jugend auch mehrfach mit dem Rad verunglückt war.

»Einmal habe ich nicht mal drauf gesessen, stell dir vor! Es war nach der letzten Schulstunde. Ich hatte es eilig, wollte das Schloss vom Hinterrad lösen, da hat mich irgendein Torfkopf von hinten geschubst, und zack, bin ich mitsamt Rad nach vorne umgekippt und habe mir am Sattel einen Schneidezahn ausgeschlagen.«

Sie ließ mich ihr makelloses Gebiss betrachten, deutete auf den verunglückten Zahn im Oberkiefer. »Man sieht überhaupt nicht, dass er überkront ist, findest du nicht auch?«, nuschelte sie dazu.

In dieser Sekunde wurde mir klar, woher der merkwürdige Bluterguss an meinem Rücken und die Beule am Hinterkopf stammten: Ich war rückwärts auf mein Rad gefallen. Und der Bluterguss am Rücken stammte von einem Pedal, das sich in meine Weichteile gebohrt hatte.

Da Theresa keine weiteren berichtenswerten Unglücksfälle mehr einfielen, erzählte ich von dem alten Mann, der so energisch behauptete, seine Frau ermordet zu haben.

»Und das Komische ist: Irgendwie lässt mich das Gefühl nicht los, dass er bei meinem Unfall dabei war.«

»Hat er dich gestoßen?«

»Das nicht. Da müssen zwei gewesen sein. Aber ich kriege es einfach nicht zusammen. In meinem Gedächtnis ist ein schwarzes Loch von mindestens einer Viertelstunde. Bist du mit dem Auto da?«

»Ja.«

»Regnet es noch?«

»Kaum.«

Dreißig Minuten später standen wir am Hainsbachweg im Heidelberger Norden und sahen uns ratlos um. Das parkähnliche Grundstück, das westlich an Dr. Kamphusens Garten grenzte, war von einem übermannshohen, robusten Zaun aus massiven Eisenstäben umgeben. An den oberen Enden reckten sich Speerspitzen, die vor langer Zeit vielleicht sogar einmal golden geglänzt hatten. Das Grundstück dahinter war schattig und wirkte ungepflegt, das Haus selbst war aus unserer Position nicht sichtbar.

»Wo?«, fragte Theresa.

Ich hob die Schultern.

»Immer noch keine Erinnerung?«

Ich schüttelte vorsichtig den Kopf. »Irgendwie beunruhigend. Man weiß, man war hier, man weiß, es ist irgendwas passiert, aber es ist einfach … gelöscht.«

Wir spazierten ein Stück am Zaun entlang die Straße hinunter. Theresa hatte sich bei mir untergehakt, um mich halten zu können, falls mir plötzlich schwindlig werden sollte. Es klappte jedoch besser als befürchtet. Die frische Luft schien mir gutzutun. Ein feuchtkalter Wind blies von Westen her, aber die Temperatur lag deutlich über dem Gefrierpunkt. Nässesatte Wolken trieben träge über uns hinweg, als suchten sie einen Landeplatz. Manchmal nieselte es ein wenig. Auf der gegenüberliegenden Seite der schmalen Straße parkten Autos. Dahinter eine hohe Mauer aus rötlichem Sandstein, über die große Bäume ihre Kronen reckten.

»Und?« Theresa ruckelte ein wenig an meinem Arm, als könnte sie dadurch mein Gehirn zurechtrütteln.

»Nichts. Nichts. Nichts.«

»Da ist ein Törchen.«

Die in den Zaun eingelassene Tür war so schmal, dass nur ein nicht allzu umfangreicher Mensch hindurchschlüpfen konnte. Theresa vermutete, sie habe früher als Dienstboteneingang gedient.

»Oder für heimliche Liebespaare.«

»Du denkst wirklich immer nur an das Eine.«

Sie lachte fröhlich. »Wie der offizielle Zugang des Anwesens sieht es jedenfalls nicht aus.«

Ich drückte probeweise die Klinke, aber das Liebestor war fest verschlossen. Der dahinterliegende Weg war von matschigem Laub bedeckt und wand sich in gemächlichen Kurven in Richtung Haus, von dem jetzt immerhin das von hohen Backsteinkaminen gekrönte graue Dach zu sehen war.

»Hier vielleicht?«, fragte Theresa.

Wieder einmal zuckte ich die Achseln.

»Da liegt etwas.« Sie bückte sich und hob ein rotes Plastikteil auf. »Könnte ein Stück von deinem Rücklicht sein. Ist es beim Sturz kaputtgegangen?«

»Ich weiß es doch nicht!«, fuhr ich sie an, mäßigte aber sofort wieder meine Stimme. »Entschuldige, ich …«

Sie drückte mir einen kräftigen Kuss auf den Mund. »Würde mich auch nervös machen, so ein totaler Blackout. Aber bald bist du wieder der Alte, du wirst sehen.«

Wir machten kehrt und gingen zurück – nun den Hang hinauf. Jetzt merkte ich, dass ich längst nicht wieder gesund war. Mein Kopf rebellierte schon nach zwei Schritten, und wir mussten immer wieder stehen bleiben, bis mein Puls sich beruhigt hatte. Der hohe Zaun endete, das Grundstück des Ehepaars Kamphusen begann. Hier gab es keine eisernen Gitterstäbe und hohe Bäume, sondern ein kniehohes Sandsteinmäuerchen und Ziergesträuch. Wir bogen auf einen etwa zwei Meter langen, breiten Pflasterweg ein, erklommen drei erstaunlich anstrengende Stufen.

Theresa lief zu ihrem kleinen goldfarbenen Skoda, den sie am Straßenrand geparkt hatte. Wenig später kam sie mit dem Blumenstrauß zurück, den wir auf der Herfahrt gekauft hatten, und der Rotweinflasche, die aus meiner Küche stammte. Ich drückte den Klingelknopf. Innen gongte es würdig und laut.

Es war die Frau, die öffnete.

»Herr Gerlach!«, rief sie strahlend. »Es geht Ihnen schon wieder besser? Und was für wunderschöne Blumen!«

Ich überreichte der für ihr hohes Alter äußerst lebhaften kleinen Dame den Strauß, Theresa gab ihr die Flasche. Nicht nur ihre Stimme klang jung, auch der Blick war wach und neugierig.

»Ich wollte mich herzlich bedanken«, sagte ich. »Es geht mir dank Ihrer Fürsorge wirklich schon wieder ganz gut. Und ich würde mir gerne mein Fahrrad ansehen.«

»Wollen Sie es nicht gleich mitnehmen?«

Dazu war Theresas Skoda zu klein. »Ich hole es, sobald ich selbst wieder Auto fahren kann«, versprach ich.

»Hier stört es nicht, keine Sorge.«

Wir gingen am Haus entlang zum breiten Garagentor. Kies knirschte unter unseren Schritten. Frau Kamphusen zückte eine Fernbedienung, das Tor schwang leise brummend auf. Mein Rad lehnte an der Seitenwand. Das Rücklicht war kaputt, und wir brauchten uns nicht zu bücken, um festzustellen, dass das, was Theresa gefunden hatte, das fehlende Teil war.

»Wer wohnt in dem großen Haus unterhalb?«, fragte ich meine Retterin.

»In der Villa? Eine Frau von Brühl.«

»Allein? In dem riesigen Anwesen?«

»Zurzeit wohl, ja.« Frau Kamphusen nickte eifrig. »Wir wissen aber wenig über sie. Man sieht sie so gut wie nie. Als wir hier vor zwanzig Jahren gebaut haben, war da unten eine Firma drin. Etwas mit Werbung haben die gemacht, mehr weiß ich nicht. Das Haus gehörte aber wohl schon damals Frau von Brühl.«

Frau Kamphusen lächelte abwechselnd Theresa und mich an. Sie schien sich zu freuen, dass ihr jemand so aufmerksam zuhörte.

»Stelle ich mir gruselig vor, ganz allein in so einem Riesending«, meinte Theresa.

»Sie hat eine Zugehfrau, die jeden Tag kommt. Sie war mehrmals verheiratet, wenn stimmt, was man hört. Aber inzwischen ist sie wohl auch in dem Alter, in dem die Männer nicht mehr Schlange stehen. Einige Zeit soll sie in Frankreich gelebt haben. Aber wie gesagt, das weiß ich alles nur vom Hörensagen. Sie hat sich nicht in der Nachbarschaft vorgestellt, als sie eingezogen ist.«

»Sagt dir der Name was?«, fragte ich Theresa, als wir wieder im Wagen saßen. »Von Brühl?«

»Nie gehört. Wie sicher bist du eigentlich, dass dich jemand gestoßen hat?«

»Überhaupt nicht. Ich habe es ja nur geträumt.«

Am Ende unserer kleinen Spazierfahrt war ich froh, wieder im warmen Bett zu liegen, gehorsam Theresas Kamillentee zu schlürfen und von ihrem selbst gebackenen Marmorkuchen zu essen, auf den sie stolz war. Ich schaffte drei dicke Stücke, lobte ihre neu erworbenen Backkünste, und sie freute sich wie ein Teenager. Schließlich verabschiedete sie sich, weil sie um halb zwei einen Termin beim Zahnarzt hatte.

»Kommst du später noch mal vorbei?«

»Später hole ich Egonchen von der Direktion ab. Wir wollen in die Stadt, ein paar Kleinigkeiten besorgen.«

Egonchen hieß mit vollem Namen Dr. Egon Liebekind und war als Chef der Heidelberger Polizeidirektion zugleich mein direkter Vorgesetzter. Ein gemütlicher und ungewöhnlich kluger Zweimeterriese, der, wie ich noch nicht lange wusste, irgendwann im Lauf seiner Ehe mit Theresa seine homosexuellen Neigungen entdeckt hatte. Aus diesem Grund hatte er – was mich sehr beruhigte – nichts dagegen einzuwenden, dass Theresa ihre sexuellen Bedürfnisse im Bett eines anderen auslebte. Früher hatte ich oft feuchte Hände gehabt, wenn ich überraschend zum Chef gerufen wurde.

Sönnchen tauchte entgegen ihrer Ankündigung nicht gegen Mittag auf, um mir die Akte zu bringen. Nachdem sie mich ordentlich lange hatte warten lassen, rief sie immerhin an und entschuldigte sich mit zu viel Arbeit auf dem Schreibtisch. Sie versprach jedoch, das ersehnte Schriftstück nach Feierabend vorbeizubringen. Ich vermutete eine erzieherische Absicht hinter der allzu durchsichtigen Aktion.

Anschließend versuchte ich, ein wenig zu lesen, ließ es aber bald wieder bleiben, da es meinen Augen nicht guttat. Einige Zeit lag ich still in meinem Bett, starrte an die Decke, wo der Lichtkreis meiner Leselampe leise zitterte, wenn ich mich bewegte. Ich fand heraus, dass ich die Richtung des Zitterns steuern konnte, indem ich mich in verschiedene Richtungen bewegte, und fand diese Beobachtung interessant. Eine Weile rang ich mit mir, ob ich das Radio einschalten sollte. Aber ich hatte heute keine Lust auf deutsche Schlager.

5

Als Sönnchen spätnachmittags an meiner Tür läutete, hatte ich gründlich gelüftet und schon ein wenig im Internet geforscht. Die Berufsbezeichnung »Filmschauspielerin« war im Zusammenhang mit Viktoria Hergarden pure Hochstapelei. Im weltweiten Netz hatte ich so gut wie nichts über sie gefunden. Wäre sie tatsächlich in nennenswerten Filmen oder auf respektablen Bühnen aufgetreten, dann hätte es irgendwo vermerkt sein müssen. Es gab Datenbanken, in denen anscheinend jeder aufgelistet war, der einmal bei einer Filmproduktion das Mikrofon gehalten, Scheinwerfer justiert oder ein Kabel abgerollt hatte. Lediglich im liebevoll gepflegten Onlinearchiv einer Viernheimer Firma für Kunststoffspritzgussteile fand ich eine kleine Notiz, in der ihr Name vorkam. Anlässlich des fünfzigjährigen Betriebsjubiläums im Jahr 1983 war eine kleine Schauspielertruppe aufgetreten und hatte eine Bühnenbearbeitung von Goethes *Wahlverwandtschaften* zum Besten gegeben. Die Liste der Darsteller umfasste nur sechs Einträge, und hinter »Ottilie« stand der Name »V. Heergarten« – vermutlich falsch geschrieben. Ob die Aufführung ein Erfolg gewesen war, konnte ich dem kurzen Text nicht entnehmen.

Der Blick, mit dem meine Sekretärin mir die enttäuschend dünne Akte in die Hand drückte, ließ eine längere Störung des Betriebsfriedens fürchten.

»Ich denk, Sie liegen im Bett?«, fragte sie anstelle einer Begrüßung.

»Wie soll ich Ihnen die Tür öffnen, wenn ich im Bett liege?«

»Sie sehen aber nicht aus, als wären Sie grad erst aufgestanden!«

Ich versuchte zu argumentieren, mich zu verteidigen, aber sie weigerte sich zuzuhören, wünschte mir kühl gute Besserung und einen langweiligen Abend mit meiner Akte und machte auf dem Absatz kehrt. Nicht einmal ein paar Blümchen hatte sie mir mitgebracht.

»Todesfallermittlung Viktoria Hergarden«, stand mit eckiger Handschrift auf dem Pappdeckel des grauen Hängeordners. In der Mappe befanden sich ein dreiseitiges, mit Maschine geschriebenes Protokoll sowie einige farbige Tatortfotos im Format 13 × 18. Am Ende waren praktischerweise auch noch Kopien des Totenscheins und des Personalausweises der Verstorbenen beigefügt.

Noch im Stehen begann ich zu lesen.

Der Anruf hatte die Heidelberger Polizeidirektion am Morgen des zehnten November 1985 erreicht, um neun Uhr vierundfünfzig. Eine Frau Elisabeth Holland hatte sich Sorgen um ihre Nachbarin gemacht, entnahm ich der ebenfalls abgehefteten Telefonnotiz. Diese Nachbarin, die im selben Haus wie die Anruferin wohnte, war nicht wie üblich gegen neun Uhr aufgestanden. Von oben hörte man keine Geräusche, auf die Türklingel reagierte sie nicht. Und im Wohnzimmer brannte Licht, wie man vom Garten aus erkennen konnte. Die letzte Zeile der Notiz lautete: »Weitergel. an KDD 9:56.« Weitergeleitet an den Kriminaldauerdienst um neun Uhr sechsundfünfzig.

Die angegebene Anschrift, Gundolfstraße, sagte mir nichts. Ich setzte mich an meinen PC und bemühte erneut das Internet. Das Haus, in dem Viktoria Hergarden gestorben war, lag im Westen Neuenheims. Ein gesichtloses Mehrfamilienhaus aus den Fünfziger- oder Sechzigerjahren wie tausend andere in dieser Stadt.

Noch etwas überprüfte ich bei dieser Gelegenheit: Ich meinte nämlich, den Namen Holland erst kürzlich gelesen zu haben. Und richtig: Bei der kleinen Theateraufführung zwei Jahre vor Viktoria Hergardens Tod hatte eine S. Holland die Charlotte gespielt. Der Vorname passte nicht, denn die Anruferin hatte Elisabeth geheißen. Aber vielleicht gab es da doch irgendeine Verbindung. Den Eduard hatte ein M. Graf gespielt, las ich bei dieser Gelegenheit, dessen Name weiter unten noch einmal auftauchte. Er hatte auch Regie geführt.

Ich fuhr meinen Klapper-PC herunter, legte mich im Bademantel aufs Bett und schmökerte weiter in der Akte. Zwei Kollegen vom Kriminaldauerdienst hatten den Ort des Geschehens um zehn Uhr vierzehn erreicht, nur zwanzig Minuten nach dem Anruf, und unverzüglich begonnen, den Fall zu besichtigen.

Ich betrachtete die Fotos, auf denen eine erschreckende Menge Blut zu sehen war. Der billige Couchtisch, auf den die junge Schauspielerin so unglücklich gestürzt war, hatte ein silbernes Metallgestell und eine dunkle Rauchglasplatte gehabt. Letztere war bei dem Sturz in Scherben gegangen, und eine dieser Scherben hatte sich in den Hals der jungen Frau gebohrt.

Sönnchen hatte recht gehabt: Viktoria Hergarden war eine attraktive Frau gewesen. Eine Frau, die außerdem jünger aussah, als sie war. Anhand der Fotos hätte ich sie auf maximal zwanzig Jahre geschätzt. An jenem unseligen Abend hatte sie ein dunkelblaues Nachthemdchen getragen, das mehr enthüllte als verdeckte, und nichts darunter. Vermutlich war sie im Begriff gewesen, zu Bett zu gehen, als sie stürzte. Ein großer Teil ihres glänzend schwarzen, vollen Haars schwamm in der Blutlache. Am schlanken Hals hing ein goldenes Kettchen mit einem Medaillon. An den bloßen Füßen Pumps mit hohen Absätzen, ebenfalls schwarz und mit Glitzersteinchen. Einer der Schuhe, der linke, lag zwei Handbreit vom Fuß entfernt auf einem kleinen weißen Flokatiteppich, der Falten warf, als wäre er auf dem glatten Fischgrätparkett verrutscht. War vielleicht dieser rutschige Teppich vom Format eines größeren Fußabtreters der Grund für den Tod der Frau? Bei der leeren Sektflasche, die Sönnchen erwähnt hatte, handelte es sich um eine Allerweltsmarke, die auch heute noch in jedem Supermarkt steht. Neben der Flasche lagen ein hohes, merkwürdigerweise ebenfalls nicht zerbrochenes Sektglas und ein welkes, dunkelrotes Rosensträußchen in einer bemerkenswert hässlichen Keramikvase. Auch, was auf den Fotos von der Einrichtung zu sehen war, entsprach nicht unbedingt dem, was man mit dem Wort »Filmschauspielerin« assoziierte.

Der Arzt hatte den Todeszeitpunkt ohne technische Hilfsmittel und langwierige Untersuchungen natürlich nur grob bestimmen können: »9.11., zw. 21:00 u. 24:00 Uhr«, hatte er notiert. Er hatte weder Würgemale noch verdächtige Blutergüsse festgestellt, keine Anzeichen auf Vergiftung noch sonst irgendetwas, das man als Hinweis auf Fremdeinwirkung hätte werten können. Bei der Todesursache hatte er sein Kreuzchen bei »nicht natürlicher Tod« gemacht. Bei den sicheren Zeichen des Todes hatte er »Totenstarre« und »Totenflecke« markiert. Die Kreuze sahen aus, als wäre er in Eile gewesen.

Die beiden Kollegen, die den Fall damals bearbeiteten, hatten in der Sache offenbar schon nach kurzer Zeit nur noch eine Routineangelegenheit gesehen. Wie Sönnchen schon am Telefon gesagt hatte: häuslicher Unfall mit Todesfolge, bei dem möglicherweise Alkohol eine Rolle gespielt hatte. Dennoch hatten die Kollegen ihren Job gründlich und gut erledigt. Im Umfeld der Toten hatten sie nichts Bemerkenswertes oder gar Verdächtiges gefunden. Sämtliche Fenster und die Balkontür waren unbeschädigt und ordentlich geschlossen gewesen. Im Schloss der Wohnungstür hatte der Schlüssel von innen gesteckt, ja, er war sogar zweimal umgedreht gewesen. Das Abus-Sicherheitsschloss ließ sich von außen nicht öffnen, las ich, wenn innen der Schlüssel steckte. An der Tür selbst waren auch unter der Lupe keine Kratzer zu entdecken, keine Druckstellen, nichts. Ein Foto dokumentierte diesen Sachverhalt.

Vor allem aber hatten die Kollegen nichts entdeckt, was auf die Anwesenheit einer zweiten Person zum Zeitpunkt des Unfalls hätte schließen lassen. Auf dem Foto mit der Sektflasche war auch ein Brief zu sehen, der ebenfalls am Boden lag. Inmitten der Scherben, halb im Blut lag das dazugehörige, achtlos aufgerissene Kuvert. Der Brief war nur wenige Zeilen lang und auf dem Foto natürlich nicht zu entziffern. An der rechten oberen Ecke befand sich das geschwungene Signet einer Firma.

Auf Seite zwei des Totenscheins hatte der Arzt als Todesursache »häuslicher Unfall« angekreuzt und handschriftlich, obwohl dafür gar kein Raum vorgesehen war, »Vermutl. Alkoholeinfl.« ergänzt. Darunter Datum, Unterschrift, Stempel. Ende eines viel zu kurzen Lebens voller unerfüllter Hoffnungen und vielleicht einer Enttäuschung zu viel. Beim Sterbedatum hatte der Arzt sich in seiner offensichtlichen Eile zunächst verschrieben, fiel mir auf, und anstelle der Neun eine Acht eingetragen, die Zahl später kräftig durchgestrichen und korrigiert.

Enttäuscht klappte ich die Akte zu und warf sie in eine Ecke. Die Kopfschmerzen, die ich vom Lesen bekommen hatte, hätte ich mir ersparen können. Inzwischen war es früher Abend geworden, halb sechs, und die Zwillinge waren nicht zu Hause. Nach dem Essen waren sie gleich wieder verschwunden, und ich hatte vergessen, wohin und wann sie zurück sein wollten. Außerdem hatte ich Hunger, stellte ich fest, und beschloss, dies als gutes Zeichen zu werten. Morgen, spätestens am Donnerstag, würde ich wieder arbeiten können, und die Zeit der quälenden Langeweile würde hinter mir liegen.

Ächzend erhob ich mich, schlüpfte in meine Hauslatschen, den Bademantel hatte ich ja noch an, schlurfte in die Küche. Die Gleichgewichtsstörungen waren eindeutig schwächer geworden.

Nach einem einsamen Abendessen, das aus Körnerbrot, Supermarktwurst und Plastikkäse bestand, fühlte ich mich gesättigt, aber nicht weniger unzufrieden als zuvor. Die Zutaten, die ich im Kühlschrank gefunden hatte, hatten die Zwillinge beschafft. Ich überlegte, ob ich mir gegen den Frust schon ein Gläschen Rotwein gönnen durfte, entschied mich jedoch dagegen. Mich ärgerte, dass mein Gedächtnis immer noch Löcher hatte wie der angebliche Emmentaler Käse, den ich soeben vertilgt hatte. Dass ich immer wieder Dinge vergaß. Sogar Dinge, die nach meinem Unfall geschehen waren.

Zurück im Schlafzimmer hob ich die fast dreißig Jahre alte Akte wieder auf und tippte versuchsweise die im Telefonprotokoll vermerkte Nummer ins schnurlose Telefon. Die Nummer der Nachbarin, die damals Viktoria Hergardens Tod angezeigt hatte. Manche Menschen zogen ja niemals um. Manche Menschen hatten auch nach Jahrzehnten noch ...

»Ja?«, meldete sich eine tonlose Frauenstimme nach mehrmaligem Tuten. »Hallo?«

Ich räusperte mich. »Frau Holland?«

»Wer ist da?«

Die Frau klang, als wäre Deutsch nicht ihre Muttersprache. »Spreche ich mit Frau Holland?«

»Wollen Sie mir nicht erst einmal sagen, wer Sie sind und worum es geht?«

»Mein Name ist Gerlach. Ich bin Polizist und ...«

Sie klang ein wenig erschrocken, als sie fragte: »Polizei?«

Nun erschrecken viele Menschen, wenn sie dieses Wort hören, und beginnen sofort, ihr Gewissen nach möglichen Missetaten zu durchforschen.

»Es geht um einen Unfall im November 1985 ...«

»Davon ... ich ... weiß nichts.«

»Sie sind aber Frau Holland?«

»Nein.«

»Ihren Namen könnten Sie aber doch ...«

»Ich weiß nichts. Auf Wiedersehen. Danke schön.«

Knack.

Dieses Mal legte ich die graue Akte ordentlich auf meinen Nachttisch. Dann löschte ich das Licht und ging in die Küche, um mir doch einen Rotwein einzuschenken. Mit dem Glas in der Hand wanderte ich ins Wohnzimmer und schaltete den Fernseher ein. Die Tagesschau hatte gerade begonnen.

Um kurz vor zehn trillerte das Telefon im Flur. Ich erhob mich seufzend. Wer rief denn zu dieser unchristlichen Uhrzeit noch an? Ich beschloss, das Gespräch anzunehmen. Meine Töchter waren unterwegs. Da wusste man nie …

Ich meldete mich mit Namen. Am anderen Ende atmete jemand.

»Gerlach?«, fragte eine helle Männerstimme, als ich schon dachte, es gäbe eine technische Störung.

»Ja, Gerlach.«

»Oh. Verwählt. Entschuldigung.«

Dann wurde aufgelegt.

Die Zwillinge tauchten eine halbe Stunde später wieder auf, merklich angeheitert und übermütig. Sie schimpften mehr der Form halber mit mir, als sie das leere Glas entdeckten. Dann erzählten sie mir von zwei Freundinnen, die Internetflatrates für ihre Smartphones hatten.

»Kostet nicht mal zehn Euro mehr, Paps«, erklärte mir Louise mit sanfter Stimme und gekonntem Augenaufschlag. »Nicht mal zwei fünfzig in der Woche!«

Auf dem Couchtisch begann das schnurlose Telefon zu randalieren. Sarah nahm es, meldete sich, wie sie es gelernt hatte, mit Vor- und Nachnamen, horchte mit krauser Stirn, legte es wieder weg.

»Irgendein Idiot, der sich verwählt hat«, kommentierte sie mit der schnellen Verachtung ihrer Jugend.

»Ein Mann?«

Sie sah mich irritiert an. »Ja. Wieso?«

»Wie hat er gesprochen?«

»Wie ein Idiot.«

»Ich meine Hochdeutsch, zum Beispiel?«

»Nö. Typisch Kurpfälzer Holzkopf.«

Für eine Sekunde war es still. Dann griff Sarah das alte Thema wieder auf: »Und das Internet geht ab wie die Hölle«, erklärte sie mit leuchtenden Augen. »Sogar Youtube-Videos kann man gucken, ganz ohne Ruckeln!«

»Paps?«, fragte Louise vorsichtig, als ich nicht reagierte.

»Zwei fünfzig pro Woche?«

Sie nickten eifrig und völlig synchron.

Warum sollte man seine Kinder nicht hin und wieder mit einer positiven Antwort überraschen?

»Ihr kümmert euch aber um alles, okay?«

»Du brauchst nur deine Kontonummer eintippen«, jubelte Sarah. Sie sprangen auf und rasten in ihre Zimmer, um einen Laptop zu holen und vermutlich die sensationelle Neuigkeit sofort über die virtuelle Welt zu verbreiten.

»Einzutippen«, seufzte ich ergeben. Aber das hörten sie natürlich nicht mehr.

Ich beschloss, mich für meine gute Tat mit einem weiteren halben Gläschen Spätburgunder zu belohnen. Meine Mädchen waren glücklich. Sie waren jung. Sie hatten keine Kopfschmerzen. Das Eintippen der Kontonummer war ein Klacks. Und im Grunde wäre jetzt ein guter Zeitpunkt gewesen, um ihnen zu eröffnen, dass sie seit Neuestem einen Bruder ... einen Halbbruder ... nannte man das überhaupt so?

Ich hörte sie in einem ihrer Zimmer lachen und giggeln. Und beschloss, das Gespräch mit meinen Töchtern auf morgen zu verschieben und ins Bett zu gehen. Schließlich war ich immer noch Rekonvaleszent und brauchte Schonung.

Wer den ganzen Tag im Bett liegt, schläft nachts oft schlecht. Zwischen wirren Träumen war ich immer wieder aufgewacht, hatte mich hin- und hergewälzt und geärgert, und schließlich war mir eine so naheliegende Idee gekommen, dass ich mich am Mittwochmorgen heftig über meine eigene Dummheit ärgerte und dann umgehend zur Tat schritt: Ich entzifferte die Namen der beiden Kripobeamten, die das Protokoll unterzeichnet hatten. KOK E. Reitzle und KHK J. Boll. Beide Namen sagten mir nichts. Vermutlich waren die Kollegen längst im Ruhestand. Wieder einmal wählte ich um kurz vor acht Sönnchens Nummer. Sie gab sich ein wenig entrüstet, drohte eher symbolisch mit Liebesentzug, sollte ich wirklich im Lauf des Tages durch ihre Tür kommen, und versprach, für mich herauszufinden, was aus den beiden Kollegen oder Kolleginnen geworden war.

Ihr Rückruf ließ so lange auf sich warten, dass nur Absicht dahinterstecken konnte.

»Ist kaum noch wer im Haus, der sich an die zwei erinnert«, erfuhr ich erst kurz vor Mittag. »Die Gerda weiß zum Glück noch ein bisschen was über die beiden. Die ist ja schon seit Anfang der Achtziger in der Direktion und hat ein unglaubliches Gedächtnis. Der erste hat mit vollem Namen Eckard Reitzle geheißen und ist ein paar Monate nach der Geschichte damals bei einem Verkehrsunfall ums Leben gekommen. Der zweite heißt Johann Boll. Der ist auch nicht mehr bei uns. Ist zweiundneunzig aus dem Dienst ausgeschieden.«

»Weiß Ihre Gerda zufällig auch, was aus dem Mann geworden ist?«

»Wir haben es über die Einwohnermeldeämter probiert. Aber bisher haben wir ihn nicht gefunden.«

»Dann warte ich einfach weiter.« Ich seufzte eine Spur zu theatralisch. »Das trainiere ich nämlich zurzeit: Warten. Ich werde jeden Tag ein bisschen besser darin.«

»Es hat damals irgendwie Theater gegeben«, fuhr meine Sekretärin mit überraschendem Eifer fort. »Beim Ausscheiden von diesem Johann Boll, meint die Gerda. Ich war seinerzeit zwar auch schon an der Direktion, bin ja auch schon seit siebenundachtzig dabei, kann mich aber an nichts mehr erinnern. Nicht mal an sein Gesicht. Seine Personalakte ist auch nicht mehr zu finden, nach so langer Zeit. Ist vermutlich irgendwann im Schredder gelandet.«

»Und wie kommen wir jetzt weiter?«

»Vielleicht kann Ihnen der Herr Runkel was dazu sagen, haben wir überlegt. Der müsste die zwei eigentlich noch gekannt haben.«

»Der ist aber leider immer noch in Reha.«

Rolf Runkel war im Dezember nicht ganz ohne mein Verschulden im Einsatz angeschossen worden und hatte die Verletzung nur mit knapper Not überlebt. Erst bei dieser Gelegenheit hatte ich erfahren, dass er außerdem einen Tumor im Kopf hatte, der jedoch glücklicherweise einige Wochen später erfolgreich entfernt werden konnte.

»Telefon werden sie in dieser Klinik in Bad Soden ja wohl haben«, meinte Sönnchen.

»Da haben Sie recht«, gab ich zu und unterdrückte einen weiteren Seufzer, damit mir Sönnchen nicht gleich mit neuen Ermahnungen kam. Mein Kopf war offenbar immer noch nicht ganz in Ordnung. »Besorgen Sie mir eine Nummer, unter der ich ihn erreichen kann?«

»Hat er denn sein Handy nicht dabei?«

Nein, ich war wirklich noch nicht wieder der, der ich vergangene Woche gewesen war. Ich hatte Runkels Mobilnummer sogar in meinem Handy gespeichert.

»Ja, ja, der Boll und der Reitzle ...«, murmelte Rolf Runkel, als er mich eine halbe Stunden später zurückrief. Er hatte gerade irgendeine wichtige Behandlung über sich ergehen lassen müssen und deshalb sein Handy vorübergehend ausgeschaltet. »An die erinnere ich mich noch, klar. Die haben viel zusammengehockt, die zwei.«

»Was können Sie mir über die beiden erzählen?«

»Oje. Wissen Sie, mein Gedächtnis ... Ich bin seinerzeit auch grad mal zwei Jahre dabei gewesen. War noch feucht hinter den Ohren, sozusagen. Was möchten Sie denn wissen?«

»Alles.«

»Dicke Kumpels sind sie gewesen, wie gesagt. Haben gern zusammen Dienst geschoben. Und ... na ja. Der Reitzle, der ist so ein Autoverrückter gewesen. Den Unfall in Italien hat er mit einem Ferrari gebaut. Ist extra mit dem Zug runtergefahren, um ihn selber im Werk abzuholen. Dass bloß kein anderer mit dem teuren Ding fährt. Und dann, auf der Autobahn hinter Bologna, ist er mit einem Affenzahn in einen Stau gerast. Weit über zweihundert soll er draufgehabt haben.«

»Ein Ferrari?«, fiel mir erst mit Verzögerung auf. »Der kostet doch ...«

»Es war kein ganz neuer. Aber werksüberholt. Hundertzwanzigtausend hat er dafür hinlegen müssen, hat's geheißen. Mark natürlich.«

»Hat er geerbt? Im Lotto gewonnen?«

»Es ist tatsächlich gemunkelt worden, er hätte geerbt. Und dann schmeißt der Depp das ganze schöne Geld für ein neues Auto aus dem Fenster, statt dass er sich ein Haus baut oder so. Aber er ist natürlich auch nicht verheiratet gewesen. Nicht mal eine halbe Stunde hat er Freude gehabt an seinem Sportwagen. Schon ein Elend, wenn man sich's überlegt.«

»Und Boll? Warum ist der später aus dem Polizeidienst ausgeschieden?«

»Eher ausgeschieden worden. Genau weiß ich's nicht. Nur so viel: Er hat auf einmal zum damaligen Chef gemusst, Wilhelmi hat der geheißen, und wie er wieder rausgekommen ist, hat er gesagt, er hat die Schnauze voll und schmeißt hin.«

»Er hat gekündigt und seine Pension sausen lassen?«

»Sonst wär er vor Gericht gekommen, hat's geheißen. Aber so richtig was Genaues hat man nie erfahren.«

»Wer könnte mehr darüber wissen?«

»Wieso interessiert Sie das eigentlich, nach so vielen Jahren?«

Ich klärte ihn ausführlich auf. Ich hatte ja jede Menge Zeit.

»Der Wilhelmi ist ein paar Jahre später in Pension gegangen und bald darauf gestorben. Lungenkrebs. Damals ist ja noch viel mehr geraucht worden als heute. Sogar in den Büros. Ich bin bei der Beerdigung gewesen und ... Da fällt mir ein: Vielleicht seine Sekretärin? Ich glaub fast, die lebt noch. Wenn ich jetzt noch wüsst, wie die geheißen hat ... Einen französischen Vornamen hat sie gehabt. Julienne oder so. Gibt's das? Ist Julienne ein Vorname?«

Vorsichtshalber notierte ich mir Runkels Erinnerungsbruchstücke und fragte nebenher meinen vom Schicksal so schwer gebeutelten Untergebenen nach seinem Befinden.

»Langweilig«, stöhnte er. »Langweilig ist einem meistens, aber seit ein paar Tagen ist es besser. Ich hab einen alten Kumpel wiedergetroffen, stellen Sie sich vor. Den Werner Schöpf. Wir sind im gleichen Sportverein gewesen, wie wir noch jung waren. Und dann hört man vierzig Jahre lang nichts voneinander, er lebt seit Ewigkeiten in Bonn, und jetzt treff ich ihn ausgerechnet hier in Bad Soden wieder. Er hat den gleichen Scheiß gehabt wie ich, auch so einen Klumpen im Kopf. Aber bei ihm war's noch ärger als bei mir. Bei ihm hat's Spitz auf Knopf gestanden.«

Ich wünschte ihm und seinem alten Sportsfreund im Namen aller Kollegen gute Genesung.

»In vier Wochen bin ich wieder an Deck, Chef«, versprach er am Ende. »Die Ärzte sagen, ich mach gute Fortschritte. Nur mit dem Gedächtnis, das ist so eine Sache. Aber sie sagen, das wird wieder – mit der Zeit.«

Damit kannte ich mich aus.

6

Juliette Baldwin lautete der Name der ehemaligen Chefsekretärin, fand Sönnchen heraus – dieses Mal in Rekordzeit. Eine Frau dieses Namens stand sogar im Heidelberger Telefonbuch. Und als ob das nicht genug wäre: Sie lebte nicht weit von mir in der Weststadt. Am Telefon blieb sie zunächst misstrauisch.

»Man hört so schlimme Sachen«, erklärte sie mir mit rauer Altfrauenstimme. »Dass sie einem erzählen, man hätte eine Reise gewonnen oder ein teures Auto.«

Schließlich, als sie ein wenig Vertrauen gefasst hatte, gelang es mir doch, sie zu einem persönlichen Gespräch zu überreden. Nachdem ich geduscht, mich zum ersten Mal seit Tagen wieder ordentlich rasiert und angekleidet hatte, war es fast zwei Uhr am Nachmittag. Ich hatte seit Stunden keine Kopfschmerzen mehr und machte mich auf den kurzen Weg.

Wieder schien mir die kalte Luft gutzutun. Der Himmel war grau verhangen, es roch nach neuem Regen. Ich schlug den Mantelkragen hoch und bewegte mich im Rentnerschritt, um meinen lädierten Kopf nicht zu sehr herauszufordern. Es klappte überraschend gut. Die Schmerzen im Kreuz waren vollkommen verschwunden, stellte ich bei dieser Gelegenheit fest.

In einem Blumengeschäft an der Rohrbacher Straße erstand ich einen kleinen Strauß gelber Tulpen, und zehn Minuten später klingelte ich an der Tür eines viergeschossigen, mäßig gepflegten Mietshauses am nördlichen Ende der Goethestraße. Inzwischen regnete es kräftig. Ich hatte mit knapper Not das Vordach erreicht, bevor die Wolken brachen. Juliette Baldwin wohnte im ersten Obergeschoss rechts und freute sich wie ein Kind über die Tulpen. Die kleine graue Frau mit flinken Augen ließ mich jedoch erst über ihre Schwelle, nachdem sie meine Visitenkarte aufmerksam beäugt und durch ihre starke Brille Wort für Wort entziffert hatte. Aus der Wohnung duftete es nach Kaffee und frisch gebackenem Kuchen.

»Sie erwarten Besuch?«, fragte ich freundlich, als ich endlich im Flur stand und meinen feuchten Mantel auszog. »Ich werde Sie wirklich nicht lange aufhalten.«

»In einer halben Stunde erst. Vivian, meine vierte Enkeltochter. Sie studiert hier in Heidelberg. Lehrerin will sie werden, am Gymnasium. Sie ist eine ganz Liebe, die Vivian. Schon, wie sie noch klein war, ist sie so ein liebes Schnuckelchen gewesen. Hat den Eltern immer nur Freude gemacht, die Vivian. Aber keine Sorge, meistens kommt sie sowieso zu spät.«

Sie beobachtete mich durch ihre dicken Brillengläser, als wäre ich ein soeben neu entdecktes Reptil, fragte, ob ich Kaffee wollte und vielleicht auch ein Stückchen vom Streuselkuchen. Beides mochte ich natürlich nicht ablehnen. Als ich den Kuchen ordentlich lobte, taute sie weiter auf und ließ mich auch einmal länger als zwei Sekunden aus den Augen.

»Der Herr Boll, ja«, sagte sie sehr langsam, als sie ihre zierliche Tasse mit spitzen Fingern abstellte. »Er war ein ... hm ... Ein schwieriger Mensch war er.«

»Wissen Sie, warum er damals Hals über Kopf ausgeschieden ist?«

»Um eine rumänische Einbrecherbande ist es gegangen.« Sie hob das Tässchen wieder an, nippte konzentriert an ihrem Kaffee, stellte es wieder ab. »Einige Tage vorher waren sie festgenommen worden, die Rumänen. Fünf Männer, alle bewaffnet. Zum Glück ist nichts passiert. Sie haben den ganzen Keller voll gehabt mit Videorekordern und teuren Stereogeräten und so weiter. Ist ja eine schreckliche Plage gewesen, mit den Rumänen, damals nach der Wende. In einem abgelegenen Bauernhaus zwischen Ladenburg und Ilvesheim hatten sie ihren Unterschlupf. Und von der Beute, von der soll später einiges gefehlt haben.«

»Und man hat vermutet, dass Boll hinter dieser Unterschlagung steckte?«

Sie nickte vorsichtig und blinzelte mich kurzsichtig an. Nickte noch einmal.

»Der Herr Wilhelmi hat aber keinen Skandal gewollt. Es ist damals sowieso viel auf uns herumgehackt worden in den Zeitungen. War eine schlimme Zeit. Der Sprengstoffanschlag auf die neue JVA in Weiterstadt, Bad Kleinen … und bei uns war auch das eine oder andere schiefgelaufen. Drum hat der alte Chef dem Herrn Boll angeboten, wenn er alles komplett zurückgibt, was er zur Seite geschafft hat, und von sich aus kündigt, dann wird er die Sache unter der Decke halten. Und so haben sie es dann auch gemacht.«

»Ich nehme an, es war nicht das erste Mal, dass Boll unangenehm aufgefallen ist.«

Wieder blinzelte sie. »Ja«, erwiderte sie dann leise. »Da haben Sie vollkommen recht. Wie gesagt, er war ein schwieriger Mensch. Aber ich habe dem alten Chef damals versprechen müssen, dass ich den Mund halte. Möchten Sie vielleicht noch ein Stück vom Kuchen?«

Ich schob meinen Teller über den Tisch. »Gerne. Er schmeckt wirklich ausgezeichnet.«

»Das macht die Sahne«, erklärte sie ernst. »Ich tu immer einen ordentlichen Schuss fest geschlagene Sahne in den Teig.«

»Was aus Boll später geworden ist, wissen Sie nicht?«

»Doch. Er hatte zwei Jahre vorher ein Haus geerbt, irgendwo im Odenwald. Seine Eltern waren kurz nacheinander gestorben. Der Vater an Krebs, meine ich. Und die Frau ein halbes Jahr später …«

Die Wohnungstür flog auf. »Hi, Omi!«, rief eine atemlose Mädchenstimme. »Bin bisschen spät, sorry.«

»Jetzt weiß ich wieder, bei ihr war es ein Herzinfarkt«, beendete Juliette Baldwin mit strahlendem Lächeln unsere gemütliche Unterhaltung und sprang auf, als wäre sie nicht auch selbst weit jenseits der Siebzig.

Während des kurzen Spaziergangs zurück zu meiner warmen Wohnung regnete es immer noch, auch wenn das Schlimmste schon vorüber war. Kurz bevor ich zu Hause war, rief Sönnchen an.

»Wir haben's rausgekriegt, Herr Gerlach. Boll wohnt in Weiten-Gesäß.«

»Frau Walldorf, auch wenn ich krank bin, finde ich, habe ich als Ihr Chef doch ein bisschen Respekt verdient …«

»Das Dorf heißt nun mal so, 'tschuldigung. Ist ein Ortsteil von Michelstadt. Da ist er auf die Welt gekommen und aufgewachsen, und jetzt lebt er wieder da. In seinem Elternhaus.«

»Und wovon lebt er?«

»Im Melderegister steht bloß: Selbstständig.«

»Dann hat er wahrscheinlich Telefon.«

»Wahrscheinlich. Obwohl viele heutzutage ja nur noch Handys haben. Im Telefonbuch ist er jedenfalls nicht zu finden und im Internet komischerweise auch nicht.«

Ein Selbstständiger ohne Internetauftritt?

»Das muss ja eine merkwürdige Beschäftigung sein, mit der der Mann sein Geld verdient.«

Ich musste zwischen zwei parkende Autos treten, da ein vielleicht zweijähriges, von der Mütze bis zu den Schuhen rosafarbenes Mädchen auf einem dieser neumodischen Laufrädchen dahergeschossen kam. Ihre Miene strahlte unerschütterliche Zuversicht und überschäumende Abenteuerlust aus. Die klein gewachsene und teuer gekleidete Mutter folgte ihrer Tochter atemlos und mit panischem Gesichtsausdruck, schob einen Kinderwagen vor sich her und rief wieder und wieder mit knappem Atem und vollkommen erfolglos nach ihrer Lisa-Kristin. Sekunden später waren sie um die nächste Ecke verschwunden. Der Wolkenbruch von vorhin hatte sich inzwischen zu einem gemütlichen Landregen herabgestuft.

Ich zog das Handy wieder heraus und wählte Sönnchens Nummer. »Noch was«, sagte ich. »Würden Sie bitte mal überprüfen, ob es in Heidelberg eine Frau namens Elisabeth Holland gibt? Von der findet man nämlich auch nichts im Internet.«

»Das ist die, die den Unfall damals gemeldet hat, richtig?«

Es existierte keine Frau mit Namen Holland im Großraum Heidelberg, erfuhr ich, als ich wieder zu Hause im Wohnzimmer saß und versuchsweise Zeitung las. Keine mit Vornamen Elisabeth und auch keine mit einem anderen Vornamen.

»Dreißig Jahre sind halt doch eine lange Zeit«, meinte Sönnchen tröstend.

Die Zeitung war von vorne bis hinten langweilig. Außerdem war Lesen immer noch zu anstrengend für meine Augen. Auf größere Entfernung sah ich dagegen schon wieder ganz gut. Und wer spazieren gehen konnte, der konnte auch Auto fahren, beschloss ich schließlich. Von Heidelberg nach Michelstadt war keine Weltreise. Bei mäßigem Verkehr höchstens eine Stunde. Okay, eine gute Stunde. Aber es war eine Spazierfahrt. Hatte nichts mit Arbeit oder Stress zu tun. Erholung pur, geradezu.

Die gemütlichste und landschaftlich schönste Strecke führte den Neckar entlang bis kurz vor Eberbach, dort links ab in Richtung Norden, über die Höhen des sagenumwobenen Odenwalds auf der gut ausgebauten, hin und wieder ein wenig kurvigen Bundesstraße. Über die Autobahn wäre ich natürlich schneller gewesen, aber ich hatte es ja nicht eilig, und die Autobahn traute ich mir noch nicht zu.

Um kurz nach vier Uhr am Nachmittag rangierte ich meinen alten Peugeot Kombi vorsichtig aus der engen Parklücke, in die ich ihn vor Tagen gequetscht hatte. Auf den Straßen herrschte angenehm wenig Betrieb. Der Berufsverkehr hatte noch nicht recht begonnen, zum Spazierenfahren lud das Wetter nicht ein, und so kam ich gut voran. Einige Zeit bummelte ich ohne Ehrgeiz hinter einem Lkw mit spanischen Kennzeichen her. Inzwischen war mir klar geworden, dass der Mann, den ich aufsuchen wollte, vermutlich – wie die meisten Berufstätigen – vor sechs Uhr abends gar nicht zu Hause anzutreffen sein würde. Außerdem hatte ich es ja aus Prinzip nicht eilig.

Alle Autos, die mir entgegenkamen, hatten schon die Scheinwerfer eingeschaltet. Auch in Dilsberg, dem romantischen Örtchen hoch über dem kurvenreichen Neckar, funkelten bereits die ersten Lichter. Der Lkw bog freundlicherweise, kurz bevor er begann, mir lästig zu werden, in ein kleines Industriegebiet ab, und für einige Zeit hatte ich die Straße ganz für mich allein.

Während ich gemächlich von Eberbach nach Beerfelden kurvte und dem einen oder anderen ungeduldigen Verkehrsteilnehmer auf die Nerven ging, riss im Westen die Bewölkung auf, der Himmel färbte sich prahlerisch rot, als ginge ein grandioser Tag zu Ende, und manchmal blendete mich die untergehende Sonne. Längst hatte auch ich die Scheinwerfer eingeschaltet.

Das Fahren klappte überraschend gut. Noch immer verspürte ich keine Anzeichen von Kopfschmerzen. Ich fühlte mich wohl, war froh, meinem Krankenzimmer entronnen und wieder unter den Lebenden zu sein. Inzwischen war es schon fast fünf Uhr, da ich in Neckarsteinach getankt und mir eine Cola gegen den Durst gegönnt hatte.

Zwischen dem Abzweig in Richtung Beerfelden und Sensbachtal hatten kluge Menschen ein großes Hinweisschild am Straßenrand aufgestellt. Darauf war ein blauer Fahrradhelm abgebildet, und darüber prangte der sinnreiche Schriftzug: » Gegen Kopfschmerzen «.

Als ich von Michelstadt noch etwa zehn Kilometer entfernt war, fiel mir auf, dass mir mit großem und gleich bleibendem Abstand ein Wagen folgte. Die runden Scheinwerfer tauchten allerdings nur auf längeren geraden Strecken in meinem Rückspiegel auf. Anfangs glaubte ich an Zufall oder Einbildung. Fast nur zum Spaß verminderte ich die Geschwindigkeit. Der andere wurde ebenfalls langsamer. Ich gab Gas, er zog nach.

Ich bog auf einen Wanderparkplatz ab, schaltete die Lichter aus und wartete. Mein mutmaßlicher Verfolger kam nicht. Ich wartete zwei, drei Minuten – immer noch nichts. Seufzend ließ ich den Motor wieder an, und schon nach wenigen Kurven war er wieder im Rückspiegel. Von dem Fahrzeug konnte ich nichts weiter erkennen, als dass es runde Scheinwerfer hatte und vermutlich kein Kleinwagen war. Vier Kilometer vor Michelstadt war ich überzeugt, dass sich wirklich jemand dafür interessierte, wohin ich unterwegs war. In meinem Magen machte sich ein ungemütliches Gefühl breit, und mein Gehirn signalisierte lebhaft, die verfluchten Kopfschmerzen könnten bald wiederkommen. Ich durfte mich auf keinen Fall aufregen. Es ist jedoch nicht leicht, gelassen zu bleiben, wenn man offensichtlich observiert wird. Nach einer scharfen Rechtskurve eine kleine Ausbuchtung. Ich bremste, hielt erneut an und wartete.

Wieder nichts.

Ich wartete länger.

Immer noch nichts.

Kopfschüttelnd fuhr ich weiter. Inzwischen war es völlig dunkel geworden. Die ersten Lichter Michelstadts tauchten auf. Hinter mir waren keine runden Scheinwerfer mehr. Dafür plötzlich kräftiger Gegenverkehr. Vielleicht Schichtende in irgendeiner Fabrik. Ich atmete auf. Vermutlich war alles doch nur Einbildung gewesen. Ein harmloser Familienvater auf dem Weg nach Hause hatte zufällig für einige Kilometer denselben Weg gehabt wie ich. Ein Wegweiser: Weiten-Gesäß rechts ab. Noch fünf Kilometer.

» Suchen Sie wen?«, fragte eine kehlige Männerstimme hinter dem hohen Maschendrahtzaun, den ich in der plötzlichen Dunkelheit mehr ahnte als sah.

Als ich mich dem Haus genähert hatte, in dem Johann Boll aufgewachsen war und heute wieder lebte, waren zwei starke Halogenscheinwerfer aufgeflammt und hatten mich geblendet. Ich war einige Schritte nach rechts gegangen, und kurz darauf waren die Scheinwerfer wieder erloschen.

»Ich will zu Herrn Boll«, sagte ich in die Richtung, aus der die Stimme gekommen war. »Johann Boll, der wohnt doch hier?«

»Da werden Sie kein Glück haben«, erwiderte der andere in mürrischem Hessisch. »Den hab ich die letzten Tage nicht zu Gesicht bekommen. Was wollen Sie denn von dem?«

»Wir kennen uns von früher, und da habe ich gedacht, ich gucke mal vorbei, wie's dem alten Johann so geht, wo ich schon in der Nähe bin.«

Der ehemalige Kripobeamte bewohnte ein bescheidenes Häuschen in einer Seitenstraße am östlichen Ortsrand. Im Licht der Halogenscheinwerfer hatte ich gesehen, dass die Außenwände des zweistöckigen Hauses mit grauen Schindeln verkleidet waren. Es duftete nach dem nahen Wald und kühlen, feuchten Wiesen. Allmählich gewöhnten sich meine geblendeten Augen wieder an die Dunkelheit. Ein paar landwirtschaftliche Geräte, die geisterhaft im Licht des eben durch die Wolken brechenden Mondes herumstanden, wirkten verlottert und verrostet.

Durch hohes Gras ging ich mit vorsichtigen Schritten auf den Nachbarn jenseits des Zauns zu. Als ich näher kam, stieg mir der beißende Gestank seiner billigen Zigarre in die Nase.

»Schönen guten Abend«, sagte ich artig.

»Hm«, machte der Nachbar und zog die Nase hoch. »Kann mich überhaupt nicht erinnern, wann der Boll das letzte Mal Besuch gehabt hätt. Woher kennen Sie den überhaupt?«

»Wir waren früher Kollegen. Lange her.«

»Und wo?«

»Sie wissen nicht, wo er früher gearbeitet hat?«

»Würd ich dann fragen?«

Mein argwöhnischer Gesprächspartner war schon im Rentenalter. Er stand auf einem frisch geharkten Kiesweg, trug grobe Kleidung und Gummistiefel. Die ausgebeulte dunkle Hose hing an breiten Trägern. Eine vermutlich handgestrickte Jacke labberte um seinen mächtigen Bauch. Ein feuchter Wind strich über die Wiesen und brachte mich zum Frösteln.

»Eine Firma in Heidelberg«, erwiderte ich entspannt.

»Gibt's inzwischen auch nicht mehr. Der Name würde Ihnen nichts sagen. Was treibt der gute alte Johann denn heute?«

Der Nachbar nahm einen langen Zug von seiner Zigarre.

»Gut? Der? Dass ich nicht lach!«

»Sie haben kein gutes Verhältnis?«

»Sie haben viele Fragen.«

Hinter mir wurde es plötzlich wieder taghell. Der andere – vollkommen kahlköpfig, wie ich jetzt feststellte – kniff die Augen zu und fluchte unterdrückt etwas von »Begegnungsmeldern« und »Scheißkatzen«.

»Die ganze Nacht geht das so«, maulte er. »Licht an, Licht aus. Licht an, Licht aus. Ich bin schon bei der Gemeinde gewesen. Aber die? Gute Worte und sonst nix!«

»Können Sie mir vielleicht sagen, wo ich den Johann um diese Zeit finde? Ich habe keine Lust, den ganzen Abend zu warten.«

»Hab Ihnen doch gesagt, der Boll ist schon länger fort. Kommt öfter mal vor, dass er für ein paar Tage fort ist, und keiner weiß, wohin und wozu. Kann mir ja auch egal sein. Wenn bloß seine mistigen Scheinwerfer nicht wären.«

»Wird in der Gegend öfter eingebrochen?«

»Hier? Ist schon Ewigkeiten nix mehr passiert. In den Neunzigern, wie überall diese Rumänenbanden rumgestromert sind, da ist mal was gewesen. Aber seitdem ...«

Die Scheinwerfer erloschen wieder. Der Nachbar seufzte und saugte an seiner Zigarre.

»Wenn er daheim ist, was treibt er dann so?«

»Fernsehen. Saufen. Wichsen. Was weiß ich. Man sieht oft das Flackern vom Fernseher. Aber vielleicht ist er auch ständig im Internet. Wie meine zwei Enkel. Siebzehn und fünfzehn und nichts wie Computerspiele und Internet im Kopf und frech wie Rotz. Wenn wir uns damals getraut hätten, mit Oma und Opa so zu reden wie die, dann hätt's von meinem Vater aber ein paar aufs Maul gegeben!«

»Keine Frau?«

»Keine Frau. Und jetzt langt's allmählich. Vielleicht fragen Sie Ihren guten alten Johann einfach selber.«

»Sie haben nicht zufällig eine Telefonnummer von ihm?«

»Ich hab seine nicht, und er hat meine auch nicht. Wenn wir reden wollen, dann haben wir den Zaun. Aber wir wollen nicht. Er nicht und ich auch nicht.«

»Wie lange ist er denn für gewöhnlich weg, wenn er unterwegs ist?«

»Wissen Sie was?« Ein letzter Zug an der Zigarre, dann wurde ihr von grober Sohle das Lebenslicht zertreten. »Sie können mich mal. Und zwar kreuzweise, wenn's recht ist.«

Der unfreundliche Nachbar hinkte schnaufend zu seiner Haustür. Ein kurzer, warmer Lichtschein, dann stand ich wieder im Dunkeln. Ich stapfte zurück zu Bolls Häuschen, dessen Grundfläche sicherlich kaum sechzig Quadratmeter betrug. Der Bewegungsmelder entdeckte mich, die Scheinwerfer flammten wieder auf. Eine mausgraue Katze huschte erschrocken um die Ecke.

Das Haus musste sehr alt sein, die Fenster waren winzig. Nur die niedrige Haustür war offensichtlich neu und einbruchsicher. Zudem waren vor den Fenstern im Erdgeschoss massive Gitter montiert, die an dem ärmlichen Anwesen reichlich deplatziert wirkten. Neben dem runden Klingelknopf kein Namensschild, nirgendwo eine Hausnummer. Der Mann, der hier lebte, legte augenscheinlich keinen Wert auf Besuch und zwischenmenschliche Kuschelwärme.

Vermutlich argwöhnisch beobachtet von der Nachbarschaft versuchte ich, durch eines der Fenster einen Blick ins Innere zu erhaschen. Aber obwohl keine Vorhänge die Sicht behinderten, war nichts zu erkennen. Inzwischen hatte der Mond sich wieder hinter Wolken verzogen. Schließlich ging ich zu meinem Peugeot zurück, wendete und machte mich auf die Rückfahrt. Ich legte keinen Wert darauf, mit den ortsansässigen Kollegen Bekanntschaft zu machen.

7

Während der einsamen Fahrt durch die Dunkelheit des Oden-walds behielt ich den Rückspiegel im Auge. Dieses Mal schien mir jedoch niemand zu folgen, und inzwischen war ich mir nicht einmal mehr sicher, ob das, was ich vor anderthalb Stun-den gesehen hatte, wirklich immer derselbe Wagen gewesen war. Meine Nerven waren überreizt. Außerdem war mir plötz-lich kalt, obwohl die Heizung meines alten Kombi sich redlich bemühte. Inzwischen waren die Kopfschmerzen mehr als nur eine Ahnung geworden. Zum Glück herrschte kaum noch Ver-kehr, sodass ich gut vorankam. Ich suchte Musik im Radio, fand jedoch nichts, was mir gefiel. Außerdem verschwand jeder Sender, sobald ich ihn endlich richtig eingestellt hatte, nach der dritten Kurve wieder.

Der Wagen mit den runden Scheinwerfern wollte mir nicht aus dem Kopf gehen. In der einen Sekunde glaubte ich an Halluzinationen, in der nächsten fand ich das, was ich wäh-rend der Hinfahrt beobachtet hatte, bedrohlich und unerklär-lich.

Als ich endlich das Neckartal erreichte, hielt ich an einer Bushaltestelle, fingerte das Handy aus der Innentasche meines Mantels, was wegen des Sicherheitsgurts nicht ganz einfach war, und wählte Sven Balkes Nummer. Trotz der späten Stunde saß er noch im Büro.

»Moin, Chef«, rief er launig. »Sie sind schon wieder fit, hat mir Frau Walldorf berichtet?«

Balke stammte aus dem hohen Norden, aus einem Dörfchen nicht weit von Bremen. Obwohl er schon lange in der Kurpfalz lebte, hörte man es bei jedem Wort.

»Fit ist was anderes«, seufzte ich. »Haben wir jemanden im Team, der Amateurfunker ist oder sich sonst irgendwie mit Funkkram auskennt?«

»Worum es geht, soll ich vermutlich nicht wissen.«

»Besser nicht. Sonst denken Sie am Ende noch, mit meinem Kopf ist irgendwas nicht in Ordnung.«

»Wäre kein Wunder, nachdem Sie so heftig draufgefallen sind.« Er lachte. Wurde aber sofort wieder ernst. Immerhin sprach er mit seinem Chef, und die Gehirnerschütterung des Chefs ist nicht lustig. »Zum Stichwort Funkkram fällt mir nur einer ein: Neugebauer von der Sippe.«

»Würden Sie mich verbinden?«

»Ob der auch so doof ist wie ich und nach sieben noch am Schreibtisch sitzt?«

»Neues von der Kellertürenbande?«

Mein Mitarbeiter verlor seine Heiterkeit. »Vor zwei Stunden haben sie wieder zugeschlagen.«

»Abends um fünf?«

»Die Jungs achten darauf, dass uns nicht langweilig wird. Dass keine Gewohnheiten einreißen. Dass kein Muster erkennbar wird.«

Die sogenannte Kellertürenbande bereitete mir schon seit Monaten Verdruss und Kopfzerbrechen. Immer benutzten sie dieselbe Masche: Sie brachen in abseits gelegene Einfamilienhäuser ein, die weit genug vom nächsten Polizeirevier entfernt lagen, dass die Täter selbst im Fall einer Alarmanlage kein Risiko eingingen. Der Einstieg erfolgte stets durch eine von außen zugängliche Kellertür, da diese meist viel schlechter gesichert waren als die Haustüren, und maximal fünf Minuten später waren sie wieder verschwunden.

»Wo?«

»Eppelheim mal wieder. Eine Villa am westlichen Ortsrand. Beute circa zwei- bis dreitausend, haben mir die Kollegen vom KDD berichtet. Das Fahrzeug war diesmal ein Audi A6, der erst heute am Nachmittag in Kaiserslautern geklaut wurde – ein Nachbar hat es gesehen. Aber immerhin haben wir diesmal so was wie eine Spur: Einer der Täter hat sich verletzt, wie er eine verschlossene Schreibtischschublade aufgehebelt hat. Wir haben Täter-DNA!«

Das machte allerdings Hoffnung.

»Das Material ist auf dem Weg zum LKA?«

»Jepp. Und jetzt versuche ich mal, Sie zu verbinden …«

Kollege Neugebauer war nicht so doof, zu so später Stunde

noch im Büro zu sitzen, aber Balke fand seine private Telefonnummer in unserer Adressdatenbank.

Ich notierte mir die Nummer, rief den jungen und zum Glück aufgeweckten Kollegen an und schilderte ihm mein Anliegen.

»Wann?«

»In einer halben Stunde?«

»Ist gebongt. Klingt spannend.«

Dreißig Minuten später stand ich zusammen mit dem funktechnisch bewanderten Kollegen neben meinem fast siebzehn Jahre alten Peugeot. Neugebauer war ein klobiger Kerl, höchstens Mitte zwanzig, mit eckigem Kopf und schütterem, weißblondem Haar. Er hielt ein zierliches Gerät in seinen Pranken, das für mich aussah wie ein billiges Transistorradio, und schaltete es so vorsichtig ein, als könnte es dabei zerbrechen. Dabei murmelte er rätselhafte Dinge wie: »Advanced sensitive Tuner« und »Fuzzy-Scanning«.

Drei bunte Leuchtdioden blinkten aufgeregt, ein schriller Pieps ertönte, und dann konnte es losgehen.

Neugebauer umrundete mit dem Gerät in der Hand langsam meinen Wagen. Hin und wieder fiepte es ähnlich wie diese neumodischen Einparkhilfen. Als er in die Nähe der Heckklappe kam, wurde das Piepen plötzlich hektisch. Er ging schnaufend in die Knie und verschwand aus meinem Sichtfeld.

»Bingo«, tönte es hohl aus der Tiefe. »Ich hab ja gedacht, Sie ... ähm, also Sie spinnen, hab ich gedacht, ehrlich gesagt.«

»Ich hatte es sogar gehofft, ehrlich gesagt.«

Augenblicke später stand er neben mir und hielt ein schwarzes Kästchen zwischen dicken Fingern, etwa von der Größe einer Streichholzschachtel, an dem ein Drähtchen baumelte – vermutlich die Antenne.

»Das war's?«, fragte ich und nahm es ebenso vorsichtig wie er zwischen Daumen und Zeigefinger.

»Nicht die allerneuste Technik, würd ich mal sagen, aber es tut seinen Dienst.«

Ich wusste nicht recht, ob ich nun erleichtert sein oder mich fürchten sollte.

»Wer klebt Ihnen denn um Himmels willen einen Peilsender ans Auto?«, fragte Neugebauer, als er den Detektor in einer der vielen Taschen seiner olivgrünen Outdoorjacke versenkte.

Ich fuhr mir mit der linken Hand durchs feuchte Haar. »Ich habe nicht die leiseste Ahnung.«

»Ihre Frau vielleicht?«

»Meine Frau ist seit drei Jahren tot.«

Er verschluckte sich an seinem Lachen. »Tschuldigung. Konnt ich ja nicht … Tschuldigung.«

»Kein Problem. Konnten Sie ja nicht wissen. Wie kommt man an ein solches Ding, und wie weit reicht es?«

»Kaufen können Sie so ein Zeug völlig problemlos im Internet. Offiziell ist das bei uns natürlich alles streng verboten. Sender plus Empfänger machen einen knappen Tausender. Der Sender allein vielleicht zweihundert, maximal zweihundertfünfzig. Das Dingelchen da hat GPS an Bord und alles. Mit dem Equipment kann Ihnen jede Oma tausend Kilometer hinterherfahren, ohne dass Sie sie je zu Gesicht kriegen.«

»Und wie weit reicht der Sender? Wie viel Abstand darf die Oma halten, ohne mich zu verlieren?«

Neugebauer sah zum wolkenverhangenen Himmel hinauf, aus dem es ein wenig nieselte. »Paar Hundert Meter? In der Stadt weniger. Auf dem platten Land mehr.«

Ein großer Volvo fuhr im Schritttempo vorbei auf der um dieser Uhrzeit in der Heidelberger Weststadt hoffnungslosen Suche nach einem freien Parkplatz.

»Und wie lange hält die Batterie?«

»Kommt drauf an. Diese Dinger schalten sich in den Sleep-Mode, sobald Sie längere Zeit anhalten. Je mehr Sie fahren, desto schneller ist die Batterie alle.«

»Bei normalem Betrieb?«

Wieder überlegte er. »Zwei, drei Wochen?«

»Und was muss ich machen, wenn ich das Ding am Auto lassen, es aber hin und wieder abschalten möchte?«

»Batterie ausbauen. Auf der Unterseite ist eine kleine Kreuzschlitzschraube, sehen Sie, da. Brauchen Sie nur einen passenden Schraubenzieher.«

»Wenn ich den nicht habe?«

»Eine Keksdose.«

»Eine Keksdose?«

»Faradayscher Käfig. Dose, auf, Sender rein, Dose zu, Ende Gelände. Faradayscher Käfig. Durch das Blech geht funktechnisch nichts durch.«

Dunkel erinnerte ich mich, vor Jahrzehnten im Physikunterricht schon einmal von diesem Phänomen gehört zu haben. Ich bückte mich, pappte den Minisender wieder ans Bodenblech, wo er durch einen kräftigen Magnet von alleine haftete. Dann drückte ich die breite Hand des hilfreichen Kollegen, lobte seine Sachkenntnis und bedankte mich in aller Form und Herzlichkeit.

»Und solche Sachen machen Sie also in Ihrer Freizeit?«

»Mein Vater war ein großer Amateurfunker vor dem Herrn und hat mir den ganzen Krempel vererbt. Erst hat's mich gar nicht interessiert. Aber jetzt hab ich Blut geleckt. Mach auch Kurse in Elektronik und so.«

»Gut zu wissen. Kann sein, dass Sie bald wieder von mir hören.«

»Und Herr Gerlach, ähm …«

Ich hatte mich schon zum Gehen gewandt. »Ja?«

»Also, dieses Jahr wär bei mir eigentlich der Oberkommissar dran …«

»Das wird klappen. Keine Sorge.«

Sein Vollmondgesicht strahlte wie das eines pappsatten Babys, als er auf sein schweres Motorrad stieg, den Helm überstülpte und den donnernden Motor anließ.

Am Donnerstagmorgen beschloss ich, wieder gesund zu sein.

»Würden Sie bitte mal versuchen, den angeblichen Mörder dieser Frau Hergarden aufzutreiben?«, sagte ich zu Sönnchen, als ich meinen Wintermantel an die Garderobe hängte. »Ich denke, er wird irgendwo in Heidelberg wohnen. Oder in der Umgebung.«

Jetzt erst bemerkte ich ihren empörten Gesichtsausdruck.

»Was machen Sie denn hier?«, fragte sie entgeistert.

»Ich arbeite hier. Haben Sie mich etwa schon vergessen?«

»Sie sind doch krankgeschrieben!«

»Ich habe mich selbst wieder gesundgeschrieben. Als Chef darf man das.«

»Gar nichts dürfen Sie! Der Arzt hat sie bis Ende der Woche krankgeschrieben, und da haben Sie daheim im Bett zu liegen!«

»Werden Sie nun versuchen, diesen Herrn Hergarden zu finden oder nicht?«

»Kommt nicht in die Tüte.«

»Sönnchen, ich bitte Sie in aller Form.«

Nun versuchte sie es auf die Fürsorgliche-Mutter-Tour: »Herr Gerlach, mit so einer Gehirnschütterung ist wirklich nicht zu spaßen!«

»Und Sie wollen sich später keine Vorwürfe machen müssen, ich weiß. Ich handle auf eigenes Risiko. Und ich bin schon ziemlich erwachsen.«

»Da habe ich meine Zweifel. Wer krank ist, der gehört ins Bett. Auch wenn er Chef ist.«

Allmählich verlor ich den Spaß an unserer Kabbelei. »Verehrte Frau Walldorf. Wenn es sein muss, kann ich meine Bitte auch als dienstliche Anweisung formulieren.«

»Sie können mir keine Anweisungen geben, weil Sie ja gar nicht da sind.«

Nun hatte ich genug. Ich ließ sie einfach sitzen und öffnete die Tür zu meinem Büro. »Dann bitte ich eben Balke darum. Oder Frau Vangelis. Oder nein, am besten Frau Krauss.«

Ich konnte mir nicht verkneifen, stehen zu bleiben und zu beobachten, wie sie reagierte. Sekundenlang starrte sie verbissen auf ihren vorbildlich aufgeräumten Schreibtisch. Dann zwang sie ein eisiges Lächeln in ihr Gesicht.

»Ich hab ein Foto aufgetrieben. Von achtundachtzig. Da ist Johann Boll drauf.«

Mit einer Bewegung, als ginge es fast über ihre Kräfte, schob sie ein großformatiges Farbfoto in meine Richtung. Es zeigte eine gemischtgeschlechtliche Gruppe, war vermutlich bei irgendeiner Feier geknipst worden. Sönnchens seit Neuestem rosarot lackierter Fingernagel deutete auf einen großen, schlanken Mann in der hinteren Reihe, der nicht übermäßig intelligent, ernst und sichtlich unzufrieden in die Linse glotzte.

»Die Gerda sagt, das ist er. Aber hundertprozentig sicher ist sie sich auch nicht. Vielleicht könnte der Kollege Runkel ...?«

»Ich werde ihn fragen. Kann ich es haben?«

»Nichts können Sie haben. Weil, Sie sind ja nicht da.«

»Sönnchen, das ist jetzt nicht mehr witzig.«

»War auch nicht als Witz gemeint.«

Da ich keine Lust auf weitere Diskussionen hatte, schloss ich die Tür zu meinem Büro heute etwas kraftvoller als sonst hinter mir.

Leider stellte sich rasch heraus, dass die Mitarbeiter, deren Namen ich eben genannt hatte, alle anderweitig beschäftigt waren, und so kümmerte ich mich am Ende notgedrungen selbst um den Verbleib des Mannes, von dem ich immer noch nur den mutmaßlichen Nachnamen kannte – Hergarden. Sönnchen hatte alle meine Termine abgesagt, ich hatte also reichlich Zeit.

Zunächst klapperte ich die Einwohnermeldeämter in Heidelberg und Umgebung ab, zog den Kreis größer und größer. In Mannheim schließlich wurde ich fündig: Dort lebte ein Mann namens Uwe Hergarden. Unter der Telefonnummer, die man mir nannte, meldete sich jedoch niemand. Anschließend rief ich noch einmal das Heidelberger Meldeamt an. Schließlich hatte Hergarden 1985 nachweislich in der Stadt gewohnt. Sämtliche Daten aus der Zeit vor 1988 lagen jedoch nur in Form von Mikrofiches vor, wurde ich aufgeklärt, und waren deshalb nicht so ohne Weiteres greifbar. Schließlich verlor ich den Spaß am Detektivspielen und gab fürs Erste auf.

Das Starren auf den kleinen Bildschirm meines Laptops tat meinem Kopf nicht gut, und Sönnchen hatte – auch wenn ich es ungern zugab – nicht ganz unrecht: Bei einem Todesfall, der so lange zurücklag, kam es auf einige Stunden mehr oder weniger nicht an. Außerdem war mir inzwischen eine Frage gekommen, die mir eigentlich schon gestern Abend hätte einfallen müssen: Wie konnte der, der mir den Peilsender ans Auto montiert hatte, überhaupt wissen, dass ich mich seit Neuestem mit Viktoria Hergardens Tod beschäftigte? Oder sollte diese merkwürdige Überwachungsaktion gar nichts mit dem Fall Hergarden zu tun haben? Den man ja bei Licht besehen nicht einmal als Fall bezeichnen konnte?

So lange ich auch rätselte und grübelte, es wollte mir keine andere Erklärung einfallen als die, dass ich unwissentlich in ein Wespennest gestochen und Menschen aufgeschreckt hatte. Menschen, die vermutlich davon ausgegangen waren, dass die Ereignisse vor dreißig Jahren längst in Vergessenheit geraten waren.

Gegen neun erschien Balke, um mir von den neuesten Entwicklungen zum Thema Kellertürenbande zu berichten, und erlöste mich aus dem Gedankenkarussell, das sinnlos in meinem Kopf rotierte.

»Mit der DNA-Analyse wird es leider dauern«, sagte er, nachdem er sich gesetzt hatte. »Das Labor ist total überlastet, und ein Einbruch hat natürlich nicht gerade Prio eins.«

Wie üblich trug er zu seinen Jeans ein T-Shirt, das heute olivgrün war und jeden Muskel seines gut trainierten Oberkörpers nachzeichnete. Balke fuhr viel Rad, natürlich immer mit Helm. Seine hellblonden Haare schienen mir heute einen halben Zentimeter länger zu sein als sonst. Wie ich wusste, schnitt er sich das Haupthaar selbst mithilfe eines Bartschneiders. Sein Blick war unternehmungslustig.

»Sie gucken, als käme noch was«, sagte ich müde.

»Stimmt.« Jetzt strahlte er. »Wir haben zum ersten Mal eine Zeugin! Der Diebstahl des Audi ist beobachtet worden. Es war auf dem Parkplatz eines Netto-Supermarkts im Osten von Kaiserslautern. Laut Aussage der Frau war der Dieb Mitte dreißig, maximal Anfang vierzig. Groß, kräftige Statur, blöde Miene und – was das Klauen von Autos betrifft – Profi. Der hat die Karre so schnell und geräuschlos geknackt, dass die Frau gar nichts davon mitgekommen hat. Erst als er weggefahren ist und sie das Kennzeichen gesehen hat, ist ihr klar geworden, dass der Audi ihrem Nachbarn gehört.«

Balke legte mir ein gut gelungenes Phantombild des Auto-knackers vor. Der Mann hatte ein markiges Gesicht und eng beieinanderliegende Augen. Dazu lange Koteletten und beneidenswert lockiges Haar.

»Wenn wir den Typ haben, dann haben wir die Bande«, meinte Balke. »Die Zeugin ist im Moment noch unten. Evalina zeigt ihr unsere Porträtsammlung. Vielleicht haben wir ja ausnahmsweise mal Glück in der Sache.«

Oberkommissarin Evalina Krauss teilte mit Balke das Büro und seit fast einem Jahr auch das Bett. Seither war er, der früher die Freundinnen schneller gewechselt hatte als manch anderer die Hemden, sehr viel ruhiger geworden. Und morgens viel ausgeschlafener.

Auf meinem Schreibtisch hatte sich in den Tagen, die ich gefehlt hatte, natürlich einiges angesammelt. Viel Unwichtiges zum Glück, manches, das sich delegieren ließ, aber leider auch Dinge, die nur ich selbst erledigen konnte. Sönnchen brachte mir zum Trost und vielleicht auch als Versöhnungsgeste eine große Tasse Fencheltee, erklärte kategorisch, Kaffee sei nichts für mich, setzte sich unaufgefordert mir gegenüber auf einen der blauen Besucherstühle.

»Geht's Ihnen wirklich wieder gut?«, fragte sie voller Besorgnis.

»Ich fühle mich, als wäre ich nicht drei Tage krank gewesen, sondern zwei Wochen in Urlaub«, behauptete ich und schlürfte tapfer den Tee, obwohl ich Fencheltee nicht ausstehen konnte.

»Sie sehen aber nicht so aus.«

»Muss nur erst wieder meinen Kreislauf in Schwung bringen. Ein Kaffee würde bestimmt dabei helfen.«

Sie überhörte meinen letzten Satz und berichtete im Telegrammstil von den Ereignissen der vergangenen Tage. Ich hörte zu und nippte nebenbei weiter an dem grauenhaft schmeckenden Aufguss, der angeblich gegen alles half. Erfreulich ruhig war es gewesen in Heidelberg. Als hätten die Verbrecher geahnt, dass der Kripochef außer Gefecht war.

»Wie läuft's mit Ihrem Christian?«, fragte ich, als ihr Bericht zu Ende war.

Wie immer, wenn die Sprache auf ihre neue Liebe kam, errötete sie bis an die Haarwurzeln.

»Ach, Herr Gerlach ...«, seufzte sie und schlug die Augen nieder.

»Also gut?«

Sie nickte verschämt.

»Ich freue mich für Sie, Sönnchen. Es ist schön, Sie glücklich zu sehen.«

»Danke«, hauchte sie. »Vielleicht wohnt dieser Herr Hergarden ja in einem Hotel?«

Aha. Sie konnte es also doch nicht lassen.

»Gut möglich.« Ich stellte meinen Becher ab. »Offiziell gemeldet ist er jedenfalls nicht. Nur in Mannheim wohnt ein Mann mit diesem Namen. Ich habe angerufen, aber da nimmt niemand ab.«

»Soll ich mich mal dahinterklemmen?«

»Das wäre lieb von Ihnen.« Ich lehnte mich zurück und schloss für einen winzigen Moment die Augen. Was ich nicht hätte tun sollen.

»Sie haben Kopfweh!«, erkannte meine hellsichtige Sekretärin sofort.

»Überhaupt nicht.«

»Sie *haben* Kopfweh. Ich seh's Ihnen an.«

»Frau Walldorf!«

»Sie fahren jetzt heim und legen sich wieder ins Bett, wo Sie hingehören!«

Jetzt hatte ich genug: »Ich fahre heim, wenn's mir passt. So. Ende der Durchsage.«

Sie hatte schon wieder den finsteren Blick von vorhin. Am Ende sah sie jedoch ein, dass sie am kürzeren Hebel saß.

»Sie glauben also, da ist doch was dran an der Geschichte?«, fragte sie und sah woandershin. »Dass er seine Frau umgebracht hat?«

»Laut Aktenlage kann er sie überhaupt nicht umgebracht haben. Aber irgendwas stimmt da nicht. Einer von den beiden

Kripobeamten, die den Fall damals untersucht haben, hat sich ein halbes Jahr später einen Ferrari gekauft. Der andere hat den Dienst quittiert und es anscheinend nicht mehr nötig zu arbeiten ...«

Die Sache mit dem Peilsender behielt ich lieber für mich, um weiteren Komplikationen aus dem Weg zu gehen.

»Und was machen wir jetzt?«

»Am besten, Sie finden für mich diesen Herrn Hergarden, und ich trinke solange Tee.«

»Sollen wir nicht machen, was die Polizei in solchen Fällen normalerweise macht?«

»Was tun wir denn normalerweise in solchen Fällen, Miss Marple?«

»Wir machen ein Phantombild. Sie haben ihn gesehen, ich hab ihn gesehen ...«

»Und dann schreibe ich ihn zur Fahndung aus und mache mich vor der halben Welt zur Lachnummer. Haha.«

»Es gibt andere Möglichkeiten.«

»Frau Walldorf, ich weiß, dass Sie mit jedem zweiten Heidelberger per Du sind. Aber der Rest, den Sie nicht kennen, das sind immer noch ziemlich viele, und außerdem ...«

»Das lassen Sie ruhig meine Sorge sein.«

8

Zehn Minuten später waren wir zu dritt, und ich musste feststellen, dass das Personengedächtnis meiner Sekretärin wesentlich besser war als meines.

»Die Nase länger, die Augen ein bisschen weiter auseinander, ja, genau so, und die Augenbrauen ...«, ratterten ihre Anweisungen wie aus einem Maschinengewehr, die die blutjunge Kollegin vom Erkennungsdienst mit ebensolcher Schnelligkeit umsetzte, während ich hie und da immerhin einen kleinen Verbesserungsvorschlag anbringen konnte. Am Ende waren wir alle zufrieden mit uns, und ich war verblüfft, nun tatsächlich das Gesicht des Mannes vor mir zu sehen, der mir vor fast einer Woche gegenübergesessen hatte. Und dann – von einer Sekunde auf die nächste – war ich mir sicher, dass dieser Mann mit den ausgeprägten Tränensäcken bei meinem Fahrradunfall anwesend war. Dass sein Gesicht sich immer wieder in meine Flashbackerinnerungen gemogelt hatte, beruhte nicht auf einem Kurzschluss irgendwelcher erschütterter Synapsen, sondern darauf, dass ich ihn tatsächlich gesehen hatte. Da waren zwei Männer gewesen, jetzt war ich mir sicher. Und der andere, der im dunklen Anzug, hatte mich gestoßen. Aber welche Rolle hatte Hergarden bei dem unerfreulichen Zusammentreffen gespielt?

»Herr Gerlach?«, hörte ich Sönnchens zaghafte Stimme.

Ich erschrak. »Ja?«

»Was er angehabt hat?«

»Angehabt?«

»Sind Sie sicher, dass Sie nicht doch besser im Bett liegen sollten? Oder vielleicht mal kurz in die Uniklinik? Die haben da ganz tolle Spezialisten für Kopfver…«

»Quatsch!«, fuhr ich ihr in die Parade. »Mir geht's super. Mir war nur gerade was eingefallen.«

Die Kollegin am Laptop betrachtete mich in einer Mischung aus Respekt und Neugierde. Wer weiß, welche Schauergeschichten Sönnchen über mein kleines Missgeschick verbreitet hatte.

»Angehabt?« Ich räusperte mich. »Keinen Mantel. Obwohl es ziemlich kalt war an dem Tag. Ein kariertes Hemd und eine schwarze Lederjacke. So eine Rockerjacke mit Fransen und vielen Taschen und ohne Ärmel. Die hat ausgesehen, als hätte er sie zum achtzehnten Geburtstag gekriegt.«

»Die Jacke hab ich auch gesehen«, bestätigte Sönnchen eifrig. »Schwarz ist vielleicht seine Lieblingsfarbe. Die Hose, die war nämlich auch schwarz.«

»Und die Schuhe. Schnürschuhe. Auch nicht mehr die Jüngsten.«

»Reich scheint er nicht zu sein«, meinte die junge Frau vor dem Laptop mit heller Stimme. Sie duftete nach einem frischen

Parfüm und trug einen langen Rock aus sehenswert buntem Stoff.

»Im Gegenteil«, bestätigte ich. »Insgesamt hat er ziemlich heruntergekommen gewirkt.«

»Und ein bisschen öfter waschen könnte er sich auch«, ergänzte Sönnchen mit gerümpfter Nase. »Da fällt mir ein: An der rechten Hand hat er einen Ring getragen. Einen goldenen Siegelring mit roter Platte oder irgendwas in der Art. Der hat echt ausgesehen, der Ring. Echt und wertvoll.«

»Brille vielleicht?«, fragte die Kollegin mit dem langen blonden Haar konzentriert, während ihre Rechte unentwegt mit der Maus herumzuckte.

Ich schüttelte den Kopf. »Definitiv nein.«

»Er hat einen aber angeguckt, als wär er ein bisschen kurzsichtig«, gab Sönnchen zu bedenken.

»Dialekt?«

Ich schüttelte den Kopf. »Akzentfreies Hochdeutsch.«

»So einen leichten Schlag ins Kurpfälzische hat er schon gehabt«, war meine eigensinnige Sekretärin überzeugt. »Außerdem hat er für mich geklungen ... wie soll ich sagen?«

»Was wollen Sie denn sagen?«

»Wie wenn er lang im Ausland gelebt hätte. Sie wissen schon.«

Ich nickte. Jetzt, wo sie es sagte ...

»Größe?«, fragte die Kollegin.

»Eins achtzig bis eins fünfundachtzig«, sagte ich.

»Mindestens eins fünfundachtzig«, sagte Sönnchen gleichzeitig.

»Statur?«

»Hager.«

»Einen krummen Rücken hat er gehabt«, wusste Frau Oberschlau. »Wenn der sich aufrecht hinstellen würd – vielleicht ist er sogar eins neunzig.«

»Na, das ist doch schon mal was.« Die duftende Kollegin klappte befriedigt ihren Laptop zu. »In zehn Minuten haben Sie das Kunstwerk im Posteingang, Herr Kriminaloberrat.«

Sönnchen gab sich Mühe, nicht allzu triumphierend zu grinsen.

» Und was machen Sie dann mit dem schönen Bild? «, fragte ich missmutig, als wir wieder unter uns waren.

» An Multiplikatoren verteilen. «

» Multiplikatoren? «

» Lassen Sie mich einfach machen «, sagte Sönnchen so milde, als spräche sie mit einem schon leicht debilen, aber ansonsten netten Greis. » Soziale Netzwerke hat's auch schon vor Facebook gegeben. Und Sie gehen jetzt wirklich heim und schonen sich. «

» Ich will mich aber nicht schonen. «

» Wenn Sie nicht brav sind, geh ich zum Dr. Liebekind und verpetze Sie. Herr Gerlach, ich kann's nur immer wieder sagen: So eine schwere Gehirnerschütterung ist eine ernste Sache. Ein Freund von meiner jüngsten Schwester, der ist mal mit dem Motorrad gestürzt. Im Hohenlohischen ist das gewesen, in der Nähe von Waldenburg ... «

Ich hob die Hand, um sie zu bremsen. Das Letzte, wonach mir heute der Sinn stand, waren weitere Horrorgeschichten und Unfallberichte. Inzwischen waren die Kopfschmerzen tatsächlich zurückgekehrt. Und sie wurden minütlich stärker.

» Ein Telefonat lassen Sie mich aber noch führen, okay? «

» Nein! «

Ich hielt den Hörer schon in der Hand, während ich im Internet die Nummer der Polizeistation Erbach suchte, die auch für Michelstadt zuständig war.

» Boll, Johann «, wiederholte eine Kollegin mit fröhlicher Stimme und hessischem Akzent. » In Weiten-Gesäß, sagen Sie? Also mir persönlich sagt der Name nichts. Aber ich frag gern mal rum ... «

Ich hörte sie lautstark in den Raum rufen. Eine dröhnende Männerstimme antwortete.

» Den Boll kenn ich, ja «, brüllte dieselbe Stimme Sekunden später in den Hörer. » Also, kennen ist zu viel gesagt. Gesehen hab ich ihn hin und wieder. Der ist ein ehemaliger Kollege, sagen Sie? «

»Schon lange her.«

»Und was wollen Sie von dem?«

»Eigentlich möchte ich ihn nur sprechen. Es geht um einen Fall, den er vor fast dreißig Jahren bearbeitet hat.«

»Dreißig Jahre?« Er lachte lautstark. Im Erbacher Revier herrschte offenbar ein gutes Betriebsklima. »Und da meinen Sie im Ernst, der erinnert sich noch?«

»Einen Versuch ist es wert. Ich bin gestern Abend bei seinem Haus gewesen. Aber er war nicht da.«

»Und was erwarten Sie jetzt von mir?«

Im Hintergrund lachte die Frau mit der sympathischen Stimme herzlich. Ich meinte, Gläserklirren zu hören.

»Das weiß ich auch nicht so genau. Wissen Sie vielleicht, was er beruflich macht?«

»Keine Ahnung.«

»Wären Sie so nett, ein bisschen bei den Nachbarn rumzuhorchen? Irgendwer muss den Mann doch kennen. Irgendwie muss der doch zu erreichen sein.«

Wieder lachte die Frau im Hintergrund. Andere fielen ein. Erst als ich auflegte, wurde mir bewusst, dass mein Gesprächspartner sich gar nicht vorgestellt hatte.

Sönnchen hatte mich während des Telefonats streng beobachtet, ersparte mir jedoch weitere Ratschläge. Die gab mir mein eigener Kopf. Und zwar mit zunehmender Deutlichkeit.

Eine Dreiviertelstunde später lag ich wieder im Bett, nachdem ich zwei Schmerztabletten hinuntergewürgt hatte.

Als ich wieder zur Besinnung kam, war es vor dem Fenster stockdunkel. Von irgendwo hörte ich gedämpftes Geklapper und Gelächter. Ich hatte fast zehn Stunden geschlafen, wurde mir erst nach einigen Sekunden klar. Die Kopfschmerzen waren verschwunden, und ich fühlte mich gesund wie seit Ewigkeiten nicht mehr. Leichtfüßig sprang ich aus dem Bett, warf elegant meinen Bademantel über die Schultern und machte mich auf die Suche nach den Menschen, die so guter Laune waren. Der Weg war nicht weit.

»Wenn er aufwacht, wird er bestimmt Hunger haben«, hörte ich durch die angelehnte Küchentür Theresas Stimme.

»Da hast du recht!«, rief ich fröhlich und trat ein.

Die Zwillinge freuten sich.

»Du siehst viel besser aus als gestern«, behaupteten sie einstimmig.

Theresa war derselben Meinung und küsste mich schmatzend auf den Mund.

Die drei waren dabei, Spaghetti mit Lachssoße zu kochen, nach einem von Theresas Lieblingsrezepten. Und mein Magen machte Freudensprünge, als mir der Duft von Estragon und Fisch in die Nase stieg.

Bald saßen wir um unseren runden Kiefernholztisch herum und schlemmten. Ich ließ mir den Teller von Theresa zweimal nachladen und lobte ihre Kochkünste, was ihr offensichtlich gefiel. Auch die Zwillinge waren begeistert. Theresa warf mir manchmal Blicke zu, die teils nachdenklich, teils so eindeutig waren, dass ich Sorge hatte, die Moral meiner Töchter könnte Schaden nehmen. Aber sie taten, als bemerkten sie nichts.

Nach dem Essen setzten wir uns zu zweit ins Wohnzimmer, und auch Theresa fand, wer so tapfer essen konnte, der könne auch ein Gläschen Rotwein vertragen. Die Zwillinge rumorten im Flur herum, streckten plötzlich die Köpfe herein, um sich zu verabschieden.

»Wir gehen in die Stadt«, erklärten sie. »Bisschen chillen.«

Dann waren sie auch schon weg, und die Wohnungstür knallte ins Schloss. Theresa rutschte zu mir herüber auf die Couch und kuschelte sich an mich.

»Du hast sie bestochen«, sagte ich und streichelte ihren Rücken.

Sie machte nicht einmal den Versuch zu leugnen.

»Wie viel hast du ihnen gegeben?«

»Zehn Euro pro Nase. Sie haben versprochen, nicht vor elf zurück zu sein.«

»Du bist völlig unmöglich.«

»Ich weiß«, hauchte sie und drückte mir einen heißen

Schlafzimmerkuss auf den Mund. Ich horchte auf meinen Kopf. Er schien keine Einwände zu haben. Seufzend begann ich, ihre Bluse aufzuknöpfen.

»Das wird das erste Mal, dass ich auf diesem Sofa mit einer Frau schlafe.«

»Irgendwann ist immer das erste Mal«, philosophierte sie verträumt, während sie an meinem Gürtel herumfummelte.

Später, als wir geduscht und wieder anständig bekleidet waren, öffnete ich feierlich die Sektflasche, die Theresa am Sonntag mitgebracht hatte. Wir saßen eng beisammen, plauderten über dies und das, und natürlich wollte Theresa wissen, weshalb ich heute schon wieder im Büro gewesen war. Ich erzählte ihr von der toten Frau in der Gundolfstraße und meiner Fahrt in den Odenwald. Fast alles erzählte ich. Nur den Peilsender unterschlug ich, ebenso wie meinen Verdacht, Hergarden könnte Zeuge meines Fahrradunfalls gewesen sein. Ich wollte sie nicht unnötig beunruhigen.

»Gundolfstraße«, sagte Theresa an meiner Schulter, »die ist bei uns gleich um die Ecke. Der Nummer nach müsste es einer von diesen Fünfzigerjahrewohnblocks sein. Und jetzt taucht nach drei Jahrzehnten aus dem Nichts der Witwer auf und behauptet, die Frau ermordet zu haben? Vielleicht hat ihn all die Jahre sein Gewissen gequält, und er will reinen Tisch machen?«

»Ich habe das Protokoll gelesen und mir die Tatortfotos angesehen. Sie war allein in der Wohnung. Er *kann* sie nicht umgebracht haben.«

Bald kamen wir überein, alte Akten alte Akten sein zu lassen und uns mehr um die Leerung der Sektflasche zu kümmern. Am Ende wäre es um ein Haar erneut zu Tätlichkeiten gekommen. Aber da war es schon weit nach zehn, und bald würden Sarah und Louise wieder auftauchen.

9

»Sie schon wieder.« Sönnchen rollte theatralisch die Augen, als ich am Freitagmorgen mein Vorzimmer betrat, ersparte mir jedoch weitere Kommentare.

»Haben Sie schon irgendwas gehört von dem Kerl mit der Lederjacke?«

»Verrat ich nicht.«

»Also nicht.«

Verdutzt sah sie in mein Gesicht. »Wie kommen Sie darauf?«

»Weil Sie im anderen Fall unmöglich den Mund halten könnten. Hat jemand aus Erbach für mich angerufen?«

Ihr »Nein« klang glaubhaft.

»Elisabeth Holland?«

»Gibt's nicht. Nirgends.«

»Würden Sie sicherheitshalber mal nachprüfen, ob es in Heidelberg einen Arzt gibt, der Hagen Baumbusch heißt?«

»Wer soll das sein?«

»Der Notarzt, der damals den Totenschein ausgefüllt hat.«

»Dieser Uwe Hergarden, der in Mannheim wohnt, kann übrigens nicht der Richtige sein.«

»Warum nicht?«

»Weil er nie verheiratet war. Da kann er ja schlecht seine Frau ... «

Es gab im Umkreis von Heidelberg niemanden mit dem Namen des damaligen Notarztes, fand Sönnchen rasch heraus. Dreißig Jahre waren eben doch eine kleine Ewigkeit. Damals war ich noch zur Schule gegangen, wurde mir bewusst. Und hatte noch keinen Schimmer gehabt, was ich mit dem Abi anfangen würde, sollte ich es überhaupt schaffen. Ich hatte es geschafft, wenn auch nicht mit Bravour. Und war bei der Polizei gelandet, weil mein Vater meinte, als Beamter werde man zwar nicht reich, habe dafür aber manche Sorgen nicht, die andere Menschen so hatten.

Sönnchen hatte mir heute ohne Widerspruch meinen Morgencappuccino gemacht. Aber sie war immer noch alles andere als herzlich zu mir. Vermutlich war sie gekränkt, weil ich ihre Fürsorge so hartnäckig ignorierte. So hielten wir an diesem Vormittag Abstand wie ein zerstrittenes Ehepaar. Irgendwann legte sie mir die unvermeidliche Unterschriftenmappe auf den Schreibtisch und verschwand wortlos wieder im Vorzimmer.

Ich ließ die Mappe liegen, weil mir plötzlich eine Idee gekommen war, griff wieder einmal zum Hörer, wählte die Nummer des Roten Kreuzes.

»Hagen Baumbusch? Wann soll das gewesen sein?«, fragte mich eine junge und für die Uhrzeit ungewöhnlich mürrische Telefonistin. »Haben Sie dreißig Jahre gesagt, oder hab ich mich verhört?«

»Knapp dreißig Jahre, habe ich gesagt.«

»Also, eine Akte habe ich nicht von dem. Ich müsste mich mal umhören.«

Ich drehte meinen Charme auf höchste Stufe: »Wäre wirklich toll, wenn Sie das für mich tun würden.«

»Sie haben Glück«, versetzte sie knurrig. »Ich hab heut nämlich meinen netten Tag.«

Fünf Minuten später rief sie zurück. »Fehlanzeige«, warf sie mir an den Kopf. »Probieren Sie's mal beim ASB.«

Dort hatte ich mehr Erfolg. Nach einigem Hin und Her hatte ich einen alten Sanitäter am Telefon, der sich noch an Dr. Baumbusch erinnerte.

»Was aus dem geworden ist? Gestorben ist der.«

»Bei einem Autounfall?«

»Wie kommen Sie darauf? Nein, der hat überhaupt kein Auto gehabt. Der war nämlich ein Grüner. Damals schon. Hat so verrückte Öko-Ideen gehabt und immer nur Grünzeug gefressen. In den Alpen ist er verunglückt. Ist nämlich für sein Leben gern geklettert, der Dr. Baumbusch. Hat er oft von erzählt, wenn wir zusammen auf dem Weg zu einem Einsatz waren. Die Natur, die hat er geliebt. Und irgendwann ist er dann am Montag nicht mehr gekommen. Hat seine geliebte Natur ihn umgebracht, sozusagen.«

»War er allein unterwegs?«

»Die Größe der Natur kann man nur erleben, wenn man allein ist, hat er immer gesagt. Er war ein sehr erfahrener Bergsteiger. Und unglaublich fit ist er auch gewesen, obwohl er schon über fünfzig war. Keiner von diesen Knallköpfen, die in Turnschuhen auf Dreitausender klettern und sich anschließend wundern, wenn sie mit kaputten Knochen in einer Gletscherspalte liegen und mit dem Hubschrauber gerettet werden müssen. Irgendwie muss er ausgerutscht sein, und an Erfahrung kann man sich eben nicht festhalten.«

»Wann war das?«

»Warten Sie ...« Ich hörte den Mann leise mit jemandem sprechen. »Im Frühjahr siebenundachtzig. April, Mai vielleicht.«

Anderthalb Jahre, nachdem Viktoria Hergarden mit ihrem Teppich ausgerutscht war.

Als ich nun doch die Unterschriftenmappe aufklappte, klingelte das Telefon. Es war die Mitarbeiterin des Einwohnermeldeamts, mit der ich gestern schon gesprochen hatte. Sie hatte inzwischen die alten Akten aus den Jahren 1985 und 1986 durchgesehen. Vicky Hergardens Ehemann hatte Heidelberg acht Wochen nach dem Tod seiner Frau verlassen und war mit unbekanntem Ziel verzogen.

»Normalerweise heißt das, dass er ins Ausland ist.«

»Wie war noch mal der Vorname?«

»Friedrich. Rufname Fred. Zweiter Vorname Otto.«

»Steht auch ein Beruf in Ihrer Akte?«

»Freischaffender Künstler und Fotograf. Das kann alles und nichts heißen.«

Sie diktierte mir noch einige Daten. Geboren 1951 in Seckenheim, besondere Kennzeichen: keine, Körpergröße: eins neunundachtzig, bisher polizeilich nicht unangenehm aufgefallen. Ich bedankte mich für ihre Hilfe. Sie lachte gurrend und zögerte einen Moment, bevor sie auflegte.

Nun arbeitete ich zügig die Unterschriftenmappe durch und erledigte im Anschluss daran gleich noch ein wenig Papierkram, während meine Gedanken ständig auf Abwegen waren.

Die komplizierten Vorgänge legte ich zur Seite, um sie am Montag zu erledigen. Und schließlich griff ich erneut zum Telefon.

»Herr Gerlach, welche Freude!«, tönte mir die Stimme von Heinzjürgen Machatscheck entgegen. »Was verschafft mir die unerwartete Ehre? Wieder mal Ärger mit der bulgarischen Mafia?«

Machatscheck war freier Journalist, schrieb für verschiedene Zeitungen und Medien und spürte bevorzugt den ganz großen Geschichten nach. Meist politischen Skandalen, bei denen es um Millionen wenn nicht Milliarden ging und Menschenleben nur noch kalkulatorische Größen waren. Machatscheck hatte den enormen Vorzug, Zugriff auf die Archive aller möglichen Verlagshäuser und Nachrichtenagenturen zu haben, die mir verschlossen blieben. Und er schien sich wirklich über meinen Anruf zu freuen.

»Ich wollte mich einfach mal wieder melden und hören, wie es Ihnen so geht«, schwindelte ich fröhlich.

»Sie sind ein miserabler Lügner, lieber Herr Kripochef. Das ist gut für den Seelenfrieden, aber leider schlecht für die Karriere. Um Ihre Frage dennoch zu beantworten: Es geht mir prima.«

»Sie haben natürlich recht. Ich hätte tatsächlich ein kleines Anliegen. Es geht um eine Geschichte, die dreißig Jahre zurückliegt.«

»Lässt sich Geld damit verdienen?«

»Ich glaube kaum.«

Ich nannte ihm den Namen Fred Hergarden.

»Er war lange im Ausland, sagen Sie?«

»Es gibt Anzeichen dafür.«

»Im Internet findet man nichts? Fotografen benutzen üblicherweise keine Pseudonyme.«

»Ich habe nicht allzu lange gesucht, zugegeben. Aber gefunden habe ich bisher nichts.«

»Will sehen, was sich machen lässt. Sie hören von mir. Kann aber ein Weilchen dauern.«

Es wurde früher Nachmittag, bis Machatscheck zurückrief. Da ich die Hand gerade am Telefon hatte, nahm ich beim ersten Klingeln ab.

»Donnerwetter«, begrüßte er mich launig. »Wusste gar nicht, dass der vielgeschmähte deutsche Beamte so reaktionsschnell sein kann.«

»Ihr vielgeschmähter Beamter ist hart am Rande des Beamtenbeleidigtseins, und das ist strafbar. Sie haben was für mich?«

»Also, die Sache ist die ...«, begann er. »Ich habe den Namen Fred Hergarden in einem Nachrichtenbeitrag der ARD aus dem Jahr 1985 gefunden.«

»Darauf haben Sie einfach so Zugriff?«

Er lachte gemütlich. »Sagen wir so: Ich habe Zugriff auf Leute, die Zugriff auf dieses Archiv haben.«

Fred Hergarden war von Beruf Kameramann. Im Spätsommer des Jahres 1985 hatte er ein Angebot der ARD angenommen, in ihrem Auftrag in Bagdad zu arbeiten. Damals hatte gerade der Krieg zwischen Iran und Irak getobt, und sein Vorgänger war während eines Drehs im Norden des Irak zusammen mit einem jungen Journalisten und einem einheimischen Fahrer unter Artilleriefeuer geraten und ums Leben gekommen. Vermutlich war die Bezahlung, die man Hergarden bot, aus diesem Grund fürstlich gewesen. So hatte er in den folgenden Monaten die meiste Zeit in Bagdad, Teheran oder sonst irgendwo im nahen Osten verbracht und seine junge Ehefrau nur alle paar Wochen für wenige Tage gesehen.

»Anfang November, als seine Frau starb, war er im Grenzgebiet im Süden unterwegs«, berichtete Machatscheck. »In der Nähe von Basra. Damals hat gerade der Noricum-Skandal gekocht.«

»Noricum?«

»Eine österreichische Waffenfabrik, die den Irak – mit Umweg über Jordanien und natürlich höchst illegal – mit modernsten 155-Millimetergeschützen beliefert hat.«

»Wie sicher ist die Information, dass er Anfang November im Irak war?«

»Warum ist das so wichtig?«

Im Hintergrund hörte ich Möwen kreischen. Der Journalist schien sich am Meer aufzuhalten. Ich fragte nicht nach, da ich ohnehin keine ehrliche Antwort erhalten hätte. Machatscheck legte großen Wert darauf, dass sein Aufenthaltsort nicht bekannt wurde. Im Lauf seines bewegten Lebens hatte er mehr als einen Mordanschlag überlebt. Einmal, damals hatten wir uns gerade erst kennengelernt, hatte man ihm das Haus angezündet, um sein darin befindliches privates Archiv und die Ergebnisse seiner aktuellen Recherchen zu vernichten. Was allerdings nicht geklappt hatte.

»Weil er vor einer Woche bei mir war«, beantwortete ich seine Frage, »und behauptet hat, er hätte am neunten November fünfundachtzig seine Frau ermordet.«

»Das ist nach Lage der Dinge unmöglich. Was ich weiß, wissen Sie jetzt ebenfalls. Mehr habe ich leider nicht zu bieten. Ich kann Ihnen höchstens noch die Nummer eines Kollegen geben, der damals mit Hergarden zusammengearbeitet hat. Vielleicht kommen Sie über den weiter. Aber das interessiert mich jetzt doch: Weshalb behauptet der Mann, er hätte seine Frau umgebracht, wenn er es doch nicht gewesen sein kann?«

»Das ist auch eine der Fragen, die mich zurzeit brennend interessieren.«

»Und das war leider eine sehr schlechte Antwort, lieber Herr Gerlach.« Machatscheck lachte wieder. »Aber mit guten Fragen fängt ja nun mal jede gute Story an. Es gibt wirklich nichts für mich zu verdienen dabei?«

»Warum sind Sie nur immer so hinter dem Geld her?«

»Weil ich mit warmen Dankesworten mein Haus nicht heizen kann. Gute Taten machen eine glatte Haut, habe ich festgestellt, aber sie machen nicht satt.«

»Wenn ich irgendeine Chance sehe, hören Sie von mir.«

»Der übliche Deal: Ich bin der Erste, den Sie kontaktieren, sobald es etwas für die Öffentlichkeit gibt? Zwölf Stunden Vorlauf, bevor Sie das Material der Meute zum Fraß vorwerfen?«

»Ganz großes Beamtenehrenwort.«

Der Name des Fernsehjournalisten, dessen Hamburger Telefonnummer Machatscheck mir diktiert hatte, war Helge Haas. Unter der Nummer meldete sich seine etwas begriffsstutzige Frau. Ich erklärte ihr, wer ich war und was ich wollte.

»Helge ist zurzeit im Ausland. Für die BBC. Mehr darf ich Ihnen leider nicht verraten.«

»Sie haben aber doch bestimmt eine Nummer, unter der ich ihn erreichen kann?«

Die durfte ich auch nicht wissen.

»Würden Sie ihm ausrichten, dass er mich bitte anrufen soll? So rasch wie möglich? Sagen Sie ihm, es geht um Fred Hergarden.«

Sie wiederholte den Namen Silbe für Silbe, ich hörte ihren Stift übers Papier kratzen.

Der Rückruf kam zu meiner Überraschung schon wenige Minuten später. Die Nummer auf meinem Display war lang, die Qualität der Verbindung miserabel.

»Freddy?«, wiederholte Helge Haas mit rauer Stimme. »Klar erinnere ich mich an Freddy.«

»Sie sollen Ende fünfundachtzig zusammen im Irak gewesen sein.«

»Das ist richtig. Die Noricum-Affäre. War ein ziemlicher Aufreger damals.«

Durchs Telefon hörte ich Verkehrslärm. Dröhnende Lkws, anhaltend hupende Autos, in einer unverständlichen Sprache zeternde Frauenstimmen, ein plärrendes Kind, mehrere kläffende Hunde. Dort, wo Haas sich aufhielt, schien es warm und lebhaft zu sein.

»Meine Frage ist: Waren Sie auch Anfang November mit ihm zusammen? Um den zehnten herum?«

Für Sekunden hörte ich nur das Rauschen und Knistern der schlechten Telefonverbindung und den großstädtischen Radau im Hintergrund. Es schien sich um eine Frau zu handeln, die in einer für mich arabisch klingenden Sprache einen Mann beschimpfte, der sich maulfaul und brummig zur Wehr setzte. Schließlich hörte ich auch wieder die Stimme des plötzlich wortkargen Journalisten.

»Muss ich nachsehen. Sie hören von mir.«

Und wieder einmal hieß es warten. Aber wieder dauerte es nicht lange.

»Ich war mit Freddy zusammen und auch wieder nicht«, sagte Haas. Dieses Mal war die Verständigung sehr viel besser. Auch der Lärm vor seinem Fenster war verstummt. Vielleicht hatte er es geschlossen. Haas sprach mit hanseatischem Akzent, bemerkte ich jetzt erst. »Glücklicherweise führe ich seit vielen Jahren so was wie ein Tagebuch. Habe vor, vielleicht später mal ein Buch daraus zu machen. Es ist damals so gewesen: Wir sind am zweiten November von Bagdad aufgebrochen. In Begleitung von zwei Fahrzeugen der irakischen Armee. Zu unserem Schutz angeblich, aber vor allem natürlich, damit wir nichts filmten, was wir nicht durften.«

»Und es ging um diese österreichischen Geschütze?«

»Es gab das Gerücht, einige davon seien an der Südfront im Einsatz. Wir hatten die Hoffnung, heimlich ein paar Bilder knipsen zu können oder ein Filmchen aus der Aktentasche zu drehen. Freddy war Meister in solchen Dingen. Einmal hat er die Exekution von fünf irakischen Deserteuren durch ein Loch in der Tasche seiner Lederjacke gefilmt.«

»Ich glaube, diese Jacke trägt er immer noch.«

»Würde ihm ähnlich sehen. Leider ist aus unserem Plan nichts geworden.«

»Warum nicht?«

»Weil die irakischen Militärs, die auf uns aufpassen sollten, komplette Idioten waren. Wir haben uns x-mal verfahren, weil sie ihre eigenen Generalstabskarten nicht lesen konnten. GPS hatte man damals ja noch nicht. Zu allem Elend waren dann auch noch ihre Informationen über den aktuellen Frontverlauf falsch, und am Ende sind wir unter Beschuss geraten. Von welcher Seite, weiß ich bis heute nicht. Das war am späten Nachmittag des fünften November, kurz vor Sonnenuntergang. Ich habe im hintersten Fahrzeug gesessen, Freddy im mittleren. Er hat dauernd aus dem Fenster gefilmt mit einer Kamera, die so winzig war, dass er sie im Ärmel verstecken konnte. Das Aufzeichnungsgerät war ein ziemlicher Klotz, aber die Irakis waren so was von dämlich, die haben die ganze Zeit nichts gemerkt. Oder vielleicht auch nichts merken wollen. Wir haben sie natürlich großzügig mit Taschengeld versorgt. Und dann ging auf einmal die Ballerei los, irgendwo mitten in der Wüste, zwischen Sanddünen und stacheligem Gestrüpp. Zum Glück war es keine Artillerie, sondern nur zwei oder drei Maschinengewehre. Das Führungsfahrzeug ist sofort in Flammen aufgegangen. Wir anderen konnten wenden und abhauen. Im Abhauen waren die Irakis nämlich Weltklasse. Das mittlere Fahrzeug, in dem auch Freddy saß, ist aber nach ein paar hundert Metern im Sand stecken geblieben, und unser Fahrer hat sich strikt geweigert anzuhalten.«

»Und dann?«

»Dann war ich wieder in Bagdad, und Freddy war weg. Wir hatten zwar Walkie-Talkies, aber die reichten nur ein paar Kilometer weit. Satellitentelefone gab's damals auch noch nicht. Zehn Tage lang hatten wir keine Nachricht von ihm. Null. Und dann, eines schönen Morgens, war Freddy auf einmal wieder da. Das war am Dreizehnten, lese ich hier.«

»Vier Tage, nachdem seine Frau gestorben war ...«

»Angeblich hatten irakische Militärs ihn festgesetzt und ihm eine Menge peinliche Fragen gestellt. Die Militärs halten uns Journalisten ja gerne für Spione.«

»Angeblich?«

»Ich habe keinen Beleg dafür, dass seine Geschichte stimmt. Auf der anderen Seite aber auch nicht wirklich Grund, daran zu zweifeln. Er war mit einem irakischen Konvoi nach Bagdad zurückgekommen. Freddy war abgemagert, todmüde und nicht gerade bester Laune. Ein irakischer Oberst hatte ihm zweitausend Dollar dafür abgeknöpft, dass er ihn laufen ließ.«

»So viel Geld hatte er dabei?«

»Hatten wir immer. Wir hatten immer eine gewisse Summe Bares dabei für den Fall, dass mal was schiefläuft.«

»Er hätte sich für das Geld ebenso gut ein Flugticket nach Frankfurt kaufen können.«

»Theoretisch ja. Praktisch wäre das höchstens über Kuwait möglich gewesen. Wobei ... von Basra nach Kuwait-Stadt sind es keine zweihundert Kilometer, und damals war die Grenze nach Süden noch offen. Der Ärger mit Kuwait fing ja erst in den Neunzigern an.«

»Wie ging die Geschichte später weiter?«

»Überhaupt nicht. Ich habe Freddy gesagt, er soll dringend in Heidelberg anrufen. Inzwischen hatte die Redaktion durchgegeben, es sei etwas mit seiner Frau. Danach ist er auf dem schnellsten Weg nach Deutschland gedüst und erst eine Woche später wiedergekommen. Ich selbst musste zurück nach Hamburg. Freddy ist in Bagdad geblieben. Wir haben uns nur noch ganz kurz gesprochen. Er war irgendwie …«

»Wie war er?«

»Verändert. Verstört. Komplett durch den Wind. Kein Wunder – nach allem, was passiert war.«

»Hat er von seiner Frau erzählt?«

»Oh ja, und wie. Angeblich war sie die schönste Frau der Welt und eine Atombombe im Bett. Er hat gerne mit ihr angegeben. Vor allem, wenn er getrunken hatte und das Heimweh ihn geplagt hat, da hat er seine Fotos ausgepackt. Manche davon waren – nun, nicht ohne. Sie war wohl recht freizügig, seine – wie hieß sie noch?«

»Viktoria.«

»Richtig. Vicky. Angeblich war sie Schauspielerin. Den Namen habe ich aber nie irgendwo gelesen oder gehört.«

War ich nun klüger als zuvor?, fragte ich mich, als ich langsam den Hörer auflegte. Ein wenig. Immerhin wusste ich jetzt, dass Fred Hergarden – zumindest theoretisch – die Möglichkeit gehabt hätte, heimlich nach Deutschland zu fliegen, dort seine Frau zu töten und wieder in den Irak zurückzukehren. Noch während ich überlegte, ob ich mein Glück noch einmal bei Machatscheck versuchen sollte, meldete sich mein Telefon erneut.

»Mir ist noch was eingefallen«, sagte Helge Haas, inzwischen hörbar in Zeitnot. »Suchen Sie mal nach einem Steffen Wiegand oder Wieland oder so ähnlich. Der war damals im selben Hotel wie wir. Für wen er gearbeitet hat, weiß ich nicht. Ich habe ihn oft mit Freddy zusammen an der Bar gesehen.«

» Und wo finde ich diesen Herrn Wiegand oder Wieland am besten?«

» Sie sind die Kripo, nicht ich. Vielleicht hilft Ihnen das weiter: Er war Journalist wie wir. Das Hotel Palestine war damals voll von Journalisten. Und die beiden haben sich in einem merkwürdigen Dialekt unterhalten. Freddy stammt doch aus der Ecke um Heidelberg, richtig? Da vermute ich, Steffen ist auch aus der Gegend.«

Und schon hatte Haas wieder aufgelegt. Vermutlich war er gerade damit beschäftigt, irgendwo in der Welt aufregende Geheimnisse aufzudecken, von denen ich demnächst in den Fernsehnachrichten erfahren würde. Ich beherzigte seinen Tipp, googelte den Namen Steffen Wiegand und wurde mit einer halben Million Treffer erschlagen. Ohne Hoffnung klickte ich einige Links an. Versuchte erfolglos, Machatscheck noch einmal zu erreichen. Starrte eine Weile trübsinnig aus dem Fenster. Was tat ich hier eigentlich? Sollte ich mich nicht besser um den Papierkram kümmern, der sich immer noch auf meinem Schreibtisch stapelte? Oder um die ungezählten Mails in meinem Posteingang?

Außerdem: Selbst wenn Hergarden damals heimlich über Kuwait nach Deutschland geflogen sein sollte – wie hätte er seine Frau ermorden können, wo doch sämtliche Fenster geschlossen waren und die Wohnungstür von innen verriegelt? Und vor allem: warum, wo er doch anscheinend so stolz auf sie war?

10

Manchmal klären sich gerade die schwierigsten Dinge ganz einfach.

Sönnchen klopfte an meine Tür. » Herr Gerlach?«

» Ja?«, brummte ich ungnädig.

» Sind Sie noch böse mit mir?«

» Ja.«

»Ich … Ich meine es doch nur gut mit Ihnen.«

»Meine Mutter hat es auch immer nur gut gemeint, wenn sie mich ins Bett gesteckt und gezwungen hat, heiße Milch mit Honig zu trinken.«

»Ihnen geht's wirklich wieder besser?«

»Mir geht's hervorragend.«

»Kann ich irgendwas für Sie tun? Ein Kräutertee …?«

»Bleiben Sie mir vom Hals mit Ihrem Kräutertee! Nein, bei dem, was ich gerade … Oder doch, warten Sie. Ich suche einen Journalisten namens Steffen Wiegand oder Wieland.«

Sie zog die Stirn in Falten. »Wenn er Weilandt heißen würde, mit ei und dt …«

»Dann?«

»Stephan Weilandt ist fast zwanzig Jahre lang Chefredakteur bei der ›Rhein-Neckar-Zeitung‹ gewesen. Den Namen kennt in Heidelberg jeder.«

Die Welt ist ein Dorf und Heidelberg nur ein winziger Teil davon.

»Dann schaffen Sie mir den Mann ans Telefon.«

Jetzt strahlte sie wieder. »Geben Sie mir fünf Minuten.«

Den ehemaligen Chefredakteur ans Telefon zu bekommen, schien doch nicht so einfach zu sein. Ich hörte sie eine ganze Weile telefonieren, während ich Akten bearbeitete, Mails beantwortete, nebenher meinen Nachmittagscappuccino schlürfte und spürte, wie das Koffein meinen Blutkreislauf belebte. »Nicht mehr bei Ihnen?«, verstand ich einmal. Ein anderes Mal: »Tut mir sehr leid für Sie. Kann mir vorstellen, was da in einem vorgeht …«

Schließlich stand sie sichtlich enttäuscht wieder in der Tür. »Bei der Zeitung ist er schon seit Jahren nicht mehr.«

»Wahrscheinlich ist er längst in Rente.«

Sie zog eine traurige Grimasse, schüttelte den Kopf. »Sie waren auffallend zugeknöpft. Da muss irgendwas gewesen sein. Er ist erst zweiundsechzig.«

»Aber er lebt noch?«

»Es gibt eine Schwester. In Zürich. Mit der hab ich telefoniert, aber sie sagt, sie hat kaum Kontakt zu ihm. Sie hat nur gewusst, dass er jetzt in Bad Wimpfen wohnt. Mit einem Mann zusammen. Er ist ... Sie wissen schon ...«

Sie senkte den Blick, als wäre ihr der Umstand peinlich. »Seinen Partner habe ich auch erreicht. Marquard heißt er. Ganz schön pampig ist er gewesen, der Herr Marquard. Hin und wieder scheint's auch bei Schwulen Ehekrisen zu geben. So bin ich jedenfalls schon lang nicht mehr runtergeputzt worden. Man kann doch schwul sein und trotzdem nett zu Frauen, oder nicht?«

Ich hielt den Hörer schon in der Hand.

»Wer?«, fragte Marquard mit eisiger Stimme. »Wer ist da?«

»Gerlach. Kripo Heidelberg.«

»Dann war das eben ...?«

»Meine beste Mitarbeiterin.«

Meine beste Mitarbeiterin begann, bis über die Ohren zu strahlen, und hoffte vermutlich, ich würde ihren neuen Feind sofort zur Vernehmung vorladen.

»Ich habe nicht verstanden – was wollen Sie denn von Stephan? Diese Sache mit dem Unfall, das muss doch irgendwann einmal ein Ende haben. Stephan hat sich schuldig bekannt, er erfüllt seine Auflagen, er hat seine Strafe bezahlt. Was wollen Sie denn nun noch?«

»Es geht nicht um einen Unfall.«

»Nicht?« Kurze Pause. »Worum dann?«

»Um einen Todesfall, der dreißig Jahre zurückliegt. Eine junge Frau ...«

»Damit hat Stephan ganz gewiss nichts zu tun.«

»Er steht nicht unter Verdacht. Ich würde nur gerne mit ihm sprechen, weil ...«

»Stephan ist nicht zu sprechen. Weder für Sie noch für sonst jemanden. War nett, mit Ihnen zu plaudern.«

Bevor ich etwas erwidern konnte, hatte er aufgelegt.

Inzwischen waren zwei SMS angekommen, stellte ich fest, als ich einen Blick aufs Handy warf. Eine von Doro, eine von Theresa. Doros Nachricht war kurz: »Hast du endlich mit ihnen gesprochen?« Die von Theresa war noch kürzer: »Heute

Abend wie üblich?« Als ich gerade beginnen wollte, mit spitzen Fingern die Antworten zu tippen, wurde ich vom Telefon unterbrochen. Sönnchens Feind war am Apparat.

»Wenn es denn wirklich so wichtig ist – wir können uns unterhalten. Aber nur von Angesicht zu Angesicht. Und Stephan wird nicht anwesend sein.«

»Wann?«

»Wann es Ihnen passt. Ich bin eigentlich immer zu Hause.«

»Morgen ist Samstag.« Ich schätzte kurz die Entfernung. »Sagen wir um elf?«

An Doro schrieb ich: »Am Wochenende rede ich mit ihnen. Diesmal wirklich ganz fest versprochen.« An Theresa: »Freu mich!!!«

Freitagabend war Theresa-Abend. Und auch wenn wir erst am Vortag zusammengewesen waren – schöne Traditionen gehörten nun mal gepflegt.

Nachdem ich meinen Aktenstapel einige Zeit feindselig gemustert hatte, was ihn jedoch nicht zum Verschwinden brachte, klappte ich den dünnen Hängeordner zum Fall Viktoria Hergarden noch einmal auf. Betrachtete – ich weiß nicht, zum wievielten Mal – die Tatortfotos. Und entdeckte auch dieses Mal nichts, was mich in irgendeiner Weise klüger machte. Die damaligen Kollegen hatten gute Arbeit geleistet, nicht nur die Tote und die unmittelbare Umgebung fotografiert, sondern auch alle möglichen Details, die irgendwann einmal vielleicht wichtig sein könnten. Die nahezu leere Sektflasche, das elegante hohe Glas mit blutrotem Lippenstift am Rand, das neckische, halb durchsichtige Nachthemdchen, den hochhackigen Schuh, der etwa zwanzig Zentimeter von dem Fuß entfernt lag, an den er gehörte …

Welche Frau trägt eigentlich Lippenstift und hohe Schuhe, wenn sie im Begriff ist, ins Bett zu gehen, und ihren Ehemann dreitausend Kilometer entfernt weiß? Eine Frau, die dennoch nicht allein in ihrem Bett liegen wird, zum Beispiel. Oder eine Frau, die mit dem Kommen ihres Mannes rechnet. Aber hätte sie dann die Sektflasche allein geleert?

Ein anderes Bild zeigte die unversehrte Wohnungstür, den

Schlüsselbund, der am Schloss baumelte, die eingehängte Sicherheitskette. Ich blätterte weiter und wieder zurück. Moment mal – ich schlug mir mit der flachen Hand an die Stirn – wie konnte die Kette eingehängt sein, wenn die Kollegen doch offensichtlich schon in der Wohnung waren? Gab es etwa einen zweiten Eingang? Über die Terrasse vielleicht? Das musste ich dringend überprüfen lassen. Das wäre ja ... Plötzlich waren meine Hände feucht.

Der Brief, der neben dem zertrümmerten Couchtisch auf dem Parkett lag, fiel mir wieder ins Auge. Ich kramte eine Lupe aus einer der unteren Schreibtischschubladen. Natürlich war auch mit Vergrößerung nichts von dem auf einer Schreibmaschine getippten Text zu entziffern. Aber das Firmenlogo in der rechten oberen Ecke, das konnte ich immerhin lesen: »HaBeFilms«.

Eine Firma dieses Namens existierte auch heute noch, wusste ich Sekunden später, und zwar in Köln. Der junge Mann, der sich nach dem ersten Tuten meldete, klang, als wäre er kolossal erfolgsorientiert und außerdem etwas in Eile. Und er amüsierte sich königlich über meine Frage.

»Nach wie vielen Jahren? Neunundzwanzig? Wir sind hier schon froh, wenn wir die Unterlagen von der vorvergangenen Woche wiederfinden!«

»Es gibt nicht so etwas wie ein Archiv bei Ihnen?«

»Sämtliche Akten und Schriftwechsel werden nach der gesetzlichen Aufbewahrungsfrist vernichtet. Falls jemand in diesem schöpferischen Chaos zufällig daran denkt, natürlich. Außerdem ist die HaBe in den drei Jahrzehnten gefühlte hundertmal umgezogen. Worum geht es überhaupt?«

»Um einen Brief aus dem November fünfundachtzig. Empfängerin war eine Frau Viktoria Hergarden.«

»Wer sollte das sein?«

»Eine offenbar ziemlich unbekannte Schauspielerin.«

»Sie haben den Brief vorliegen?«

»Leider nein. Ich sehe ihn nur auf einem Foto, und das Einzige, was ich lesen kann, ist das Emblem Ihrer Firma.«

»Ist der Text eher lang oder eher kurz?«

»Drei Zeilen.«

»Dann wird es eine Absage gewesen sein.«

»Das würde bedeuten, sie hätte sich bei Ihnen beworben?«

»Wahrscheinlich eine Blindbewerbung. So was haben wir hier häufig. Und da kommt mir, hm, hm, hm, gerade ein vielleicht gar nicht mal so dummer Gedanke ...«

Ich hörte meinen Gesprächspartner eifrig mit Papier rascheln.

»Gab's damals eigentlich schon PCs?«, fragte er nebenbei.

»Waren gerade erst erfunden, wenn ich mich richtig erinnere.«

»Diese mausgrauen Blechkisten mit fünf Megabyte Festplatte?«

»Ungefähr so, ja.«

»Aber noch kein Internet, nehme ich an?«

»Das kam zehn Jahre später, glaube ich.«

»Wir führen hier nämlich eine Datenbank, müssen Sie wissen, in der sämtliche Darsteller landen, die sich bei uns bewerben. Falls man mal nach etwas Speziellem sucht, für eine bestimmte Rolle. Wirklich gebraucht hat man das zwar eher selten, aber mit schönen alten Gewohnheiten soll man ja nicht ohne Not ... Neunzig ... Neunundachtzig ... Hm, hm, hm ... Da scheint eine arme Praktikantin als Strafarbeit die ganzen ollen Kamellen in die EDV eingepflegt zu haben, bevor das Zeug geschreddert ... Fünfundachtzig ... Bingo! Es geschehen tatsächlich noch Zeichen und Wunder, selbst in diesem Megachaos, das Sie irrtümlich als Firma bezeichnen.«

»Wie läuft das eigentlich, wenn man sich bei Ihnen bewirbt?«

»It depends. Die meisten wollen einfach nur Filmstar werden und bewerben sich querbeet. Das ist natürlich Blödsinn, die kriegen oft nicht mal Antwort. Frau Hergarden hatte sich auf ein bestimmtes Projekt beworben, sehe ich hier. Schönes Mädel, übrigens. Wenn auch ein wenig nichtssagend, das Gesichtchen. Es ging um die *Lindenstraße*. Die ersten drei Staffeln hat die HaBe damals produziert. Die allererste Folge ist zwar erst im Dezember fünfundachtzig ausgestrahlt worden.

Aber es wird schon vorab Presse gegeben haben, denke ich. Oder sie hatte auf anderem Wege Wind davon bekommen und wollte einfach mal ihr Glück versuchen. Sie glauben nicht, was Schauspieler alles anstellen, um ins Geschäft zu kommen. Wir kriegen Tag für Tag Berge von Briefen und E-Mails von angehenden Oscargewinnern, die ganz kurz vor ihrem großen Durchbruch stehen ...«

Eine Karriere beim Film war vermutlich auch der Lebenstraum der jungen Vicky Hergarden gewesen. Dann wieder einmal die große Hoffnung auf eine Rolle beim Fernsehen und die – wer weiß wievielte – Enttäuschung. Womöglich war auch der erwartete Liebhaber nicht aufgetaucht, Frust, Wut, zu viel Sekt und ein tückischer kleiner Teppich auf spiegelglattem Parkett ...

Sönnchen schreckte mich aus meinen trübsinnigen Phantasien.

»Ich mach dann Schluss für heute«, erklärte sie. In ihren Augen blitzte die Vorfreude auf ein schönes Wochenende mit ihrer neuen Liebe.

»Haben Sie schon was von Hergarden gehört?«, fragte ich übellaunig.

»Bisher noch nicht. Aber das wird schon, Sie werden sehen.«

»Wissen Sie was?«, sagte ich kurz entschlossen. »Verteilen Sie unser schönes Phantombild doch einfach an sämtliche Reviere im Umkreis von ... sagen wir fünfzig Kilometern. Nicht festnehmen, nicht ansprechen, nur melden, falls er irgendwo gesehen wird.«

»Sie meinen, jetzt gleich? Ich wollt eigentlich ...«

»Zehn Minuten, Frau Walldorf, ich bitte Sie. So lange wird Ihr Christian noch ohne Sie zurechtkommen.«

Um fünf beschloss auch ich, es für heute gut sein zu lassen. Anstatt den Weg nach Hause einzuschlagen, wandte ich mich jedoch in Richtung Norden. Ich überquerte den Neckar in der Abenddämmerung, erreichte Neuenheim, fand nach kurzem Suchen die Gundolfstraße und nach wenigen Schritten auch schon die richtige Hausnummer. Es handelte sich um ein drei-geschossiges, gut instand gehaltenes Mehrfamilienhaus, in dem mindestens zwanzig Parteien lebten. Die Balkonverklei-dungen waren himmelblau gestrichen, der Eingang befand sich auf der Hinterseite, die Haustür war geschlossen. Hier hatte also vor dreißig Jahren das Ehepaar Hergarden gewohnt. Und vielleicht wohnte auch heute noch jemand von damals im Haus. Ich drückte aufs Geratewohl einen der untersten Klin-gelknöpfe, und Augenblicke später surrte freundlich der Tür-öffner. Innen musste ich einige Stufen hinaufsteigen und wurde am oberen Ende der kleinen Treppe von einem rüstigen älteren Herrn mit liebenswürdiger Miene und silbergrauem Haar erwartet.

Ich überreichte ihm mein Kärtchen. Irgendwo im Haus wurde mit Knoblauch und Frutti di Mare gekocht, und mir lief sofort das Wasser im Mund zusammen.

»Wir hatten noch nie mit der Polizei zu tun«, sagte der freundliche Mann, an dessen offen stehender, hellgrau la-ckierter Wohnungstür ein weißes Schildchen mit dem Namen Wischnewski pappte. »Dürfte ich das Kärtchen als Andenken behalten?«

Die Freude gönnte ich ihm. »Es geht um einen Todesfall, der sich in diesem Haus vor fast dreißig Jahren ereignet hat.«

Herr Wischnewski trug eine ordentlich gebügelte Anzug-hose, ein weißes Hemd, eine dunkelblaue Krawatte und ele-gante graue Pantoffeln aus weichem Leder. »Damals haben wir noch nicht hier gewohnt, sondern im Norden oben. In Großburgwedel, falls Ihnen das etwas sagt.«

Von einem Ort dieses Namens hatte ich noch nie gehört.

»Gibt es jemanden im Haus, der sich vielleicht noch er-innern könnte?«

»Fragen Sie Frau Tröndle im ersten OG«, sagte er mit plötz-lich gesenkter Stimme und bedeutungsvollem Blick zur Decke. »Aber sagen Sie ihr um Himmels willen nicht, dass ich Sie ge-schickt habe, sonst werden Sie womöglich der nächste Todes-fall in diesem Haus.«

»Direkt über Ihnen?«, fragte ich leise.

Er nickte lebhaft, schenkte mir noch einen mitfühlenden Blick und schloss leise die Tür. Ich stieg die sauber gefegte Treppe weiter hinauf und drückte den nächsten Klingelknopf. Die Tür sprang so schnell auf, als hätte die Bewohnerin dahinter gelauert.

»Schickt er Sie?«, fragte eine magere alte Dame mit finsterem Verschwörerblick. »Was hat er Ihnen erzählt? Dass ich seinen Hund vergiftet habe? Oder seine langweiligen Petunien? Sind Sie von der Polizei?«

Offenbar verfügte die Dame trotz ihres Alters über ein vorzügliches Gehör.

»Aber nein«, sagte ich mit dem strahlendsten Lächeln, das ich am Freitagabend zustandebrachte, und wiederholte mein Sprüchlein: »Es geht um einen Todesfall, der sich in diesem Haus vor fast dreißig Jahren ereignet hat.«

Sie trug eine seegrünfarbene Strickjacke mit Schalkragen zu einem scheußlich bunt geblümten Kleid. Und an den Füßen Wanderstiefel mit dicken Sohlen und grobem Profil.

»Das wundert mich nicht.«

»Sie haben damals schon hier gewohnt?«

»Ich wohne hier, seit das Haus steht.«

»Vielleicht wäre es besser, das drinnen zu besprechen?«, raunte ich mit Blick nach unten. Das Argument überzeugte sofort.

»Kommen Sie nur«, wisperte sie. »Er muss ja wirklich nicht alles mitkriegen.«

Zwei Minuten später saß ich in einem gut geheizten, etwas plüschig eingerichteten Wohnzimmer vor einer Tasse grünem Tee, der nach Heu schmeckte.

»Seit wann genau wohnen Sie hier?«, fragte ich Frau Tröndle.

»Schon immer, sagte ich doch schon. Zur Welt gekommen bin ich zwei Straßen weiter. 1948.« Offenbar war sie jünger, als sie aussah. »Wie wir hier eingezogen sind, war das Haus nagelneu und ich gerade mal acht Jahre alt. Und wenn der Herr im Erdgeschoss nicht irgendwas dreht, werde ich auch hier sterben. Aber wer weiß, was er als Nächstes ausheckt?

Vielleicht findet man mich morgen irgendwo im Straßengraben mit durchgeschnittener Kehle? Oder zerhackt im Keller verbuddelt?«

»So schlimm?«

»Der da unten ist kein Mensch, auch wenn er immer so freundlich tut. Der Ikarus ist der, der Pförtner der Unterwelt! Der Gott des Gemetzels!«

Nach meiner Erinnerung war Ikarus zwar eher das Gegenteil des Türstehers der Hölle gewesen, aber ich wollte nicht vom Thema abkommen.

»Erinnern Sie sich noch an das Ehepaar Hergarden?«

»Selbstverständlich.« Sie nickte heftig, betrachtete mich wohlwollend mit lebhaften kleinen Augen. »Sehr nette Leute. Aber hier wohnen eigentlich nur nette Leute. Außer *ihm* eben ... ein Schnäpschen vielleicht zum Tee?«

Ich lehnte dankend ab. Sie erhob sich schnaufend, holte aus einer Vitrine hinter der Tür ein Schnapsglas und eine große Flasche ohne Etikett, schenkte sich eine glasklare Flüssigkeit ein und leerte das Gläschen in einem Zug. Erst dann setzte sie sich wieder und sah mich neugierig an.

»Erinnern Sie sich noch an den Tag, als man Frau Hergarden tot in ihrer Wohnung gefunden hat?«

»Schreckliche Geschichte«, seufzte sie bewegt. »Eine so nette, ruhige Frau.«

Von unten erklang Klaviermusik. Gut gespielte Klaviermusik. Schubert, wenn ich nicht irrte.

»Hören Sie das?«, fragte Frau Tröndle mit vor Verzweiflung halb erstickter Stimme. »So geht das jeden Tag, den der Herrgott werden lässt! Pling-pling-pling. Je-den Tag! Er will mich in den Wahnsinn treiben mit seinem Geklimper. Und er wird es schaffen, ich weiß es. Soll ich Ihnen sagen, was ich jeden Tag an Tabletten ...?«

Nun verstand ich, wozu sie in der Wohnung Wanderstiefel trug. Sie versuchte nämlich, den begabten Pianisten durch kräftiges Trampeln aus dem Takt zu bringen. Das Klavier wurde lauter. Das Getrampel auch.

»Hatten Sie guten Kontakt mit Ihren damaligen Nachbarn?«, fragte ich mit lauter Stimme. »Wo genau haben sie denn gewohnt?«

Sie wies in Richtung Treppenhaus. »Gegenüber. Sehr nette Leute. Ich habe mit allen im Haus guten Kontakt. Ich habe mit niemandem Probleme. Mit niemandem. Außer mit ...«

»Damals muss auch eine Frau Holland im Haus gewohnt haben.«

»Warten Sie ... Holland, sagen Sie? Ja, natürlich! Das war so eine hübsche Blondine, nicht wahr? Sehr feine Frau. Immer hilfsbereit und immer für ein Schwätzchen zu haben. Damals hat man natürlich noch mehr Zeit gehabt. Damals musste noch nicht alles mit Düsenjägergeschwindigkeit gehen wie heute.«

Ich gab ihr seufzend recht.

»Noch ein Tässchen Tee?«

»Das wäre schön, danke.«

»Und immer noch kein Schnäpschen?«

»Wirklich nicht. Danke.«

Sie schenkte umsichtig nach. Füllte auch ihre Blümchen-tasse wieder auf. Stellte die schon etwas angestoßene Kanne im Meißener Stil auf das reich verschnörkelte Messingstöv-chen zurück. Schenkte sich auch ihr Schnapsglas noch einmal voll.

»Sie wissen nicht zufällig, was aus Frau Holland geworden ist?«

Die alte Dame nippte adrett an ihrem Tee und sah mir dabei immer wieder und vor Neugierde sprühend in die Augen. Und trampelte unentwegt weiter. »Wer?«

»Frau Holland. Die freundliche Blonde aus dem Erdge-schoss.«

»Im Erdgeschoss wohnt doch *er*!«

»Auf der anderen Seite? Die gegenüberliegende Wohnung.«

»Da wohnt seit Neuestem eine Frau Holland?«

Die Musik im Erdgeschoss brach ab. Frau Tröndle trat noch einige Male kräftig aufs Parkett, als hätte sie den Schluss-akkord zu geben, und Herr Wischnewski legte daraufhin mit einem schwungvollen und äußerst laut gespielten Boogie-

Woogie los. Nun kam meine Gastgeberin mit dem Trampeln nicht mehr nach. Über uns begann ein großer, offenbar unmusikalischer Hund zu bellen. Das Haus stammte aus der Nachkriegszeit und war nicht besonders gut isoliert.

Ich bemühte mich, noch lauter zu sprechen.

»Vor dreißig Jahren ...«

»Was war da? Damals habe ich nämlich schon hier gewohnt. Ich bin ja in dieser Wohnung praktisch auf die Welt gekommen, und wenn Ikarus nichts dagegen unternimmt ...«

Mir fiel auf, dass die alte Frau ständig auf die Uhr sah.

»Erwarten Sie Besuch?«, fragte ich.

»Meine Putzfrau«, erwiderte sie mit bedeutendem Blick. »Aber sie kommen ja immer zu spät, diese Putzfrauen. Sind heutzutage alles Russinnen. Oder Polinnen. Mein Sohn bezahlt sie, damit ich's ein bisschen leichter habe. Aber sie bestehlen einen. Lassen Sachen verschwinden. Manchmal bringen sie sie später zurück und verstecken sie irgendwo in der Wohnung, wo man sie nach Monaten wiederfindet. Die meisten kommen nach zwei, drei Wochen sowieso nicht mehr. Weil sie ein schlechtes Gewissen haben. Weil sie eine alte Frau bestehlen.«

»Hergarden?« Ich unternahm einen letzten Versuch. »An den Namen erinnern Sie sich aber noch?«

»Sie haben ihn doch vorhin selbst erwähnt.« Frau Tröndle sah mir forschend ins Gesicht. »Haben Sie Probleme mit dem Gedächtnis? Mein Schwager, bei dem hat es nämlich auch schon mit Mitte vierzig angefangen. Wie der sechzig war, hat er nicht mal mehr seine Frau erkannt. Was haben Sie gefragt?«

»Das Ehepaar Hergarden. Die Frau war Schauspielerin.«

»Die wohnen schon ewig nicht mehr hier. Nach Hirschberg sind die gezogen, Anfang der Neunziger schon. War auch gut so. Zwei schreckliche Kinder haben sie nämlich gehabt. Schrecklich ungezogene Kinder. Ein Haus haben sie sich gekauft. Irgendwo bei Hirschberg. War ihnen hier nicht mehr fein genug. Noch ein Tässchen Tee vielleicht?«

Ich lehnte dankend ab und erhob mich. Im Erdgeschoss spielte man jetzt Bach. Die Goldberg-Variationen. Frau

Tröndle trampelte mit beiden Füßen, dass das Geschirr im Schrank klapperte und klirrte. Oben bellte wieder der Hund.

Das Parkett in Frau Tröndles Wohnung hatte anders ausgesehen als das auf meinen Fotos, wurde mir bewusst, als ich die Treppe hinabstieg. Neuer. Vermutlich war es irgendwann ausgetauscht worden.

Der Abend mit Theresa verlief freudlos. Sie war wortkarg und gedrückter Stimmung – was bei ihr hin und wieder vorkam und wofür es keinen besonderen Grund brauchte. Dieses Mal hatten wir uns wieder in unserem Liebesnest in der Ladenburgerstraße verabredet. Eine kleine Zweizimmerwohnung, die wir eigens zu dem Zweck angemietet hatten, einen Ort zu haben, wo wir zusammen sein konnten. Den Lichtblick dieses Abends bildete der Saxophonist in der Wohnung über unserer. Viele Monate war er verschwunden gewesen, und plötzlich war er wieder da. Improvisierte auf seinem Instrument, als spiele er nur für uns. Auch er schien traurig zu sein.

Theresas schlechte Laune führte ich auf den ausbleibenden Verkaufserfolg ihres neuen Buchs zurück. Fragen dazu beantwortete sie ausweichend. Nicht einmal beim heute etwas mühsamen Sex wollte die übliche Begeisterung aufkommen.

»Das wird schon noch«, versuchte ich sie zu aufzumuntern, nachdem wir uns geliebt hatten. Ich hatte mich ein wenig gebremst, damit mein Kreislauf nicht zu sehr in Schwung geriet. Immer noch lauerten irgendwo ganz weit hinten in meinem Kopf die verfluchten Schmerzen.

»Meinst du?«, fragte Theresa und sog lustlos an ihrer Zigarette.

»Das Buch ist gerade mal zwei Monate auf dem Markt.«

»Es hat bisher nicht eine Besprechung gegeben! Und dann dieses Wetter! Die Kälte, die ewige Dunkelheit. Da muss man ja depressiv werden.«

Der Saxophonist versuchte sich an einem heiteren Thema, brach jedoch bald wieder ab.

Seufzend schmiegte Theresa sich an mich. Ich streichelte sie still und hatte eine – wie ich fand – geradezu geniale Idee.

»Theresa, du musst ans Licht. Du bist eindeutig ein Fall von Winterdepression. Morgen ist Samstag, die Sonne soll ein bisschen scheinen. Hast du schon was vor?«

Fragend sah sie mich von der Seite an. »Warum?«

Ich kratzte sie hie und da ein wenig am Rücken. Das liebte sie und brachte sie normalerweise zuverlässig zum Schnurren. Heute schnurrte sie nicht. Heute seufzte sie nur. Sah ihrer Zigarette beim Qualmen zu.

»Hättest du Lust auf einen kleinen Landausflug?«

»Ein Ausflug?«, fragte sie müde zurück. »Wohin denn?«

»Nach Bad Wimpfen zum Beispiel?«

Plötzlich entschlossen drückte sie ihren erst halb gerauchten Glimmstängel aus. »Warum nicht.« Nicht einmal die Zigaretten schienen ihr heute zu schmecken.

»Du kommst auf andere Gedanken. Denkst nicht ständig an dein Buch. Erinnerst du dich überhaupt noch an das Hotel in … wie hat der Ort geheißen? War nur zwei, drei Kilometer von Bad Wimpfen entfernt.«

»Heinsheim.« Nun lächelte sie doch ein wenig in trauriger Erinnerung an unseren allerersten Ausflug mit Übernachtung im Luxushotel und grandiosem Sex in der Nacht und dem ersten richtigen Krach unserer damals noch taufrischen Beziehung.

»Was hältst du davon, wenn wir dort zu Mittag essen? Ein bisschen alte Erinnerungen auffrischen?«

»Mal sehen«, sagte sie, erhob sich und stolzierte splitternackt in Richtung Bad. Theresa war nicht schlank, aber ich fand sie gerade deshalb schön. Die großen, sanften Brüste, die kräftigen, geraden Beine, die stolze Haltung. Die honigblonden Locken wippten im Rhythmus ihrer entschlossenen Schritte. Mir wurde bewusst, dass man sogar den eleganten Schwung eines Rückgrats lieben kann.

11

»Du bist sicher, dass du fahren kannst?«, fragte Theresa am Samstagvormittag. Wir waren in meinem unverwüstlichen Peugeot unterwegs auf der Bundesstraße in Richtung Osten. Wie vom Wetterbericht versprochen, hatte es über Nacht aufgeklart. Vielleicht würden wir im Lauf des Tages sogar für längere Zeit die Sonne sehen. Um halb zehn waren wir aufgebrochen. Soeben kamen die ersten Häuser Eberbachs in Sicht. Die Straße schwenkte in Richtung Süden.

»Mir geht's wirklich prima, Theresa. Und du bist nur zum Vergnügen dabei und damit du dein schönes Gesicht in die Sonne hältst.«

»Was genau treibt dich eigentlich nach Bad Wimpfen?«, fragte sie, ohne auf meine Schmeichelei einzugehen.

»Vor allem natürlich wunderschöne Erinnerungen ...«

Sie zog eine Miene, als hätte sie Zahnschmerzen. »Wir waren doch damals gar nicht dort.«

Weil sie nicht die richtigen Schuhe dabeigehabt hatte und wir deshalb unseren kleinen Spaziergang von Heinsheim nach Bad Wimpfen schon vor der Hälfte abbrechen mussten. Unsere Unternehmung war schließlich mit giftigen Worten, stürmischem Türenknallen und eisigem Schweigen geendet.

»Aber immerhin fast.« Ich streichelte ihr linkes Knie, das heute in einer dunkelgrauen Armani-Jeans steckte.

»Und zweitens?«, fragte sie ungerührt.

»Okay, ich will dort kurz mit jemandem reden.«

»Arbeitest du eigentlich immer, oder hast du ab und an auch mal frei?«

Dieser Tag begann nicht gut.

Theresa starrte ab sofort auf die Straße, die in vielen Kurven den gemächlichen Windungen des Neckars folgte. Die Sonne zog es in Anbetracht von Theresas Laune vor, sich wieder zu verkrümeln. Das mächtige Schloss Zwingenberg kam in Sicht, an dem vor Zeiten vermutlich nicht viele Lastkähne ungeplündert vorbeigekommen waren. Meine Göttin interessierte sich heute – obwohl studierte Historikerin – nicht für Geschichte. Bald darauf die Burg Hornberg, wo das Raubein Götz von Berlichingen einst gelebt hatte. Meine Liebste interessierte sich nicht für alte Ritter mit ungehobelten Manieren.

Ich warf hin und wieder einen Blick in den Rückspiegel. Was meiner kratzbürstigen Liebsten nicht lange verborgen blieb, obwohl sie mich hartnäckig keines Blickes würdigte.

»Weshalb siehst du dauernd in den Spiegel?«

»Nur so. Eine dumme Angewohnheit.«

»Wird dein Gespräch im Bad Wimpfen lange dauern?«

»Höchstens eine Viertelstunde. Und anschließend haben wir den ganzen Tag für uns. Jetzt freu dich doch einfach mal!«

»Die Sonne scheint überhaupt nicht.«

»Das ändert sich bald, du wirst sehen.«

»Heute morgen hat der Wetterbericht für den Nachmittag Regen angekündigt.«

»An Wetterberichte glaube ich nur, wenn sie gut sind.«

Auch mein erneuter Vorschlag, im ehrwürdigen Schlosshotel Heinsheim zu Mittag zu speisen, fand keine Gnade.

»Dann essen wir eben woanders, kein Problem. Hast du Lust auf Italiener?«

»Was ist das eigentlich für ein Ding?« Sie wies auf das kleine schwarze Kästchen, das auf dem Armaturenbrett lag und an dem ein knapp zehn Zentimeter langes Drähtchen baumelte.

»Eine Art Sender. Erkläre ich dir später.«

»Du bist heute wirklich merkwürdig, Alexander. Willst du nicht vielleicht doch mal zu einem guten Neurologen gehen? Nicht, dass ich dich für verrückt halten würde, aber ...«

Nun war ich es, der plötzlich schlechte Laune hatte. »Ich finde, ich benehme mich ganz normal, und auf gar keinen Fall brauche ich einen Neurologen.«

»Du bist ... so angespannt.«

»Dasselbe könnte ich von dir sagen.«

Bisher hatte ich keinen Wagen entdecken können, der mit konstantem Abstand hinter uns herfuhr. Aber es war natürlich möglich, dass sie mehrere Fahrzeuge benutzten und sich abwechselten. Außerdem konnten sie uns durch den Peilsender auf weiten Strecken bequem ohne Sichtverbindung folgen.

»Und wieso liegt eine Keksdose auf dem Rücksitz?« Theresa griff nach hinten und schüttelte die hübsch bedruckte Dose misstrauisch, die früher einmal schwedische Haferkekse enthalten hatte. »Die ist ja leer!«

»Wir werden sie später noch brauchen. Und jetzt entspann dich einfach und genieße die Aussicht.« Mein letzter Satz hatte alles andere als freundlich geklungen, wurde mir bewusst, als es zu spät war.

Die Sonne wagte nun doch einen neuen Anlauf, und die blauen Flecke am Himmel wurden von Minute zu Minute größer. Im Radio sang Nancy Sinatra »Summer Wine«.

»Ich habe meine Sonnenbrille vergessen«, stellte Theresa fest.

Ein Traktor mit einem Anhänger voller Mist behinderte eine Weile den Verkehr. Theresa rümpfte die hübsche Nase und fand, er stinke. Sobald es ohne Lebensgefahr möglich war, überholte ich. Bei Gundelsheim überquerten wir den Neckar, durchfuhren schweigend Heinsheim. Theresa ignorierte eisern die Wegweiser zum Schlosshotel.

Bald tauchten die spitzen Türme der stolzen Kaiserpfalz Bad Wimpfen über dem Horizont auf. Die Straße auf dieser Seite des Flusses war schmal und wand sich auf den letzten Metern vor unserem Ziel in engen Serpentinen den Berg hinauf. Dann endlich das Ortsschild, und zehn Minuten später stellte ich vor dem Haus, in dem Stephan Weilandt und sein Lebensgefährte wohnten, den Motor ab. Haus und Garten machten nicht den Eindruck, als legten die Bewohner Wert auf Äußerlichkeiten. Neben einem verdorrten Rosenbusch lag ein Gartenzwerg auf dem Bauch, aus dessen Rücken ein Messergriff ragte.

Theresa hatte ich am Eingang der Fußgängerzone abgesetzt mit dem Versprechen, mich in spätestens zwanzig Minuten zu melden.

Ich drückte den Klingelknopf, neben dem keine Namen standen. Sekunden später wurde die taubenblau lackierte Holztür geöffnet. Jörg Marquard war ein sportlicher, schlanker Mann in den Fünfzigern mit markantem Kinn und militärisch kurz geschnittenem Haar. Er betrachtete mich mit schmalen Augen und mahlendem Kiefer.

»Wir haben telefoniert«, sagte ich.

»Wegen Stephan, ich weiß.«

Er tat einen resignierten Atemzug und blickte mich an wie einen lästigen Staubsaugervertreter, der nicht einsehen will, dass er hier kein Geschäft machen wird. »Treten Sie doch ein.«

Offensichtlich ärgerte er sich, mich überhaupt eingeladen zu haben. Mein erster Eindruck war Enge. Das Haus war entschieden übermöbliert. Außerdem investierte hier jemand enorm viel Zeit und Liebe darauf, unkonventionelle Gemütlichkeit zu schaffen. In jeder Ecke standen und lagen teils kostbare, teils ganz wertlose Dinge herum. Strohblumensträuße neben kunstvoll gearbeiteten expressiven Plastiken. Ein irgendwo gefundener, merkwürdig geformter Ast neben Teddybärchen, die zu Füßen uralter und dick vergoldeter Kerzenständer hockten und ein Schwätzchen zu halten schienen. An den Wänden überall Bilder neben, unter und über anderen Bildern. Auch hier eine verwegene, aber keineswegs geschmacklose Mischung. Nichts passte wirklich zusammen, und genau das schien das Konzept zu sein. Ich fühlte mich in der ersten Sekunde wohl und geborgen.

»Kaffee?«, fragte Marquard in einem Ton, der keinen Zweifel daran ließ, dass er lediglich die Anstandsregeln eines kultivierten Gastgebers befolgte.

»Gerne. Danke.«

Solange ich seinen Kaffee trank, würde er mich nicht vor die Tür setzen. Während der Hausherr in der Küche hantierte, betrachtete ich einige der Gemälde an der Wand. Auf den meisten waren Landschaften dargestellt. Karge Landschaften. Wüsten, Steppen, Flussniederungen mit tiefem Horizont. Erst nach einer Weile entdeckte ich die immer wieder gleiche schwungvolle Signatur: »SteWe«. Stephan Weilandt.

Marquard erschien mit zwei großen, dampfenden Tassen. Der Kaffee duftete ungewöhnlich gut. Wir nahmen Platz auf zwei geschnitzten Stühlen, die aussahen wie aus einem Kloster entwendet.

»Nun?«, sagte er und sah mir offen, wenn auch nicht freundlich ins Gesicht.

Ich erzählte ihm von Fred und Viktoria Hergarden. »Ihr Partner war zum Zeitpunkt ihres Todes zusammen mit dem Ehemann in Bagdad.«

»Damals waren wir noch nicht zusammen. Aber ich weiß natürlich, dass Steph früher viel unterwegs war. Er hat die halbe Welt gesehen und allerhand Abenteuer überlebt. Ich habe die Jahreszahlen nicht im Kopf. Aber Bagdad, das sagt mir etwas, ja.«

»Seit Neuestem besteht nun der Verdacht, dass der Ehemann der Mörder der Frau sein könnte. Und deshalb würde ich gerne mit Herrn Weilandt reden.«

Marquard sah mir stumm ins Gesicht, als wartete er auf die Fortsetzung.

»Ich habe Sie gestern so verstanden, dass Ihr Lebensgefährte in der Vergangenheit ein wenig Ärger mit der Polizei gehabt hat ...«

»Ein *wenig* Ärger?« Seine Miene wurde noch eine Spur distanzierter. »Es war die totale Katastrophe. Stephan – er ist ...« Marquard schluckte und senkte den Blick. »Steph ist drogenabhängig. Kokain. Hat er sich im fernen Osten angewöhnt. Inzwischen ist er aber clean. So gut wie clean. Deshalb ist er auch nicht hier. Er macht zurzeit eine Therapie. Nicht die erste, leider. Und dieser Unfall ... Er war auf der Landstraße nach Neudenau unterwegs. Muss am Steuer eingeschlafen sein. Es gab zwei Tote. Und er hatte schon damals keinen Führerschein mehr.«

»Wo macht er die Therapie?«

»Nicht weit von hier. In Münzesheim, im Kraichgau.«

Ich bat ihn, dort anzurufen, weil ich keine Lust hatte, begleitet von einer schlecht gelaunten Theresa sinnlos durch die Gegend zu kutschieren.

Mein Gastgeber zögerte, erhob sich schließlich, um sein Handy zu holen. Das Handy war weiß, und die Rückseite zierte ein angebissenes Äpfelchen. Das Telefonat dauerte nur wenige Sekunden.

»Er wird mit Ihnen reden«, sagte er, als er sein iPhone achtlos auf den Tisch warf. »Heute Nachmittag, vierzehn Uhr. Im Moment haben sie irgendeine Maßnahme. Sie malen Aquarelle. Und um zwölf gibt es Essen.«

»Er malt sehr gut, habe ich gesehen.«

Jörg Marquard sah mich mit bitterer Miene an. In seinem Gesicht zuckten Muskeln. Schließlich traten Tränen in seine Augen. Ich trank meinen Kaffee aus, erhob mich, er nach kurzem Zögern ebenfalls. An der Haustür schüttelten wir stumm und fest Hände. In der Ferne schlug eine Kirchturmuhr zwei Mal. Halb zwölf. Immer noch schien die Sonne.

»Du bist sicher, dass es hier nach Münzesheim geht?« Theresa hatte entdeckt, dass ihr Hightechhandy, das sie erst seit wenigen Wochen besaß, auch als Navi zu gebrauchen war. Nun war sie irritiert, weil ich kurz vor dem Ortsende von Kirchhardt rechts abbog. »Mein Telefon möchte geradeaus in Richtung Eppingen.«

»Dein Telefon kann gerne über Eppingen fahren«, erwiderte ich gereizt. »Ich persönlich fahre lieber über kleine Straßen, weil ich das schöner finde. Und nach Münzesheim finde ich immer noch ohne Computer.«

In Bad Wimpfen hatten wir einen eiligen Spaziergang im Nieselregen gemacht, den blauen Turm umrundet, den Ruinen der Stauferpfalz einen Blitzbesuch abgestattet und anschließend bei einem Italiener, den zum Glück die übellaunige Blonde an meiner Seite ausgewählt hatte, klebrige Nudeln gegessen. Dabei hatte ich entdeckt, dass Theresa nicht nur gut Französisch und Englisch sprach, sondern auch noch so viel Italienisch, um mit dem sizilianischen Koch einen lautstarken und sehr authentisch klingenden Streit über die richtige Zubereitung von Spaghetti arrabiata vom Zaun zu brechen.

Die Sonne hatte für diesen Tag endgültig den Dienst quittiert, und der Regen schien sich auf Dauer eingerichtet zu haben.

Die nächsten Kilometer spielten wir das in Paarbeziehungen so beliebte Spiel »Wer als Erster den Mund aufmacht, hat verloren«, gondelten schmale und kurvige Landstraßen entlang, durchquerten Dörfer, deren Namen ich noch nie gehört hatte, und ich behielt den Rückspiegel im Auge. Die Nebenstrecken hatte ich nicht gewählt, weil ich sie schöner fand, sondern um eventuelle Verfolger zu irritieren und aus der Reserve zu locken.

Hin und wieder meinte ich, einen Wagen zu entdecken, den ich am Vormittag schon einmal gesehen hatte. Aber nie war ich mir wirklich sicher, und immer war er zu weit entfernt, als dass ich wenigstens den Typ hätte bestimmen können. Als wir Odenheim erreichten, öffnete Theresa endlich den verkniffenen Mund und erklärte frostig, sie müsse mal. Klein. Und zwar sofort.

»Wir sind in zehn Minuten da.«

»In zehn Minuten ist es zu spät.«

Vermutlich verspürte sie ihr dringendes Bedürfnis schon seit geraumer Zeit, war jedoch zu stolz gewesen, es zuzugeben.

»Hast du gewusst, dass hier ganz in der Nähe Hagen von Tronje den tapferen Helden Siegfried gemeuchelt hat? Im Nibelungenlied heißt das Dorf zwar Odenhain und liegt im Odenwald ...«

»Dein tapferer Held ist mir schnurz, und außerdem werde ich in Kürze deine Polster durchnässen. Aber es ist schließlich dein Wagen ...«

»Ich halte, sobald ich kann.«

Mitten im Ort bog ich links ab, und bei der nächsten sich bietenden Gelegenheit, als keine Häuser mehr in Sicht waren, fuhr ich an den Straßenrand und zog die Handbremse. Theresa verschwand hinter einem vor Nässe tropfenden Busch. Als sie Sekunden später wieder auftauchte, war ihr Blazer feucht, die Frisur hinüber und ihre Laune am absoluten Nullpunkt.

»So, jetzt kommt die geheimnisvolle Dose zum Einsatz«, erklärte ich betont heiter. Ihr Schnauben klang ungefähr so freundlich wie das von Siegfrieds Lindwurm. Aber immerhin,

sie griff nach hinten, angelte die Keksdose vom Rücksitz, überreichte sie mir, ohne den Blick von der kurvigen Straße zu wenden. Ich nahm im Fahren den Deckel ab, warf den Peilsender
hinein, drückte den Deckel wieder auf, legte Theresa die Dose
in den Schoß.

»Mit deinem neuen Superhandy kannst du doch bestimmt
auch Filme drehen.«

»Selbstverständlich. Wenn ich wüsste, wie.«

»Würdest du es mir kurz ausleihen?«

»Was willst du denn filmen in dieser trostlosen Einöde?«

Inzwischen fuhren wir wieder durch Wald. Ein Wanderparkplatz kam in Sicht, ich bremste, setzte zurück, sodass der
Wagen halb unter Bäumen stand und von der Straße aus nicht
gleich zu sehen war, stellte den Motor ab.

»Das Ding in der Dose ist ein Peilsender, den mir jemand
ans Auto geklebt hat«, erklärte ich, während ich mich hastig
durch die Menüs des Handys tippte.

»Heißt das, wir werden …?«

»Wir werden möglicherweise verfolgt, ja.«

Sie starrte mich für zwei Sekunden sprachlos an, dann half
sie mir eilig, den Videomodus zu finden und zu aktivieren. Ich
hielt das Handy so, dass die Linse knapp über das Lenkrad
hinwegsah.

»Und was wird das nun?«, wollte Theresa hörbar unent-
spannt wissen.

»Erkläre ich dir gleich.«

Und dann warteten wir.

Eine Krähe tapste auf der Straße herum und suchte nach
Essbarem. Schwere Regentropfen zerplatzten auf der Motor-
haube meines Wagens. Schwaden von Nässe trieben über
die Wiesen. Ein Wetter, um den Gashahn aufzudrehen. Nach
einer kleinen Ewigkeit und einigen theatralischen Seufzern
vom Beifahrersitz tauchte aus Richtung Odenheim ein weißer
Lieferwagen auf, der merkwürdige Klappergeräusche machte
und eine bläuliche Wolke hinter sich her zog. Ihm folgte ein
feuerrotes Mercedes Cabrio, dessen Fahrer keine Eile zu haben schien. Und dahinter ein dunkler Volvo Kombi, der das

klapperndes Verkehrshindernis offensichtlich unbedingt über-
holen wollte, jedoch wegen der vielen Kurven und gelegentlichen Gegenverkehrs nicht konnte. Dann kam lange nichts
mehr.

»Und?«, fragte Theresa, als ich ihr das Handy zurückgab
und den Motor wieder anließ. »Zufrieden?«

»Ich weiß noch nicht.«

»Mir ist kalt, Alexander. Meine Haare sind nass. Mein Blazer ist nass. Meine Schuhe sind nass. Ich werde mir den Tod
holen, wenn ich nicht sofort einen starken Kaffee kriege!«

»Kannst du mir das Video per Mail schicken, wenn wir wieder in Heidelberg sind?«

»Nein.«

»Warum nicht?«

»Weil ich nicht weiß, wie man es aus dem dämlichen Ding
herausbekommt, darum. Und weil du mir allmählich tierisch
auf den Geist gehst mit deiner Geheimniskrämerei. Wer verfolgt uns denn nun? Der weiße Lieferwagen oder der rote
Mercedes?«

»In fünf Minuten sind wir am Ziel, und dann kriegst du
deinen Kaffee, und später, auf der Rückfahrt, werde ich dir
alles haarklein erklären, versprochen.«

»Ich bin gespannt wie ein Regenwurm.«

»Diesen dämlichen Spruch habe ich seit mindestens einem
Vierteljahrhundert nicht mehr gehört.«

Sie gab sich redlich Mühe, aber es gelang ihr doch nicht
ganz, ein Lächeln zu unterdrücken.

12

»Der Fred, ach ja, der war schon 'ne Marke«, sagte Stephan
Weilandt.

Wir spazierten durch den asiatischen Garten des Münzes-
heimer Therapiezentrums, der heute nur spärlich besucht war.
Auf den letzten Kilometern hatte der Regen überraschend auf-

gehört. Die feuchten Wolken über uns hatten es plötzlich eilig, sich zu verziehen, und hie und da blinzelte schon wieder ein wenig trübe Sonne durch die Ritzen des steingrauen Himmels. Theresa hatte sich sofort in die Cafeteria der weitläufigen Anlage zurückgezogen und sich einen doppelten Cognac sowie einen dreifachen Espresso bestellt. Cognac hatte man allerdings nicht im Angebot.

Der Mann, den ich so dringend hatte sprechen wollen, war untersetzt, beäugte die Welt mit treuherzigem Hundeblick und trug einen beeindruckenden Kugelbauch vor sich her. Erst nachdem wir einige Sätze gewechselt hatten, wurde mir klar, dass der alte Journalist keineswegs so harmlos und gemütlich war, wie er bei flüchtigem Hinsehen wirkte.

»Fred war für die ARD in Bagdad. Ich war solo und habe nach Storys Ausschau gehalten, die sich zu Geld machen ließen. Fred und seine Leute wollten immer an die Front. Ich war mehr auf Hintergrundgeschichten aus, für die leichte Presse. Hübsche Mädchen, die kleine Kätzchen retten, schöne Mütter, die ihre gefallenen Söhne beweinen, solches Zeugs. Das andere war mir viel zu gefährlich. Ich war nie ein Held und wollte auch keiner werden. Heldenmut ist in meinen Augen nichts weiter als eine besonders dumme Form von Phantasielosigkeit.«

»Hergarden hat das Risiko nicht gescheut?«

»Im Gegenteil. Der wollte die harten Geschichten. Am liebsten pfeifende Kugeln im O-Ton. Er war auch der Einzige, der fast immer mit einer Waffe am Gürtel herumgelaufen ist. Sie waren immer mal wieder für ein paar Tage weg und haben irgendwo gedreht, und dann haben sie wieder wochenlang in diesem verfluchten Hotel Palestine gehockt und gewartet, dass irgendwo irgendwas passiert. Abends haben wir gesoffen und manchmal gepokert und wieder gesoffen und …«

»Hin und wieder bestimmt auch geredet.«

»Das auch, natürlich. Aber ich wollte etwas anderes sagen. Wir waren Männer. Wir waren solo, Sie verstehen, was ich meine. Die schärfsten Huren finden Sie ja komischerweise in den muslimischen Städten.«

»Ich dachte, Sie sind …«

Er kicherte albern. »Ich kann schon auch mit Mädchen was anfangen, keine Sorge. Denen da unten steckt *Tausendundeine Nacht* immer noch im Blut. Und in der Bar vom Palestine – ich will's mal so ausdrücken: Das islamische Verhüllungsgebot für Frauen hat da definitiv nicht gegolten. Da war so eine Rothaarige. Ich kann Ihnen sagen ...«

»Hergarden war verheiratet.«

»Und hat seine Frau ... wie hat sie noch geheißen?«

»Viktoria.«

»Vicky, richtig. Alle vier Wochen hat er sie für zwei, drei Tage gesehen. Aber sagen Sie erst mal: Weshalb fragen Sie mich überhaupt nach diesen uralten Sachen?«

Wieder einmal erzählte ich meine Geschichte.

»Vicky ...?« Weilandt sah mich in einer Mischung aus Amüsement und ungläubigem Schrecken an. »Umgebracht? Fred?«

»Sie glauben es nicht?«

Er wandte den Blick ab. Schnaufte. Einige Schritte gingen wir schweigend. Eine geschwungene, knallrot lackierte Holzbrücke kam in Sicht. Rechts ein Pavillon in einem kleinen See, der aus Japan importiert zu sein schien.

»Wer weiß schon, wozu Menschen fähig sind?«, sagte der alte Journalist schließlich wie zu sich selbst. »Fred ist schon ein verrückter Hund gewesen. Ein Abenteurer. Und er konnte ganz schön zornig werden, wenn etwas nicht nach seinem Kopf ging.«

Das konnte ich bestätigen.

»Hergarden soll damals Anfang November in der Nähe von Basra unterwegs gewesen sein.«

»Das mag schon sein.«

Ein altes, weißhaariges Ehepaar kam uns eng umschlungen entgegen. Die Frau war kräftig und schien ihren ausgemergelten Mann stützen zu müssen. Sie sprach leise und tröstend auf ihn ein. Er nickte hin und wieder mit abwesender Miene und leerem Blick.

»Sie erinnern sich nicht?«

»Ich sagte doch, die waren immer wieder mal an der Front

unterwegs. Irgendwo, wo's kracht und brennt und man aufregendes Material schießen kann. Material, das die Leute in den Nachrichten sehen wollen.«

»Hergarden war damals für mehrere Tage verschwunden, während der Rest des Teams schon wieder in Bagdad war.«

»Ach, diese Geschichte. Jetzt entsinne ich mich, ja.«

»Abends an der Bar hat er doch bestimmt davon erzählt.«

»Vicky«, murmelte Weilandt mit schmalen Augen und blieb stehen, den Blick in die Ferne gerichtet. »Von der hat er mir ständig was vorgeschwärmt. Was für eine Wahnsinnsfrau sie war. Was für ein Feger im Bett. Manchmal war es nicht zum Aushalten.«

»Hat er sie geliebt?«

»Wie verrückt. Manchmal dachte ich, zu sehr. Abstand hält ja bekanntlich die Liebe jung.«

»Können Sie sich daran erinnern, wie er damals wieder aufgetaucht ist?«

Weilandt nickte zögernd. »Ich bin mir nicht sicher ...«

»Vermutlich hat er noch am selben Tag erfahren, dass seine Frau tot ist.«

Wieder nickte er bedächtig. »Am Abend hat er auf einmal wieder an der Bar gesessen. Dabei hatten wir alle schon gedacht, den hat's erwischt. Den sehen wir nicht wieder.«

»Wirkte er verändert?«

»Was denken Sie denn? Er war gerade erst dem Sensenmann von der Schippe gesprungen. Seine Frau war tot. Er hat es erst seit ein paar Minuten gewusst, als ich mich neben ihn gesetzt habe. Einen Whisky nach dem anderen hat er gekippt. Ganz blass ist er gewesen. Ganz blass.«

»Die Geschichte hat ihm zugesetzt?«

»Zugesetzt?« Weilandt lachte bitter. »Sie sind gut. Für Fred war die Welt explodiert. Stellen Sie sich das doch mal vor: Da ist man eben noch haarscharf mit dem Leben davongekommen, und das Erste, was man hören muss ...«

»Wie würden Sie seine Reaktion nennen? Traurig? Wütend? Erschrocken?«

»Erschrocken? Natürlich. Traurig auch, ja. Wütend in dem

Fall eher nicht. Verstört. Völlig verstört war er. Man hat überhaupt kein vernünftiges Wort mit ihm reden können. Erst wollte er nicht, und bald war er so besoffen, dass er nicht mehr denken konnte. Jeder Mensch reagiert anders auf eine solche Nachricht. Freddy – ich denke, vielleicht war er doch wütend. Tief drin. Muss er ja. Erst wollte er es gar nicht glauben. Dachte, die anderen wollten ihn verkohlen. Die haben manchmal derbe Späße gemacht. Dann wollte er unbedingt wissen, was genau passiert war. Hat immer wieder versucht, in Deutschland anzurufen. Aber die Iraner hatten gerade mal wieder ein Bömbchen auf irgendeine Vermittlungszentrale geschmissen. Oder war's ein Sprengstoffanschlag? Jedenfalls hat er keine Verbindung gekriegt und ist schier wahnsinnig geworden vor Aufregung und Verzweiflung. Ich hatte keine Ahnung, was passiert war. Niemand hatte eine Ahnung. Die einzige halbwegs verlässliche Information war: Die Frau ist tot. Am nächsten Tag wollte Fred so schnell wie möglich heim, wegen der Beerdigung und allem. War aber nicht so leicht. In ganz Bagdad hat kein Telefon funktioniert. Erst am übernächsten Tag hat er dann endlich einen Flug nach Damaskus erwischt. Und dann war er wieder mal für eine Woche weg.«

Das alte Paar kam uns zum zweiten Mal entgegen. Dieses Mal schwieg die Frau, und der Mann sprach murmelnd. Ob zu sich selbst oder zu seiner Begleiterin, war nicht zu erkennen.

»Und Sie glauben also nicht, dass er selbst seiner Frau etwas angetan haben könnte?«

Weilandt sah mich verständnislos an. »Wie hätte das zugehen sollen?«

»Er war mehrere Tage verschwunden. Er hätte von Kuwait aus nach Frankfurt fliegen können …«

»Aber das ist doch kompletter Unfug!«

»Was macht Sie so sicher?«

»Weil ich zwei Tage später – da war Fred schon in Deutschland – mit einem Franzosen gesprochen habe, der mit demselben Transport aus Basra gekommen war wie er. Und der hat Freds Geschichte bestätigt. Den Franzosen hatten die Irakis sogar vier Wochen lang festgehalten, bis er es geschafft hat, das Lösegeld aufzutreiben. Und außerdem ... «

»Außerdem?«, fragte ich, als der Journalist nicht weitersprach.

»Es war ... Ich muss nachdenken. Genau: Wie Fred wieder zurück war aus Deutschland, nach der Beerdigung, da hat er behauptet, jemand hätte sie umgebracht, seine Vicky. Ich will sagen ... «

Wieder blieb er stehen.

»Hat er einen Namen genannt?«

»Ich meine, ja. Aber den weiß ich nun wirklich nicht mehr. Was ich aber weiß: Fred war bei der Polizei gewesen, in Heidelberg, und hat den Mann ganz offiziell angezeigt, den angeblichen Mörder. Und er war immer noch fuchsteufelswild, weil die den Kerl nicht gleich verhaften wollten.«

»Bei der Polizei war er? Dann müsste es doch ...«

Dann müsste es ein Protokoll geben. Eine Gesprächsnotiz wenigstens. Irgendetwas. Aber es gab nichts. Zumindest in der Akte Viktoria Hergarden war diese Anzeige definitiv nicht gewesen. Ich hatte sie oft genug durchgeblättert.

»Er war irgendwas beim Fernsehen«, fiel Weilandt ein, als wir unseren Spaziergang fortsetzten.

»Wer?«

»Der Kerl, der angeblich Freds Frau auf dem Gewissen hat. Fred war übrigens überzeugt, dass der seine kleine Vicky gepimpert hat. Sie hatten wohl auch einen mörderischen Krach deswegen gehabt, als Fred sie das letzte Mal gesehen hat. Damals hat sie ihm angeblich hoch und heilig versprochen, dass sie Schluss macht mit dem anderen. Zwei, maximal drei Wochen vor ihrem Tod war das. Der Streit, meine ich. Der Streit und das Versprechen.«

»Fahr da vorne mal rechts ran«, sagte Theresa, als wir wieder in Richtung Heimat unterwegs waren. »Bitte.«

Ich ging vom Gas, fuhr auf den kleinen Parkplatz, den sie erspäht hatte. Zog die Handbremse. Sah ihr ins Gesicht.

»Was ist?«

»Das wollte ich dich fragen.«

»Du hast schlechte Laune. Seit Tagen schon. Weil dein Buch sich nicht verkauft.«

Sie schüttelte den Kopf mit den honigblonden, inzwischen wieder getrockneten Locken. »Alexander. Lass bitte den Unsinn.«

»Unsinn?«

»Ja, ich bin nicht gerade glücklich mit den Verkaufszahlen. Ja, es nervt mich, dass keiner dieses verflixte Buch lesen will. Aber wenn hier jemand für schlechte Stimmung sorgt, dann bist du es.«

»Ich? Ich bin vollkommen entspannt. Geht es um die Aktion mit der Keksdose? Ich kann dir alles erklären, es ...«

»Es geht um eine SMS, die du mir gestern Nachmittag geschrieben hast. Du wirst am Wochenende mit irgendwem reden ...«

Ach herrje! Und vermutlich hatte ich an Doro geschrieben, wie sehr ich mich auf den Abend freute ...

Theresa hatte sich schon einiges zusammengereimt. »Ich nehme an, es hat mit einer gewissen Doro zu tun. Du bist seit Wochen manchmal so merkwürdig abwesend. Ständig geht dir etwas im Kopf herum, worüber du nicht reden willst. Du wirst nervös, wenn sie anruft. Bitte, was läuft da, Alexander? Sag ehrlich: Muss ich mir Sorgen machen?«

»Wir beide müssten mal reden«, hatte in Doros SMS gestanden, die sie mir Anfang Januar schickte. In den Tagen und Wochen davor hatte ich mir das Hirn zermartert, ob ich vielleicht der Vater ihres Sohnes Henning war. Neun Monate vor seiner Geburt hatte ich eine einzige Nacht mit ihr verbracht. In einem Hotelzimmer, bei diesem verflixten Klassentreffen. Das Ganze hatte ich längst vergessen oder gut verdrängt, bevor ich sie Mitte Dezember völlig überraschend wiedersah. Henning war sogar mit meinen Töchtern in einer Klasse, und so kannte ich ihn schon eine ganze Weile. Wie man die Freunde seiner Kinder eben so kennt. Zunächst hatte Doro meine Hoffnungen und Befürchtungen zerstreut mit der Bemerkung, Henning sei ein Siebenmonatsbaby gewesen. Und dann, zwei Wochen später, aus heiterem Himmel ihre SMS.

Schon zwei Tage später hatten wir uns getroffen. An einem Samstagvormittag, in einem ruhigen Bistro in Rohrbach. Nur wenige hundert Meter von Doros großer und kostbar eingerichteter Wohnung entfernt. Im Radio war etwas von Nazareth gelaufen, das wusste ich noch, und es hatte die ganze Zeit nach Blumenkohl gerochen.

»Er ist mein Sohn, nicht wahr?«, hatte ich ohne jede Einleitung gefragt, und sie hatte mit verlegen gesenktem Blick genickt.

»Warum hast du behauptet, er sei zu früh auf die Welt gekommen?«

»Ich wollte …« Sie kaute auf der kirschrot bemalten Unterlippe. Schluckte. »Ich wollte kein Durcheinander haben. Nicht noch mehr Durcheinander. Aber es … es geht nicht. Henning hat ein Recht darauf zu wissen, wer sein Vater ist. Vor allem, wo er dich doch … Sascha hat ihn als sein Kind angenommen.«

»Dein Mann weiß aber, dass er nicht Hennings Vater ist?«

Wieder nickte sie. Immer noch hielt sie den Blick gesenkt. »Es hat ihm nichts ausgemacht. Und er war Henning ein guter Vater. Ein wenig kühl vielleicht, manchmal. Nicht so herzlich, wie er hätte sein sollen, manchmal. Sascha ist mehr so der Kopfmensch. Mit dem Herzen … mit dem Herzen hat er es nicht so.«

Ihr Mann und Hennings juristischer Vater hatte die beiden erst vor wenigen Monaten verlassen. In seiner Sekretärin meinte er eine Frau gefunden zu haben, die sein Herz mehr ansprach.

»Und nun findest du auf einmal, Henning soll die Wahrheit wissen?«

»Wie?« Sie blinzelte mich irritiert an.

»Du wolltest vorhin etwas sagen. Aber dann hast du angefangen, von deinem Ex zu reden.«

»Er ist nicht mein Ex. Wir sind getrennt. Nicht geschieden.«

»Hoffst du immer noch?«

»Ich hoffe nicht. Ich bin nicht dumm. Ich weiß, wenn ich verloren habe.«

»Und warum lasst ihr euch nicht scheiden?«

»Darum.«

»Du willst nicht darüber reden?«

»Nicht mit dir.«

»Kann es sein, dass du nicht recht weißt, was du willst?«

Ihr Blick irrte ab. »Das könnte sein, ja. Ich muss erst mit mir ins Reine kommen.«

»Und wie machen wir jetzt weiter?«

»Wenn du einverstanden bist, dann werde ich es ihm sagen.«

»Natürlich bin ich einverstanden. Warum nicht?«

»Ich dachte ... deine Mädchen? Was werden sie davon halten, wenn ihr Freund auf einmal ihr Bruder ist?«

»Sie sind keine Kinder mehr, erklären sie mir dreimal am Tag. Sie werden es verkraften.«

»Wir sollten es ihnen gleichzeitig sagen. Ich möchte nicht, dass Henning es hintenherum erfährt. Ich will es ihm selbst sagen.«

»Du hast ihm gegenüber ein schlechtes Gewissen.«

»Natürlich. Vielleicht. Ein bisschen.«

»Wir haben nichts Unrechtes getan.«

»Möchtest du erfahren, dass du das Ergebnis eines One-Night-Stands bist? Dass dein Vater gar nicht dein Vater ist?«

Ich hob die Schultern. Ließ sie wieder sinken. Spielte mit einem Bierdeckel. »Irgendwann muss er es erfahren. Er wird im Juli achtzehn. Und wer weiß, vielleicht freut er sich ja sogar ein bisschen.«

Sie sah mich ausdruckslos an und schlug nach einigen Sekunden die wasserblauen Augen nieder. »Mag sein. Er und Sascha – sie haben sich nie gut verstanden. Obwohl Sascha sich wirklich Mühe gegeben hat. Im Rahmen seiner Möglichkeiten. Henning mag dich ... sehr.«

»Freut mich zu hören. Ich ihn übrigens auch.«

»Er hat großen Respekt vor dir, weißt du das? Er findet, du hast einen coolen Beruf. Ja, ich glaube, er wird sich freuen.«

»Dann ist doch alles prima.«

»Weißt du eigentlich, wie stolz deine Töchter auf dich sind?«

»Was?« Nun war ich doch überrascht.

Sie nickte ernst. »Du bist der Größte, Tollste, Klügste für sie.«

»Wenn das wirklich so ist, dann halten sie es mir gegenüber sorgfältig geheim.«

Sie schmunzelte wehmütig. »Henning hätte auch immer gerne einen Vater gehabt, den er für den Größten hätte halten können. Vor dem er Respekt hätte haben können ...«

»War es wirklich so schlimm?«

»Nein. Du hast recht. Und was vergangen ist, ist vergangen, und jetzt ist jetzt. Wann wirst du es ihnen sagen?«

»Demnächst.«

Das war vor vier Wochen gewesen. Oder waren es schon fünf? Tausend Anläufe hatte ich genommen. Aber immer war irgendetwas dazwischengekommen.

»Alexander«, hatte Doro ernst gesagt, »lass dir bitte nicht zu viel Zeit. Ich glaube, Henning ahnt etwas. Er hat mir in letzter Zeit so merkwürdige Fragen gestellt. Wann und wie ich Sascha kennengelernt habe und noch mehr in diese Richtung.«

Anschließend hatten wir lange geschwiegen. Hin und wieder an unseren Tassen genippt. Jeder hatte seinen Gedanken nachgehangen, seinen widersprüchlichen Gefühlen nachgespürt. Doro hatte ständig in ihrem milchigen Kräutertee herumgerührt. Ich hatte aus dem Fenster gesehen auf eine Straße, wo wenig los war. Samstag war es gewesen. Später Vormittag. Und jetzt hatte ich also einen Sohn. Mein Leben würde sich dadurch nicht ändern. Das meiner Töchter ebenso wenig. Nichts würde sich ändern, und doch würde nichts so sein wie früher.

Im Radio lief jetzt ein melancholisches Stück von Lana del Rey.

Theresas inquisitorischer Blick ruhte immer noch auf mir.

»Nein, du musst dir keine Sorgen machen«, beantwortete ich schließlich ihre Frage. »Ich habe ein Kind mit ihr.«

»Ein Kind?«, schnappte sie. »Dann ... darf man also gratulieren?«

»Das Kind ist ein Sohn und heißt Henning und wird im Juli volljährig. Und ich weiß es selbst erst seit ein paar Wochen. Meine Töchter wissen es noch gar nicht. Mein Sohn weiß auch noch nicht, wer sein Vater ist. Dass ich sein Vater bin. Sein leiblicher Vater.«

»Achtzehn ist er schon?«

»Es war ein Klassentreffen. Es war eine einzige Nacht. Davor war nichts, und danach war nichts. Damals war ich noch nicht mal verheiratet. Und jetzt bin ich Vater eines fast erwachsenen Sohnes und weiß nicht, wie ich damit klarkommen soll.«

Theresa sah mich eine Weile ausdruckslos an. »Wieso freust du dich nicht einfach?«, fragte sie schließlich. »Wieso machst du ein solches Geheimnis um diese Geschichte?«

»Das ist nicht so einfach, wie du es dir vorstellst. Doro drängt die ganze Zeit, dass ich endlich mit den Zwillingen reden soll. Damit sie mit Henning reden kann. Aber immer ist irgendwas ...«

»Ich kann dir sagen, was ist: Du traust dich nicht.«

»Wahrscheinlich hast du recht. Doro meint, Henning würde seit Langem ahnen, dass sein Vater nicht sein Vater ist. Aber sie traut sich auch nicht, ihm reinen Wein einzuschenken.«

»In welchem Jahrhundert lebt diese Dame eigentlich? Weiß der offizielle Vater schon, dass du plötzlich aus der Versenkung aufgetaucht bist?«

»Sie leben getrennt.«

»Versucht sie, dich ...«

»Theresa, bitte, mach jetzt keine Witze«, unterbrach ich sie müde. »Mir ist im Moment wirklich nicht zum Lachen. Aber falls es dich beruhigt: Sie ist absolut nicht mein Typ.«

»Das beruhigt mich tatsächlich.« Plötzlich neigte sie sich zu mir herüber und küsste mich zärtlich auf den Mund. Ich drehte den Kopf weg und sah zum Seitenfenster hinaus in eine hoffnungslos verregnete, trostlos graue Winterlandschaft.

»Du bist ein Sensibelchen.« Theresa schien mit einem Mal

blendender Laune zu sein. »Das liebe ich an dir, weißt du das? Dass du nicht so ein Haudrauf bist.«

»Und was mache ich jetzt?«

»Jetzt fährst du auf dem schnellsten Weg nach Hause und redest endlich mit deinen Töchtern.«

»Willst du ... Würdest du dabei sein?«

»Nein, Alexander.« Sie lachte fast bei der Vorstellung. »Das ist eine Sache zwischen dir und deinen Mädchen. Sie werden dich schon nicht zerreißen.«

13

»Krass«, lautete Sarahs Kommentar, nachdem ich meine Beichte abgelegt hatte.

Louise musterte mich mit großen Augen, als würde sie in meinem Gesicht nach Spuren alter Leidenschaft suchen.

»Es war ein One-Night-Stand. Und ich habe eure Mutter damals noch nicht mal gekannt.« Was nicht ganz der Wahrheit entsprach, aber nun ja ...

»Das haben wir schon begriffen«, sagte Sarah langsam, und Louise nickte dazu.

»Ihr seid irgendwie ... Überrascht euch das denn gar nicht?«

Sie schüttelten erst zögernd, dann entschieden die gerstenblonden Köpfe. Seit Neuestem hatten sie Locken, nachdem sie sechzehn Jahre lang glattes Haar gehabt hatten. Theresa hatte mir erklärt, Mädchen in einem gewissen Alter müssten unbedingt Locken haben, falls sie vorher keine hatten. Die, die von Natur aus lockig waren, kauften sich im Gegenzug irgendwelche Glätteisen, um sie loszuwerden. Ich fand, dass Locken meinen Mädchen nicht standen. Aber das durfte ich nicht sagen, sonst wurden sie wütend.

»Henning hat schon lang gewusst, dass sein Daddy nicht sein Daddy ist.«

»Doro sagt, er ahnt irgendwas, aber gewusst ...«

»Doch, er hat's gewusst. Sie hat sich mal verplappert. Hat

gesagt, sie hätte seinen Daddy auf einer Party in Berlin kennengelernt. Henning hat später mit seiner Oma gequatscht und rausgefunden, wann seine Mom in Berlin war. Und dann hat er sich ausgerechnet, dass seine angeblichen Eltern sich erst sechs Monate vor seiner Geburt kennengelernt haben. Henning ist in Mathe der Klassenbeste.«

Louise sah mich fast mitleidig an. Vielleicht, weil sie drauf und dran waren, meine Illusionen zu zerstören. »Und wie er uns das erzählt hat, haben wir natürlich überlegt, wer sein richtiger Vater sein könnte. Wir haben entdeckt, dass du und seine Mom in einer Klasse wart ...«

»Und dann haben wir alte Fotos von dir gefunden, und – na ja ...«

»Wann war das?«

Sie grinsten sich kurz und stolz an. »Vor einem Jahr, ungefähr.«

Plötzlich wirkten meine Töchter sehr erwachsen. »Erst wollten wir's nicht glauben. Aber wie Henning dann im Krankenhaus war, und du die ganze Zeit so komisch drauf warst ...«

»Das heißt, ihr wisst schon seit einem Jahr ...?«

»Wissen tun wir's erst seit grad eben.«

»Und was sagt ...« Ich musste schlucken, obwohl ich einen ganz trockenen Mund hatte. »Was sagt Henning dazu?«

»Der findet's cool. Er hat seinen Daddy noch nie leiden können.«

»Der Typ ist voll das Angeberarschloch«, urteilte Louise mit der Gnadenlosigkeit ihrer pubertierenden Unschuld. »Porsche und fette Uhr und Armani und so.«

»Und was machen wir jetzt?«, fragte ich nach einigen still verstrichenen Sekunden. Bis zu diesem Augenblick hatte ich noch keinen Gedanken daran verschwendet, was sein würde, wenn endlich alle Bescheid wussten.

»Das ist doch klar«, meinte Louise. »Jetzt machen wir 'ne richtig fette Neue-Familie-Party. Mit Henning und Doro ...«

»... und Theresa natürlich.«

Ich nahm die Brille ab und rieb mir die müden Augen. Das konnte ja heiter werden. Es würde mit Sicherheit die seltsamste

Familienfeier meines Lebens werden. Aber irgendwie gefiel mir die Idee.

»Genau«, sagte ich und setzte die Brille wieder auf. »So machen wir es.«

»Und wir kriegen auch ein Glas Sekt«, verkündete Louise.

»Mindestens eins«, ergänzte Sarah mit strahlenden Augen.

»So viel ihr mögt«, sagte ich und fühlte mich auf einmal, als könnte ich fliegen, wenn ich nur wollte. »Schließlich kriegt man nicht jeden Tag Familienzuwachs.«

Am Montagmorgen galt mein ersten Anruf dem Heidelberger Grundbuchamt. Dort erfuhr ich nach dem Austausch einiger Unfreundlichkeiten mit einem schlecht gelaunten älteren Herrn, dass das Haus an der Gundolfstraße einer Berliner Immobilienfirma gehörte, die es vor sechzehn Jahren von einer Erbengemeinschaft gekauft hatte. Es kostete mich fast eine Stunde herauszufinden, dass diese Erbengemeinschaft aus drei Geschwistern bestand, von denen zwei bereits verstorben waren. Die einzige noch lebende frühere Besitzerin wohnte heute in einem Altersheim in Alzey und wusste nichts über die Menschen, die vor drei Jahrzehnten das später von ihr geerbte Mietshaus bewohnt hatten. Die Telefonnummer der Berliner Immobilienverwaltung fand ich dagegen rasch. Auch in Berlin war man montäglich schlecht gelaunt. Und natürlich wusste man ebenfalls nichts von irgendwelchen Mietern, die vor dem Eigentümerwechsel in der Heidelberger Immobilie gehaust hatten.

Anschließend saß ich frustriert an meinem Schreibtisch und zog Bilanz.

Was hatte ich?

Einen nicht auffindbaren alten Mann, der plötzlich behauptete, seine Frau ermordet zu haben, und allem Anschein nach unzurechnungsfähig war.

Ein Polizeiprotokoll, das vermutlich unvollständig, wenn nicht sogar in Teilen falsch war.

Zwei ehemalige Kollegen, die den Fall damals bearbeitet hatten und von denen heute einer tot und der andere verschwunden war.

Aussagen diverser Personen, deren Informationen über den Todesfall aus dritter Hand stammten.

Die nicht auffindbare, weil vermutlich unterschlagene Anzeige Fred Hergardens gegen den angeblichen Mörder seiner Frau.

Einen Totenschein, in dem das Datum zunächst falsch eingetragen worden war und dessen Unterzeichner das Ereignis ebenfalls nicht lange überlebt hatte.

Eine Nachbarin, die seinerzeit die Leiche fand, nach allen amtlichen Unterlagen jedoch niemals in Heidelberg gelebt hatte.

Alles in allem: ein löchriges Gespinst aus wackeligen Vermutungen, lückenhaften Ermittlungsergebnissen und verschwommenen Erinnerungen.

Bei Licht besehen, hatte ich nichts.

Zeit, die Sache endlich zu vergessen.

Andererseits …

Andererseits hielt es jemand aus unerfindlichen Gründen plötzlich für nötig, mich zu überwachen. Zu beobachten, wohin ich fuhr. Natürlich war immer noch denkbar, dass der Peilsender schon vor Wochen und in einem ganz anderen Zusammenhang an meinem Wagen befestigt worden war. Allerdings wäre dann vermutlich längst die Batterie leer gewesen, er hätte nicht mehr gepeilt und gesendet, und ich hätte das winzige Ding niemals gefunden. Offenbar hatte ich unabsichtlich und unwissentlich in ein Wespennest gestochen und dort für enorme Aufregung gesorgt. Ein uraltes Wespennest, von dem niemand geahnt hatte, dass es noch bewohnt war.

Ich schrieb Theresa eine neckische Guten-Morgen-wie-hast-du-geschlafen-SMS und fragte an, ob es ihr schon gelungen war, ihrem Handy das kurze Video von Samstag zu entlocken. Die Antwort kam rasch. Sie hatte sehr gut geschlafen, war auf dem Weg ins Bad und später in die Stadt zum Frisör, und nein, das Video war immer noch nur im Handy gespeichert.

Den Samstagabend hatte ich nach dem Gespräch mit meinen Töchtern vor dem Fernseher verbracht und – da ich aufregende Filme zurzeit nicht gut vertragen konnte – mir eine ebenso bunte wie kindische Fernsehshow angesehen. Den vollständig verregneten Sonntag hatte ich verschlafen und vertrödelt. Es war kaum hell geworden an dem Tag. Am Abend hatte es sogar ein wenig geschneit. Wenn diese Viktoria Hergarden wirklich Schauspielerin gewesen war, hatte ich mir beim Dösen überlegt, was lag da näher …

Die Telefonnummer des Heidelberger Stadttheaters fand ich rasch.

»Hergarden?«, fragte die Sekretärin des Intendanten gedehnt, bei der ich nach einigem Hin und Her gelandet war. »Wann soll das denn gewesen sein?«

Als sie »fünfundachtzig« hörte, sagte sie mit Pathos: »Oje! Damals war ich noch in Bremen und habe Latein gepaukt fürs Abi.«

Mehrfach wurde ich verbunden. Am Ende landete ich bei einer alten Dame, die am Theater seit Ewigkeiten als Souffleuse arbeitete.

»Die Viktoria«, sagte sie in strengem Ton. »Ja, an die kann ich mich noch erinnern.« Sie klang nicht, als wären es schöne Erinnerungen. »Aber gekannt habe ich sie eigentlich kaum.«

»Wer könnte denn …?«

»Da müsste ich … Ich überlege … Simone vielleicht … Aber haben Sie bitte ein wenig Geduld. Schauspieler stehen für gewöhnlich nicht so früh auf wie Sie und ich.«

Das Exemplar der Bühnenkünstler, das mich eine halbe Stunde später anrief, zählte offenbar nicht zu den notorischen Langschläfern.

»Simone Kranich«, stellte sich eine Frau mit rauchiger Stimme vor. »Ich war Mitte der Achtziger einige Jährchen in Heidelberg engagiert. Gott im Himmel, ist das lange her! Zurzeit bin ich in Bochum, von wo ich Sie auch anrufe.«

»Und Sie kennen den Namen Viktoria Hergarden?«

Ihr gedehntes »Ja« klang, als hätte sie sie mehr als nur gekannt.

»Fred Hergarden?«

»Freddy? Aber natürlich!« Hier klang schon mehr Sympathie mit. »Freddy hat ja sooo an seiner Vicky gehangen. Sieht man nicht oft im Leben, so eine richtig große, dicke Liebe. Wissen Sie eigentlich, wie und wo Freddy und Vicky sich kennengelernt haben?«

»Ich weiß bisher so gut wie gar nichts.«

»Freddy war ja immer und ewig in Geldnot, als freiberuflicher Kameramann. Mal hatte er einen Job, meist hatte er keinen. Und in Hannover gab es seinerzeit eine kleine Filmproduktion. Eine, die im Gegensatz zu vielen anderen im Geld schwamm. Die Lolly Movies, Gesellschaft mit beschränkter Haftung.«

»Ich ahne, was Sie andeuten wollen ...«

»Nichts will ich andeuten. Vicky hat fröhlich auf breiten Betten herumgevögelt, und Fred hat die Kamera drauf gehalten und geschwitzt und vermutlich bald nicht mehr gewusst, wohin mit seiner Geilheit.«

»Sie soll ihm nicht so treu gewesen sein, wie man es bei der großen Liebe erwartet.«

Das fand sie zum Lachen. »Ach Gottchen, Herr ...«

»Gerlach.«

»Sie haben eine angenehme Stimme, wissen Sie das?«

»Äh ...«

»Eine männliche Stimme, in die man sich am Telefon verlieben kann als Frau. Sind Sie groß?«

»Ja. Aber ...«

»Schlank?«

»Ich arbeite daran.«

Inzwischen hatte ich Bilder von Frau Kranich im Internet gefunden. Professionelle Fotos, wie sie Theaterfotografen schießen. Eine herbe Schönheit, in deren Gesicht einige schlimme Erfahrungen ihre Spuren gezeichnet hatten. Andere Bilder stammten von Partys. Auf diesen sah sie zwanzig Jahre älter aus als auf den offiziellen, und meist versuchte sie in angetrunkenem Zustand mit der Kamera zu flirten.

»Sie sind aber nicht dick, ja?«

»Frau Kranich, bitte ...«

Wieder das gurrende Lachen. »Schon begriffen. Der Herr ist in festen Händen.«

» Wir waren dabei, dass Frau Hergarden neben ihrer Ehe ein Verhältnis gehabt haben soll. «

» Eines? « Sie kicherte.

» Mehrere? «

» Ich weiß natürlich nicht alles. Da gab es zum Beispiel einen Musiker. Den Namen weiß ich nicht mehr. Jens? Nils? Der war ja so was von verschossen in die niedliche kleine Vicky. Sie hatte etwas an sich, das hat die Männer angezogen wie ein Hundehäufchen die Schmeißfliegen. «

» Jemand sagte mir, einer ihrer Liebhaber sei beim Fernsehen gewesen. «

» Das kann eigentlich nur Marcel gewesen sein. War damals auch am Theater und ein gefürchteter Schürzenjäger. Marcel und Freddy waren dicke Freunde. Haben sich noch vom Studium her gekannt und später sogar einige Zeit im selben Haus gewohnt. Freddy mit seiner Vicky und Marcel mit dieser Giftnudel, deren Namen auszusprechen ich mich bis heute weigere. Das Haus hat übrigens der Unaussprechlichen gehört. Sie war reich von Geburt. Marcel hatte eine blendende Partie gemacht. Bis das mit Vicky passierte. Danach war es plötzlich aus mit der Freundschaft. Freddy war dann ja auch bald weg. Auf Dauer. Im Ausland irgendwo. «

» Und dieser Marcel hatte also mit dem Fernsehen zu tun? «

» Damals noch nicht. Aber er hatte etwas am Laufen. Er war nämlich nicht nur gelernter Schauspieler, sondern hatte auch eine Ausbildung als Regisseur. Als Darsteller war er nicht übel, aber das Bühnenspiel war ihm nicht kreativ genug. Außerdem wollte er Chef sein und sich nicht von dahergelaufenen Idioten über die Bühne scheuchen lassen. Hat ja dann später auch geklappt mit dem Fernsehen. Aber der Einstieg war nicht leicht für ihn. Er hat sich allen möglichen Produktionen angedient. Wieder und wieder. Als Regisseur oder zur Not auch erst mal als Darsteller. Im Grunde war er wirklich nicht schlecht auf der Bühne. Er hat es nur gehasst, Text zu lernen und Anweisungen zu befolgen. Vicky wollte übrigens auch auf Teufel komm raus zum Film. Sie war ehrgeizig wie eine Rasierklinge. Vielleicht ist das die Erklärung. «

»Die Erklärung wofür?«

»He!«, rief sie. »Jetzt habe ich Sie! Sie sind ja überhaupt nicht dick! Sie sind ... Sie sind Chef der Kriminalpolizei, ist das richtig?«

Offenbar saß auch Frau Kranich vor einem aufgeklappten Laptop.

»Wofür wäre Frau Hergardens Ehrgeiz die Erklärung?«

Simone Kranich wurde wieder ernst: »Marcel war seinerzeit als Regisseur für die zweite Staffel der ›Lindenstraße‹ im Gespräch. Bei der ersten Staffel hatte es Ärger gegeben, und noch bevor die Serie gestartet wurde, war klar, dass ein neuer Regisseur her muss.« Sie verstummte mit einem Seufzer, als sei sie vorübergehend in angenehmen Erinnerungen versunken.

»Ich sehe immer noch nicht den Zusammenhang.«

»Der Zusammenhang ist ganz einfach: Ich denke, er hatte Vicky versprochen, ihr eine kleine Rolle zu verschaffen. Und den Rest können Sie sich denken, wenn Sie über ausreichend schmutzige Phantasie verfügen. Bei Ihrer Stimme kann man als Frau wirklich ins Träumen kommen, Herr Gerlach ...«

»Sie wollen andeuten, dass unter Schauspielern wirklich so lose Sitten herrschen, wie der gemeine Mann wie ich es sich vorstellt?«

»Na, Sie! Gemein klingen Sie ja nun gar nicht. Und was ich sagen will: Junge Schauspielerinnen tun fast alles, um voranzukommen. Einige Male mit einem Mann zu schlafen, ist da ein kleines Opfer. Und mit Marcel zu schlafen, war überhaupt kein Opfer. Wenn ich Ihnen erzählen würde, in wie vielen Betten wie vieler alter Säcke ich schon geschwitzt habe, Sie würden den Glauben an das Gute im Menschen verlieren. Obwohl, glaubt man als Kripochef überhaupt noch an das Gute im Menschen?«

In diesem Punkt konnte ich sie beruhigen.

»Marcel und Fred Hergarden waren also befreundet und haben im selben Haus gewohnt ...«

»Und Freddy hatte schon länger den Verdacht, dass Marcel

was mit Vicky am Laufen hatte. Er hat sie ja auch zu oft allein gelassen. Eine schöne Frau soll man nicht ohne Aufsicht lassen ... «

Ich erzählte ihr von Hergardens Besuch bei mir und seiner merkwürdigen Selbstanzeige. »Haben Sie eine Erklärung dafür, dass er plötzlich behauptet, er hätte seine Frau umgebracht? Obwohl er zu der Zeit nachweislich im Irak war?«

»Freddy? Vicky umgebracht? Was für ein Unfug! Und weshalb denn? Zufällig weiß ich, dass Vicky ihren Bettgeschichten ein Ende machen wollte. Wir haben uns zwei oder drei Tage vor ihrem Unfall am Theater getroffen. Ich meine, wir hätten gerade die *Maria Stuart* geprobt. Vicky war nicht engagiert. Sie hatte die Dummheit begangen, mit dem damaligen Intendanten Streit anzufangen. Trotzdem hat sie regelmäßig vorbeigeschaut und herumgeschnüffelt in der Hoffnung, wieder ins Geschäft zu kommen. Manchmal wird jemand krank. Oder erleidet einen Unfall. Aber dann hatte sie ja selbst diesen schrecklichen Unfall.«

»Und bei dieser Gelegenheit hat sie Ihnen erzählt, sie wollte ihr Verhältnis beenden?«

»So direkt nicht, nein. Sie hat durchblicken lassen, dass Freddy mächtig Stress macht. Und dass er nicht ganz unrecht hatte mit seinem Misstrauen. Dass ihr Leben ein wenig aus dem Ruder gelaufen war und dass sie aufräumen muss. So hat sie es ausgedrückt, das weiß ich noch: dass sie aufräumen muss.«

»Hergarden hat also nichts Genaues gewusst?«

»Er hatte nur einen mehr oder weniger begründeten Verdacht. Zwei, drei Wochen zuvor war er für einige Tage in Heidelberg gewesen. Auf Heimaturlaub, sozusagen. Und bei dieser Gelegenheit müssen die beiden Hübschen sich tüchtig in die Wolle gekriegt haben. Freddy hat Vicky vermutlich auf den Kopf zugesagt, was er denkt, und aufs fotogene Mäulchen gefallen war sie ja nun nicht. Dass Fred in Bagdad sitzt, hat sie ihm vorgeworfen, und es sich gut gehen lässt, und dass es da ja wohl auch hübsche Frauen gibt, auf die eine Fernsehkamera Eindruck macht. Am Ende haben sie dann groß Versöhnung gefeiert, und wie er Vicky das nächste Mal gesehen hat, da war sie schon tiefgekühlt.«

»Noch mal zu diesem Marcel – wie hieß er eigentlich mit Nachnamen?«

»Graf. Marcel hat gerne den Schurken gegeben. Das war seine Paraderolle. Mein Fach war damals die junge Naive. Heute spiele ich meist die alte Naive.« Ihr Lachen klang, als bräuchte sie zu viele Zigaretten, um über den Tag zu kommen.

»Darf ich mir Ihre Nummer notieren für den Fall, dass mir noch weitere Fragen einfallen?«

Jetzt lachte sie wieder, nachdem sie in den vergangenen Minuten ernst geblieben war.

»Sie dürfen sich von mir notieren, was Sie mögen. Meine Maße sind: 93-67-97. Größe: eins vierundsiebzig. Körbchengröße: C. Und falls der Zufall Sie einmal nach Bochum verschlagen sollte – ich habe bei Weitem nicht mehr so viele Vorstellungen wie früher …«

»Allerletzte Frage: Dieser Marcel Graf, können Sie mir sagen, was aus dem geworden ist? Wie ich ihn erreichen kann?«

»Den kennen Sie nicht?«

»Sollte ich?«

»Sie sehen nicht oft fern, wie?«, fragte sie milde. »*Grafs Abend*, na?«

»Ist das nicht eine von diesen Samstagabendrateshows?«

»Eine Rateshow weniger. Eher eine Mischung aus seichter Unterhaltung und dämlicher Talkshow. Früher war es mal eine ganz erfolgreiche Sache. Aber inzwischen ist das Format auf dem absteigenden Ast, hört man. Wenn Sie ihn sprechen möchten, rufen Sie am besten beim ZDF an.«

»Würden Sie ihm zutrauen, einen Mord zu begehen?«

»Marcel? Ein Mord?« Sie klang, als hätte diese Vorstellung sie ernsthaft erschreckt. Wieder blieb es für Sekunden still. Im Hintergrund hörte ich Verkehrsrauschen. Die dröhnende Hupe eines großen Lkw. Simone Kranich schien verkehrsgünstig zu wohnen. »Marcel war immer ehrgeizig bis zum Erbrechen«, fuhr sie schließlich zögernd fort. »In unserem Gewerbe gehören brennender Ehrgeiz und ein hypertrophes Selbstbewusstsein zur Grundausstattung. Selbstzweifel gönnt man sich höchstens mal abends nach dem dritten Glas Rotwein.« Sie legte eine Pause ein. Offenbar rauchte sie auch während des Gesprächs. »Ohne Ehrgeiz hätte er es nicht so weit gebracht. Aber geht er deshalb über Leichen? Nein, das traue ich ihm nicht zu. Nein.«

»Neigt er zum Jähzorn? Ist er leicht reizbar?«

»Wie Marcel heute ist, kann ich nicht sagen. Aber damals? Jähzornig? Hm … reizbar war er, wenn man ihn kritisiert hat. Wissen Sie, es gibt zwei Typen von Schauspielern: Die einen brauchen nach einer schlechten Kritik einen Psychiater. Die anderen brennen darauf, dem Kritiker den Hals umzudrehen. Marcel zählte eindeutig zu Kategorie zwei. Und das meine ich wörtlich. Einer Schreiberin vom ›Mannheimer Morgen‹ hat er tatsächlich mal in aller Öffentlichkeit eine geschallert, nachdem sie gewagt hatte, ihn einen selbstverliebten Narzissten zu nennen. Und damit – nach meiner bescheidenen Ansicht – exakt ins Schwarze getroffen hatte. Bei der nächsten Premierenparty war die junge Dame wieder dabei. Dem Aussehen nach war sie noch Studentin. Marcel hatte wieder eine Hauptrolle und wohl auch schon einiges intus. Sie hat versucht, ihm Komplimente zu machen, hatte wohl auch ein schlechtes Gewissen. So was kommt sogar bei Kritikern manchmal vor, dass sie einsehen, wenn sie den Bogen überspannt haben. Und da hat er ihr eine gelangt. Kommentarlos und mit Anlauf. Das hat ihm bei den anderen Schreiberlingen so viel Respekt eingebracht, dass er anschließend in allen Feuilletons über den grünen Klee gelobt wurde. Nur im ›Mannheimer Morgen‹ nicht. Die haben überhaupt nichts über die Premiere gebracht. Ich meine, es war *Charleys Tante*. Ich war die Kitty. Marcel hatte sein geliebtes Bärtchen abnehmen müssen, um als Tante durchzugehen. Aber ohne Bart sah er sogar noch besser aus als mit.«

14

»Ein Kollege aus Erbach«, sagte Sönnchen, die – nach dem Klang ihrer Stimme zu schließen – ein schönes Wochenende hinter sich hatte. »Sie hätten ihn angerufen.«

»Also dieser Boll«, begann der dröhnende Kollege, der sich diesmal als Polizeihauptmeister Schneevogt vorgestellt hatte, »kein Mensch kennt den richtig. Aber ich hab immerhin rausfinden können, wie er seine Kohle verdient.«

»Erreicht haben Sie ihn aber nicht?«

»Der ist nie daheim. Eine Nachbarin hat mir gesagt, sie hätte ihn schon seit Wochen nicht mehr gesehen. Das sei bei dem aber normal, sagt sie. Das liegt nämlich an seinem Beruf.«

»Was ist denn nun sein Beruf?«

»Ich weiß nicht recht, wie ich's am besten sagen soll. Also, wenn eine Firma wen einstellen will, meistens sind das große Firmen, und sie haben Zweifel an dem seinen Angaben oder den Zeugnissen, dann beauftragen sie den Boll, und der findet dann raus, ob das alles seine Richtigkeit hat. Oder wenn einer dauernd krank ist, und die Firma hat Zweifel, ob das stimmt. So Sachen.«

»Dann wäre er eine Art Privatdetektiv?«

»So kann man's wohl nennen, ja. Er hat aber komischerweise kein Gewerbe angemeldet. Und die Nachbarin weiß auch nicht, für wen genau der arbeitet.«

»Er hat bestimmt ein Auto.«

»Einen elf Jahre alten Daimler fährt er. C-Klasse, silbergrau.«

Ich notierte das Kennzeichen, das mit ERB begann.

»Jedenfalls, der Nachbarin hab ich eingeschärft, falls er wieder auftaucht, soll sie mich sofort anrufen. Und ihm nichts davon sagen, natürlich.«

»Wunderbar«, sagte ich. »Das haben Sie sehr gut gemacht.«

Schneevogt lachte so herzhaft, dass ich den Hörer ein Stück vom Ohr halten musste. »Wenn's doch für einen guten Zweck ist!«

Nun tat ich das, was ich eigentlich schon vor dem Anruf hatte tun wollen: Ich suchte und fand die Telefonnummer des ZDF im Internet.

»Herrn Graf möchten Sie sprechen?« Die Frau am Telefon klang, als hätte ich sie um die Durchwahlnummer des Papstes gebeten. »In welcher Angelegenheit denn bitte?«

Ich stellte mich vor, worauf ihre Heiterkeit erlosch. »Was ich kann …«, sagte sie langsam, und ich hörte Papier rascheln. »Ich kann Ihnen die Handynummer seiner persönlichen Assistentin geben. Die sind zurzeit in Ludwigshafen, um die Sendung am kommenden Samstag vorzubereiten. Sie wird nämlich aus Ludwigshafen ausgestrahlt, und das ist doch nicht weit von Heidelberg, oder irre ich mich?«

Es dauerte noch einen Augenblick, bis sie gefunden hatte, wonach sie suchte.

»Olivia Opelt. Sie haben was zu schreiben?«

Frau Opelt nahm nach dem zweiten Tuten ab.

»Ja?«, sagte sie hektisch. »Was ist denn jetzt noch?«

Wieder einmal nannte ich meinen Namen.

»Gerlach? Und was …?«

»Ich bin Leiter der Heidelberger Kriminalpolizei und würde gerne Herrn Graf in einer persönlichen Angelegenheit sprechen. Es wird bestimmt nicht lange dauern.«

»Machen Sie Witze? Haben Sie eine Vorstellung, was hier los ist? In fünf Tagen soll die Show laufen, und hier sieht es aus wie nach einem Atomkrieg! Es ist doch jedes Mal dieselbe Sch… Worum geht es denn? Kripo? Sagten Sie eben Kripo?«

»Worum es geht, würde ich ihm gerne selbst sagen.«

Im Hintergrund dröhnten Hammerschläge.

»Aber doch nicht so herum!«, hörte ich meine Gesprächspartnerin schreien. »Das Rote muss nach oben! Nach oben, versteht ihr denn nicht?«

Die Hammerschläge brachen ab. Jemand fluchte. Eine Klarinette spielte schnelle Läufe dazu.

»Sorry«, sagte Olivia Opelt nun wieder ins Handy. »Irgendwann schmeiße ich einfach alles in die Ecke und suche mir einen normalen Job. Einen, bei dem man jeden Tag pünktlich um fünf Feierabend hat.« Es folgten zwei tiefe Atemzüge. »Okay«, sagte sie dann ruhiger. »Sie sind also die Kripo, und Sie möchten Marcel sprechen. Okay. Ich werde sehen, was ich für Sie tun kann. Sind Sie in den nächsten Stunden unter dieser Nummer erreichbar?«

Ich gab ihr sicherheitshalber meine Handynummer, da ich keine Lust verspürte, den ganzen Abend an meinem Schreibtisch zu sitzen und auf den Rückruf eines alternden Showstars zu warten, der vermutlich nie kommen würde.

»Ich hab ihn!«, jubelte Sönnchen, als sie am frühen Nachmittag in mein Büro platzte. »Hab ich's nicht gesagt? Ich hab ihn!«

Ich war gerade in eine Akte vertieft gewesen und sah erst mit Verzögerung auf. »Wen haben Sie?«

»Diesen Verrückten mit der Lederjacke.«

Ich nahm die Brille ab. »Hergarden?«

Sie nickte aufgeregt. »In Dossenheim wohnt er zurzeit, in einem Privathaus, wahrscheinlich hat er ein möbliertes Zimmer. Zwei Kollegen haben ihn grad erst vor ein paar Minuten auf der Straße erkannt. Anhand des Phantombilds, das wir zusammen gemacht haben! Sie sagen, er sei ziemlich betüdelt gewesen und hätt überhaupt nicht gemerkt, dass sie ihm gefolgt sind.«

»Haben sie ihn angesprochen?«

»Sie haben doch ausdrücklich angeordnet: Nicht ansprechen, bloß melden.«

»Und jetzt ist er zu Hause?«

»Sie sagen, er ist in einem Haus verschwunden. Und er hat einen Schlüssel gehabt. Und er hat ziemlich geschwankt. Wie's scheint, hat er ordentlich einen über den Durst getrunken.«

Ich klappte mit Genuss meine Akte zu. »Da fahre ich doch gleich mal hin. Bin sehr gespannt, was der Herr mir zu erzählen hat.«

»Sie fahren jetzt nirgendwohin, Herr Gerlach. Sie haben nämlich um drei einen Termin bei der Staatsanwaltschaft.«

Seufzend sank ich in meinen Chefsessel zurück. Griff mir an die Stirn. »Wenn ich Sie nicht hätte, Sönnchen ...«

Sie strahlte mich an. »Da täten Sie manchmal ganz schön dumm gucken, gell?«

Bei dem Termin mit der Leitenden Oberstaatsanwältin Frau Dr. Steinbeißer ging es wieder einmal um die leidige Geschichte, die mich schon seit Monaten Nerven kostete: die Kellertürenbande. Die – aus unseren spärlichen Ermittlungsergebnissen zu schließen – jungen Männer, die mal zu zweit, mal zu dritt zur Tat schritten, hatten bisher entschieden mehr Glück als Verstand gehabt. So viel Glück, dass ich inzwischen sogar befürchtete, sie könnten über einen Informanten bei der Polizei verfügen, der sie über unsere Pläne und Aktivitäten auf dem Laufenden hielt.

Meine Leute konnten unmöglich den ganzen Großraum Heidelberg überwachen. So hatte ich in der Vergangenheit immer wieder Schwerpunktaktionen angeordnet, bestimmte Stadtviertel oder Orte verstärkt befahren lassen. Und immer hatten die Täter zuverlässig am anderen Ende ihres Aktionsgebiets zugeschlagen.

Das Gespräch mit der Chefin der Staatsanwaltschaft verlief wie erwartet und befürchtet – ich durfte mir einige Ermahnungen und unangenehme Fragen anhören, musste gestehen, dass mir allmählich die Ideen ausgingen und dass ich letztlich, wie so oft, auf einen gnädigen Zufall hoffen musste, der uns früher oder später fast immer zur Seite sprang.

»Irgendwann ist auch die Glückssträhne der Kellertürenbande zu Ende«, lautete mein Schlusswort, als wir uns über ihren wie immer sauber abgeräumten und staubfreien Schreibtisch aus rötlich schimmerndem Holz hinweg die Hände reichten.

Frau Dr. Steinbeißer seufzte und nickte und seufzte noch einmal. Dann wünschte sie mir viel Glück.

Das Haus, in dem Fred Hergarden zurzeit angeblich wohnte, lag fast am oberen Ende des Schlüsselwegs, eines Sträßchens in Dossenheim, das in Richtung Osten den Hang hinaufführte.

Der Name an der Klingel des einfachen, aber gepflegten Hauses aus der Nachkriegszeit lautete passenderweise Häusler. Ich drückte den blitzsauberen Kunststoffknopf. Augenblicke später klappte innen eine Tür, schlurfende Schritte näherten sich, die billige Haustür wurde geöffnet. Vor mir stand eine kugelrunde Frau mit würdig-ernster Miene.

»Ja?«, sagte sie misstrauisch. »Was ist?«

Ich ließ sie meinen Dienstausweis sehen und stellte mich vor. »Vielleicht gehen wir lieber hinein. Es muss ja nicht die ganze Nachbarschaft ...«

Sie warf sichernde Blicke die schmale, lückenlos vollgeparkte Straße hinauf und hinab und ließ mich eilig ein. Weiter als bis in den Hausflur kam ich allerdings nicht.

»Geht's wieder mal um die Parkerei? Mein Mann und ich können doch nichts dafür, dass unsere Mieter Autos haben!«

»Ich suche diesen Mann hier.« Ich zeigte Frau Häusler, die mir kaum bis zur Brust reichte, das Phantombild.

»Der hat doch gar kein Auto.«

»Es geht auch nicht um sein Auto.«

»Nicht?« Sie sah verdattert zu mir hinauf. »Worum geht's dann?«

»Das würde ich ihm gerne selber sagen.«

»Andauernd gibt's Theater wegen den Autos von unseren Gästen. Aber wo sollen die denn parken, wenn nicht am Straßenrand, frag ich Sie? Andere Leute parken doch auch am Straßenrand, und da holt auch keiner die Polizei.«

Die Hausherrin trug einen braunen, fast knöchellangen Rock und eine sandfarbene, schon ein wenig ausgebleichte Bluse. Am rechten Ringfinger glänzte ein fetter Ehering. Es roch nach Kurzgebratenem.

»Kann ich Herrn Hergarden sprechen?«

»Der ist nicht da. Er ist vorhin kurz dagewesen, hat vielleicht irgendwas geholt oder gebracht, und dann ist er wieder weggegangen.«

»Wann wird er wiederkommen?«

»Mein Mann und ich fragen unsere Gäste nicht, wohin sie gehen und wann sie zurückkommen.«

»Aber seit wann er bei Ihnen wohnt, können Sie mir bestimmt sagen.«

Sie sah zur Decke. Blinzelte beim Rechnen. »Mitte Januar. Zwei Wochen. Nein, drei. Kinder, wie die Zeit vergeht! Bald haben wir schon wieder Frühling.«

»Ich hoffe es«, seufzte ich.

»Wir vermieten hier übrigens ganz legal. Das ist alles ordentlich angemeldet und wird ehrlich versteuert. Nicht, dass es wieder Gerede gibt. Mein Mann war nämlich früher Beamter. Beim Heidelberger Bauordnungsamt. Hier bei uns ist alles legal, da gibt es nichts. Da können die Nachbarn schwätzen, so viel sie wollen.«

»Daran habe ich keine Zweifel. Könnte ich irgendwo auf Ihren Mieter warten?«

»Wir haben hier keine Wartezimmer. Und in sein Zimmer kann ich Sie ja nicht lassen, auch wenn Sie von der Polizei sind. Ein Stück die Straße runter liegt das Hotel Heidelberger Tor. Da können Sie warten. Und was zu essen kriegen Sie auch.«

»Rufen Sie mich an, wenn er wieder auftaucht?«

Nur widerstrebend nahm sie meine Visitenkarte entgegen, versprach dann aber doch, sich zu melden. Ich verließ das gastliche Haus, ging die Straße hinunter bis zu dem Hotel, das sie mir genannt hatte. Im Erdgeschoss gab es ein kleines Restaurant, das um diese Uhrzeit noch fast leer war. Ich wählte einen Tisch am Fenster, von dem ich die Straße im Auge behalten konnte. Die Coca-Cola-Uhr über der Theke zeigte halb sechs, und draußen war es schon wieder dunkel geworden. Ausnahmsweise regnete es nicht, und so hatte ich am frühen Abend endlich mein Rad am Hainsbachweg abgeholt und nach Hause gebracht. Einige bunte Luftschlangen an den Lampen taten kund, dass demnächst die närrische Zeit begann, aus Sicht der Polizei die Hochsaison der Schlägereien und Alkoholvergiftungen. Ich bestellte mir einen Pfefferminztee.

Um halb sieben war etwa die Hälfte der Tische besetzt. Die meisten der Gäste schienen sich und das Personal zu kennen. Die beiden Bedienungen, die sich so ähnlich sahen, dass sie Schwestern hätten sein können, hatten gut zu tun. Ständig wurde Bier und Wein und Essen bestellt. In der Küche wurde tüchtig geklappert und geschimpft. Im Gastraum herrschte ordentliche Fröhlichkeit.

Um halb acht war es richtig voll geworden, und ich bestellte mir nun doch etwas zu essen, nachdem die Bedienung zum dritten Mal und zunehmend besorgt gefragt hatte, ob ich denn wirklich gar keinen Hunger hätte.

»Einen Straßburger Wurstsalat bitte.«

»Vielleicht ein Bierchen dazu?«

»Nein, danke.«

»Ein Viertele von unserem Hauswein? Wir haben einen Lützelsachsener Grauburgunder aus biologischem ...«

»Noch einen Pfefferminztee bitte.«

Sie notierte meine Bestellung mit gerunzelter Stirn und fand die Kombination offenbar befremdlich.

Ab acht wurde es allmählich wieder ruhiger. Der Wurstsalat war gut gewesen, und durch meine Phantasie geisterte jetzt immer öfter das Bild eines gut gekühlten Glases Lützelsachsener Grauburgunder aus biologischem Anbau. Ungefähr hundert Mal hatte ich schon überprüft, ob mein Handy funktionierte, ob es genug Strom und ausreichend Empfang hatte.

Um kurz vor neun bestellte ich mir ein Viertel vom Hauswein.

Um halb zehn sah ich endlich Fred Hergarden die Straße hinaufwanken. Ich erkannte ihn schon, als er noch im Schatten zwischen zwei Straßenlaternen war, an den schlackernden Bewegungen der langen Arme und Beine. Groß war er und ungewöhnlich hager. Und Sönnchen hatte wieder einmal recht gehabt: Er hielt sich schlecht. Der Kopf hing an seinem krummen Rücken. Als er ins Licht der nächsten Laterne trat, erkannte ich auch die zerschlissene Jeans, die schwarze Lederjacke ohne Ärmel. Hergarden schien wirklich betrunken zu sein. Ich winkte der Bedienung und bat um die Rechnung.

Als ich in die kalte Winterluft hinaustrat, sah ich Hergarden gerade in den Vorgarten des Ehepaars Häusler abbiegen. Kurze Zeit später begann mein Handy aufgeregt zu vibrieren.

»Jetzt ist er da«, raunte die Vermieterin. »Er ist oben.«

Eine halbe Minute später stand ich selbst vor der Haustür, die sich ganz von allein öffnete.

»Er ist in seinem Zimmer«, flüsterte die steuerehrliche Vermieterin mit konspirativem Blick zur Decke. »Treppe rauf, die erste Tür rechts.«

Ich stieg die schmale, auf manchen Stufen knarrende Treppe hinauf und klopfte an die Tür, hinter der es keuchte und rumpelte. Fred Hergarden öffnete, starrte mich zwei Sekunden lang argwöhnisch und ein wenig kurzsichtig an. Sein Mundgeruch schlug mir entgegen. Ich zwang mir ein Lächeln ab.

»Ach, Sie sind das«, sagte er, als hätte er seit Tagen mit meinem Kommen gerechnet. »Haben Sie es sich doch noch überlegt?«

»Darf ich reinkommen?«

»Wird sich wohl nicht vermeiden lassen.« Er lachte trocken, hustete.

»Sie wollten *mich* sprechen«, versetzte ich leicht verärgert. »Nicht umgekehrt.«

Ich schloss die gut geölte Tür hinter mir. Das Zimmer war winzig, bot gerade Platz für ein schmales Bett, einen Schrank, ein Tischchen am Fenster und zwei billige Stühle. Die Wände waren nachlässig mit Raufaser tapeziert und matschgrau gestrichen. Früher war es vermutlich ein Kinderzimmer gewesen.

Hergarden deutete auf einen der Stühle, sank ächzend auf sein Bett, das quietschend protestierte. Die Lederjacke hatte er noch an.

»Was macht der Kopf?«, fragte er mit gesenktem Blick.

»Sie waren also wirklich dabei?«

Überrascht sah er auf.

»Ich war eine Weile bewusstlos«, erklärte ich. »Gehirnerschütterung. Partielle Amnesie.«

Er nickte, als würde er das kennen.

»Warum waren Sie da?«, fragte ich. »Am Hainsbachweg?«

»Meine Sache.«

»Herr Hergarden, Sie waren bei mir und haben behauptet,

Sie hätten Ihre Frau umgebracht. Einen Tag später sehe ich Sie wieder, werde niedergeschlagen und bin eine Woche krank. Da finde ich schon, dass mich die Sache etwas angeht.«

»Niedergeschlagen stimmt nicht.« Er grinste müde. »Aber Sie sind ganz schön hingeknallt. Ihr Rad hat Sie zu Fall gebracht. Sonst wäre nichts passiert, aber das hat Sie zum Stolpern gebracht.«

»Und deshalb will ich wissen, was da los war.«

Hergarden saß vorgebeugt da, die Unterarme auf den Oberschenkeln, und atmete schwer. Es schien ihm nicht gut zu gehen. Erst jetzt fiel mir auf, dass ich keinen Alkohol roch. Allerdings hatte ich natürlich selbst schon ein Viertel Wein getrunken.

»Ich ...«, begann er nach Sekunden. Schnaufte noch ein Weilchen mit mahlendem Kiefer. »Muss erst mal aufs Klo. Mir ist auf einmal ...«

Mühsam stemmte er sich hoch, schwankte kurz, schüttelte den Kopf mit dem fettigen grauen Pferdeschwänzchen, hielt sich am Schrank fest, tappte zwei Schritte in Richtung Tür und fiel dann ohne einen Laut in sich zusammen.

Ich sprang auf, um ihm zu helfen, was aber in der Enge des Zimmers nicht einfach war. Er war bei Bewusstsein, stellte ich fest, als ich mich über ihn beugte, litt jedoch unter starker Atemnot. Ich zerrte ihn in Richtung Bett, er half mit, so gut es ging, sein Atem ging keuchend, als hätte er Asthma. Zwischendurch schluckte er immer wieder so heftig, dass der vorstehende Adamsapfel hüpfte. Endlich lag er auf dem Bett. Ich drehte den schweren Körper sicherheitshalber in Seitenlage und knöpfte die Lederjacke auf und den oberen Teil des blassblauen Hemds, das aussah, als gehörte es zu einer Uniform. Es dauerte Minuten, bis sein Atem sich wieder beruhigte. Auch der Adamsapfel kam allmählich zum Stillstand. Die Augen hielt er geschlossen.

»Danke«, nuschelte er schließlich. »Es ist zum Kotzen.«

»Was fehlt Ihnen denn?«

Er machte eine hilflose Handbewegung zur Brust. »Das ... Herz.«

»Brauchen Sie einen Arzt?«

Er schüttelte matt den Kopf. Seine Stimme war jetzt kaum noch zu hören. »Pillen«, keuchte er. »Schublade.«

Das Nachttischchen. Ein Fläschchen, halb voll mit rosaroten Tabletten. Auf dem Tisch eine Wasserflasche und ein Glas. Ein wenig von dem Wasser lief auf die bunte und vermutlich von der Hausfrau eigenhändig genähte Tagesdecke. Dann war die Medizin hinuntergewürgt, und Hergarden atmete wieder normal.

»Geht's wieder?«

Er nickte kaum merklich. Sein knochiger Körper entspannte sich mehr und mehr, und auf einmal – ohne jeden Übergang – war er eingeschlafen.

Ich blieb neben seinem Bett sitzen. Kam zu dem Schluss, dass ein Arzt hier wohl nicht nötig war. Er hatte seine Medizin, war also vermutlich in ärztlicher Behandlung, und ich war nicht sein Kindermädchen. Auf dem Nachttisch, in dessen Schublade ich die Pillen gefunden hatte, stand ein Foto in silbernem Rahmen. Eine junge, dunkelhaarige Frau. Strahlend lächelnd, fast überirdisch schön. Viktoria Hergarden, vermutlich professionell retuschiert, seit fast dreißig Jahren tot und offenbar immer noch geliebt.

Hergardens Gesichtsmuskeln zuckten hin und wieder, als würde er träumen. Er schmatzte. »Sie machen ja sowieso nichts«, hörte ich ihn plötzlich murmeln. Offenbar schlief er doch nicht.

»Wer? Ich?«

Wieder schmatzte er. Es dauerte lange mit der Antwort, die schließlich keine war. »Ich krieg sie schon noch dran, die Sau. Auch ohne Sie. Ich krieg ihn schon.«

»Wen kriegen sie? Marcel Graf?«

»Und wenn es das Letzte ist, was ich in diesem Scheißleben ...«

»Wen kriegen Sie?«

Ich erhielt keine Antwort. Jetzt schien er wirklich eingeschlafen zu sein. Ich blieb noch einige Minuten sitzen. Dachte an Theresa und unseren verunglückten Samstagsausflug.

Nutzte die Zeit, um ihr eine besonders freundliche Hab-schöne-Träume-mein-Schatz-SMS zu schreiben.

Hergarden drehte sich im Schlaf auf den Rücken und begann zu schnarchen. In der Ferne schlug eine Kirchturmuhr Viertel nach zehn, und allmählich hatte ich meine Zweifel, dass ich hier heute noch etwas erfahren würde. Inzwischen war auch ich müde und kam aus dem Gähnen nicht mehr heraus. Ich zückte eine Visitenkarte, schrieb auf die Rückseite: »Bitte rufen Sie mich an. Ich will Ihnen helfen« und steckte sie an den unteren Rand des Bilderrahmens. Dann löschte ich das Licht, schloss die Tür leise von außen und ging.

Noch auf der Treppe begann mein Handy wieder zu surren. Es war Marcel Graf persönlich, der mich anrief, stellte ich fest, als ich vor die Tür trat und den Knopf drückte.

»Herr Gerlach, ich grüße Sie!«, rief der berühmte Showstar, als wäre ich ein lange vermisster Freund. »Olivia sagte, Sie wollten mich sprechen. Ich habe zwar nicht übermäßig viel freie Zeit, aber …«

Ich bedankte mich für den Rückruf und fragte, ob ihm der Name Fred Hergarden etwas sagte.

»Freddy? Na klar. Von dem habe ich seit Ewigkeiten nichts gehört. Was ist mit ihm? Ist er etwa wieder zu Hause in seiner alten Heimat, der Herumtreiber?«

»Er war vor anderthalb Wochen bei mir und hat mir merk-würdige Sachen erzählt.«

»Merkwürdige Sachen?«

»Es ging um den Tod seiner Frau.«

»Vicky? Ach du lieber Gott. Diese Geschichte wird mich wohl bis ins Grab verfolgen.«

Er lachte. Aber seine Stimme hatte sich um eine Winzigkeit verändert. Die joviale Heiterkeit war einer gespielten Fröh-lichkeit gewichen.

»Ich möchte das Thema ungern am Telefon besprechen«, sagte ich, während ich die Tür meines Peugeot aufschloss und einstieg. »Könnten wir uns morgen im Lauf des Tages irgend-wann für eine halbe Stunde treffen? Wenn es sein muss, komme ich gerne zu Ihnen nach Ludwigshafen.«

»Morgen, nein, das ist ganz schlecht. Hier kocht die Hölle. Jedes Mal denke ich wieder, dieses Mal geht es schief. Dieses Mal läuft die Show auf einem Trümmerfeld. Bisher hatte ich noch jedes Mal unrecht. Aber dieses Mal bin ich überzeugt, wir gehen unter am Samstag. Mit Pauken und Trompeten.«

»Wann passt es Ihnen dann?«

»Ist es denn so wichtig, dass es nicht Zeit hat bis nach meinem Untergang?«

»Ich fürchte, ja.«

»Sie fürchten? Nun denn ...« Graf schnaufte. Räusperte sich. »Warum nicht gleich? Sagen wir, in einer halben Stunde? Würde das gehen?«

»Wo finde ich Sie?«

»Wie heißt der Schuppen hier?«, fragte Graf jemanden im Hintergrund. »Pfalzbau«, sagte er dann. »Wir sind mindestens noch bis Mitternacht hier. Fragen Sie einfach nach Olivia.«

15

Die Autobahn in Richtung Mannheim war fast leer. Zur Abwechslung nieselte es wieder einmal. Die Scheibenwischer meines betagten Peugeot quietschten empört. Im Westen, über Mannheim und Ludwigshafen, glühte der Himmel rot vom Widerschein der nächtlichen Lichter. Im Radio lief Countrymusik. Bald tauchte die SAP-Arena am Rand der Autobahn auf. Strahlend erleuchtet, der Parkplatz voller Autos. Offenbar lief dort gerade eine gut besuchte Veranstaltung. Eine Weile ging es durch die Mannheimer Innenstadt, aber auch hier herrschte nur wenig Verkehr. Dann tauchte die Rheinbrücke nach Ludwigshafen im Regendunst auf. Im Norden glühte der Himmel stärker als zuvor. Die BASF, der größte Chemiekomplex der Welt. Ein festlich erleuchtetes Kreuzfahrtschiff glitt lautlos unter mir hindurch in Richtung Rotterdam. Ich fragte mich, wer wohl auf die absurde Idee kam, im Februar eine Kreuzfahrt auf dem Rhein zu unternehmen.

Zehn Minuten später erreichte ich das prosaisch »Pfalzbau« genannte Veranstaltungszentrum Ludwigshafens. Die Tiefgarage war geschlossen, ich fand jedoch einen halblegalen Parkplatz in einer Seitenstraße und schloss den Wagen ab im Vertrauen darauf, dass ich im Fall eines Strafmandats auf Sönnchens Charme und Verhandlungsgeschick rechnen konnte. Auf der Freifläche vor dem großen Gebäude standen ohne erkennbare Ordnung viele Fahrzeuge herum. Große Sattelzüge, kleine Lkws, Lieferwagen, Kombis mit und ohne Aufschrift, mehrere dunkle Limousinen. Auf einigen der Wagen prangte das Emblem des Zweiten Deutschen Fernsehens.

Das sachliche Kongress- und Kulturzentrum im Stil der Sechzigerjahre hatte für mich viel Ähnlichkeit mit einem modernen Bahnhof. Hinter den riesigen Glasflächen schimmerte dämmriges Licht.

Nicht nur die Tiefgarage, auch der Haupteingang des Gebäudes war verschlossen. Ich war gerade dabei, die Nummer von Grafs Assistentin in meinem Handy zu suchen, als ich zwei Männer im Blaumann bemerkte, die eine Seitentür öffneten und eilig im Haus verschwanden. Ich machte mich durch lautes Rufen bemerkbar. Sie hielten mir die Tür auf, grinsten solidarisch, stellten keine Fragen. Auf ihren breiten Rücken prangte der Name einer Münchner Bühnenbaufirma.

Das weitläufige Foyer war nur notdürftig beleuchtet. Die warme Luft roch muffig und verbraucht, als hätten sich vor Kurzem noch sehr viele Menschen hier aufgehalten. Aus der Ferne hörte ich Lärm. Ich folgte den beiden Bühnenbauern, die irgendwelche schweren Geräte mit sich schleppten, deren Sinn sich mir nicht erschloss. Die Männer unterhielten sich ungeniert in breitem Bayerisch, schimpften zünftig auf das Chaos, die wie üblich katastrophale Organisation, den indiskutablen Zeitplan. Es klang jedoch heraus, dass sie Marcel Graf bewunderten und die Show am kommenden Samstag vor dem Fernseher miterleben würden. Wir liefen breite Treppen hinauf. Auch die beiden Bayern kamen ins Schnaufen und hörten auf zu reden.

Der Lärm wurde stärker. Schließlich passierten wir eine

schwere Doppeltür, und ich betrat einen großen, dicht bestuhlten Saal. Die grell erleuchtete Bühne war das Zentrum von Chaos und Lärm. Unzählige Menschen wimmelten dort herum, und bis jetzt war nicht einmal zu erahnen, was das Ganze in wenigen Tagen darstellen sollte. Nicht weit von mir stritt ein drahtiger Mann, der die fünfzig schon eine Weile hinter sich hatte, mit einem athletisch gebauten Anzugträger. Soweit ich verstand, ging es darum, dass eine Ballettgruppe am nächsten Morgen mit den Bühnenproben beginnen sollte, woran angesichts des Bauzustands der Kulissen nicht zu denken war. Der Anzugträger rauchte ein langes Zigarillo, antwortete wortkarg und ließ den anderen fühlen, wer die Show bezahlte.

Ich ging durch den Mittelgang des Saals nach vorne, erreichte den fast schulterhohen Bühnenrand. In der Mitte gab es eine provisorische Treppe. Ich wagte jedoch nicht, die Großbaustelle zu betreten, aus Sorge, von einem herunterfallenden Teil oder einem übermotivierten Handwerker erschlagen zu werden. Überall wurde gebrüllt, geschraubt, geklopft und geflucht. Da ich niemanden entdecken konnte, der zu Grafs engerem Umfeld zu gehören schien, wählte ich nun doch die Nummer seiner Assistentin. Dieses Mal nahm sie erst nach dem fünften oder sechsten Tuten ab. War hörbar konsterniert, da ihr Chef sie nicht über meinen Besuch informiert hatte. Aber sie beruhigte sich rasch wieder. Offenbar war sie unangenehme Überraschungen gewohnt.

»Ich komme«, sagte sie. »Geben Sie mir eine Minute.«

Während ich wartete, versuchte ich, die Menge der Leute zu schätzen, die auf der Bühne herumwerkelten. Ich kam auf etwas über dreißig. Irgendwer stellte fest, dass eine römische Säule wieder demontiert werden musste, da vor ihr etwas anderes hätte aufgebaut werden müssen. In der rechten Ecke wurde ein längliches Gerät zusammengeschraubt, das ich für einen Kamerakran hielt. Die Minute war um, Olivia Opelt erschien nicht. Die Säule wurde unter derben Flüchen gekippt, was nicht ungefährlich aussah, und ein Stück zur Seite gerollt. Im Hintergrund brummte ein kleiner Gabelstapler herum.

Endlich öffnete sich eine Seitentür des Saals, und eine etwa dreißigjährige Frau mit dunklem, kurz geschnittenem Haar, eckiger Brille mit schwarzem Rand und kraftvollen Bewegungen trat heraus. Sie sah sich hastig um, entdeckte mich, winkte ohne zu lächeln.

Ich ging zu ihr hinüber. Sie kam mir einige Schritte entgegen. Ihr Händedruck war beeindruckend, und jede ihrer Bewegungen ließ mich spüren, dass Zeit hier noch mehr Geld bedeutete als anderswo. Sie war klein, eins fünfundsechzig vielleicht und trug einen knielangen dunkelblauen Rock zu einer hellblauen Bluse. Trotz ihrer Kleinheit flache Schuhe. Unter dem linken Arm hielt sie ein Klemmbrett, auf dem einige zerfledderte Listen befestigt waren. Aus der Nähe wirkte sie angespannt und müde.

»Wir sind gerade ein wenig im Stress, wie Sie sehen«, erklärte sie, als sie die Tür hinter uns schloss und der Baustellenlärm schlagartig leiser wurde.

»Ich möchte nicht miterleben, was für Sie großer Stress ist.«

Sie lachte höflich und führte mich einen langen, kahlen Gang entlang. Ein Schild an der Wand wies den Weg zu den Garderoben.

»Die Bühnenbauer haben zwei Tage zu spät geliefert, und jetzt klemmt es mal wieder hinten und vorne. Obwohl wir immer reichlich Pufferzeiten einplanen, irgendwas geht ja todsicher jedes Mal schief, aber diesmal wird es wirklich eng. Was wollen Sie denn von Marcel?«

»Es geht um einen ehemaligen Freund von Herrn Graf.«

»Und deshalb kommt die Kriminalpolizei?«

»Es ist ein bisschen kompliziert und außerdem persönlich.«

Wir durchquerten eine weitere Tür und betraten das Reich der Garderoben. Hier herrschte Ruhe und ein unangenehmer Geruch nach fettiger Schminke und tausend Sorten Menschenschweiß. Die meisten Türen standen offen. Die Räume dahinter waren dunkel.

»Wenn Sie hier bitte kurz warten würden.« Frau Opelt knipste irgendwo Licht an und winkte mich in ein leer stehendes Kämmerchen. Vermutlich eine Umkleide für Nebendarsteller. »Ich gebe Marcel Bescheid.«

Sie zog die Tür hinter sich ins Schloss und ließ mich allein.

Der Raum mochte zwölf Quadratmeter messen. An der rechten Längswand reihten sich eine schmale Liege, ein wackliges Tischchen, ein einfacher Sessel. Gegenüber ein großer Schminktisch mit einem enormen Spiegel, der – wie in alten Filmen – mit Glühbirnen umrandet war. Ich drückte versuchsweise den dazugehörigen Schalter und betrachtete kurz das müde Gesicht eines in nicht allzu ferner Zukunft fünfzig Jahre alten, hoch gewachsenen Kerls, dessen Mantel wieder einmal in die Reinigung gehörte. Ich schaltete das gnadenlose Licht wieder aus und setzte mich in den unerwartet hart gepolsterten Sessel. Erhob mich wieder, um die Tür zu öffnen, da mir der Raum sonst zu eng und beklemmend war. Anschließend setzte ich mich auf die Liege, lehnte mich an die weiß gestrichene Wand. Betrachtete ein Theaterplakat an der anderen Wand. »Die Entführung aus dem Serail«, aufgeführt vor fünf Jahren. Damals vielleicht ein rauschender Erfolg. Oder eine gute Seele, der diese karge Zelle zu trostlos erschienen war, hatte auf die Schnelle nichts Besseres gefunden.

Der Showstar ließ standesgemäß auf sich warten. Inzwischen war es schon kurz vor elf, und bald merkte ich, dass ich wirklich so müde war, wie ich eben im Spiegel ausgesehen hatte. Hoffentlich dauerte das hier nicht bis Mitternacht. Irgendwo murmelten ruhige Stimmen. Weit entfernt das dumpfe Wummern der Bühnenbauer. Als ich schon kurz davor war einzuduseln, klappte auf dem Flur eine Tür, und Augenblicke später kamen zwei wichtig aussehende Jeansträger an meinem Zimmerchen vorbei, ohne mich zu bemerken.

»… das dritte Mal in Folge«, sagte der eine gerade. »Sorry, aber wir sind ja nun nicht die Wohlfahrt.«

»Er hat dem Sender Millionen eingebracht! Hunderte von Millionen, über die Jahre!«

»Na, na. Nun übertreiben Sie mal nicht.«

Die beiden blieben einige Meter von mir entfernt stehen, dämpften die Stimmen.

»Im Leben jedes Künstlers gibt es Zeiten, wo es aufwärtsgeht, und Zeiten, in denen geht es abwärts.« Der Mann sprach das Wort »Künstler« aus, als wäre es eine Beleidigung. »Und zurzeit geht's leider nur noch abwärts mit ihm. Nichts auf der Welt währt ewig. Sorry.«

»Eine Durststrecke. Nichts weiter, eine Durststrecke. Wir sind dabei, das Konzept zu modernisieren.«

»Was wollen Sie denn da modernisieren? Sein Publikum stirbt ihm weg, das ist sein Problem. Oder ist inzwischen einfach zu verkalkt zum Fernsehen. Wir brauchen junges Blut. ›Wetten dass‹ hat es uns doch vorgemacht. Und Gottschalk war noch keine vierundsechzig.«

»Marcel hat immer noch fast fünf Millionen Zuschauer.«

»Dreieinhalb vor acht Wochen. Davor drei Komma acht, vier Komma null, drei Komma neun. Es geht aber nicht nur um die absoluten Zahlen, der Trend ist es, was uns Sorgen …«

Eine Tür quietschte. Die beiden verstummten und gingen weiter.

Sekunden später betrat Marcel Graf mit dem strahlenden Lächeln eines großzügigen Gastgebers die kleine Garderobe. Ich kannte sein Gesicht inzwischen von diversen Fotos im Internet. Auf keinem hatte er annähernd so alt gewirkt wie in Wirklichkeit.

»Herr Gerlach!«, rief er voller Wärme und Herzlichkeit. »Bitte verzeihen Sie, dass Sie warten mussten.« Er hatte einen besitzergreifenden Händedruck, trug einen maßgeschneiderten, fast weißen Anzug über einem dunkelblauen Hemd mit offenem Kragen und duftete nach einem für Beamte wie mich gewiss unerschwinglichen Herrenparfüm. Die leichten Slipper an seinen Füßen stammten vermutlich von einem italienischen Schuhmacher. »Um den alten Freddy geht es also.«

Mit energischer Geste packte er das Sesselchen, setzte sich. Ich sank wieder auf die Liege, von der ich eben hochgeschreckt war.

»Wie geht's meinem alten Freund denn?«

»Aktuell leider nicht so gut.«

»Er ist aber wieder in Deutschland? Dumme Frage, ent

schuldigen Sie. Sie sagten ja vorhin, er sei bei Ihnen gewesen. Er ist hoffentlich nicht krank?«

»Ich fürchte, doch. Aber deshalb bin ich nicht hier. Sollten wir nicht vielleicht die Tür …?«

Graf winkte ab. Fuhr sich mit den Fingern durch die grau melierten, noch beneidenswert fülligen Locken. Sein Gesicht und sein Körper waren rundlicher, als ich erwartet hatte. »Hier ist niemand mehr außer uns.«

Ich überlegte, ob sein Haar echt war oder ob er ein Toupet trug.

»Frau Opelt?«

»Olivia gehört zur Familie, sozusagen. Also, was kann ich für Sie tun?«

»Erinnern Sie sich an den neunten November 1985?«

»Vicky?«

»Richtig.«

»Den Tag werde ich nicht so leicht vergessen. Behauptet Freddy etwa immer noch …?«

Er brach ab, sah mich mit schrägem Kopf amüsiert an.

»Was meinen Sie?«

»Na ja, dass ich sie sozusagen … auf dem Gewissen habe?«

»Er hat das damals schon behauptet?«

Seine Miene wurde abrupt ernst. »Ich verstehe gerade nicht ganz. Ich dachte, das sei der Grund, weshalb wir hier sitzen?«

»Mir gegenüber hat Herr Hergarden behauptet, er hätte seine Frau selbst umgebracht.«

»Was ist das denn für ein Quatsch?«

»Ich nehme an, er will die Ermittlungen wieder in Gang bringen. Und das klappt in Deutschland nur, wenn neue Sachverhalte auftauchen. Die Wiederaufnahme eines Verfahrens ist bei uns keine einfache Sache. Da reichen neue Aussagen nicht. Und damals hat er also behauptet, Sie seien schuld an ihrem Tod?«

Graf sah mich so forschend an, als vermutete er eine Heimtücke in meiner Frage. »Das haben Sie aber doch … vermutlich in Ihren Protokollen gelesen?«

»Nach meinen Protokollen war es zweifelsfrei ein Unfall. Die Ermittlungen meiner damaligen Kollegen und die Leichenschau des Notarztes haben keinerlei Hinweise auf Fremdeinwirkung ergeben.«

»Na, immerhin ... Aber er ... Freddy, war er nicht sogar bei der Polizei? Hat er mir gegenüber so dargestellt. Allerdings ...« Graf atmete tief aus und ein, wandte den Blick zur Decke, als wäre dort ein Teleprompter montiert, von dem er seinen Text ablesen konnte. »Ich habe mich damals schon gewundert, weshalb die Polizei mich nicht einmal kontaktiert hat. Das heißt, eigentlich habe ich mich nicht wirklich gewundert. Ich dachte, sie haben sein Geschwätz vielleicht einfach nicht ernst genommen. Was ja auch vollkommen richtig war. Dann ist er ja bald wieder nach Bagdad geflogen. Und – meines Wissens – nie wieder nach Deutschland zurückgekehrt. Zumindest nicht auf Dauer.«

»Ihrem ehemaligen Freund ... Das kann man so sagen?«

Graf nickte bedächtig, den väterlichen Blick jetzt wieder auf mein Gesicht gerichtet.

»Ihrem ehemaligen Freund geht es schlecht. Er ist offenbar schwer krank. Erst vorhin habe ich ihn gesehen und kurz gesprochen. Und bei dieser Gelegenheit hat er eine Bemerkung gemacht, die mich ein wenig beunruhigt.«

»Hat er mir wieder mal gedroht?« Der Fernsehstar lachte gemütlich.

»So hat es tatsächlich geklungen, ja. Ihren Namen hat er allerdings nicht genannt. Sie nehmen das nicht ernst?«

»Ach Gottchen, lieber Herr Gerlach. Freddy hat schon damals getönt, er würde mich irgendwann umbringen. Freddy hat ein – wie soll man sagen? – etwas explosives Gemüt. Und seine Vicky hat er nun mal über alles in der Welt geliebt.«

»Wie kommt er darauf, Sie könnten an ihrem Tod schuld sein?«

»Das müssten Sie ihn schon selbst fragen.«

»Er hat Ihnen gegenüber keine Gründe genannt?«

»Nein.« Nun senkte er zum ersten Mal den Blick. Betrachtete seine perfekt manikürten Hände. »Damals dachte ich, mein Gott, der arme Kerl, erst wird er im Irak entführt und muss Todesängste ausstehen, und nach seiner Rettung ist das Erste, was er hören muss, seine Herzallerliebste ist tot. Die beiden Süßen hatten ja leider keine ganz einfache Beziehung. Aber wo gibt es das schon – einfache Beziehungen?« Graf schwieg für einige Sekunden. Leise hörte ich wieder entfernte Hammerschläge. »Er ist völlig durchgedreht damals. Er war am Ende seiner Kräfte und Nerven. Da kommt man schon mal auf verrückte Ideen. Nein, ich habe das zu keiner Zeit wirklich ernst genommen.«

»Er hat Ihnen damals angeblich auch vorgeworfen, ein Verhältnis mit seiner Frau zu haben.«

Graf nickte so befriedigt, als hätte er genau jetzt mit genau dieser Wendung des Gesprächs gerechnet. »Ich fürchte, das wirft er mir heute immer noch vor.«

»Und was sagen Sie dazu?«

Jetzt sah er mir wieder in die Augen. Sein Blick war auf einmal kalt.

»Herr Gerlach, bitte, was soll das jetzt?« Er machte eine wohl dosierte Pause, und seine Stimme klang leicht gereizt, als er weitersprach: »Vicky war jung und ... gnadenlos ehrgeizig. Zudem war sie die meiste Zeit allein. Hat sich zu Tode gelangweilt ...«

»An Langeweile ist sie definitiv nicht gestorben.«

»In gewisser Weise vielleicht doch. Sie hat zu viel getrunken. Wäre sie nüchtern gewesen an dem vermaledeiten Abend, würde sie vermutlich noch leben. Ich bezweifle allerdings, dass sie die Karriere gemacht hätte, von der sie träumte.«

»Und Sie hatten also keine sexuelle Beziehung mit ihr?«

Er lächelte zufrieden. Schüttelte den Kopf. »Nicht, dass sie mir keine Avancen gemacht hätte. Nicht, dass sie nicht attraktiv gewesen wäre. Aber ich habe mich beherrschen können. Außerdem war ich verheiratet.«

Graf, der in den vergangenen Minuten langsam in sich zusammengesunken war, straffte plötzlich den Rücken. Setzte eine energische Miene auf. Sah mir wieder in die Augen. Aller Charme, jegliche Liebenswürdigkeit waren aus seinem Blick gewichen. Mir gegenüber saß plötzlich ein glasharter Geschäftsmann.

»Ich weiß zwar nicht, warum ich Ihnen das überhaupt erzähle, aber in Gottes Namen: Ja, ich war meiner Frau untreu. Ja, ich habe damals hin und wieder auch mit anderen Frauen geschlafen. Wir waren alle ziemlich verrückt seinerzeit. Von AIDS hatten wir noch nichts gehört. Vicky wusste natürlich, dass ich mit der HaBeFilms in Verhandlungen stand. Und sie hätte so gut wie alles getan, um ins Fernsehen zu kommen.«

»Und das haben Sie nicht ein wenig ausgenutzt?«

Graf seufzte, als würde er allmählich an meinem Verstand zweifeln. »Nein, ich habe es nicht ein wenig ausgenutzt. Sollte es allerdings wegen meiner diversen anderen Ehebrüche zur Verurteilung kommen, dann werde ich meine Strafe mit Haltung auf mich nehmen.«

»Darum geht es hier nicht. Und das wissen Sie auch.«

Er wurde übergangslos wieder milder. »Was sollen diese alten Geschichten? Ich habe Vicky nichts getan. Ich war an dem Tag ja nicht einmal in Heidelberg.«

»Wo waren Sie dann?«

»Ist das ein Verhör?«

»Selbstverständlich nicht.«

»Es fühlt sich aber so an.«

Ich zuckte die Achseln und lächelte so freundlich, wie ich konnte.

»Köln«, brummte Graf. »In Köln war ich. Bin erst am nächsten Abend zurückgekommen. Und da erst habe ich erfahren, dass sie tot ist.«

»Von Ihrer damaligen Frau sind Sie inzwischen geschieden.«

»Und von zwei anderen Frauen auch. Mein Beruf macht es nicht leicht, eine stabile Beziehung zu führen, wie Sie sich vielleicht vorstellen können.«

»Ihre damalige Ehefrau hat am nächsten Morgen den Tod von Frau Hergarden gemeldet?«

»Steht das denn nicht in Ihren Protokollen? Ich dachte immer, bei der Polizei wird alles aufgeschrieben.«

»Im Protokoll steht, eine Frau Holland hätte angerufen.«

»Holland war ihr Mädchenname. Später hat sie ihn als Künstlernamen geführt. Und Sabeth klinge interessanter als Elisabeth, fand sie. Außerdem war sie beim Publikum bereits als Sabeth Holland bekannt, als wir uns zusammentaten. Wenn man sie mal so richtig auf die Palme bringen wollte, dann musste man sie ›Lisa‹ nennen.«

»Was macht sie heute?«

Er hob die weichen Schultern, lächelte mich erschöpft an. »Wir haben seit Jahrzehnten keinen Kontakt mehr. Nach unserer Trennung ist sie ins Ausland gegangen. Nach Frankreich. Seither …?«

»Wie heißt sie jetzt?«

»Auch das weiß ich leider nicht, Herr Gerlach.« Offensichtlich war ihm inzwischen mein Name wieder eingefallen. »Wir haben seit damals keinerlei Kontakt mehr.«

»Arbeitet sie immer noch als Schauspielerin?«

Reichlich ungeniert sah er auf seine elegante Uhr mit Lederarmband, die nicht annähernd so kostbar aussah, wie sie vermutlich war. Meine Audienz neigte sich dem Ende zu. Ich erhob mich, er tat mit einer halben Sekunde Verzögerung dasselbe. Reichte mir – plötzlich wieder strahlend – die Hand.

»Passen Sie in den nächsten Tagen ein bisschen auf sich auf«, sagte ich ernst. »Ich fürchte, Ihr alter Freund ist ziemlich schlecht auf Sie zu sprechen.«

»Ich habe zwei sehr erfahrene und fähige Leibwächter, die bestens auf mich aufpassen«, erwiderte Marcel Graf mit breitem Lächeln. »Ohne mich gibt's am Samstagabend nämlich keine Show im ZDF, sondern vermutlich eine alte Rosamunde-Pilcher-Schnulze.«

Wir sahen uns in die Augen, drückten immer noch Hände, als würden wir einen lautlosen Wettstreit austragen. In diesem Moment der Stille meinte ich im Flur ein Rascheln zu hören. Als ich jedoch hinter dem alternden Fernsehstar durch die Tür trat, war niemand zu sehen. Meinen Weg zum Ausgang fand ich allein.

Die Luft draußen schien kälter geworden zu sein. Was vielleicht an dem unangenehmen Wind lag, der aufgekommen war. Dafür hatte der Nieselregen aufgehört, der den Tag so trostlos gemacht hatte. Ich zog den Kopf zwischen die Schultern, stopfte die Hände in die Manteltaschen und sah zu, dass ich zu meinem Wagen kam. Eilig überquerte ich die Freifläche, hastete an etwa zwanzig am Straßenrand geparkten Autos entlang, dann hatte ich den Peugeot erreicht, fummelte den Schlüssel aus der Manteltasche, schloss auf, zögerte. Ich lief einige Schritte zurück. Der dritte Wagen hinter meinem war ein schon etwas betagter Mercedes der C-Klasse. Silbergrau. Das Kennzeichen begann mit »ERB« und kam mir bekannt vor. Ich merkte es mir und ging – nun etwas langsamer – zu meinem französischen Oldtimer zurück.

Zehn Minuten später war ich wieder auf der Autobahn und freute mich an dem bisschen Wärme, das aus den Lüftungsschlitzen drang. Inzwischen zeigte die Uhr halb zwölf. Die Großveranstaltung in der SAP-Arena war zu Ende, der Parkplatz bis auf wenige Autos leer, das riesige Gebäude selbst dunkel.

Im Radio liefen Oldies. Die Beatles wieder einmal.

16

Als Erstes kümmerte ich mich am Dienstagmorgen um das Kennzeichen des Mercedes, den ich in der Nacht zuvor in Ludwigshafen gesehen hatte. Meine Erinnerung hatte mich nicht getrogen – der Wagen war zugelassen auf einen gewissen Johann Boll, wohnhaft in Weiten-Gesäß im Odenwald, den ehemaligen Kripobeamten, der damals den Todesfall Vicky Hergarden aufgenommen hatte.

Konnte das ein Zufall sein?, fragte ich mich, als ich mich in die Rückenlehne meines Sessels sinken ließ. Gewiss nicht. Hatte Boll also irgendwie mit Graf zu tun? Wahrscheinlich. Oder sollte jemand anders den seltsamen Detektiv beauftragt haben, den Fernsehstar auszuspionieren? Fred Hergarden womöglich? Ich weiß nicht, aus welchem Grund, aber in diesem Augenblick fiel mir das Video auf Theresas Handy wieder ein.

»Ich dachte, das hat sich erledigt«, erklärte meine Göttin hörbar unausgeschlafen.

»Würdest du es gleich mal versuchen?«

»Nachdem ich im Bad war.« Sie gähnte ausführlich. »Wenn ich etwas versuche, bevor ich im Bad war, dann endet das üblicherweise in einer Katastrophe.« Sie gähnte noch einmal. »Beim letzten Mal wollte ich mir nur einen Tee kochen und hätte um ein Haar die Küche in Brand gesetzt.«

Was bedeutete, dass mit dem Video vor zehn Uhr nicht zu rechnen war. Schriftsteller sollte man sein, dachte ich nun ebenfalls gähnend, während ich den ersten Cappuccino des Tages schlürfte. Am besten ein Schriftsteller, der von seiner Kunst nicht leben muss.

Auf Fred Hergardens Anruf wartete ich an diesem Vormittag vergeblich. Ich ärgerte mich, weil ich ihn nicht nach seiner Handynummer gefragt hatte, als er noch ansprechbar war. Mehrere Versuche, seine Vermieter telefonisch zu erreichen, führten ins Nichts. Einen Anrufbeantworter schien es dort nicht zu geben. Ansonsten geschah an diesem Morgen wenig, und ich nutzte die ungewohnte Ruhe, um Akten durchzuarbeiten, Urlaubsanträge, Dienstreiseanträge, Benzinrechnungen und Vernehmungsprotokolle mit meinem Autogramm zu versehen. Beim Studium eines Protokolls, das Sven Balke angefertigt hatte, kam mir eine Idee. Es ging um ein eher harmloses Ehedrama in Ziegelhausen. Die Frau hatte ihren Mann schon seit Jahren verdächtigt, ein Verhältnis mit einer Arbeitskollegin zu haben. Er hatte dies ebenso hartnäckig geleugnet. An einem Abend vor wenigen Tagen war der Konflikt eskaliert, und am Ende war die siebenundfünfzigjährige Frau mit einem Ausbeinmesser auf ihren Gatten losgegangen und hatte ihn am Oberarm verletzt. Nachbarn hatten die Polizei gerufen. Der Mann – also das Opfer – hatte die Polizisten jedoch mit wüsten Worten wieder fortgeschickt und sich geweigert, Anzeige zu erstatten. Er hatte heftig geblutet, aber standhaft behauptet, sich selbst geschnitten zu haben. Balke war am nächsten Tag zum Ort des handgreiflichen Ehestreits gefahren, um die Sache formal abzuschließen.

Eines dieser alltäglichen Dramen, wie sie sich regelmäßig irgendwo hinter den zugezogenen Vorhängen des Bürgertums ereignen. Der Mann hatte auch Balke gegenüber bestätigt, dass er nicht juristisch gegen seine Frau vorgehen werde. Mein Mitarbeiter hatte alles protokolliert und von den beiden Beteiligten unterschreiben lassen, bevor er wieder zurück nach Heidelberg gefahren war. Im Grunde eine Szene für die so genannten Realityshows, mit denen das Privatfernsehen kostengünstig die Nachmittage füllte und von denen manche Menschen offenbar nicht genug bekommen konnten. Vielleicht, weil sie dabei andere Menschen beobachten konnten, denen es noch dreckiger ging als ihnen selbst. Fernsehserie – das war das Stichwort, das mich zum Telefon greifen ließ.

»HaBeFilms, mein Name ist Ansgar Schön, was darf ich für Sie tun?«, flötete dieselbe Jungmännerstimme, mit der ich bereits in der vergangenen Woche gesprochen hatte.

»Es geht noch mal um die ›Lindenstraße‹. Wir hatten wegen Viktoria Hergarden telefoniert.«

»Sie sind der Kripomensch, richtig?«

»Meine heutige Frage lautet: Bei Ihnen hatte sich damals auch noch eine andere Person beworben. Marcel Graf.«

»Der Marcel Graf, an den ich jetzt denke?«

»Ja. Als Regisseur. Mich interessiert, ob er an einem bestimmten Tag einen Besprechungstermin bei der HaBeFilms hatte.«

»Etwa auch 1985?«

»Ich weiß, es ist eine verrückte Idee. Aber es passieren ja auch manchmal die verrücktesten Dinge.«

»Aber sooo verrückt ...?«

»Es gibt doch bestimmt Personen bei Ihnen, die schon länger dabei ist?«

»Der Älteste im Team ist Jörg. Er war damals ... lassen Sie mich rechnen ... er dürfte damals elf gewesen sein. Eventuell auch schon zwölf.«

»Ausgeschiedene Mitarbeiter, zu denen Sie noch Kontakt haben?«

»Das könnte schon eher ... Momentchen mal kurz. Hm, hm, hm. Es ist vielleicht eine schräge Idee, aber wir lieben hier ja schräge Ideen ...«

Ich lauschte einer leisen und unverständlichen Unterhaltung. Vermutlich hielt der dynamische junge Mann die Hand vors Mikrofon.

»Hansi«, sagte er dann mit wieder klarer Stimme. »Hansi hat den Laden in den Siebzigern gegründet und gegen alle Tücken der Branche und Widerstände der Banken groß gemacht. Seit er die Firma vor acht Jahren vertickt hat, lebt er in seiner Finca auf Malle. Ich habe hier eine Handynummer. Hansi Bertram.«

Auch der ehemalige Firmeninhaber schien verrückte Ideen zu mögen. Vor den Fenstern meines Büros schien es ein wenig heller zu werden.

»Marcel Graf?«, wiederholte Bertram mit sonorem Bass. »Nein, beim besten Willen nicht. Aber ›Lindenstraße‹, Heidelberg, da klingelt irgendwas ...«

Im Hintergrund zwitscherten Vögel. Wasser gluckste. Vermutlich stand mein Gesprächspartner in Shorts und Poloshirt am Rand seines bläulich schimmernden Pools und hielt ein hohes Glas in der gut gebräunten Rechten, während sich neben ihm eine prächtige Schwarzhaarige mit lasziver Sorgfalt die Nägel lackierte.

Ich hörte mich seufzen.

»Gleich hab ich's«, sagte Bertram. »Warten Sie nur. Gleich hab ich's. Auf mein Gedächtnis ist ... war bisher immer ...«

Wieder hörte ich es eine Weile zwitschern und plätschern.

»Ein Regisseur. Graf hätte fast als Regisseur bei uns angefangen. Wir waren uns praktisch schon handelseinig, aber dann ist irgendwas vorgefallen ...«

»Es geht mir darum, ob er am Abend des neunten November fünfundachtzig einen Termin bei Ihnen hatte?«

»Einen Termin?«

»Das behauptet er, und es wäre für mich aus bestimmten Gründen wichtig ...«

»Graf war ein vielversprechendes Talent. Und wir sind ihm sehr entgegengekommen. Sehr. Aber aus irgendeinem Grund hat sich die Sache dann zerschlagen. Bei den Verhandlungen war ich selbst nicht dabei. Wegen dieses Termins ... Ich müsste telefonieren. Melde mich wieder, ja?«

Der Filmproduzent im Ruhestand meldete sich nicht wieder. Stattdessen sein ehemaliger Kompagnon und Geschäftsführer. Dieses Mal hörte ich im Hintergrund kein Vögelgezwitscher, sondern eine gequält klingende Blockflöte.

»Es geht um den neunten November.«

»Das hat mir Hansi schon erläutert. Aber da kann ich Ihnen beim besten Willen nicht weiterhelfen. Ich habe tonnenweise Papier geschreddert, als ich in den Ruhestand ging. Das ging damals ja fast alles per Fax. Damals war das Telefax ja noch brandneu, mein Gott, und heute wissen die jungen Leute schon nicht mal mehr, was das ist. Was da im Hintergrund so jämmerlich piept, ist übrigens kein sterbender Schwan, sondern mein Enkelchen. Tills Mutter will partout nicht wahrhaben, dass ein Kind auch unmusikalisch sein kann.«

Es wäre ja auch zu schön gewesen.

»Sie sehen also keine Chance ...?«

»Leider. Beim besten Willen. Wir hatten damals mehrere Bewerbungen aus dem Raum Heidelberg, erinnere ich mich noch. War eine regelrechte Welle.«

»Eine davon war Viktoria Hergarden.«

»An den Namen erinnere ich mich nicht mehr. Aber es war eine Frau. Es war ... warten Sie. Sie hat Eindruck auf mich gemacht, damals. War zweimal zum Vorsprechen bei uns gewesen, und um ein Haar hätte es geklappt. Blond war sie. Strohblond, richtig? Und etwas rundlich, richtig?«

»Das kann nicht Frau Hergarden gewesen sein.«

»Ich war – nachdem meine Frau tot ist, darf ich es ja sagen – ich war mit ihr essen, und es wurde ein – nun ja – in jeder Hinsicht unterhaltsamer Abend.«

»Jetzt bräuchte ich nur noch den Namen.«

»Sie hatte so einen lustigen Dialekt. Pfälzisch, obwohl sie gar nicht aus der Pfalz stammte ...«

»Kurpfalz vielleicht? Hat sie aus Heidelberg gestammt?«

Die Blockflöte verstummte mit einem finalen Kreischen.

»Rosalie! Jetzt hab ich's. Rosalie. Der Nachname ... Jo... Jonas, vielleicht? Johann? Geben Sie versuchsweise mal ›Rosalie‹ bei Google ein und ›Theater‹.«

Der Tipp des pensionierten Geschäftsführers führte mich in Sekunden zum Ziel. In Heidelberg lebte zwar keine Schauspielerin mit Namen Rosalie. Dafür aber eine Rosa Jordan, geboren 1959. Sie wohnte in der Schiffgasse, keine zweihundert Meter vom Theater entfernt. Sogar eine Telefonnummer war in den Dateien des Meldeamts vermerkt. Eine fünfstellige Nummer, wie nur Heidelberger Ureinwohner sie besaßen.

Sönnchen streckte den Kopf herein, um mich daran zu erinnern, dass Essenszeit war und man sich auch angenehmeren Dingen widmen konnte als längst vergessenen Todesfällen.

»Sagt Ihnen der Name Rosalie Jordan etwas?«, fragte ich spontan.

Meine Sekretärin bekam runde Augen.

»Die Schauspielerin? Die kennt in der Altstadt jeder. Keine Ahnung, welches zurzeit ihre Stammkneipe ist. In den meisten hat sie ja Hausverbot.«

Ich lehnte mich zurück und verschränkte die Hände im Genick.

»Das Haus, in dem sie lebt, hat sie von ihren Eltern geerbt. Der Vater war auch ein armer Schlucker beim Theater. Ich meine aber, er war nicht Schauspieler, sondern Kulissenmaler. Die Mutter hat aus einer reichen Professorenfamilie gestammt. Die Rosa war das einzige Kind und hat später das Mietshaus in der Schiffgasse geerbt.«

»Hat sie in den Kneipen Hausverbot, weil sie ihre Zeche nicht bezahlt?«

»Das weniger. Den größten Teil von ihrem Haus hat sie an Studenten vermietet. Finanziell kommt sie zurecht, denke ich. Aber sie ist ein fürchterliches Lästermaul. Früher oder später gibt's überall Stunk, wo sie auftaucht.«

Die Tür schloss sich. Ich wählte die fünfstellige Nummer der streitbaren Schauspielerin, aber es wurde nicht abgenommen. Draußen dunkelte es schon wieder, obwohl erst Mittag war. Fred Hergarden hatte sich noch immer nicht gemeldet. So rief ich wieder einmal die Vermieter an, und dieses Mal war jemand zu Hause. Herr Häusler war nicht weniger unwirsch als seine Gattin und erklärte mir nach einigen Schimpftiraden auf die Nachbarschaft, Hergarden habe gegen zehn das Haus verlassen und sei bislang nicht wieder aufgetaucht. Ob er ein Handy mit sich führte, war dem Vermieter nicht bekannt.

»Hat er gesagt, wie lange er bei Ihnen wohnen bleiben will?«

»Die Miete hat er bis Ende des Monats im Voraus bezahlt. Wir kassieren immer im Voraus. Sie glauben nicht, was heutzutage für Menschen ...«

Ich bedankte mich und legte auf.

Rosalie Jordan öffnete mir erst, nachdem ich mehrmals kräftig gegen ihre Tür geklopft hatte. Nach einigen vergeblichen Versuchen, sie anzurufen, hatte ich beschlossen, ihr einen unangemeldeten Besuch abzustatten. Aber auch das war nicht so einfach, hatte sich herausgestellt, da die Klingel nicht funktionierte. Bis vor die Wohnungstür der alten Schauspielerin war ich nur vorgedrungen, weil eine kleine Studentin mit asiatischem Gesicht aus dem Haus gekommen war und mich mit respektvoller Verbeugung und ohne irgendwelche Fragen eingelassen hatte. Das Haus hatte schon von außen einen ungepflegten Eindruck gemacht. Von den blassgrün gestrichenen Fensterläden blätterte die Farbe, und auch der Verputz zeigte Verfallserscheinungen. Der Hausflur war lange nicht mehr gefegt worden.

Rosalie Jordan zog die Tür nur so weit auf, dass sie gerade eben hinausspähen konnte. Aus kurzsichtigen Augen starrte sie mich feindselig an.

»Ja?«, sagte sie. »Was gibt's denn Dringendes?«

Ich stellte mich vor. Lächelte tapfer. »Es geht um Viktoria Hergarden.«

»Die ist doch schon ewig tot.«

»Und ich würde Ihnen gerne ein paar Fragen dazu stellen.«

»Ich weiß nichts. Wieso denn auf einmal?«

»Ihr Mann ist wieder aufgetaucht.«

»Freddy?«

Ich nickte und lächelte weiter.

»Und?«

»Dürfte ich vielleicht reinkommen?«

Ihr Blick war immer noch misstrauisch. Aber schließlich gab sie die Tür frei. »Falls die Unordnung Sie stört – Sie dürfen gerne aufräumen.«

Die Erdgeschosswohnung, die ich betrat, war ein finsteres, nach Alkohol und Schimmel stinkendes Loch voller Müll und leerer Flaschen. Die Bewohnerin steckte in einer fleckigen Jogginghose, die ihr über die Jahre zwei Nummern zu weit geworden war. Darüber schlabberte ein ebenfalls viel zu großer grauer Rollkragenpullover. Das hellblonde Haar war über die Jahre weiß und dünn geworden.

Während ich vor dem Haus auf das Schnarren des Türöffners wartete, hatte ich mir das bunte Klingelschild mit den unzähligen, überwiegend ausländischen Namen angesehen. In dem Haus lebten außer der Besitzerin noch fünf Wohngemeinschaften, von denen jede nach meiner Schätzung fünf- bis siebenhundert Euro Miete bezahlte. Das Haus wirkte nicht, als würde Geld für die Instandhaltung verschwendet, und die leeren Flaschen, die in der Küche herumstanden, hatten keine Luxusgetränke enthalten. Was also machte die Frau mit ihrem vielen Geld?

Wir setzten uns an einen verschmierten Tisch in der Küche, dem Raum, der von allen der vermüllteste zu sein schien. Ich zwang mich, den Gestank zu ignorieren, und achtete darauf, nirgendwo anzustoßen und nichts zu berühren. Ein uralter Kühlschrank dröhnte friedlich vor sich hin.

»Und?«, fragte Rosalie Jordan mit kalter Stimme. »Was ist nun mit Freddy?«

»Er behauptet, er hätte seine Frau umgebracht.«

»Hä? Was raucht der denn seit Neuestem für ein Kraut?«

»Ich vermute, er verdächtigt in Wirklichkeit einen anderen.«

»Wäre nichts Neues.«

»Hat er das damals auch schon getan?«

Sie nickte gelangweilt. Spielte mit einem Glas, in dem noch bräunliche Reste der einsamen Party vom Vorabend klebten. »Ja. Hat er.«

Ihre Gesichtsfarbe changierte zwischen Grau und Gelb. Im Mundwinkel klebte noch ein wenig Lippenstift. Die Alkoholfahne war atemberaubend.

»Was wissen Sie darüber?«, fragte ich, da sie offenbar nicht vorhatte, von sich aus zu reden.

»Er hat Marcel verdächtigt. Oder Sabeth, seine Frau. Er hat die fixe Idee gehabt, Marcel hätte seine Vicky gefickt. Und Sabeth hätte das dann logischerweise gewusst und sich bestimmt nicht gerade gefreut. Sie haben ja im selben Haus gewohnt, die vier.«

»Stimmt es, dass Graf etwas mit Frau Hergarden hatte?«

Sie grinste mich schelmisch an und ließ dabei zwei Zahnlücken sehen. »Vicky hat's jedenfalls behauptet. Wollte mich wahrscheinlich eifersüchtig machen, das dreckige, kleine Luder.«

»Sie waren auch … an Herrn Graf interessiert?«

»Jede war an Marcel interessiert. Bin aber leider nicht sein Typ gewesen. Obwohl ich damals noch ein bisschen besser ausgesehen habe als heute, auch wenn es kaum zu glauben ist.«

»Fred Hergarden hat damals Herrn Graf verdächtigt, am Tod seiner Frau schuld zu sein.«

Sie nickte betont gelangweilt. Schenkte klaren Schnaps ins trübe Glas, nahm einen ordentlichen Schluck. Alles, ohne mich eine Sekunde anzusehen.

»Und halten Sie das für glaubhaft?«

»Dass Marcel Vicky …?« Wieder grinste sie. Machte mit dem Zeigefinger eine Bewegung über die Kehle. »Klar halte ich das für glaubhaft. Jeder Mensch ist zu einem Mord fähig. Das Schicksal muss ihn nur tüchtig genug in den Schwitzkasten nehmen. Bei Sabeth bin ich mir nicht so sicher, ob die so was gepackt hätte. Wenn Vicky an Gift gestorben wäre, dann okay. Aber so, mit roher Gewalt und Blut und allem ...« Sie schloss die Augen und atmete einige Male tief ein und aus, als kämpfte sie gegen einen Schmerz an. »Hat es nicht geheißen, es sei ein Unfall gewesen? Ist nicht sogar die Polizei da gewesen und hat alles offiziell bestätigt?«

»Das ist richtig. Meine Kollegen, die den Fall damals untersucht haben, sind zu dem Schluss gekommen, dass Frau Hergarden allein war und unglücklich gestürzt ist.«

»Sie war besoffen, nicht?«

»Dafür gibt es keine Beweise. Allerdings war da eine leere Sektflasche. Und nur ein Glas dazu.«

Sie sah an meinem rechten Ohr vorbei auf einen trübseligen grauen Hof hinaus. »Ich weiß nur, dass sie behauptet hat, was mit Marcel zu haben, und dass sie ihm angeblich irgendwann den Laufpass gegeben hat und dass sie zwei Tage später tot war.«

Der Kühlschrank schaltete sich klappernd aus, als wollte er diese Aussage bestätigen.

»Wissen Sie, warum Frau Hergarden das Verhältnis – angeblich – gelöst hat?«

»Braucht man seit Neuestem einen Grund, um sich zu trennen?«

»In meinen Kreisen normalerweise schon.«

»In Ihren Kreisen?« Sie lachte schrill. »Sie sind wahrscheinlich eher so der solide Typ. Wie war noch der Spruch? Wer zweimal mit demselben pennt, gehört schon zum Establishment. Wir waren jung. Wir wollten Spaß haben. Und in Künstlerkreisen hat diese Kreuz- und Querfickerei ja sowieso irgendwie zum guten Ton gehört. Es gab die Pille. Von AIDS hat man noch nichts gewusst ...«

»Hat Hergarden damals mit Ihnen über den Tod seiner Frau gesprochen?«

»Und wie! Er ist ja erst eine Woche nach dem sogenannten Unfall hier aufgekreuzt. In Afrika war er gewesen oder in Indien, was weiß ich. Er war fix und alle, wie er hier aufgekreuzt ist. Total runter mit den Nerven. Und gleich am nächsten Tag war ja schon die Beerdigung. Ich bin nicht hingegangen. Ich kann so was nicht. Marcel und Sabeth waren dabei. Keine gute Idee. Am offenen Grab soll's um ein Haar eine Schlägerei gegeben haben, weil Freddy Marcel an die Gurgel wollte. Sabeth ist dazwischen und hat sie auseinandergekloppt, habe ich später gehört. War wohl alles mächtig peinlich, und danach haben sie nicht mehr miteinander geredet. Kein Wort. Nie.«

Eine schmale schwarze Katze kam mit steil aufgerichtetem Schwanz durch die Küchentür geschlichen, beäugte mich unschlüssig, machte schließlich wieder kehrt.

»Sie haben also mit Hergarden gesprochen?«

»Sag ich doch«, erwiderte Rosalie Jordan unwirsch und nahm einen weiteren Holzfällerschluck aus ihrem Glas. Sie konnte nicht annähernd so alt sein, wie sie aussah. »Am Abend nach der Beerdigung ist er bei mir gewesen. Hier, an diesem Tisch, hat er gehockt und sich ausgekotzt.«

Ich beugte mich so weit vor, wie es ging, ohne mit dem Tisch in Kontakt zu kommen. »Und was genau hat er gesagt? Das ist jetzt wichtig.«

»Dass Vicky seine große Liebe war. Und dass Marcel sie gefickt hat. Und dass er schuld ist an ihrem Tod. Und dass er Marcel am liebsten umbringen würde. ›Du bist selber schuld‹, hab ich zu ihm gesagt. ›Hättest besser auf sie aufpassen müssen. Nicht ständig in der Weltgeschichte rumgondeln. Auf läufige Hündinnen muss man ein Auge haben‹, hab ich ihm gesagt, ›sonst hat man bald eine Hundezucht.‹«

»Hat er irgendeinen glaubhaften Grund genannt für seine Behauptung, Herr Graf hätte seine Frau auf dem Gewissen?«

Der Kühlschrank sprang wieder an.

»So direkt nicht. Es war ein großes Hin und Her. Erst hieß es, es würd ihn nicht wundern, wenn … Nach dem dritten Whisky war er überzeugt, dass Marcel es war. Beim sechsten sind ihm auf einmal wieder Zweifel gekommen.«

»Das ist alles mehr als vage …«

Sie zuckte die knochigen Schultern unter dem grauen Pulli.

»Ich kann's nicht ändern. Vielleicht hat er in den vielen Jahren seither nachgedacht, und jetzt ist er überzeugt, dass Marcel es war? Vielleicht hat er irgendwas erfahren, was er damals noch nicht gewusst hat? Wobei ich mir nicht vorstellen kann, wie man in Afrika ... Oder war's doch Indien?«

»Er ist viel rumgekommen, soweit ich weiß.«

»Irgendwas muss da jedenfalls passiert sein. Sonst würde er ja wohl nicht nach dreißig Jahren auf einmal wieder aufkreuzen.«

»Er scheint krank zu sein.«

Diese Neuigkeit machte wenig Eindruck auf sie. »Vielleicht will er Ordnung schaffen in seinem Leben? Alte Schulden eintreiben?«

Nun war ich es, der die Achseln hob. »So etwas Ähnliches habe ich auch schon gedacht.«

Das Gespräch begann, sich im Kreis zu drehen. So kam ich nicht weiter. Für einige Sekunden blieb es still. Erst jetzt entdeckte ich, dass die schwarze Katze im Halbschatten des Flurs stand und mich nicht aus den grünen Raubtieraugen ließ.

»Ich weiß nicht mehr so genau, was er an dem Abend alles gelabert hat«, murmelte Rosalie Jordan, die plötzlich am Ende ihrer Kräfte zu sein schien. »In Begleitung von einer Flasche Black and White ist er aufgekreuzt. War seinerzeit unsere Lieblingslimonade, Black and White.«

Ich lehnte mich zurück und unterdrückte einen Seufzer. Es war sinnlos, was ich hier tat. Stochern in zähem, undurchdringlichem Nebel, noch dazu mit einem viel zu kurzen Stock. Auf dem Tisch vor mir standen die Reste eines kargen Frühstücks. Ein Kaffeebecher, der offensichtlich schon lange nicht mehr mit klarem Wasser in Berührung gekommen war, ein Teller voller Krümel und Butterspuren. Ein Glas, in dem noch ein Rest Orangensaft stand.

Okay, ein allerletzter Versuch: »Sie halten es also für ausgeschlossen, dass Herr Graf ein Verhältnis mit Frau Hergarden hatte?«

»Völlig ausgeschlossen. Eine von Freddys Schnapsideen.«

»Hergarden scheint davon überzeugt gewesen zu sein.«

»Warum fragen Sie nicht einfach Marcel?«

»Das habe ich schon getan. Er streitet es ab.«

»Haben Sie mit ihm telefoniert? Wo in der Weltgeschichte treibt er sich denn rum zurzeit?«

»In Ludwigshafen. Ich bin gestern Abend bei ihm gewesen.«

Dass ihr alter Bekannter so nah war, überraschte sie. Ich erzählte ein wenig von meinem Gespräch, und sie fragte, wie Graf heute aussah.

Ich fragte mich, ob es nicht allmählich an der Zeit war, mich zu verabschieden.

»Ziemliche Scheiße, was?«, meinte Rosalie Jordan mitfühlend, der meine ratlose Miene nicht entgangen war. »Warum tun Sie sich das überhaupt an? Wen juckt es heute noch, mit wem eine gewisse Vicky vor einem halben Jahrhundert in der Kiste war und wie sie ums Leben gekommen ist? Ist das nicht sowieso alles verjährt?«

»Mord verjährt nicht. Und irgendetwas ist faul an der Geschichte.«

»Was?« Jetzt war sie plötzlich wach. »Was ist faul?«

Dass der Polizeibericht von damals voller Fehler und Lücken war. Dass jemand mich vor die Brust gestoßen hatte und ich wie ein Mehlsack umgekippt und auf den Hinterkopf geknallt war. Dass jemand einen Peilsender an meinen Wagen montiert hatte. Dass die Anzeige nicht zu finden war, die Hergarden angeblich damals bei der Polizei gemacht hatte.

»Ich weiß es nicht«, sagte ich und rieb mir mit beiden Händen das Gesicht. »Mehr so ein Gefühl.«

»Gefühle muss man ernst nehmen«, sagte die Schauspielerin. »Gefühle sind das Allerwichtigste im Leben. Das bisschen Verstand obendrüber, das kann man vergessen. Es gibt nicht viel, was ich in meinem Scheißleben gelernt habe. Aber das, das ist hängen geblieben.«

Ich widerstand meinem Fluchtdrang. »Kommen wir zu Frau Holland.«

»Sabeth.«

»Sie hat die Tote am nächsten Morgen gefunden.«

»Wenn man sie ärgern wollte, musste man sie Lisa nennen.«

»Hat sie von der angeblichen Geschichte zwischen Vicky und ihrem Mann gewusst?«

»Davon bin ich überzeugt. Wissen Sie, was meine Mutter immer zu mir gesagt hat? Rosamädchen, hat sie gesagt, lass die Finger von schönen Männern. Einen schönen Mann hast du nie für dich allein.«

Irgendwo über uns begann Musik zu wummern. Rosalie Jordan verzog das faltige Gesicht zu einer leidenden Grimasse. »Geht das schon wieder los!«, murmelte sie. »Ich schmeiß sie raus. Irgendwann schmeiß ich das ganze Drecksspack raus ...« Sie sah mich mit verlorenem Blick an. »Die Chinesen sind alle so freundlich und leise und fleißig. Aber diese Chaoten im Zweiten, die führen sich auf, dass es der Sau graust.«

Nachdem wir noch eine Weile gemeinsam den Technobässen gelauscht hatten, straffte sie sich und fuhr fort: »Sabeth ist jähzornig gewesen. Marcel ist mehr als einmal mit der Sonnenbrille rumgeschlichen, weil er ein blaues Auge hatte.«

»Sie wollen andeuten, sie hat ihn geschlagen?«

»Nicht nur einmal. Alle haben es gewusst. Alle.«

»Wirklich gesehen hat es aber niemand?«

Sie zögerte mit der Antwort. Blickte in ihr schon fast wieder leeres Glas. »Solche Sachen machen die Runde. Man kann nicht sagen, wer es in die Welt gesetzt hat. Aber es hat gepasst, irgendwie. Sie war ihm über. Sabeth war Marcel über. Die hat sich von ihm nichts gefallen lassen.«

»Wissen Sie, was aus ihr geworden ist?«

»Hab mal gehört, sie hätte wieder geheiratet. In Frankreich irgendwo.«

»Eine große Karriere als Schauspielerin hat sie offenbar nicht gemacht.«

»Große Karriere hat nur Marcel gemacht. Sabeth hat es ja auch gar nicht nötig gehabt. Deren Wiege war mit Tausendern ausgepolstert. Für Sabeth ist die Schauspielerei nur ein netter Zeitvertreib gewesen. Da war keine Leidenschaft, wenn sie auf der Bühne stand. Und Leidenschaft kommt ja nun mal von Leiden. Sabeth ist es immer zu gut gegangen.«

»Sie hat geerbt?«

»Nach dem Tod ihrer Eltern hat sie mehr Geld auf dem Konto gehabt, als ein Mensch in einem Leben verpulvern kann. Dazu hat sie dieses Riesenhaus geerbt. Allein von dem, was das wert war, kann man ganz schön lange leben.«

»So riesig fand ich das Haus nun auch nicht.«

»Vielleicht haben Sie nicht richtig hingeguckt?«

Ich überlegte, was ich noch fragen könnte, aber es wollte mir nichts mehr einfallen. Die Katze starrte mich immer noch aus dem Dämmerlicht an und machte mich allmählich nervös. Über uns dröhnten die Bässe, dass das Geschirr im alten Küchenbüfett klirrte. Mein Blick schweifte umher. Chaos, überall. Schmutz, verkrustete Teller, manche schon angeschimmelt, leere Flaschen. Hauptsächlich Whisky, aber auch Cognac, Korn. Rosalie Jordan schien nicht wählerisch zu sein, was ihre Betäubungsmittel betraf. Wie konnte ein Mensch so leben und nicht verzweifeln? Auf dem obersten Brett eines Standregals voller verstaubter Kochbücher, Plunder und Vergessenem entdeckte ich eine Pillenschachtel, halb verdeckt von einem schmutzigen Lappen.

»Atrip…«, entzifferte ich. Der Rest war wegen des Lappens nicht zu sehen. Der verkrachten Schauspielerin war mein Blick nicht entgangen.

»Tja«, sagte sie mit schiefem Grinsen und hob wieder einmal die knochigen Schultern. »Atripla. Bisher hilft's noch.«

»Das … das konnte ich natürlich nicht …«

Ihr Lächeln kippte weg. »Ich sag doch, von AIDS haben wir damals noch nichts gewusst. Manche hat's erwischt, andere nicht. Manche haben eine Krankenversicherung, andere nicht. Kein Grund zum Heulen. Wir Schauspieler sind eine zähe und leidensfähige Spezies.«

Ich schluckte. Was sagt man in einer solchen Situation? »Das tut mir wirklich leid«, sagte ich.

»Muss Ihnen nicht leidtun. Meine Schuld. Mein Problem.«

»Wer könnte noch etwas von damals wissen?«, fragte ich, als ich mich wieder gefasst hatte. »Hat es noch andere Männer gegeben, die mit Frau Hergarden …? Jemand hat mir etwas von einem Musiker erzählt …«

»Klar hat's die gegeben«, erwiderte sie, nun wieder in der alten Bissigkeit. »Ich kann Ihnen aber bestimmt keine komplette Liste liefern. Das hätte wahrscheinlich nicht mal Vicky selber gekonnt.« Sie lachte, als hätte sie einen schmutzigen Witz erzählt. Die Katze war auf einmal verschwunden, obwohl ich hätte schwören können, dass sie vor einer Sekunde noch da gewesen war. »Aber warten Sie, einer fällt mir ein. Wie hat der noch …« Ihre Stirn wurde kraus, das linke Auge schmal. »Ein Musiker. Nils. Nils Irgendwas.«

»Ein Orchestermusiker?«

»Trompete, wenn ich mich nicht irre. Auf jeden Fall Blech. Ein Adonis. Nie wieder habe ich so einen schönen Mann gesehen.«

»Mehr wissen Sie nicht über diesen Nils?«

»Anfangs habe ich dumme Kuh geglaubt, er ist schwul.« Wieder grinste sie ihr schiefes Grinsen. »Und wie ich begriffen habe, dass ich falschliege, da hatte Vicky ihn sich schon geschnappt.«

»Sie haben keine Idee, wie der Nachname …?«

Jetzt sah sie mir wieder ins Gesicht. Ihr Blick war mit einem Mal fast freundlich. »Allzu viele Nilse wird's nicht geben unter den Trompetern dieser Welt, was?« Abrupt verfinsterte sich ihre Miene wieder. »Haben Sie schon mit der Kranich geredet? Simone?«

Ich nickte.

»Und?«

»Sie konnte mir nicht viel sagen.«

»Wundert mich nicht – blöd, wie sie nun mal ist. Was macht sie heute?«

»Sie ist in Bochum am Theater.«

»Große Rollen?«

»Wohl eher nicht.«

Meine Antwort schien sie zu befriedigen. »Hübsche Fresse, aber dumm wie Bohnenstroh. Das hat sie ja auch immer gespielt: dumme Weiber. Was anderes konnte die nicht.«

»Und Frau Holland?«

»Die hätte gut sein können. Aber ich hab's ja schon gesagt: Der ist es einfach zu gut gegangen.«

»Klingt alles ziemlich schrecklich, was Sie vom Theaterleben erzählen«, sagte ich, als ich mich müde lächelnd erhob. »Nichts als Neid und Intrigen und Eifersucht ...«

»Theater?« Sie musterte mich von unten her, als hätte ich etwas unfassbar Dummes gesagt. In ihrem Mundwinkel hing ein wenig Speichel. »Theater ist das Größte und Schönste, was es gibt auf dieser Welt! Theater, das ist Glück und Leid und Drama! Alles abwechselnd echt oder gespielt, wobei man das manchmal gar nicht so genau auseinanderhalten kann. Theater, das ist Leben im Quadrat. Wenn bloß die lieben Kollegen und Kolleginnen nicht wären ...«

Rosalie Jordan reichte mir die Hand zum Abschied.

Ich ergriff sie, obwohl sie schmutzig war.

»Ich hab sie gut leiden können, die Vicky«, sagte sie leise, als wir an der Tür waren. »Sie hat nicht immer nur an sich gedacht wie die meisten anderen. Aus dem Osten hat sie gestammt, aus Leipzig, wenn ich mich nicht täusche. Wie sie mit ihren Eltern rüber ist, da war sie gerade mal fünfzehn. Vicky hat das Soziale im Blut gehabt. Ich kenne das, mein Vater war auch Kommunist, bis er mit siebenundachtzig gestorben ist. Vicky hat sich in der Gewerkschaft engagiert, hat Plakate geklebt und Flugblätter verteilt, während die anderen an ihren Karrieren gefeilt haben.«

Von oben wummerte immer noch Musik, die im Treppenhaus noch deutlicher zu hören war als in der Küche der alten Schauspielerin. Wenige Schritte bevor ich die Haustür erreichte, wurde sie von außen aufgestoßen, und drei junge Männer – alle in bunten Jeans und wetterfesten Jacken – kamen mir entgegen. Zusammen schleppten sie zwei Bierkästen und einige Plastiktüten. Ihrem fröhlichen Gespräch entnahm ich, dass sie sich auf eine Party freuten, die demnächst steigen würde. Sekunden später trat ich aufatmend in die kalte, klare Februarluft hinaus.

Nils. Trompeter. Na wunderbar.

Wahrscheinlich hatte der Mann die Musik vor zwanzig Jahren an den Nagel gehängt oder war nach Amerika ausgewandert oder hatte geheiratet und den Namen seiner Frau angenommen. Andererseits hatte Rosalie Jordan nicht ganz unrecht: Nils war wirklich kein häufiger Name, und den Vornamen wechselt man in Deutschland nicht. Allzu viele gute Trompeter gab es vermutlich auch nicht.

Frustriert machte ich mich auf den Weg zurück zur Direktion. Inzwischen war meine Mittagspause zu Ende gegangen. Ich war hungrig, was ich für ein gutes Zeichen hielt, denn Appetit ist ein Zeichen für Gesundheit. Außerdem regnete es wieder, was kein gutes Zeichen war, denn ich hatte meinen Schirm im Büro gelassen.

»Sie werden sich noch den Tod holen!«, lautete denn auch die herzliche Begrüßung meiner heute wieder einmal nicht so gut gelaunten Sekretärin. »Aber Sie wollen es ja so.« Dann murmelte sie noch etwas, was klang wie: »Männer!«

»Frau Walldorf«, erwiderte ich, während ich den nassen Mantel neben meinen trockenen Schirm hängte. »Vielleicht nehmen Sie zur Kenntnis, dass eine Gehirnerschütterung nichts mit Erkältung und Viren zu tun hat.«

»Wie Sie meinen«, sagte sie, ohne mich anzusehen. »Sie sind der Chef, und Chefs haben bekanntlich immer recht.«

»Und deshalb könnten Sie ruhig ein bisschen netter zu mir sein.«

Schweigend zog sie eine Schublade ihres Schreibtischs auf, kramte darin herum, knallte einen kleinen Reiseföhn vor mich hin.

»Ist das nett genug?«

Vorsichtshalber verzog ich mich in mein Büro und schloss die Tür hinter mir.

»Männer!«, hörte ich sie noch einmal sagen. Dieses Mal laut und verständlich.

Das Internet kannte nur einen Nils Wülker, der zwar Trompeter, aber zu jung war, um der zu sein, den ich suchte. Auch die Sekretärin des städtischen Theaters war dieses Mal ratlos. Beim Einwohnermeldeamt war man am ratlosesten und glaubte anfangs sogar an einen Scherzanruf. Schließlich erhob ich mich wieder und öffnete die Tür zum Vorzimmer.

»Sönnchen, wollen wir uns nicht wieder vertragen? Wir sind doch erwachsene Menschen.«

»Wenn Sie meinen.«

Immer noch weigerte sie sich hartnäckig, mir in die Augen zu sehen.

»Das mit dem Föhn war wirklich sehr nett von Ihnen.«

»Sie haben ihn ja nicht mal benutzt!«

»Ich hatte erst noch was zu erledigen.«

»Ach so.«

»Wollen Sie gar nicht wissen, was?«

»Nein.«

Ich setzte mich auf den Stuhl neben ihrem Schreibtisch, um auf Augenhöhe mit ihr zu sein. Es wollte mir jedoch nicht gelingen, ihren Blick einzufangen.

»Ich entschuldige mich für alles, was ich Ihnen jemals angetan habe ...«

Sie schwieg. Blinzelte. Und Augenblicke später hielt ich zu meiner Verblüffung meine von Schluchzern geschüttelte Sekretärin im Arm und hoffte, dass jetzt niemand hereinplatzte. Nach einiger Zeit beruhigte sie sich wieder. Schniefte und hustete noch ein wenig. Dann sprang sie unvermittelt auf.

»Kaffee?«

»Wäre super.«

»Ich brauch jetzt auch einen.«

Mit hängenden Schultern hantierte sie an der Kaffeemaschine. Dann saßen wir zusammen, nippten stumm an unseren Bechern. Ich an einem Cappuccino, sie an etwas, das sie Café au lait nannte und in das sie drei Löffel Zucker rührte.

»Und jetzt erzählen Sie endlich.«

»Wir haben uns so gestritten.«

»Worum?«

»Weiß ich nicht mehr.«

»Dann rufen Sie ihn an.«

»Im Leben nicht.«

»Er muss anrufen?«

»Natürlich.«

»Soll ich versuchen zu vermitteln?«

»Unterstehen Sie sich!«

»Vielleicht wartet er darauf, dass Sie anrufen?«

»Soll er. Kann er lange warten.«

»Wenn ich mal ganz offen sein darf, als Chef: Sie benehmen sich wie eine beleidigte Dreizehnjährige.«

»Weiß ich.«

»Und das finden Sie in Ordnung?«

»Nein. Aber ich … Ich weiß doch auch nicht.«

Ich erhob mich, nahm meinen Becher und sagte: »Ich gehe jetzt an meinen Schreibtisch und mache die Tür hinter mir zu. Und wenn ich in zehn Minuten wieder herauskomme, dann will ich sehen, dass Sie wieder lachen wie sonst immer.«

Sie nickte trostlos. Nippte an ihrer Milchbrühe. Schniefte wieder.

»Das war eben eine dienstliche Anweisung, Frau Walldorf!«

»Okay, Herr Chef.« Sie nickte tapfer. »Ist okay.«

Für zwei, drei Minuten blieb es mäuschenstill im Vorzimmer. Dann hörte ich, wie sie den Hörer abnahm und wieder auflegte und wieder abnahm und noch einmal auflegte. Schließlich räusperte sie sich, wie sie sich immer räusperte, bevor sie jemanden anrief. Glücklicherweise schien ihr Christian zu Hause zu sein, den ich noch immer nicht zu Gesicht bekommen hatte, wie mir jetzt erst bewusst wurde. Offenbar war er auch gesprächsbereit, denn als ich nach exakt zehn Minuten die Tür wieder öffnete, drückte sie den Hörer immer noch ans Ohr und strahlte mich an wie eine Fünfjährige den Weihnachtsmann.

Kurze Zeit später kam sie herein und wollte sich bedanken. »Weiß gar nicht, was in mich gefahren ist …«

»Das ist völlig normal, wenn man verliebt ist.«

»Danke, dass Sie mir ins Gewissen geredet haben. Wie kann ich das wiedergutmachen?«

»Da habe ich eine prima Idee …«

Augenblicke später telefonierte sie wieder, wie früher lachend und kichernd, und knapp drei Stunden später, nachmittags um kurz vor vier, hatte sie ihn aufgespürt: Nils Hedin, heute Inhaber einer chemischen Reinigung im schönen Landau an der südlichen Weinstraße.

»Von der Musik bin ich geheilt«, sagte der ehemalige Konzerttrompeter mit weicher Stimme am Telefon. »Die idiotischen Arbeitszeiten, die ewige Ungewissheit, wenn man wieder mal ohne Engagement dasteht. Ständig liest man, dass wieder irgendwo ein Orchester aufgelöst wird. Überall wird gespart und gespart und gespart. Als Allererstes natürlich immer an der Kultur. Wer interessiert sich heute noch für so unnütze Dinge wie Musik …«

»Es geht um eine Frau, die Sie einmal gekannt haben sollen. Viktoria Hergarden.«

»Vicky? Gütiger Gott! Wie lange ist das denn her?«

»Fast dreißig Jahre.«

Hedin schwieg lange. Schließlich erklärte er mit tonloser Stimme: »Dazu will ich nichts sagen, bitte entschuldigen Sie.«

»Es geht nicht darum, was damals zwischen Ihnen und Frau Hergarden war. Es geht …«

»Nein. Nein. Ich … weiß ja nicht mal … Nein.«

»Wenn ich zu Ihnen nach Landau komme?«

»Nein. Das ist Vergangenheit. Das ist … vorbei ist das. Vorbei.«

»Wollen Sie gar nicht wissen, warum ich mich nach so langer Zeit mit der Sache beschäftige?«

Sein nächstes »Nein« klang endgültig. Er legte auf.

Von Theresa war inzwischen eine lange Mail gekommen. Eine halbe Ewigkeit hatte sie sich mit dem Video herumgeärgert. Die zur Übertragung notwendige Software auf ihrem Laptop behauptete hartnäckig, das Handy nicht zu erkennen. Theresa vermutete, es liege vielleicht am Verbindungskabel.

Nicht einmal ihrer in technischen Dingen versierten polnischen Putzfrau war es gelungen, dem bockigen Hightech-Handy das kurze Filmchen zu entlocken. Außerdem wollte sie wissen, ob wir unseren Abend auf den nächsten Tag verschieben könnten. Sie fühlte sich nicht gut.

Fred Hergarden hatte sich immer noch nicht gemeldet.

17

Wie ich gehofft hatte, zählten Hergardens Vermieter zu den Menschen, die man morgens um acht schon anrufen kann.

»Der ist in der Nacht gar nicht heimgekommen!«, lautete die alarmierende Auskunft von Frau Häusler am Mittwochmorgen. »Die ganze Nacht ist er sonst nie fortgeblieben!«

»Sein Gepäck ist aber noch da?«

»Müsst ich nachsehen. Wenn Sie einen Moment dranbleiben wollen ...«

Ein Moment kann ganz schön lang sein. Ich hörte die alte Frau abwechselnd schnaufend und Verwünschungen murmelnd die Treppe erklimmen. Hörte Stufen knarren. Hörte einen großen Schlüsselbund klimpern, ein altes Schloss knacken.

»Ist noch da«, keuchte sie endlich. »Das Gepäck. Er hat ja auch bloß die Tasche dabei.«

»Wann ist er weggegangen?«

»Gestern am Vormittag. Ich bin um neun beim Arzt gewesen. Und wie ich weggegangen bin, da hab ich ihn oben rumpeln gehört. Leise ist der Herr nämlich nicht. Wie ich später heimgekommen bin, das muss so um elf rum gewesen sein, da ist's oben still gewesen.«

»Hat er vielleicht Ihrem Mann gesagt, wohin er wollte?«

»Der sagt einem ja nie irgendwas. Grad, dass er einem mal einen guten Tag wünscht. Meinen Sie, es ist ihm was passiert?«

»Aber nein. Ich müsste ihn nur dringend sprechen.«

»Auf seinem Nachttisch, da liegt ... eine Visitenkarte liegt da. Von der Polizei. Gerlach, sind Sie das?«

»Ja.«

»Kriminal...oberrat. Mein Gustav ist auch Beamter gewesen. Beim Bauordnungsamt. Der hat's auch bis zum Oberrat gebracht. Jetzt ist er natürlich in Pension.«

»Mein Vater war früher auch Beamter.«

»Sagen Sie bloß! Vielleicht kennen Ihr Herr Vater und mein Gustav sich sogar?«

»Er war nicht in Heidelberg. Und er war beim Finanzamt.«

Sönnchen öffnete die Tür, um mir mit glänzenden Augen einen guten Morgen zu wünschen.

»Bin heut ein bisschen spät, weil ...«

»Kein Problem«, sagte ich großmütig, während ich den Hörer auflegte. »Sie bleiben ja oft genug länger.«

Kurz darauf hörte ich sie auf ihrem Schreibtisch herumkramen und leise telefonieren und manchmal noch leiser lachen. Offenbar hatte man eine vergnügliche Nacht gehabt.

Die Fahrt von Heidelberg nach Landau dauerte fast anderthalb Stunden. Der Regen war gerade so stark, dass keine Geschwindigkeit des Scheibenwischers richtig war. Immerhin war die A5 heute ausnahmsweise staufrei. Dafür stockte der Verkehr vor der Rheinbrücke bei Karlsruhe, an der offenbar wieder einmal etwas repariert werden musste. Nils Hedin hatte mich um kurz vor neun angerufen und kleinlaut einem Treffen zugestimmt.

»Aber auf keinen Fall hier in meinem Haus!«

»Wir können uns treffen, wo Sie wollen und wann Sie wollen.«

»So wichtig ist es?«

»Sagen Sie mir, wo ich hinsoll, und ich fahre sofort los.«

Er hatte noch ein wenig herumgedruckst. »Meine Frau ... Sie möchte bestimmt nichts hören von dieser Sache damals ... Aber heute fährt sie mit einer Freundin in Weißenburg zum Shoppen. Es gibt hier in der Nähe ein ruhiges Café ... Wäre elf Uhr für Sie okay? Dann könnte ich anschließend einkaufen und Mittagessen machen, bis die Kinder aus der Schule kommen.«

Während der Fahrt rief ich Theresa an. Ein richtiges Gespräch wollte jedoch nicht in Gang kommen. Sie behauptete, das Wetter schlage ihr aufs Gemüt. Ich behauptete, sie habe schlechte Laune wegen des ausbleibenden Verkaufserfolgs ihres Buchs. Sie gab mir so einsilbig recht, dass es höchstens die halbe Wahrheit sein konnte.

»Hab ich irgendwas falsch gemacht? Geht es um Doro?«

»Nein.«

»Geht es um Henning?«

Theresa konnte keine Kinder bekommen, obwohl sie sich immer welche gewünscht hatte. Da war der Verdacht nicht ganz abwegig, sie sei bedrückt, weil mir ein drittes Kind mehr oder weniger in den Schoß gefallen war.

»Aber nein.«

»Meine Töchter wollen eine große Party feiern. Wegen Henning. Du bist natürlich herzlich eingeladen.«

»Wie schön.«

»Kriegst du deine Tage?«

An Stelle einer Antwort stöhnte sie auf.

»Du willst nicht darüber reden?«

Keine Antwort ist oft auch eine Antwort.

Nils Hedin war auch heute noch ein schöner Mann. Kein Muskelprotz, kein Alphatier, sondern von schlanker Gestalt mit geschmeidigen Bewegungen, elegant angegrauten Schläfen, seidigen Wimpern und einem Mund, der mich an klassische Götterstatuen denken ließ. Außerdem hatte er damals in Heidelberg nicht Trompete gespielt, sondern Oboe.

»Eine Ewigkeit her«, sagte er heiser, als er mir eine schmale, feuchte Hand reichte. »Ich bin damals bald weg. Weg von Heidelberg, nach dieser … Geschichte.«

Er hatte auf mich warten müssen, denn infolge des Staus bei Karlsruhe war ich eine Viertelstunde zu spät in Landau angekommen. Glücklicherweise zählte er jedoch zu den seltenen Menschen, denen Warten nichts ausmacht. Schon bei unseren kurzen Telefonaten war mir aufgefallen, dass er beim Sprechen immer wieder lange Pausen machte und manche Sätze nicht zu Ende sprach.

Er hatte einen Tisch an der Wand gewählt, der weit von der Theke entfernt war. Wir setzten uns. Vor ihm stand ein schon halb geleertes Glas gelbe Limonade. Das modern eingerichtete Café am östlichen Rand der Altstadt war nur schwach besucht. Neben der Heizung saßen zwei weibliche Gäste jenseits der besten Jahre und unterhielten sich angeregt über eine gemeinsame Bekannte, die kürzlich einen zwanzig Jahre älteren Mann geheiratet hatte. In einer Ecke saß ein pummeliger junger Mann und tippte mit konzentrierter Miene auf der Tastatur eines winzigen Laptops herum. Aus unsichtbaren Lautsprechern kam leise Kaufhausmusik. Es duftete nach Kaffee und frischem Kuchen. Die Bedienung baute sich vor mir auf und sah mich, Kuli und Blöckchen in der Hand, drohend an.

»Sie sollen damals eine enge Beziehung zu Frau Hergarden gehabt haben«, begann ich, nachdem ich mangels besserer Ideen wieder einmal Tee geordert hatte.

»Das ist richtig, aber ... hoffentlich kein Verbrechen.« Hedin seufzte und sah auf seine Musikerhände. »Vicky war sehr – wie sagt man? – lebenslustig. Und Freddy war so ...«

Er knetete seine gelenkigen Finger und hielt den Blick der dunklen Augen gesenkt, als müsste er wegen seiner längst verjährten Liebe immer noch ein schlechtes Gewissen haben. Als ich mein Handy auf den Tisch legte, entdeckte ich, dass während der Fahrt eine SMS gekommen war.

»... viel im Ausland, ich weiß.«

»Vicky sagte mal, sie unterscheidet zwischen seelischer Treue und körperlicher Treue. Letztere hielt sie für eine moderne Form von ... Leibeigenschaft.«

»Darf ich fragen, wie lange das ging?«

»Erst möchte ich Sie etwas fragen.« Zum ersten Mal sah er mir ins Gesicht. Sein Blick war traurig. »Nämlich, weshalb Sie das Ganze auf einmal so interessiert.«

Ich klärte ihn in knappen Worten auf.

»Ermordet?«, fragte er, als ich geendet hatte, und senkte den Blick wieder. »Aber ... von wem denn?«

»Das weiß ich nicht. Es gibt Anhaltspunkte dafür, dass Herr Hergarden Marcel Graf verdächtigt.«

»Marcel?« Hedin lachte erschrocken auf, brach sofort wieder ab. »Was ist das denn für eine verrückte ... Marcel?«

»Sie haben mir noch nicht gesagt, wie lange das ging zwischen Ihnen und Frau Hergarden.«

»Angefangen hat es im Sommer. Etwa einen Monat, bevor Freddy in den Irak geflogen ist. Es ging bis etwa ... knapp zwei Wochen vor ihrem Tod. Nicht mal ein halbes Jahr, insgesamt. Die plötzliche Trennung war ein ... schlimmer Schlag für mich. Nur für mich. Vicky war da anders. Obwohl sie so lebenslustig war, hatte Vicky nicht viele richtige Freunde. Vielleicht war sie ein wenig zu verbissen hinter ihrer Karriere her. Auf der anderen Seite war sie aber nicht so intrigant wie manche ... Wenn ich da nur an die süße Rosalie denke. Und Simone. Das waren vielleicht zwei Biester. Wie Gift und ... Wenn die zwei sich um dieselbe Rolle bemüht haben, und das kam öfter vor, es hätte einen wahrhaftig nicht gewundert, wenn sie sich gegenseitig vergiftet ...«

»Kann es sein, dass Frau Hergarden neben der Beziehung zu Ihnen auch noch mit anderen Männern ein Verhältnis hatte?«

Hedin nickte zögernd und mit hartnäckig abgewandtem Blick. Die beiden Damen neben der Heizung unterhielten sich inzwischen über Unterleibserkrankungen.

»Mit Marcel. Auf den waren sie alle scharf, die Mädchen. Jeder hat gespürt ... Marcel wird es schaffen. Aus dem wird mal was. Der kann einem nützlich sein. Dass er als Fernsehclown enden würde, hat ja niemand ahnen können. Aber wie kommt denn nun die Polizei nach so vielen ... Jahren darauf, dass es doch kein Unfall ...?«

»Dafür gibt es verschiedene Gründe. Und es ist bisher nicht mehr als ein Verdacht.«

»Es hieß doch, sie sei ausgerutscht und ...?«

»Auf einem kleinen Flokatiteppich. Und sie war wohl betrunken.«

Hedin nickte gedankenverloren. Die Gelenke seiner langen Finger knackten. Der junge Mann in der Ecke gönnte sich eine schöpferische Pause und ein zweites Kännchen Filterkaffee.

»Diesen Teppich kenne ich gut«, sagte Hedin so leise, als vertraute er mir ein jahrzehntelang gehütetes Geheimnis an. »Habe mir selbst mal fast das ... Handgelenk gebrochen, als ich damit weggerutscht bin. Ich habe ihr gesagt, sie soll das Ding in den Müll tun, bevor noch ein Unglück passiert. Da hat sie gelacht und gesagt, auf dem Teppich hat sie ihre Unschuld verloren. Der Teppich bleibt.«

»Sie waren öfter in ihrer Wohnung?«

»Ich habe gesagt, dann leg doch wenigstens so eine Antirutschmatte unter den blöden Lappen, bevor du dir noch den Hals brichst. Habe ihr sogar so ein Ding besorgt, und wir haben sie dann zusammen feierlich ... installiert, und dann haben wir den Teppich ... sozusagen neu eingeweiht.« Er lächelte in wehmütiger Erinnerung und errötete ein wenig.

»Sie haben sich immer in ihrer Wohnung getroffen?«

»Vicky war auch manchmal bei mir. Aber bei ihr war es natürlich ... schöner. Viel schöner. Und größer auch. Ich hatte ja nur ein winziges und im Winter eiskaltes Ein-Zimmer-Loch unterm Dach in Ziegelhausen. Das Einzige, was ich bezahlen konnte, und vermutlich war mein ganzes Appartement kleiner als ... Vickys Wohnzimmer. Die hatten es schon mondän, die vier da draußen in Neuenheim.«

Ich dachte an das Wohnzimmer der alten Frau Tröndle mit den Wanderschuhen, das vermutlich dieselben Maße hatte wie das der gegenüberliegenden Wohnung und bestimmt nicht größer war als zwanzig Quadratmeter. Nils Hedin musste wirklich eine sehr beengte Behausung gehabt haben. Oder blind gewesen sein vor Liebe.

»War dieses Antirutschdings denn nicht mehr da?«, wollte er wissen.

»Soweit ich weiß, nein. Allerdings kenne ich die ganze Situation natürlich nur von Fotos.«

»Aber wieso ...?« Hilflos hob er die Achseln. »Na ja. Vicky, sie war so … unberechenbar. Wahrscheinlich hat es ihr Spaß …«

»Was wollen Sie sagen? Was könnte ihr Spaß gemacht haben?«

»Ihren eigenen Kopf zu haben. Sich über … Vorschläge anderer hinwegzu…«

Wieder versank er in Gedanken. Nippte an seiner Limonade. Die beiden Damen neben der Heizung bezahlten lautstark und rauschten davon.

»Ich war gerne da«, fuhr der ehemalige Musiker träumerisch fort. »Es waren … lustige Nächte mit Vicky. Sie hatte eine unglaubliche Phantasie, wenn Sie verstehen, was … Und eine Menge Erfahrung auch. Sie war älter als ich, fünf Jahre. Wenn ich ehrlich sein soll …«

»Sie war Ihre erste Frau?«

Er nickte demütig. »Und für lange Zeit auch die letzte.«

»Sie haben sie … sehr geliebt?«

Jetzt sah er mir wieder ins Gesicht. »Glauben Sie, dass es so etwas gibt? Dass einem die Liebe das Herz brechen kann? So fühlt es sich an. Immer noch. Nach so langer …«

»Mein Gott.«

»Glauben Sie mir, ich war damals drauf und dran, mich …« Sein dunkler Blick irrte wieder ab. Die Linke griff unbewusst nach dem rechten Handgelenk.

»Ich muss leider noch einmal darauf zurückkommen: Halten Sie es für vorstellbar, dass Marcel Graf Frau Hergarden getötet hat?«

»Warum sollte er so etwas tun?«

»Sie glauben aber, dass Frau Hergarden auch mit ihm ein Verhältnis hatte?«

»Ich weiß es.«

»Woher?«

»Von Rosalie. Ich habe Vicky dann … einfach gefragt. Da hat sie gelacht. Mich ausgelacht und gefragt, was ich denn wollte. Wie sie gemerkt hat, was in mir vorging, hat sie gesagt, ich sei im … Bett tausendmal … besser als alle anderen. Aber wahrscheinlich hat sie das zu jedem gesagt.«

»Und umgekehrt?«

»Wie umgekehrt?«

»Hat Herr Graf von Ihrer Beziehung zu Vicky gewusst?«

Schon zum zweiten Mal hatte ich sie Vicky genannt.

»Natürlich. Marcel und Sabeth hatten ihr Schlafzimmer direkt unter Vickys. Wir haben manchmal das Kind gehört, wenn es nachts geweint hat. Da werden die auch uns gehört haben. Vicky hat … immer ein ziemliches … Geschrei … wenn Sie …«

»Grafs hatten ein Kind?«

Verwirrt sah er mich an. »Wieso nicht?«

Ja, warum eigentlich nicht?

»Ein Mädchen oder ein Junge?«, fragte ich automatisch.

»Ein Junge, soweit ich weiß. Ich habe ihn aber nie gesehen. Er soll …«

»Er soll …?«

»Irgendwie …« Wieder knetete er die langen Finger. »Irgendwie krank … soll er gewesen sein. Mehr weiß ich nicht.«

»Wissen Sie, was aus dem Kind geworden ist?«

»Es wird bei der Mutter geblieben sein, als Marcel und Sabeth sich … Vicky hat manchmal Bemerkungen … Keine schönen … Bemerkungen. Sie hat Kinder gehasst. Nein, nicht gehasst. Sie konnte einfach nichts mit ihnen anfangen. Marcel war aber auch nicht gerade ein Mustervater. Nie hat er von seinem Sohn erzählt. Oder Fotos gezeigt, wie andere. Vielleicht war es auch gar nicht sein Sohn. Vielleicht hat Sabeth den Kleinen mit in die Ehe … Ich weiß nicht …«

Die Bedienung lehnte am Tresen und betrachtete mit finsteren Blicken abwechselnd unsere leeren Gläser und die Uhr an der Wand. Der Mann mit dem Laptop packte so schnell und lautlos seine Sachen zusammen, als wäre er plötzlich auf der Flucht.

»Können Sie sich noch an den Namen des Jungen erinnern?«

Nils Hedin schüttelte deprimiert den Kopf. »Vicky hat ihn immer nur ›das Kind‹ genannt. Sie konnte manchmal schrecklich herzlos sein.«

» Sie haben angedeutet, dass es Frau Hergarden war, die die Beziehung beendet hat. «

» Ganz plötzlich, ja. Es hatte wohl einen wüsten ... Streit mit Freddy gegeben. Er war da gewesen. Für ein paar Tage. In den Zeiten konnten wir uns nicht sehen, wenn Freddy da war. So ... locker war sie dann doch nicht. Und wie er wieder weg war, war plötzlich alles anders. Und ein paar Tage später war es dann zu Ende. Fredy muss ziemlich ausgerastet sein. «

» Genaueres wissen Sie aber nicht? «

Kopfschütteln. » Nur, dass sie plötzlich anders war. Verschlossener. Ernster. «

» Von wem haben sie es erfahren? «

» Was? «

» Dass die beiden Streit hatten. «

» Von ... Rosalie. Rosalie war die Quatsch- und Tratschzentrale des Heidelberger Theaters. «

» Und nachdem es zu Ende war, haben Sie Heidelberg verlassen? «

» Ich habe sie hunderttausend Mal angerufen. Aber Vicky war nicht der Typ Frau, den man zu etwas überreden ... Sie war ... «

Die Bedienung hatte das Interesse an uns verloren und betrachtete nun eingehend ihre pink lackierten Fingernägel.

» Um ehrlich zu sein, ich habe erst nach der ... Trennung begriffen, wie wichtig sie für mich war. Vorher war alles Glückseligkeit, Abenteuer, Lust gewesen. Es war mir völlig ... gleichgültig, dass sie verheiratet war, dass es keine Zukunft für uns gab. Dass es noch andere gab. Wir waren zusammen, und das genügte. Ich war so jung, damals. Und leider ... auch unglaublich dumm. Ich war für Vicky wohl doch nur ... ein Bettvergnügen. Ein Dildo, an dem praktischerweise ... ein Mann hing. «

» Wann genau haben Sie die Stadt verlassen? «

» Zwei Tage vor ihrem Tod. Völlig idiotisch. Ich hatte noch einen Vertrag bis Jahresende. Den habe ich nicht erfüllt. Aber ich musste ... weg, ich musste einfach. Habe meine sieben, acht Sachen gepackt. Alles, was ich damals besaß, konnte ich bequem auf einen Rutsch zum Bahnhof tragen. In Frankfurt habe ich eine billige Souterrainwohnung gefunden. In Praunheim draußen. Dort gab es eine Jazzband, bei der ich einsteigen konnte. Ich hatte nicht mal weniger Geld als früher.«

»Oboe in einer Jazzband?«

»Ich spiele auch Trompete.«

Also doch.

»Wie stand eigentlich Frau Graf beziehungsweise Frau Holland zu der Situation? Wusste sie, dass ihr Mann fremdging?«

»Ich habe Sabeth eigentlich immer nur am Theater gesehen. Gesprochen haben wir nie miteinander. Sie hat mich ... einfach nicht zur Kenntnis genommen. ›Die Queen‹ haben wir sie genannt. So hat sie sich gegeben: als königliche Hoheit. Bei *Maria Stuart*, zum Beispiel, da war in der ersten Sekunde klar, wer die Maria spielen wird. Und keine der anderen Mädchen hat ihr die Rolle streitig gemacht. Wir haben alle ... Respekt vor ihr gehabt.«

»Sie soll aus wohlhabendem Haus gestammt haben.«

»Ihre Eltern hatten in Mannheim eine Firma. Keine kleine Firma. Die haben ihre Brüder geerbt, wenn ich mich richtig erinnere.«

Viktoria Hergardens ehemaliger Liebhaber hatte in den letzten Minuten immer öfter auf sein Handy gesehen. Es war offensichtlich: Meine Zeit mit ihm war abgelaufen.

Wir erhoben uns, und ich legte einen Schein auf den Tisch, der die unfreundliche Bedienung abrupt in eine strahlende Gastgeberin verwandelte. Sie hielt uns sogar mit einer kleinen Verbeugung die schwere und aufwendig verzierte Glastür auf.

»War sie eine gute Schauspielerin?«, fragte ich Nils Hedin im Hinausgehen.

»Sabeth?« Zum ersten Mal seit Beginn unseres Gesprächs lachte er. »Sie selbst war sehr von sich überzeugt. Wie alle Schauspieler. Sie war auch nicht schlecht. Aber im Grunde konnte sie eben nur eine einzige Rolle: Sabeth Holland, die Queen. Ich habe ihren Namen später nie wieder gehört. Vielleicht hat sie die Schauspielerei aufgegeben. Wie so viele. Und sich einen verlässlicheren Mann gesucht als Marcel. Nach

Vickys Tod ist die ganze Truppe irgendwie ... explodiert. Vicky war tot, Freddy weit weg, Sabeth ist nach Frankreich gezogen, Marcel ist nach Köln gegangen. Dort soll er später auch wieder geheiratet haben.«

»Was aus Frau Holland geworden ist, wissen Sie nicht?«

»Sollte doch kein Problem sein, die zu finden. Das Haus? Das muss es doch noch geben?«

»Natürlich gibt es das noch. Ich war sogar dort. Heute leben aber keine Schauspieler mehr da, und das Anwesen gehört seit Jahren einer Berliner Immobilienfirma. Die haben es von einer Erbengemeinschaft gekauft.«

»Von einer Erbengemeinschaft? Heißt das ...?«

Erst jetzt wurde mir bewusst, was das bedeutete. »Das heißt, sie ist vermutlich tot«, sagte ich erschrocken. Oder sie hatte das Haus nach der Scheidung verkauft.

Hedin stand mit hängenden Armen vor mir und sah auf seine billigen Schuhe. »Sabeth ... also auch«, murmelte er kopfschüttelnd.

»Dreißig Jahre sind eine lange Zeit.«

»Sabeth war damals ... neunundzwanzig. Heute wäre sie ... achtundfünfzig. Kein Alter, um tot zu sein, finde ich.«

18

Als ich ins Auto stieg, war es Viertel nach zwölf, und Theresas SMS fiel mir wieder ein. Sie klang völlig anders als befürchtet:

»Jubel, jubel!!!«, schrieb sie. »Das Buch!!!! RUF MICH AN!!!!!!!!«

Als ich wieder auf der Autobahn war, drückte ich die Kurzwahl mit der Nummer eins. Meine Liebste war völlig aus dem Häuschen. »Die Zeit« hatte ihr neues Buch besprochen. Und zwar äußerst wohlwollend.

»Ach was, wohlwollend. Über den grünen Klee haben sie es gelobt!«

»Erscheint ›Die Zeit‹ nicht erst am Donnerstag?«

»Ja, ja, natürlich. Aber sie haben die Rezension vorab an den Verlag geschickt, und ich, ich bin so aufgeregt, und jetzt ... jetzt habe ich völlig vergessen, was ich noch sagen wollte.«

»So kenne ich dich ja gar nicht«, meinte ich und lachte.

»Können wir uns heute Abend sehen? Hast du Zeit? Bitte-bittebitte, hab Zeit!«

Zwei Stunden später stand ich zum zweiten Mal vor Rosalie Jordans Haustür. Sie hatte mich offensichtlich belogen, als sie behauptete, Marcel Graf habe kein intimes Verhältnis mit Vicky gehabt. Und nun hätte ich zu gern erfahren, warum.

Nachdem ich wieder zweimal erfolglos den Klingelknopf gedrückt hatte, schnappte die Tür von alleine auf. Eine walkürenhafte Rothaarige mit alabasterweißem Gesicht blinzelte in die Helligkeit und hielt mir mit finsterer Miene die Tür auf. Ich drückte den Lichtschalter, was jedoch außer einem dumpfen Klacken in der Ferne nichts weiter bewirkte.

Die Klingel der verkrachten Schauspielerin funktionierte immer noch nicht. So klopfte ich wieder gegen die Tür. Nichts geschah. Ich klopfte noch einmal. Dieses Mal hörte ich ein Kratzen von innen sowie das vorwurfsvolle Maunzen der Katze. Ich versuchte es ein drittes Mal. Das Miauen der Katze wurde lauter und klang sehr kläglich. Schließlich ging ich zum Hinterausgang, durch den man in den betonierten Hof gelangte. Die altersschwache Holztür klemmte und quietschte zum Erbarmen, war jedoch nicht verschlossen. Das erste Fenster rechts musste das Küchenfenster sein. Praktischerweise stand sogar eine Kletterhilfe bereit, ein noch recht gut erhaltener Esszimmerstuhl aus Eichenholzimitat, der in den Sechzigerjahren in gewissen Kreisen modern gewesen sein mochte. Ich rückte ihn unters Fenster, stieg vorsichtig hinauf und spähte hinein. Von weiter oben dröhnte Rapmusik, wie ich sie in letzter Zeit oft aus den Zimmern meiner Mädchen hörte. Das Wort, das im Text am häufigsten vorkam, war »Motherfucker«.

Es dauerte einige Sekunden, bis ich in der Dunkelheit hinter der schmutzige Scheibe etwas erkennen konnte. Den Tisch sah ich, an dem ich gestern gesessen hatte, darauf das Glas, das die Bewohnerin benutzt hatte. Die Schnapsflasche dagegen schien eine andere zu sein. Der Stuhl, auf dem ich gesessen hatte, stand etwas entfernt vom Tisch. Der andere war umgekippt. Am Boden zwei Füße in braunen Socken aus grober Wolle. Der dazugehörige Körper war durch den Tisch verdeckt. Ich sprang von meinem Aussichtsplatz und suchte das Handy in den Manteltaschen.

»Viel kann ich nicht sagen«, erklärte mir der Notarzt zwanzig Minuten später. Die altersschwache Wohnungstür hatte dem Mann vom Schlüsseldienst keinen ernst zu nehmenden Widerstand geleistet. Die kleine schwarze Katze war völlig ausgehungert gewesen und beim Anblick der hereinstürmenden Fremden in Panik geraten. Am Boden neben der toten Quatsch- und Tratschzentrale des Heidelberger Theaters lag ihr Telefon. Vielleicht hatte sie in ihren letzten Sekunden noch versucht, Hilfe zu rufen.

Der übergewichtige und fast zwei Meter große Arzt richtete sich schnaufend auf und massierte sein breites Kreuz.

»Sie dürfte seit zwölf, vierzehn Stunden tot sein. Sie sagten was von HIV?«

Ich deutete auf die Tablettenpackung, die noch an derselben Stelle lag wie bei meinem letzten Besuch. Von der offenen Cognacflasche auf dem Tisch fehlte knapp ein Viertel des Inhalts. Im Glas war noch ein winziger Rest. Obwohl wir sofort alle Fenster aufgerissen hatten, stank es nach verwesendem Müll, Katzenkot und Menschenurin.

»Kann natürlich alles Mögliche sein«, meinte der Arzt. »Aber Herzversagen halte ich für die wahrscheinlichste Todesursache. Die Symptomatik, offensichtlich Alkohol, ihr schlechter Allgemeinzustand ...«

Mit ihm zusammen waren zwei Rettungssanitäter gekommen, ein noch sehr junger, kräftiger Mann und eine mütterliche Frau in den Vierzigern. Sie hatte inzwischen Katzenfutter gefunden und das kleine schwarze Raubtier versorgt. Es klopfte an der Tür. Zwei Kollegen vom Kriminaldauerdienst traten vorsichtig ein und sahen mich fragend an.

»Nach allem Anschein natürliche Todesursache«, sagte ich zu den beiden, und der Arzt nickte beifällig dazu. »Sie können gleich wieder abziehen.«

»Alles klar, Chef«, sagte der Ältere der beiden erleichtert. »War ja auch nicht mehr die Jüngste, die Dame.«

»Na denn«, seufzte der Arzt und öffnete seinen schweren Koffer. »Wenn aus Ihrer Sicht nichts dagegen spricht, mache ich den Papierkram fertig.«

Ich zögerte, ohne zu wissen, weshalb. Betrachtete die offene Cognacflasche auf dem Tisch, die zahlreichen neben dem umgefallenen Stuhl stehenden und liegenden leeren Flaschen. Das billige Becherglas mit einem Fingerbreit brauner Flüssigkeit darin. Der Arzt sah mich auffordernd an. Ich zögerte immer noch.

»Wir haben nicht ewig Zeit«, erinnerte er sanft.

»Okay«, sagte ich schließlich. »Füllen Sie den Totenschein aus.«

Der junge Sanitäter zückte ein Handy vom Format eines kleinen Flachbildfernsehers. »Ich telefonier schon mal nach dem Leichenwagen.«

»Was für ein Scheißleben«, meinte die Frau mit Blick in die Runde. »Aber von Cognac hat sie was verstanden, das muss ich sagen.«

Die Katze hatte fertig gefressen und strich ihr schnurrend um die Beine. Sie packte das Tier unter der Brust und hob es achtsam hoch. »Böse Sache, was, kleiner schwarzer Kater? Jetzt wirst du wohl umziehen müssen.«

»Am besten, Sie nehmen ihn gleich mit«, schlug ich vor.

Sie sah mich überrascht an. Nickte dann langsam, nahm das kleine Tier auf den Arm und lächelte es an. »Meine Tochter löchert mich eh schon die ganze Zeit.« Der Kater schien sich sofort wohl zu fühlen bei seiner neuen Chefin. »Und mein Mann wird sich wahrscheinlich scheiden lassen.«

Ich räusperte mich und sagte: »Ich sehe mich hier noch ein bisschen um. Vielleicht gibt es Angehörige.«

»Sie bleiben hier, bis die Bestatter kommen?«

Ich nickte.

»Na dann.« Der Arzt hatte inzwischen die amtlichen Unterlagen ausgefüllt, die in Deutschland am Ende eines Lebens auszufüllen sind, und alles farblich sortiert auf dem Küchentisch deponiert. Kurze Zeit später war ich allein mit der Toten.

Das Schlafzimmer war rasch erledigt. Dort gab es nichts zu entdecken, was mir hätte nützlich sein können. Auch hier ein trostloser Anblick: das Bett zerwühlt, das Laken vermutlich seit Monaten nicht gewaschen. In den Schränken überreichlich Material für die Kleidersammlung. Vieles wirkte, als hinge es schon seit zwanzig Jahren auf demselben Bügel. Auf dem Nachttischchen lag ein aufgeschlagenes Taschenbuch älteren Datums mit dem Einband nach oben: *Lynch* von Jürgen Lodemann. Sie hatte erst zehn Seiten gelesen.

Im Flur stand einsam eine kleine, überraschend hübsche Kommode mit zierlich gedrechselten Beinen. In der Schublade fand ich einige persönliche Dinge: einen grünen Reisepass, Bundesrepublik Deutschland, schon vor einer halben Ewigkeit abgelaufen. Einige vermutlich unbezahlte Rechnungen, eine Mahnung von den Stadtwerken, eine zweite von einem medizinischen Labor über zweihundertdreiundfünfzig Euro mit Androhung des gerichtlichen Mahnverfahrens. Zuunterst lag der Prospekt einer Firma namens »Flying Pizza«, die es vermutlich längst nicht mehr gab. Auf der Kommode ein Heidelberger Telefonbuch aus dem Jahr 1998. Keine Briefe, keine Ansichtskarten, keine Notizen. Ich schob die Schublade wieder zu und nahm das schnurlose Telefon zur Hand, das jemand aufgehoben und auf die Kommode gelegt hatte. Klickte das Telefonbuch durch, sah mir die zuletzt gewählten Nummern an. Den letzten Anruf, bei dem eine Verbindung zustandegekommen war, hatte Rosalie Jordan am Vortag getätigt, anderthalb Stunden, nachdem ich mich verabschiedet hatte. Eine Nummer in Mannheim.

An der Garderobe hing ein lappiger Wollmantel mit ausgebeulten Taschen. In der rechten eine Fahrkarte aus einem der Automaten der Deutschen Bahn. In der linken Streichhölzer und ein wenig Kleingeld. In den Innentaschen Flusen und Krümel und ein Kugelschreiber mit dem Werbeaufdruck einer Apotheke. Daneben hing eine Windjacke, die ebenfalls schon bessere Zeiten gesehen hatte. Dort fand ich das Portemonnaie der alten Dame. Es enthielt knapp fünfzig Euro überwiegend in Scheinen, ihren Personalausweis, der sogar noch gültig war, eine EC-Karte von der Sparda-Bank. Kein Zettel mit einer Telefonnummer, die im Notfall anzurufen war, keine vergessene Visitenkarte, kein Adressbüchlein. Wie konnte ein Mensch so einsam leben?

Ich betrat das zweite Zimmer der Wohnung, das als Wohnraum und – wenn man so wollte – Arbeitszimmer gedient hatte. Hier war es lausig kalt und überraschend aufgeräumt. An der Längswand stand ein altertümliches moosgrünes Plüschsofa mit stilistisch perfekt dazu passendem Eichentisch, mitten im Raum ein verschlissener Ohrensessel, der wirkte, als stammte er aus einer Theaterrequisite des vorvorigen Jahrhunderts. Am Fenster ein kleiner Schreibtisch, auf dem sich Unerledigtes und Vergessenes türmte. An der Wand gegenüber dem Sofa ein Regal, vollgestopft mit Büchern. Ich überflog die Titel. In erster Linie Romane der modernen Klassik, dazwischen Künstlerbiografien, Memoiren bekannter und weniger bekannter Schauspieler. Darüber ein nachlässig gerahmter Kunstdruck. Traurig verblasste Sonnenblumen von van Gogh. Nirgendwo ein Fernseher, fiel mir auf.

Eine Staubschicht auf allem machte deutlich, dass dieser Raum lange nicht genutzt worden war. Die Luft war stickig und trocken, die Temperatur nicht weit über dem Gefrierpunkt.

Lustlos kramte ich in den Papierstapeln auf dem Schreibtisch. Werbung, weitere Arzt- und Laborrechnungen, Mahnungen, abgestempelte Rezepte mit schwindelerregenden Beträgen darauf. Dazwischen immer wieder Kontoauszüge. Auch hier nichts Persönliches, kein Notizbuch mit Adressen oder Telefonnummern, nichts.

Es klopfte lautstark an der Wohnungstür. Die grauen Männer mit dem Zinksarg waren da.

Unser Abend war ein einziges Fest aus Gelächter und Geblödel, aus Sekt und funkensprühender Zärtlichkeit und atemlosem Sex. Der Misserfolg ihres Buchs schien zentnerschwer auf Theresas Autorinnenseele gelastet zu haben.

»So ist es seit Ewigkeiten nicht mehr gewesen«, stellte ich fest, als wir endlich verschwitzt, betrunken und zu einem unlösbaren Knoten verschlungen auf unserer Matratze zur Ruhe kamen.

»So kann es nicht immer sein«, schnurrte sie unendlich zufrieden. »Man würde verrückt werden davon.«

»Und die Nachbarn vermutlich auch.«

Über uns improvisierte wieder der Saxophonist, der heute ebenfalls sehr viel besser gelaunt zu sein schien als beim letzten Mal.

Theresas heiße Rechte war schon wieder auf dem Weg nach unten. Ich hielt sie fest. Sie kicherte wie ein übermütiger Teenager, gab endlich Ruhe. Ich erzählte ihr von Nils Hedin und seiner unglücklichen Liebe. Einer Liebe, die ihn selbst drei Jahrzehnte nach Vickys Tod immer noch in den Klauen hielt.

»Wenn man Pech hat«, philosophierte meine erschöpfte Göttin, »dann ist Liebe das Schlimmste und Gemeinste, was einem das Leben antun kann. Wenn sie nicht gestorben wäre, dann wäre er wahrscheinlich nach einiger Zeit froh gewesen, sie loszuwerden.«

19

Als ich am Donnerstagmorgen beim Frühstück saß, dachte ich über die beiden Paare in Neuenheim nach, deren buntes Zusammenleben so grauenvoll geendet hatte. Wie oft war ausgerechnet die Liebe, das Schönste und Größte, was uns das Leben zu bieten hat, Anlass für Mord und Totschlag? Wie oft gingen Beziehungen und Existenzen in Trümmer, weil der Mensch zur Treue nicht gemacht ist? Wie oft schlug das größte

Glück in ein noch größeres Unglück um? Die Literatur der Welt quoll über von diesen uralten und immer wieder neuen Geschichten.

Ich genoss die Minuten der Ruhe vor Tagesbeginn. Das Radio spielte leise Musik. Die Zwillinge hatten wieder einmal erst zur zweiten Stunde Unterricht und lagen noch in ihren Betten. Ich schlürfte meinen Cappuccino und sah zu, wie sich der Himmel vor den Fenstern allmählich rosa färbte. Offenbar sollte ausnahmsweise wieder ein schöner Tag werden. Natürlich dachte ich auch an Theresa, lächelte in mich hinein. Heute war der neunzehnte Februar. Nur noch gut vier Wochen bis zum Frühlingsanfang. Im Radio spielten die Dire Straits *Brothers in Arms*. Ich drehte es lauter, setzte mich wieder an den Tisch. Lange hatte mir kein Cappuccino so gut geschmeckt.

Bald würden die ersten warmen Tage kommen, die Terrassen in der Innenstadt würden sich über Mittag wieder bunt bevölkern. Für die nächsten Tage hatte der Wetterbericht allerdings ein letztes Aufbäumen des Winters angedroht. Sogar Schnee sollte es noch einmal geben, selbst in der Kurpfalz, einer der wärmsten Regionen Deutschlands. Im Radio erzählte ein etwas zu gut gelaunter Sprecher eine alberne Geschichte, in der es um ein gestohlenes Auto ging, dessen Motor bereits an der nächsten Ampel schlappgemacht hatte. Ausgerechnet eine Streifenwagenbesatzung hatte den schwitzenden Dieben geholfen, den Wagen an den Straßenrand zu schieben.

Ich streckte die Beine von mir, wärmte mir die Finger an meiner Tasse. Selten hatte ich weniger Lust auf Büro und Arbeit gehabt als an diesem Morgen. Ich beschloss, mir noch ein Glas Orangensaft zu gönnen, bevor ich mich auf den Weg in die Tretmühle machte.

Im Radio brach die Musik ab.

Eine aufgeregte Frauenstimme: »Soeben wurde bekannt, dass auf den beliebten Fernsehstar Marcel Graf vor wenigen Minuten ein Mordanschlag verübt wurde. Die Tat ereignete sich in der Heidelberger Innenstadt, in der Nähe des Hotels, in dem Herr Graf zurzeit Quartier bezogen hat. Dem Vernehmen nach hat er den Anschlag jedoch glücklicherweise überlebt.

Über die Schwere seiner Verletzungen ist derzeit noch nichts bekannt. Sobald wir weitere Einzelheiten erfahren, werden wir Sie unverzüglich informieren ...«

Schon begann mein Handy zu surren. Eine Kollegin vom Kriminaldauerdienst war geistesgegenwärtig genug, mich sofort anzurufen. Graf hatte wenige Minuten vor sieben Uhr zu Fuß sein Heidelberger Hotel verlassen, um – ohne Begleitung – seinen offenbar üblichen Morgenspaziergang zu machen. Am Neckarufer war ein groß gewachsener Unbekannter mit einem Messer in der Hand über ihn hergefallen, hatte ihm zahlreiche Stich- und Schnittwunden zugefügt, aber schlussendlich war es Graf gelungen, den Täter in die Flucht zu schlagen. Während des kurzen Telefonats hörte ich Motorenbrummen und das Martinshorn des Einsatzwagens, in dem die Anruferin saß. Die Verbindung war schlecht.

»... erst vor zehn oder fünfzehn Minuten oder so ... sind auf dem Weg zum Tatort ... schon unterwegs ins Klinikum ... wahrscheinlich nicht lebensgefährlich ... vorläufig nicht vernehmungsfähig ... keine Zeugen ... was wir bisher wissen, hat mir vor einer Minute der Rettungssanitäter am Telefon erzählt.«

»Wer hat den Notarzt gerufen?«, fragte ich, während ich in meine Schuhe schlüpfte. »Graf selber?«

»Soweit ich weiß, ja«, erwiderte die Kollegin mit gepresster Stimme. Reifen quietschten. »Im Moment blickt aber noch keiner so richtig durch.«

»Aber er lebt.«

»Scheint so.«

Ich zog die Wohnungstür hinter mir zu und lief die Treppe hinab.

»... keine inneren Organe verletzt«, war das Letzte, was ich hörte, bevor wir auflegten.

Als ich zwölf Minuten später den Ort des Anschlags erreichte, war ein Teil des Uferwegs bereits mit Flatterband abgesperrt, und meine Finger waren steif vor Kälte. Um so schnell wie möglich am Tatort zu sein, hatte ich mich zum ersten Mal seit meiner unfreiwilligen Rolle rückwärts wieder aufs Fahrrad gewagt. Unterwegs hatte ich feststellen müssen, dass es über Nacht zwar aufgeklart hatte, die Temperatur jedoch kräftig gefallen war. Auf manchen Pfützen hatte sogar dünnes Eis geglitzert, und von Westen her ging ein eisiger Wind, der die hektischen Atemwölkchen von meinem Mund riss.

Der Anschlag auf Marcel Graf hatte sich am nördlichen Neckarufer ereignet, etwa hundert Meter westlich der Theodor-Heuss-Brücke, anderthalb bis zwei Kilometer von seinem Hotel entfernt, dem Europäischen Hof an der Friedrich-Ebert-Anlage. Ein asphaltierter Fußweg verlief hier parallel zum Flussufer, nur zwei Schritte vom strudelnden braunen Wasser entfernt. Wegen des vielen Regens der vergangenen Tage führte der Neckar Hochwasser. Es roch nach kommendem Schnee.

Um den Kopf der Kollegin, mit der ich vor wenigen Minuten telefoniert hatte, leuchteten rote Locken in der Morgensonne. Sie war klein und kräftig, war in Begleitung eines Kollegen vom KDD und zweier uniformierter Beamter des Reviers Mitte gekommen und hüpfte wegen der Kälte von einem Fuß auf den anderen. Gleichzeitig versuchte sie, ihre Hände durch eifriges Reiben und Pusten warm zu halten. Einer der Uniformierten rauchte. Er musterte mich aus schmalen Augen.

»Wieder mal ohne Helm unterwegs, Herr Gerlach?«, fragte er grinsend. »Na, na ...«

Mein Helm hing seit Neuestem griffbereit an der Garderobe, wie ich es mir vorgenommen hatte. Dummerweise hatte ich jedoch bei meinem Alarmstart vorhin vergessen, ihn mitzunehmen.

»Graf ist auf dem Weg ins Krankenhaus?«, fragte ich und blies ebenfalls in meine Hände, um sie wieder zum Leben zu erwecken.

Die rothaarige Kollegin nickte eifrig. »Wie wir gekommen sind, sind sie gerade losgefahren. Wir haben erst mal nur abgesperrt. Spusi müsste jeden Moment auftauchen.«

Über Grafs Gesundheitszustand war noch immer nicht mehr bekannt, als dass er am Leben war. Da das Uniklinikum buchstäblich nur wenige Meter entfernt lag, war er inzwischen vermutlich schon in guten Händen.

»Soweit ich sehen konnte«, fuhr die vor Kälte zitternde Kollegin fort, »hat er nicht so wahnsinnig viel Blut verloren. Seine Sachen, die haben allerdings schon wüst ausgesehen.«

»Haben Sie mit ihm sprechen können?«

Sie schüttelte den Kopf. An den Wurzeln ihrer roten Locken schimmerte die natürliche dunkelbraune Farbe durch. »Der Arzt ist ein aufgeregter Jungspund gewesen und hat ein Theater gemacht, als wäre sein Patient der liebe Gott persönlich und außerdem schon so gut wie tot.«

Ich zückte mein Handy, wählte mit kältesteifen Fingern die Nummer des Klinikums und fragte mich zur Abteilung für Unfallchirurgie durch. Herr Graf werde zurzeit ärztlich versorgt, beschied man mir kühl. Ob man heute schon einer Befragung durch die Polizei zustimmen könne, würde man mich zu gegebener Zeit wissen lassen. Als Nächstes drückte ich die Direktwahltaste zu Klara Vangelis, meiner besten und zuverlässigsten Mitarbeiterin. Wie erwartet, war sie um Viertel vor acht schon im Büro. Mit wenigen Worten brachte ich sie auf den aktuellen Stand.

»Wir bilden eine Soko, und Ihnen würde ich gerne die Leitung übertragen.«

»Wen kann ich kriegen?«

»Jeden, der verfügbar ist. Das wird eine Staatsaktion, die viel Fingerspitzengefühl verlangt. Sie sollten umgehend zum Tatort kommen und sich selbst ein Bild machen. In einer Stunde kann ich Ihnen sagen, wen ich Ihnen für die Soko geben kann.«

»Hatten wir schon einmal ein so prominentes Opfer?«

»Ich fürchte, nein. Jedes Käseblättchen Europas wird uns auf die Finger schauen.«

Als ich wieder auf mein Rad stieg und meine Abneigung gegen warme Handschuhe und Pudelmützen verfluchte, quietschten Bremsen. Es war jedoch nicht die dringend erwartete Spurensicherung, sondern ein Übertragungswagen des SWR. Ich sah zu, dass ich fortkam.

Sönnchen saß schreckensblass an ihrem Schreibtisch, als ich mein Vorzimmer betrat.

»Sie haben es also auch schon gehört?«, fragte ich und hängte meinen Mantel auf.

Sie starrte mich an, als könnte sie den Gesundheitszustand Grafs von meiner Nase ablesen. »Im Radio reden sie von nichts anderem mehr. Und auch noch praktisch vor unserer Haustür!«

»Wird wohl nichts werden mit der Show am Samstag. Gucken Sie sich so was eigentlich an?«

»Natürlich!«, erwiderte sie entgeistert. »Jede Folge!«

Nach allem, was ich inzwischen wusste, zählte meine Sekretärin vermutlich zu Grafs jüngsten Fans.

»Er ist so ... charmant. Und lustig auch. Lustig, ohne anderen wehzutun. Das, was heutzutage modern ist, kann ich nicht aushalten. Das ist mir alles zu bunt, zu schräg, zu schmutzig und vor allem viel zu laut. Über die Witze kann ich auch nicht lachen, weil ich sie entweder nicht versteh, oder weil sie mir zu dumm oder zu unanständig sind. Haben Sie mit ihm geredet?«

»Am Montag.«

»Persönlich?«

»Wenn es kein Double war.«

»Und? Wie ist er so?«

»Nett.«

»Nett?«

»Verehrte Frau Walldorf, ich bin ein Mann, wie Sie vor Kurzem noch sehr richtig festgestellt haben. Darum bin ich vermutlich nicht ganz so empfänglich für seinen Altherrencharme.«

»Der Jüngste ist er wirklich nicht mehr«, gab sie zu und wandte endlich den Blick ab. »Aber mir gefällt's trotzdem. Letztes Mal hat er die Mireille Mathieu als Überraschungsgast gehabt.«

»Die lebt noch?«

»Also bitte!«, rief sie entrüstet. »Sie sollten ...«

Ihr Telefon ersparte mir den Rest.

Sönnchen hörte kurz zu, sagte: »Moment, er steht mir gegenüber«, und reichte mir den Hörer kommentarlos.

»Jetzt ist er endgültig weg!«, tönte die empörte Stimme der Vermieterin in Dossenheim. »Gestern Abend ist er noch mal da gewesen und hat seine Tasche geholt. Mein Mann und ich, wir sind im Kino gewesen, und wie wir um halb elf heimkommen, da liegt der Schlüssel auf dem Schuhschränkchen unter dem Spiegel. Und die Tasche ist weg. Und nicht mal ›Auf Wiedersehen‹ hat er gesagt!«

»Wann er da war, wissen Sie aber nicht?«

»Doch. Kurz nach der Tagesschau. Mit dem Auto ist er gekommen, hab ich von einer Nachbarin gehört.«

»Mit einem Taxi?«

»Kein Taxi. Ein Mercedes. Die Frau Knobel von schräg gegenüber hat ihn gesehen. Mit einem Mercedes ist er vorgefahren. War aber kein ganz großer. Eher so ein mittlerer, meint die Frau Knobel. Seit ihr der Mann weggestorben ist, guckt sie viel aus dem Fenster. Achtundvierzig ist er bloß geworden, der Herr Knobel. Lehrer ist er gewesen, an der Berufsschule in Bergheim, und da kriegt der einen Herzinfarkt! Ist mit dem Rad von der Schule heimgefahren, der Knobel ist ja bei jedem Wetter mit dem Rad gefahren und hat so auf seine Gesundheit geachtet und nie Alkohol getrunken und nicht geraucht und immer nur Bio gegessen. Und dann? Bums. Mit achtundvierzig.«

»Kann Frau Knobel den Mercedes ein bisschen genauer beschreiben? War es vielleicht eine C-Klasse? Welche Farbe?«

»Die Frau Knobel versteht nichts von Autos. Die haben selber nie eins gehabt. Bloß Fahrräder. Weiß gar nicht, von was die jetzt lebt, nachdem der Mann tot ist. Fürs Aus-dem-Fenster-Gucken kriegt sie ja nichts bezahlt, und die Pension von ihrem Mann, das wird nicht viel sein, nach grad mal zwanzig Dienstjahren. Mein Mann, der ist ja auch Beamter gewesen, und der meint, mehr als tausend Euro kann sie nicht haben zum Leben. Aber gut, kein Auto, das Haus ist abgezahlt, sie hat einen großen Garten hinten raus und baut Gemüse ...«

»Was weiß sie denn nun von dem Mercedes?«

»Müsst ich fragen.«

»Fragen Sie bitte auch, ob sie sich das Kennzeichen gemerkt hat.«

»Sie meinen, das Nummernschild?«

»Genau.«

»Ich flitz schnell zu ihr rüber. Wird ein paar Minuten dauern.« Und schon hatte sie aufgelegt.

Es dauerte am Ende über eine Viertelstunde, bis Hergardens ehemalige Vermieterin wieder anrief. Vermutlich hatte man noch ein Schwätzchen halten müssen.

»Hell war der Mercedes, meint sie.«

»Silbergrau vielleicht?«

»Kann sie nicht genau sagen. Es ist ja schon Nacht gewesen. Und jetzt hat der bis Monatsende die Miete gezahlt und lässt das schöne Zimmer einfach leer stehen. Aber gut, ist ja schließlich sein Geld ...«

»Und das Kennzeichen?«

»Hat sie nicht gesehen.«

Sönnchen hatte gehört, dass ich zu Ende telefoniert hatte, und streckte den Lockenkopf durch die Tür. »Der Herr Runkel hat vorhin angerufen. Sie sollen ihn bei Gelegenheit zurückrufen.«

Erst hatte ich Wichtigeres zu tun. Theresa hatte an diesem Morgen schon drei SMS geschickt, hatte ich gerade entdeckt. Eine um halb acht, als sie sich auf den Weg zum Bahnhof machte, um dort ein druckfrisches Exemplar der »Zeit« zu ergattern. Sie hatte das Blatt zwar abonniert, aber auf den Briefträger zu warten, hätte sie an den Rand eines Nervenzusammenbruchs gebracht. Die zweite Nachricht war um zehn nach acht gekommen. Der Artikel war groß und lobend und noch viel schöner, als sie gehofft hatte. Die dritte Nachricht war erst wenige Minuten alt und kündigte eine Mail an, an die sie die inzwischen eingescannte Kritik gehängt hatte. So weit reichten ihre technischen Kenntnisse offenbar ...

Der Verkaufsrang ihres Buchs bei Amazon war bisher nicht wie erwartet gestiegen, sondern über Nacht sogar noch weiter abgesackt. Ich schrieb zurück, dass der typische »Zeit«-Leser vermutlich erst abends seine Zeitung aufschlug und viele erst am Wochenende das Feuilleton studierten.

Gehorsam öffnete ich die Mail, überflog den zweispaltigen Artikel, der wirklich äußerst wohlwollend war, tippte eine zweite Kurznachricht, um Theresa nicht zu enttäuschen. Kurz überlegte ich, bei Amazon zum ersten Mal im Leben ein Buch zu ordern, um den Verkaufsrang ein wenig nach oben zu treiben. Aber ich hatte die Finger noch nicht auf der Tastatur, als das Handy schon wieder brummte.

»Können wir uns über Mittag sehen?«, schrieb die aufgedrehte Bestsellerautorin. »Irgendwo eine Kleinigkeit zusammen essen? Ich platze, wenn ich nicht bald mit jemandem anstoßen kann.«

Ich versprach, es irgendwie möglich zu machen und mich im Lauf des Vormittags wieder zu melden.

20

»Graf wird von seinen Bodyguards komplett abgeschirmt«, berichtete Sven Balke bei der kurzfristig anberaumten Fallbesprechung. Inzwischen war es halb zehn geworden, und die erste Aufregung hatte sich schon ein wenig gelegt. Draußen schien eine prächtige Wintersonne, als gäbe es Grund zum Feiern. »Sie haben seinen Leibarzt aus Wiesbaden eingeflogen und lassen nicht mal die Klinikärzte an ihn ran. Der einzige Mensch, den man ans Telefon kriegt, ist seine Assistentin, und das Mädel ist ein verdammt zäher Knochen. Die Klinikärzte sind übrigens ziemlich angepisst, weil man sie in ihrem eigenen Haus mehr oder weniger kaltgestellt hat. Aber anscheinend haben Grafs Leute das direkt mit dem Chefarzt gedealt.«

Wir saßen zu dritt in meinem Büro, Klara Vangelis, Sven Balke und ich, und versuchten eine erste Bestandsaufnahme.

Vangelis hatte getan, was man als Chef an guten Mitarbeitern am meisten schätzt: Sie hatte selbst gedacht und noch auf dem kurzen Weg zum Tatort per Handy einige Mitstreiter akquiriert. Balke war auf dem Weg von seiner Wohnung in Schlierbach in die Heidelberger Innenstadt gewesen, wie fast jeden Tag per Rennrad, und sie hatte ihn zum Hotel Europäischer Hof umgeleitet, wo Graf Quartier bezogen hatte. Evalina Krauss hatte sie zum Uniklinikum dirigiert, wo sie sich zurzeit noch aufhielt und versuchte, für uns Informationsschnipsel zu sammeln.

»Die Täterbeschreibung passt auf Hergarden«, stellte ich fest. »Graf hat sie zum Glück dem Notarzt geben können, bevor er bewusstlos wurde.«

Vangelis tippte auf ihrem Handy herum, legte es dann auf den Schreibtisch. »Das ist der Anruf. Sieben Uhr neun.«

»Hilfe!« quäkte die panische Stimme des Fernsehstars aus dem winzigen Lautsprecher. »Hilfe, ich werde ...« Ein unterdrückter Schrei, etwas wie das Knurren eines großen Hundes, Keuchen, dann nicht zu deutende Geräusche. »Überfall! Ich werde überfa...! Am ...« Wieder Kampfgeräusche, Keuchen. »Am Neckar auf Höhe des ... des ...« Ein Schrei aus voller Kehle. Wieder das merkwürdige Knurren. »Auf Höhe des ...«

Dann brach das Gespräch ab.

»Ich nehme an, Sie haben sich das schon in etwas besserer Qualität angehört?«, fragte ich Vangelis.

Sie nickte. »Man erkennt deutlich Grafs Stimme. Eine zweite Stimme ist nicht auszumachen. Da ist nur dieses Knurren.«

»Um zehn nach sieben war's noch dunkel«, wusste Balke. »Ich bin um fünf vor halb aus dem Haus, und da ist es gerade hell geworden.«

»Wie hat man Graf so schnell finden können?«, fragte ich.

»Er hat nach einer halben Minute noch einmal angerufen und seine genaue Position durchgegeben. Der Notarzt war drei Minuten später schon da.«

»Die konnten ja praktisch zu Fuß gehen«, meinte Balke gallig. »In die Klinik hätten sie ihn tragen können. Wieso wohnt der Typ eigentlich in Heidelberg, wenn sein Job in Ludwigs-hafen ist?« Der Ton seiner Frage ließ keine Zweifel aufkom-men, wie gering seine Sympathie für Graf und dessen Gewerbe war. »Sind ihm die Hotels da nicht fein genug?«

»Vielleicht alte Anhänglichkeit«, sagte ich achselzuckend und referierte im Telegrammstil die Vorgeschichte. Ich erzählte von Fred Hergarden und Johann Boll und von Hergardens Verdacht gegen Graf und reichte unser Phantombild herum.

»Klingt relativ eindeutig.« Vangelis sah Balke an, und der nickte mit abwesender Miene dazu, während er etwas in sein Smartphone tippte. »Damit wäre Hergarden unser Hauptver-dächtiger?«

»Die Täterbeschreibung – wenn man das so nennen kann, was Graf von sich gegeben hat – passt jedenfalls.«

»Ein Mann. Groß. Hager«, las sie mit gerunzelter Stirn aus ihrem Notizbuch vor. »Wenn die beiden früher befreundet waren, warum hat Graf ihn dann nicht erkannt?«

Das war ein bedenkenswerter Einwand. »Sie haben sich dreißig Jahre nicht gesehen«, überlegte ich laut. »Es war dun-kel. Graf war völlig überrascht …«

»Außerdem ist die Beleuchtung am Uferweg westlich von der Brücke mehr als mies«, erklärte Balke. »Da stehen keine Lampen. Da wird höchstens ein bisschen Licht von der Brücke gewesen sein.«

»Wieso geht der Mann ausgerechnet an so einer Stelle spa-zieren?«, warf ich in die Runde. »Ich habe ihn am Montag noch ausdrücklich gewarnt. Und dann läuft er ausgerechnet in die finsterste und einsamste Ecke Heidelbergs und lässt sich überfallen.«

Balke steckte sein Handy ein, das noch größer zu sein schien als der Vorgänger.

»Wir schreiben Hergarden offiziell zur Fahndung aus«, sagte ich in Richtung Vangelis. »Bis vorgestern hat er in Dos-senheim in einem Privatzimmer gewohnt. Im Moment hat er wahrscheinlich keine feste Bleibe in Deutschland.«

»Dumm, dass es keine Augenzeugen gibt«, sagte sie. »Eine Joggerin hat Graf vielleicht zwanzig Sekunden vor dem Angriff getroffen, aber nicht erkannt. Zwei Ohrenzeugen, die zu Fuß auf der Brücke unterwegs waren, haben zwar Gebrüll gehört, sich aber nichts weiter gedacht. Sie glaubten, es wären Obdachlose, die Streit hatten.«

»Und diese Frühsportlerin hat nichts gehört? Oder vielleicht eine zweite Person gesehen?«

»Sie hatte die Stöpsel ihres MP3-Players in den Ohren. Wegen einer zweiten Person ist sie sich unsicher.«

»Das heißt?«

»Sie meint, jemand könnte hinter einem Baum gestanden haben. Vielleicht ein Mann beim ... nun ja, Pinkeln, hat sie sich gedacht und absichtlich nicht hingesehen.«

Ich wandte mich an Balke. »Hat Graf eigentlich jeden Morgen einen Spaziergang gemacht?«

»Das Hotelpersonal sagt, ja. Sein persönliches Fitnessprogramm, hat er ihnen mal erklärt. Eine halbe Stunde stramm spazieren gehen, anschließend ein bisschen im Pool rumplanschen, dann ein gesundes Frühstück mit viel Obst und Früchtetee. Scheint Vegetarier zu sein. Es heißt, er sei ein großer Freund von Regelmäßigkeit. Jeden Morgen Glockenschlag Viertel vor sieben ist er mit dem Lift runtergekommen, hat gnädig in die Runde gegrinst und ist losmarschiert. Immer die gleiche Runde.«

»Bei jedem Wetter?«

»Bei jedem Wetter.«

»Traut man ihm gar nicht zu, wenn man ihn so sieht. Und er war immer allein unterwegs?«

»Er braucht das, hat er den Leuten an der Rezeption erzählt. Er hat ständig so viele Menschen um sich, dass er hin und wieder mal eine Stunde ohne Gesellschaft und Wachhunde braucht. Er geht absichtlich so früh los, weil es da noch dunkel ist und ihn niemand erkennt.«

»Das heißt, der Täter musste sich nur hinter einen Baum stellen und warten ...«

»Scheint ja ein ziemlicher Trottel zu sein«, schnaubte Balke. »Dieser Fernsehmensch ist zwar groß und geht regelmäßig spazieren, aber der Fitteste ist er bestimmt nicht. Außerdem ist er über sechzig, war unbewaffnet und unvorbereitet. So einen überwältigt normalerweise ein Zwölfjähriger. Zur Not ohne Messer.«

»Vermutlich war es Hergardens erster Mordversuch.«

»Hoffentlich auch sein letzter.«

Als das Gespräch sich im Kreis zu drehen begann, beendete ich die Veranstaltung mit der dringenden Bitte an Vangelis, mich ständig auf dem Laufenden zu halten.

Die beiden erhoben sich. Meine letzte Frage galt Balke: »Neues von der Kellertürenbande?«

Er zog eine schiefe Grimasse, hob die Hände und schlug kräftig auf seine strammen Biker-Oberschenkel. »Wir stecken mal wieder fest. Auf das Phantombild von dem Typen, der den Audi geklaut hat, gab es bisher null Reaktion. Und die DNA-Analyse dauert und dauert ...«

Inzwischen war mir Rolf Runkel wieder eingefallen. Er nahm schon vor dem ersten Tuten ab, sodass zunächst eine kleine Verwirrung entstand.

»Ah, Sie sind's, Chef«, stellte er dann erfreut fest. »Schön, dass Sie anrufen.«

»Was kann ich für Sie tun?«

Er wurde verlegen. »Das klingt jetzt vielleicht ein bisschen komisch, aber ... Im November, beim Einbruch in Bammental, ist diesem Rechtsanwalt doch eine Armbanduhr geklaut worden. Eine Patek Phillipe Calatraviata oder so ähnlich.«

»Und?«

»Könnten Sie die Seriennummer feststellen und mir vielleicht eine kurze SMS schicken?«

»Haben Sie die Uhr etwa gefunden?«

»Es wär zu verrückt, aber ...«

Es klopfte, und eine Zehntelsekunde später polterte Sönnchen herein mit vor Aufregung roten Bäckchen. »Im Dritten bringen sie grad eine Sondersendung! Der Chefarzt von der Unfallchirurgie sagt, Graf ist außer Lebensgefahr!«

»Schön, dass wir es auch erfahren«, sagte ich und wünschte Runkel weiter gute Genesung.

»Seine Assistentin haben sie auch interviewt. Die kennen Sie doch, nicht wahr? Sie meint, die Show am Samstag muss auf jeden Fall abgesagt werden. Die arme Frau ist völlig fertig mit den Nerven. Hat nicht viel gefehlt, und sie hätte vor der Kamera geweint.«

»Ist Graf bei Bewusstsein?«

»Am Ende hat sie gesagt, er freut sich, dass er noch lebt, und lässt seine Fans und Freunde schön grüßen. Und er bedankt sich für die überwältigende Anteilnahme. Wie man hört, werden da Lieferwagen voller Blumen angeliefert. Und so ein läppischer Mordanschlag, sagt er, ist noch lange nicht das Ende seiner Karriere und seiner Show.«

»Das hat er so gesagt?«

»Das hat seine Assistentin so gesagt.«

21

Gegen Mittag gab es eine erste kleine Erfolgsmeldung. Klara Vangelis ließ es sich nicht nehmen, sie mir persönlich zu überbringen: »Wir haben das Messer gefunden. Der Täter hat es unmittelbar nach dem Anschlag in den Neckar geworfen.«

»Nach Fingerspuren brauche ich wohl nicht zu fragen.«

»Da liegen Sie richtig. Das Messer ist billige Kaufhausware. Die Spusi sagt, es sei neuwertig, vermutlich erst kürzlich gekauft. Ich lasse gerade die Geschäfte im Umfeld abtelefonieren, die so etwas führen. Die Chancen sind nicht groß, aber wer weiß ...«

Damit schien unsere Erfolgssträhne aber auch schon wieder zu Ende zu sein. Ich bat sie, mir die Seriennummer der teuren Armbanduhr zu besorgen, die bei dem Einbruch der Kellertürenbande im November verschwunden war. Wenige Minuten später rief Sven Balke an. Sie hatte die Aufgabe an ihn weitergereicht.

»Eine Patek Philippe Calatrava Gold war das. Über dreizehntausend Mücken kostet so ein Teil!«, erklärte er empört.

»Für eine Scheißarmbanduhr, die auch nur die Zeit anzeigen kann!«

»Jeder hat seinen eigenen Spleen, für den er sein Geld aus dem Fenster wirft.«

»Solange Menschen solche Beträge für Tinnef ausgeben können, während andere ihr Fressen aus Müllcontainern suchen müssen, ist mit dieser Gesellschaft irgendwas nicht in Ordnung.«

Er diktierte mir die Seriennummer der verschwunden Edeluhr. Ich schrieb Runkel die gewünschte SMS und machte mich auf den Weg in die Innenstadt, um Theresa im Café Extrablatt zum Lunch zu treffen.

Das Messer stammte aus der Haushaltsabteilung von Kaufhof, fand Vangelis im Lauf des Nachmittags heraus. Dort lief zurzeit eine Sonderverkaufsaktion: Küchenmesser verschiedenster Größen aus fernöstlicher Produktion, jedes nur ein Euro neunundneunzig. Von der Sorte, die der Täter benutzt hatte, waren allein in den letzten sieben Tagen neunzehn Stück verkauft worden.

Schon im Lauf des Vormittags hatte die Sonne sich mehr und mehr verzogen. Düstere Wolken zogen auf, vor den Fenstern wurde es minütlich kälter und windiger. Erste Graupelschauer gingen nieder. Und unsere Ermittlungen kamen nicht voran. Hergarden war trotz der intensivierten Fahndung nicht zu finden, weitere Zeugen waren nicht aufzutreiben, hilfreiche Spuren am Tatort nicht zu entdecken. Der Weg, auf dem Marcel Graf seinen Spaziergang unternommen hatte, war asphaltiert, sodass auch keine Schuhabdrücke oder dergleichen auszumachen waren. Hoffnungen setzten wir in Blut- und Gewebespuren, die sich an Grafs Händen finden lassen mussten. Niemand lässt sich mit dem Messer abstechen, ohne sich handfest zur Wehr zu setzen. Aber die Ärzte ließen uns nicht an ihn heran. Die Gesundheit des Patienten stehe an erster Stelle, wurde mir immer wieder beschieden, und Herr Graf sei durch den Mordanschlag physisch und psychisch stark angegriffen.

Der heimtückische Anschlag auf den prominenten Show-master war natürlich Aufmacherthema aller Onlinemedien, Radio- und Fernsehnachrichten. Man erging sich in Spekulationen über mögliche Hintergründe und denkbare Motive des Täters. Bewunderte Graf für seine Tapferkeit, bemitleidete ihn nach Kräften, rätselte, ob die beliebte Samstagabendshow jemals wieder auf den Bildschirmen erscheinen würde. Die Station des Uniklinikums, wo man das Opfer mehr oder weniger unter Verschluss hielt, wurde von Mikrofonen und Kameras belagert. Sogar Hubschrauber knatterten hin und wieder über dem Gelände, mit Kameramännern, die durch lange Objektive heruntergelassene Jalousien filmten. Ich konnte sie bei geschlossenen Fenstern durch die Luft rattern hören. Jeder, der auch nur am Rande mit der Station zu tun hatte, wurde interviewt. Selbst das nur gebrochen Deutsch sprechende Reinigungspersonal war nicht sicher vor der jagdfiebrigen Meute.

Die Polizei verfolge mehrere Spuren, hieß es immer wieder, halte sich jedoch aus ermittlungstaktischen Gründen bedeckt. Harmlose Spaziergänger am Neckarufer gerieten zu ihrer Verblüffung ins Zentrum des Medieninteresses, durften vor schweren Kameras wahlweise Abscheu, Empörung oder Mitgefühl äußern. Ein kleines Mädchen mit braunen Zöpfen, vielleicht acht Jahre alt, erzählte artig, seine Omi sei sehr traurig. Fast so traurig wie damals im Sommer, als der Opi starb. Sönnchen hielt mich ständig auf dem Laufenden.

»Auf Twitter gibt's alle paar Minuten die letzten Neuigkeiten«, wusste sie zu melden.

»Twitter?«

Mein Kopf war infolge der zwei Gläser Sekt, die ich auf Theresas Erfolg geleert hatte, noch etwas langsam. Theresa war ausgelassen und albern gewesen, hatte gesprüht vor guter Laune, kaum etwas gegessen, und sich im nächsten Moment Sorgen gemacht, weil ihr immer noch keine Idee für ihr drittes Buch gekommen war.

»Man muss mit der Zeit gehen, Herr Gerlach«, meinte meine verliebte Sekretärin und lachte über meine verdutzte Miene.

»Das Messer kann er sich schon vor Wochen beschafft haben«, spekulierte Balke bei der hoffentlich letzten Besprechung des Tages. »Wer weiß, wie lange er schon auf eine passende Gelegenheit gelauert hat.«

»Vielleicht hat er es geklaut«, meinte Vangelis frustriert. »Oder in Hamburg gekauft oder im Ausland. Jedenfalls ist hier wohl leider Ende der Fahnenstange …«

Außer einigen mikroskopisch kleinen Blutspuren vom Opfer hatte unser Labor an der mit Neckarwasser gründlich gewaschenen Tatwaffe nichts Verwertbares gefunden. Eventuell vorhandene Fingerabdrücke hatte der Täter natürlich gründlich abgewischt, wenn er nicht ohnehin Handschuhe getragen hatte. Noch immer waren außer der Joggerin keine ernst zu nehmenden Zeugen aufgetaucht. Hergarden – inzwischen war ich überzeugt, dass er der Angreifer war – hatte den Ort seiner Tat verflucht geschickt ausgewählt.

»Und jede Menge Glück hat er außerdem gehabt«, maulte Balke. »Normalerweise treten sich um die Uhrzeit am Neckarufer die Jogger auf die Hacken.«

»Wie weit sind wir denn mit den Anruflisten von Frau Jordan?«

Nach dem Anschlag auf Marcel Graf hatte ich Balke gebeten, sich darum zu kümmern. Man konnte ja nie wissen …

Wortlos und mit immer noch mürrischer Miene schob er mir einen Computerausdruck über den Tisch. »Viel telefoniert hat sie ja nicht. Auf der Vorderseite sind die abgehenden Anrufe der letzten vier Wochen aufgelistet, auf der Rückseite die Anrufer. Hat sie kein Handy gehabt?«

»Ich habe zumindest keines gefunden.«

Ich überflog die wirklich kurze Liste von Rosalie Jordans Telefonkontakten und blieb an der letzten Position hängen.

»Null-sechs-zwei-eins, das ist doch …«

»Mannheim«, sagte Balke.

»Und Ludwigshafen«, ergänzte ich und war schon dabei, die Nummer in meinen Laptop zu tippen.

»Pfalzbau«, murmelte ich zunächst verständnislos. Im nächsten Moment war mir alles sonnenklar: »Sie hat Graf angerufen. Neunzig Minuten, nachdem ich bei ihr war.«

Ich drehte das Blatt um. Bei den Anrufern tauchte mehrfach meine eigene Nummer in der Liste auf. Zuletzt eine Handynummer. Dienstagabend, dreiundzwanzig Uhr vier. Das Gespräch hatte fast eine Viertelstunde gedauert.

»Diese Handynummer interessiert mich«, sagte ich und schob Balke die Liste zurück. »Der Anruf war vermutlich kurz vor ihrem Tod.«

Balke warf einen Blick auf die Liste, zog die blassblonden Brauen hoch, sagte: »Augenblick mal.«

Sekunden später wussten wir, dass die Handynummer Marcel Graf gehörte. Durch meinen Kopf wirbelten Gedanken wie das alte Herbstlaub vor den Fenstern im Wintersturm. »Das wäre ... Das heißt ja ...«

Sönnchen brauchte nur wenige Augenblicke, um Namen und Telefonnummer des Bestattungsunternehmens herauszufinden, das Rosalie Jordans sterbliche Überreste verwahrte. Ich ordnete eine Obduktion an.

»Die Spurensicherung soll sich die Wohnung vornehmen. Und zwar heute noch.«

Als ich abends nach Hause kam, saßen die Zwillinge vor dem Fernseher, zwischen sich eine große Tüte Popcorn, und guckten mit großen Augen *Germany's next Topmodel*.

»Oma hat angerufen«, sagte Louise, ohne den Blick vom bunten Bildschirm zu wenden.

»Was wollte sie?«

»Hat sie nicht gesagt. Du sollst sie anrufen. Es ist aber nicht dringend.«

»Morgen«, seufzte ich und gähnte. »Für heute habe ich genug telefoniert. Außerdem muss ich jetzt erst mal was essen.«

Als ich zu Abend gegessen hatte, war es schon fast neun. Ich gesellte mich mit einem Glas Wein in der Hand zu meinen Töchtern, wurde ermahnt, leise zu sein, und fragte mich wieder einmal, wer sich eigentlich solche Sendungen ausdachte und warum die Feministinnen dieser Welt das Studio nicht längst in Brand gesteckt hatten. Schon nach zehn Minuten war ich eingenickt. Das Letzte, was ich von Deutschlands nächsten Topmodels sah, war ein Rotz und Wasser heulender und wie eine Prostituierte aufgeputzter Teenager.

In der Nacht riss mich das Handy aus dem ersten Tiefschlaf. Der Radiowecker zeigte null Uhr dreiundzwanzig. »Unbekannter Teilnehmer«, las ich auf dem Display, nachdem ich meine Brille gefunden und auf die Nase bugsiert hatte. Unschlüssig ließ ich es noch einige Male brummen, dann drückte ich den grünen Knopf.

»Ja?«, sagte ich und räusperte mich. »Hallo?«

Ich hörte schweren Atem und – sehr leise, wie aus weiter Ferne – Männergebrüll. Dann brach das Gespräch ab. Vermutlich verwählt. Oder einer dieser Spaßvögel, denen es Vergnügen bereitet, andere Menschen um ihre hart verdiente Nachtruhe zu bringen. Ich warf das Handy wieder neben den Wecker, die Brille dazu, und drehte mich auf die andere Seite. Aber nun konnte ich nicht mehr einschlafen. Meine Gedanken kreiselten um Hergarden, Graf, Rosalie Jordan, Vicky. Meine immer wirrer werdenden Überlegungen und Gedankenkurzschlüsse führten zu keinem sinnvollen Ende, sondern nur zu immer neuen Fragen ohne Antworten.

22

Am Freitagmorgen erwartete mich eine schlechte Nachricht, als ich unausgeschlafen und nicht allzu gut gelaunt mein Vorzimmer betrat. In der Nacht hatte es kräftig geschneit, die Temperatur war noch weiter gefallen, und ich war für den Wintereinbruch zu leicht angezogen.

Sönnchen hielt den Hörer noch in der Hand.

»Sie haben ihn.«

»Wen?«, fragte ich brummig und fegte mit der bloßen Hand den Schnee von meinen Schultern. Draußen schneite es immer noch, aber zum Glück nicht mehr so stark wie in der Nacht.

»Hergarden. Er hat sich in der Nacht vor den Zug geschmissen. In der Nähe von Neulußheim.«

Ich erstarrte. »Wann genau?«

»Es war ein Güterzug. Um kurz nach zwei hat der Lokführer den Unfall an die Betriebsleitung gemeldet.«

Der nächtliche Anruf war eine halbe Stunde früher gewesen. Sönnchen legte den Hörer so zögernd auf, als würde erst dadurch Hergardens Unglück unwiderruflich. »Der Zug hat ihn fast dreihundert Meter mitgeschleift, bevor er zum Stehen gekommen ist.« Sie schauderte bei der Vorstellung. »Er muss furchtbar aussehen.«

»Ist die Identifizierung verlässlich?«

»Er hat seinen Ausweis in der Tasche gehabt.«

»Der Lokführer, ist der vernehmungsfähig?«

»Steht noch unter Schock.«

»Sobald man mit dem Mann reden kann, will ich es wissen, okay?«

»Der Kollege Runkel hat übrigens schon wieder angerufen«, sagte Sönnchen tonlos. »Diesmal hat er geklungen, als wär's wirklich wichtig.«

Zunächst setzte ich mich jedoch mit meinem Handyprovider in Verbindung. Man zierte sich zunächst ein wenig, aber fünf Minuten später kannte ich die Nummer des Handys, von dem der nächtliche Anruf gekommen war. Es handelte sich um eine Prepaidnummer, die erst vor drei Wochen vergeben worden war. Auf den Namen eines gewissen Fred Hergarden.

Anschließend wählte ich die Nummer von Rolf Runkel, der immer noch in Bad Soden seine Rehabilitation betrieb.

»Morgen, Chef!«, rief er ungewohnt gut gelaunt. »Schön, dass Sie sich gleich melden!« Ich hörte Tellerklappern. Offenbar saß man beim Frühstück. »Ich glaub fast, jetzt haben wir sie am Sack!«

»Die ... Kellertürenbande?«

»Ich hab Ihnen doch von Horst erzählt? Der jetzt in Bonn wohnt?«

»Hm.«

»Der Horst hat nämlich so eine superteure Armbanduhr …«
Jetzt saß ich senkrecht in meinem Sessel.

»Sagen Sie bloß …«

»Hat er von seinem Sohn zum Sechzigsten gekriegt, im Februar erst. Angeblich gebraucht gekauft auf einer Auktion. Aber die Seriennummer …«

»… ist die von der Uhr aus Bammental?«

»Der Sohn wohnt in Saarbrücken. Haben Sie was zum Schreiben?«

Um halb zehn meldete Sönnchen, sie habe den Lokführer in der Leitung.

»Brabetz hier.« Der bedauernswerte Mann sprach mit dünner Stimme und leichtem sächsischem Akzent. »Sie wollten mich sprechen? Ich habe doch schon alles Ihren Kollegen erzählt.«

»Ich habe auch nur eine einzige Frage: Wie war das genau, letzte Nacht? Was haben Sie gesehen?«

»Nichts«, erwiderte der Mann leise. »Nichts habe ich gesehen. Man guckt ja nicht dauernd auf die Gleise. Das hält man ja gar nicht aus, vor allem nachts hält man das nicht aus. Man guckt nur nach den Signallichtern. Und wenn es auch noch schneit, dann ist es sowieso eine Katastrophe. Da sehen Sie ja nichts im Licht als Schnee, Schnee, Schnee. Stundenlang. Es hat einfach bums gemacht, und ich war mir nicht mal sicher … Hätte ja ebenso gut ein Tier sein können … Ich habe ganz automatisch die Bremse reingehauen und die Betriebsleitung angerufen. Ich habe so gehofft, dass es ein Tier war. Ein Reh. Ein Hirsch. Eine ausgebüxte Kuh, von mir aus. Das hatte ich nämlich schon mal: eine Kuh. Aber irgendwie habe ich dieses Mal gleich so ein Gefühl gehabt … Dass es diesmal was Schlimmes ist. Ich bin erst ausgestiegen, als Ihre Kollegen gekommen sind. Und die haben mir dann gesagt, es ist ein Mensch gewesen. Ein Mann wahrscheinlich. Keine Kuh. Ein Mann. Wieso kann so einer sich nicht bitte irgendwo aufhängen? Oder den Gashahn aufdrehen? Am liebsten würde ich den Beruf an den Nagel hängen. Ich habe Kinder, zwei Mädels und zwei Jungs …«

Es gelang mir erst im dritten Anlauf, den Redefluss des verzweifelten Familienvaters zu unterbrechen. Ich bedankte mich mit warmen Worten und wünschte dem bemitleidenswerten Lokführer alles Gute. Anschließend bat ich Sönnchen, mir einen der Kollegen ans Telefon zu schaffen, die in der Nacht als Erste vor Ort gewesen waren. Obwohl diese sich nach Ende ihrer Schicht schlafen gelegt hatten, musste ich nur wenige Minuten warten, bis ich die raue Stimme eines gewissen Hauptkommissar Ehrmann vom Polizeirevier Hockenheim hörte.

»Die Meldung ist um kurz nach zwei reingekommen. Von der Bahnbetriebsleitung in Mannheim. Wir sind zu dem Zeitpunkt nur zu zweit gewesen im Revier, weil das andere Team mit einem Verkehrsunfall zu tun gehabt hat. In der vergangenen Nacht hat's ja ständig irgendwo gekracht, wegen dem Schnee. Wir sind dann gleich raus, und zehn Minuten später waren wir vor Ort. Da war's genau achtzehn nach zwei.«

»Haben Sie die Stelle gefunden, wo der Mann sich auf die Schienen gelegt hat?«

»Der Zug ist kurz vor der Brücke gestanden, wo die L 723 die Bahnlinie kreuzt. War Richtung Mannheim unterwegs. Und es hat die ganze Zeit geschneit wie verrückt.«

Das war keine Antwort auf meine Frage.

»Haben Sie die Stelle gefunden und gesichert? Gerade weil es geschneit hat, könnten da noch Spuren sein.«

»Darum haben sich die Kollegen von der Kripo gekümmert. Wir haben nur den Rettungswagen alarmiert, dem Lokführer einen Kaffee spendiert und die Kripo gerufen. Das ist jetzt der Fünfte, der sich auf die Schienen schmeißt, in den drei Jahren, die ich in Hockenheim bin. Wieso können die sich nicht einfach irgendwo im Warmen aufhängen? Oder von mir aus irgendwas einwerfen …«

Neulußheim gehörte zum Zuständigkeitsbereich der Polizeidirektion Heidelberg. So waren die Dienstwege kurz. Die beiden Beamten vom KDD, die den Fall in der Nacht übernommen hatten, schliefen jedoch und waren klug genug gewesen, ihre Handys stumm zu stellen.

Eine halbe Stunde später stapfte ich in Begleitung von Sven Balke an den Bahngleisen nördlich von Neulußheim durch gut zwanzig Zentimeter hoch liegenden Neuschnee. Die dicken Wolken waren zwischenzeitlich nach Osten weitergezogen, und eine höhnische Sonne beschien die weiße Bescherung. Über die weiten Felder im Westen pfiff ein widerlich kalter Wind und blies uns harte Schneekristalle ins Gesicht. Mein Wintermantel bot dem Wind keinen nennenswerten Widerstand, ganz zu schweigen von der Hose. Die Halbschuhe mit Ledersohle waren für die Witterung absolut ungeeignet. Schon bei den ersten Schritten fühlte ich Schnee eindringen.

Balke hatte zwischenzeitlich mit irgendjemandem bei der Deutschen Bahn telefoniert.

»Die sind imstande, aus der Geschwindigkeit und den Witterungsverhältnissen den Punkt relativ genau zu berechnen, wo der Lokführer die Bremse reingehauen hat«, berichtete er stolz. »Ungefähr hier muss es gewesen sein.«

Die Stelle, wo wir uns befanden, lag wenige Meter nördlich von der Unterführung, wo die B 36 unter der Bahnlinie hindurch verlief. Hier führte ein schmaler Fahrweg von einem nicht geräumten Sträßchen zu den Schienen hinunter, von denen uns nur noch eine Leitplanke trennte.

»Hier ist die einzige Stelle, wo man relativ problemlos an die Gleise rankommt«, meinte Balke, der den Fellkragen seiner dick gefütterten Outdoorjacke hochgeschlagen hatte. »Zum Glück schneit es nicht mehr. Aber dieser Scheißwind verweht alle Spuren.«

»Deshalb wollte ich so schnell wie möglich hier sein«, erwiderte ich missmutig. »Mit jeder Stunde werden die Spuren schwächer. Falls es überhaupt noch welche gibt, natürlich.«

Wir stiegen über die Leitplanke und traten näher an die Gleise heran. Die Oberleitung sirrte. Offenbar näherte sich ein Zug.

»Da habe ich wenig Hoffnung, sorry, Chef. Es hat schon vor Mitternacht angefangen zu frieren. Und der Wind hat den Schnee so stark verweht, dass wir mit Fußspuren …«

Ein ICE brauste an uns vorbei in Richtung Süden und wirbelte einen Blizzard auf, der uns fast von den Füßen riss.

»Was für ein Kackjob!«, schimpfte Balke, als der Zug vorbei war und er seine Kapuze wieder loslassen konnte.

Fred Hergardens Körper war durch den Zusammenprall mit dem Güterzug so stark verunstaltet, hatte ich inzwischen erfahren, dass etwaige Anzeichen von Fremdeinwirkung kaum noch nachzuweisen sein würden. Falls es auf dem Gleisbett Blutspuren geben sollte, dann hatte der Schnee sie gnädig verdeckt.

»Wann genau hat es angefangen zu schneien?«

Balke sah mit schmalen Augen um sich. »Erst hat es nur geregnet. Ungefähr ab sechs hat es dann zunehmend geschneit. Richtig übel ist es erst nach Mitternacht geworden, als der Schnee …«

Er stockte, bückte sich, blies den lockeren Schnee von etwas, das einen Meter neben den Gleisen in einem flachen Graben lag. »Sehen Sie mal«, sagte er dann.

Ich sah einen Schuh. Einen Männerschuh. Einen schwarzen Slipper aus festem Leder. Wie es aussah, schon einige Jährchen alt und häufig getragen.

»Der liegt noch nicht lange hier«, meinte mein aufmerksamer Mitarbeiter und begann, mit der bloßen Hand den Schnee rund um das Fundstück zur Seite zu schieben. »Wäre er gestern Abend schon hier gewesen, wäre er nämlich festgefroren.« Unter dem Schnee kam eine dünne, vereiste Schicht zum Vorschein.

»Wie ist Hergarden hergekommen?« Ich sah um mich. »Mit einem Auto offenbar nicht. Sonst müsste hier irgendwo eines stehen.«

Balke richtete sich auf, rückte seine Kapuze zurecht, um die ich ihn inzwischen heftig beneidete. »Vielleicht hatte er sich ein Zimmer in Neulußheim genommen? War aufgewühlt? Konnte nicht einschlafen?«

»Und macht einen zwei Kilometer langen Nachtspaziergang im Schneeregen?«

»Hergarden hatte keine Übung darin, Leute abzustechen, nehme ich an. So was kann auch härtere Typen um den Schlaf bringen. Vielleicht wollte er sich abreagieren. Müde laufen. Ihm war klar, dass wir ihn früher oder später schnappen würden. Im Radio hatte er gehört, dass Graf den Anschlag überlebt hat. Und dann ...«

Und dann hatte ihn die Sinnlosigkeit seines Daseins überwältigt?

Noch während er sprach, hatte Balke sein iPhone gezückt und begonnen, aus verschiedenen Perspektiven Fotos von dem einsamen schwarzen Schuh zu knipsen. Für die letzte Aufnahme kniete er sich sogar heldenhaft in den Schnee. Bevor er den Auslöser drückte, zögerte er, sagte: »Ups!«, und steckte eilig das Handy ein. Er beugte sich so weit vor, dass seine Nase fast den gefrorenen Boden berührte.

»Sehen Sie sich das mal an!«

Obwohl ich wenig Lust dazu verspürte, kniete ich mich ebenfalls nieder – man kann sich als Chef ja vor seinen Leuten keine Blöße geben. Dann sah ich es auch: den Abdruck einer groben Sohle in der Eisschicht, ungefähr zehn Zentimeter von dem verlorenen Schuh entfernt. Schuh und Abdruck passten nicht zusammen. Die Sohle des verlorenen Slippers war so glatt wie die der Halbschuhe, in denen meine inzwischen tiefgefrorenen Füße steckten.

»Größe dreiundvierzig«, schätzte Balke mit krauser Stirn.

»Höchstens vierundvierzig. Der Slipper ist siebenundvierzig.« Er sprang auf und rieb sich die Hände. Bei mir dauerte es ein wenig länger, bis ich wieder in der Senkrechten war. Inzwischen fühlten meine Ohren sich an, als würden sie zersplittern, wenn man sie unsanft berührte.

»Hergarden hat große Füße gehabt«, sagte ich langsam. »Das ist mir schon beim ersten Gespräch aufgefallen.«

Ich zog mein Handy aus der Innentasche meines Mantels und wählte mit steifen Fingern die Nummer des Gerichtsmedizinischen Instituts der Universität Heidelberg. Die Assistentin,

218

die ich dort erreichte, war zum Glück mit einem flinken Verstand gesegnet und außerdem keine Freundin komplizierter Amtswege. Rasch war geklärt, dass der verlorene Schuh von Fred Hergardens rechtem Fuß stammte.

»Er war nicht allein«, sprach ich aus, was wir beide längst dachten.

»Und den Schuh hat er nicht verloren, als die Lok ihn erfasst hat, sondern als man ihn auf die Gleise geschleppt hat«, ergänzte Balke.

»Einen erwachsenen Mann trägt man nicht kilometerweit«, überlegte ich laut. Wie viel mochte Hergarden gewogen haben? Achtzig Kilo? Er war nicht dick gewesen, aber ziemlich groß. »Irgendwo in der Nähe müssten Spuren von Autoreifen zu finden sein.«

Aus Richtung Süden rumpelte ein langer Güterzug heran und machte für einige Sekunden jedes Gespräch unmöglich. Balke machte mehr aus Langeweile noch einige Aufnahmen von dem Sohlenabdruck.

Als der Güterzug vorbei war, rauschte eine Regionalbahn in Richtung Süden und veranstaltete das nächste Schneegestöber.

Ich schüttelte mich. Sah Balke an. Er sah mich an. Seine Nasenspitze war weiß vor Kälte. In seinen blonden Augenbrauen klebten Schneeflocken und gaben ihm das verwegene Aussehen eines Polarforschers.

»Im Grunde«, sagte ich und schüttelte mich. »Im Grunde ist das hier ja nicht unser Job.«

23

Als Balke auf den Parkplatz der Polizeidirektion einbog, war es schon kurz vor zwölf, ich spürte allmählich meine Füße wieder, und das Handy meines Mitarbeiters klingelte. Er schaffte es, gleichzeitig rückwärts einzuparken und zu telefonieren.

»Danke«, sagte er am Ende. »Vielen herzlichen Dank. Super Arbeit, Kollegin!«

Er zog den Schlüssel ab und grinste mich an. »Saarbrücken. Rübes Tipp war goldrichtig.«

»Das heißt, mit der Kellertürenbande werden wir künftig keinen Stress mehr haben?«

»Der Sohn von Rübes Schulfreund ist Mitglied der Hells Angels. Er scheint nicht direkt mit den Einbrüchen zu tun zu haben, aber die Uhr stammt definitiv aus dem Bruch in Bammental. Zurzeit quetschen sie den Kerl noch aus. Ist wohl eine harte Nummer. Behauptet jetzt, er hat das Teil von einem Unbekannten in einer Kneipe gekauft, an die er sich nicht mehr erinnern kann. Außerdem hat er natürlich keinen blassen Dunst gehabt, dass die Uhr so wertvoll ist. Aber sie haben inzwischen in seiner Wohnung noch andere Sachen aus der Beute sichergestellt, und allmählich wird er weich.«

Auch meine Schuhe waren weich. Außerdem völlig durchnässt, stellte ich auf dem kurzen Weg zur Kantine fest. Meine frisch getauten Ohren brannten und kribbelten.

»Wie läuft's mit der toten Schauspielerin?«, wollte Balke gut gelaunt wissen.

»Ich warte auf den Bericht aus der Gerichtsmedizin. Äußere Verletzungen hat sie definitiv nicht.«

»Irgendwer läuft da Amok«, überlegte Balke, als wir uns mit hellgrauen, von der Spülmaschine noch ein wenig feuchten und angenehm warmen Tabletts in den Händen in die Essensschlange einreihten. »Gibt's überhaupt jemanden in dieser alten Geschichte, der noch am Leben ist und nicht im Krankenhaus liegt? Was ist mit Grafs geschiedener Frau?«

»Die ist seit zwanzig Jahren tot, wie es aussieht.«

»Sicher?«

Unser Unterbewusstsein ist um vieles intelligenter als wir selbst und hat zudem unglaubliche Mengen an Informationen und Erfahrungen gespeichert. Nur behält es sein Wissen gerne für sich oder rückt zu den unpassendsten Zeitpunkten damit heraus. Irgendetwas in meinem Kopf hatte die Antwort auf unsere Fragen längst gefunden, wurde mir in diesem Moment bewusst. Dieses Etwas weigerte sich jedoch bislang, sein Wissen zu veröffentlichen.

»Eigentlich«, sagte ich zögernd. »Eigentlich ist das sicher, ja. Ihr Haus in der Gundolfstraße wurde von der Erbengemeinschaft verkauft und ...«

»Sie haben Zweifel?«

Ich zuckte ratlos die Achseln. »Irgendwas ist komisch, aber ich kann es noch nicht greifen.«

»Soll Evalina sich mal ans Telefon hängen, um rauszufinden, was aus der Frau geworden ist? Die hat gerade ein wenig Luft.«

Als ich Blechbesteck und eine dünne Papierserviette auf mein Tablett legte, fiel mir der logische Fehler in der Geschichte auf. Das, was mich die ganze Zeit schon irritiert hatte. Balke brauchte im Gegensatz zu mir nicht Tage, sondern nur wenige Sekunden dazu.

»Erbengemeinschaft heißt doch, sie hat entweder mehrere Kinder gehabt ...«

»Oder es gibt noch andere Verwandte. Mit einem Mitglied dieser Erbengemeinschaft habe ich sogar selbst telefoniert, aber ...« Aber das war kurz nach meinem Unfall gewesen, als ich noch nicht wieder Herr meiner Sinne war.

Inzwischen waren wir in der Essensschlange so weit vorgerückt, dass wir uns entscheiden mussten. Weil Freitag war, gab es Fisch. Weil nicht jeder Fisch mochte, war die Alternative Wiener Schnitzel vom Schwein. Dazu die üblichen Pommes und Salat.

»Schniposa«, sagte Balke befriedigt und griff ohne Zögern zu. Ich zierte mich kurz, wählte dann ebenfalls das Schnitzel.

»Da muss ich gleich mal nachhaken«, sagte ich kopfschüttelnd. »Zurzeit passieren mir ständig solche Sachen.«

»So eine Gehirnerschütterung ist kein Spaß, Chef. Und wenn ich Ihnen einen Tipp geben darf ...«

»Sprechen Sie das Wort ›Helm‹ aus, und Sie sind ab Montag für die Überwachung des ruhenden Verkehrs in Ziegelhausen zuständig.«

Balke sah mich aus schmalen Augen nachdenklich an. »Irgendwas wollte ich noch sagen, aber ... Worüber hatten wir eben gesprochen?«

Noch bevor ich das Altersheim in Alzey anrufen konnte, in dem die letzte Überlebende der Erbengemeinschaft heute ihre eintönigen Tage verbrachte, meldete sich ein Mitarbeiter des Kriminaltechnischen Labors am LKA in Stuttgart bei mir.

»Definitiv vergiftet also?«, fragte ich sicherheitshalber, nachdem ich dem kurzen Bericht gelauscht hatte.

»Irgendwas war in dem Cognac. Was es war, weiß ich noch nicht.« Der Techniker atmete schwer und klang erkältet. »Ich habe eine Probe des Glasinhalts per Express nach Wiesbaden zum BKA geschickt. Ich hoffe, die Ergebnisse noch im Lauf des Nachmittags auf den Tisch zu kriegen.«

Da ich den Hörer schon in der Hand hielt, rief ich unserer eigenes Labor an, das natürlich nicht annähernd so üppig ausgestattet war wie das in Stuttgart.

»An der Flasche sind logischerweise Fingerspuren von der Toten, aber ...« Ein Niesanfall unterbrach die Kollegin, die ebenfalls erkältet zu sein schien. Ich wünschte Gesundheit.

»Danke. Und noch von mindestens drei oder vier weiteren Personen. Einer davon ist vermutlich ein Mann.«

»Bis wann kann ich mit Ergebnissen rechnen?«

»Heute noch«, seufzte die Frau zwei Stockwerke tiefer ergeben und nieste zur Bekräftigung zweimal. »Und noch was: Ich verstehe zufällig was von Cognac. Mein Freund sammelt nämlich alten Cognac. Und diese Flasche ... Die Frau hat ja eigentlich nicht ausgesehen, als wäre sie reich gewesen.«

»Sie wollen andeuten, der Cognac war teuer?«

»Sauteuer sogar«, erwiderte die Laborantin. »Für einen zwölf Jahre alten Château de Montifaud müssen Sie ganz schön tief in die Tasche langen. Wenn Sie ihn im normalen Handel überhaupt kriegen. Ich schätze, für so ein Fläschchen müssen Sie fast einen Hunni hinlegen.«

Während des kurzen Gesprächs hatte ein Piepston einen wartenden Anrufer gemeldet. Ich drückte die Taste mit dem roten Hörer und nahm das Gespräch an. Es war einer der armen Kollegen, die in den vergangenen Stunden neben den Bahngleisen bei Neulußheim Schnee geschippt hatten.

»Also …«, begann er grimmig. »Die Sohlenabdrücke haben wir in der Eisschicht ungefähr zwanzig Meter zurückverfolgen können. Dann hören sie urplötzlich auf.«

Im Hintergrund brummte ein Motor. Vermutlich war man auf dem Weg zurück ins gut geheizte Büro.

»Da hatte der Täter wahrscheinlich sein Auto stehen«, vermutete ich.

»Zwei. Zwei sind's gewesen. Es sind verschiedene Profile. Und mit dem Auto liegen Sie richtig. Wir haben Reifenspuren sichergestellt. Geht gleich ins Labor. Ich hoffe, da ist um die Uhrzeit noch einer.«

»Das darf auf gar keinen Fall bis Montag liegen bleiben!«, fuhr ich den armen Kerl an. »Auch wenn Freitagnachmittag ist, das duldet keinen Aufschub!«

Er stöhnte gequält. »Ich geb's gleich weiter, versprochen. Wie's aussieht, ist das ein großer Wagen gewesen. Das waren mindestens Zweihundertfünfzehner-Reifen. Und ich hab jetzt gleich Feierabend. Übers Wochenende geht's mit meiner Frau und dem Ältesten zusammen nach Paris. Hab schon vor Wochen die Fahrkarten gekauft, für den TGV, und meine Frau freut sich seit einer halben Ewigkeit auf den Eiffelturm und alles. Das versaut mir keiner. Da kann von mir aus mitten in der Altstadt ein Flugzeug abstürzen. Ich bin in acht Stunden in Paris.«

Fahrkarte. Wieder so ein Stichwort, das in meinem Kopf eine Kette von Assoziationen auslöste. Nachdem ich dem Kollegen ein schönes und hoffentlich sonniges Wochenende an der Seine gewünscht hatte, drückte ich die Direktwahl zum Chef der Spurensicherung.

»Eine Fahrkarte?«, fragte er.

»Im Mantel an der Garderobe, ich glaube, in der linken Tasche.«

»Ich sag meinen Leuten, sie sollen nachsehen.«

Nun war endlich Gelegenheit, in Alzey anzurufen. Es dauerte ein Weilchen, bis die alte Frau ans Telefon kam.

»Holland?«, fragte sie mit dünner Stimme und völliger Verständnislosigkeit.

»Oder Graf?«

»Sie hatte zwei Namen?«

»Sie war verheiratet. Holland war ihr Mädchen- und Künstlername.«

»Sie war Künstlerin?«

»Schauspielerin.«

»Mir ist weder der eine noch der andere Name bekannt. Unsere Familie heißt Kornhaupt. Meine Mutter war eine geborene Hertz. Und mein Mann, Gott hab ihn selig, hat Müller geheißen. Schlicht und einfach Müller. Und so heiße ich jetzt auch.«

Herzhaft fluchend knallte ich den Hörer auf den Apparat. Ich war tagelang einer falschen Spur gefolgt.

Es ging gar nicht um das Haus an der Gundolfstraße.

Die in unseren Akten vermerkte Anschrift war falsch.

Wieder einmal nahm ich mir den alten grauen Hängeordner vor. Die Telefonnotiz vom zehnten November fünfundachtzig. Elisabeth Holland, las ich zum x-ten Mal, Gundolfstraße. Im Protokoll, auf dem Totenschein, überall dieselbe Adresse. Erst als alle drei Papiere nebeneinanderlagen, fiel mir etwas auf: Es war überall dieselbe Handschrift. Die Telefonnotiz, die Einträge im Totenschein und sogar eine der beiden Unterschriften unter dem maschinengeschriebenen Protokoll stammten ganz offensichtlich von ein und derselben Person. Von Johann Boll. Jetzt, wo ich es endlich sah, konnte ich mir nicht mehr erklären, warum mir das nicht gleich zu Beginn aufgefallen war.

Und noch etwas fiel mir ins Auge: Die Ergänzung des Arztes auf der zweiten Seite, die Tote habe vermutlich unter Alkoholeinfluss gestanden, war mit einer anderen Handschrift geschrieben als der ganze Rest. Mit einer typischen, kaum leserlichen Arztklaue. Ich warf die graue Mappe auf den Tisch zurück und meine Brille hinterher. Jetzt war mir klar, was damals abgelaufen war: Boll und sein Kollege hatten dem Arzt angeboten, ihm den lästigen Schreibkram abzunehmen, vermutlich, während dieser noch dabei war, den Leichnam zu inspizieren. Dann hatten sie auch in ihrem Protokoll – und zwar mit Sicherheit nicht aus Versehen – die Anschrift eingetragen, die in Vicky Hergardens Personalausweis stand und offenbar falsch war. Vermutlich war das Ehepaar Hergarden irgendwann innerhalb der Stadt umgezogen und hatte versäumt oder sogar absichtlich unterlassen, dies dem Einwohnermeldeamt mitzuteilen. Auch, dass nicht der Arzt, sondern Boll die Daten auf den Totenschein geschrieben hatte, war nicht ungewöhnlich. Ich hatte so etwas selbst schon mehr als einmal erlebt: Der Fall ist klar, alle wollen die lästige Sache so rasch wie möglich hinter sich bringen. Man will fort, man hat Wichtigeres und Besseres zu tun. Man unterstützt sich gegenseitig, so gut es geht, um das Verfahren abzukürzen. Daran war nichts Ungewöhnliches und nichts Ehrenrühriges. Und schließlich hatte Boll, um die Sache wasserdicht zu machen, auch noch die Telefonnotiz ausgetauscht, was kein großes Problem war, denn die wurden in einem allgemein zugänglichen Ordner im Führungs- und Lagezentrum aufbewahrt. Er hatte die Notiz herausgenommen, weil er sie angeblich für irgendetwas brauchte, und später einen anderen, von ihm selbst ausgefüllten Vordruck zurückgebracht.

Viktoria Hergarden war nicht in dem Haus an der Gundolfstraße gestorben. Was nur bedeuten konnte – ja, was eigentlich?

Ich fiel in meinen Sessel zurück. Eines war nun endgültig klar: Ihr Tod war kein Unfall gewesen. Hier waren in großem Stil die Fakten gefälscht worden. War vielleicht auch der Arzt an dem Deal beteiligt gewesen? Denn irgendeine Art von Deal musste es gegeben haben. Welchen Grund sollten zwei Polizisten haben, Karriere und Pensionsansprüche aufs Spiel zu setzen, wenn nicht die Erwartung einer großzügigen Belohnung? Einer Belohnung, für die man sich einen gebrauchten Ferrari kaufen konnte zum Beispiel? Vermutlich hatten sie zuvor den Tatort so verändert, dass das Ganze am Ende nicht nach dem aussah, was es in Wirklichkeit eben doch gewesen war: nach einem Mord. Aus diesem Grund hatte es auch so lange gedauert, bis der Notarzt kam. Man hatte ihn erst gerufen, als alles gewissenhaft präpariert war.

Man hatte Zeit gebraucht.

Zeit, um Spuren zu verwischen.

24

Eine Stunde später hielt ich die Fahrkarte aus Rosalie Jordans Manteltasche in Händen. Sie war für die Strecke Ludwigshafen Hauptbahnhof nach Heidelberg gültig und abgestempelt am Dienstagnachmittag um siebzehn Uhr siebenunddreißig. Die alte Schauspielerin war mit einem S-Bahn-Zug der Deutschen Bahn unterwegs gewesen, entnahm ich dem Zangenabdruck des Zugbegleiters mit der telefonischen Unterstützung eines auch am späten Freitagnachmittag noch gut gelaunten und geduldigen Mitarbeiters der Deutschen Bahn. Was hatte sie in Ludwigshafen gewollt? Einen alten Bekannten treffen, natürlich. Einen alten Bekannten, der sie knapp sechs Stunden später anrief, nachts um kurz nach elf, von seinem Hotelzimmer aus. Und wenig später war sie tot gewesen.

»Sie bringen ein Interview!«, jubelte Sönnchen im Vorzimmer. »Wollen Sie es sehen?«

»Mit Graf?«

»Im ZDF bringen sie ein Interview. Live!«

Marcel Graf sah blass und mitgenommen aus. Halb aufgerichtet, aber sichtlich kraftlos lag er in seinem blütenweiß bezogenen Krankenbett. Beide Hände und Unterarme waren dick verbunden. Auf der rechten Wange klebte ein enormes Pflaster, und auch an der Stirn und am linken Ohr schien es ihn erwischt zu haben. Um seine Mundwinkel geisterte trotz seiner zahlreichen Verletzungen schon wieder das verschmitzte Lächeln, das alle acht Wochen Millionen Frauenherzen zum Schmelzen brachte.

»Wie geht es Ihnen heute, Marcel?«, fragte eine mitfühlende Sprecherin aus dem Off. »Unsere Zuschauer machen sich große Sorgen um Sie. Und wir, Ihre Kollegen und Freunde, selbstverständlich auch.«

Das Lächeln wurde eine winzige Spur breiter, fiel dann in sich zusammen, als hätten Schmerz und Erinnerung den Patienten in die Realität seines Elends zurückgerissen.

»Nun ja«, erwiderte er heiser, räusperte sich lange und erfolglos. »Den Umständen entsprechend, wie man so treffend sagt.«

»Sie haben immer noch große Schmerzen?«

»Es lässt sich aushalten. Man gibt mir ja alle möglichen Mittel. Ich bin hier in guten Händen. In einer der besten Kliniken Deutschlands, wenn nicht gar Europas und ...« Die tapfere Stimme erstarb.

In einer Klinik, in deren Personal er offenbar nicht das geringste Vertrauen setzte.

»Sehen Sie sich in der Lage, unseren Zuschauerinnen und Zuschauern den Mordanschlag zu schildern?«

»Sie werden verstehen, dass ich nicht gerne daran zurückdenke. Allein die Erinnerung ...«

»Ihre Fans und Verehrerinnen wären sicher glücklich ...«

Graf räusperte sich erneut. Sein unruhiger Blick fand keinen festen Punkt im Raum. »Im Grunde ... Ich kann kaum etwas sagen. Er ist von hinten gekommen. Es war dunkel. Ein Mann, so viel ist sicher. Ein großer, hagerer Mann. Erst habe ich ein Geräusch gehört. Das hat mir vermutlich das Leben gerettet. Ich habe mich instinktiv umgewandt ...«

»Nicht auszudenken, wenn Sie ... Mein Gott!«

Der Patient schloss kurz die Augen. Nickte matt. »Deshalb hat der erste Stich mich am Oberarm erwischt und nicht im Rücken. Ich habe seinen Arm gepackt. Mit aller mir zur Verfügung stehenden Kraft versucht, das Messer von mir wegzuhalten. Mich dabei an allen möglichen Stellen verletzt, geschnitten, gestochen. Ich habe seltsamerweise überhaupt keinen Schmerz gefühlt. Nicht im Geringsten. Es stimmt tatsächlich, was man sagt. Man fühlt nichts in einer solchen Situation. Es war ein Kampf auf ... auf Leben und Tod. Mehr Tod als Leben ...«

»Sie haben um Ihr Leben gefürchtet?«, lautete die selten dämliche nächste Frage.

»Man denkt nicht in einer solchen Situation. Man fürchtet sich nicht einmal. Man kämpft. Wie ein Tier. Ja, wie ein Tier. Da sind nur noch Instinkte. Triebe. Der Trieb zu überleben. Irgendwie zu überleben.«

»Haben Sie um Hilfe geschrien?«

»Zeugen sagen Ja. Ich selbst weiß nichts davon. Man reagiert völlig automatisch. Ich weiß nur, dass ich mit ihm gerungen habe. Gekämpft.«

»Wie lange ging das so?«

»Sekunden? Minuten? Mir kam es vor wie eine Ewigkeit.«

»Und dann?«

»Ich bin gestolpert und gefallen. Dachte, jetzt ist es aus. Das ist es also nun, das Ende. So schnell. So schäbig, im Dreck … Aber plötzlich hat er von mir abgelassen und ist weggelaufen.«

»Was können Sie unseren Zuschauerinnen und Zuschauern über den Täter sagen?«

»Groß war er. Glücklicherweise nicht allzu muskulös. Es war meine Rettung, dass er nicht so kräftig war. Sonst läge ich jetzt nicht hier, sondern …« Wieder schluckte der Showstar. Zwinkerte. Zwang die Augen wieder auf. Sah mit verlorenem Blick haarscharf an der Kamera vorbei. »Mundgeruch hat er gehabt, daran kann ich mich merkwürdigerweise erinnern. Es war so schrecklich. So schrecklich …«

Die Szene brach ab. In der nächsten Einstellung stand die Journalistin, von der man bisher nur die Stimme gehört hatte, vor dem hohen Glas-und-Beton-Gebäude des Heidelberger Krebsforschungszentrums – vermutlich weil es repräsentativer aussah als die äußerlich etwas renovierungsbedürftige Chirurgische Klinik – und hielt ein Mikrofon mit Windschutz in der Hand. Von den Bäumen im Hintergrund tropfte es. Offenbar taute der Schnee schon wieder weg.

»An dieser Stelle haben wir das Interview auf Geheiß der Ärzte abbrechen müssen. Ich darf Ihnen von Marcel Graf noch die allerbesten Grüße ausrichten und das Versprechen, dass seine Show weitergehen wird. Dass er sich nicht entmutigen lassen wird durch die Wahnsinnstat eines Geisteskranken. Solange er stehen und sprechen kann, darf ich Ihnen sagen, so lange wird *Grafs Abend* leben.«

Sönnchen schniefte ein wenig und knüllte ihr Taschentuch.

»Interviews kann der Herr schon wieder geben. Aber für eine kurze Vernehmung fehlt ihm die Kraft«, maulte ich.

»Er ist nun mal ein Fernsehmensch«, gab Sönnchen mitfühlend zu bedenken. »Sagen Sie, was Sie wollen. Für mich ist er ein Held. Um ein Haar wär er gestorben, und als Allererstes denkt er an seine Zuschauer.«

»Wahrscheinlich denkt er zuallererst an das viele Geld, das ihm am Samstag durch die Lappen geht.«

Ein Blick voll flammender Verachtung traf mich.

»Am Vormittag sind sie übrigens im Haus gewesen, die vom Fernsehen«, berichtete meine bewegte Sekretärin nach kurzer Pause kühl. »Drei Männer und die Frau, die man grad gesehen hat. Sie haben unseren Pressesprecher interviewt. Mit Ihnen wollten sie auch reden. Aber Sie waren ja bei Neulußheim.«

»Glück muss der Mensch haben.«

Das Telefon rief mich zurück an meinen Schreibtisch und auf den Boden der Tatsachen. Inzwischen war es halb vier geworden.

»Wegen der Reifenspur soll ich Sie anrufen«, sagte die verschnupfte Laborantin, mit der ich erst vor einer Stunde gesprochen hatte. »Das war zur Abwechslung mal leicht. Es ist ein Michelin Sommerprofil, Niederquerschnitt. Zugelassen bis zweihundertzwanzig Stundenkilometer. Manche Mercedestypen haben den Typ serienmäßig drauf. Aber auch der Audi A8. Und die großen Volvos.«

Volvo …

Volvo?

Das Filmchen von Theresas Handy fiel mir wieder ein, das immer noch in ihrem Handy schlummerte, weil meine Göttin zwei linke Hände hatte, sobald sie es mit Technik zu tun bekam.

Noch bevor ich einen Finger rühren konnte, klingelte schon wieder das Telefon. Dieses Mal war eine ältere Mitarbeiterin der Spurensicherung am Apparat, die schon kurz vor der Pensionierung stand und für ihre übermenschliche Geduld und Akribie bekannt war. Und für eine gewisse Vorliebe für das Plusquamperfekt.

»Ich hab was!«, verkündete sie stolz. »Bargeld. Fünftausend Euro. Die alte Hexe hatte das Geld verflixt gut versteckt gehabt. Im Gefrierschrank war es gewesen. In einer Packung Buttergemüse, die auf den ersten Blick ausgesehen hatte, als wäre sie noch zu gewesen. Geschickt gemacht, muss ich sagen. Geschickt gemacht.«

»Sind Fingerspuren auf den Scheinen?«

»Jede Menge. Aber ob wir das heut noch schaffen …«

»Es muss sein. Tut mir leid.«

»Eigentlich hab ich aber in zwanzig Minuten Wochenende.«

»Bitte!«

»Na gut. Aber versprechen kann ich nichts!«

Man brauchte nicht viel Phantasie, um zu erraten, woher die runde Summe in Rosalie Jordans Tiefkühlvorräten stammte. Am Dienstagnachmittag war sie nach Ludwigshafen gefahren, vermutlich angeregt durch das Gespräch mit mir, und hatte Graf zur Rede gestellt. Sie verlangte Geld für ihr Schweigen – was immer es da zu verschweigen geben mochte. Wie hatte er ihr das Geld zukommen lassen? Wen hätte er mit einer so heiklen Aufgabe betraut? Warum hatte er sie spätnachts angerufen?

Ich drückte die Direktwahl zu Klara Vangelis und bat sie, mir die Überwachungsvideos aus dem Hotel zu besorgen, die es mit Sicherheit gab.

»Wenn wir Glück haben, sind die Bänder aus der Nacht von Dienstag auf Mittwoch noch nicht überschrieben.«

»Bänder benutzt man heute kaum noch«, wurde ich aufgeklärt. »Heute wird das auf Festplatten gespeichert, und die haben Kapazität für Wochen.«

»Ich will wissen, ob Graf in der Zeit vor Mitternacht das Hotel noch mal verlassen hat.«

Die nächste Nummer, die ich wählte, war eine Handynummer.

»Opelt«, hörte ich die matte Stimme von Grafs Mädchen für alles.

Ich nannte meinen Namen.

»Ich weiß«, erwiderte sie tonlos. »Mein Handy kennt Sie inzwischen.«

»Können wir uns irgendwo ein paar Minuten in Ruhe unterhalten?«

»In Ruhe?« In ihrem Lachen schwang eine Spur Hysterie mit. »Machen Sie Witze?«

»Ich kann mir vorstellen, was bei Ihnen zurzeit los ist.«

»Nein, das können Sie bestimmt nicht. Aber egal. Worum geht es?«

»Wo können wir uns treffen?«

»Am liebsten überhaupt nicht, ehrlich gesagt. Ich bin zurzeit in Ludwigshafen und versuche, irgendwie den Weltuntergang aufzuhalten.«

»Sie kommen im Lauf der nächsten Stunden vermutlich nicht nach Heidelberg?«

»Gewiss nicht, nein.«

»Dann komme ich zu Ihnen. Sagen wir, in einer Stunde?«

Sie atmete zwei, drei Mal tief ein und aus. »Wenn es wirklich sein muss, okay. Kommen Sie, wann Sie mögen. Es passt sowieso nie. Rufen Sie mich an, wenn Sie in der Nähe sind, ja? Dann können wir einen Treffpunkt vereinbaren. Ich weiß im Moment nicht, wo mir der Kopf steht ...«

25

Wir trafen uns im sparsam beleuchteten Foyer des Ludwigshafener Pfalzbaus, in dessen großem Saal am morgigen Samstagabend Marcel Grafs Show ausfallen würde. Olivia Opelt kam die Treppe herabgelaufen, nachdem sie mich zehn Minuten hatte warten lassen, und wirkte wie kurz vor dem finalen Zusammenbruch.

»Es ist die Hölle«, seufzte sie, als sie mir die Hand reichte und dann sofort auf einen der herumstehenden Stühle sank. »Stress mit dem Produktionsleiter, Stress mit dem Bühnenbauer, Superstress mit dem Sender, alle fünf Minuten ruft wer von der Presse an, und jetzt auch noch Sie …«

»Wie geht es Herrn Graf? Gibt es Neuigkeiten?«

»Besser als befürchtet, aber alles andere als gut. Marcel ist eine Kämpfernatur, aber …« Sie zuckte die schmalen Schultern. Sah durch ihre schwarz umrandete Brille an mir vorbei.

»Einen Mordanschlag steckt niemand so einfach weg.«

»Weshalb wollten Sie mich denn nun so dringend sprechen?«

»Es geht um eine Schauspielerin, die Herrn Graf aus früheren Zeiten kennt.«

»Davon gibt es einige.«

»Sagt Ihnen der Name Rosalie Jordan etwas?«

»Jordan?« Ihre Miene blieb gleichgültig. »Nie gehört. Weshalb?«

»Sie war am Dienstagnachmittag hier und hat ihn getroffen.«

»Am Dienstag? Das wüsste ich. Man kann hier nicht einfach aufkreuzen, um mitten in den Vorbereitungsarbeiten mit Marcel ein Pläuschchen über alte Zeiten zu halten. Möglich, dass sie hier war. Aber sie hat ihn bestimmt nicht gesprochen.«

»Er hat sie wenige Stunden später angerufen. Aus dem Hotel, nehme ich an, um kurz nach elf. Sie haben fast eine Viertelstunde geredet.«

»Mit wem Marcel telefoniert, wenn er allein ist, weiß ich natürlich nicht. Um diese Zeit war ich auf meinem Zimmer und habe versucht, wenigstens die wichtigsten Mails des Tages abzuarbeiten.«

»Wissen Sie, ob Herr Graf danach das Hotel noch einmal verlassen hat?«

»Wie sollte ich?«

»Sie hätten es doch vermutlich erfahren?«

»Wir sind nicht im selben Hotel. Ich habe mir etwas hier in der Nähe gesucht. So bin ich flexibler und kann mich am Tag mal eine halbe Stunde hinlegen, wenn gerade nichts brennt. Seine beiden Beschützer, die kriegen es mit, wenn er weggeht ...«

»Stehen die die ganze Nacht vor seiner Tür, wenn er im Hotel ist?«

Sie lächelte erschöpft, fuhr sich durchs kurze schwarze Haar. »Das nicht. Aber sie haben ihre Zimmer direkt neben Marcel. Wenn er weggeht, gibt er ihnen normalerweise Bescheid. Sagt, wo er hingeht und wann er zurück sein wird. So ist es vereinbart, und bisher hat er sich immer an die Regeln gehalten, soweit mir bekannt ist.«

Immer, wenn sie von ihrem Chef sprach, veränderte sich der Ton ihrer Stimme ein wenig, fiel mir auf. Wurde eine Spur weicher, sanfter. Sie schien ihn sehr zu verehren.

»Die Personenschützer begleiten ihn also nicht ständig?«

»Sonst wäre dieser fiese Anschlag ja wohl nicht möglich gewesen, nicht wahr? Marcel will das nicht. Er ist nicht der Bundespräsident, sagt er, sondern nur der allseits beliebte Fernsehonkel. Wer sollte ihm Böses wollen? Haha.«

»Warum braucht er überhaupt Bewachung? Ist das üblich in Ihrer Branche?«

»Nein, das ist gar nicht üblich. Es hat Drohungen gegeben, in letzter Zeit. Ernst zu nehmende Drohungen, offenbar.«

»Von wem?«

»Das weiß ich nicht. Anonym, vermute ich. Marcel wollte nicht darüber sprechen. Er findet den ganzen Aufwand maßlos übertrieben. Er mag es überhaupt nicht, wenn ein solches Gewese um seine Person gemacht wird. Aber der Sender hat darauf bestanden.«

»Ich nehme an, der Sender bezahlt das Ganze auch?«

»Ich denke doch.«

»Er hat also nicht mit Ihnen darüber gesprochen, ob er am Mittwochabend nach elf noch einmal das Hotel verlassen hat?«

»Definitiv: nein.« Ihr Blick wurde unruhig. Sie sah auf die große Uhr über dem Treppenaufgang. »Marcel war am Dienstagabend restlos alle und wollte sich sofort ins Bett legen. Es war ein endlos langer Tag gewesen. Außerdem hatte er Kopfschmerzen vom ewigen Reden und Kreuzschmerzen vom langen Stehen. Er hat Probleme mit den Bandscheiben in letzter Zeit und ... Nein, ich kann mir beim besten Willen nicht vorstellen, dass er so spät noch einen Ausflug unternommen hat. Wohin auch immer. Wo hätte er diese Frau ...?«

»Jordan. Rosalie Jordan.«

»Wo hätte er sie denn getroffen?«

»In ihrer Wohnung, nehme ich an. Die liegt keine fünfhundert Meter vom Hotel entfernt. Außerdem ...« Ich zögerte. Mir war unklar, ob ich die Bombe schon platzen lassen sollte. Aber die Gelegenheit war günstig. Sie war nervös, weil sie wieder an die Arbeit wollte. Sie dachte, das Gespräch sei zu Ende. Saß schon aufrecht, bereit, aufzuspringen.

»Außerdem?«

»Frau Jordan ist in derselben Nacht ermordet worden.«

Sie fiel wieder auf den Stuhl zurück. Ihre bernsteinfarbenen Augen waren plötzlich riesengroß.

»Ermordet? Ja ... aber ... wie denn?«

»Vergiftet.«

»Und jetzt denken Sie ...?«

»Außerdem hatte sie fünftausend Euro im Gefrierschrank versteckt.«

Ihr Blick wurde noch ungläubiger.

»Wollen Sie ... Sie wollen mich verscheißern, ja?«

»Sehe ich so aus? Die Scheine werden zurzeit auf Fingerabdrücke untersucht.«

Und ich war rasend gespannt auf das Ergebnis.

Olivia Opelt schlug die Augen nieder und nickte verstört. War mit den Gedanken plötzlich weit weg. Dann wurde ihr Blick wieder klar. Sie richtete sich zum zweiten Mal auf, sah mir offen ins Gesicht.

»Sonst noch ...?«

»Ich bräuchte etwas, worauf Herrn Grafs Fingerabdrücke sind. Ein Glas, das er in der Hand gehalten hat, eine Flasche. Sie müssen das natürlich nicht tun. Ich bitte Sie nur darum. Falls Sie meine Bitte nicht erfüllen, werde ich allerdings in

einer halben Stunde mit einem richterlichen Durchsuchungsbeschluss hier stehen.«

Sie nickte unbefangen.

»Kommen Sie. Marcel wird nichts dagegen haben, da bin
ich mir sicher.«

Minuten später hatte ich ein benutztes Wasserglas aus Grafs
Garderobe in einem Spurenbeutel verstaut. Olivia Opelt begleitete mich sogar bis zum Ausgang. Dieses Mal war ihr Händedruck deutlich fester als bei der Begrüßung.

»Eine Menge Autos da draußen«, sagte ich mit Blick auf die
große Freifläche vor dem Gebäude. »Gehören die alle zu
Ihnen?«

»Die meisten sind von unseren Hilfstruppen. Unsere sind
die, bei denen ZDF auf den Türen steht.«

»Welcher ist Ihrer?«

»Der dunkle Kombi da drüben.«

»Der Volvo? Da steht aber nichts von ZDF.«

»Es ist mein eigener. Mein Dienstwagen ist in der Werkstatt.
Irgendwas mit dem Getriebe.«

Das Kennzeichen des Volvo begann mit »MZ« für Mainz.

Als ich den Motor meines Wagens startete, liefen gerade die
Achtzehn-Uhr-Nachrichten. Natürlich wurde ausführlich über
Marcel Grafs Schicksal berichtet. Neuigkeiten gab es keine.
Der Verkehr war dicht – Freitagabend, Rushhour vor dem
Wochenende. Da es kein großer Umweg war und ich noch ein
wenig Zeit hatte, beschloss ich, kurz im Uniklinikum vorbei-
zuschauen. Vielleicht schaffte ich es ja wider Erwarten doch,
Graf einige Fragen zu stellen.

Ein großer Lift brachte mich hinauf zu der Station der Chir-
urgischen Klinik, wo Marcel Graf gesund gepflegt wurde. Sein
Zimmer lag ganz am Ende des hell erleuchteten Flurs, an dessen einer Wand sich fast über die ganze Länge Sitzbänke reihten. An der anderen Wand standen zwei leere Krankenbetten.
Grafs Zimmer war leicht daran zu erkennen, dass auf einem
einsamen Stuhl vor der Tür ein knochiger Mann in dunklem
Anzug saß. Der Anzug stand dem durchtrainierten Kerl unge-

fähr so gut wie ein Zebrafell einem Pinguin. Ansonsten war der Flur menschenleer. Als ich näher kam, erhob der Leibwächter sich langsam und sah mir mit wachsamem Blick entgegen. Auf den letzten zehn Schritten zückte ich meinen Dienstausweis. Er nahm mir das Kärtchen aus der Hand, studierte es von beiden Seiten, verglich sogar das Foto mit meinem Gesicht, reichte es mir zurück, ohne dass seine misstrauische Miene sich im Geringsten verändert hätte. Er hatte das hagere Gesicht einen Marathonläufers. Oder eines Mannes, der bei der Bundeswehr jede Ausbildung durchlitten hat, die aus Männern Kampfmaschinen macht.

»Herr Graf wünscht keine Besuche«, erklärte er mit verblüffend heller Stimme und fränkisch rollendem R. »Tut mir leid.«

»Fünf Minuten würden mir reichen.«

»Herr Graf wünscht keine Besuche. Tut mir leid.«

»Kann er mir das nicht selber sagen?«

»Herr Graf wünscht keine Besuche«, wiederholte er mit der Sturheit eines Roboters, der nichts anderes gelernt hat. Sein Ton war zuletzt eine Spur ungeduldiger geworden, der Blick finsterer. »Noch so eine dumme Frage, und du kriegst eine aufs Maul«, sagte dieser Blick.

In der Tür zu einem Zimmer etwa in der Mitte des Flurs erschien der blond gelockte Kopf einer Frau in den besten Jahren. Ich meinte, ein flüchtiges Lachen zu sehen, bevor sie wieder verschwand.

Wortlos steckte ich meinen Ausweis ein und machte kehrt. Ich ging an den leeren Betten vorbei, klopfte an die Tür, aus der vor Sekunden die Blonde geguckt hatte, und trat ein, ohne auf ein Herein zu warten. Die Frau – vermutlich eine Krankenschwester – trug einen weißen Kittel über grüner Jacke und Hose und war damit beschäftigt, am Arm eines ausgemergelten Greises eine neue Infusion zu setzen. Sie sah auf und musterte mich fragend.

»Ich würde gerne den Stationsarzt sprechen.«

Sie antwortete mit slawisch klingendem Akzent, jedoch in fehlerfreiem Deutsch: »Dr. Haller ist kurz weggegangen. Er wird gleich wieder da sein. Wollen Sie bitte draußen warten? Sie sehen … «

Wie angekündigt erschien der Arzt, kaum dass ich auf einer der Bänke Platz genommen hatte. Er mochte einige Jahre jünger sein als ich und zog das rechte Bein ein wenig nach. Sein müder Blick ließ auf schlimme Erfahrungen und ein für seinen Beruf zu weiches Herz schließen. Das dunkle Haar war millimeterkurz geschnitten, der Zehntagebart schon leicht angegraut. Sein Händedruck war trocken und fest.

»Ich nehme an, es geht um …?« Ein vielsagender Blick zum Ende des Flurs ersetzte den Schluss des Satzes. »Gehen wir doch in mein Zimmer.«

Er führte mich einige Schritte weiter in Richtung Lift, hielt mir die Tür zu einem geräumigen Büro auf. Den Raum dominierten zwei Schreibtische, die kein bisschen ordentlicher waren als mein eigener. In der Ecke hinter der Tür ein runder Tisch, zwei, drei regellos herumstehende Stühle. An der gegenüberliegenden Wand eine schmale, weiß bezogene Liege. Auf dem Tisch stand ein Stövchen mit einer beinahe leeren gläsernen Teekanne und eine verkrustete Tasse. Das Teelicht war erloschen, auf dem verbliebenen Tee schwammen schwärzliche Schlieren. Der Arzt schloss sorgfältig die Tür hinter uns.

»Zu trinken kann ich Ihnen leider nichts anbieten«, sagte er. »Der Tee ist wahrscheinlich schon gesundheitsschädlich.« Sein Lächeln war freundlich und offen.

Wir setzten uns an den Tisch. Er schob das Stövchen samt Kanne zur Seite, damit nichts zwischen uns stand, und begann zu sprechen, bevor ich eine Frage stellen konnte.

»Ich kann Ihnen nichts sagen«, sagte er. »Hier rufen alle paar Minuten irgendwelche Journalisten an und halten unsere Leute von der Arbeit ab. Aber auch denen können wir keine andere Antwort geben.«

»Können Sie nicht, oder dürfen Sie nicht?«

Er atmete tief ein. Sah mir mit vorgeneigtem Kopf von unten her ins Gesicht. »Niemand wird mir in diesem Haus den Mund verbieten. Aber ich unterliege der ärztlichen Schweigepflicht wie jeder andere auch.«

»Ich wollte Sie nicht nach Details zu Grafs Gesundheitszustand fragen.«

Der Blick seiner dunkelbraunen Augen ging auf Wander-
schaft. »Selbst wenn ich dürfte, ich könnte Ihnen nichts sagen.
Sie lassen uns ja nicht zu ihm. Was ich ein starkes Stück finde,
ehrlich gesagt. Eine Abmachung zwischen dem ZDF und der
Klinikleitung. Herr Graf wird von seinem eigenen Arzt versorgt.«

»Ist so etwas üblich?«

»Ganz und gar nicht.«

Jetzt ruhte sein wohlwollender Blick wieder auf meinem
Gesicht.

»Zu seinen Verletzungen können Sie mir auch nichts sagen?«

»Alles, was ich weiß, haben Sie schon ein paar Mal im Radio
gehört. Es wird ja pausenlos berichtet. Inzwischen gibt es
sogar eine Facebook-Seite, habe ich eben erfahren, auf der
behauptet wird, er sei tot, und der Sender halte es geheim, um
ihn durch ein Double zu ersetzen.«

»Wer hat gestern Morgen die Erstversorgung gemacht?«

»Der Notarzt.«

»Wer hat ihn hier in Empfang genommen?«

»Ich. Aber da war er schon verbunden.«

»War er ansprechbar?«

»Er war bei Bewusstsein. Aber sehr schweigsam. Wenn er
etwas gesagt hat, dann wirres Zeug.«

»Hat er einen Namen genannt?«

»Nein. Sie meinen, er hätte den Täter erkannt?«

»Wäre ja denkbar.«

Der Arzt schüttelte nachdenklich den Kopf mit den braunen
Borsten. »Er hatte alle Symptome eines posttraumatischen
Schocks. Symptome wie im Lehrbuch ...«

»Herr Dr. Haller, wenn ich ehrlich sein darf ...«

»Das dürfen Sie unbedingt.«

»Sie wirken auf mich wie ein Mensch, der zu gerne etwas
sagen würde, es aber nicht darf.«

Sein Lächeln wurde noch eine winzige Spur stärker. »Sie
sind ein guter Menschenkenner, Herr Gerlach.«

Er erhob sich langsam, trat mit leicht hinkendem Schritt ans Fenster, die Hände auf dem Rücken, stand einige Sekunden schweigend da. Er stand da wie eine Aufforderung, wurde mir endlich klar.

Ich räusperte mich. »Waren seine Verletzungen … lebensbedrohlich?«

Der Arzt sprach mit dem Fenster, was ihm das Antworten vielleicht leichter machte. »Nein.«

Welches war die Frage, die er hören wollte?

»Waren die Verletzungen … waren sie so, wie Sie es nach Lage der Dinge erwartet hätten?«

Dieses Mal musste ich eine Weile auf die Antwort warten.

»Das ist natürlich schwer einzuschätzen«, sagte der Arzt schließlich leise. »Er hatte Schnittwunden an allen möglichen Stellen. Dort, wo man sie erwarten würde, in einem solchen Fall.«

»Es war also nichts Ungewöhnliches an diesen Verletzungen?«

Wieder musste ich warten, während Dr. Haller mit seinem Gewissen rang. »Ich weiß nicht, wie ich es am besten ausdrücken soll. Sie waren mir … ein bisschen zu … Genau wie Sie sagen – so, wie man sie erwarten würde.«

Mit einem Ruck wandte er sich um und sah mir wieder ins Gesicht. Sehr ernst, mit einem Mal. »Vor einem halben Jahr hatte ich einen jungen Burschen hier. Achtzehn oder neunzehn Jahre alt, aus Beerfelden. Es war ein heißer Samstagabend, Hochsommer, und wie üblich hatten wir gut zu tun in der Notaufnahme. Es hatte wohl Streit um ein Mädchen gegeben, eine kleine Schubserei, und dann hat sein Kontrahent ein Messer gezückt.«

Er verstummte und kam mit gesenktem Blick zum Tisch zurück. Setzte sich wieder. Füllte linkisch trüben Tee in seine schmutzige Tasse. Nippte daran. Schüttelte angewidert den Kopf. Dann sah er entschlossen auf.

»Der Bursche damals hatte Schnittwunden am Oberschenkel, am Unterbauch, an der Brust natürlich, an beiden Unterarmen, im Gesicht, an der rechten Hand, an der linken Hand und ich weiß nicht, wo sonst noch überall.« Er machte eine kurze Pause, um die Wichtigkeit des Folgenden zu unterstreichen. »Auch an vielen Stellen, wo man sie nicht erwarten würde.«

Ich nickte.

Er nickte ebenfalls.

Und lächelte plötzlich wieder.

Was man alles sagen kann, ohne es auszusprechen.

26

Kurze Zeit später stand ich wieder vor den Edelstahltüren der beiden Aufzüge. Es dauerte nur wenige Sekunden, dann ertönte auch schon der sanfte Gong, die Doppeltüren glitten lautlos auseinander, ein bulliger, großer Mann in dunklem Anzug trat heraus, ging an mir vorbei, ohne mich zu bemerken. Ich betrat den Lift, drückte den zweituntersten Knopf und hatte plötzlich Herzrasen. Er war es! Kein Zweifel – der Mann im dunklen Anzug, der mich vor fast zwei Wochen gestoßen und zu Fall gebracht hatte! Hastig drückte ich alle Knöpfe von oben nach unten. Der Lift stoppte auf dem nächsten Geschoss, ich stürzte heraus, raste die Treppe hinauf, aber als ich den Flur wieder betrat, war der andere schon nicht mehr zu sehen. Ich hastete zu Dr. Hallers Zimmer, klopfte kurz, riss die Tür auf. Das Zimmer war leer. Ich öffnete die nächste Tür. Die übernächste. Dort traf ich auf die blonde Schwester.

»Eine kurze Frage«, sagte ich atemlos.

Sie musterte mich halb bestürzt, halb belustigt. »Ja?«

»Grafs Leibwächter. Einen davon habe ich vorhin getroffen, den Schlanken. Wie sieht der andere aus?«

»Der? Ein Klotz von einem Kerl. Immer in Anzug und Krawatte. Nicht sehr gesprächig.«

»Wie groß ist er?«

»Ungefähr wie Sie. Eins neunzig vielleicht. Aber fast doppelt so breit. Und unfreundlich wie ein Ochse. Der schmale sagt wenigstens mal guten Tag oder nickt einem freundlich zu. Der andere … unmöglich.«

Während der kurzen Fahrt zur Polizeidirektion wurde mir bewusst, dass ich das runde und ein wenig dumm wirkende Gesicht des zweiten Leibwächters noch ein drittes Mal gesehen hatte. Nicht nur vor zehn Minuten, und als er mir den Stoß vor die Brust versetzte, sondern …

Sönnchen war vernünftigerweise längst ins Wochenende geflüchtet, als ich atemlos in mein Vorzimmer stürmte. Ich durchstöberte mit fliegenden Fingern den beneidenswert kleinen Papierstapel auf ihrem Schreibtisch, fand nicht, was ich suchte. Aber glücklicherweise besaß auch sie ein Handy.

»Das Foto?«, fragte sie verdutzt. »Natürlich ist das noch … Warten Sie … Gucken Sie mal in die unterste Schublade links. Das ist meine Ablage für alles, wo ich nicht weiß, wohin damit. Müsste ziemlich weit oben liegen.«

Sekunden später hielt ich das alte Gruppenfoto aus dem Jahr 1988 in Händen. Johann Bolls Gesicht war ein wenig zu gewöhnlich, und er war damals ein Vierteljahrhundert jünger gewesen, sodass ich ihn nicht mit hundertprozentiger Sicherheit wiedererkannte. Dennoch war ich sofort überzeugt, dass er es war – Grafs zweiter Bodyguard war kein anderer als Johann Boll, der ehemalige Polizist. Und plötzlich passte vieles zusammen: Sein Mercedes in Ludwigshafen, die Tatsache, dass er damals die Untersuchungen zu Vicky Hergardens Tod geführt und dabei vermutlich auch mit Marcel Graf zu tun hatte. Sehr langsam legte ich das alte Foto auf den Schreibtisch meiner Sekretärin. Die Puzzleteilchen begannen allmählich, ein Bild zu formen.

Am Monitor meines Laptop pappte eines von Sönnchens gelben Klebezettelchen mit einer Wiesbadener Telefonnummer und dem Vermerk »dringend!!!«. Glücklicherweise hatte auch beim BKA das Wochenende noch nicht für jeden begonnen.

»Es ist wegen diesem Glas …«, begann die Chemikerin des

Bundeskriminalamts in rustikalem Pfälzisch und ohne große Umschweife. »Ich sitz bloß noch hier, weil ich auf Ihren Rückruf warte.«

Die toxikologische Untersuchung hatte ergeben, dass das Glas auf Rosalie Jordans Küchentisch Gamma-Hydroxybuttersäure enthielt, ein Mittel, das in höheren Dosen als Schlafmittel oder Narkotikum Verwendung fand. Und in geringer Dosierung als Partydroge.

»Bei starker Überdosierung kann es zu Atemstillstand kommen. Bei der Frau war eine Menge Alkohol im Spiel. Außerdem war sie auch noch krank. Das alles zusammen ... Da muss die Dosierung gar nicht so hoch sein.«

»Wie kommt man an das Zeug ran?«

»Offiziell nur über den Pharmahandel. Aber seit es als Liquid Ecstasy gedealt wird, kriegen Sie das Dreckszeug praktisch überall. Den Bericht hab ich schon fertig. Den kriegen Sie in zehn Sekunden. Und dann ist finito für diese Woche.«

Während ich telefonierte, hatte an meinem Apparat ein Lämpchen zu blinken begonnen. »Krauss«, las ich auf dem Display, als ich auflegte, und drückte – immer noch im Stehen – die Rückruftaste.

»Es geht um diese Frau Holland«, begann Oberkommissarin Evalina Krauss mit erschöpfter Stimme. »Sie sind noch da?«

»Sonst hätte ich wahrscheinlich das Telefon nicht abgenommen.«

Für dumme Scherze war sie heute nicht mehr zu haben. »Hätten Sie zehn Minuten?«

»Wenn es um Frau Holland geht, habe ich auch eine Stunde.«

»Ist ein ziemliches Stück Arbeit gewesen«, seufzte die junge Kollegin mit der praktischen aschblonden Kurzhaarfrisur, als sie sich setzte. »Sie und ihr Mann haben sich ungefähr ein Jahr nach dem Unglücksfall getrennt ...«

»Der alles Mögliche war, aber ganz bestimmt kein Unglücksfall ...«

»Nicht?« Sie sah mich verwirrt an. Offenbar war sie nicht auf dem Laufenden. Aber das machte nichts.

»Wegen dieses sogenannten Unfalls hat es in den letzten Tagen zwei Tote und einen wahrscheinlich vorgetäuschten Mordanschlag gegeben.«

»Ach was ...?«

Ich entspannte mich. »Egal jetzt. Was ist aus Frau Holland geworden?«

»Wie gesagt, sie haben sich dann bald getrennt. Der Mann ist nach Köln gezogen. Die Frau hat das Haus vermietet und ist nach Frankreich. Hat mich Stunden gekostet, da weiterzukommen. Aber dann hat es doch geklappt, und ab da war es einfacher: Sie hat einen französischen Filmschauspieler geheiratet, Jean Bressault, falls Ihnen das was sagt ...«

Ich schüttelte den Kopf.

»Na ja, so berühmt ist er auch wieder nicht gewesen. Bei Perpignan haben sie gewohnt, im Süden unten, die Liebe hat aber bloß sechs Jahre gehalten ...«

Elisabeth Holland hatte in den Jahren in Frankreich nicht weniger als dreimal geheiratet und sich bald wieder getrennt. Nach dem Filmstar war der Bürgermeister eines Städtchens an der Côte d'Azur gekommen und schließlich ein Provinzpolitiker in Bordeaux.

»Und jedes Mal ist sie hinterher ein bisschen reicher gewesen als vorher. Ihr Haus hier in Neuenheim ist die ganze Zeit vermietet gewesen. An eine Firma, irgendwas mit Modeschmuck.« Krauss gähnte, murmelte eine Entschuldigung. »Diese Firma gibt's aber nicht mehr.«

»Frau Holland ist jetzt wieder in Deutschland?«

»Seit 2008. Da hat sie einen reichen Bankier in Kronberg geheiratet. Viel älter als sie und anscheinend auch nicht mehr ganz gesund. Diesmal hat man sich nicht geschieden, sondern er ist vor zwei Jahren gestorben. Und jetzt hat sie wahrscheinlich noch viel mehr Geld. Und seit vergangenem Jahr wohnt sie wieder in ihrem alten Haus.«

»Jetzt bin ich mächtig gespannt ...«

Verwundert sah die Oberkommissarin auf. »Wieso?«

»Weil im Totenschein eine falsche Adresse gestanden hat.«

»Sie heißt jetzt von Brühl.«

Diesen Namen hatte ich schon einmal gehört. Vor einer halben Ewigkeit und in einem ganz anderen Zusammenhang, aber ...

In meinem Kopf purzelten die Gedanken und Assoziationen durcheinander. »Die Villa, natürlich! Die Villa!«

»Ludolf-Krehl-Straße«, las Krauss von ihrem linierten Zettel ab. »Das ist ganz am nördlichen Rand von Neuenheim. Danach kommt ein bisschen Grün, und dann fängt schon Handschuhsheim an.«

»Das passt nicht. Mein Unfall war am ... Moment ...« Ich trommelte mit den Fingern auf meiner Schreibtischplatte herum. »... am Hainsbachweg.«

»Ihr Unfall? Was hat der denn damit zu tun? Ich versteh grad nicht ...«

»Können Sie auch nicht.«

Sekunden später hatte ich die Lösung des Rätsels im Internet gefunden: Das Parkgrundstück lag zwischen zwei Straßen. Der offizielle Zugang zu Elisabeth von Brühls herrschaftlichem Anwesen lag an der Ludolf-Krehl-Straße. Nach Norden, zum Hainsbachweg gab es lediglich das Törchen, vor dem ich meinen Zusammenstoß mit Boll und Hergarden gehabt hatte.

Krauss beobachtete meine hektische Klickerei ratlos.

»Alles klar, Chef?«, fragte sie besorgt.

»Sonnenklar.« Ich sank in die Lehne zurück, rieb mir die Augen. »Hergarden ist vorne nicht reingekommen. Er wollte aber unbedingt zu Frau von Brühl. Und Grafs Leibwächter ... wieso war der überhaupt dort? Na, egal. Jedenfalls ist Hergarden vorne herum nicht aufs Grundstück gekommen, und da hat er es eben durch den Hintereingang versucht. Boll hat ihn aber erwischt. Sie haben sich gestritten, und dann bin ich dazugekommen ...«

»Ich versteh bloß noch Bahnhof.«

»Macht nichts. Danke für die tolle Arbeit. Haben Sie wirklich prima gemacht, danke. Sie können dann jetzt Wochenende machen.«

»Und im Totenschein hat also die falsche Adresse gestanden?«

»Die, wo das Ehepaar Hergarden früher gewohnt hat, nehme ich an. Sie müssen irgendwann in die Villa der Frau von Brühl gezogen sein, die damals natürlich noch Holland geheißen hat, und waren zu faul, sich umzumelden. Oder sie haben es einfach vergessen.«

Der Blick von Evalina Krauss wurde immer verwirrter. »Das passiert öfter, als man denkt.«

»Na, jedenfalls können Sie jetzt heimgehen. Noch mal danke. Sie haben mir wirklich sehr geholfen.«

Sie erhob sich, sah mich unsicher an, verstand immer noch nicht, wieso sie mich mit der Erledigung einer Routineangelegenheit in solchen Aufruhr versetzt hatte, freute sich aber dennoch über mein Lob.

»Weiß man eigentlich, was aus ihrem Kind geworden ist?«, fragte ich, als die Kollegin schon in der Tür stand.

»Ein Kind?«, fragte sie verständnislos mit der Klinke in der Hand.

»Ich habe gehört, das Ehepaar Graf hätte ein Kind gehabt. Es soll krank gewesen sein.«

»Vielleicht ... ist es gestorben?«

Ich schloss kurz die Augen. Nickte schließlich.

Sekunden später war ich wieder allein. Inzwischen war es halb acht geworden und auch für mich Zeit, endlich Schluss zu machen.

27

Die einzige vernünftige Erklärung für Johann Bolls Anwesenheit bei der Villa im Norden Heidelbergs war, dass auch sein Chef dort gewesen war, überlegte ich, während ich die Weststadt im Schleichtempo nach einem freien Parkplatz durchkreuzte. Das erklärte auch, dass Hergarden sich dort herumgetrieben hatte. Hatte Graf seiner geschiedenen Frau einen

Besuch abgestattet? Weshalb nicht? Man hatte sich vermutlich nicht im Streit getrennt. Er hatte für einige Tage in Heidelberg zu tun. Warum nicht mit der Ex einen Kaffee trinken?

Der Schnee war im Lauf des Tages fast völlig weggetaut. Nur in einigen dunklen Ecken lagen noch schmutzige Reste der weißen Pracht vom Vormittag. Die Temperatur war seit Mittag gestiegen und stieg immer noch. Das Wetter spielte Achterbahn mit uns.

Endlich entdeckte ich eine Parklücke, mindestens dreihundert Meter von meinem Zuhause entfernt. Von Westen her ging ein träger, feuchter Wind, stellte ich beim Aussteigen fest. Bald würde es wieder Regen geben. Und schon, als ich den Wagen abschloss, begann es zu schütten, als hätte der Himmel nur auf mich gewartet.

»Es kam vorhin in den Nachrichten«, hörte ich Theresa gut gelaunt verkünden, als ich die Wohnungstür öffnete. Ich hängte meinen durchnässten Mantel an die Garderobe. Im Wohnzimmer wurde gelacht.

»Ehrlich?«, fragte Doros Stimme ungläubig. »Er will sich das wirklich antun?«

»Dieser Fernsehopa, den sie am Neckar abgestochen haben?«, wollte Sarah wissen. »Hi, Paps! Schön, dass du doch noch kommst.«

Sie reichte mir ein gut gefülltes Sektglas, Theresa drückte mir von der anderen Seite einen Kuss auf den Mund.

»Also, Sarah ...«, sagte Doro mahnend.

»Ist doch wahr. Die machen einen Zirkus um den alten Sack, als wär er der Bundespräsident oder so was.«

»Stimmt«, fiel Henning vor Aufregung und Verlegenheit ein wenig zu großspurig ein. »Ich hab's im Internet gelesen. Der will das echt durchziehen.«

Wir stießen reihum an und tranken.

»Was will er durchziehen?«, fragte ich.

»Na, die Show morgen.«

»Vor ein paar Stunden hieß es noch, er sei schwer verletzt.«

»Unglaublich, nicht wahr?«, fand auch Doro. »Ich habe

Bilder von ihm gesehen, wie er im Bett liegt, von oben bis unten verbunden, und trotzdem will er morgen Abend ... Wirklich unglaublich!« Zur Bekräftigung nahm sie einen tüchtigen Schluck aus ihrem Sektglas.

Theresa war in Jeans und einem grünen Pulli zur großen Feier erschienen, dessen Farbe vorzüglich zu ihrem rotblonden Haar passte. Moment, rotblond? War sie vorgestern nicht noch ...? Sie war am Montag beim Frisör gewesen, fiel mir ein. Ich durfte auf keinen Fall vergessen, ihr später ein Kompliment zu machen. Doro dagegen hatte noch dieselbe Haarfarbe wie vor zwanzig Jahren, war in einem etwas zu feierlichen Kleid mit langem Rock erschienen und fühlte sich sichtlich overdressed. Die Kinder – nein, die Jugendlichen natürlich – sahen aus wie immer. Meine Töchter trugen Jeans mit Löchern, die jeden Tag größer zu werden schienen, Henning Jeans ohne Löcher.

Die drei hatten den Nachmittag über Kanapees präpariert, Obstsalat geschnippelt, mit meiner telefonischen Beratung Sekt und Säfte eingekauft und unser Wohnzimmer sogar mit einigen etwas verloren wirkenden Luftschlangen dekoriert. Im CD-Spieler rotierte eine hektische Scheibe, die eher den jüngeren Teil des Publikums ansprach. Immerhin schien das Wort »Motherfucker« nicht vorzukommen.

Theresa angelte sich ein Schnittchen von der großen Platte – Lachs mit einem Klecks Sahnemeerrettich und einer Scheibe Ei – und biss beherzt zu. Dann sah sie meine Älteste an. »Du hast übrigens völlig recht, Sarah. Die Nachrichtensprecherin hat sich aufgeführt, als würde der Weltfrieden von dieser Show abhängen.«

Sie prostete mir zu, lächelte warm und sah mir tief in die Augen. Doro tat, als bemerkte sie es nicht, und besichtigte nun ihrerseits das Angebot an Fingerfood.

»Dieser Obstsalat sieht ja köstlich aus«, verkündete sie. »Den habt ihr wirklich ganz alleine gemacht?«

»Mama!« Henning verdrehte die Augen. »Obstsalat konnte ich schon mit acht!«

»Echt jetzt?« Louise, die eine halbe Stunde jünger war

als ihre Schwester, musterte ihn, als sähe sie ihn zum ersten Mal.

»Hübsch habt ihr es hier«, stellte Doro fest, als sie sich ein Schälchen Obstsalat genommen hatte und noch einen winzigen Klecks Sahne obenauf tat. Sie war nervös. Wir alle waren nervös. Nur Theresa nicht. Aber für sie war die Situation ja auch nicht weiter kompliziert. Zudem sonnte sie sich im Glanz ihres neuen Status als Erfolgsautorin. Der Verlag meldete Nachbestellungen in sensationellem Umfang, hatte sie am frühen Abend per SMS berichtet. Die zweite Auflage war in greifbarer Nähe. Eine dritte nicht ausgeschlossen.

»Sie sind also Schriftstellerin?«, wollte Doro zwischen zwei Obststückchen wissen, als könnte sie meine Gedanken lesen.

Theresa gesellte sich zu ihr, und Augenblicke später unterhielten sich die Damen prächtig. Doro gickelte. Theresa lachte glucksend. Hoffentlich war nicht ich das Thema dieses ebenso angeregten wie vertrauten Gesprächs. Die Zwillinge alberten mit ihrem neuen Halbbruder herum. Ich vertilgte Kanapees, da ich hungrig war, und irgendwann stand plötzlich Henning neben mir.

»Hi«, sagte er.

»Na?«, sagte ich.

»Jetzt muss ich ja wohl Alexander zu dir sagen.«

»Das ist das Mindeste.«

Wieder fiel mir auf, wie ähnlich er mir sah. Dieselbe kräftige Nase, fast dieselbe Größe, sogar dieselbe Körperhaltung.

»Schon komisch irgendwie«, sagte Henning verlegen.

»Wir werden uns dran gewöhnen.«

Zum ersten Mal in den zwei Jahren, die ich ihn nun schon kannte, sahen wir uns richtig in die Augen. Lächelten vorsichtig. Hoben unsere Gläser und stießen an.

»Ich freu mich«, sagte Henning leise. »Echt!«

»Ich mich auch.«

Gegen zehn löste die Party sich überraschend plötzlich auf. Doro wollte nach Hause, die Zwillinge waren irgendwo zu irgendetwas eingeladen, was ausnahmsweise keine Geburtstagsfeier zu sein schien, und Henning musste sie unbedingt begleiten. Und mit einem Mal war ich mit Theresa allein. Wieder sah sie mir tief in die Augen, stellte achtsam ihr Glas ab und fiel mir mit Macht und Anlauf um den Hals.

»Ende des offiziellen Teils«, flüsterte sie mir feucht ins Ohr.

Ich drückte sie fest an mich.

»Hast du meine Töchter schon wieder bestochen?«

»Sie hatten sowieso was vor. Ich kann die ganze Nacht bleiben.«

»Ich habe ein ziemlich schmales Bett.«

»Liebe geht in der kleinsten Kiste, wenn man jung und gelenkig ist.«

Minuten später waren wir, obwohl weder jung noch übermäßig gelenkig, allein auf der Welt, trieben eng umschlungen durch ein Universum voller Hitze und Wollust und interessierten uns nicht mehr für irdische Gemeinheiten und Affären. Kein Mord, keine Intrige konnte so dringend sein, dass die Aufklärung nicht bis morgen Zeit hatte.

Als wir wieder auf der Erde gelandet waren und Theresas unverzichtbare Zigarette danach glimmte, sprachen wir dann doch über Marcel Graf, und es stellte sich heraus, dass auch meine Göttin seine Show kannte.

»Ich bin nicht gerade ein Fan, aber um sich einen Abend angenehm zu vertreiben, reicht es allemal.«

Sie wollte wissen, wie weit wir mit der Aufklärung des Mordanschlags am Neckar waren, und staunte über meine Antwort.

»Er hat das alles nur vorgetäuscht, meinst du?«

»Ich bin mir sogar ziemlich sicher. Aber ich werde es ihm vermutlich nicht beweisen können. Der angebliche Täter ist tot, brauchbare Zeugen gibt es keine. Verwertbare Spuren – Fehlanzeige.«

»Ganz schön clever«, meinte sie. »So ein Theater zu veranstalten …«

»Clever ist er, das ist wohl wahr. Aber ich bin auch nicht dumm. Ich werde ihn grillen, dass ihm Hören und Sehen vergeht, sobald er die Klinik verlässt.«

»Wie willst du das anstellen? Willst du ihn gleich festnehmen?«

»Das überlege ich mir morgen. Jetzt habe ich Feierabend.«

Bevor ich eine Entscheidung traf, musste ich mir ohnehin Rückendeckung bei der Staatsanwaltschaft holen, damit am Ende nicht ich selbst der Gegrillte war.

Theresa drückte gemächlich ihre Zigarette aus und rückte wieder näher, was auf dem schmalen Bett jedoch kaum möglich war. Ihre heiße Rechte näherte sich schon wieder der kritischen Zone.

»Sie sind unmöglich, Frau Liebekind«, sagte ich.

»Ich weiß«, seufzte sie. »Das liebst du ja so an mir.«

Ihre zärtlichen Bemühungen blieben vergeblich. Ich überlegte, ob das damit zu tun hatte, dass ich mich unaufhaltsam meinem fünfzigsten Geburtstag näherte. Theresa fand das eine vollkommen idiotische Überlegung und meinte, ich würde einfach zu viel arbeiten. Bald qualmte ihre zweite Zigarette, ich holte aus dem Kühlschrank eine noch halb volle Flasche Sekt, und wir sprachen weiter über die aktuellen Ereignisse. Theresa interessierte sich vor allem für die Beziehung der beiden Frauen in der Neuenheimer Villa.

»Natürlich war die Ehefrau eifersüchtig«, erklärte sie rigoros. »Wenn sie ihren Marcel geliebt hat, dann hat sie die andere aufs Blut gehasst. Freie Liebe – das sind doch leere Sprüche.«

Ich gab ihr recht und füllte die Gläser wieder auf. Während ich in der Küche war, hatte Theresa im Wohnzimmer einige dicke Kissen geholt, sodass wir bequem im Bett sitzen konnten. Wir stießen zum x-ten Mal an diesem Abend an, nicht ohne uns dabei gebührend tief in die Augen zu sehen. Theresa war nicht von der Überzeugung abzubringen, sich beim Anstoßen nicht in die Augen zu sehen, bedeute sieben Jahre schlechten Sex. Und das Risiko wollte natürlich niemand eingehen.

Schließlich landeten wir beim plötzlichen Erfolg ihres Buchs.

»Das Tolle ist, das erste läuft auf einmal auch wieder besser«, berichtete sie vergnügt.

»Du bist wie verwandelt seit dieser Besprechung.«

Sie streichelte gedankenverloren meine Brust, nippte an ihrem Glas. »Das Dumme ist nur, jetzt muss ich mir wirklich schleunigst Gedanken über das nächste machen.«

Ihre Hand geriet schon wieder auf Abwege.

»Ich kann nicht mehr«, sagte ich und versuchte, sie wegzuschieben.

Sie küsste mich heiß und fordernd und schnurrte: »Wir werden sehen, Herr Kriminaloberrat.«

Endlich bekam ich ihre Hand zu fassen. »Ich bin trotzdem dafür, dass du künftig jede Woche so eine tolle Besprechung kriegst.«

»Zwei«, hauchte sie selig lächelnd. »Mindestens zwei.«

28

»Wie bitte?«, fuhr mich Olivia Opelt am Samstagmorgen per Telefon an. »Was ist? Erstens liegt Marcel immer noch in der Klinik, und zweitens ...«

»Gestern Abend hieß es noch, die Show findet statt.«

Sie klang, als wäre sie gerade schnell gelaufen. Atmete hektisch. War unkonzentriert. Vielleicht hatte ich tatsächlich eine morgendliche Joggingrunde unterbrochen.

»Das hat Marcel in diesem verflixten Interview gesagt, ja, aber leider etwas vorschnell«, keuchte sie. »Und nicht so, wie er später zitiert wurde. Wörtlich sagte er: ›Ich will nicht völlig ausschließen, dass die Show trotz allem irgendwie stattfinden könnte.‹ Was die Medien anschließend daraus gemacht haben, dafür können wir nichts. Dafür kann er nichts.«

»Das heißt, sie findet also nicht statt?«

»Das heißt, wir wissen es einfach noch nicht, Himmel noch mal! Wir sind mit dem Aufbau zu neunundneunzig Prozent fertig, die letzten Proben laufen. Von uns aus kann es losgehen.«

»Wenn Ihr Chef Fernsehinterviews geben kann, dann kann

er doch auch fünf Minuten mit mir sprechen und mir ein paar einfache Fragen beantworten.«

Der Atem der jungen Frau beruhigte sich allmählich.

»Das entscheidet der Arzt, nicht ich«, erwiderte sie, jetzt ein wenig freundlicher. »Gestern Abend war Marcel guter Dinge. Aber er hatte eine schlimme Nacht. Körperlich ist er schon wieder – nun ja, fit zu sagen, wäre natürlich übertrieben. Glücklicherweise sind seine Verletzungen doch nicht so schwer, wie es anfangs aussah. Aber die Seele ...«

»Posttraumatischer Schock, ich weiß. Der Arzt hat mich schon aufgeklärt.«

»Welcher Arzt?«, fragte sie sofort.

»Einer der Stationsärzte.«

»Der weiß nichts. Der kann gar nichts wissen. Obwohl posttraumatischer Schock es wohl ganz gut trifft. Wie auch immer, ich kann Ihnen beim besten Willen nicht sagen, ob wir in zwölf Stunden auf Sendung sein werden oder pleite und alle sturzbetrunken. Technisch ist alles bereit. Nun müssen wir sehen, wie es weitergeht.«

Ich legte das Telefon auf den Küchentisch. Es war halb acht, und ich war schon seit einer Stunde glockenwach, während Theresa immer noch selig schlummerte und hin und wieder kleine, zufriedene Geräusche machte, die nach angenehmen Träumen klangen. Auch ich hatte erstaunlich gut geschlafen, auf meinem schmalen Bett zusammengekuschelt mit einer nackten und raumgreifenden Theresa. Die Zwillinge waren viel zu spät heimgekommen, hatte ich im Halbschlaf gehört, und würden sich vor Mittag nicht blicken lassen.

In der halben Stunde, die ich vorhin neben Theresa nicht gewagt hatte, mich zu rühren, hatte ich über die Frage nachgedacht, warum Graf und seine Frau nach Vickys Tod solchen Wert auf Anonymität gelegt hatten. Darauf, dass ihre Adresse nicht in den amtlichen Dokumenten auftauchte. Die einzige Antwort, die mir einfallen wollte, war und blieb: Weil sie etwas zu verbergen hatten. Ihr Motiv war die Angst der Schuldigen vor Entdeckung gewesen. Diese Angst war so groß gewesen, dass sie sogar die beiden Polizisten bestochen hatten.

Mit erheblichen Summen, denn sonst hätten die beiden sich nie und nimmer auf den Handel eingelassen. Das Risiko der Entdeckung war enorm gewesen, die Folgen einer solchen Pflichtverletzung für die Beamten existenzbedrohend. Das war überhaupt ein schwacher Punkt in meinen Überlegungen: Wie konnten die beiden Schuldigen wissen, dass die Kripobeamten bestechlich waren? Oder waren sie in ihrer Verzweiflung das Risiko eingegangen, hatten es einfach versucht? Wo ohnehin alles in Scherben lag, konnte es schlimmer nicht werden. Dass Graf in jener unseligen Nacht tatsächlich in Köln war, wie er behauptete, hatte ich keine Sekunde geglaubt, würde es aber nach so langer Zeit kaum widerlegen können.

Boll und sein Kollege hatten damals bereits kurz nach dem Anruf vor der Tür der Villa in Neuenheim gestanden. Bei einem ungeklärten Todesfall zaudert der Kriminaldauerdienst nicht lange. Da herrscht Alarmstufe rot, denn jede vergeudete Minute kann der Täter nutzen, um Spuren zu vernichten oder sich weiter vom Tatort zu entfernen. Sie hatten den Fall eingehend besichtigt, stellte ich mir vor, und vermutlich rasch erkannt, was geschehen war – dass es sich nicht um einen Unfall handeln konnte. Graf und seine reiche Frau hatten auf die beiden eingeredet, gejammert, gefleht, gebettelt. Den Kripobeamten irgendeine blümchenreiche Mitleidsgeschichte aufgetischt, schließlich Geld angeboten, mehr Geld, als ein Polizist auf ehrliche Weise in vielen Jahren verdienen kann, und am Ende war man sich offenbar einig geworden. Man hatte den Tatort so verändert, dass alles nach dem aussah, was der Notarzt später attestierte: nach einem häuslichen Unfall mit Todesfolge. Das Fälschen der Anschrift in den amtlichen Dokumenten war am Ende nur noch eine Kleinigkeit gewesen. Das minimale Risiko, dass der Arzt den Schwindel bemerken würde, hatte man in Kauf genommen. In diesem Fall hätte man sich immer noch auf ein Versehen herausreden können.

Als später Hergarden in der Polizeidirektion auftauchte und Graf des Mordes beschuldigte, war er natürlich bei den Beamten gelandet, die den Fall bearbeitet hatten. Und für die war es ein Leichtes gewesen, die Anzeige anschließend im Papierkorb verschwinden zu lassen.

So weit die Theorie.

Aber woher die Beweise nehmen?

Es gab auf der Welt nur drei Menschen, die mir diese liefern konnten: Johann Boll, Marcel Graf und seine geschiedene Frau, Elisabeth von Brühl. An Graf kam ich vorläufig nicht heran, Boll würde alles leugnen, und die Frau konnte ich um diese Uhrzeit noch nicht belästigen. Die würde sich vermutlich am ehesten überrumpeln lassen, überlegte ich. Sie war das schwächste Glied in der Kette. Graf dagegen war ein ausgebufftes Schlitzohr, Boll kannte als ehemaliger Polizist unsere Tricks und Schliche.

Ich erhob mich, machte mir einen schönen großen Cappuccino mit extra viel Schaum, setzte mich wieder. Draußen war es schon hell. Die Nächte wurden wieder kürzer. Mit etwas Glück würde heute sogar ein sonniger Tag werden.

Wie mochte es weitergegangen sein, nachdem der Arzt sich damals verabschiedet hatte? Graf hatte sich bei den beiden kooperativen Polizisten herzlich bedankt und jedem einen Packen Geldscheine in die Hand gedrückt. Ein Leichenwagen war gekommen und hatte Vicky Hergardens sterbliche Überreste abgeholt. Womöglich hatten Boll und sein Kollege – wie hatte er noch geheißen? Reitzle, richtig – zu Beginn einige Fotos geschossen, die den Tatort in seinem ursprünglichen, unveränderten Zustand zeigten. Und die man später, viel später, vielleicht für eine hübsche kleine Erpressung nutzen konnte.

Reitzle hatte seinen plötzlichen Reichtum dazu genutzt, sich mit einem italienischen Sportwagen das Leben zu nehmen. Oder – der Gedanke war mir noch gar nicht gekommen – sollte bei diesem Verkehrsunfall etwa jemand nachgeholfen haben? Um einen Zeugen zu beseitigen, der leichtsinnig wurde? Oder einen Erpresser? Wenn ja, warum lebte Boll dann noch? Und wurde sogar von Graf als Leibwächter engagiert? In einer Vertrauensstellung also? Kein Mensch kommt näher an einen Prominenten heran als seine Bodyguards.

Inzwischen hatte es die Morgensonne über die Dächer der Häuser auf der anderen Straßenseite geschafft und wärmte mein Gesicht. Ich nippte an meinem Cappuccino, der inzwischen auf Trinktemperatur abgekühlt war. Sollte ich doch gleich heute mein Glück bei Elisabeth von Brühl versuchen, alias Sabeth Holland? Ich sah auf die Uhr: bald halb neun. Immer noch zu früh für einen Überraschungsbesuch. Andererseits, bis ich Zähne geputzt, geduscht und mich rasiert hatte …

Die Sonne beschien mich freundlich, als ich den Neckar per Rad – und dieses Mal mit Helm – in Richtung Norden überquerte. Einige Wolkenschleier hielten sich noch, aber auch die würden hoffentlich im Lauf der nächsten Stunden verschwinden. Der Verkehr war noch spärlich. Fußgänger mit Hunden strebten zum Philosophenweg hinauf. Ein weißer Paketwagen fegte um eine Ecke, bremste quietschend. Ich fühlte mich ausgeschlafen und tatendurstig. Theresa war nicht aufgewacht, als ich mich leise angekleidet hatte.

Zehn Minuten später stand ich vor dem hohen und schon leicht angerosteten Gittertor zum Park der dunklen Villa, in der nirgendwo Licht oder andere Spuren von Leben zu erkennen waren. Neben dem zweiflügligen Tor für Gäste, die standesgemäß mit dem Wagen vorfuhren, gab es auch eine Tür für niederes Volk wie mich. Ich drückte den Klingelknopf, der am Pfosten daneben angebracht war, aber nichts geschah. Ich drückte noch einmal, dieses Mal länger. Wieder nichts. Ich spähte eine Weile zwischen den massiven Eisenstäben hindurch. In den Bäumen freuten sich Vögel auf den kommenden Frühling. Es roch nach modrigem Laub und feuchtem Kompost. Irgendwo in meinem Rücken lachte ein unsichtbarer Mann schallend. Ein schweres Motorrad wurde probeweise angelassen und gleich wieder ausgemacht.

In dem großen Haus regte sich noch immer nichts. Nur aus einem der Kamine schien ein wenig heller Rauch aufzusteigen. Aber der konnte von der Heizung stammen, die vermutlich auch arbeitete, wenn niemand zu Hause war. Aber vermutlich war Frau von Brühl daheim und legte einfach keinen Wert auf unangemeldeten Besuch zu früher Stunde. Oder sie war durch ihren ehemaligen Mann vorgewarnt und stellte sich tot, was ich für die wahrscheinlichste Variante hielt. Auch meine Hoffnung, sie beschäftige vielleicht Personal, das ich ein wenig mit Fragen löchern könnte, schien sich nicht zu erfüllen.

Als auch auf mein drittes Läuten keine Reaktion erfolgte und mir allmählich kalt wurde, schwang ich mich wieder aufs Rad und strampelte nach Hause zurück.

Kurz vor der Neckarbrücke trillerte das Handy in meiner Manteltasche. Ich fuhr brav an den Straßenrand, hielt, nahm es ans Ohr. Auch Telefonieren auf dem Rad ist nämlich verboten. Bis vor zwei Wochen hatte ich mich allerdings nicht groß darum geschert.

Es war Sven Balke. »Das Auto neben den Bahngleisen ist wahrscheinlich wirklich ein Volvo gewesen«, eröffnete er mir aufgeräumt. »Ein Zeuge hat gestern Mittag beim Hockenheimer Revier Anzeige erstattet. Ihm ist in der Nacht um kurz nach zwei ein dunkler V70 Kombi in die Quere gekommen. Ist mit einem Affentempo auf die B 36 eingebogen und hat ihn um ein Haar gerammt. Und zwar keine fünfhundert Meter von der Stelle, wo sie Hergarden auf die Gleise geschmissen haben. Der Volvo ist trotz Schneetreiben und glatter Straßen angeblich wie ein Verrückter gefahren.«

»Wie verlässlich ist dieser Zeuge?«

»Schwer zu sagen. Aber die Uhrzeit passt perfekt. Ich habe noch mal mit den Leuten von der Bahn telefoniert. Auf dem Gleis ist um ein Uhr fünfzig ein Güterzug durch, und da hat die Leiche noch nicht auf den Schienen gelegen. Der nächste, der, der Hergarden dann erwischt hat, war um zwei Uhr sieben.«

»Hat er sich das Kennzeichen gemerkt?«

»Das wäre natürlich cool.« Balke lachte aufgekratzt. Offenbar hatte nun auch ihn das Jagdfieber gepackt. »Aber es hat ja leider wie blöd geschneit. Die Sicht war hundsmiserabel.«

Ich brauchte unbedingt das Video von Theresas Smartphone, überlegte ich, als ich weiterradelte. Das Gerät steckte vermutlich in ihrer Handtasche, und die lag irgendwo in meinem Schlafzimmer am Fußboden. Als ich den Bismarckplatz erreichte, hielt ich erneut an und wählte Hennings Nummer. Erfreulicherweise war mein Halbsohn schon wach und klar im Kopf.

»Logo kann ich das machen, Alexander.« Mein Vorname ging ihm noch ein wenig holprig über die Lippen. »Aber ich lieg noch in der Kiste. Müsste erst duschen. Ein paar Kabel zusammensuchen ...«

»Duschen kannst du später bei uns.«

»Sooo wichtig ist es?«

Theresa war wach, als ich nach Hause kam, saß mit nackten Füßen und gut gelaunt in der Küche vor einer Müslischüssel voller Milchkaffee. Bekleidet war sie im Wesentlichen mit dem Hemd, das ich gestern getragen hatte.

Sie strahlte mich an. »Wie war Ihre Nacht, Herr Kriminaloberrat?«

»Selten war eine Nacht schöner, Frau Bestsellerautorin.«

Und selten hatte ich sie glücklicher gesehen. Ich beugte mich zu ihr hinunter und küsste sie auf den vollen, heute noch ungeschminkten Mund. Sie roch noch ein wenig nach Bett und Liebe. Ihr Kuss war eindeutig. Ich löste mich lachend von ihr.

»Erst mal haben wir jetzt Wichtigeres zu tun, Gnädigste.«

»Was gibt es Wichtigeres als die Liebe?«, schmollte sie mit gekonntem Kulleraugenblick.

»Ich brauche dein Handy.«

29

Um halb elf saßen wir zu dritt in der Küche um Hennings großen Laptop herum. Theresa trug inzwischen meinen Morgenmantel und meine Hausschuhe. Henning murmelte Computerchinesisch, probierte mit flinken Fingern drei verschiedene Datenkabel aus, musste noch rasch eine Software herunterladen, bevor sein Computer sich bequemte, mit Theresas neuem Samsung-Handy in Kontakt zu treten. Dann ging plötzlich alles sehr schnell.

»Drei, zwei, eins, meins«, sagte mein Halbsohn befriedigt und startete das Video.

»Es geht um einen Volvo Kombi«, erinnerte ich ihn.

»Das hast du jetzt schon drei Mal gesagt, Alexander«, erwiderte Henning heiter. Dieses Mal war das »Alexander« schon ganz flüssig gekommen.

Eine Weile betrachteten wir zu dritt die Kühlerhaube meines Peugeot im Nieselregen, die nässeschwarze, schmale Straße, den trüben, tief hängenden Winterhimmel, die Krähe, die hoheitsvoll auf der Fahrbahn herumstolzierte und hie und da pickte. Sogar Ton gab es, nachdem Henning eine Taste gedrückt hatte.

»Und was wird das nun?«, hörten wir Theresa nörgeln.

»Erkläre ich dir gleich«, antwortete meine zugegeben auch etwas angespannte Stimme.

Die Krähe wurde unruhig, flatterte empört krächzend auf. Das Brummen eines Diesel näherte sich. Der weiße Lieferwagen mit der Qualmwolke durchquerte das Bild. Unmittelbar dahinter das rote Mercedes-Cabrio.

Und ich hatte mich nicht getäuscht: Einen Wimpernschlag später folgte der schwarze oder dunkelgraue Volvo, der zu gerne überholt hätte, sich wegen der vielen Kurven jedoch nicht traute. Henning stoppte das Video, spulte zurück und wieder vor. Aber das Kennzeichen war beim besten Willen nicht zu entziffern, der Fahrer oder die Fahrerin nicht einmal zu sehen. Das Kürzel für den Zulassungsort schien zwei Buchstaben zu haben, kamen wir überein, aber nicht einmal das war zweifelsfrei auszumachen.

»Auf keinen Fall nur einen«, war Henning überzeugt. »Aber warte mal kurz …«

Während er mit Höllengeschwindigkeit etwas im Internet suchte, erklärte er halblaut, was er vorhatte: »Irgendwo gibt's die geknackte Version von einer Software von Pixelfrogs. Du guckst jetzt mal bitte kurz weg, Alexander.«

Das »Alexander« war jetzt schon ganz selbstverständlich gewesen. Junge Menschen lernen so schnell.

»Und was kann diese Software?«

»Ah, da. Wusst ich's doch. Augenblick ...« Als er das Programm wenige Sekunden später startete, erfuhr ich, worum es ging: »Pixelfrogs sitzt in Palo Alto, und normalerweise machen die Bildauswertung fürs Pentagon und wahrscheinlich auch die NSA. Alles supergeheim, logischerweise. Aber sie haben auch schon zivile Sachen gemacht. Automatische Erkennung von Autokennzeichen zum Beispiel. Tollcollect benutzt die Software auch. Die können noch das verdreckteste Nummernschild lesen, indem sie einfach zig Bilder aus einem Video übereinanderlegen und dann mit irgendwelchen statistischen ... Bingo!«

»Mainz«, sagte ich, längst nicht mehr überrascht.

»Passt das?«, fragte Theresa.

»Das passt sogar perfekt.«

Sie sprang auf und küsste mich hastig auf den Mund. »Ich muss in die Dusche. Wir wollen heute nach Frankfurt ins Städel. Eine Munch-Ausstellung.«

Auch Henning hatte es auf einmal eilig, sich zu verabschieden, und packte seine Sachen zusammen. Meine Töchter hatte ich noch nicht zu Gesicht bekommen an diesem sonnigen Vormittag.

Als ich wieder allein war, wählte ich die Nummer des Telefons auf Balkes Schreibtisch. Er war jedoch nicht zu erreichen. Ich versuchte es auf dem Handy. Dort war besetzt. Wenige Minuten später rief er in bester Laune zurück.

Unser Gespräch dauerte nur wenige Sekunden. Dann hatte ich die Bestätigung: Was ich vor Minuten auf dem Computermonitor gesehen hatte, war das Kennzeichen von Olivia Opelts anthrazitgrauem V70 Kombi.

»Ich rede mit der Staatsanwaltschaft«, entschied ich.

»Die Frau kann nie und nimmer Hergardens Leiche auf die Gleise gewuppt haben. Auch wenn der Typ nicht viel auf den Rippen hatte. Und die Fußabdrücke, das waren keine ...«

»Natürlich hat sie es nicht selbst gemacht«, unterbrach ich

ihn. »Aber ich weiß auch schon, wen sie dafür eingespannt hat.«

»Graf scheidet ja leider aus«, meinte Balke. »Dem würde ich zu gern und vor möglichst vielen Kameras Handschließen anlegen.«

»Warten Sie ab. Vielleicht haben Sie das Vergnügen heute noch.«

»Sie denken wirklich, er hat Vicky Hergarden auf dem Gewissen?«

»Entweder er oder seine Frau. Vielleicht auch beide zusammen.«

Bei meiner vorgesetzten Behörde stieß ich nicht auf Begeisterung.

»Wenn das schiefläuft, Herr Gerlach ...« Der Staatsanwalt, der das Pech hatte, Wochenendbereitschaft zu haben, stöhnte abgrundtief. »Wenn diese Samstagabendshow ausfällt, und wir können Herrn Graf später nichts beweisen, dann wird das ZDF uns auf siebenstelligen Schadenersatz verklagen.«

»Das heißt, die Show findet nun doch statt?«

»Hören Sie kein Radio? Marcel Graf ist der Held des Tages. Sehen Sie denn Verdunklungsgefahr?«

Inzwischen saß ich – Samstag hin oder her – wieder an meinem Schreibtisch. »Bei Graf eher nicht. Dafür bei seiner Assistentin und seinen Leibwächtern umso mehr.«

»Nur damit ich auch alles richtig verstanden habe: Ihre Beweise sind bisher eine Reifenspur und ein Zeuge, der nachts im Schneetreiben einen Volvo gesehen hat?«

Wenn man es so zusammenfasste, dann klang das wirklich nicht überwältigend. Auch der Staatsanwalt spürte meine plötzliche Unsicherheit.

»Schaffen Sie mir belastbares Material bei, Herr Gerlach«, sagte er milde. »Und dann telefonieren wir noch mal an, ja?«

In einer so verzwickten Situation wie der, in der ich in diesen Stunden steckte, gibt es im Grunde nur zwei Handlungsoptionen: Entweder man hält still, um den Gegner in Sicherheit zu wiegen, und hofft, dass er früher oder später leichtsinnig wird.

Oder aber man kommt früh aus der Deckung, stichelt und nervt, um ihn nervös zu machen und zu Fehlern zu verleiten. Auf die Gefahr hin, dass der eine oder andere Gegner dann plötzlich auf Nimmerwiedersehen verschwunden ist. Noch während ich das Für und Wider der beiden Möglichkeiten abwog, klingelte wieder einmal mein Telefon.

»Professor Gericke«, stellte sich ein Mann undefinierbaren Alters mit selbstbewusster Stimme vor. »Privatdozent am Institut für Rechtsmedizin. Es geht um die Leichensache Hergarden.«

»Ich bin ganz Ohr.«

»Um es kurz und knapp zu sagen, denn schließlich ist ja Wochenende: Der Mann war schon tot, als der Zug ihn überfahren hat. Vermutlich schon eine bis zwei Stunden.«

»Und woran ist er gestorben?«

»Nach dem ersten Augenschein: Herzinfarkt. Er hat offenbar schon länger an einer chronischen Koronarinsuffizienz gelitten.«

»Er hat was am Herzen gehabt«, konnte ich bestätigen. »Er litt unter starker Atemnot.«

»Eines der gängigen Symptome. Im fortgeschrittenen Stadium ist das Risiko eines Infarkts beträchtlich.«

»Aber wer um Himmels willen wirft einen Menschen vor den Zug, der an einem Herzinfarkt gestorben ist?«, fragte ich nach einer Denksekunde.

»Diese Frage fällt wohl eher in Ihr Ressort«, meinte der Privatdozent kühl.

»Wäre es denkbar, dass er ... Dass es zum Beispiel eine Schlägerei gegeben hat, in deren Verlauf sein Herz schlappgemacht hat?«

»Das ist sogar sehr gut denkbar. Starker Stress ist häufig der letzte Auslöser eines Infarkts.«

»Dann müsste er Verletzungen haben, die nicht durch den vorgetäuschten Selbstmord verursacht worden sind.«

»Da kann ich Ihnen möglicherweise sogar weiterhelfen. Der Tote hat deutliche Strangmarkierungen an den Handgelenken.«

»Er war gefesselt, als er starb?«

»So sieht es aus. Nach dem ersten Blick durchs Mikroskop mit einem älteren und ziemlich schmutzigen Hanfseil.«

»Spuren von einem Kampf? Abwehrverletzungen?«

»Unter den Fingernägeln war nichts zu finden außer Schmutz, der auch vom Bahndamm stammen könnte. Wird ein Weilchen dauern, bis wir hier klarer sehen. Ansonsten ... nicht leicht zu sagen beim beklagenswerten Zustand des Leichnams. Die meisten Verletzungen, die ich dokumentiert habe, sind ihm unzweideutig postmortal beigebracht worden.« Der Privatdozent hustete zweimal kräftig, fuhr dann fort: »Soll ich Ihnen meinen vorläufigen Bericht schon mal zukommen lassen? Den offiziellen werden Sie frühestens am Mittwoch kriegen, weil zwei unserer Schreibkräfte wegen grippaler Infekte außer Gefecht sind. Und außerdem wird mir meine Frau den Krieg erklären, wenn ich nicht in Kürze nach Hause komme.«

Ich wusste zwar nicht, inwiefern mir der schriftliche Bericht weiterhelfen konnte, aber sicher war sicher. Minuten später piepte eine Mail, an der ein kurzes Word-Dokument hing. Ich überflog es, ohne dabei wirklich klüger zu werden, schloss es wieder. Öffnete es erneut, weil mich etwas irritiert hatte, las den in Stichworten abgefassten Text ein zweites Mal, der zahllose offene und geschlossene Knochenfrakturen, mehr oder weniger tiefe Schnittwunden und großflächige Abschürfungen auflistete. Wieder entdeckte ich nichts Auffälliges. Ich schloss die Datei erneut, aber das unzufriedene Gefühl in meinem Bauch blieb. Schließlich las ich den von medizinischen Fachausdrücken strotzenden Text ein drittes Mal, Wort für Wort für Wort, und nun endlich entdeckte ich, was nicht stimmte: Es stand gleich in der ersten Zeile – der Vorname des Toten lautete Uwe. Nicht Fred.

Glücklicherweise erwischte ich Professor Gericke noch in seinem Büro.

»So steht es im Totenschein: Uwe Hergarden. Möglicherweise ein Fehler Ihrer Kollegen?«

Der Kollege vom Kriminaldauerdienst, mit dem ich kurz darauf telefonierte, war nicht amüsiert über meine Unterstellung, er oder einer seiner Mitstreiter hätte den Vornamen falsch notiert. Es hatte mich mehrere Anrufe gekostet, ihn an die Leitung zu bekommen. Schließlich hatte ich ihn zu Hause in seinem Bastelkeller erreicht. Er führte einen konsonantenreichen Namen, der ungefähr wie »Krwzcyck« klang.

»Also erstens stellen nicht wir den Totenschein aus, sondern der Arzt«, belehrte er mich grimmig.

»Das ist mir sonnenklar, aber …«

»Gar nix aber. Den Namen von dem Arzt hab ich mir natürlich nicht gemerkt. Der war vom Roten Kreuz, den finden Sie leicht …«

»Ich will Ihnen ja auch gar nichts …«

»Und zweitens hab ich selber den Ausweis von dem Toten in der Hand gehabt. Und er hat halt nun mal Uwe geheißen, ich kann's nicht ändern. Sein Perso müsste bei den Akten sein.«

Fünf Minuten später hielt ich das Kärtchen in der Hand: Uwe Hergarden, geboren am siebten Januar 1949, wohnhaft in der Leutweinstraße in Mannheim-Rheinau. Damit war er zwei Jahre älter als Fred Hergarden. Es kostete mich einige Telefonate herauszufinden, dass die zwei Männer Brüder waren. Beide in Viernheim zur Welt gekommen, wo die Eltern bis 1961 gewohnt hatten. Die Mutter war Ende der Fünfzigerjahre gestorben. Der Vater, der zeitlebens als Krankenpfleger gearbeitet hatte, hatte bald eine neue Frau gefunden und war zusammen mit ihr und den beiden heranwachsenden Söhnen nach Mannheim gezogen, in das Haus in Rheinau, wo Uwe Hergarden bis vor zwei Tagen noch gelebt hatte.

All dies bedeutete, dass Fred Hergarden noch am Leben war, sich jetzt irgendwo versteckt hielt und wahrscheinlich sehr, sehr wütend war. Und das wiederum bedeutete, dass Marcel Graf in höchster Gefahr schwebte.

Das Passfoto war fast zehn Jahre alt, aber so viel konnte ich doch erkennen: Die Brüder sahen sich ähnlich. Fred schien mir im Gesicht ein wenig schmaler zu sein als Uwe. Aber die Augenpartie, die Tränensäcke, der mürrische Mund, die hohe Stirn, das schüttere Haar – die beiden hätten fast als Zwillinge durchgehen können. Auch die Personenbeschreibungen

wichen nur unwesentlich voneinander ab: Größe eins siebenundachtzig bei Uwe, eins neunundachtzig bei Fred, Statur in
beiden Fällen hager.

30

Ich beschloss, von meinen zwei Handlungsoptionen, die mir
gleich gut oder schlecht erschienen, einfach beide zu wählen.
Jede ein bisschen. Deshalb ordnete ich an, vor die Villa in Neuenheim einen Streifenwagen mit zwei Beamten zu stellen, um
zu zeigen, dass ich das dreißig Jahre alte Spiel durchschaute.
Deshalb nahm ich Boll und seinen Mitstreiter nicht fest,
obwohl die beiden mit Sicherheit an Uwe Hergardens Ableben
maßgeblichen Anteil hatten. Und deshalb rief ich wieder einmal Grafs durchtriebene Assistentin an.

»Ja?«, meldete sie sich in ihrer üblichen Atemlosigkeit.
»Herr Gerlach?«

»Ich muss Ihren Chef sprechen. Dieses Mal ist es wirklich
dringend.«

»Völlig ausgeschlossen. Wir gehen in acht Stunden auf Sendung. Und Marcel ist immer noch sehr geschwächt. Nein, tut
mir leid, wirklich völlig ausgeschlossen.«

Nicht einmal die Polizei kann einen Menschen zwingen, für
seine Sicherheit zu sorgen. So erklärte ich ihr, dass der Tote auf
den Gleisen nicht der war, für den wir ihn zunächst gehalten
hatten. Diese Nachricht brachte sie dann doch ein wenig aus
der Fassung.

»Er ... Er ist nicht tot?«

»Er lebt. Und er ist ganz bestimmt nicht besonders gut
gelaunt.«

Sie zögerte lange. »Marcel wird von zwei Leibwächtern
beschützt«, sagte sie schließlich mit tonloser Stimme. »Bestens
ausgebildeten und bewaffneten Leibwächtern, die ihren Job
verstehen.«

»Sagen Sie Ihrem Chef trotzdem, was geschehen ist. Dass er

auf sich aufpassen soll. Nachdem nun auch noch sein Bruder tot ist, dürfte Hergarden zu allem fähig sein.«

Sie hatte ihre Fassung schon zurückgewonnen. »Er wird nicht fähig sein, in Marcels Nähe zu gelangen«, erklärte sie fest. »Und ich werde ihn auch nicht informieren. Jede Irritation kann in seiner Verfassung eine erneute Krise auslösen. Wir müssen das heute Abend durchziehen. Wir *müssen* einfach.«

»Koste es, was es wolle?«

»Ja, koste es, was es wolle.«

»Hergarden könnte sich unters Publikum mischen.«

»Das Publikum wurde schon vor Monaten ausgewählt und handverlesen. Wir gehen da schon unter normalen Umständen kein Risiko ein. Ohne Eintrittskarte kommen Sie nicht einmal ins Foyer, geschweige denn in den Saal. Aber – falls es Sie beruhigt – ich werde das Personal an den Eingängen sicherheitshalber noch einmal instruieren, dass sie die Augen dieses Mal besonders gut offen halten sollen. Hätten Sie vielleicht ein Foto? Ich könnte es verteilen lassen.«

Mein Vorschlag, einige bewaffnete Polizisten in Zivil unters Publikum zu mischen, wurde rundweg abgelehnt.

»Solange Marcel im Gebäude ist, ist er sicher«, meinte Olivia Opelt. »Alle Plätze sind vergeben. Und wir können hier wirklich keine weitere Unruhe brauchen.«

»Leicht zu übersehen ist Hergarden zum Glück nicht, bei seiner Größe. Ein aktuelles Foto habe ich nicht, aber immerhin ein brauchbares Phantombild. Außerdem kann ich Ihnen das Passfoto des toten Bruders zukommen lassen. Die beiden sehen sich ähnlich.«

»Tun Sie das bitte.«

»Und sagen Sie Ihrem Chef wenigstens, ich möchte ihn sprechen, sobald die Sendung vorbei ist.«

»Zu gegebener Zeit ja, versprochen. Er wird Sie anrufen.«

»Einer der Leibwächter ist Johann Boll, richtig?«

»Das … das sind interne Informationen, die ich nicht weitergeben darf.«

»Frau Opelt, ich habe ihn gesehen. In der Klinik.«

»Weshalb fragen Sie dann?«

»Weil ich von Ihnen gerne eine Bestätigung hätte.«

»Ich bin nicht befugt, solche internen Informationen herauszugeben. Aber ja, es ist Boll.«

»Und der andere?«

»Tut mir leid.«

»Die Nummer der Personalabteilung des ZDF, die dürfen Sie doch bestimmt herausgeben.«

»Die finden Sie im Internet. Aber Sie werden dort niemanden erreichen. Heute ist auch in Mainz Samstag.«

Mein nächster Anruf galt dem Polizeipräsidium in Ludwigshafen. Ich erklärte dem diensthabenden Beamten lang und breit die Lage und bat ihn, wenigstens den Veranstaltungsort von außen im Auge zu behalten.

»Verdeckt oder offen?«

»So offen, wie Sie wollen. Stellen Sie ruhig ein paar Streifenwagen um das Gebäude herum.«

»Wir haben heute Großkampftag. In Mannheim drüben spielen die Adler gegen die Grizzly Adams aus Wolfsburg.« Sein Ton ließ keinen Zweifel daran, dass er nur zu gerne Augenzeuge dieses Eishockeyspiels gewesen wäre. »Wir müssen dreißig Leute abstellen. Wo soll ich da bitte schön das Personal hernehmen, um jetzt auch noch auf diesen Fernsehfuzzi aufzupassen?«

»Lassen Sie sich was einfallen.«

Er lachte sarkastisch. »Lassen Sie sich was einfallen, Sie sind gut! Wenn diese Bewachung irgendwas bringen soll, dann brauche ich mindestens zehn Zweierteams in Uniform und am besten noch mal zehn in Zivil, die sich unters Volk mischen. Soll ich die Leute aus dem Hut zaubern, oder wie?«

»Ich werde dafür sorgen, dass Sie Verstärkung von uns kriegen. Graf ist in Lebensgefahr. Stellen Sie unbedingt auch ein paar Leute an die Zugänge von der Tiefgarage zum Foyer.«

»Denken Sie eigentlich, wir sind hier blöd? Weil Ludwigshafen zur Pfalz gehört, oder was?«

»Natürlich nicht«, seufzte ich erschöpft. »Aber ich halte die Tiefgarage nun mal für besonders kritisch. Außerdem natürlich die Hinter- und Seiteneingänge. Was weiß ich, wie Hergarden sich verkleidet. Vielleicht kommt er im Monteursanzug mit Werkzeugkasten oder als Musiker mit Geigenköfferchen unterm Arm oder als Pizzalieferant ... «

» Sie glauben im Ernst, der will den umlegen? So mitten während der Show? «

» Verstehen Sie, der Mann ist vollkommen verzweifelt. Er hängt nicht mehr am Leben, und das macht ihn so gefährlich. «

» Ist er bewaffnet? «

» Eine Schusswaffe hat er meines Wissens nicht. Aber ein Messer lässt sich leicht besorgen. «

» Weiß Graf und seine Bagage, dass wir auf ihn aufpassen werden? «

» Nein. Und er wird es auch nicht gut finden. Und das ist mir schnurzpiepegal. «

Ich wählte noch einmal die Nummer des Kollegen mit den vielen Konsonanten.

» Waren Sie im Haus von Uwe Hergarden? «

Inzwischen hatte sich seine Empörung schon ein wenig gelegt. » Klar sind wir da gewesen. Wir haben geguckt, ob es wen gibt, der benachrichtigt werden muss. Aber wir haben nichts gefunden. Wieso? «

» Ist Ihnen dort irgendwas aufgefallen? «

» Dass der Herr kein großer Freund von Ordnung gewesen ist, das ist mir aufgefallen. Da hat's ja ausgesehen, schlimmer als bei Hempels unterm Hundekissen ... «

» Spuren von einem Kampf? «

» Wieso denn jetzt von einem Kampf? Was ist denn überhaupt los? «

» Es sieht aus, als wäre er nicht selbst vor den Zug gesprungen. «

» Ach was. « Kurze Denkpause. » Nein, da war nichts von einem Kampf. Aber bei dem Durcheinander kann man natürlich leicht was übersehen. Und wie wir dort waren, sind wir ja noch von Selbstmord ausgegangen. Sie meinen also, den ... den hat wer umgebracht? «

» Als der Zug ihn überfahren hat, war er schon eine Weile tot. Wer hat den Schlüssel zum Haus? «

»Liegt in meiner Schreibtischschublade oben links. Brauchen Sie ihn heute noch?«

»Ich brauche ihn jetzt sofort.«

Es kostete mich einige Überredungskünste und Schmeicheleinheiten, aber schließlich willigte er ein, in einer Stunde vor Uwe Hergardens Haustür auf mich zu warten. Mit dem Schlüssel in der Hand.

Die einzige Erklärung für den vorgetäuschten Selbstmord, überlegte ich während der Fahrt nach Mannheim, war eine Verwechslung. Jemand aus Grafs Gefolge hatte Fred Hergarden einen ordentlichen Schrecken einjagen wollen. Dafür kamen eigentlich nur die Leibwächter infrage. Sie hatten ihr Opfer gefesselt, vielleicht mit einer Waffe bedroht, aber vermutlich nicht in der Absicht, ihn zu töten. Der erste große Fehler der beiden war gewesen, dass sie sich den falschen Bruder vorgeknöpft hatten. Der zweite, dass dieser ihnen unter den Händen weggestorben war. Um die Tat zu vertuschen, hatten sie das Opfer ihrer Dummheit anschließend ins Auto verfrachtet und einige Kilometer vom Tatort entfernt vor den Zug geworfen. Es war schon nach Mitternacht gewesen, es hatte stark geschneit, die Gefahr, bei dieser vollkommen idiotischen Aktion beobachtet zu werden, war gering gewesen.

Olivia Opelt verfügte weder über das Gemüt noch über die Körperkräfte für eine solche Tat. Als Anstifterin kam sie jedoch durchaus in Frage. Und als Autoverleiherin natürlich auch.

Ich angelte mein Handy vom Beifahrersitz und suchte die Telefonnummer von Klara Vangelis aus dem Telefonbuch. Wie nicht anders zu erwarten, war auch sie heute im Büro.

»Ich brauche den Namen des zweiten Leibwächters von Graf. Und am besten auch noch ein bisschen was zu seinem Lebenslauf.«

»Den bezahlt das ZDF, nehme ich an?«

»Davon gehe ich aus. Aber in der Verwaltung ist heute natürlich niemand zu erreichen. Ich habe es schon versucht.«

31

Dreißig Minuten später stellte ich vor Uwe Hergardens Haus am westlichen Ende der Mannheimer Leutweinstraße den Motor ab. Der Kollege mit dem unaussprechlichen Namen erwartete mich bereits. Er war für seine kräftige Stimme überraschend klein gewachsen, überragte die einhundertsechzig Zentimeter, die man in Baden-Württemberg bei der Einstellung zur Polizei vorweisen muss, sicherlich nicht weit.

Wir schüttelten kollegial Hände und betraten die gepflasterte Fläche vor der Garage. Nicht weit entfernt summten Industrieanlagen und brummten Lkws. Die Tür des bescheidenen und nachlässig gepflegten Häuschens machte keinen wehrhaften Eindruck. Das schmale Vorgärtchen zwischen Haus und Straße zierte verdorrtes Unkraut. Ein lange nicht mehr geschnittener Rhododendron wirkte nicht so, als wollte er noch einmal Knospen treiben. Auch die anderen Häuser, die die schmale Straße säumten, sahen nicht nach großem Wohlstand aus.

Der stämmige Kollege schloss auf, zerriss die beiden Polizeisiegel, die über und unter dem Türgriff pappten. Wir betraten Uwe Hergardens nach Kohl und feuchter Wäsche riechendes Reich.

»Rechts geht's zur Küche. Geradeaus ins Wohnzimmer. Die Schlafzimmer sind oben.«

»Die Schlafzimmer?«

»Insgesamt drei. Eines mit Doppelbett und zwei ehemalige Kinderzimmer. Von dem Doppelbett ist nur eines bezogen. Das eine Kinderzimmer hat er als Hobbyraum benutzt. Er hat Schmetterlinge gesammelt und Käfer und so. Das ganze Zimmer hängt voll davon. Das zweite Zimmer hat er als Gästezimmer benutzt.«

Ich blieb stehen. Sah ihn an. »Ist da etwa auch das Bett bezogen?«

»Komischweise ja. Aber da ist wenigstens die Bettwäsche sauber.«

»Wer da übernachtet hat, wissen Sie aber nicht?«

»Hier ist keiner gewesen, als wir gekommen sind.« Er seufzte gequält. »Wir haben zweimal geläutet, bevor wir die Tür haben öffnen lassen. Wir haben gedacht, der hat sich vor den Zug geschmissen, und haben geguckt, ob wir irgendwo eine Adresse finden, einen Namen von jemanden, den man anrufen kann. Der ihn identifiziert und sich später um die Beerdigung kümmert und alles. Das war doch keine Staatsaktion.«

Wir drehten eine Runde durchs Erdgeschoss, besichtigten eine Küche, die im Stil der Siebzigerjahre eingerichtet war. Lediglich der Herd mit Cerankochfeld war neueren Datums. Auch eine Spülmaschine gab es, die jedoch nicht zu funktionieren schien, denn in einem Abtropfgestell neben der Spüle standen einige saubere Teller, Tassen und Gläser. An dem billigen Tisch mit Chrombeinen standen nur drei Stühle. Stühle mit roten Kunstledersitzen, wie sie vor fünfzig Jahren aus der Mode gekommen waren.

Auch das wegen der heruntergelassenen Rollläden dunkle Wohnzimmer versprühte den Charme vergangener Jahrzehnte. Es stank nach kaltem Zigarettenrauch und abgestandenem Bier. Ich drückte den Lichtschalter. Eine Deckenlampe mit bunten Stoffschirmchen sorgte für trübe Helligkeit. Das einzig Wertvolle in diesem Zimmer schien ein Flachbildfernseher von rekordverdächtigen Ausmaßen zu sein.

»Die Blumen, gucken Sie mal!«, sagte der Kollege ehrfurchtsvoll. »Darf ich die Rollläden hochziehen, damit die nicht eingehen?«

Nie zuvor hatte ich so große und stolz blühende Orchideen gesehen.

»Diese Dinger sind so was von zimperlich«, sagte der andere, während er die schweren Holzlamellen am Gurt nach oben zerrte. »Hab's auch mal eine Weile damit versucht. Aber wenn man die bloß mal schief anguckt oder zu laut hustet, schon fangen sie an zu kümmern.«

Auf dem Couchtisch standen vier leere und eine halb volle Flasche Eichbaum Kellerbier, daneben zwei beinahe leer getrunkene Glaskrüge von Paulaner, an deren Rändern eingetrockneter Schaum klebte. Am Rand des Tischs stapelte sich eine beachtliche Sammlung Fußballzeitschriften, ein vier Wochen altes Exemplar des »Mannheimer Morgen« und ein auf acht Feldern ausgefüllter Lottoschein.

»Stellen Sie sich vor, der hat vielleicht am Mittwoch sechs Richtige gehabt, und jetzt wird er es nicht mal mehr erfahren«, grübelte der Kollege.

»Er war nicht allein hier«, stellte ich fest.

»Nach einem Kampf sieht's aber nicht aus, das müssen Sie zugeben.«

Ich knipste das Licht wieder aus. Unter der Garderobe im Flur lag ein großer tannengrüner Knopf. Mein Begleiter bückte sich und hob ihn auf.

»Könnte von einer Strickjacke stammen«, meinte er sachkundig. »Von einer grünen Strickjacke. So eine hat er nämlich angehabt.«

»Können Sie auf die Schnelle rausfinden, ob da ein Knopf fehlt?«

Bereitwillig zückte er sein Handy.

Während er telefonierte, stieg ich die Treppe zum Obergeschoss hinauf, öffnete dort eine Tür nach der anderen. Das eiskalte Doppelzimmer mit dem verwaisten zweiten Bett. Der Hobbyraum, dessen Wände mit verglasten Kästen gepflastert waren, in denen Schmetterlinge und Käfer in allen denkbaren Größen und Farben ihre Pracht entfalteten. Das im Gegensatz zum ersten Raum hoffnungslos überheizte Gästezimmer mit zerwühltem Laken und zerknülltem Kissen. Im moosgrün gekachelten Bad eine kalkverkrustete Dusche, ein Duschvorhang voller Schimmelflecken, eine Badewanne, in die sich vor einer gründlichen Behandlung mit Scheuerpulver und Essigreiniger kein Mensch freiwillig gelegt hätte, ein dagegen halbwegs sauberes Waschbecken, in dem Spuren von Zahnpasta und einige kurz geschnittene graue Haare klebten.

»Gucken Sie sich das mal an!«, rief der Kollege aus dem Schlafzimmer des toten Hausbesitzers.

Er stand vor einem Nachttischchen aus Kirschbaumimitat und starrte in die Schublade. In der rechten Hand hielt er ein Tuch, um keine Fingerabdrücke zu hinterlassen. Ich zog einen der Latexhandschuhe über die rechte Hand, die ich für solche Anlässe immer in der Manteltasche hatte. In der Schublade befanden sich neben einigen Kondomen mit vermutlich längst abgelaufenem Haltbarkeitsdatum ein zerfleddertes Pornoheftchen im Format DIN A5, ein fleckiger Lappen, der sicherlich einmal Teil eines Feinrippunterhemds gewesen war, und eine Schachtel Pistolenmunition. Ich nahm sie heraus. Fünfzig Schuss stand auf der Packung. Sie war halb leer.

»Neun Millimeter Makarov«, sagte der Kollege ehrfurchtsvoll. »Damit richtet man schon was aus.«

»Die Frage ist, gibt es auch eine Waffe dazu?«

Er wies auf die Schublade. »Auf dem Lappen da, das sind keine Wichsflecken.«

Er hatte recht, es schienen Ölflecken zu sein. Ich legte die Munitionsschachtel zurück an ihren Platz und drückte meinen Rücken durch. »Wenn da eine Waffe war, dann weiß ich, wer sie jetzt hat. Was sagen eigentlich die Nachbarn?«

»Nichts. Mit denen hat noch keiner geredet. Bis vor einer Stunde ist es ja noch ein Selbstmord gewesen. Wir haben gedacht, früher oder später tauchen Angehörige auf, die uns was über den Typ sagen können. Ob er depressiv gewesen ist, ob er getrunken hat oder Geldsorgen gehabt hat. Das übliche Elend halt bei so was. Mit den Nachbarn werden Sie nicht viel Glück haben. In der Gegend hier wohnen fast nur alte Leute. Nach Mitternacht kriegen die nichts mit.«

»Alte Leute haben oft einen leichten Schlaf.«

Er nickte und seufzte. »Bei mir geht's auch schon los. Zehnmal die Nacht pissen, und jedes Mal fünf Tropfen.«

Hintereinander stiegen wir die schmale Treppe wieder hinab. Das Handy meines Begleiters jubelte eine Opernarie.

»Die Strickjacke«, sagte er Sekunden später in meinem Rücken. »Da fehlt tatsächlich ein Knopf. Die Farbe passt.«

Ein abgerissener Knopf war natürlich noch lange kein Beweis für Gewaltanwendung. Aber es war immerhin ein Hinweis. Ich betrat ein zweites Mal die Küche, trat auf das Pedal des orangefarbenen Mülleimers mit braunem Klappdeckel und entdeckte auch dort nichts Interessantes. Er war vollkommen leer.

»Was suchen Sie eigentlich?«, wollte der Kollege wissen.

»Zum Beispiel irgendwas, womit sie ihn gefesselt haben.«

»Sie meinen, die haben den hier im Haus durch die Mangel gedreht? Wieso?«

»Wo sonst?«

»Und dann fällt der einfach tot um. Dumm gelaufen, kann man da nur sagen.«

Wieder legte ein Handy los. Dieses Mal war es meines.

»Der zweite Leibwächter heißt Patrick Wunderlich«, berichtete Klara Vangelis. »Geboren 1981 in Erlangen. Nach der Mittleren Reife zwölf Jahre Bundeswehr, zuletzt Hauptfeldwebel und Zugführer.«

»Welche Truppe?«

»Panzerpioniere. Drei Auslandseinsätze: zweimal Kosovo, jeweils für ein halbes Jahr, später einige Monate Afghanistan. Da hat er aber anscheinend eine ruhige Kugel geschoben.«

»Wann ist er ausgeschieden?«

»Vor zwei Jahren. Zuletzt war er in Straubing stationiert. Anschließend längere Zeit arbeitslos. Dann hat ihn eine Firma für Securitydienstleistungen in Landshut eingestellt, die unter anderem auch Personenschutz im Angebot hat. Und die hat ihn dann an das ZDF ausgeliehen.«

»Arbeitet Boll auch für diese Securityfirma?«

»Von Boll wissen die Leute beim ZDF überhaupt nichts. Die Dame, mit der ich gesprochen habe, meint, Graf bezahlt Boll aus eigener Tasche. Vielleicht, weil er sich mit nur einem Wachhund nicht sicher fühlt.«

»Wann hat er eigentlich Personenschutz verlangt?«

»Vor knapp vier Wochen. Es hat Drohungen gegeben.«

»Von wem und womit?«

»Anonym. Mehr wusste meine Gesprächspartnerin auch nicht. Graf habe nur angedeutet, es handle sich um eine alte Geschichte und er müsse für ein paar Wochen vorsichtig sein.«

»Die Polizei ist nicht eingeschaltet worden?«

»Nein.«

»Warum nicht?«

»Das wissen vermutlich nur ein paar Menschen in den oberen Etagen des ZDF und Herr Graf selbst.«

»Im Keller sind wir noch nicht gewesen«, sagte der kleine Kollege, der während meines kurzen Telefonats die nikotingelbe Decke der Küche angestarrt hatte. »Links rum. Die Tür neben dem Klo.«

Im Keller stank es nach fauligem Gemüse, und es sah aus, als hätte jemand die komplette Einrichtung einer vierköpfigen Familie hineingestopft und anschließend vergessen. Lediglich im Heizungsraum, wo eine überraschend moderne Gaszentralheizung vor sich hin summte, war ein wenig Platz. Aber auch hier machte nichts den Eindruck, als wäre kürzlich etwas Aufregendes geschehen.

»Da muss noch ein Raum sein«, entdeckte mein eifriger Begleiter, der eine Gasse durch das Gerümpel gefunden hatte. »Da ist noch eine Tür.«

Die Tür, die er meinte, führte in einen kleineren Raum, der nach hinten zum Garten lag. Hier standen vollgestopfte Metallregale an den Längswänden. Knapp unter der Decke befand sich ein vergittertes Fensterchen, durch das ein wenig graue Helligkeit hereindrang. In einer Ecke waren leere und unglaublich verstaubte Obstkisten bis an die Decke gestapelt. Und an der Wand gegenüber der Tür stand ein einsamer Küchenstuhl mit rotem Polstersitz. Wir gingen vor dem Stuhl in die Hocke. Der Kollege zückte eine kleine, verblüffend starke LED-Taschenlampe, leuchtete herum. Am staubigen Boden waren fast überall frische Fußabdrücke zu erkennen. Abdrücke von Männerschuhen mit grobem Profil.

»Hier muss die Spurensicherung rein«, entschied ich.

Unter dem Stuhl entdeckte ich feine Fussel. An eine Lupe hatte mein Begleiter leider nicht auch noch gedacht, aber wir wurden uns auch ohne Vergrößerung rasch einig: Es handelte sich um millimeterkurze Fasern von einem alten Hanfseil.

»Der Fleck, da am Stuhlbein, das könnte Blut sein«, spekulierte er. »Besonders viel Mühe haben die sich ja nicht gegeben, dass man nichts findet.«

»Das waren keine Profis. Und sie haben wahrscheinlich nicht vorgehabt, ihn umzubringen.«

»Die werden schön blöd geguckt haben, wie der auf einmal tot war.«

Wir stiegen die steile Betontreppe wieder hinauf und traten kurz drauf ins Freie. Mein Begleiter schloss ab und erneuerte mit geduldigen Bewegungen die Siegel. Ich bat ihn, umgehend die Mitarbeiter der Spurensicherung zu alarmieren. »Ich brauche Täterspuren. Hautschuppen, Haare, Textilfasern, alles. Im Keller finden sie bestimmt jede Menge davon.«

Er versprach, die Anweisung sofort weiterzugeben.

»Was basteln Sie eigentlich in Ihrer Freizeit?«, fragte ich, um ihm eine Freude zu machen.

Da begann er zu strahlen. »Nachbauten von Formel-1-Rennwagen. Maßstab eins zu zehn. Mit allen Funktionen. Meine Fernsteuerung ist voll digital und hat zwölf Kanäle!«

»Fährt man auch Rennen damit?«

»Das gibt's tatsächlich. Aber ich mach da nicht mit, dazu sind mir meine Autos viel zu schade. Ich gehe manchmal auf Ausstellungen. Hab schon zweimal den ersten Preis gemacht!«

Ich nickte anerkennend, und wir verabschiedeten uns wie alte Kampfgefährten, die schon viel zusammen erlebt hatten.

Er stieg in seinen sichtlich neuen Toyota Prius und schnurrte fast lautlos davon. Ich blieb zurück und sah mich um.

32

Vor einem vergilbten Haus an der gegenüberliegenden Straßenseite sammelte ein nicht mehr junger, magerer Mann dürres Laub und Papierschnipsel vom Gehweg und versuchte dabei angestrengt so auszusehen, als würde er nicht demnächst vor Neugierde platzen. Ich wechselte die Straßenseite und stellte mich vor. Mit einem großen Seufzer richtete er sich auf, sah mich an und gab sich überrascht.

»Was die Leute alles wegschmeißen«, sagte er mit theatralischer Geste auf den blitzsauberen Gehweg. »Die ganze Zeit könnt man nur den Dreck von anderen Leuten wegmachen. Als hätte man nichts Besseres zu tun.«

»Sie haben den Herrn Hergarden doch bestimmt gekannt«, eröffnete ich das Gespräch.

»Der ist tot, stimmt das?«

Ich nickte.

»Und warum ist die Polizei da? Ich meine, es sterben doch jeden Tag Leute. Ist irgendwas nicht in Ordnung?«

»Danach sieht es leider aus.«

»Es heißt, er hat sich umgebracht.«

»Inzwischen gibt es Verdachtsmomente dafür, dass jemand dabei nachgeholfen hat.«

»Sie meinen ... also ... Er ist umgebracht worden?«

Der Nachbar strich sich mechanisch das schüttere, senffarbene Haar aus der Stirn. »Ich wohn hier seit über dreißig Jahren, wissen Sie. Die Eltern haben das Haus gebaut, da war ich elf. Vorher haben wir in Heidelberg drüben gewohnt. Und der Uwe ... also der Herr Hergarden ... der hat schon seit Anfang der Sechziger hier gewohnt. Dem seinem Vater sein Haus ist ein bisschen früher fertig gewesen als das von meinen Eltern. Damals haben sie ja praktisch die ganze Straße neu hochgezogen. Aber was erzähl ich eigentlich ... Sie sind wirklich von der Polizei?«

Ich zeigte ihm meinen Dienstausweis und machte enormen Eindruck damit.

»Kennen Sie diese Heidelberg-Krimis von ...?«

»Ich lese keine Krimis.«

Der Nachbar zwinkerte mich so ungläubig an, als wäre dies eine unverzeihliche Bildungslücke.

»Er hat allein hier gelebt?«

Ein empörter Blick aus grauen Augen. »Er hat ja niemand gehabt! Geheiratet hat er nicht, die Eltern tot, der Bruder irgendwo in weiter Ferne. Die zwei haben sich auch nicht so gut vertragen, hat er mir mal erzählt. Viel von sich erzählt hat er sonst ja nicht. Nur von dem Bruder, dass der im Ausland gewesen ist. Im Libanon und in Syrien und Jordanien. Er soll eine Libanesin geheiratet haben. Früher ist der Kameramann beim Fernsehen gewesen. Später nicht mehr. Der Uwe hat gemeint, sein Bruder macht da im Osten irgendwelche krummen Geschäfte, und irgendwann würde ihn jemand abknallen deshalb. Was genau, hat er aber auch nicht gewusst. Jedenfalls hat er mit dem nichts zu tun haben wollen. Mit meiner Schwester, das funktioniert ja auch nicht so. Seit ich arbeitslos bin, höre ich von der bloß noch Vorwürfe und schlaue Ratschläge. Vorwürfe und Ratschläge, von morgens bis abends.«

»Kann es sein, dass der Bruder in den letzten Tagen aufgetaucht ist?«

Die grauen Augen wurden groß. »Hab sogar gesehen, wie er angekommen ist.« Der hagere Nachbar zupfte aufgeregt den Saum seines schmutziges T-Shirts zurecht. »Im Januar ist das gewesen. Auf einmal steht der da drüben und läutet. Ich denk noch, was läutet der Uwe denn jetzt an seiner eigenen Tür, weil, eigentlich war der nämlich in Urlaub ...«

»Wann genau war das?«

Der Mann hob die knochigen Schultern. »Vor drei Wochen ungefähr? Der Uwe war erst zwei, drei Tage vorher losgefahren. Nach Spanien.«

»Mitte Januar?«

»Es gibt da irgendeine Art von Mistkäfern, im Norden, und die fängt man am besten im Winter, fragen Sie mich nicht. Mit dem Auto ist er gefahren. Und vorgestern ist er wieder heimgekommen. Oder war's schon am Mittwoch? Jedenfalls, auf einmal steht das Auto wieder da, und ich weiß, aha, der Uwe ist wieder daheim. Ich hab ihm dann gleich gesagt, dass jemand bei ihm geläutet hat. Und da hat er gemeint, das kann nur sein Bruder gewesen sein.«

»Die beiden Brüder haben sich ziemlich ähnlich gesehen, nicht wahr?«

»Aber wie! Wenn sie nicht zwei Jahre auseinander gewesen wären, man hätt die zwei glatt für Zwillinge halten können.

Obwohl der Uwe ein paar Zentimeter kleiner gewesen ist als der Fred. Fred heißt er nämlich, der Bruder. Aber das hat man nur gesehen, wenn sie quasi nebeneinandergestanden haben. Wo ist der eigentlich hin, der Bruder?«

»Das wüsste ich auch gerne. Ist er in den letzten Tagen drüben gewesen?«

Der Nachbar nickte wichtig. »Der Fred hat ihm einen Zettel in den Briefkasten geschmissen mit seiner Telefonnummer. Und den Uwe hat tatsächlich wer umgebracht? Ausgerechnet jetzt, wo er auf einmal nicht mehr allein ist auf der Welt ... Da fällt mir ein, vielleicht war's der Bruder?«

»Das halte ich für unwahrscheinlich. Außerdem waren es zwei.«

»Ja, ja«, seufzte der hagere Mann und sah mit grauem Blick ins Weite. »Man guckt in den Menschen nicht rein, was?«

»Hat er sich denn gefreut, als sein Bruder auf einmal wieder da war, nach so vielen Jahren?«

»Erst nicht so. Er hat ihn dann wohl angerufen, und gleich am nächsten Tag ist er wieder da gewesen, der Fred. Ich hab nicht alles verstanden, was sie an der Tür geredet haben, aber Wiedersehensfreude ist was anderes. Am Ende hat er ihn dann doch reingelassen, und dann haben sie den ganzen Abend im Wohnzimmer gehockt und Bier getrunken und später Pizza gegessen. Die Pizza muss der Uwe aus dem Gefrierschrank geholt haben, und Bier hat er ja immer genug im Keller gehabt. Der hat lieber aufs Essen verzichtet als auf sein geliebtes Feierabendbierchen.«

»Was war er eigentlich von Beruf?«

»Bäcker. Hat aber dann aufhören müssen. Mehlallergie, mit zweiundfünfzig. Am Herz hat er's auch gehabt. Hat ja aber auch gequarzt, dass einem vom Zugucken schlecht werden konnt. Manchmal hab ich den Qualm bis hier rüber gerochen. Zwei Packungen am Tag hat der mindestens durchgezogen. Wie oft hab ich ihm gesagt, Uwe, du bringst dich noch um damit. Wo er doch ein schwaches Herz gehabt hat ...«

»Wissen Sie noch, an welchem Abend das war, als der Bruder aufgetaucht ist?«

»Am Mittwoch? Genau, jetzt hab ich's wieder: Am Mittwochabend ist er auf einmal drüben gestanden. Nehme an, der Uwe hat ihn angerufen, und da ist er gleich gekommen. Am nächsten Vormittag sind sie zusammen weg, mit dem Uwe seinem Mercedes. Haben seine Sachen geholt, weil, Gepäck hat er ja erst nicht dabeigehabt, der Bruder, wie er gekommen ist. Und später, wie's dunkel war, haben sie dann wieder … im Wohnzimmer … bis der Uwe … Meine Fresse, das muss in der Nacht gewesen sein, wo …?«

»Sie haben nicht mitbekommen, dass er später am Abend noch mal das Haus verlassen hat? War nach Mitternacht Unruhe auf der Straße?«

»Gar nichts hab ich mitgekriegt. Ich geh immer um halb zwölf ins Bett, und dann schlaf ich wie ein Stein. Ich hab alle möglichen Krankheiten, hier zwickt's, und da zwickt's und im Rücken sowieso. Aber schlafen kann ich wie ein Faultier. Du musst einen geregelten Tag haben, wenn du keinen Job hast, erklärt mir meine Schwester immer, sonst kommst du auf den Hund.«

Irgendwo in der Nähe schlug eine Kirchturmuhr scheppernd zweimal.

Noch sechs Stunden und fünfzehn Minuten, bis »Grafs Abend« begann.

Während der Rückfahrt zur Direktion rief ich noch einmal in Ludwigshafen an, um dem Einsatzleiter mitzuteilen, dass Fred Hergarden mit größter Wahrscheinlichkeit eine Schusswaffe mit sich führte und man entsprechende Vorsichtsmaßnahmen treffen sollte. Dort war man noch dabei, aus der Umgebung Personal zusammenzuziehen, und die Laune meines Ansprechpartners war nicht besser geworden seit unserem letzten Telefonat.

»An Heidelberg habe ich eine offizielle Anfrage geschickt«, erklärte er mir knurrig. »Aber bisher ist nicht mal eine Antwort gekommen.«

»Ich kümmere mich gleich darum. Sie kriegen, was wir irgendwie entbehren können.«

»Na hoffentlich. Meine Leute sind nämlich auch froh, wenn sie mal ein freies Wochenende haben.«

Die Zuschauer wurden erst eine Dreiviertelstunde vor Beginn der Show ins Gebäude gelassen, erfuhr ich. »Dann werden die eine halbe Stunde lang bespaßt und müssen üben, auf Kommando zu lachen und zu klatschen. Wissen Sie überhaupt, wie diese Fernsehfritzen die Leute im Publikum unter sich nennen?«

Nein, das wusste ich nicht.

»Klatschvieh! Da sind die Leute stolz, dass sie einmal im Leben im Fernsehen kommen, und ziehen sich fein an und freuen sich wochenlang einen Wolf, und dann ... Klatschvieh! Ich weiß überhaupt nicht ...«

»Hergarden ist in einer Verfassung, in der ihm alles egal ist«, unterbrach ich seine verständliche Empörung. »Wahrscheinlich gibt er Graf jetzt auch noch die Schuld am Tod seines Bruders.«

Und lag damit vielleicht nicht ganz daneben.

Nachdem ich das Handy auf den Beifahrersitz zurückgelegt hatte, überlegte ich, was ich tun würde, wäre ich Fred Hergarden. Graf innerhalb des Pfalzbaus aufzulauern, war praktisch unmöglich, das hatte ich inzwischen eingesehen. Der Showstar wurde perfekt abgeschirmt, der Garderobenbereich war für nicht Autorisierte unerreichbar, schon um Graf das liebe »Klatschvieh« vom Hals zu halten. Selbst eine Waffe in den Saal zu schmuggeln, war nach Lage der Dinge ausgeschlossen. Später allerdings, nach der Show, würde Graf in der Tiefgarage in einen Wagen steigen, um sich zum Hotel fahren zu lassen. Auch dort gab es wieder eine Tiefgarage mit Lift direkt zur Etage, wo seine Suite lag.

Tiefgaragen waren nicht gut.

Tiefgaragen waren unübersichtlich, schlecht beleuchtet, hatten meist mehrere Ein- und Ausgänge. Zudem würde sich in Ludwigshafen dort unten nach der Veranstaltung eine Menge Menschen aufhalten. Aufgekratzte, gut gelaunte Menschen, ein großes Durcheinander von Fahrzeugen, die alle zur Ausfahrt drängelten – eine Horrorvorstellung für jeden Personenschützer. Ich beschloss, die Kollegen zu bitten, unmittelbar nach der Sendung ein besonders scharfes Auge auf den Fernsehstar zu haben und ihn wenn irgend möglich festzuhalten, bis die Tiefgarage sich geleert hatte, ob es diesem nun in den Kram passte oder nicht.

Während Grafs nächtlicher Fahrt von Ludwigshafen nach Heidelberg würde es für Hergarden eher schwierig sein, etwas zu unternehmen. Außer, er eröffnete unterwegs das Feuer auf Grafs Wagen. An einer roten Ampel zum Beispiel, irgendwo in Mannheim. Auf die Gefahr hin, dass die Leibwächter zurückschossen, was diese sicherlich tun würden. Beide waren im Besitz eines Waffenscheins. Beide schossen wahrscheinlich besser als der potenzielle Attentäter. Obwohl Hergarden im nahen Osten möglicherweise einige Erfahrung mit Handfeuerwaffen gesammelt hatte.

Ich überlegte, ob es Umwegstrecken gab, wo Grafs Wagen nicht so oft würde anhalten müssen. Das Problem, das wirklich große Problem bei allem war: Fred Hergarden hing nicht mehr am Leben. Er wollte jetzt nur noch eines, Rache. Der Albtraum jedes Personenschützers.

Vielleicht im Hotel?

Natürlich im Hotel!

Wäre ich Fred Hergarden, dann würde ich mir Zutritt zu Grafs derzeit verwaister Suite verschaffen, was sicherlich nicht einfach, aber auch nicht unmöglich war. Dort könnte ich dann stundenlang und seelenruhig warten, bis mein Todfeind auftauchte. Schon hielt ich das Handy wieder in der Hand.

33

Olivia Opelt konnte sich nur mit Mühe das Lachen verkneifen. Sie klang sehr viel entspannter als noch vor wenigen Stunden.

»Sie wollen was?«

»Sie haben mich schon richtig verstanden.«

»Nun gut. Ich werde Marcel Ihren Vorschlag unterbreiten. Aber ich kann mir nicht vorstellen, dass er gesteigerten Wert darauf legt, seine Räume von der Polizei filzen zu lassen.«

»Sie haben verstanden, dass Hergarden im Besitz einer Schusswaffe ist? Und vermutlich auch damit umgehen kann?«

»Herr Gerlach, ganz ehrlich, wir wissen Ihre Fürsorge zu schätzen. Es ist wunderbar, dass es Menschen wie Sie gibt, die ihre Aufgabe selbst am Wochenende so ernst nehmen. Aber Sie brauchen sich wirklich keine Sorgen zu machen. Herr Graf wird bestens bewacht.«

»Können Sie mir wenigstens versprechen, dass die Suite von den Leibwächtern durchsucht wird, bevor …«

»Ja, das kann ich Ihnen versprechen, ja. Sie können wirklich ganz unbesorgt sein. Inzwischen haben wir übrigens auch die Polizei in den Saal gelassen. Momentan suchen sie nach Sprengstoff, mit Hunden. Marcel ist noch niemals so gut bewacht worden wie heute. Überall werden Polizisten herumstehen, hat mir Ihr Kollege eben erklärt. Ein ausgesucht unsympathischer Zeitgenosse übrigens. Ich habe versucht, ihm klarzumachen, dass wir im Saal während der Show keine uniformierte Polizei akzeptieren können. Aber der Mann ist ungefähr so sensibel wie ein Ochsenhorn. Ich nehme an, den habe ich Ihnen zu verdanken?«

Warum tat ich mir das eigentlich an?, fragte ich mich, als ich das Handy zu Seite schmiss, wobei es vom Sitz abfederte und irgendwo im Fußraum landete. Warum machte ich mir Gedanken um das Wohlbefinden eines Menschen, der so offensichtlich keinen Wert auf meine Fürsorge legte?

Der zweite Albtraum jedes Personenschützers: ein Subjekt, das gar nicht beschützt werden will.

Zehn Minuten später stellte ich meinen unverwüstlichen Peugeot auf dem heute fast leeren Parkplatz der Heidelberger Polizeidirektion ab und lief die Treppen hinauf zu dem Büro, wo Vangelis saß. Sie hatte dasselbe gedacht wie ich.

»Im Grunde haben wir keine Chance«, sagte sie, als ich eintrat, und lächelte mir erschöpft entgegen. »Wie wollen wir jemanden beschützen, der nicht kooperiert? Und gleichzeitig in einem solchen Maß exponiert ist wie Graf?«

Ich griff mir einen Besucherstuhl und setzte mich rittlings darauf.

»Wenn Sie Hergarden wären«, sagte ich. »Sie wollen Graf an den Kragen. Und wenn es das Letzte ist, was Sie in Ihrem Leben tun. Sie wollen, dass er tot ist. Wie Vicky. Wie Ihr Bruder. Wie würden Sie es machen? Und wo würden Sie sich bis dahin verstecken?«

Sie lehnte sich zurück, sah zur Decke, schloss die dunklen Augen. »Verstecke gibt es Tausende. Ich nehme an, er hat einen Wagen?«

»Der Mercedes seines Bruders steht vor dem Haus. Aber er kann natürlich einen Leihwagen …«

Sie beugte sich vor, ergriff einen Stift, machte sich eine Notiz. »Das werde ich gleich mal abfragen lassen.«

»In einem Hotel wird er sich nicht verstecken. Er kann sich an drei Fingern ausrechnen, dass wir als Erstes die Hotels abklappern.«

»Verwandte? Alte Freunde?«

»Er hat sein halbes Leben im Ausland verbracht.«

»Auch aus dem Ausland kann man heutzutage Freundschaften pflegen.«

Ich sah auf die Uhr: halb drei. »Es gibt einfach zu viele Möglichkeiten. Vielleicht, wenn wir viel Glück haben, läuft er einer Streife in die Arme. Aber ich fürchte, dazu ist er nicht dumm genug. Er hat sich drei Jahrzehnte lang in Krisengebieten aufgehalten, wo scharf geschossen wurde. Er weiß, wie man überlebt und wie man sich verteidigt.«

»Wo ist Graf jetzt?«

»Ich nehme an, im Pfalzbau.« Noch einmal sah ich auf die Uhr, weil ich schon wieder vergessen hatte, was ich eben gesehen hatte. Es war immer noch halb drei. Ich berichtete Vangelis, was ich über die Sicherheitsmaßnahmen des Senders wusste.

»In den Saal schafft er's also eher nicht«, sagte sie. »Schon gar nicht ohne Eintrittskarte.« Vangelis atmete durch die Zähne ein und aus. »Was macht Graf nach der Sendung?«

»Nach After-Show-Party ist ihm heute bestimmt nicht zumute. Er wird sich so schnell wie möglich ins Hotel fahren lassen.«

»Was ist mit seinem Zimmer?«

»Er hat eine standesgemäße Suite. Aber wir dürfen nicht rein. Und ich kriege keinen Durchsuchungsbeschluss, bei der momentanen Faktenlage.«

»Im Europäischen Hof ist er abgestiegen?« Klara Vangelis griff zum Hörer, telefonierte kurz auf Griechisch mit jemandem, notierte sich eine Nummer, telefonierte wieder auf Griechisch, notierte sich eine weitere Nummer. Zwei Minuten später legte sie auf.

»Fahren wir hin«, sagte sie mit unbewegter Miene und erhob sich. »Die Tochter einer meiner Cousinen hat früher dort im Housekeeping gearbeitet. Sie hat immer noch Kontakt zu einigen der Angestellten. Einer davon hat eine Codekarte, mit der man in jedes Zimmer kommt.«

Große Hotels haben den Vorteil, dass das Personal niemals die Gesichter aller Gäste kennen kann. Wenn man mit selbstbewusster Miene und angeregt plaudernd an der Rezeption vorbeischlendert, wird man nicht nach seinem Namen gefragt. Vangelis hatte zudem das Handy am Ohr und telefonierte halblaut mit dem Mann, der uns zwei Stockwerke weiter oben erwartete. Einer der Gold-und-Spiegel-glänzenden Aufzüge stand offen und brachte uns lautlos hinauf.

Der Hotelangestellte, mit dem wir verabredet waren, trug einen hellgrauen Anzug und hatte fast weißblondes Haar. Er wechselte einige launige Worte mit Vangelis, die ich nicht verstand. Offenbar war er trotz der hellen Haare ebenfalls Grieche. Man lachte. Wir schüttelten Hände. Er öffnete eine Tür, und wir betraten ein Treppenhaus, das nicht annähernd so nobel war wie der Rest des Fünfsternehotels. Wir mussten bis ganz nach oben, zur Penthousesuite. Die beiden unterhielten sich weiter und lachten viel. Ich verstand nicht ein Wort und fühlte mich in diesen Sekunden weniger als Chef denn als geduldeter Mitläufer.

Dann standen wir wieder auf dickem Teppichboden, der jegliches Geräusch aufzusaugen schien. Eine Codekarte, ein Pieps, und wir betraten Marcel Grafs derzeitiges Reich. Atemberaubender Luxus umgab uns. Glänzendes Parkett, edles weißes Mobiliar, Licht überall. Wir befanden uns direkt unter dem Dach, fast alle Wände waren schräg, aber dem Innenarchitekten war es gelungen, den Eindruck zu erzeugen, als wäre dieser Umstand gewollt. Die Suite war vermutlich doppelt so groß wie meine eigene Vierzimmeraltbauwohnung.

»Voilà«, sagte der Grieche strahlend zu mir. »Hier wären wir.«

Das Erste, woran mein Blick hängen blieb, waren drei noch originalverpackte Cognacflaschen auf einem Sideboard. Alle von der Marke, die ich zuletzt auf Rosalie Jordans Küchentisch gesehen hatte. Daneben protzte ein riesiger Blumenstrauß, von dem schon das eine oder andere Blütenblatt abgefallen war.

»Im Prinzip kommt jeder zumindest bis vor die Tür«, sagte ich zu dem Griechen, dessen Vorname Andreas zu sein schien.

Er nickte zuvorkommend. »Wenn Sie durch die Tiefgarage kommen, müssen Sie an zwei Überwachungskameras vorbei. Aber auf die Monitore sieht kaum mal jemand. Schon gar nicht, wenn an der Rezeption Stoßzeit ist. Wenn Sie erst mal im Lift sind, kommen Sie problemlos bis ins dritte OG. Erst für das letzte Stockwerk brauchen Sie dann die Codekarte zur Suite, damit hier oben nicht Kreti und Pleti auf dem Flur herumläuft.«

»Aber übers Treppenhaus kommt man problemlos hinauf.«

Er rieb seine schlanken Hände aneinander, als wäre ihm kalt. »Da hängt natürlich auch wieder eine Kamera, aber wie schon gesagt ...«

»Wenn Herr Graf hier ist, stehen dann gewöhnlich seine Leibwächter vor der Tür?«

»Soweit ich weiß, nein. Die beiden haben Zimmer auf demselben Stock, und ich habe noch nie einen hier stehen sehen.«

Er zuckte lächelnd die Achseln unter dem perfekt sitzenden Jackett und rieb sich immer noch die Hände.

Einen anderen Weg als Lift und Treppenhaus gab es nicht, stellten wir fest.

»Wenn er ein gutes Gewehr mit Zielfernrohr hätte«, überlegte Vangelis mit Blick auf die breite Glastür zur Dachterrasse. Wir traten hinaus in die Sonne, die schon seit dem Morgen schien. Der Tag war fast so schön wie der Samstag vor zwei Wochen, als das ganze Elend begann.

»Da braucht er aber ein verdammt gutes Gewehr«, stellte ich fest, nachdem ich in die Runde geschaut hatte. »Und dann müsste er immer noch Präzisionsschütze sein.«

»Graf wird spätabends vermutlich nicht mehr auf die Terrasse gehen.«

»Es sei denn, er raucht.«

Wir sahen uns nach dem obligatorischen Aschenbecher um. Natürlich gab es gleich zwei. Einen Standaschenbecher direkt links neben der Glastür und einen weiteren auf dem sehenswerten Rattantisch, der aussah wie ein umgedrehter und in den Terrassenboden gerammter Kegel. Beide wirkten nicht, als wären sie schon einmal benutzt worden. Aber vermutlich wurden Aschenbecher in einem Haus wie diesem stündlich gereinigt und desinfiziert.

Wir gingen wieder hinein.

»Wir stellen zwei gute Leute ins Treppenhaus«, entschied ich. »Und Graf frage ich nicht um Erlaubnis.«

»Die Direktion müsste man aber schon ...«, warf der Mann im hellen Anzug ein.

Das Büro des Hoteldirektors, eines smarten Mannes Anfang vierzig mit unruhigen Glupschaugen, wirkte auf mich wie ein hanseatisches Seefahrtskontor. Das Gespräch verlief überraschend problemlos.

»Unser Gast wird wirklich nichts davon bemerken?«

»Meine Leute werden so diskret wie nur irgend möglich sein.«

»Sie verstehen, dass wir Herrn Graf in keiner Weise beunruhigen möchten.«

»Er wird sie nicht einmal zu Gesicht bekommen. Sie werden sich die meiste Zeit eine halbe Treppe tiefer aufhalten. Von dort kriegt man besser mit, wenn weiter unten eine Tür zum Treppenhaus geöffnet wird.«

Er zögerte, zwinkerte, zögerte. Sein Rasierwasser war atemberaubend.

»Ich möchte auch nicht, dass morgen früh das halbe Personal Bescheid weiß ...«

»Auf der anderen Seite möchten Sie bestimmt auch keine Schießerei erleben. Und morgen früh eine halbe Hundertschaft Polizisten, die Ihre Suite auseinandernehmen, und daneben eine Menge Fernsehkameras, die ihnen dabei zusehen.«

Mit saurer Miene willigte er schließlich ein. Vangelis hatte schon das Handy am Ohr.

34

Inzwischen war es halb vier geworden, die Sonne versank schon wieder hinter den hohen Häusern, die die Straßen säumten. Keine fünf Stunden mehr bis zu *Grafs Abend*.

»Na dann«, sagte Vangelis, als sie in die Bergheimer Straße einbog. »Nicht vor der Show, nicht während der Show, nicht im Hotel ...«

»Bleibt noch: während der Fahrt nach Heidelberg. Das ist vielleicht unsere Schwachstelle.«

»Und wenn er sich einfach Zeit lässt? Wartet, bis sich die Aufregung wieder gelegt hat? Wir können Graf nicht ewig bewachen.«

»Hergarden hat keine Zeit. Er will es hinter sich bringen. Und außerdem: In dem Moment, in dem Graf Heidelberg verlässt, ist er nicht mehr unser Problem.«

»Die Waffe des Bruders war übrigens nicht angemeldet. Wir wissen nicht, um was für einen Typ es sich handelt.«

»Die Munition im Nachttisch war fünfzehn Jahre alt. Aber funktionieren wird sie vermutlich noch.«

Wenig später saßen wir uns in meinem Büro gegenüber. Im Haus war es still. Durchs Fenster fiel ein letzter Streifen Sonne. Wurde rasch schmaler. Verlosch schließlich ganz. Die Fahndung nach Fred Hergarden war nach wie vor erfolglos.

Nur zur Sicherheit, nur um wirklich nichts zu versäumen, rief ich noch einmal in Ludwigshafen an. Dort hatte man inzwischen mit einiger Mühe die für den Abend notwendigen Kräfte akquiriert. Eine Menge Kolleginnen und Kollegen musste wieder einmal ein freies Wochenende in den Wind schreiben und ihrem Überstundenkonto weitere Stunden hinzufügen. Viele wurden von Revieren aus dem Umland abgezogen. Auch Heidelberg stellte acht Beamte zur Verfügung. Ich widerstand dem Wunsch, selbst im Pfalzbau nach dem Rechten zu sehen. Was dort zu tun war, würde in den kommenden Stunden von anderen getan werden.

»Und nun?« Klara Vangelis sah auf die kleine silberne Uhr an ihrem Handgelenk. Mir wurde bewusst, dass sie zu den wenigen Menschen zählte, die noch Armbanduhren trugen. Seit jeder ein Handy mit sich führte, schienen Armbanduhren plötzlich aus der Mode gekommen zu sein.

»Fahren Sie nach Hause, und gehen Sie mit Ihrem kleinen Konstantin spazieren. Jetzt können wir nur noch warten und hoffen.«

»Meine Mutter war schon mit ihm an der frischen Luft.«

»Dann spielen Sie mit ihm. Wie alt ist er denn inzwischen?«

»Knapp fünf Monate.«

»Wie die Zeit vergeht.« Ich stemmte mich hoch. »Ich mache jetzt Schluss. Es hat keinen Sinn, hier herumzusitzen. Mein Handy bleibt an.«

Nun gut, die Musik war ein wenig gewöhnungsbedürftig, aber zu meiner Überraschung gefiel mir Marcel Grafs Show fast von Beginn an. Es war nicht die im Fernsehen heute übliche Hektik, keine ständigen Licht- und Perspektivenwechsel, keine rasenden Kamerafahrten, die einen schwindlig machten, keine zotigen Witze zu Lasten von Menschen, die sich nicht wehren konnten. Das Publikum klatschte an den richtigen Stellen, lachte brav über Grafs Eröffnungsscherz, dessen Pointe ich nicht verstand.

Die Bühne war völlig dunkel, ein einziger Spot ruhte auf dem Hauptdarsteller, der einsam wirkte im gnadenlosen Licht, verloren. An seiner Stirn klebte ein extragroßes Pflaster, sein rechter Arm hing kraftlos in einer Schlinge, das Lächeln wirkte gezwungen, als er das Publikum im Saal und vor den Bildschirmen zu Hause begrüßte. Er spielte seine Rolle mit bewundernswerter Präzision: der bescheidene Held, der noch sehr erschöpft ist von seiner Großtat, aber dennoch klaglos seine Pflicht erfüllt. Zwei Tage, nachdem er mit knapper Not einen Mordanschlag überlebt hat.

»Nie habe ich mich so sehr gefreut, hier vor Ihnen zu stehen«, sagte er und griff mit der linken Hand wie zufällig an das Pflaster.

Tosender Beifall.

»Ich muss Sie um Verständnis bitten für mein lädiertes Aussehen und die umfangreichen Sicherheitsmaßnahmen, die nun leider Gottes ...«

Rasender Beifall.

»Sicherheitsmaßnahmen, die ich persönlich für etwas ... nun ja ... übertrieben halte. Andererseits verstehe ich selbstverständlich die Sorgen der Menschen, die die Verantwortung tragen müssen. Wir dürfen nicht zulassen, dass einzelne Verrückte über unser aller Leben ...«

Exorbitanter Beifall.

Die Kamera schwenkte über den Saal, zoomte wichtig dreinschauende Polizisten heran, verweilte kurz auf dem hübschen Gesicht einer kleinen, dunkelhaarigen Kollegin, die die Uniformmütze verwegen schräg auf dem Kopf und ein freches Lächeln im Gesicht trug. Hatte es nicht geheißen, man wünsche auf keinen Fall Polizei im Saal? Bestimmt ein später Regieeinfall. Und die Dunkelhaarige war vermutlich keine Kollegin, sondern eine junge Schauspielerin, die man zu Dekorationszwecken in eine Uniform gesteckt hatte.

Das Licht wurde heller, Musik setzte ein. »I did it my way«, gesungen von einer überschlanken Rothaarigen mit enormer

Stimme, deren Namen ich nie zuvor gehört hatte. »I did what I had to do and saw it through without exemption.« Eine kleine Balletttruppe legte dazu eine beeindruckend perfekte Show hin. Nichts an diesem makellosen, farbenfrohen Bild ließ ahnen, dass die Bühne noch vor wenigen Tagen ein Trümmerfeld gewesen war. »I faced it all and I stood tall and did it my way.«

Dann war plötzlich Graf wieder da, begrüßte unter verdutztem Beifall seinen ersten Gast: den Chef der Ludwigshafener Polizeidirektion, Manfred Vogel, den ich sogar persönlich kannte. Man setzte sich – jeder mit einem Rotweinglas in der Hand – aufs berühmte gelbe Sofa, stieß an, nippte an den Gläsern, und Graf schaffte es mit wenigen Worten, eine entspannte Atmosphäre zu schaffen. Fast, als säße man als heimlicher Dritter mit dabei, bei diesen zwei angeregt plaudernden Menschen.

»Herr Vogel, eine Frage, die mich schon lange – und ganz besonders heute beschäftigt: Gibt es so etwas wie böse Menschen?«

Vogel zog ein nachdenkliches Gesicht und musste sich zweimal räuspern, bevor er ein Wort herausbrachte. »Das ist ein Thema, auf die die Menschheit bis heute keine endgültige Antwort gefunden hat. Was ist das denn überhaupt: böse?«

»Jesus sagt: Liebe deine Feinde. Wenn dir jemand auf die rechte Wange schlägt, halte ihm auch deine linke hin. Was nun nicht heißen soll, dass ich den Mann, der mich kürzlich überfallen hat, auffordern möchte ...«

Der Rest seines Satzes ging in Gelächter und Beifall unter.

Vogel hatte inzwischen zu einer brauchbaren Antwort gefunden. »Unser Strafgesetzbuch kennt das Prinzip der Rache schon lange nicht mehr, was im Prinzip ja heißt ...«

»Strafe nützt letztlich nur dann, wenn sie zur Besserung des Täters beiträgt. Zu seiner Resozialisierung, wie man heute so schön sagt ...«

So ging es eine Weile hin und her. Graf zeigte sich väterlich verständnisvoll, weitsichtig, alles andere als rachelüstern, was ihm weitere Sympathiepunkte und noch mehr Beifallsstürme einbrachte. Dann gab es wieder Musik und anschließend eine Spaßnummer mit einem Pfälzer Original, dessen Namen ich ebenfalls nicht kannte. Logischerweise ging es meist um Wein und ein kleines bisschen auch um jugendfreien Winzersex. Das dankbare Klatschvieh krümmte sich stellenweise vor Lachen. Mein Handy surrte auf dem Couchtisch.

Olivia Opelt: »Nur, falls es Sie interessiert: Wir haben eben die zehn Millionen gerissen!«

»Über zehn Millionen Zuschauer?«

»Das hatten wir seit fünf Jahren nicht mehr! Und das Tollste – bisher gibt es kaum Schwund. Die Leute bleiben dran. Trotz des etwas hakeligen Themas. Und der Oberhammer: Im Ersten läuft parallel der neue James Bond, und die haben zwei Millionen weniger als wir!«

Vom zweiten Gast des Abends kannte ich immerhin den Namen: Agneta Björndal, Skandalnudel des leichten schwedischen Films der Siebzigerjahre. Die Filme, an denen sie mitgewirkt hatte, trugen Titel wie *Drei Schwedinnen an der Riviera* oder *Drei Schwedinnen in Paris*. Frau Björndals Paraderolle war das durchtriebene Dummchen vom nordschwedischen Bergland gewesen. Sie war gut im Geschäft bis zu dem Tag, als sie um ein Haar Opfer eines Mordanschlags wurde. Eines Mordanschlags aus heiterem nordischem Himmel. Auf einer Schäreninsel vor Stockholm, in einem Örtchen, wo niemand je auf die Idee gekommen wäre, die Haustür abzuschließen, wenn er für ein paar Tage mit seinem Boot aufs Festland fuhr. Wo seit Menschengedenken außer kleineren Ehestreitereien nichts vorgefallen war. Die damals schon nicht mehr ganz junge Schauspielerin hatte stilgerecht nackt in einem Liegestuhl vor ihrem natürlich ochsenblutrot gestrichenen Sommerhäuschen gelegen, als ein Mann das Feuer auf sie eröffnete. Ein Mann, den man heute als Stalker bezeichnen würde. Buchstäblich Hunderte von Briefen hatte er seiner Angebeteten geschrieben. Liebesbriefe, Gedichte, halbe Romane. Sie hatte ihm – was im Nachhinein ein Fehler war – anfangs einige Male knapp, aber höflich geantwortet. Später nicht mehr. Frau Björndal wurde von drei Kugeln aus einem sechsschüssigen Revolver getroffen. Zwei Schüsse gingen daneben. Die letzte Patrone hatte der Täter für sich selbst aufgespart. Heute war Agneta Björndal zweiundsiebzig Jahre alt und noch immer gezeichnet von ihrer persönlichen Apokalypse, die damals von einer Sekunde auf die nächste über sie hereingebrochen war.

Inzwischen war mir klar geworden, was Grafs Konzept war: Thema des Abends war der Mordanschlag auf ihn selbst. Er und seine Leute hatten es geschafft, innerhalb von vielleicht vierundzwanzig Stunden eine völlig neue Sendung auf die Beine zu stellen. Man sprach zunächst über die Schauspielerei. Lachte zusammen über die Torheiten, die man damals begangen hatte. Aber natürlich landete man bald beim Thema: Wie geht es einem Menschen, den jemand töten wollte? Wie wird man mit so etwas fertig?

»Überhaupt nicht«, erwiderte die Schauspielerin, die fast perfekt Deutsch sprach und, wie ich bald merkte, alles andere als dumm war. »Mit so etwas wird man niemals wirklich fertig. Auch heute noch fahre ich manchmal nachts aus dem Schlaf und bin schweißgebadet.«

Dieses Mal hielt man keine Weingläser in der Hand. Vielleicht trank die Schwedin keinen Alkohol.

»Hasst du den Täter?«

»Hassen?« Sie sah Graf erstaunt an. »Vielleicht wäre es einfacher, wenn ich ihn hassen könnte. Aber für mich ist der Mann ein armer, zutiefst unglücklicher Mensch gewesen. Vielleicht trage ich ja mit den Rollen, die ich damals spielte, auch ein wenig Schuld an dem Drama. Er war verliebt. Hoffnungslos und zutiefst unglücklich verliebt. Mir ist ein Unglück geschehen, verstehst du? Könnte ich einen Baum hassen, gegen den ich auf winterlichem Glatteis gerutscht bin?«

»Das ist eine bewundernswerte Einstellung, Agneta.«

»Ich finde, es ist die normalste Einstellung der Welt, Marcel. Das Alte Testament ist seit zweitausend Jahren Geschichte.«

Man kam wieder zur Schauspielerei. Erinnerte sich an die Wenigen, die man noch kannte, und vergaß nicht der Unzähligen zu gedenken, die sich mit gelegentlichen Engagements und vielen Nebenjobs über Wasser hielten. Kurz bevor es begann, ein wenig langatmig zu werden, strahlte Graf seinen Gast an und bedankte sich für das interessante Gespräch.

»Möchtest du dem Publikum noch etwas sagen, Agneta?«

Sie wirkte überrascht. Verwirrt. Offenbar war die Frage nicht abgesprochen. »Etwas sagen?«, murmelte sie. »Ja ... Ich ... Es gibt etwas, das ich bis heute nicht begreife. Ich habe noch nie darüber gesprochen. Aber es geht und geht mir nicht aus dem Kopf. Carl, so hieß er ...«

»Du nennst deinen Beinahe-Mörder beim Vornamen?«

»In Schweden nennen wir uns alle beim Vornamen. Carl hat sich in den Kopf geschossen ... und die Polizei hat den ... die Waffe erst nach Tagen ... im Wasser ... fast fünfzig Meter von der Stelle entfernt, wo er stand ...«

»Das heißt, er hat quasi noch im Tod die Waffe weggeworfen?«

Sie nickte fahrig. »Und ich frage mich jede Nacht vor dem Einschlafen, wozu? Jede Nacht. Wozu hat er das getan? Und so weit? Fünfzig Meter, das ist doch sehr weit? Oder ist sie vielleicht irgendwie durch den Rückstoß ...? Ist so etwas möglich? Es ist vollkommen dumm, ich weiß, aber diese Kleinigkeit, sie lässt mir einfach keine Ruhe.«

Dieses Mal blieb der Saal völlig ruhig. Das Licht auf die gelbe Couch verdämmerte. Musik setzte wieder ein. Auch ich war sprachlos. Versuchte, mir die Szene vorzustellen. Ein Mann, der fünf Schüsse auf die unglückliche Liebe seines Lebens abgegeben hat, auf die schöne Frau, die er niemals, niemals besitzen würde. Die letzte Kugel hat er sich durch die Schläfe gejagt. Und dann wirft er – vermutlich im Zusammenbrechen – die Waffe ins Meer. Nein, auch ich konnte mir keinen Reim darauf machen.

Irgendwann wurde mir bewusst, dass ich diese Sendung, die ich mir unter normalen Umständen nie im Leben angetan hätte, rundum genoss. Graf war ein Genie darin, sich in Sekundenbruchteilen auf einen neuen Gesprächspartner einzustellen, sich im richtigen Moment zurückzunehmen und den anderen reden zu lassen, das Thema exakt dann zu wechseln, wenn es zwei Sätze später langweilig geworden wäre, einem Gespräch immer wieder einen originellen Schwenk zu geben, der niemals gekünstelt wirkte. Und zehn Millionen liebten den Mann an diesem Abend für das, was er tat. Dafür, dass es ihn gab. Am Ende konnte ich nicht anders: Ich musste ihn ein wenig bewundern.

Als die letzte Musik lief und die Balletttruppe noch einmal alles gab, zeigten die Kameras ein ehrlich begeistertes Publikum, glückliche Menschen, die größtenteils stehend klatschten, lächelnde Polizisten, denen sichtlich zu warm war in ihren Uniformen, die verschmitzt und zugleich geschmeichelt in die Kamera grinsende Nicht-Kollegin, die man einfach mögen musste. Und ich? Ich fühlte mich pudelwohl und bestens unterhalten.

Wieder surrte mein Handy.

»Gegen Ende haben wir ein wenig abgebaut«, berichtete Grafs Assistentin ausgelassen. »Aber sogar in der letzten Minute lagen wir immer noch über neun Millionen. Damit wäre mancher *Tatort* glücklich!«

»Sagen Sie Ihrem Chef, es hat mir sehr gefallen.«

»Oh, das sage ich ihm gerne. Er wird sich freuen, das weiß ich. Und das meine ich ehrlich. In unserem Geschäft ist man ja leider nicht so oft ehrlich. Außerdem ...«

»Ja?«

»Bitte verzeihen Sie, wenn ich in den letzten Tagen nicht immer nett zu Ihnen war. Wir haben hier unter einem irrsinnigen Druck gestanden. Ich hoffe, Sie sind nicht allzu sauer auf mich.«

»Ich war und bin nicht sauer. Aber es ist noch nicht zu Ende. Sagen Sie Ihrem Chef bitte, sein Publikum würde ihn mehr als je zuvor vermissen, wenn ihm etwas zustoßen sollte.«

»Heute Abend war der Durchbruch. Ein Neustart. Ein völlig anderes Konzept, ernst, mit Tiefgang – und es hat voll eingeschlagen. Wir sind alle so unsagbar erleichtert. Was Sie nicht wissen ...«

»Doch, ich weiß es. Ihre Sendung stand auf der Kippe.«

»Ich hätte mir zum Quartalsende einen neuen Job suchen können. Und viele andere mit mir. Jetzt werden wir erst mal eine riesengroße Flasche Sekt knallen lassen. Falls Sie Lust und Durst haben ...«

Ich verzichtete dankend. »Aber Sie könnten mir einen Gefallen tun.«

»Der wäre?«

»Schicken Sie mir eine SMS, wenn er im Hotelzimmer ist?«

»Das mache ich. Fest versprochen. Und ... danke noch mal. Für alles. Ich möchte Ihren Job nicht haben.«

»Ich Ihren auch nicht.«

Wir verabschiedeten uns heiter. Als wäre alles schon zu einem guten Ende gekommen.

35

Die SMS piepste erst nachts um Viertel nach zwölf. Ich hatte schon geschlafen, jedoch ständig auf den erlösenden Ton gewartet. Die Sektflasche schien wirklich groß gewesen sein.

»Sind angekommen«, schrieb Grafs Assistentin. »Alles in bester Ordnung.«

Ich war gerade wieder beruhigt eingedämmert, als mein Handy sich erneut meldete. Dieses Mal war es keine Kurznachricht, sondern ein Anruf von unbekannter Nummer. Ich ärgerte mich, weil ich wieder einmal vergessen hatte, den Quälgeist leise zu stellen, hatte den Daumen schon auf dem roten Knopf, drückte schließlich doch den grünen.

»Ich bin's«, sagte eine heisere Stimme. »Sie wissen schon.«

»Wo stecken Sie? Wir müssen unbedingt reden.«

»Können wir. Machen wir. Ich bin bei ihm. Er sitzt hier neben mir. Und es geht ihm nicht besonders, ehrlich gesagt.«

Jetzt saß ich senkrecht und hellwach im Bett. Mein Puls hämmerte.

Etwas war schiefgegangen.

Etwas war katastrophal schiefgegangen.

»Graf?«

»Wer sonst? Kommen Sie, aber schnell. Nicht, dass er mir vor Angst noch krepiert. Wie mein Bruder. Nicht, dass er die Fliege macht, bevor er Ihnen gesagt hat, was er zu sagen hat.«

»Ich ... muss ... Ich habe schon geschlafen. Muss mich erst anziehen. Geben Sie mir eine Viertelstunde.«

»Viertelstunde reicht nicht. Wir sind nicht in Heidelberg.«

»Nein? Wo denn?«

»In Ludwigshafen. Hotel Excelsior. Zimmer zwölf null fünf. Und jetzt machen Sie hin. Sieht wirklich schon ein bisschen schlapp aus, der Herr Fernsehstar.«

»Machen Sie keinen Unsinn!«

Fred Hergarden lachte trocken. »Ich habe mein Leben lang Unsinn gemacht. Aber heute nicht. Heute mache ich endlich mal was richtig Vernünftiges.«

»Ich will ihn sprechen.«

Zwei Sekunden später hörte ich Marcel Grafs erschöpfte Stimme, die jeden Klang verloren hatte.

»Herr Gerlach, bitte«, krächzte er. »Er hat ... er hat eine Pistole. Er ist völlig ... ich ...«

»Genug«, schnarrte Hergarden. »Keine Tricks, verstanden? Die Knarre ist voll geladen, neun Schuss, und glauben Sie mir, ich weiß, wo man drücken muss.«

Als ich zwei Minuten später die Treppe hinabstürmte, trillerte mein Handy erneut. Olivia Opelt.

»Gott sei Dank, dass Sie Sie endlich ...«, schrie sie. »Ich habe schon zehnmal ... aber es war dauernd ...«

»Hergarden, ich weiß es schon.«

»Er ist im Hotelzimmer!«

»Ich dachte, sein Zimmer ist in Heidelberg?«

Ich hatte das untere Ende der Treppe erreicht, riss die Haustür auf. Kalte Luft stürzte mir entgegen. Tat mir gut. Machte mich hoffentlich endgültig wach.

»Es ... Es ist mein Zimmer«, schluchzte Grafs Assistentin. »Ich ... Wir glaubten ...«

Ich rannte den Gehweg hinunter zu meinem Wagen.

»Liege ich richtig mit dem, was ich jetzt vermute?«

»Ja.«

»Haben Sie schon die Polizei informiert?«

»Ich dachte, ich rufe gleich Sie an. Dann muss ich nicht so viel erklären, dachte ich.«

Inzwischen hatte ich den Peugeot erreicht, bekam den Schlüssel erst beim dritten Anlauf ins Schloss, fiel auf den Sitz, startete mit der rechten Hand den Motor, während die linke das Handy hielt.

»Wo sind Sie jetzt?«

»Im Flur. In Sicherheit. Er ... er hat mich ... rausgeschickt und ...«

»Ich brauche zwanzig Minuten«, rief ich. »Wenn ich mich über sämtlichen Verkehrsregeln hinwegsetze. Muss jetzt auflegen. Bleiben Sie erreichbar.«

Sekunden später bog ich mit quietschenden Reifen auf die Lessingstraße ein. Glücklicherweise war mein Kombi das einzige Auto weit und breit. Klara Vangelis nahm dieses Mal erst nach dem zehnten Tuten ab und klang verschlafen. Was sich innerhalb der nächsten Sekunden änderte.

»Ich brauche alles, was Sie auftreiben können, das volle Programm. Sie unternehmen nichts, bevor ich da bin.«

»Was haben Sie vor?«

»Das überlege ich mir, wenn ich auf der Autobahn bin. Versuchen Sie eine Stelle zu finden, von wo man in das Zimmer hineinsehen kann.«

»Das Excelsior ist ein Hochhaus. Zwölfhundertfünf dürfte ziemlich weit oben sein.«

»Versuchen Sie es trotzdem.«

»Ich organisiere Ihnen Begleitschutz, damit Sie nicht am Ende noch von einer Streife gestoppt werden.«

Drei Minuten später saß ich in einem Streifenwagen mit Blaulicht, der mit über zweihundert Stundenkilometern über die Autobahn in Richtung Westen jagte. Einer weiterer folgte uns mit einigem Abstand. Weit im Westen glühte der Himmel, als loderte dort ein Großbrand. Bald schon das Ortschild, ein dritter Streifenwagen war plötzlich vor uns, Mannheimer Kollegen, Ortskundige, übernahmen die Führung. In halsbrecherischem Tempo ging es durch die glücklicherweise menschenleere Stadt, ich wurde hin- und hergeworfen wie ein Gepäckstück, überall gelb blinkende Ampeln, hie und da Nebelschwaden, ein einsames Taxi, kreischende Reifen, die enge Kurve zur Konrad-Adenauer-Brücke.

Keine fünf Minuten später setzte der Streifenwagen vor uns den Blinker und bremste, dass es qualmte.

Ein schmaler, rechts und links von Betonwänden begrenzter Parkplatz. Viele dunkle Autos. Links ein Hochhaus.

Das Excelsior.

Vor dem hell erleuchteten Eingang standen mehrere Polizeifahrzeuge, alle mit funkelnden Blaulichtern. Überall Kollegen in Uniform. Als ich aus dem Wagen sprang, war ich umringt von erwartungsvollen, erschrockenen, ratlosen Gesichtern.

»Ich gehe rein«, rief ich in die Runde, ohne stehen zu bleiben. Jeder hier wusste, wer ich war.

»Ist das nicht zu riskant?«, fragte der Ranghöchste der Ludwigshafener Kollegen, ein beleibter Hauptkommissar, der mir die Glastür aufhielt. »Es heißt, er ist bewaffnet.«

»Ist er auch. Aber ich denke nicht, dass es für mich gefährlich ist.«

»Der Mann ist ein Desperado.«

Ja, das war Hergarden wohl: ein Mensch ohne Hoffnung. Das machte ihn gefährlich, aber nicht skrupellos.

»Vor der Tür oben stehen schon ein paar von uns. Das Horchgerät müsste jeden Moment kommen. Damit können wir wenigstens durch die Tür mithören.«

»Sie halten still, bis ich laut und deutlich: ›Totale Scheiße!‹ sage.«

»Totale Scheiße?«, fragte er verblüfft. »Das ist das Codewort für den Zugriff?«

»Was Besseres fällt mir auf die Schnelle nicht ein.«

Gleißendes Licht. Weicher Teppichboden.

An der Rezeption ein blasses, schmales Mädchengesicht.

Die Tür zum rechten Aufzug stand offen.

36

»Wer ist da?«, fragte Hergardens raue Stimme hinter der Tür.

»Gerlach«, antwortete ich nicht weniger heiser.

»Damit Sie es wissen: Er hat den Pistolenlauf am Kopf. Ich schließe jetzt auf. Machen Sie irgendeinen Blödsinn, und das ZDF hat einen Quotenbringer weniger.«

»Ich bin allein. Ich bin unbewaffnet. Ich mache keinen Blödsinn.«

»Und ich bin kein Idiot. Sie sind nicht allein. Versuchen Sie bloß nicht, mich zu verarschen.«

Leise Geräusche an der Innenseite der Tür.

Das Schloss knackte.

Die Tür öffnete sich einen Spalt.

Ich schob sie vorsichtig auf, trat ein. Im Zimmer war es dämmrig. Nur ein Lämpchen neben dem breiten Bett spendete Licht. Die weinroten Samtvorhänge waren zugezogen. Hergarden war – während ich eintrat – bis zur gegenüberliegenden Wand zurückgewichen, hielt seinen ehemaligen Freund als Schutzschild vor sich, den Unterarm um dessen Hals gepresst, und drückte die Mündung einer schweren Automatic an Grafs Schläfe. Mein Blick zuckte durch das verglichen mit der Suite im Europäischen Hof fast karge Zimmer. Ein zerwühltes, breites Doppelbett, edel dunkelblau bezogen, eine Champagnerflasche, zwei noch halb volle Sektschalen auf einem Tischchen. Muffige Schlafzimmerluft. Der Duft von Olivia Opelts Frühlingsparfüm schwebte noch in der Luft.

Ich hob die leeren Hände in Schulterhöhe und sagte ruhig: »Ich will keinen Stress. Wir finden eine Lösung. Machen Sie keinen Unsinn!«

»Schließen Sie ab!«, erwiderte Hergarden grob.

Ich gehorchte.

»Setzen Sie sich hin!«

»Wo?«

»Nehmen Sie den Stuhl da, setzen Sie sich mit dem Rücken an die Tür, und rühren Sie sich nicht!«

Mich an der Tür zu platzieren war ein verflucht kluger Schachzug. Hergarden hatte sich seinen Plan offenbar gründlich überlegt. Ich gehorchte mit gemessenen Bewegungen. Ruhe verbreiten, Deeskalation, das war jetzt das erste Ziel.

Als ich saß, ließ Hergarden seine schwitzende Geisel so plötzlich los, dass diese vorübergehend das Gleichgewicht verlor. Graf plumpste auf die Kante des Betts, hielt sich keuchend an dem runden Tischchen fest, auf dem der Champagner stand. Die Flasche schwankte, fiel jedoch nicht. Hergarden behielt ihn ständig im Blick, während er sich auf einen Polsterstuhl setzte, die Pistole immer auf die Stirn seiner Geisel gerichtet. Die Waffe war entsichert, das konnte ich selbst auf die Entfernung und bei schlechter Beleuchtung erkennen. Die stickige Luft machte das Atmen schwer. Graf schnaufte, als hätte er soeben einen Dauerlauf absolviert, rieb sich den Hals, hustete, röchelte und hustete wieder. An der Stirn und am rechten Ohr klebten immer noch Pflaster. Die Armbinde schien er schon nicht mehr nötig zu haben.

»Du machst vielleicht einen Scheiß, Freddy«, brachte er endlich heraus. »Noch ein bisschen fester, und du hättest mich erwürgt, Himmel noch mal!«

Das war entschieden der falsche Ton für einen Mann in seiner Lage.

»Wäre nicht schade drum«, versetzte Hergarden giftig. »Und ab jetzt hältst die Fresse. Heute redest du ausnahmsweise mal nur, wenn du gefragt wirst.«

»Was wollen Sie?«, fragte ich ihn so jovial, als wollte ich ihm sein Auto abkaufen.

In meinem Rücken hörte ich leise Kratzgeräusche. Vermutlich schob jemand das Mikrofon und hoffentlich auch eine dieser winzigen Kameras unter der Tür hindurch. Ich rutschte ein wenig auf meinem Stuhl herum, um die Geräusche zu überdecken. Aber Hergarden saß wohl zu weit entfernt, als dass er es hätte hören können.

»Was wollen Sie?«, fragte ich ein zweites Mal.

Hergarden warf mir einen bösen Seitenblick zu. Dann fixierte er wieder Graf. »Reden soll er.«

»Was denn?« Graf hatte seine Stimme wiedergefunden.
»Was willst du hören, verdammt?«

»Das weißt du ganz genau«, brummte Hergarden und
hob seine Waffe noch ein wenig höher. »Die Wahrheit
will ich hören. Sag einfach nur einmal im Leben die Wahrheit.«

Graf starrte auf seine bloßen Füße. Er trug nur die Hose
eines rot-beige karierten und offensichtlich frisch gebügelten
Seidenpyjamas. Sein Oberkörper war bis auf einige erstaunlich kleine Pflaster nackt. Die Haut schlaff und fahl wie die
eines sehr alten Mannes. Da war nichts mehr von der Kraft
und Frische, die er noch vor wenigen Stunden versprüht hatte.
Seine plötzlich sehr schütteren Haare waren wirr und feucht
vom Angstschweiß, das Gesicht zerknautscht, die Miene
wechselte ständig zwischen Fassungslosigkeit und Wut. Offenbar trug er in der Öffentlichkeit wirklich ein Toupet. Angst
schien er nicht zu haben.

Während der rasenden Fahrt hierher war mir klar geworden, was der kindische Plan gewesen war: Graf und seine
Assistentin, die offenbar zugleich sein Betthäschen war, hatten
den dunklen Mercedes allein nach Heidelberg geschickt und
waren mit dem Volvo die wenigen hundert Meter zu dem
Hotel gefahren, wo sich Olivia Opelts Zimmer befand. Hier,
hatten sie gedacht, würde Hergarden sie nicht finden, hier
wären sie in Sicherheit. Auch vor aufdringlichen Reportern,
die dem frisch aufpolierten Star spätestens beim Frühstück
auflauern würden. Aber Hergarden war schlauer gewesen, als
wir alle gedacht hatten.

Graf atmete einige Male tief ein und aus, als würde er sich
auf einen Auftritt vorbereiten. Schluckte. Sagte schließlich mit
kaltem Blick in den Lauf der Waffe: »Du bist das größte Arsch-
loch, das die Welt je gesehen hat, Fred. Und jetzt tu endlich
dieses blöde Ding weg.«

Mir stockte der Atem.

Die Pistole zitterte ein wenig. Hergarden knirschte so laut
mit den Zähnen, dass sogar ich es hören konnte. Aber er
drückte nicht ab. Er hatte sein Ziel noch nicht erreicht. »Du

hast sie umgebracht«, presste er nach Sekunden heraus. »Los, sag es endlich! Gib es endlich zu!«

»Überhaupt nichts gebe ich zu. Sie ist über ihre eigenen Füße gestolpert, blöd und besoffen, wie sie war. Außerdem, du hättest sie vielleicht nicht so oft allein lassen sollen, wenn du sie so geliebt hast, wie du behauptest.«

»Ich musste doch! Das Geld ... Wir haben das Geld gebraucht, das weißt du ganz genau. Bagdad war meine Chance, wir konnten ja nicht mal mehr die Miete ... wenn du und Sabeth uns nicht ...«

»Du warst immer ein Loser, Fred«, sagte Graf ruhig und geduldig, den Blick jetzt auf Hergardens verzerrtes Gesicht gerichtet. »Du warst ein Loser, du bist ein Loser und du wirst immer ein Loser bleiben. Und – nur der Ordnung halber, und weil die Polizei zuhört: Es stimmt nicht, ich habe sie nicht umgebracht. Die Kripo hat damals eindeutig festgestellt, dass es ein Unfall war.«

»Du hast sie gevögelt!«

In Grafs linkem Mundwinkel zuckte ein böses, verächtliches Lächeln, als er zischte: »Deine Vicky hat sich von jedem vögeln lassen, der was zu sagen und einen Schwanz zwischen den Beinen hatte. Auch das weißt du.«

»Jetzt mal bitte ganz langsam«, mischte ich mich ein. »Wir sind doch vernünftige ...«

»Du bist so eine Drecksau!« Hergarden brachte kaum noch die Zähne auseinander. Die Mündung der Pistole hatte sich in den letzten Sekunden Millimeter für Millimeter Grafs Stirn genähert. Jetzt berührte sie ihn fast. Und sie zitterte bedenklich. Graf blieb scheinbar völlig ruhig. »Du bist so eine unglaubliche, so eine ... eiskalte ... Drecksau.«

»Immer mit der Ruhe«, versuchte ich erneut mein Glück. »Man kann doch über alles reden. Wir sind doch erwachsene Menschen.«

Aber niemand hörte mir zu.

Grafs Blick war jetzt eiskalt.

»Drück doch ab, du Schwächling! Mach endlich ein Ende! Aber das kannst du nicht, was? Dazu fehlt dir der Mumm, oder? Mit einer Knarre rumfuchteln und große Reden schwingen, das kannst du. Aber wenn's ernst wird, dann bleibst du der Loser, der du immer warst.«

Hergardens Rechte wurde hart. Ich hörte auf zu atmen. Der Zeigefinger krümmte sich, und ich erwartete jede Sekunde den Knall. Aber ich konnte das Signal zur Stürmung des Zimmers nicht geben, da die Leute vom SEK mich hätten über den Haufen rennen müssen, um hereinzukommen. Außerdem konnte jetzt jede Bewegung, jedes Geräusch, jedes Wort Grafs Tod bedeuten. Die Wangenmuskeln des Fernsehstars waren angespannt, der Blick jedoch völlig ruhig und konzentriert. Hinter mir blieb es still. Auch jenseits der Tür hielt man vermutlich den Atem an. Grafs Blick war nicht einmal unfreundlich. Mit einer eisigen, spöttischen Ruhe und einem winzigen Grinsen im Mundwinkel saß er da und erwartete seinen Tod. Der nicht kam. Hergardens Zeigefinger entspannte sich allmählich wieder. Sekunden verstrichen. Hergarden drückte nicht ab. Das Zittern der Waffe in seiner Hand wurde schwächer.

»Du bist so ...«, flüsterte er und ließ die Pistole sinken. »Du warst immer schon ... Du hast sie gevögelt. Weil du gewusst hast, ich bin weit weg, du hast freie Bahn. Vicky war einsam, ja verdammt, einsam ist sie gewesen. Sie war euch dankbar, weil wir bei euch unterkriechen konnten. Vor allem Sabeth war sie dankbar. Dir nicht. Dir hat das Haus ja nicht gehört. Du, du hast immer nur alle ausgenutzt. Alle. Auf allen bist du rumgetrampelt. Du warst ja immer der Größte. Marçel Graf, der kommende Superstar. Dass ich nicht lache. Dass ich nicht lache!«

»Dann lach doch«, versetzte Graf mit Eiseskälte. »Lachen soll gesund sein. Tu dir keinen Zwang an.«

»Du hast sie gevögelt, wie du jede gevögelt hast, die die Beine breitgemacht hat, um ein bisschen weiter nach oben zu kommen. Wie viele sind schon mit dir ins Bett gestiegen für ein bisschen Karriere?«

»Man kann nicht nur im Bett vögeln, Fred. Solltest du in deinem Alter allmählich wissen. Obwohl, wahrscheinlich hast du nicht mehr allzu viel Erfolg bei den Frauen, so versifft, wie du aussiehst ...«

»Aber für deine Assistentin, da ist dir das Bett dann doch ...«

»Draußen ist es kalt, Fred. Und ich gebe zu, ich bin auch nicht mehr der Jüngste. Ich mag's gerne bequem, ja.«

Die Mündung des Pistolenlaufs näherte sich erneut Grafs Stirn. Der Zeigefinger krümmte sich wieder. »Wie viele, frage ich dich!«

»Hunderte? Ich habe sie nicht gezählt.« Graf wusste längst, dass er gewonnen hatte. »Verstehst du, deine Vicky war nur eine von Hunderten.«

Die beste Methode, einen Menschen zu töten, ist, es sofort zu tun. Mit Anlauf sozusagen. Ohne zu zögern. Ohne zu überlegen. Mit jeder Sekunde, die man zögert, wird die Schwelle höher, die man übersteigen muss.

»Du gibst es also zu?«, flüsterte Hergarden fassungslos. »Du hast sie ...?«

»Aber selbstverständlich habe ich sie.« Graf klang jetzt geradezu entspannt, obwohl die todbringende Pistolenmündung wieder seine Stirn berührte. »Und glaub bloß nicht, sie hätte sich lange bitten lassen. Sie wollte ins Fernsehen, und dafür hätte sie alles getan.«

»Du ...!«, keuchte Hergarden. »Du ...!«

Graf schien geradezu Spaß daran zu finden, den gehörnten Ehemann zu quälen. »Ja, ich habe sie gefickt. Von vorne und von hinten. Und – falls dich das tröstet – Vicky ist verdammt gut gewesen im Bett. Aber wem sage ich das.« Sekunden starrten sich die ehemaligen Freunde in die Augen. Hergarden zutiefst verzweifelt. Hoffnungslos. Offensichtlich nicht fähig, seinem Zeigefinger das Kommando zum Abdrücken zu geben. Graf ruhig und spöttisch.

»Ich hab sie gefickt, deine Vicky«, wiederholte er, als spräche er mit einem Kind, das die simpelste Wahrheit nicht begreifen kann. »Wie oft willst du es denn noch hören? Ich – habe – sie ...«

»Fresse«, presste Hergarden heraus. »Noch ein Wort, und ...«

Grafs Ton veränderte sich plötzlich: »Fred, jetzt hör mir mal bitte zu: Ich habe sie nicht umgebracht. Keine Ahnung, wen sie in der Nacht im Bett gehabt hat. Ob sie überhaupt wen im Bett gehabt hat. Die Polizei sagt, sie war allein. Und falls das nicht stimmen sollte – ich war's definitiv nicht, der's ihr in der Nacht besorgt hat. Ich war nämlich in Köln. Frag Sabeth. Sie wird es dir bestätigen. Ich war in Köln wegen der *Lindenstraße*. Vicky hat so gehofft, ich verschaffe ihr eine kleine Rolle. Ständig ist sie um mich rumgeschwänzelt, hat mir Kulleraugen gemacht, ist mir um den Bart gegangen. Hat aber leider nicht geklappt mit ihrer Rolle, wie du weißt. An dem Tag war die Absage gekommen. Darauf hat sie wahrscheinlich ein paar Gläser zu viel gekippt, und am Ende ist sie über ihre eigenen Füße gestolpert. Und das ist die ganze verdammte Scheißgeschichte. Hör mir genau zu, Freddy, ich war's nicht! Verstehst du meine Worte? Ich! War's! Nicht! Es war ein Unfall. Einfach nur ein dummer, blöder, ganz und gar unnötiger Unfall.«

»Es war kein Unfall! Im Leben nicht!«

»Wie kommst du denn darauf?«

»Der Flokati. Die Polizei hat mir Fotos gezeigt. Ich bin nicht gegangen, bis ich wenigstens die Fotos gesehen hatte. Und der kleine Flokati, der hat immer vor dem Fernseher gelegen und nie im Leben dort, wo Vicky dann … angeblich …«

Aus Hergardens Körper wich allmählich jede Anspannung. Er würde nicht schießen. Die Schwelle war zu hoch geworden. Es war vorbei. Und auch Graf wusste es. Seine Taktik war aufgegangen. Er war jedoch klug genug, nicht zu triumphieren. Ich wagte nicht einmal, mich zu räuspern. Ich musste diese verfluchte Automatic aus Hergardens Hand bekommen. Um ihn anzuspringen, war die Entfernung zu groß. Ich hätte quer durchs Zimmer hechten müssen, und in der Sekunde, die ich dazu brauchen würde, konnte alles Mögliche geschehen. Ich konnte auch nicht den Rambos vom Sondereinsatzkommando, die hoffentlich einen halben Meter hinter meinem Rücken Stellung bezogen hatten, freie Bahn geben. Auch die würden Zeit brauchen. Nicht viel. Aber zu viel.

Hergarden entspannte sich wieder. Aber er nahm die Waffe nicht herunter. Starrte jetzt am Kopf seines Feindes vorbei ins Nirgendwo. Im faltigen Gesicht zuckten alle möglichen Muskeln. Sein Atem ging flach und schnell. Er hatte versagt, wurde ihm in diesen ewigen Sekunden klar. Wieder einmal. Er war genau das, was Graf gesagt hatte: ein Verlierer. Auch Graf spürte die Veränderung. Und er trat sofort nach.

»Du bist nun mal ein Loser, Fred«, sagte er, nun fast freundlich und ohne jede Spur von Hohn. »Alles, was du anfasst, wird zu Scheiße. Das war damals so, das ist heute so und – na ja … Es wird wohl leider so bleiben.«

Jetzt zitterte die Waffe wieder. Hergarden sah Graf wieder in die Augen. Der erwiderte den Blick. Hielt ihm mühelos stand. Begann schließlich sogar zu grinsen. Hergarden nahm die Waffe langsam von der Stirn seines Todfeindes. Ließ sie jedoch nicht sinken.

»Lassen Sie das!«, brüllte ich, als ich endlich begriff, dass es eine Planänderung gegeben hatte. »Das ist doch totale Scheiße!«

Ich ließ mich samt Stuhl zur Seite kippen, um nicht von den Kollegen vom SEK zertrampelt zu werden. Sekundenbruchteile später krachte es überall. Die Tür flog mir in den Rücken. Gebrüll. Getrampel. Dann plötzlich Stille.

»Shit!«, sagte jemand leise. »So eine gottverdammte verkackte Scheiße!«

Hergarden lag am Boden, der halbe Hinterkopf fehlte. Aber nicht die schwarz vermummten Polizisten hatten geschossen. Er hatte die Waffe gegen sich selbst gerichtet. Da die Vorhänge dunkelrot waren, war hinter ihm überhaupt kein Blut zu sehen.

Graf starrte auf den Toten zu seinen Füßen. Den Toten, der einmal vor sehr langer Zeit sein Freund gewesen war. Jetzt war er käseweiß im Gesicht. Schwankte. Kippte vornüber.

»Obacht!«, rief jemand.

Der Kollege, der am nächsten stand, fing den halbnackten alten Mann auf. Zu zweit legten sie ihn aufs Bett. Deckten ihn zu.

»Wo bleibt der Arzt?«, fragte eine befehlsgewohnte Männerstimme vom Flur her.

»Waffen sichern und entladen«, befahl eine andere.

Der Arzt war schon da. Untersuchte Graf eilig und routiniert.

»Ein leichter Schock«, sagte er, als er sich wieder aufrichtete. »Wir bringen ihn sicherheitshalber ins Krankenhaus zur Beobachtung.«

Erst jetzt entdeckte ich, dass Grafs Gesicht über und über mit Blutspritzern besprenkelt war. Als hätte er plötzlich, mitten im Winter, Sommersprossen bekommen.

»Bringen Sie ihn nach Heidelberg«, sagte ich mit noch etwas unsicherer Stimme. »Ich will ihn morgen in meinem Zuständigkeitsbereich haben.«

Dann wählte ich mit bebenden Fingern die Nummer von Klara Vangelis, berichtete, was geschehen war. »Graf ist vorläufig festgenommen. Stellen Sie ihm zwei Kollegen vor die Tür. Und, das ist ganz wichtig: Er darf auf keinen Fall telefonieren. Und er kriegt auch keinen Besuch, außer ich habe es ausdrücklich genehmigt.«

»Mit welcher Begründung nehmen wir ihn fest?«

Ja, mit welcher Begründung? Immer noch hatte ich keinerlei Beweise gegen Graf in der Hand.

»Sagen wir erst mal: Er steht unter Mordverdacht. Und es besteht Verdunklungsgefahr. Außerdem lassen Sie bitte sofort seine beiden Leibwächter festnehmen.«

Gegen die hatte ich genug in der Hand: Verdacht auf Freiheitsberaubung in Tateinheit mit Körperverletzung mit Todesfolge. Außerdem Vertuschung einer Straftat und gefährlicher Eingriff in den Bahnverkehr. Und spätestens am Montag, wenn die Spurensicherer ihr Material ausgewertet hatten, würde ich auch genug Beweise zur Begründung eines Haftbefehls für Marcel Graf in Händen haben.

»Außerdem …« Um ein Haar hätte ich sie vergessen. »Frau Opelt. Anstiftung plus Beihilfe zu einer schweren Straftat.«

37

Es war elf Uhr am Sonntagvormittag, als ich Marcel Graf wiedersah. Ich hatte einige Stunden unruhig geschlafen, von wirren Träumen gestört und wieder und wieder geweckt. Immerhin hatte ich keine Albträume gehabt. Die würden in den folgenden Nächten kommen.

Als Erstes hatte ich nach dem Aufwachen auf meinem Handy eine schlechte Nachricht entdeckt: Johann Boll war verschwunden. Nach Aussage seines inzwischen festgesetzten Kollegen war er in der Nacht gar nicht erst mit nach Heidelberg gefahren, sondern in seinen Mercedes gestiegen und mit unbekanntem Ziel davongefahren. Das war ärgerlich, aber nun nicht mehr zu ändern.

Trotz der unruhigen Nacht fühlte ich mich erholt, als ich Grafs Krankenzimmer betrat, dessen Tür heute nicht von seinen Bodyguards, sondern von zwei uniformierten Polizisten bewacht wurde. Ich fühlte mich, als läge eine große, schwierige Sache endlich hinter mir. Graf war wach und ansprechbar. Der diensthabende Oberarzt hatte nichts gegen ein kurzes Gespräch einzuwenden.

»Es stimmt«, sagte Graf, nachdem wir Hände geschüttelt hatten. »Fred hatte leider recht. Ich habe sie getötet. Ich habe Vicky getötet. Aber es war kein Mord. Soweit ich das als juristischer Laie beurteilen kann, war es nicht einmal Totschlag.«

Für das, was er in der vergangenen Nacht durchgemacht hatte, sah er schon wieder erstaunlich frisch aus. Der Mann war härter, viel härter, als man vermutete, wenn man ihn als netten Plauderonkel im Fernsehen sah. Klara Vangelis stand schräg hinter mir. Wie üblich im selbst geschneiderten Designerkostüm.

»Ist es okay, wenn meine Kollegin bei unserem Gespräch dabei ist?«

»Nein« erwiderte Graf in einem Ton, der jede Diskussion sinnlos machte. »Sie können aber gerne ein Band mitlaufen lassen, wenn es Ihnen hilft.«

Was nun folgen würde, war noch keine offizielle Vernehmung, sondern ein informelles Gespräch, bei dem Graf die
Regeln diktierte. So gab ich Vangelis einen Wink. Sie verließ
das geschmackvoll eingerichtete Erste-Klasse-Krankenzimmer,
ohne eine Miene zu verziehen, und schloss die schallgedämmte
Tür von außen.

»Warum?«, fragte ich, während ich einen Stuhl aus hellem
Holz neben das Bett stellte und das Diktiergerät auf den
Nachttisch platzierte. »Warum haben Sie Vicky Hergarden
getötet?«

»Ich wollte die Beziehung beenden«, erwiderte Graf leise
und mit Blick zur Decke. »Ich musste dem Irrsinn ein Ende
machen. Die Geschichte lief völlig aus dem Ruder. Das wollte
ich ihr sagen. Das habe ich ihr gesagt, an dem Abend. Sie ist
sofort ausgerastet, damit hatte ich gerechnet. Aber dann ist
sie ... Vicky ist ausfällig geworden. Sehr ausfällig. Das konnte
sie nämlich verdammt gut, andere beleidigen, mit Worten nie-
dermachen. Außerdem hatte sie wirklich getrunken. Das ist
die Wahrheit. Sie hatte zu viel getrunken. Wie so oft.«

»Sie waren also nicht in Köln?«

Graf blinzelte. Schüttelte den Kopf. Atmete schwer.

»Nicht dass Sie denken, ich hätte sie verführt. Umgekehrt
war es. Als sie hörte, dass ich eventuell in die *Lindenstraße*
reinkomme, hat sie plötzlich an mir geklebt wie eine Zecke.
Wie eine überaus attraktive Zecke. Vicky wollte nach oben.
Mit allem, was sie zu bieten hatte, hat sie gekämpft. Aber sie
war schlecht. Als Schauspielerin. Im Bett nicht.«

Wieder musste ich ein Weilchen auf die Fortsetzung warten.

»Am Ende ist sie sogar tätlich geworden«, fuhr Graf endlich
fort, auch nach fast drei Jahrzehnten immer noch fassungslos.
»Völlig hysterisch. Hat geschrien und gekreischt und um sich
geschlagen. Unwürdig. Schrecklich war es. Unwürdig und
schrecklich.«

»Und Sie haben sie von sich gestoßen?«

Er nickte mit altem Grauen im Gesicht. »Ich musste mich ja
irgendwie wehren. Ja, ich habe sie weggestoßen. Sie ist gestolpert. Es war keine Absicht. Ich wollte nur nicht, dass sie mir

das Gesicht zerkratzt. Unten war Sabeth. Wie sollte ich ihr erklären …?«

»Ihre Frau hat es gewusst?«

»Wir hatten das, was man eine offene Zweierbeziehung nannte. Damals dachten wir, Treue sei eine Erfindung der Kirche, damit ihre Schäfchen nicht auf abwegige Gedanken kommen. In den höheren Kreisen hat man es mit der Treue ja nie so genau genommen. Da ist es immer schon kreuz und quer gegangen. Lesen Sie nur die Bibel.«

»Auch in Fürstenhäusern soll es hin und wieder gute Ehen gegeben haben.«

Endlich sah Graf mich an. Ernst und ratlos. »Gute Ehen sind so selten wie gute Menschen.«

»Wie ging es dann weiter?«

»Wie es weiterging? Ich habe festgestellt, dass Vicky tot war. Da war so unglaublich viel Blut. Ihr Hals …«

»Ich habe Fotos gesehen. Aber vielleicht wäre sie zu retten gewesen. Sie hätten einen Krankenwagen rufen müssen. Sie haben sie verbluten lassen.«

»Sie war nicht zu retten. Und eine Halsschlagader kann man nicht abdrücken, so viel verstehe sogar ich von Medizin. Es sei denn, man will den Verletzten erwürgen.«

»Sie hätten einen Arzt rufen müssen. Einen Krankenwagen.«

»Ja, Sie haben wahrscheinlich recht. Aber ich … ich war in Panik. Unten war Sabeth. Ich wusste mir nicht zu helfen. Und ich war mir sicher, dass Vicky nicht mehr zu retten war. Das Blut hat nur wenige Sekunden gespritzt, dann hat es schon aufgehört. Alles hat aufgehört. Puls, Atmung, einfach alles. Das Leben.«

»Und dann haben Sie Frau Hergarden einfach liegen lassen und sind nach unten gegangen.«

Graf senkte den Blick.

»Das war mindestens unterlassene Hilfeleistung.«

»Und längst verjährt.«

»Sie sind auch später nicht auf die Idee gekommen, die Polizei zu rufen, sondern haben das Ihrer Frau überlassen.«

»Ich hatte am nächsten Tag einen wichtigen Termin in Köln.

Einen wirklich wichtigen Termin. Musste schon morgens um sechs am Bahnhof sein. Sabeth meinte, ich solle mich nicht aufregen. Sie würde sich im Lauf des Vormittags um alles kümmern. Sabeth hat Vicky ... nun ja ... nicht gerade gehasst, aber ... Im Grunde war sie wohl doch ziemlich eifersüchtig.«

»Und Sie sind am nächsten Morgen seelenruhig nach Köln gefahren ...«

»Seelenruhig ist hier das völlig falsche Wort, Herr Gerlach. Ich war fix und fertig. Hatte praktisch nicht geschlafen in der Nacht. Entsprechend toll ist der Termin dann auch gelaufen. Auf gut Deutsch: Ich habe es vergeigt. Gründlich vergeigt.«

»Und um alles Weitere hat sich dann Ihre Frau gekümmert. Dass die Polizei kam. Dass der Arzt gerufen wurde, seltsam spät, übrigens. Dass eine falsche Anschrift ins Protokoll kam ...«

Erstaunt sah er auf. »War das so?«

Seine Überraschung schien echt zu sein. Aber wer konnte das wissen bei einem so ausgefuchsten Schauspieler?

Er schloss die Augen. »Wir ... Sabeth und ich ... wir haben nie wirklich über diese Nacht gesprochen. Es ging dann ja auch bald auseinander. Die Beziehung, es ging einfach nicht mehr. Nicht mit dieser Vorgeschichte. Vicky stand immer zwischen uns. Jede Sekunde. Ich habe später aus Köln ein anderes Angebot bekommen. Nicht so groß wie die *Lindenstraße*, aber doch interessant. Habe mir dort eine kleine Wohnung genommen, in Deutz draußen. Wir haben uns ohne Streit getrennt. Ohne ... fast ohne Tränen. Sabeth hielt nichts mehr in Heidelberg. Sie hat das Haus vermietet und ist nach Südfrankreich gezogen. Sie liebte immer schon die Wärme. Das Meer. Ich glaube, es ging ihr dort recht gut. Mit diesem ... wie hieß er noch?«

»Bressault. Jean Bressault.«

»Richtig, Jean. Mit ihm hatte sie mehr Glück als mit mir.«

»Soweit ich weiß, hat die Ehe nicht lange gehalten. Und alle folgenden auch nicht.«

Graf schwieg mit einer Miene, als hätte er meinen Einwand überhaupt nicht gehört.

»Andere Frage, im Grunde nicht wichtig, aber es interessiert mich persönlich: Was haben Sie am siebten Februar in Ihrem alten Haus in Neuenheim gemacht?«

»Am Siebten?«, fragte er gedehnt und sah mich plötzlich konzentriert an.

Offensichtlich hatte ich ihn auf dem falschen Fuß erwischt.

»Ich … Natürlich! Sabeths Geburtstag. Wo ich schon mal in der Gegend war, dachte ich, schau ich auf ein Gläschen Sekt vorbei und bringe ihr ein paar Blumen. Seit sie Witwe ist – es geht ihr nicht besonders. Sie ist ein wenig einsam in dem riesigen kalten Kasten.«

Wer viele Worte macht, versucht meist, etwas zu verschweigen, hatte ich schon früh in meiner Polizistenausbildung gelernt.

»Warum haben Sie all das in der vergangenen Nacht nicht gesagt?«

»Mit Freds Pistole am Kopf?« Graf schwieg für Sekunden. »Ich lasse mich nun mal nicht gern erpressen.«

»Er könnte noch leben.«

Mit großen, ernsten Augen sah er mir ins Gesicht. »Und ich könnte jetzt tot sein. Wer weiß, ob er mir geglaubt hätte. Wer weiß, ob er nicht erst recht durchgedreht wäre, wenn er die banale Wahrheit gehört hätte. Sie werden mich jetzt hoffentlich nicht des Totschlags bezichtigen.«

»Natürlich nicht.« Ich lehnte mich zurück. Sah dem Fernsehstar ins plötzlich wieder todmüde Gesicht. Vor der Tür unterhielten sich zwei Männer lautstark. Einer lachte. Eine Frau mit harten Absätzen tackerte den Flur entlang.

»Kommen wir zu einem anderen Thema.« Ich schlug die Beine übereinander. »Der Name Rosa Jordan sagt Ihnen etwas?«

Dieses Mal blieb Graf entspannt. »Natürlich.«

»Ich habe eine Videoaufzeichnung gesehen, aus dem Foyer des Europäischen Hofs. Darauf sind Sie deutlich zu sehen, wie Sie am Mittwochabend eine halbe Stunde vor Mitternacht das Hotel verließen.«

Das war ganz und gar gelogen, denn dieses Video, falls es

jemals existiert hatte, war längst gelöscht, hatte ich erst während der Herfahrt von Klara Vangelis erfahren. Graf sah mich überrascht an und war plötzlich wieder hellwach. Ich hatte auf die richtige Karte gesetzt. Und der Mann war ein Chamäleon.

»Auch ich habe ein Recht auf ein wenig Freiraum, Herr Gerlach. Ich will nicht ständig in einem goldenen Gefängnis leben. Und deshalb gehe ich manchmal ohne Bewachung spazieren, wie Sie ja wissen. Manchmal gehe ich ganz allein und inkognito in eine Bar oder eine schäbige Kneipe und trinke ein Bierchen oder ein Glas Wein.«

»Bevor Sie Ihr Hotelzimmer verlassen haben, haben Sie eine Viertelstunde lang mit Rosalie Jordan telefoniert.«

»Ist das verboten?«

»Ich bin sicher, Sie waren anschließend bei ihr.«

Er lächelte. »Davon haben Sie aber kein Video?« Sein Lächeln erlosch so schnell, wie es erschienen war. »Wir kennen uns von damals.«

»Und Sie wollten alte Erinnerungen auffrischen.«

»Natürlich nicht. Sie hat Geld von mir verlangt. Sie hat mich erpresst.«

»Womit?«

»Sie waren bei ihr, hat sie mir erzählt.«

»Das stimmt.«

»Haben ihr von Fred erzählt. Von seinem Verdacht gegen mich. Und da hat die liebe kleine Rosa gedacht, sie versucht einfach mal ihr Glück bei mir.«

»Und Sie haben ihr Geld gegeben. Auf einen Anruf hin?«

»Sie ist schon am Nachmittag in Ludwigshafen aufgetaucht. Aber ich konnte nicht mit ihr sprechen. Wir waren mitten in den ersten Stellproben. Olivia hat ihr dann in meinem Namen versprochen, dass ich mich melde. Fünftausend Euro wollte sie, hat sie mir durch Olivia ausrichten lassen. Dabei hat sie überhaupt nichts gewusst. Aber sie ist ein armes Schwein, die kleine Rosa, das alte Lästermaul. Und ich habe ein zu weiches Herz. Ich kann Menschen nicht leiden sehen.«

»Sie *war* ein armes Schwein.«

Grafs Blick wurde sofort konzentriert. »Weshalb war?«

»Sie ist tot. Erzählen Sie nicht, Sie wüssten nichts davon.«

»Ich ... Tot? Ich weiß wirklich nichts. Aber ... wie?«

Er schaffte es sogar, ein wenig zu erblassen. Entweder, er war wirklich ein genialer Schauspieler. Oder ich war auf der falschen Fährte.

»Sie ist vergiftet worden. Mit einem Cognac, an dessen Flasche meine Leute Ihre Fingerabdrücke gefunden haben. Auf dem Video ist zu sehen, dass Sie eine längliche Tasche bei sich hatten. Eine dieser Geschenktaschen, in die man Flaschen steckt. Und wenn ich das noch anmerken darf: In der vergangenen Nacht hatte ich nicht den Eindruck, Sie hätten ein zu weiches Herz. Sie haben Ihren ehemaligen Freund getötet. Mit Worten in den Selbstmord getrieben.«

Graf sank zurück in sein Kissen und stöhnte abgrundtief. »Ich habe um mein Leben geredet, Herr Gerlach, ich bitte Sie! Er oder ich – das waren die Alternativen. Und die, die es dann letztlich geworden ist, ist mir wesentlich sympathischer als die andere. Außerdem hätte er sich vermutlich ohnehin erschossen. So oder so.«

Damit lag er vermutlich nicht einmal falsch. »Sie haben Frau Jordan also nicht nur Geld mitgebracht, sondern auch eine Flasche Cognac«, fuhr ich fort.

»Ich bekomme ständig Cognac geschenkt, Château de Montifaud, seit ich einmal in einem Interview behauptet habe, das sei meine Lieblingsmarke. Dabei trinke ich überhaupt keinen Alkohol. Ich habe Sie vorhin belogen. Ich trinke kein Bier und keinen Wein und erst recht keinen Cognac. Meine Imageberater sind aber der Ansicht, Askese passe nicht zu mir. Sie meinen, das Publikum sieht mich lieber als Bonvivant.«

»Im Fernsehen habe ich beobachtet, wie Sie einen pfälzischen Dornfelder genossen haben. Sie haben ihn sogar ausdrücklich gelobt.«

»Product Placement. In meinem Glas war aber kein Rotwein, sondern leicht verdünnter Johannisbeersaft.«

»Und da haben Sie also Frau Jordan einfach eine von Ihren Flaschen mitgebracht.«

»Sie hat schon immer gesoffen. Auch am Telefon klang sie nicht mehr nüchtern, vorsichtig ausgedrückt. Und in dem Cognac soll Gift gewesen sein?«

»Liquid Ecstasy.«

»Ich wüsste nicht mal, wo man so etwas bekommt.«

»Sie wollen mir aber jetzt bitte nicht erzählen, der Cognac sei schon vergiftet gewesen, als er in Ihren Besitz kam.«

Graf hob in Zeitlupe die weichen Schultern. Sah nachdenklich auf seine verwelkten Hände. »Ich habe einfach eine der Flaschen gegriffen, die auf dem Sideboard herumstanden, habe sie aus der Geschenkverpackung genommen, die Tragetasche lag praktischerweise gleich daneben. Ich weiß nicht, woher diese Flasche stammt. Und ich habe sie vorher nicht angerührt, das müssen Sie mir glauben. Ich habe sie am Hals gepackt und in die Tasche gestopft in der Hoffnung, Rosalie dadurch milde zu stimmen. Ich wollte mit ihr reden. Und ich wollte sie beruhigen. Das Telefongespräch verlief ... etwas unangenehm.«

Soweit es die Fingerabdrücke betraf, hatte er leider recht. Die Spuren, die meine Spezialisten an der Flasche gefunden hatten, stammten von Graf, der sie eingepackt, und von Rosa Jordan, die sie entgegengenommen und vermutlich umgehend geöffnet hatte. Die Person, die die Flasche in den Geschenkkarton gesteckt hatte, trug dabei vermutlich Handschuhe, um das kostbare Glas nicht zu beschmutzen.

»Die fünftausend Euro hatten sie einfach so herumliegen?«

»Olivia hat mir das Geld im Lauf des Nachmittags besorgt.«

»Hat Frau Jordan die Flasche in Ihrem Beisein geöffnet?«

»Sie hat mir sogar ein Gläschen angeboten. Aber ich habe nur so getan, als würde ich trinken, und den Inhalt in ihre schmierige Spüle geschüttet, als sie einen Moment nicht hinsah.«

»Da haben Sie ja Glück gehabt!«

»Herr Gerlach, lassen Sie bitte den Zynismus.« Wieder schloss Graf die Augen. »Sie können jeden in meiner Umgebung fragen, jeden. Ich rühre seit zwanzig Jahren keinen Alkohol mehr an. Ich hatte einige Zeit ein ... gewisses Problem damit. Und es gab nur zwei Möglichkeiten: entweder der Schnaps oder ich.«

»Führen Sie Buch über die Absender der Geschenke, die Sie erhalten?«

»Andrea, meine Sekretärin. Sie verschickt auch hübsche Dankeschönkarten mit meiner Unterschrift. Meiner von Andrea gut gefälschten Unterschrift, selbstredend. Ich hätte viel zu tun ...«

»Was geschieht üblicherweise weiter mit den Sachen?«

»In der Regel wird das Zeug weiterverschenkt. Das meiste ohne mein Zutun. Die eine oder andere Flasche habe ich auch schon persönlich Journalisten überreicht. Die Interviews klingen freundlicher, wenn der Schreiberling beim Formulieren an einem zwölf Jahre alten Cognac nippen darf.«

»Sie haben die Flasche also persönlich vom Sideboard genommen und ausgepackt? Niemand sonst hat sie vorher angefasst?«

Mattes Kopfschütteln. »Ich war allein an dem Abend. Auch später.«

»Warum haben Sie sie überhaupt aus dem Karton genommen?«

»Weil sie sonst nicht in meine Tasche gepasst hätte.«

»Hat Frau Opelt von dieser ... merkwürdigen Erpressung gewusst?«

»Natürlich. Sie hat Rosa am Nachmittag abgewimmelt. Mit handfester Unterstützung von Johann. Johann Boll, einer meiner beiden Bewacher. Rosa kann ... konnte recht starrköpfig sein. Durch Olivia habe ich erfahren, was Rosa wollte. Sie hatte Olivia aufgetragen, sie wolle mich am selben Tag noch sprechen, sonst geht sie am nächsten Morgen zur Polizei. Die ganze Sache war vollkommen idiotisch. Ich bin überhaupt nur darauf eingegangen, weil ich sie vom Hals haben wollte. Das Letzte, was wir brauchten, war ein Skandal. Es hätten sich genug Revolverblättchen mit Freuden auf die Story gestürzt, das dürfen Sie mir glauben. Also habe ich Olivia gebeten, Rosa auf den späten Abend zu vertrösten – und mir fünftausend Euro zu besorgen.«

»Wie lange sind Sie in der Nacht bei Frau Jordan geblieben?«

»Zehn Minuten. Höchstens fünfzehn. Sie war schon betrunken, als sie mir die Tür öffnete. Dieser unglaubliche Dreck überall. Die Katze ist mir ständig um die Hosenbeine gestrichen, und ich hasse Katzen. Rosa hat gekeift und gezetert und mich verhöhnt. Von oben hat die ganze Zeit Musik gedröhnt, und ich habe mich selbst dafür verflucht, dass ich mich überhaupt auf diesen Unfug eingelassen habe. Im Grunde war sie nur eifersüchtig auf meinen Erfolg, den ich mir natürlich erschlichen und erschwindelt habe und der absolut nichts mit meinen Fähigkeiten … und so weiter.«

»Sie waren nicht besonders guter Stimmung, als Sie sich verabschiedet haben?«

»Ganz im Gegenteil. Ich habe ihr von Herzen den Tod gewünscht. Und das habe ich ihr auch gesagt: ›Verrecke endlich‹, habe ich gesagt. ›Verrecke in deinem Dreck. Ich will dich nie wiedersehen.‹«

»Wie hat sie reagiert?«

»Sie hat hysterisch gelacht und gesagt, wir zwei hören noch voneinander, Marcel. Öfter, als dir lieb ist. Wart's nur ab.«

Ich gönnte Graf einige Sekunden Pause, bevor ich sagte: »Kommen wir zum letzten Thema für heute: dem Donnerstagmorgen.«

Er kniff die bereits geschlossenen Augen noch fester zu. »Dazu ist alles gesagt, was ich sagen kann. Er kam von hinten. Er war groß. Er war ein Mann. Er hatte ein Messer.«

Es juckte mich in den Fingern, ihn noch ein wenig zu quälen, zu sticheln, zu pokern. Aber schließlich entschied ich mich, in diesem Punkt nicht nachzuhaken. Der Mann war trotz seiner Erschöpfung viel zu schlau, um sich in Widersprüche verwickeln zu lassen. Bevor ich nicht wenigstens etwas Ähnliches wie einen Beweis in Händen hatte, würde ich in diesem Punkt nicht weiterkommen.

Ich erhob mich. Graf öffnete die Augen, sah mich an, als hätte er mit dem Leben abgeschlossen. Sein Händedruck war kühl, schwach und trocken.

Zum Abschied lächelte er dann doch noch einmal sein berühmtes Samstagabendlächeln. »Ich fürchte, jetzt brauche ich ein wenig Ruhe. Es war ein anstrengendes Gespräch. Aber ich danke Ihnen trotzdem dafür. Jetzt ist mir wohler.«

38

Das erste Gespräch mit Patrick Wunderlich, dem früheren Soldaten, brachte kaum etwas Neues zutage. Ich hatte ihn in den Vernehmungsraum der Polizeidirektion bringen lassen, und dieses Mal war Klara Vangelis dabei.

»Wo ist Ihr Kollege?«, lautete meine erste Frage.

Die Fahndung nach Boll lief bereits seit der Nacht, war bisher allerdings erfolglos. Das machte mir jedoch keine Kopfschmerzen. Er hatte weder Zeit noch Gelegenheit gehabt, sein Untertauchen vorzubereiten. Er würde sich irgendwo mit Geld versorgen müssen. Er würde in Hotels seinen Ausweis zeigen müssen. Eine Frage von ein, zwei, maximal drei Tagen.

Wunderlich nahm im Sitzen Haltung an, als wäre er immer noch Soldat und ich sein Vorgesetzter. Sein Blick war unsicher, fast ängstlich.

»Das weiß ich leider nicht, Herr Gerlach. Herr Graf hat uns nach der Veranstaltung allein nach Heidelberg zurückgeschickt. Das hat uns ein wenig gewundert. Ich habe den Mercedes gefahren. Herr Boll hat seinen eigenen Wagen genommen und gesagt, er hätte noch etwas zu erledigen und würde später nachkommen. In Heidelberg bin ich dann gleich zu Bett gegangen. Erst als heute Nacht Ihre Kollegen an meine Tür geklopft haben, habe ich erfahren, dass er einen anderen Weg gewählt hat.«

»Sie können sich vorstellen, weshalb ich Sie beide gerne sprechen möchte?«

Der ehemalige Soldat nickte. »Diese Sache mit Hergarden. Ich war dabei. Aber ich habe nichts gemacht. Praktisch nichts gemacht habe ich.«

»Natürlich nicht.«

»Es war Herr Boll. Es war seine Idee. Mit Frau Opelt zusammen hat er das ausgeheckt. Wir wollten dem mal einen tüchtigen Schrecken einjagen. Mehr wollten wir nicht.«

»Woher wussten Sie überhaupt, wo er war? Wir haben tagelang nach ihm gesucht und ihn nicht gefunden.«

»Herr Boll hat gute Verbindungen. Er hatte ja schon vor Wochen mit Herrn Hergarden zu tun gehabt. Der war immer wieder aufgekreuzt und wollte Ärger machen. Und da hat Herr Boll dann Erkundigungen eingezogen. Herr Graf hat den Mann von früher gekannt und manches über ihn gewusst. Wo er aufgewachsen war und so weiter. Daher wussten wir bald, dass er einen Bruder in Mannheim hatte. Da lag die Vermutung nahe …« Er hob die kantigen Schultern, lächelte verkrampft.

»Und wie lief das Ganze ab?«

Wunderlich redete wie ein Wasserfall. Offenbar hatte ihm die Geschichte schwer zu schaffen gemacht. »Frau Opelt hatte uns ihren Wagen geliehen. Herr Boll mochte seinen eigenen nicht nehmen.«

»Warum?«

»Das weiß ich nicht. Er hat gesagt, damit fällt er vielleicht zu sehr auf. Wir haben geläutet, Hergarden hat uns die Tür geöffnet. Er war noch wach, obwohl schon fast Mitternacht war. In Pantoffeln und einer grünen Strickjacke hat er uns die Tür geöffnet …«

Der Rest war exakt so abgelaufen, wie ich es mir zusammengereimt hatte. Sie hatten den vermeintlichen Fred Hergarden in den Keller geschleppt, dort auf einen der Küchenstühle gefesselt, ihn angebrüllt, mit Fäusten bedroht, jedoch angeblich nicht mit Waffen. Und irgendwann war er plötzlich blass geworden und in sich zusammengesackt.

»Herr Boll hat vorgeschlagen, den Leichnam verschwinden zu lassen. Ich war nur dabei, sozusagen. Das war nicht richtig, das ist mir klar. Das war ein Verbrechen. Ich bin bereit …«

»Sie haben also ausschließlich auf Bolls Anweisungen gehandelt?«

»Das war dumm von mir, ich weiß.« Wieder das militärisch knappe Nicken. »Herr Boll hat den Mann angebrüllt. Dass er Herrn Graf endlich in Ruhe lassen soll. Dass wir wissen, dass er Herrn Graf mit dem Messer angegriffen hat, und dass er froh sein soll, dass wir nicht zur Polizei gehen. Das konnten wir natürlich nicht, zur Polizei gehen.«

»Warum nicht?«

»Weil Herr Graf es uns ausdrücklich verboten hat. Er wollte nichts mit der Polizei zu tun haben. Und Herr Boll hat auch gesagt, das hat keinen Sinn. Das müssen wir so regeln.«

»In welcher Beziehung stehen Graf und Boll?«

»Das weiß ich nicht. Aber sie kennen sich von früher. Von viel früher. Mehr wollte Herr Boll dazu nicht sagen.«

»Und dann ist Ihr Opfer in Ohnmacht gefallen ...«

»Und wie Herr Boll ihn geschüttelt hat, da war er tot.«

»Und Sie haben es nicht für nötig gehalten, einen Arzt zu rufen?«

»Ich schon. Herr Boll war dagegen. Er hat gemeint, das bringt nur Ärger, und dem Mann ist eh nicht mehr zu helfen, und außerdem glaubt uns kein Mensch, dass wir gar nichts dafür können. Unsere einzige Chance war, den Leichnam irgendwie ... verschwinden zu lassen.«

»Und dabei haben Sie natürlich auch nur ein ganz klein wenig mitgeholfen.«

Inzwischen standen Schweißperlen auf der Stirn des ehemaligen Hauptfeldwebels, dessen Leibwächterkarriere nach so kurzer Zeit schon wieder zu Ende war. Niemand stellt einen vorbestraften Personenschützer ein.

»Auch das ist richtig, Herr Gerlach. Genau so war es. Wir haben ihm einen Mantel und Schuhe angezogen. Ich habe mitgeholfen. Getragen hat ihn Herr Boll. Ich habe die Türen aufgehalten und den Kofferraum geöffnet und so weiter.«

»Wie sind Sie dann auf die Idee gekommen, ihn vom Zug überfahren zu lassen?«

»Herr Boll meinte, eine Leiche spurlos verschwinden zu lassen, sei schwierig. Er meinte, wir lassen es besser wie Selbstmord aussehen. Er hat eine Stelle gekannt, wo man das gut machen konnte. Dummerweise hat es die ganze Zeit fürchterlich geschneit. Wir haben uns drei- oder viermal verfahren, bis wir die Stelle endlich fanden.«

Ich sah Klara Vangelis an. Auch sie hatte keine weiteren Fragen. Ich drückte den Knopf am Mikrofon.

»Wissen Sie eigentlich, dass Sie den falschen Herrn Hergarden auf die Schienen geworfen haben?«, war meine letzte Frage, schon im Stehen.

Nein, Patrick Wunderlich hatte es nicht gewusst. Er war bis zu dieser Sekunde davon ausgegangen, dass sie den Richtigen erwischt hatten.

Ich erklärte ihm, dass ich einen Haftbefehl gegen ihn beantragen würde. Und dass er mit viel Glück mit einer Bewährungsstrafe davonkäme.

Auch mein Gespräch mit Olivia Opelt war kurz und ohne Überraschungen. In ihrem Blick war keine Angst, keine Neugierde auf das, was nun kam. Nur noch Müdigkeit und grenzenlose Erschöpfung.

»Im Zuge der ganzen Geschichte hat mindestens zweimal Ihr Volvo eine Rolle gespielt«, begann ich.

Sie sah auf. »Soll ich vielleicht einfach …?«

Ich nickte.

Sie senkte den Blick und begann zu reden, als hätte sie sich seit Ewigkeiten nichts anderes gewünscht.

»Es begann alles damit, dass Johann am Samstag vor zwei Wochen erzählt hat, neben Hergarden sei noch ein zweiter Mann in Neuenheim aufgetaucht, der Ärger machen wollte. Und dass er Sie gestoßen hat. Ich selbst war nicht dabei.«

»Hergarden war Ihnen aber schon früher auf die Nerven gegangen, nehme ich an.«

»Wenn, dann habe ich nichts davon mitbekommen. Ich vermute, der Umstand, dass Marcel plötzlich Personenschutz brauchte, hatte mit seinem Auftauchen zu tun. Ich selbst habe den Namen Hergarden zum ersten Mal im Zusammenhang mit Ihrem Erscheinen gehört. Wir haben dann überlegt, wer Sie sein könnten. Was Sie mit Hergarden zu schaffen haben.

Marcel hat von alldem nichts erfahren. Wir mussten jede Aufregung von ihm fernhalten. Die Show – es durfte einfach nicht schiefgehen. Und dann ist doch alles schiefgegangen, was überhaupt nur ... Und am Ende auch wieder nicht. Ich ... Es ist ... «

»Sie sind müde.«

»Müde?« Sie lächelte wehmütig und mit feuchten Augen. Immer noch hielt sie den Blick gesenkt. »Es gibt kein Wort für meinen Zustand.«

»Sollen wir vielleicht später ...?«

»Nein.« Sie schüttelte heftig den Kopf. »Ich will ... Ich muss jetzt reinen Tisch machen. Vorher kann ich ohnehin nicht schlafen.«

»Der Peilsender an meinem Auto war vermutlich Bolls Idee?«

»Als Sie zwei Tage später bei Marcels geschiedener Frau angerufen und sich nach Vickys Tod erkundigt haben ...«

»Ich habe mit einer Angestellten gesprochen.«

»Die es natürlich Frau von Brühl sofort weitererzählt hat. Und die hat dann wiederum sofort Marcel angerufen. Und damit wusste er Bescheid. Er hat gesagt, er lässt uns freie Hand. Er will nichts wissen. Er will nur seine Ruhe haben, bis nach der Show.«

»Was ja dann nicht ganz geklappt hat.«

»Nein, wahrhaftig nicht.« Sie biss sich auf die Unterlippe, kniff die Augen zu. Riss sie wieder auf. »Johann hat anhand Ihrer Telefonnummer nicht herausfinden können, wer Sie sind. Patrick hat bei Ihnen angerufen, um Ihren Namen herauszufinden. Dummerweise hatten die beiden sich nicht abgesprochen, sodass Johann kurz darauf auch noch bei Ihnen angerufen hat.«

Den zweiten Anruf hatte Sarah entgegengenommen, erinnerte ich mich. »Typisch Kurpfälzer Holzkopf«, hatte ihr Kommentar gelautet.

»So begann es«, fuhr Frau Opelt fort, »und in diesem Stil ging es weiter. Erst mal waren wir sehr erschrocken, als wir hörten, Sie sind von der Kripo. Haben alles Mögliche gedacht.

Wir wussten nicht, und ich weiß bis heute nicht, was dieser Herr Hergarden eigentlich wollte, was da eigentlich vorgefallen war. Nur, dass Vicky wohl seine Frau war und irgendwie ums Leben gekommen ist. Johann schien mehr zu wissen, wollte aber nicht mit der Sprache heraus.«

Olivia Opelt verstummte. Kaute wieder auf der schmalen Unterlippe. »Er hat dann vorgeschlagen, wir sollten Sie beobachten. Herausfinden, was Sie vorhaben. Er hatte all solche Sachen wie Peilsender und Wanzen in seiner Detektivausrüstung. Mir war zu dem Zeitpunkt alles recht, solange es nur mit der Show voranging. Er hat Ihnen also einen solchen Sender an den Wagen montiert, und einer von uns musste immer in der Nähe bleiben und aufpassen, ob Sie losfahren. Ich habe Johann meinen Wagen geliehen. Seinen wollte er nicht nehmen. Warum, weiß ich nicht. Vielleicht wollte er das Bezingeld sparen. Er ist Ihnen gefolgt. Und das Erste, was er sehen musste, war ...«

»Dass ich zu seinem Haus gefahren bin.«

»Er war sehr aufgeregt, als er zurückkam. Johann ist ja sonst die Ruhe selbst. Ein Bär. Gutmütig. Manchmal auch ein wenig trottelig. Aber nicht ungefährlich.«

»Und Sie wussten immer noch nicht, worum es bei der ganzen Sache ging.«

»Nur, dass es etwas in Marcels Vergangenheit gab, worauf er nicht stolz war und was uns nichts anging. Mir hat es genügt zu wissen, dass Marcel in Gefahr schwebt. Und damit die Show und mein Job, alles. Was wir brauchten, was wir mehr als alles andere brauchten, war Ruhe.«

Vor den Fenstern des Vernehmungsraums, der im Erdgeschoss lag, fuhren kurz nacheinander zwei Streifenwagen mit eingeschalteten Blaulichtern davon. Von irgendwoher duftete es nach Kaffee.

»Sie sind mir auch einmal gefolgt, richtig?«

Olivia Opelt nickte. »Am Samstag vor einer Woche. In der Zeit davor hatten Sie ja Ihren Wagen nicht bewegt. Ich blieb immer so weit hinter Ihnen, dass Sie mich nicht bemerken konnten. Unterwegs, irgendwann am Nachmittag, hatte ich plötzlich kein Signal mehr. Johann meinte, die Batterie des Senders sei vielleicht alle gewesen. Aber zu dem Zeitpunkt wussten wir schon mehr als genug. Es war klar, Sie würden keine Ruhe geben. Die Bombe würde früher oder später hochgehen.«

»Und Sie haben weiter versucht, Ihren Chef aus allem herauszuhalten.«

Sie schloss die Augen. »Bald danach hatte sich das ja dann erledigt.«

»Als ich persönlich bei ihm aufgetaucht bin.«

Ihr Nicken war kaum noch wahrzunehmen. Sie war am Ende ihrer Kräfte. »Von diesem Moment an war klar, dass wir auf den Abgrund zusteuern. Der Tiefpunkt war der Donnerstag. Dieser Mordanschlag ... Da dachte ist, das war's. Finito.«

Plötzlich sah sie wieder auf. »Sie glauben mir doch?«

»Ja.« Ich räusperte mich und lehnte mich zurück. Der Kaffeeduft irritierte mich. Aber für Kaffee war später noch Zeit.

»Ein anderer Punkt: Frau Jordan.«

»Die verrückte Alte?«

»Was wissen Sie darüber?«

»Nur, dass sie am Dienstag plötzlich da war und ein Mordsgezeter angestimmt hat. Sie wollte unbedingt Marcel sprechen. Johann und ich haben versucht, sie loszuwerden. Aber richtig handgreiflich konnten wir ja nicht werden, so alt und klapperig, wie sie war. Schließlich bin ich nach hinten gegangen, um Marcel zu fragen, was wir mit ihr anstellen sollen. Sie wollte Geld von ihm. Fünftausend. Warum, wisse er schon. Ich sollte nur den Namen Vicky erwähnen, dann wisse er schon.«

»Als wir zum ersten Mal darüber sprachen, haben Sie behauptet, Frau Jordan nie gesehen zu haben.«

Sie nickte demütig. Rückte ihre schwarze Brille zurecht, die auf einmal viel zu groß zu sein schien für ihren Mädchenkopf. »Das tut mir sehr leid. Aber es ... Ich ...«

»Wo waren Sie in der darauffolgenden Nacht?«

»In meinem Hotelzimmer, wie ich gesagt habe. Das ist die Wahrheit. Sie müssten anhand meiner Mails leicht feststellen können, dass ich bis weit nach Mitternacht gearbeitet habe. Ich habe mit dem Tod dieser Frau nichts zu tun. Bitte glauben Sie mir. Ich ... ich könnte so etwas doch gar nicht.«

Ich drückte den Knopf am Mikrofon. »Ja, ich glaube Ihnen. Sie dürfen jetzt gehen. Ich werde Sie vielleicht noch einmal brauchen. Halten Sie sich bitte die nächsten Tage zur Verfügung.«

Erstaunt, erschrocken und sehr verletzlich sah sie zu mir auf. »Ich bin nicht verhaftet?«

39

»Ich sehe nur zwei Möglichkeiten«, sagte Sven Balke bei der spontan einberufenen Fallbesprechung am frühen Sonntagnachmittag. »Erstens: Der Cognac war schon gedopt, als Graf ihn bekommen hat. Oder er hat die Tropfen selbst reingetan. Die Alte wird sich ja nicht selbst vergiftet haben.«

Vangelis nickte konzentriert. »Ich habe von Grafs Sekretärin eine Liste mit den Absendern der Flaschen bekommen, die in der Suite standen. Bin aber noch nicht dazu gekommen, alle zu prüfen. Vielleicht hat jemand von den Spendern ja Grund, Graf zu hassen?«

Ich nahm den Laborbericht zur Hand, den ich bisher nur flüchtig überflogen hatte. »Die Konzentration der Tropfen war nicht tödlich«, sagte ich. »Selbst, wenn das Glas randvoll war, hätte die Menge nicht gereicht, sie umzubringen. Bei der Dosis hätte sie höchstens in Tiefschlaf fallen dürfen.«

»Am Anfang kriegt man von dem Zeug ja erst mal nur gute Laune«, wusste Balke – vielleicht aus eigener Erfahrung. »Deshalb nennt man es ja auch Partydroge. Erst, wenn's mehr wird, wird es kritisch. Man schläft ein, kann sich später an nichts erinnern. Wird es noch mehr, dann ... na ja.« Er hob die muskulösen Schultern. Ließ sie wieder sinken. »Die Alte war nicht gerade bei guter Gesundheit, nicht wahr?«

Ich nickte zerstreut. »Das ist noch milde ausgedrückt.«

Partydroge. Wieder einmal löste ein Wort etwas in mir aus.

Etwas, das ich noch nicht greifen konnte. Partydroge ... Ich kam nicht darauf.

»Die ganze Geschichte ist gleich in mehrfacher Hinsicht merkwürdig«, sagte ich langsam. »Erstens müsste Graf schon ausgesucht dämlich sein, seiner alten Freundin einen vergifteten Cognac aus seiner Sammlung mitzubringen. In einer Flasche, auf der auch noch seine Fingerabdrücke sind. Zweitens waren die Tropfen ja offenbar so schwach dosiert ...«

Partydroge. Plötzlich wurde mir klar, welche Assoziation das Wort in mir ausgelöst hatte. Und noch etwas wurde mir klar. »Die Konzentration im Glas«, hatte die Laborantin am Telefon gesagt. Ich blätterte zurück und brauchte nur wenige Sekunden, um zu finden, was ich bisher übersehen hatte.

»Wir wissen gar nicht, ob in der Flasche auch Tropfen waren!« Seufzend warf ich den Bericht auf den Tisch. »Vielleicht war das Zeug nur im Glas.«

»Dann käme Graf also doch als Täter infrage.«

»Im Prinzip ja, aber trotzdem ...«

Partydroge. Plötzlich ging mir das sprichwörtliche Licht auf. Ich griff zum Telefon.

»Es gibt doch noch eine dritte Möglichkeit,«, sagte ich, während ich darauf wartete, dass am anderen Ende abgenommen wurde.

»Die wäre?«, fragte Balke verblüfft.

Ich hatte die Direktwahltaste zum Polizeirevier Heidelberg Mitte gedrückt, das sich praktischerweise im Haus befand.

»Es geht um ein Haus in der Schiffgasse.« Ich nannte der Kollegin die Nummer. »Hat es da in der jüngeren Vergangenheit Klagen gegeben?«

»Klagen?«, wiederholte sie und lachte. »Das ist doch diese Bruchbude mit den ganzen Studi-WGs, nicht wahr?«

»Richtig.«

»Da steppt jede zweite Nacht der Bär. Meistens ruft irgendwann die Hausbesitzerin an. Die wohnt im Erdgeschoss und würde ihre Mieter am liebsten abknallen. Manchmal sind's auch die Nachbarn. Wenn's besonders hoch hergeht, klingelt hier zehnmal in der Nacht das Telefon.«

»Hat es auch in der Nacht von Dienstag auf Mittwoch geklingelt?«

»Dienstag ... Momentchen ... Oje. Diesmal war's mal ausnahmsweise nicht die Vermieterin, sondern jemand aus dem Haus gegenüber. Der erste Anruf war um null Uhr achtzehn. Der zweite um null Uhr siebenunddreißig und der dritte zehn Minuten später. Wir sind dann mit zwei Wagen hin und haben die Fete zwangsweise beendet. Bin selber dabei gewesen. Wir haben sogar mit Festnahme drohen müssen, bis die endlich Ruhe gegeben haben. Komplett zugedröhnt mit irgendwelchen Pillchen oder hackevoll besoffen. Völlig außer Rand und Band sind die gewesen. Man konnt fast neidisch werden, wie das da abgegangen ist ...«

Wenig später läutete ich wieder einmal an der Tür des ungepflegten Hauses, in dem Rosalie Jordan gelebt hatte und gestorben war. Dieses Mal war ich nicht allein gekommen. Sven Balke begleitete mich und außerdem zwei uniformierte Beamte von der Schutzpolizei.

»Eins-a-Wohnlage für Studenten«, meinte Balke gut gelaunt. »Zwanzig Schritte bis zur Mensa. Da lässt sich's leben.«

Die Mensa befand sich im ehemaligen Marstall, einem historischen Gebäude mit dicken Mauern, das tatsächlich nur wenige Meter entfernt in Richtung Neckar lag.

Ich drückte der Reihe nach alle Klingelknöpfe von unten nach oben, da ich nicht genau wusste, wohin ich eigentlich wollte. Augenblicke später surrte der Türöffner gleich mehrmals. Ich wies die beiden Uniformierten an, an der Haustür Posten zu beziehen und niemanden hinein oder heraus zu lassen. Balke folgte mir die Treppe hinauf. Ins zweite OG wollte ich, so viel wusste ich. Dort erwartete uns eine sehr unausgeschlafene junge Frau mit schreiend grüner Borstenfrisur. An den knochigen Beinen trug sie lilafarben schillernde Leggins, oben herum ein schlabberiges hellgraues T-Shirt mit der Aufschrift »Fake!«, durch das sich deutlich ihre Brustwarzen abzeichneten. Zu meiner Verwunderung entdeckte ich keinerlei Metall in ihrem Gesicht.

»Ja?«, fragte sie misstrauisch.

»Sie haben in Ihrer Wohnung in der Nacht von Dienstag auf Mittwoch eine Party gefeiert.«

»Wieso?« Ihre Stimme klang voll und rauchig. Wenn sie Wert darauf gelegt hätte, hätte sie eine attraktive junge Frau sein können. »Die Bullerei war doch schon da. Gibt's wieder mal 'ne Anzeige, oder watt?«

Ich hielt der jungen Frau, die unüberhörbar aus Berlin stammte, meinen Dienstausweis unter die Nase.

Ihre Augen wurden zu Schlitzen. »Wer hat sich diesmal beschwert?«

»Dürften wir kurz hereinkommen?«

»Nö.«

»Sie legen Wert darauf, die Sache offiziell zu machen?«

»Ich lege auf jar nüscht Wert. Ich will nur nicht, dass die Polente in meine Wohnung rumschnüffelt.«

»Es ist Ihre Wohnung?«

»Mietvertrag läuft uff mein' Namen. Aber ich hab die Erlaubnis unterzuvermieten. Die Alte vermietet ja gerne an WGs. Bringt am meisten, und geldgeil ist die ja jewesen wie 'ne alte Nutte.«

»Ihr Verhältnis zur Vermieterin war nicht das beste?«

Sie lachte. »Sind Sie immer so witzig drauf?«

»Wie viele Personen leben in dieser Wohnung?«

»Mit mir zusammen vier. Zwee Jungs, zwee Mädels. Und wat wird det nu?«

Balke zupfte mit amtlicher Miene das Smartphone aus einer der Taschen seiner engen Jeans. Die junge Frau beobachtete ihn dabei mit Interesse und Wohlwollen.

»Jetze kommen Sie mit Blaulicht und Tatütata, oder wat?«, fragte sie, wieder an mich gewandt.

»Jetzt komme ich mit einem Durchsuchungsbeschluss.«

»Dann kommen Sie eben in Gottes Namen rein.«

Mit einem Mal sprach sie akzentfreies Hochdeutsch.

Eine Minute später saßen wir in einer verblüffend aufgeräumten, hochmodern eingerichteten und keineswegs billig ausgestatteten Küche.

Die Mieterin hatte sich rittlings und demonstrativ entspannt auf einen Stuhl gesetzt. Ihre Füße waren nackt. Die Farbe der Zehennägel passte zu der der struppigen Haare. Der Ausschnitt ihres T-Shirts war so weit, dass ich mit einigen Verrenkungen vermutlich ihren Bauchnabel hätte sehen können. Aber diese Taktik kannte ich zur Genüge.

»Sie wissen, dass Frau Jordan tot ist?«

Anstelle einer Antwort plinkerte sie einmal mit den mascaraverschmierten Augenlidern. Offenbar war man in der vergangenen Nacht nicht zum Abschminken gekommen.

»Wissen Sie auch, wie sie gestorben ist? Sie ist vergiftet worden. Mit Liquid Ecstasy.«

Mehr brauchte ich nicht zu sagen. Die junge Frau wurde erst blass, dann rot. »Mit Li…?« Sie verschluckte sich. Hustete ausführlich. »Det kann gar nich … Verdammich. Ick muss …«

»Wer von Ihnen war es?«

Sie wechselte wieder ins Hochdeutsch. »Ich muss erst mit den anderen reden. Warten Sie bitte fünf Minuten im Treppenhaus? Ich verspreche auch, keinen Scheiß zu machen. Ehrlich!«

»Sie werden mit niemandem reden. Sie sind alle miteinander vorläufig festgenommen. Den Rest klären wir in der Polizeidirektion.«

»Ich war's aber nicht.«

»Wer von Ihnen es war, werden wir anhand der Spuren feststellen, die wir unten in der Wohnung sichergestellt haben.«

»Ich war's nicht allein.«

Die drei verschlafenen Gestalten, die nach und nach in der Küche auftauchten, sahen abenteuerlich aus. Der Kopf des zweiten Mädchens war praktisch kahl rasiert, das runde, mit Pickeln übersäte Gesicht an den unmöglichsten Stellen gepierced, die schläfrigen Augen dick schwarz umrandet. Die beiden Männer waren von der Sorte, von deren Anblick man als Vater geschlechtsreifer Töchter Albträume bekommt. Aber sie waren friedlich. Vermutlich stammten alle vier aus guten Familien, waren wohlerzogen, obwohl sie sich jede Mühe gaben, diesen Umstand zu verbergen. Außerdem hatten sie sich abgesprochen.

»Wir wissen nicht, wer es war«, behauptete die Berlinerin, als alle versammelt waren. »Wir waren alle zusammen unten. Wegen der Fete. Es hat ja jedes Mal todsicher Stress gegeben. Als ob es kein Oropax gäbe auf der Welt. Wir wollten das diesmal in Frieden regeln. Also sind wir runter und haben brav angeklopft, sie war ja sogar zu geizig, ihre Klingel reparieren zu lassen, und irgendwie sind wir auf die Idee gekommen ...«

»Ihrer Vermieterin ein paar Tropfen einzuflößen.«

Sie nickte. »Wir wollten nur, dass sie mal gute Laune kriegt und später gut schläft.«

»Sie können es nicht alle vier gewesen sein. Einer muss das Fläschchen in der Hand gehalten und die Tropfen ins Glas geträufelt haben. Oder wollen Sie mir etwa einreden, jeder von Ihnen hätte ein bisschen ...?«

Wieder nickte sie. »Jeder von uns hat ein kleines bisschen was in ihr Glas getan, während die anderen sie abgelenkt haben. War überhaupt nicht schwer. Sie war ja schon sturzbetrunken. Hat ständig rumgekreischt, sie schmeißt uns raus. Am nächsten Morgen kriegen wir alle die Kündigung.«

»Sie wissen, dass ich weiß, dass Sie lügen?«

»Ich lüge nicht. Wir waren es alle vier. Jeder ein bisschen.«

»Studiert zufällig jemand von Ihnen Jura?«

Einer der Jungs, der, der am abgefucktesten aussah, hob träge die linke Hand.

»Offenbar haben sie gut aufgepasst in Ihren Vorlesungen über Strafrecht.«

Er ließ den Kopf hängen, als würde die Müdigkeit ihn jeden Moment vom Stuhl reißen.

»Sie sind vorläufig festgenommen«, erklärte ich wütend. »Packen Sie ein paar Sachen zusammen. Falls Sie das Bedürfnis verspüren, können Sie selbstverständlich einen Anwalt anrufen.«

»Der Anwalt bin ich«, erklärte der Jurastudent träge und gähnte.

»Das nennt man dann wohl groben Unfug mit Todesfolge«, brummte Balke auf dem Weg nach draußen.

»Der Staatsanwalt wird es eher schwere Körperverletzung nennen.«

»Die Kids können einem fast leidtun. Ein Leben verschissen wegen eines solchen Mists.«

40

Es war noch nicht zu Ende.

Am Sonntagabend um kurz nach siebzehn Uhr stand ich zum zweiten Mal vor dem verschlossenen Tor zum Park der Villa, die dieses Mal nicht vollkommen dunkel war. Hinter mehreren Fenstern war Licht zu sehen. Der Streifenwagen, den ich am Vortag herbeordert hatte, war so geparkt, dass er vom Haus gut zu sehen war. Die beiden Kollegen, die sich bisher darin gelangweilt hatten, standen hinter mir.

Die Vernehmungen der vier jungen Leute aus der Wohngemeinschaft waren zäh, unangenehm und unergiebig gewesen. Sie blieben stur bei ihrer Darstellung, dass alle gleich schuldig waren am Tod von Rosalie Jordan. Mit den üblichen Tricks und Drohungen waren sie nicht zu übertölpeln. Wieder und wieder hatten sie ihren abgesprochenen Text abgespult. Am Ende würden sie vermutlich mit einer kleinen Freiheitsstrafe auf Bewährung davonkommen. Dass die vier den Tod der alten Frau nicht beabsichtigt hatten, glaubte ich ihnen sogar. Nur für einen der Studenten konnte es kritisch werden. Als vorbestrafter Jurist würde er nicht leicht eine angemessene Stellung finden.

Dieses Mal hatte mein Läuten Erfolg.

»Ja?«, tönte eine dünne Stimme aus der Sprechanlage. Die Stimme, die ich schon einmal am Telefon gehört hatte.

Ich nannte meinen Namen und mein Anliegen.

Der Türöffner schnarrte. Die Scharniere des Tors kreischten gequält, als ich es aufdrückte. Die schlecht beleuchtete

Kiesauffahrt zum Haus war ungepflegt. Überall welkte Unkraut.

Die Frau, die den Türöffner betätigt hatte, trug eine blütenweiße Schürze und ein neckisches Häubchen im dunklen Haar.

»Frau von Brühl lässt bitten«, erklärte sie mit einem bühnenreifen Knicks.

Ich wurde durch ein Vestibül geführt, in dem teures Schuhwerk unordentlich herumstand und diverse, vermutlich ebenfalls kostbare Mäntel an schmiedeeisernen Haken hingen, durchquerte eine geräumige Halle, landete schließlich in einer veritablen Bibliothek voller verstaubter Regale aus dunklem Holz und alter Bücher. Es roch, als wäre hier das Leben vor Jahren zum Stillstand gekommen.

Die Haushälterin hatte die hohe dunkelbraune Kassettentür zur Halle sofort wieder geschlossen und mich mit einer gemurmelten Entschuldigung allein gelassen. Eine andere Tür stand zur Hälfte offen. Im Nachbarraum sah ich einen kunstvoll gedrechselten Esstisch, ein Cello an der Wand, einen filigranen Notenständer ohne Noten. Ich setzte mich auf einen der beiden herumstehenden Ledersessel mit hoher Lehne. Sprang wieder auf, trat ans Fenster, sah in den verwilderten, in der trügerischen Dunkelheit des frühen Winterabends nur noch schemenhaft erkennbaren Park hinaus.

Vor einer halben Stunde hatte mir Balke freudestrahlend einen Durchbruch gemeldet: Der Hells Angel in Saarbrücken hatte endlich ausgepackt und die Namen der Täter genannt. Insgesamt sieben Männer waren in wechselnder Besetzung zu den Raubzügen in die Kurpfalz aufgebrochen. Im Keller des Anführers, der als Einziger in Heidelberg aufgewachsen war, hatten unsere Kollegen ein regelrechtes Lager voller Diebesgut gefunden. Der Verkauf der Beute war zum größten Teil über das französische eBay-Portal gelaufen.

Irgendwo im Haus hörte ich leise Frauenstimmen. Dann Schritte draußen, die Tür schwang auf, die Hausherrin trat ein.

Nein, Elisabeth von Brühl trat nicht ein, sie trat auf.

Mir fiel nur ein halbvergessenes Wort ein, um diese Frau zu

beschreiben: Grandezza. Das entspannte Selbstbewusstsein jahrhundertealten Adels. Obwohl sie das »von« ja erst vor wenigen Jahren erheiratet hatte und von Adel keine Rede sein konnte. Dennoch diese freundliche, überaus dezente, ja fast liebevolle Verachtung für Menschen niederen Standes.

»Bitte verzeihen Sie, dass Sie warten mussten«, sagte die Hausherrin mit voller Altstimme, als sie mir die ungeschmückte Rechte reichte. »Ich habe sehr schlecht geschlafen in der letzten Nacht. Deshalb habe ich mir erlaubt ... Aber kommen Sie doch. Setzen wir uns nach nebenan. Darf Anna Ihnen einen Tee bringen?«

Kalt war es in diesem Haus. Wie hatte Graf die Villa genannt? Einen alten Kasten. An jedem Möbelstück, an jedem Teppich, jeder Tapete war zu sehen und zu spüren, dass das Anwesen verkam. Dass nicht genug Geld da war, um es zu erhalten. Nein, am Geld konnte es nicht liegen, nach allem, was ich über Frau von Brühl wusste. Hier fehlte es nicht an Barem, hier fehlte es an Interesse und Liebe zu den Dingen, die sie umgaben. Oder an Energie, sich damit zu befassen. Dennoch oder vielleicht gerade deshalb flößte jedes alte Gemälde an der Wand, jedes einzelne Möbelstück Respekt ein.

»Wie geht es ihm?«, fragte die fast einen Meter achtzig große ehemalige Schauspielerin über die Schulter. Sie trug ein schlichtes, gewiss maßgeschneidertes Kleid aus einem weichen Stoff, der ihrer üppigen Figur schmeichelte. Ihr schulterlanges braunes Haar fiel in weichen Locken. Nicht nur an den Händen trug sie keinerlei Schmuck. Da waren auch keine Ohrringe, keine Ketten, nichts. »Ich weiß leider nur sehr ungefähr, was vergangene Nacht geschehen ist. Sie lassen einen ja nicht einmal mit ihm telefonieren. Ist er schwer verletzt?«

»Er ist zum Glück überhaupt nicht verletzt. Herrn Graf steht noch ein wenig unter Schock und ist natürlich sehr erschöpft. Die letzten Tage waren auch für einen Mann seines Kalibers ein wenig heftig.«

Wir setzten uns auf eine mit schokoladenbraunem Leder bezogene Couchgarnitur, die um einen wuchtigen Holztisch herum gruppiert war. Frau von Brühl hatte die hohen Sprossenfenster im Rücken.

»Und was führt Sie nun zu mir, Herr Gerlach?«, fragte sie mit etwas mühsamer Liebenswürdigkeit.

»Die Suche nach der Wahrheit.«

»Welcher Wahrheit?«

»Ich möchte wissen, was in diesem Haus am neunten November 1985 geschehen ist. Auch wenn es inzwischen strafrechtlich nicht mehr von Belang sein dürfte. Ich möchte es einfach wissen. Nennen wir es eine Art Berufskrankheit.«

»Warum haben Sie nicht Marcel gefragt?«

»Das habe ich getan. Aber er sagt mir nicht die Wahrheit.«

»Und nun denken Sie, ich …?«

»Ich wage es zu hoffen.«

»Welchen Grund sollte ich haben?«

»Vielleicht werden Sie sich anschließend besser fühlen?«

Sie sah zur Decke. Zögerte. In ihrem apart geschnittenen Gesicht arbeitete es. Ihr rechtes Auge war eine Winzigkeit kleiner als das linke, was ihre reife Schönheit auf seltsame Weise noch verstärkte. Schließlich sah sie mir wieder ins Gesicht. Sie hatte ihre Entscheidung getroffen.

»Nun denn«, begann sie und atmete tief ein. »Marcel war an jenem Abend in Köln. Bei einer Filmproduktionsfirma. Er war schon am frühen Nachmittag zum Bahnhof gefahren.«

»Die HaBeFilms. Ich habe mit den Leuten gesprochen.«

»Ich war allein im Haus. Nein, natürlich nicht allein. Oben war ja Vicky. Fred war irgendwo im Nahen Osten unterwegs. Geld verdienen, das die beiden so dringend brauchten. Sie waren aus ihrer Wohnung geflogen, weil sie nicht einmal mehr die Miete bezahlen konnten.«

»Sie wussten, dass Ihr Mann und Frau Hergarden …?«

»Selbstverständlich wusste ich.« Kurz nagte sie an der Unterlippe. »Marcel und ich sind sehr offen mit solchen Dingen umgegangen. Dachten, Treue, das sei etwas für das Bürgertum. Fürs gemeine Volk. Wir, die Gotteskinder, lebten auf einem anderen Stern, haben wir uns eingebildet. Wir waren frei, wollten uns entfalten, selbst verwirklichen, in jeder Beziehung. Selbstverwirklichung, das war überhaupt unser Lieblingswort. Inzwischen scheint es ein wenig aus der Mode gekommen zu sein.«

»Aber es hat nicht funktioniert.«

Sehr langsam und sehr endgültig schüttelte sie den Kopf. »Es hat ganz und gar nicht funktioniert. Es gab Tage, da konnte ich recht gut damit umgehen. An anderen Tagen habe ich nur gelitten. Still gelitten, natürlich. Man wollte sich ja keine Blöße geben, als Gotteskind.«

»Und Frau Hergarden haben Sie vermutlich gehasst.«

Sie schwieg lange. Betrachtete ihre Hände, die locker in ihrem Schoß lagen. Ihr Kleid reichte bis über die Knie und wirkte auf mich irgendwie englisch. Es war nichts Besonderes, aber es stand ihr ungemein gut, da es in seiner Schlichtheit ihr aristokratisches Gesicht noch besser zur Geltung brachte. Ich habe es nicht nötig, meinen Reichtum zur Schau zu stellen, verkündete ihr Aufzug. Du weißt auch so, dass ich dich kaufen könnte, wenn ich nur wollte.

»Mit der Zeit ja«, gestand sie leise. »Ich habe Vicky nie besonders gemocht. Sie war mir zu … verzeihen Sie, es fällt mir kein treffenderes Wort ein … zu vulgär. Marcel wollte, dass die beiden hier einziehen. Er und Fred waren alte Freunde. Noch vom Studium her. Außerdem war ihm das Haus zu groß und zu still. Er war sie nicht gewohnt, diese Stille. Marcel stammte aus einfachen Verhältnissen. Seine fünfköpfige Familie war in einer Vierzimmerwohnung aufgewachsen. Später hat er dann in einer Studenten-WG gelebt, übrigens mit Fred zusammen. Und dann plötzlich das hier. Erst später ist mir aufgegangen, dass hinter seiner Hilfsbereitschaft vielleicht noch ein ganz anderes Motiv gesteckt haben könnte.«

»Lief die Beziehung zu Frau Hergarden schon, als die beiden hier einzogen?«

»Das weiß ich bis heute nicht. Ich denke aber, ja. Sie müssen sich vorstellen, hier war es nie so wie in normalen Ehen. In normalen Ehen weiß man immer, wo der andere gerade ist, was er tut, mit wem er zusammen ist. Abends und an den Wochenenden unternimmt man etwas gemeinsam, sieht fern, spielt Spiele. Bei uns wusste man selten ganz genau, wo der andere steckt. Ich hatte Proben, Marcel einen Vorsprechtermin oder Vertragsverhandlungen. Ich hatte am Abend Vorstellung, er am nächsten Morgen eine andere Verpflichtung. Wir waren nicht so oft zusammen, wie man sich das bei einem jungen Paar vorstellt.«

»Und an jenem Abend war Ihr Mann also in Köln ...«

»Oben war es still. Manchmal hörte ich den Fernseher, hin und wieder Schritte. Ihre albernen Stöckelschuhe, die sie sogar zu Hause trug. Vermutlich, damit ich nicht vergaß, dass sie da war. Damit ich meine Blamage keine Sekunde verdrängen konnte. Ich hatte an dem Abend keine Lust auf Ablenkung. Sonst habe ich oft Musik gehört, wenn ich allein war. So laut, dass sie nicht mehr durchdrang. Oder Cello gespielt. Damals habe ich noch viel gespielt. Jetzt schon seit Jahren nicht mehr. Ich ... Aber ... aber an dem Abend – ich weiß nicht – ich konnte auf einmal keine Geräusche ertragen. Auch nicht die Schritte oben – ich wusste, sie sitzt da, hat vielleicht noch am Vormittag mit Marcel ... Trinkt ein Gläschen Sekt auf ein paar aufregende Liebesstunden ... Telefoniert vielleicht mit ihm. Ich habe einige Male versucht, ihn im Hotel zu erreichen. Aber sein Apparat war ständig besetzt.«

»Und irgendwann sind Sie nach oben gegangen ...«

Sie nickte mit ausdrucksloser Miene, jetzt tief in Gedanken und Erinnerungen versunken. Sah endlich auf und in meine Augen. »Ja, Sie haben recht. Ich bin nach oben gegangen. Oder besser: Etwas ist mit mir nach oben gegangen. Ich hatte keinen Plan. Ich habe nicht überlegt. Etwas hat mich einfach diese Treppe hinaufgetrieben. Ich habe an ihre Tür geklopft. Sehr unsanft. Wie üblich war nicht abgeschlossen. Ich habe ihre Stimme gehört. Ich bin eingetreten. Und da saß sie. Auf dem billigen roten Sofa, in ihrem primitiven Nylonnegligé, die ach so schönen Beine hochgezogen, hat mich angegrinst. Angegrinst. Sie hatte ein so ... ordinäres Grinsen. ›Hallo, Sabeth‹, höre ich sie noch sagen, und dabei hat sie ganz langsam und sehr ostentativ den Hörer aufgelegt. Sie hatten oben so ein grünes Telefon mit Wählscheibe und schwarzer Ringelschnur.

Wie man das früher eben hatte. Und ich war sicher, sie hatte noch vor einer Sekunde mit Marcel gesprochen. Geflirtet. Ihm Schweinereien ins Ohr geflüstert. Vermutlich hatte sie noch nicht einmal geduscht, seit sie mit ihm ... Sein Zug ging um drei. Da war ich noch im Theater gewesen. Abends hatte ich spielfrei. Und sie hat mich angegrinst. Wusste, dass ich wusste, dieses miese ... miese Flittchen.«

Sie brach ab. Schloss die Augen. Atmete schwer.

»Und weiter?«

»Das Grinsen ist ihr dann rasch vergangen. Ich konnte nicht mehr anders. Habe sie angeschrien. Sie hat zurückgeschrien. Wie zwei hysterische Weiber haben wir uns gegenseitig die schlimmsten Gemeinheiten an die Köpfe geworfen. Sie ist aufgesprungen. Hat die leere Sektflasche nach mir geworfen, die auf dem Couchtisch stand. Daneben zwei Gläser. Zwei. Ich weiß nicht mehr ... Ich bin auf sie los. War kräftiger als sie. Größer auch. Und auf einmal so unfassbar wütend. Etwas ist aus mir herausgebrochen, was sich über Monate aufgestaut hatte. So wütend war ich. Und dann lag sie plötzlich da. Ich ... Ich kann nicht sagen, was genau vorgefallen ist. Aber es war kein Mord. Es war keine Absicht dabei. Kein Plan.«

»Juristisch haben Sie nichts mehr zu befürchten, denke ich. Im schlimmsten Fall war es Körperverletzung mit Todesfolge und damit verjährt.«

»Was all die Jahre in meinem Kopf vor sich gegangen ist, war weitaus schlimmer als jede Strafe hätte sein können. All die durchwachten Nächte. All die Selbstvorwürfe. Bitte glauben Sie mir: Ich war nie wieder wirklich glücklich seitdem. Bitte glauben Sie mir das. Nie wieder war ich wirklich und von Herzen glücklich seit jener katastrophalen Nacht.«

»Wie ging es weiter?«

»Ich bin davon. In heller Panik. Die Treppe hinab. Ein Wunder, dass ich mir nicht den Hals gebrochen habe. Habe wieder versucht, Marcel anzurufen, vor der letzten Ziffer aufgelegt. Wir hatten auch noch so ein Wählscheibentelefon. Aber unseres war beige, und es hatte eine unendlich lange Schnur. Ich liebte es, beim Telefonieren im Haus spazieren zu gehen. Damals kannte man ja noch nicht all diese Funkdinge, die es heute gibt. Ich habe mir ein Glas Cognac eingeschenkt. Ein großes Glas. Und in einem Zug geleert. Ich habe die Hundertzehn gewählt und wieder aufgelegt. Irgendwann bin ich dann wieder hinauf. Habe ein wenig Ordnung gemacht. Wie eine Idiotin versucht, Spuren zu beseitigen. Mich immer wieder überzeugt, dass sie tatsächlich nicht mehr atmete. Dass sie wirklich und wahrhaftig tot war. Dabei hätte ein Blinder mit seinem Krückstock ertastet, dass sie tot war. Mausetot. Ich habe das zweite Sektglas gespült, das ohne Lippenstift, und in den Schrank gestellt. Ich habe das zerwühlte Bett gemacht, nach Spuren von Marcel gesucht, Haare aufgesammelt. Die Sektflasche, die sie nach mir geworfen hatte, war merkwürdigerweise nicht zerbrochen. Ständig war mir übel. Ich denke, ich habe mich auch zwei oder drei Mal erbrochen. Ich ... ach ... «

»Sie haben vermutlich nicht viel geschlafen in der folgenden Nacht. «

»Ich habe überhaupt nicht geschlafen. Fast wahnsinnig geworden bin ich bei dem Gedanken, dass sie da oben liegt. In ihrem Blut. Dass ich sie gestoßen habe. Dass etwas geschehen muss. Irgendetwas, das nicht dazu führt, dass ich ins Gefängnis muss. Die irrsinnigsten Pläne habe ich gewälzt. Dass ich sie die Treppe hinunterschleife, in den Kofferraum packe, irgendwo ins Wasser werfe, ihr vorher Steine an die Füße binde. Dass ich der Polizei erzähle, Einbrecher seien im Haus gewesen. Dass ich vorher natürlich entsprechende Spuren erzeugen muss. Damit es glaubhaft ist. Mit schmutzigen Männerschuhen durchs Haus latschen, Türen aufbrechen, Schubladen durchwühlen ... All solche blödsinnigen Dinge habe ich gedacht. Es war die schlimmste Nacht meines Lebens. Und ich hatte eine Menge schlimmer Nächte, das dürfen Sie mir glauben. «

»Und Ihren Mann haben Sie nicht erreicht? «

»Doch. Später. Morgens, gegen vier wird es gewesen sein. Da habe ich ihn endlich angerufen. « Sie nickte wie in Trance. »Er hat mich beruhigt. Mir meine Ängste ausgeredet. Endlich konnte ich wieder klar denken. Ich habe gefühlt, dass er mich immer noch liebte. Dass ich ihm wichtiger war als die ... die da oben. Sie machen sich keine Vorstellung, wie gut das tat.«

»Die Einsamkeit ist oft das, was Straftätern am meisten zu schaffen macht.«

»Ist das so? Nun ja, bei mir war es gewiss so. Marcel hat mir empfohlen, noch einmal nach oben zu gehen und alles so aussehen zu lassen, als wäre sie gestürzt. Ein Unfall sollte es sein. Und es war gar nicht so schwer. Wir sind es genau durchgegangen, Schritt für Schritt. Ich bin immer wieder nach unten, habe mit ihm telefoniert, dann wieder nach oben. Bis alles genau gestimmt hat. Dann musste ich warten, bis Tag war. Und noch länger. Es war unerträglich. Unerträglich. Un-erträglich.«

»Nach meinem Protokoll haben Sie um kurz vor zehn die Polizeidirektion angerufen.«

»Das mag stimmen, ja. Marcel hatte mir eingeschärft, was ich sagen muss. Dass man von oben nichts hört. Dass ich geläutet habe. Dass man von draußen Licht im Wohnzimmer sieht. Das mit dem Licht ist uns erst sehr spät eingefallen. Dass das natürlich an bleiben musste. Ich hatte es immer automatisch ausgemacht, wenn ich das Zimmer oben verließ. Aber das musste natürlich an sein. Alles andere wäre ... wäre ja ...«

»Manches von dem, was dann passiert ist, ist gelinde gesagt merkwürdig. Es sind zwei Kripobeamte gekommen. Etwa zwanzig Minuten nach Ihrem Anruf.«

Sie musterte mich aufmerksam. Nickte.

»Die haben sich vermutlich alles angesehen und Fotos gemacht.«

Wieder nickte sie.

»Aber den Arzt haben sie erst geschlagene zwei Stunden später gerufen.«

»Tatsächlich?«

»Der Totenschein ist erst um zwölf Uhr fünfundvierzig ausgestellt worden. Und außerdem wurde eine falsche Anschrift eingetragen.«

»Von alldem weiß ich nichts. Ich habe mich da nicht eingemischt. Ich war hier unten. Die ganze Zeit. Hier. Auf diesem Sofa. Ich habe sie oben rumoren gehört. Und Schritte. Hin und wieder ist jemand die Treppe heruntergekommen, und ich dachte, jetzt ... Aber er ist nur zum Wagen, oder was auch immer, und später wieder hinauf. Irgendwann kam ein Arzt. Das ist richtig. Er trug eine rote Jacke. Ich weiß noch, wie ich ihn sagen hörte, er habe Schwierigkeiten gehabt, die Adresse zu finden. War wohl etwas in Eile.«

»Und dreißig Jahre später ist einer der beiden Polizisten Leibwächter Ihres damaligen Mannes. Und der zweite hat sich in Italien tot gefahren mit einem Ferrari, den er sich nie und nimmer hätte leisten können von seinem Beamtengehalt.«

Sie musterte mich verstört. Versuchte, meine Gedanken zu erraten. Den plötzlichen Schwenk zu verstehen. Es dauerte eine kleine Ewigkeit, bis das, was ich eben gesagt hatte, ihr Bewusstsein erreichte.

»Dafür können Sie wohl schlecht mich verantwortlich machen. Oder Marcel.«

»Wie viel haben Sie den beiden bezahlt?«, fragte ich geradeheraus.

Sie schlug die Augen nieder. Zögerte viel zu lange. Über ihr Gesicht irrlichterten die widersprüchlichsten Gefühle. Angst, Entschlossenheit, Wut. Wut auf ihre Konkurrentin, die ihr nach so langer Zeit immer noch Ärger bereitete. Wut auf mich, der nach so vielen Jahren alles wieder aufwühlte. Schließlich sprach sie mit gesenktem Blick weiter.

»Johann ... Ich habe ihn gekannt. Von früher.«

»Johann Boll?«

»Sein Vater war bei meinem Vater angestellt. Wir hatten eine große Fabrik in Mannheim. Die Holland Kabelwerke. Ihr Vater hatte sie gegründet. Und der Vater von Johann hat dort gearbeitet. Er hatte mit der Produktion zu tun. Was genau, weiß ich nicht. Jedenfalls eine Vertrauensposition. Vater hat große Stücke auf den alten Herrn Boll gehalten. Sie hatten auch privat hin und wieder Kontakt. Er war zusammen mit seiner Frau hin und wieder bei uns zum Essen. Und deshalb habe ich Johann gekannt.«

»Das heißt, Sie haben nicht gleich die Polizei angerufen, sondern erst einmal Ihren alten Freund?«

»Am frühen Morgen schon. Ich war so erleichtert, als er gleich ans Telefon ging. Als ich seine Stimme hörte. Er ist dann auch sofort gekommen. Mir war rasch klar, dass er es nicht umsonst tun würde. Er sagte, allein kann er gar nichts machen, aber er hätte einen Kollegen, mit dem man reden könne. Dann hat er sich alles genau angesehen, noch das eine oder andere Detail korrigiert. Der Schuh, der so dekorativ von Vickys Fuß gerutscht war, zum Beispiel, das war seine Idee. Und der kleine Teppich, auf dem sie angeblich ausgeglitten war. Anschließend, als alles fertig war, ist er ganz normal zur Arbeit gefahren. Vorher hatte er mir noch eingeschärft, was ich tun musste. Und zwei Stunden später war er wieder hier. Mit dem Kollegen zusammen. Den habe ich gleich nicht gemocht. Seine Augen. Er war so ... kalt. Kalt und berechnend. Hat sofort versucht, den Preis hochzutreiben. Anzügliche Bemerkungen gemacht. Bis Johann ihn zurechtgewiesen hat.«

»Wie viel haben die beiden bekommen?«

»Hundertfünfzigtausend. Mark. Jeder. Zehntausend noch am selben Tag. Den Rest vier Wochen später, nachdem alles gut ausgegangen war. Ich kann nichts dafür, dass dieser Narr sich dann gleich einen Sportwagen kauft. Und sich damit auch noch zu Tode fährt.«

»Vielleicht war das sogar Ihr Glück. Ich bin mir nicht sicher, ob er lange den Mund gehalten hätte.«

»Ich auch nicht. Ich habe ihn von Beginn an nicht gemocht. Was ist aus Johann geworden? Wird er bestraft werden?«

»Für diese alte Geschichte nicht mehr. Aber er hat genug anderes auf dem Kerbholz. Zurzeit ist er flüchtig. Und wie ging das mit dem Arzt? Was haben die beiden ihm erzählt?«

»Ich war nicht dabei. Sie haben zuvor lange beratschlagt, oben. Der Arzt musste sein, das war klar. Und es musste natürlich jedes Detail stimmen, damit er die Version mit dem Unfall glauben würde.«

»Warum die falsche Adresse?«

»Das war Johanns Idee. Wegen des Skandals. In Vickys Ausweis stand glücklicherweise noch die alte Anschrift. Sie und Fred waren zu faul gewesen, sich umzumelden. Sie wollten ja auch nur vorübergehend bei uns wohnen. Jedenfalls stand in ihrem Ausweis noch die alte Anschrift, und Johann meinte, das wäre doch geschickt. Weil so später kein Verdacht auf uns fallen könne. Warum der Arzt nichts davon bemerkt hat, weiß ich nicht. Vielleicht hat er auch Geld bekommen. Vielleicht war er nur leichtgläubig. Mir war alles gleichgültig an dem Tag, wenn nur die Tote da oben endlich verschwand und ich wieder meine Ruhe hatte.«

Sie verstummte. Sah ins Leere. Ihr Atem ging stoßweise. Ich lehnte mich zurück und gönnte ihr ein wenig Zeit und Ruhe. Schließlich erhob ich mich, trat an eines der hohen Fenster und sah mit den Händen auf dem Rücken in den Park hinaus, von dem jetzt kaum noch etwas zu sehen war. Unendlich groß und geheimnisvoll schien er auf einmal zu sein. Nur ganz fern waren vereinzelte Lichter zu sehen. Lichter anderer Häuser. Glücklicher Häuser, vielleicht.

41

Aber es war noch immer nicht zu Ende.

»Wie kommt es, dass Ihr damaliger Mann mir heute Vormittag mehr oder weniger dieselbe Geschichte erzählt hat?«, fragte ich und beobachtete ihr Spiegelbild in der Fensterscheibe.

»Hat er das?« fragte sie mit matter Stimme zurück, ohne eine Regung zu zeigen. Von ihrem anfänglichen Stolz war nichts mehr übrig geblieben.

»Allerdings hat in seiner Version er Frau Hergarden gestoßen und nicht Sie.«

Immer noch keine sichtbare Reaktion. »Er will mich schützen. Er wollte mich schon damals schützen. Marcel kann sehr ritterlich sein. Aber meine Version ist die Wahrheit.«

»Wann haben Sie Geburtstag, Frau von Brühl?«

Jetzt reagierte sie. Ihr Spiegelbild richtete sich abrupt auf.

»Wie bitte?«

»Wann ist Ihr Geburtstag?«

Ohne ihr Gesicht zu sehen, spürte ich ihre Verwirrung. Ihre hektischen Gedanken. Ihre Angst.

»Am ... dreißigsten ... dreißigsten Juli. Aber ... weshalb?«

»Und wer hat am siebten Februar Geburtstag?«

»Wie ...? Was ...? Ich verstehe nicht.«

Ich wandte mich um, ging langsam an meinen Platz zurück, setzte mich, sah sie an.

»Sie sind eine großartige Schauspielerin«, sagte ich leise. Auch im Raum war es jetzt sehr dämmrig. Nur in der Ecke neben der Tür brannte eine einsame Wandlampe. »Aber eine gute Lügnerin sind Sie nicht.«

Sie starrte mich an, als hätte man ihr ein Messer in den Rücken gerammt.

»Ich ... verstehe ... immer noch nicht.«

»Sie verstehen mich sehr gut. Wer hat am siebten Februar Geburtstag?«

Wilde Panik loderte in ihrem Blick. Uraltes Grauen. Wir kamen der Wahrheit näher.

»Am ...? Wie ...? Was soll denn diese Frage?«

»Ihr ehemaliger Mann sagte mir, er hätte Sie am siebten Februar besucht, gestern vor zwei Wochen, um mit Ihnen auf Ihren Geburtstag anzustoßen. Ich selbst hatte übrigens die Ehre, mir bei dieser Gelegenheit eine Gehirnerschütterung zuzuziehen, an der Ihr alter Freund Johann Boll tatkräftig mitgewirkt hat.«

»Eine Gehirnerschütterung?«

»Wer hat am siebten Februar Geburtstag, Frau von Brühl? Ich werde nicht gehen, solange ich keine Antwort habe.«

Langsam wich alle Kraft erst aus ihrer Miene, dann aus ihrem Körper. Sie senkte den Blick in Zeitlupe. Suchte immer noch in höchster Aufruhr nach einem Ausweg. Nach einer Fluchtmöglichkeit. Und musste endlich einsehen, dass diese Suche vergeblich bleiben würde.

»Raoul«, gestand sie fast unhörbar leise.

»Ihr Sohn.«

Sie nickte kaum merklich.

»Er war es, nicht wahr? Ihn decken Sie die ganze Zeit. Sie und sein Vater. Für Ihren Sohn haben Sie damals dreihunderttausend Mark ausgegeben und unvorstellbar viel Leid auf sich genommen und dreißig Jahre lang gelogen. Warum?«

»Es wäre gut gegangen«, murmelte sie tonlos. »Es ist gut gegangen. Wenn Sie nicht gekommen wären …«

»Ich bin aber gekommen. Ich bin hier. Fred Hergarden ist auch gekommen und wollte endlich die Wahrheit erfahren. Er ist in der vergangenen Nacht gestorben – mit der falschen Wahrheit im Kopf.«

»Er hat mich angerufen.«

»Hergarden?«

»Er hat mich vor etwa vier Wochen angerufen. Sagte, er sei wieder in Deutschland und wolle, dass Marcel endlich bestraft wird. Er dachte von Anfang an, Marcel sei der Schuldige. Er sagte, er würde keine Ruhe geben, bis alles geklärt war. Und wenn sonst niemand etwas unternehmen sollte in der Sache, dann solle Marcel sich vor ihm in Acht nehmen.«

»Wie war das nun mit Ihrem Sohn?«

»Raoul war elf«, flüsterte sie. »Elf Jahre alt.«

»Wo ist er heute?«

»In einem Heim in Mosbach. Es geht ihm gut dort. Er fühlt sich sehr wohl.«

»Seit wann?«

»Seit damals. Ich … Ich bin eine schrecklich schlechte Mutter.«

»Unsinn.«

»Aber doch! Ich bin nie, nie, nie damit klargekommen, dass mein Kind … nicht normal sein sollte. In der Schwangerschaft war doch alles in Ordnung gewesen. In unserer Ehe war – damals – alles in Ordnung. Mit mir war alles in Ordnung. Alle meine Verwandten haben gesunde Kinder bekommen. Soweit sie überhaupt Kinder bekommen haben, natürlich. Bei der letzten Ultraschalluntersuchung, bei den Blutproben, alles, alles war immer in bester Ordnung. Und dann, bei der Geburt ... irgendwas ist schiefgegangen. Und wie ich wieder zur Besinnung kam, da waren sie alle so seltsam. Raoul sei auf der Intensivstation, erklärte man mir. Nur vorübergehend. Nur eine Vorsichtsmaßnahme. Auch Marcel hat so merkwürdig getan. Und niemand wollte mit mir reden. Niemand. Angeblich nur eine Vorsichtsmaßnahme. Welche Ängste ... Und dann der Schock. Sauerstoffmangel. Während der Geburt. Viel zu lange. Marcel meinte später, wir müssten den Arzt verklagen. Oder die Klinik. Oder alle beide. Aber das war natürlich Unsinn. Alles Unsinn. Er war wütend. So wütend. Dann meine Mutter. Diesen Blick hätten Sie sehen müssen, als sie es erfahren hat. ›Wieder mal typisch‹, sagte dieser Blick. Sie hatte sich einen kraftstrotzenden Mann geangelt, der das Familienunternehmen erst richtig groß machte, und vier proppengesunde Kinder in die Welt gesetzt. Drei Söhne, alles Musterknaben. Nur die Tochter, ach herrje. Einen Luftikus geheiratet, nichts Gescheites gelernt, und nun auch noch das ... Meine wunderbaren Brüder haben die Firma nach Papas Tod übrigens sehr zügig zugrunde gerichtet. Ich selbst habe dieses Haus und etwas Geld geerbt, und ... aber das tut ja nichts zur Sache. Erst nach sechs Wochen durften wir unseren kleinen Sohn mit nach Hause nehmen. Körperlich war er völlig normal. Nur die Reflexe. Alles war so langsam bei ihm. Ich habe ihn natürlich trotzdem geliebt. Natürlich. Er war so süß. So klein. So warm. Aber mit den Jahren ... Es wurde immer schwieriger mit ihm. Es ging einfach nicht voran. Mit elf Jahren, als ... es geschah, hat er nachts immer noch Windeln tragen müssen. Immer haben wir ein Kindermädchen gebraucht. Später sogar zwei, die sich abwechselten, weil wir ja oft auch abends nicht da waren. Und er konnte so entsetzlich wütend werden. So unvorstellbar wütend, wenn etwas nicht so lief, wie er sich das in seinem kleinen kranken Kopf vorgestellt hatte. Er konnte so dickköpfig sein. Zum Verzweifeln dickköpfig. Und dann doch wieder so lieb. So anschmiegsam. Nichts war normal in unserem Leben. Ich bin nicht auf Spielplätze mit ihm gegangen wie die anderen Mütter. Er musste immer hier spielen. Allein. Im Park oder im Haus. Platz war ja zum Glück reichlich. Ich habe ihm seinen eigenen Spielplatz eingerichtet. Schaukel, Wippe, Sandkasten, alles. Ich habe mich versteckt. Uns versteckt. Mein Kind versteckt. Irgendwann wurde mir bewusst, dass ich zwei Leben führte: das der heimlichen Mutter, die sich für ihr Kind schämt, für das Versagen ihres Körpers schämt. Und das der Schauspielerin. Ja, ich war gut. Ja, ich hätte es vielleicht zu etwas gebracht. Aber Raoul. Immer wieder Raoul. Nicht einmal in Urlaub fahren konnten wir mit ihm ...«

»Und vor zwei Wochen war sein Geburtstag.«

Sie nickte, als käme meine Stimme aus ihrem Kopf.

»All die Jahre, gleichgültig, wo ich war – zu seinem Geburtstag war ich immer bei ihm. Wenigstens das. Und dieses Mal dachten wir, da Marcel ohnehin in Heidelberg war und ich wieder in diesem Haus lebe, holen wir ihn doch her. Wir haben Raoul bringen lassen. In das Haus, wo er seine Kindheit verbracht hat.«

»Hat er sich gefreut?«

»Ich weiß es nicht. Es ist schwer zu durchblicken, was in ihm vorgeht. Manchmal hatte ich den Eindruck, er erkennt etwas wieder. Sein Kinderzimmer, in dem heute keine Möbel mehr stehen. Die Küche, die sich natürlich auch verändert hat. Den Park, wo früher seine Schaukel stand. Wir haben Kuchen gegessen. Raoul – er muss immer noch gefüttert werden. Mit vierzig Jahren. Es war ein runder Geburtstag und ... fast nicht zu ertragen. Ich war so froh, als es vorbei war.«

»Auf seine Weise hat er sich gefreut, da bin ich mir sicher.«

Sie nickte mit gesenktem Blick. Mir war nicht klar, ob sie meine Worte verstanden hatte.

»Und wie war es nun damals wirklich, in jener unseligen Novembernacht?«

Jetzt sah sie auf, mir gerade in die Augen. Aufgewühlt. Verstört. Und aus tiefster Seele erleichtert, dass sie endlich reden konnte. Die Wahrheit sagen durfte. Endlich.

»Es war alles, wie ich es geschildert habe. Marcel in Köln, Vicky oben. Die Geräusche. Raoul hat geschlafen. Es war immer ein Elend, bis er endlich einschlafen konnte. Er hatte eine solche Unruhe in sich. Und Kraft auch schon. Wie er klein war, da war alles noch einfacher. Aber er kam allmählich in die Pubertät, viel zu früh – und ich weiß nicht – mit jedem Tag wurde er unerträglicher. Ich saß hier, auf dieser Couch, fühlte mich wieder einmal hundeelend. Schuldig. Verzweifelt. Und oben dieses Flittchen, das mit meinem Mann telefonierte. Mit dem Vater meines Sohnes. Dem Vater, den ich gerade jetzt so dringend gebraucht hätte. Zum Reden. Wenigstens zum Reden.«

»Sie sind nach oben gegangen …«

»Und wir haben gestritten. Sie hat gegrinst. Dieses ewige, ewige Schlampengrinsen. Die dumme Verachtung der Siegerin. Aber es war dann nicht ich, die tätlich wurde, sondern sie. Und auf einmal stand Raoul in der Tür mit offenem Mund und blödem Blick. Seinen ekligen Teddybär unterm Arm, dieses verfilzte, stinkende Ding, das er keine Sekunde loslassen konnte, das man niemals waschen durfte. Er hatte uns gehört. War aufgewacht. Und nun stand er da. Mit sabberndem Mund. Und hat nichts begriffen. Nur, dass sie böse auf mich war. Vicky hat ihn erst gar nicht gesehen, hat mich weiter herumge-schubst, verspottet, ausgelacht. Raouls Schrei werde ich nie vergessen. Den zornigen Schrei eines Menschen, der nicht sprechen kann, nur lallen. Er hat sich einfach auf sie gestürzt, ein fetter Knirps, kaum halb so groß wie sie, hat sie aus vollem Lauf umgerannt. Nicht einmal angefasst hat er sie. Einfach mit der Schulter in den Bauch, den Teddy immer unterm Arm, ganz fest im Arm, sie stolpert, schreit, fällt, und aus. Und aus.«

Elisabeth von Brühl, die Queen, sah mir immer noch starr in die Augen, ohne mich wahrzunehmen. Lange war es still. Ein müdes Vögelchen zirpte vor den hohen, zugigen Sprossenfens-tern.

Schließlich sagte sie ein drittes und letztes Mal: »Und aus.«

Nachwort und Danksagung

Liebe Leserin, lieber Leser,

um es gleich zuzugeben und bösen E-Mails zuvorzukommen: Die dunkle Villa werden Sie in Heidelberg vergeblich suchen. Und schon gar nicht steht sie dort, wo ich sie hingedichtet habe. Nicht immer richtet sich die Realität nach der Phantasie des Autors, und manchmal ist das vielleicht auch ganz gut so. Wenn es gar nicht passen will oder soll, dann nennt man das dichterische Freiheit. Und auch wenn ich gewiss kein Dichter bin, diese Freiheit nehme ich mir trotzdem.

An dieser Stelle möchte ich mich – am Ende des zehnten Bands der Gerlach-Reihe – endlich einmal in aller Form bedanken. Bedanken, bei Ihnen, liebe Leserinnen und Leser, ohne deren Begeisterung und Treue es diese Bücher längst nicht mehr gäbe. Danke aber auch an die vielen, vielen Menschen, die mitgeholfen haben, dass die Bücher so wurden, wie sie am Ende oft wider alle Erwartung dann doch geworden sind. Bücher sind Teamwork, ob man es glaubt oder nicht.

Danke an all diejenigen, die mich auf Fehler hingewiesen haben – ein finsteres Kapitel im Leben eines Autors, denn was ist schlimmer, als wenn man die Schuld nicht jemand anderem in die Schuhe schieben kann?

Danke an meine langjährige Lektorin Annika Krummacher und die aufmerksamen Korrekturleser des Piper Verlags, die fehlende Kommata, peinliche Tippfehler und grausige logische Unstimmigkeiten finden und so unglaublich viel dazu beitragen, dass das Buch noch ein wenig besser wird. Denn besser kann es immer werden. Ein Buch ist niemals fertig. Man muss nur irgendwann aufgeben, weil die Druckerei wartet.

Ein ganz besonderes Dankeschön gilt schließlich den vielen Mitarbeiterinnen und Mitarbeitern der Heidelberger Polizeidirektion, die mit nicht nachlassender Geduld auch meine blödesten Fragen beantworten. Stellvertretend für viele möchte ich Herrn Polizeihauptkommissar Norbert Schätzle nennen, den Leiter der Pressestelle, sowie den Leitenden Polizeidirektor Bernd Fuchs, oberster Chef der Polizeidirektion, der selbstverständlich nicht die allergeringste Ähnlichkeit mit Egon Liebekind hat und mit stoischem Humor und unerschütterlichem Wohlwollen die Früchte meiner manchmal allzu überschäumenden Phantasie erträgt. Und, noch etwas: Seine Ehefrau heißt natürlich nicht Theresa!